The

QUEST

for the

HISTORICAL
MUHAMMAD

The

QUEST

for the

HISTORICAL
MUHAMMAD

EDITED AND TRANSLATED BY

IBN WARRAQ

Prometheus Books

59 John Glenn Drive
Amherst, New York 14228-2197

Published 2000 by Prometheus Books

Inquiries should be addressed to
Prometheus Books, 59 John Glenn Drive, Amherst, New York 14228–2197.
VOICE: 716–691–0133, ext. 207.
FAX: 716–564–2711.
WWW.PROMETHEUSBOOKS.COM

10 09 08 07 06   8 7 6 5 4

Library of Congress Cataloging-in-Publication Data

The quest for the historical Muhammad / edited and translated by Ibn Warraq.
        p.   cm.
    Includes bibliographical references.
    ISBN-13: 978-1–57392–787–1 (alk. paper)
    ISBN-10: 1–57392–787–2 (alk. paper)
    1. Islam—Controversial literature. 2. Muòammad, Prophet, d. 632.
I. Ibn Warraq.

BP169.Q47   2000
297.6'3—dc21   99–054420
                                                                      CIP

Printed in the United States of America on acid-free paper

To

Diana and Roy

"The vivid transparence that you bring is peace."

Contents

Preface

There was a time when scholars and other writers in communist eastern Europe relied on writers and publishers in the free West to speak the truth about their history, their culture, and their predicament. Today it is those who told the truth, not those who concealed or denited it, who are respected and welcomed in these countries. . . .

Historians in free countries have a moral and professional obligation not to shirk the difficult issues and subjects that some people would place under some sort of taboo; not to submit to voluntary censorship, but to deal with these matters fairly, honestly, without apologetics, without polemic, and, of course, competently. Those who enjoy freedom have a moral obligation to use that freedom for those who do not possess it.

Bernard Lewis, *Islam and the West* (Oxford), 1993

I have written the introduction to the present anthology, first, with a view to helping nonspecialists familiarize themselves with not only the names of historians, Muslim and non-Muslim, but also as many of the technical and semitechnical terms that they were likely to encounter on reading this volume, and indeed any articles or monographs on Islamic history in general (further supplemented by a glossary at the end of the book). Second, I had hoped to give sufficient background to put the current debates, between the revisionists and traditionalists about the origins of Islam, in their intellectual context. However, it should be read in conjunction with Ibn Rawandi's excellent survey (chapter 2), where he discusses certain scholars and issues purposely left out by me to avoid unnecessary repetition. There is nonetheless bound to be a certain amount of overlap.

9

In the preface to T. E. Lawrence's *Seven Pillars of Wisdom*, A. W. Lawrence reprinted a series of questions by the publisher and Lawrence of Arabia's answers concerning the printing of *Revolt in the Desert*, an abridgement of the *Seven Pillars*. An exhausted proofreader first poses the question about the inconsistencies in the spelling of proper names, to which Lawrence replies in an off-hand manner, "Arabic names won't go into English, exactly, for their consonants are not the same as ours, and their vowels, like ours, vary from district to district. There are some 'scientific systems' of transliteration, helpful to people who know enough Arabic not to need helping, but a washout for the world. I spell my names anyhow, to show what rot the systems are."[1]

The proofreader then gives the following example of inconsistent spellings, "Sherif Abd el Mayin of slip 68 becomes el Main, el Mayein, el Muein, el Mayin, and el Muyein," to which Lawrence replies, "Good egg. I call this really ingenious."[2]

Only genuises can flout rules in such a cavalier manner; lesser mortals have to follow them and show some sort of respect for the readers. I have tried hard to be consistent, but without the proper software and trilingual secretaries the task occasionally proved too much for me, so I ask the reader's, and above all the Islamologists', indulgence if an occasional "Zaid" slips through instead of "Zayd," or "Ibn Sad" instead of "Ibn Sa'd," "Wakidi" instead of "Waqidi," "al Walid" instead of "al-Walid," and particularly of the inconsistencies in the transliteration of whole Arabic sentences in the thousand or more footnotes. As Lawrence says, the only people who will notice the inconsistencies, especially in the footnotes, are the very people who will understand what the translator and transliterator was getting at anyway.

I am very fortunate that many scholars from Belgium, Canada, Egypt, France, Germany, Great Britain, India, Israel, and the United States gave me countless suggestions of immense value, and criticized my introduction in great detail. Many provided photocopies of articles and even manuscripts of books they themselves were working on that would otherwise have been difficult to obtain. I was truly touched that so many distinguished scholars with so much of their own teaching and research to attend to, nonetheless, took the time to reply to my questions with tolerance and patience for my ignorance.

I should have liked to have given the names of these scholars, but not wishing to compromise them or the august institutions at which they teach in any way, and not to involve them in any controversy or polemics, I, with much, much regret, decided it best not to.

Of course, it remains for me to stress that the opinions expressed and any errors in the introduction are entirely my responsibility.

Ibn Warraq, June 1999

NOTES

1. T. E. Lawrence, *Seven Pillars of Wisdom* (London: Jonathan Cape, 1940), p. 19.
2. Ibid., p. 20.

EDITORIAL NOTE

The challenge in putting together a collection such as this lies in the fact that there is no universally accepted transliteration scheme for Arabic. Quite often there is little consistency in the way authors transliterate Arabic words and terms into English, resulting in various forms for the same thing: Islam's holy book might be spelled Kor'án, Kur'an, Qurân, Qur'an, Coran, Koran, and so on, while the name of Islam's prophet could be transliterated as Mahomet, Mohammed, Muhammad, and so forth. To leave such diverse forms of these names and many other Arabic terms would only confuse the reader. Therefore, every effort has been made to ensure that a consistent spelling conforming with modern usage is employed throughout.

Islam's sacred text is thus represented by its most recognizable form—Koran—even though Qur'an, preferred by scholars, is closer to the actual Arabic pronunciation. The name of Islam's prophet is also consistently spelled Muhammad. The symbol ' represents the Arabic *'ayn*, while the symbol ' represents the Arabic *hamza*; all other diacritical marks have been eliminated.

In addition, English punctuation and capitalization have generally been made to conform to modern usage based on the fourteenth edition of the *Chicago Manual of Style*.

PART ONE

INTRODUCTION

Chapter 1

Studies on Muhammad and the Rise of Islam

A Critical Survey

Ibn Warraq

E rnest Renan believed that, "in place of the mystery under which the other religions have covered their origins [Islam] was born in the full light of history;[1] its roots are on the surface. The life of its founder is as well known to us as that of any sixteenth-century reformer. We can follow year by year the fluctuations of his thought, his contradictions, his weaknesses" (see page 110 in this volume). This view has been vigorously attacked by formidable modern scholars, whose conclusions are lucidly presented by Ibn Rawandi in his following essay, "Origins of Islam: A Critical Look at the Sources." The other essays equally cast doubt on the reliability of the Muslim sources, that Renan, and in more recent years, Montgomery Watt, have taken at their face value; indeed, this whole anthology can be seen as an implicit criticism of this optimistic view of our historical evidence for the rise of early Islam. Renan's views are still shared by some scholars and laymen alike. Here is how Salman Rushdie, echoing Renan's very words, voiced a very common opinion:

> And what seemed to me to be really interesting was that [Islam] was the only one of the great world religions that existed as an event inside history. You couldn't say that about Christianity, because our records of Christianity date from about a hundred years after the events they represent. It's a really long time. The degree of authority one can give to the evangelists about the life of Christ is relatively small. Whereas for the life of Muhammad, we know everything more or less. We know where he lived, what his economic situation was,

15

who he fell in love with. We also know a great deal about the political circumstances and the socioeconomic circumstances of the time.[2]

One of Renan's achievements was to liberate scholars and enable them to freely "discuss the origins of Christianity as dispassionately and as 'scientifically' as those of any other religion."[3] And it is with supreme irony that we read today his preface to the thirteenth edition of *The Life of Jesus* (1867), where he pleads for the right to examine scientifically the Gospels, the same right that, he claims, Islamologists avail themselves of when examining the Koran and the Hadith;[4] or when we read in *L'Avenir de la Science* (The Future of Science, 1890), where he hopes the day will arrive when writing a history of Jesus will be as free as the writing of the history of Muhammad![5]

Of course, Renan is interesting in his own right as a historian of religion. The present essay in this volume, the first English translation, was written in 1851, twelve years before his more celebrated *Life of Jesus*. Renan is an infinitely more subtle and sensitive thinker than the rather racist bigot[6] presented to us by certain "antiorientalist" writings. Those who expect to find only rationalist mockery or Voltairean skepticism will be surprised to discover instead "reverence towards religion, a sensitivity to legends, sympathetic awareness of the perennial human need for faith."[7] A shallowness in his own capacity for belief did not preclude a profundity of religious understanding and knowledge.[8]

Renan, not uncritical in his attitude to the Muslim sources, was able to appreciate the difference between "the historical value of the chronicles of the Arab historians and the collection of legends spawned by the Persian imagination" (see page 130 in this volume). Nearly thirty years before Goldziher's pioneering research on the Hadith, Renan was able say that, although Bukhari himself had reduced 20,000 Hadith to just 7,225 that seemed to him genuine, "without being accused of recklessness, European criticism could assuredly proceed to an even more strict selection." Similarly, Renan says of the Koran, "the integrity of a work committed to memory for a long time is unlikely to be well preserved; could not interpolations and alterations have slipped in during the successive revisions?" Having made these token gestures of skepticism, Renan in the end accepts the Muslim accounts on their own terms: "However, it cannot be denied that these early accounts show a lot of features of the true character of the Prophet, and are distinguished, in a clear-cut manner, from the collection of pious stories solely imagined for the edification of their readers. The veritable monument of the early history of Islam, the Koran, remains absolutely impregnable, and suffices in itself, independently of any historical accounts, to reveal to us Muhammad. . . . [N]othing could attack the broad authenticity of this book [the Koran]."

Basing himself on these Muslim sources, Renan then proceeds to draw an exceedingly favorable portrait of the Prophet, while recognizing his moral failings: "On the whole, Muhammad seems to us like a gentle man, sensitive, faithful, free from rancor and hatred. His affections were sincere, his character in general was inclined to kindness. . . . Neither ambition nor religious rapture had dried up the personal feelings in him. Not at all akin to this ambitious, heartless and machiavellian fanatic [depicted by Voltaire in his drama *Mahomet*]." Renan is at pains to defend Muhammad from possible criticisms: "As to the features of the life of Muhammad which, to our eyes, would be unpardonable blots on his morality, it would be unjust to criticize them too harshly. . . . It would also be unjust to judge severely and with our own considered ideas, the acts of Muhammad, which in our days would be called swindles." The Prophet was no imposter, Renan asserts: "It would be to totally lack a historical sense to suppose that a revolution as profound as Islam could be accomplished merely by some clever scheming, and Muhammad is no more explicable by imposture and trickery than by illuminism and religious fervor." Being a religious humanist, Renan valued Islam, and religion in general, "because it manifested what was divine in human nature,"[9] and seemed to answer the deepest instincts of human nature; in particular it answered the needs of seventh-century Arabia, an idea taken up in modern times by Montgomery Watt.

In adumbrating Renan's thought on religion in general and Islam in particular, I do not wish to necessarily endorse everything he says. Indeed, I do not find his analyses always compelling or correct. Renan contradicts himself when he tells us that Islam somehow answered the needs of seventh-century Arabia while at the same time insisting that "I do not know if there is in the entire history of civilization a spectacle more gracious, more attractive, more lively than that offered by the Arab way of life before Islam . . . unlimited liberty of the individual, complete absence of law and power, an exalted sense of honor, a nomadic and chivalrous life, humour, gaiety, roguishness, light, impious poetry, courtly love." Why bring Islam into this idyllic picture then? Renan tells us that, even after the arrival of Islam, outside a small group of Arabs, there was nothing particularly religious about the movement. As Patricia Crone has argued, "the fact is that the tradition knows of no malaise in Mecca, be it religious, social, political or moral. On the contrary, the Meccans are described as eminently successful; and Watt's[10] impression that their success led to cynicism arises from his otherwise commendable attempt to see Islamic history through Muslim eyes."[11] As for the spiritual crisis, there was no such thing in sixth-century Arabia. Islam was successful because it offered the Arabs material rewards in the here and now—military conquests with all the attendant material advantages: loot, women, and land.

Otherwise, Renan's essay is full of insights and pithy sayings like the following:

> Persecution, in effect, is the first of the religious pleasures; it is so sweet to the heart of man to suffer for his faith, that this attraction suffices sometimes to make him believe. This is what Christian consciousness has wonderfully grasped in creating these admirable legends where so many conversions take place through the charm of torture. (See p. 158 in this volume.)

> If the zeal of an imperious temperament clinging frantically to dogma, in order to hate at his leisure, must be called faith, then 'Umar [the Second Caliph, 634 C.E.] really was the most energetic of believers. No one has ever believed with more passion, no one has ever got more angry in the name of the unquestionable. The need to hate often leads loyal, crude, and unsubtle characters into faith, for absolute faith is the most powerful pretext for hatred, the one to which one can abandon oneself with the clearest conscience. (See p. 141 in this volume.)

We end these reflections on Renan by noting some of his views that are surprisingly modern. Renan remarks that all the dogmas of the Muslim creed floated in uncertainty right up to the twelfth century, a thesis developed with extraordinary rigor by John Wansbrough in modern times. Renan concludes his essay with the following observation:

> It is superfluous to add that if ever a reformist movement manifests itself in Islam, Europe should only participate in it by the influence of a most general kind. It would be ungracious of her to wish to settle the faith of others. All the while actively pursuing the propagation of her dogma which is civilization, she ought to leave to the peoples themselves the infinitely delicate task of adjusting their own religious traditions to their new needs; and to respect that most inalienable right of nations as much as of individuals, the right to preside oneself, in the most perfect freedom, over the revolutions of one's conscience. (See pp. 163–64 in this volume.)

These are hardly the words of a cultural imperialist. Nor does Renan believe that Islam is unchanging or essentially incapable of changing: "Symptoms of a more serious nature are appearing, I know, in Egypt and Turkey. There contact with European science and customs has produced freethought sometimes scarcely disguised. Sincere believers who are aware of the danger do not hide their disquiet, and denounce the books of European science as containing deadly errors, and subversive of all religious faith. I nevertheless persist in believing that if the East can surmount its apathy and go beyond the limits that up to now it was unable to as far as rational speculation was concerned, Islam will not pose a serious obstacle to the progress of the modern mind. The lack of theological centralization has always left a certain degree of religious liberty to Muslim nations."

However, Renan's views never remained immutably fixed; to think that he had just one set of monolithic beliefs obstinately held throughout his career is just the very "orientalist" attitude that certain "antiorientalists" accuse Renan of. During his visits to the Middle East, in 1860 to 1861 and later in 1865, Renan witnessed what he felt was the moral, cultural, and scientific stagnation of Muslims, and his ideas changed accordingly; Renan now felt it was one's duty to liberate Muslims from Islam, to which he attributed all their backwardness in his lecture *Islamisme et a Science* given in 1883:

> Muslims are the first victims of Islam. Many times I have observed in my travels in the Orient that fanaticism comes from a small number of dangerous men who maintain the others in the practice of religion by terror. To liberate the Muslim from his religion is the best service that one can render him.

The rights established by Renan and other nineteenth-century European scholars to examine critically and scientifically the foundations of Islam—whether of the Koran or the life of the Prophet—have been squandered in a welter of ecumenical sentimentality resulting in a misplaced concern for the sensibilities of Muslims. For instance, very recently in an essay entitled "Verbal Inspiration? Language and Revelation in Classical Islamic Theology,"[12] Professor Josef van Ess expressed his respect for the tender susceptibilities of Muslims by stopping, being a non-Muslim himself, his critical analysis out of respect for the way that Sunni Islam treats the history of thought! Mohammed Arkoun very sensibly replied that such an attitude was unacceptable scientifically, for historical truth concerns the right of the human spirit to push forward the limits of human knowledge; Islamic thought, like all other traditions of thought, can only benefit from such an epistemological attitude.[13] Besides, continues Arkoun, Professor van Ess knows perfectly well that Muslims today suffer from the politics of repression of free thought, especially in the religious domain. Or to put it another way, we are not doing Islam any favors by shielding it from Enlightenment values.

I have already noted how and why western scholarship has moved from objectivity to Islamic apologetics pure and simple;[14] a trend remarked in 1968 by Maxime Rodinson:

> In this way the anticolonialist left, whether Christian or not, often goes so far as to sanctify Islam and the contemporary ideologies of the Muslim world. . . . A historian like Norman Daniel has gone so far as to number among the conceptions permeated with medievalism or imperialism, any criticisms of the Prophet's moral attitudes, and to accuse of like tendencies any exposition of Islam and its characteristics by means of the normal mechanisms of human history. Understanding has given way to apologetics pure and simple.[15]

Professor Montgomery Watt has been taken to task in recent years by scholars for his overoptimistic attitude to the Islamic sources of the history of early Islam. Their arguments against Watt have been superbly summarized below by Ibn Rawandi. I, however, have severely criticized Watt for other reasons: for his protective and ultimately patronizing and insincere stance to Islam and Muslims, a position that goes beyond dispassionate scholarship and veers between Islamic apologetics on the one hand and condescension on the other. Watt's bad faith (*mauvaise foi*) is in evidence when he writes in the preface to his celebrated biography of Muhammad, "in order to avoid deciding whether the Koran is or is not the Word of God, I have refrained from using the expressions 'God says' and 'Muhammad says' when referring to the Koran, and have simply said 'the Koran says.' "[16]

Bernard Lewis has remarked that such measures have tended to make the discussions of modern orientalists "cautious and sometimes insincere." That is putting the matter kindly. Professor Watt is a devout Christian, an ordained priest, in fact, who does not believe that the Koran is the Word of God. But the curious fact is that this maneuvering has not endeared him to thoughtful Muslims, who ask why Watt obstinately refrains from converting to Islam if it is such a wonderful religion as he claims. The irony of a Christian cleric apologizing for the most anti-Christian of religions is not missed by the Muslims. Here is what Hussein Amin, an Egyptian intellectual, diplomat, and liberal practicing Muslim, has to say about Watt:

> Watt defends Islam and her Prophet better than the most zealous Muslims. . . . However, in our opinion, there is in his position a profoundly incomprehensible contradiction, such that we prefer in certain ways the biography by Muir,[17] which has the advantage of honestly coming out in its true colors.[18]

Hussein then quotes several examples of Watt's rather dishonest attempts to ingratiate himself with Muslims[19]—the maneuvering referred to above. Hussein ends with the following quote from Watt and then comments on it:

With the greatly increased contacts between Muslims and Christians during the last quarter of a century, it has become imperative for a Christian scholar not to offend Muslim readers gratuitously, but as far as possible to present his arguments in a form acceptable to them. Courtesy and an eirenic outlook certainly now demand that we should not speak of the Koran as the product of Muhammad's conscious mind; but I hold that the same demand is also made by sound scholarship.[20]

Despite all our admiration for the works of W. Montgomery Watt, this position seems to us, in a word, incomprehensible and unacceptable. First of all why should there be a connection between the present development of links between Islam and the West, and the necessity for the Westerners to judge the Prophet fairly, even to exalt his merits, . . . ? If there is in Europe a mounting interest in the Arab cause, which is evident for example in the proliferation of Islamic cultural festivals, or in the relatively large number of copies printed of contemporary Arab writers, perhaps we shall soon be studying the impact of the global energy crisis on the writing of the biography of the Prophet in oil-consuming countries!

All that is, in the end, not very surprising. On the other hand what is more surprising, and which grieves us more deeply, is to see Muslims besottedly applauding any old Western author, including those without a specialist knowledge of Islam such as Gustave le Bon or Carlyle, who defends the Prophet, and inversely, take exception to those who denigrate him. There is nothing to be proud of in the praise of the former, nor any reason to get excited about the calumnies of the latter. Why be proud of praise which results more often from the atheism of the author and his desire to shock his compatriots, to prove his independence of thought or his objectivity, even to safeguard his material interests or to draw closer to the Muslim states . . . ?

The moment has come for Muslims to write a new biography of the Prophet . . . which does not leave out "that which could offend certain readers."

No, Muslims do not need patronizing liberals to meet them "halfway"! Muslims need to write, for example, an honest biography of the Prophet that does not shun the truth, least of all cover it up with the dishonest subterfuge of condescending Western scholars. However, as Rodinson points out, writing in 1963, most Muslim biographers of the Prophet lack any critical sense whatsoever: "Numerous works in Arabic appear each year evidencing blind confidence in sources that are several centuries later than the events which they report. The accounts found in our Muslim sources of events which occurred at the beginning of Islam do indeed require special methodological study, for the process of oral transmission constitutes a problem whose implications have not yet been fully explored."[21] But, as Rodinson hastens to add in a footnote, this "is in no way a question of an incapacity congenital to the 'Arab spirit.' Many contemporary Arab authors have given us excellent historical studies and remarkable critical editions which in all points conform to the rules of historical and philological method. However, in the present state of affairs and for precise sociological reasons, the biography of Muhammad is a subject that is taboo and is permitted only when written as apologetic and edifying literature."[22]

Rodinson gives us an admirable survey of the writings of Arab scholars, which are quite worthless from the scientific point of view: "[F]or complex sociological reasons, the larger part of [the] educated bourgeois public [in the Middle East] rejected the scientific enthusiasm of the preceding generation and returned to the faith of the ancestors. This explains the immense popularity of the biography of the Prophet published in 1935 by the writer and politician, Muhammad Husain Haykal. . . . In an easy and modern style, Haykal retraces the life of the Prophet, writing a 'scientific study according to the modern western method' " (5th ed., p. 18). But if this "scientific method" leads him to reject a certain number of miracles attributed (at a late date) to the Prophet and to interpret some of them in "natural" fashion, it also leads him to affirm the foundations of the Muslim faith. He undertakes a critical study of the sources but only for the purpose of attacking certain narratives preserved by Muslim tradition that appear offensive to the modern conception of the Prophet. It is a skillful reconstruction of the life of Muhammad suited to the needs of a modern apologetic, "but it is far from being scientific in its viewpoint." In an even more damning footnote, Rodinson specifies all the shortcomings of Haykal's decidedly unscientific methodology; "one might mention as typical passages the attack on the narrative of the 'satanic verses' inspired in Muhammad by the devil" (Haykal, pp. 160–67), and the reconstruction of the history of the "revolt" of the wives of the Prophet (pp. 447ff.). The work is interspersed with discussions that are purely apologetic and with attacks against "the Orientalists" of whom he mentions only the popular work of Dermenghem and especially the work of the American author, Washington Irving, written in 1849. Occasionally, there are opportune silences, as, for example, the murder of Ka'b b. al-Ashraf (pp. 278ff.); he passes over in silence the incitement to murder by Muhammad (Ibn Hisham, p. 550). There are even some falsifications: according to Haykal [p. 339], the Jews of Qurayza chose "as though they were blinded by fate" the arbiter Sa'd b. Mu'adh who was going to decide in favor of their massacre; however, according to the early sources it was Muhammad who made that decision."[23]

Rodinson continues his survey of Arabic works: "At about the same time, the Egyptian savant, Ahmad Amin [father of Hussein Amin, discussed above], in a book entitled Fajr al-Islam (the Dawn of Islam, Cairo, 1929) commenced an extensive history of Arab and Muslim civilization. However, he carefully avoided the difficult and dangerous area of the biography of the founder."[24] The Egyptian man of letters, Taha Husain, had got into a great deal of trouble in 1926 for his work, *Fi'sh-Shi'r al-Jahili,* in which he questioned the historical veracity of the Koran. Charged with blasphemy, he was forced to withdraw his book, and lost his university post. But in 1933, "Taha Husain quickly came around to a less threatening approach; following the literary style of Jules Lemaitre, he wrote delightful narratives in the margin of the sira (the traditional life of Muhammad) [in *Ala Hamish as Sira,* Cairo, 1933]. The talented essayist Abbas Mahmud al-Aqqad, a man of fascist sympathies, assumed the apologetic stance in a more virulent, 'updated' manner, but also with less caution. *From the scientific point of view one may disregard such works.* "[25] The one exception seems to have been the Arab Marxist, Bandali Jawzi,[26] who "did raise the question of the historical forces at work in the rise of Islam, and he did so without recourse to the principle of divine intervention."[27]

Rodinson was writing of the twenties and thirties, but unfortunately things have not improved a great deal, as can be seen by the embarrassment caused in Cairo in the 1980s by Hussein Amin himself with his gentle but courageous skepticism. Nothing could illustrate with greater irony the fact that not much has changed for the better since Rodinson wrote his survey in 1963 than the fate of *Mohammed,* the celebrated biography of the Prophet by Maxime Rodinson himself, first published in 1961.[28] Despite the fact that Rodinson's very conventional biography has been available in Egypt for over twenty years, it was withdrawn in May 1998 from the curriculum of the American University in Cairo's History of Arab Society course after complaints from a newspaper columnist, Salah Muntaser of the government-run newspaper, *Al-Ahram,* and the ministry of higher education. According to the Minister, Mufeed Shehab, the book contained "fabrications harmful to the respected prophet and to the Islamic religion,"[29] even though Rodinson had grounded his work solidly and entirely on Muslims sources. Rodinson had upset Muntasser by suggesting that Muhammad had been influenced by Jews and Christians, and by explicitly avowing that he (Rodinson) did not believe the Koran was the word of God. Perhaps Muntasser had in mind the following passage in Rodinson's work: "May any Muslims who happen to read these lines forgive my plain speaking. For them the Koran is the book of Allah and I respect their faith. But I do not share it and I do not wish to fall back, as many orientalists have done, on equivocal phrases to disguise my real meaning. This may perhaps be of assistance in remaining on good terms with individuals and governments professing Islam; but I have no wish to deceive anyone. Muslims have every right not to read the book or to acquaint themselves with the ideas of a non-Muslim, but if they do so, they must expect to find things put forward there which are blasphemous to them. It is evident that I do not believe that the Koran is the book of Allah."[30]

While Rodinson is to be commended for his frankness, his statement quoted above amounts to an apology, and I wonder if he has entirely avoided a certain moral ambiguity in his position, rather like the health warnings on packets of cigarettes. In any case, his position has not done his work any good in Egypt.

THE SOURCES AND THEIR RELIABILITY

A. Literary Sources: Sira and Maghazi

If we were to examine Fuat Sezgin's *History of Arabic Literature*,[31] we would get a falsely optimistic picture of the sources for the history of pre-Islamic Arabia, the life of Muhammad, and the rise of Islam and its history up to the year 1000 C.E., since Sezgin gives the name of some seventy historians. Alas, the writings of these historians are not extant, and we only know them through quotations of them by later historians.[32]

Our knowledge of early Islam and its founder rests on the writings we call sira and *al-Maghazi*, and also the Koran, Koranic exegesis (tafsir), and the Hadith (the traditions).

Sira, in our context, means "biography" or "the life and times of." "The sira," *sirat rasul allah* or *al-sira al nabawiyya* have been the most commonly used names for the traditional account of the Prophet's life and background.[33] *Sira* even came to mean, in the end, the account of Muhammad's life and background as transmitted by Ibn Hisham on the basis of the work by Ibn Ishaq.[34]

According to the definition in the *Encyclopedia of Islam*, second edition, "*al-maghazi* (also *maghazi 'l-nabi, maghazi rasul allah*), a term which, from the time of the work on the subject ascribed to al-Waqidi (d. 207/823), if not earlier, has signified in particular the military expeditions and raids organized by the Prophet Muhammad in the Medinan period."[35] But this term in the end also acquired a broader sense and seems to have been used more or less synonymously with the term sira.

Stefan Leder has usefully summarized the several fields of Arabic literature that deal with early Islamic history, and introduces us to the various Arabic terms that we use in this domain, which are indispensable for any understanding of Muslim historical writing:

Prophetic tradition (Hadith), which contains countless reports about sayings and deeds of Muhammad; Koranic commentaries (tafsir), where revelation is related to the life of the Prophet; historiography, and finally adab literature, which displays the ideal of refinement and unites entertaining and didactic tendencies.

Historiographical literature about early Islamic times is divided mainly according to historical periods. Material on the life of the Prophet (sira), the military campaigns directed by the Prophet or his Companions (*maghazi*), and the conquests (*futuh*), as well as particular cases (*waqa, maqtal*) are kept distinct, although not entirely separate. Biographically organized works (*tabaqat*) and collections of hadith may include all of these materials. Narratives about the pre-Islamic battle-days (*ayyam al-arab*) are often considered to be the predecessors of and model for Arabic historiographical narration; this seems questionable, however, since the extant textual evidence cannot claim an origin prior to other branches of literature about early Islamic times.

The historiographical and biographical compilations, works on poets and poetry, and those which treat linguistic matters, are to a great extent compilations of short texts. These include simple statements, utterances of authoritative scholars, saints, or statesmen, reports of events, and—sometimes rather complex—stories about historical events and personalities. These texts, which may vary in length from one line to several pages are designated by the term *khabar* (pl. *akhbar* [*akhbari* pl. *akhbariyun* = the collector and/or compiler of *akhbar*]).[36]

Here it would perhaps be appropriate to include the terms *qussas* and *qisas*. Qisas denotes particularly the genre of tales and myth relating to the prophets of the Koran or the Old Testament, but is also used to designate other stories that indulge in dramatic effects and colorful descriptions, all derived from the style of popular storytellers, *qussas*.[37]

I shall be begin with a list[38] of the most prominent historians giving both their Islamic (A.H.) and Common Era dates, for this enables us to see immediately how near, or more frequently, how far they are from the events they describe.

1. Aban b. 'Uthman al-Bajali (ca. 20/640–100/718). He was the son of the murdered caliph 'Uthman, and took part in the campaign against his father's slayers. He seems to have written a book on *maghazi*, which has not survived. Neither Ibn Ishaq nor al-Waqidi cite him.[39]

2. 'Urwa b. al-Zubayr b. al-Awwam (23/643–94/712). He was a cousin of the Prophet, and considered an authority on the early history of Islam. It is uncertain whether he wrote a book, but there are many traditions that have been handed down in his name by Ibn Ishaq, Ibn Sa'd, and al-Tabari. For this reason he is often referred to as the founder of Islamic history.

3. Shurabil b. Sa'd (d. 123/740). Little is known about him, though it

appears he wrote a *maghazi* book. However, many later writers considered him unreliable and thus he is seldom quoted.

4. Wahb b. Munabbih (34/654–110/728). He seems to have been a South Arabian of possibly Persian origin with a deep knowledge of Jewish and Christian scriptures and traditions. Wahb wrote the *Kitab al-Mubtada,* which inspired many Muslim versions of the lives of the prophets. However, much was attributed to him for which he was not responsible. Wahb collected the *maghazi,* and this has been confirmed by the discovery of a fragment of the lost work on papyri written in 228/842, the so-called Heidelberg papyrus. Wahb himself did not know of the use of isnads, that is the chain of transmitters of a particular tradition. Ibn Ishaq, Ibn Sa'd, al-Tabari, and al-Waqidi do not use Wahb for the life of the Prophet but for the beginnings of Christianity in South Arabia.[40]

5. Asim b. 'Umar b. Qtada al-Ansari (d. ca. 120/737). He lectured in Damascus on the *maghazi* of the Prophet and his Companions, and probably committed his lectures to writing, though this is much disputed by skeptics who point out that this claim is based on later writings. He does not always cite his authorities or isnads. Ibn Ishaq seems to have attended al-Ansari's lectures.

6. Muhammad b. Muslim b. Shihab al-Zuhri (51/671–124/741). He was a member of a distinguished Meccan family of Zuhra, of which he wrote a history. He is sometimes credited with a book of *maghazi,* but Zuhri's compilations were probably confined to collections of traditions of the Prophet and his companions of which he very assiduously collected a vast number.[41] His students took down notes of his lectures which have survived; Ibn Ishaq often cites him as an authority. However, skeptics point out that the claim that Zuhri used writing are based on later historians, and thus cannot be accepted uncritically.

7. Abdullah b. Abu Bakr b. Muhammad b. 'Amr b. Hazm (d. 130/747 or 135/752). He was one of Ibn Ishaq's most important informants. There is no evidence of any book by Abdullah, and he does not seem to have bothered with isnads when passing down traditions to his hearers.

8. Abu'l-Aswad Muhammad b. 'Abdu'l-Rahman b. Naufal (d. 131/748 or 137/754). He wrote a book of *maghazi* that seems to remain faithful to Urwa b. al-Zubayr in its essentials.

9. Musa b. 'Uqba (ca. 55/674–141/758) A fragment of his work has survived and was published by Sachau in 1904, the so-called Berlin manuscript.[42] Many distinguished traditionists felt his book was the most important and trustworthy of all, rivaling that of his contemporary Ibn Ishaq, and yet, surprisingly, not much of his work has survived. Ibn Ishaq himself never mentions him, though he is quoted by later historians like al-Tabari, al-Waqidi, and others. Musa for his part leaned heavily on al-Zuhri, much idealizing the Prophet.

10. Ibn Ishaq (ca. 85/704–150/767).[43] He is one of our main authorities on the life and times of the Prophet. His family was involved in transmissions of Hadith and Ibn Ishaq followed suit. He left Medina where he was born for good, probably because of the enmity of certain people like the traditionist Malik b. Anas; he eventually settled in Baghdad. Apart from the *Sira* he is also credited with a *Kitab al Khulafa* (sometimes called *Ta'rikh al-khulafa'—A History of the Caliphs)* and a book of *Sunan.* His reputation seems to have varied considerably among the early Muslim critics; some found him very sound (e.g., al-Zuhri, who spoke of him as "the most knowledgeable of men in *maghazi*"), while others regarded him as a liar in relation to Hadith (e.g., al-Athram, Sulayman al-Taymi, and Wuhayb b. Khalid).[44] However, it is of the utmost importance to realize that the *Sira* of Ibn Ishaq is *not* extant in its original form, and is not preserved as a single work. It has been preserved in two recensions, one by Ibn Hisham (d. 218/833; see below) and another by Yunus b. Bukayr (d. 199/814–815); each text seems to vary from the other. Other parts of Ibn Ishaq's work have been quoted by Muhammad b. Salaam al-Harrani (d. 191/807) and thirteen other students, compilers, and historians who had heard his lectures in various towns like Medina, Kufa, Basra, and so on. Thus, the lost original of Ibn Ishaq's work has to be restored or recovered from at least fifteen different versions, excluding that of Ibn Hisham (with the towns where the individuals heard Ibn Ishaq's lectures:[45]

a. Ibrahim b. Sa'd, 110/728–184/800, Medina
b. Ziyad b. 'Abdullah al-Bakkai, d.183/799, Kufa
c. 'Abdullah b. Idris al-Audi, 115/733–192/807, Kufa
d. Yunus b. Bukayr, d.199/815, Kufa
e. 'Abda b. Sulayman, d.187/802 or 188/803, Kufa
f. 'Abdullah b. Numayr, 115/733–199/814, Kufa
g. Yahya b. Said al-Umawi, 114/732–194/809, Baghdad
h. Jarir b. Hazim, 85/704–170/786, Basra
i. Harun b. Abu'Isa, Basra?
j. Salama b. al-Fadl al-Abrash, d. 191/806, Ray
k. Ali b. Mujahid, d. ca.180/796, Ray
l. Ibrahim b. al-Mukhtar, Ray
m. Sa'id b. Bazi
n. 'Uthman b. Saj
o. Muhammad b. Salama al-Harrani, d. 191/806

These facts have led many scholars to conclude that "there has hardly been any written standard text by Ibn Ishaq himself and that we depend on his transmitters, whose texts should be studied synoptically, in all their variants."[46] Sellheim, on the other hand, has tried to discern three layers of sources in Ibn Ishaq, an original layer reflecting historical reality, a second layer reflecting legendary material about the Prophet, and a top layer reflecting the political tendencies of Ibn Ishaq's own time.[47] Passages left out by Ibn Hisham in his edition have been quoted by later historians like al-Tabari, al-Azraki, and at least ten others. Ibn Ishaq placed the Prophet Muhammad in the tradition of the earlier prophets, which makes him the pivot of world history by adding a history of the caliphs.[48]

11. Ma'mar b. Rashid (d.154/770). His *Kitab al-Maghazi* is preserved within the *Musannaf* of Abd al-Razzak b. Hammam al-San'ani (126/744–211/827). Rashid gathered much of his material from al-Zuhri.

12. Abu Mikhnaf Lut b.Yahya 'l-Azdi (d. 157/774). He is said to have written over thirty historical treatises, and much of his work is quoted by both al-Tabari and Baladhuri. But many writings that were attributed to him are now known to be later forgeries.

13. Sayf b. 'Umar (d. ca. 180/796). He was al-Tabari's principal source for the early Arab conquests and the history of the Caliphate down to the death of 'Ali. The great German scholar, Julius Wellhausen (1844–1918) wrote a devastating critique of Sayf's work in his *Prolegomena zur altesten Geschichte des Islams* (1899), and Sayf's reputation has not been high ever since. Wellhausen places Sayf in what he calls the "artificial" tradition of Arab historical writing, which was full of "tendentious distortions and fictitious tales invented for their literary impact."[49]

14. Yunus b. Bukayr (d. 199/815). As noted above, Yunus is important for his recension of Ibn Ishaa's work, though his version differs from the familiar versions. But what is often forgotten is that Yunus "transmitted materials which do not go back to Ibn Ishaa at all. Yunus was a sira compiler in his own right, whose *Ziyadat al-Maghazi* was quoted by al-Bayhaki, Ibn Kathir and several others."[50]

15. Ibn Hisham (d. 218/833 or 213/828). Born in Egypt, he spent his entire life there. Although he wrote a book on South Arabian antiquities, *Kitab al-Tidjan*, that has survived down to our times, Ibn Hisham is, of course, more famous for his edition of the *Sira* of Ibn Ishaq. Ibn Hisham derived his knowledge of the latter's work from Ziyad al-Bakka'i (d. 183/799), a pupil of Ibn Ishaq who lived mostly in Kufa, but may have travelled to Iraq to study.[51] Al-Bakkai made two copies of Ibn Ishaq's work, one of which reached Ibn Hisham, "whose text, abbreviated, annotated, and sometimes altered, is the main source of our knowledge of the original work."[52]

16. Al-Waqidi (130/747–207/822–23). He wrote over twenty works of a historical nature, but only the *Kitab al-Maghazi* has survived as an independent work. Waqidi's authorities include Musa b. 'Uqba, and he made extensive use of

Ibn Ishaq's work. He was a Shiite, and his zeal for 'Ali is revealed in the details in his history. He is especially important for having established the chronology of the early years of Islam. He is frequently cited by al-Tabari, who also relied upon him for variant narratives. Both Ibn Ishaq and al-Waqidi's reputations have suffered in recent years as a consequence of the trenchant criticisms by Patricia Crone, especially in *Meccan Trade and the Rise of Islam*, pp. 203–30), where she argues that much of the classical Muslim understanding of the Koran rests on the work of storytellers and that this work is of very dubious historical value. These storytellers contributed to the tradition on the rise of Islam, and this is evident in the steady growth of information: "If one storyteller should happen to mention a raid, the next storyteller would know the date of this raid, while the third would know everything that an audience might wish to hear about it."[53] Then, comparing the accounts of the raid of Kharrar by Ibn Ishaq and al-Waqidi, Crone shows that al-Waqidi, influenced by and in the manner of the storytellers, "will always give precise dates, locations, names, where Ibn Ishaq has none, accounts of what triggered the expedition, miscellaneous information to lend color to the event, as well as reasons why, as was usually the case, no fighting took place. No wonder that scholars are fond of al-Waqidi: where else does one find such wonderfully precise information about everything one wishes to know? But given that this information was all unknown to Ibn Ishaq, its value is doubtful in the extreme. And if spurious information accumulated at this rate in the two generations between Ibn Ishaq and al-Waqidi, it is hard to avoid the conclusion that even more must have accumulated in the three generations between the Prophet and Ibn Ishaq."

17. Ibn Sa'd (d. 230/844–45). Ibn Sa'd was al-Waqidi's secretary, and relied considerably on his master's work for his own *Kitab al Tabakat al Kabir*, which is considered the first major biographical dictionary.

18. Al-Baladhuri (d. 279/892). He seems to have been a close friend of the caliphs Mutawwakkil and Musta'in. He studied in Damascus and Emesa, and in Iraq under Ibn Sa'd. Al-Baladhuri is now famous for his two historical works, *Futuh al-Buldun* and *Ansab al-Ashraf*. The former is a history of Muhammad beginning with his wars against the Jews, Mecca, Ta'if, and then the subsequent Arab conquests from the Maghrib to Persia. The latter begins with the sira of the Prophet, and continues with the history of the Abbasids, and so forth. He seems to have relied upon Ibn Ishaq and Ibn Sa'd, among others.[54]

19. 'Ali b. Muhammad al-Mada'ini (d. ca. 225/840). He was a very important source for the Arab conquests of Iran.

20. Al-Tabari (ca. 224 or 225/839–311/923). Born in Tabaristan, he traveled extensively in Egypt, visited Raiy, Basra, and Kufa, but eventually settled down

in Baghdad. A considerable polymath, al-Tabari devoted much time to history, fiqh, the Koran, poetry, grammar, and even mathematics and medicine. His commentary on the Koran, *Djami al Bayan fi Tafsir al Kuran*, or simply *Tafsir*, has survived, and is of great importance since al-Tabari gathered together "ample material of traditional exegesis and thus created a standard work upon which later Kuranic commentators drew; it is still a mine of information for historical and critical research by western scholars."[55] Even more important is al-Tabari's *History of the World, Tarikh al-Rusul wa 'l-Muluk*, beginning with the prophets, patriarchs, and rulers of the early period, and ending precisely at 303 (July 915). Al-Tabari derived much of his material from oral traditions, but also literary sources like the works of Abu Mikhnaf, and of course the *Sira* of Ibn Ishaq, the writings of al-Waqidi, Ibn Sa'd, and so on.

Characteristics of Sira Texts

Although the above historians had differing approaches to the writing of the life of the Prophet and the rise of Islam, certain broad common themes seem to emerge. They all want to defend, embellish, and "build up the image of Muhammad in rivalry to the prophets of other communities, to depict him as a statesman of international stature, to elaborate on Kuranic texts and create a chronological framework for them, to record the deeds of the early Muslims, . . . and to set standards for the new community."[56]

Most of them recount recount details of the raids, military expeditions, and eighty political assassinations carried out by the Prophet and his companions, with many romanticized deeds of heroism, single combats, and so on. Many give the genealogies (*nasab*, pl. *ansab*) of the various clans and individual Companions who took part in the events. It is also very clear as was probably first pointed out by C. H. Becker,[57] and more recently John Wansbrough[58] that large parts of the sira were inspired by the Koran; some texts merely paraphrase a Koranic passage. There are abundant examples of what are called the "occasions of revelation" (*asbab al-nuzul*), that is, accounts of the particular occasion when a certain passage was revealed. For example, when the Prophet was mocked the verse "Apostles have been mocked before you . . ." (sura 6, verse 10) was revealed.

C. H. Becker speaks of "exegetical elaborations of Koranic allusions," and he is probably referring to the many sira texts that expand on a Koranic passage rather like a Jewish midrash; for example, the episode of the "Satanic Verses" recounted in al-Tabari is an elaboration of sura 22, verse 52. There are quite long narratives in the sira that are rather flimsily built on various verses in the Koran.[59]

The sira tried to place the Prophet Muhammad among the prophets of old and to assert the identity of Islam among the other, older religions of Judaism, Christianity, and Manichaeism; in so doing, it extensively mined the already existing repertoire of symbols, myths, and structures and put them to use for the Muslims' own newly emerging system of belief. The twelve tribes of Israel and the twelve disciples of Jesus are paralleled, for example, by the twelve leaders appointed, at al-Aqaba, by Muhammad from the Ansar, the Helpers (that is, those citizens of Medina who rallied to Muhammad after his flight from Mecca).[60] The sira also contains stories of miracles brought about by God through Muhammad, or by Muhammad himself as proofs of his prophethood. The sira incorporates speeches and sermons of the Prophet, but also "documents" such as treaties, letters putatively written by Muhammad to foreign rulers, and above all the so-called "Constitution of Medina," which is an agreement between Muhammad and the "believers and Muslims of Quraysh and Yathrib, and those who follow them, join them and strive alongside them" including Jewish groups.[61]

B. Manuscripts, Papyri[62]

1. Khirbat al-Mird Papyrus, early second/eighth century. This papyrus contains just eight lines about the Battle of Badr, studied by Grohmann.
2. Chicago Papyrus (Oriental Institute, ms. no. 17635), late second/eighth century. This papyrus deals with Badr, Bi'r Ma'una, and the B. al-Nadir
3. The Berlin Manuscript, fourth/ninth century. Published by Sachau in 1904, this manuscript contains a short text of Musa b. Ukba (ca. 55/674–141/758).
4. The Heidelberg Manuscript, early third/ninth century, refers to the meeting at al-Akaba, the conference of Kuraysh, the Hijra, and the expedition against Khatham, which has an isnad, a chain of transmitters, going back to Wahb b. Munabbih.

Thus only the Khirbat al-Mird papyrus of eight lines, dating from the early second/eighth century, is from the pre-Abbasid period. Otherwise we only have citations once-removed or more.

C. Non–Muslim Sources[63]

1. John of Nikiou (seventh century). Coptic Bishop; author of an account of the Arab conquest of Egypt, of which an Ethiopic translation survives. He describes the Muslim yoke as being "heavier than the yoke which had been laid on Israel by Pharaoh." (*Chronique de Jean, Eveque de Nikiou*, edited and translated by Hermann Zotenberg, Paris, 1879; *The Chronicle of John, Bishop of Nikiu*, translated R. H. Charles, London, 1916.)

2. Sebeos (Sepeos) (late seventh century). Armenian Bishop. Author of a *History of Heraclius*, which starts at the end of the fifth century, bringing the story up to 661, his own times. (*Histoire d' Héraclius*, translated by F. Macler, Paris 1904.)

3. Khuzistan Syriac Chronicle (written in the 670s). Mentions Muhammad as ruler of the Arabs. (*Chronica Minora*, edited by I. Guidi, Louvain, 1903–1907)

4. Patriarch Sophronius of Jerusalem[64] (written 634–38). Speaking of the Arab invaders as godless barbarians, the text gives a gruesome picture of the atrocities, but sees it all as a punishment for the sins of the Christians. (*Patrologia Graeco-Latina*, edited J. P. Migne, Paris 1857–66.)

5. Doctrina Iacobi (ca. 636). This is a Greek anti-Jewish tract, in which we find that Muhammad is presented as being alive at the time of the conquest of Palestine, that is, two years after his death according to the Muslim tradition. The Prophet is reported as preaching the advent of "the anointed one who is to come," that is, the coming of the messiah. (F. Nau,"La Didascalie de Jacob," in *Patrologia Orientalis*, edited by R. Graffin and F. Nau, Paris 1903.)

6. Sahdona the Nestorian (written in mid-seventh century). Talks of the Arab invasion in catastrophic terms. (Martyrius [Sahdona], *Oeuvres spirituelles*, vol. 1 edited and translated by A. de Halleux [CSCO, Scroprores Syri, vols. 86 ff] Louvain 1960.)

7. Bar Penkaye (late seventh century). A Nestorian Christian writing in Syriac that has some interesting details about the early Arab conquests, but significantly does not mention the existence of any sacred book among the Arabs. (*Sources syriaques*, edited and translated by Alphonse Mingana, Leipzig, n.d.)

8. Jacob of Edessa (late seventh century). Sees the Arab invasions as divine punishment of the Christians. (*Scholia on passages of the Old Testament*, edited and translated by G. Philips, London 1864.)

9. Pseudo-Methodius (late seventh century). His "apocalypse" also talks of the Ishmaelite (Arab) yoke. (*Vatican codex Syr. 58*, see M. Kmosko, "Das Ratsel des Pseudomethodius," *Byzantion*, 1931.)

10. Theophilus of Edessa (d. 785). A Maronite historian who wrote a chronicle extending from Creation to the Abassid revolution and the collapse of the Umayyad caliphate. As his work has been lost, Theophilus's work is only known to us through citations from later writers like Bar Hebraeus, Michael the Syrian, and Dionysius (842). He later served as astronomer to the Abassid caliph al-Mahdi, and translated Homer into Syriac.

11. The Apocalypse of Samuel al-Qalamun (eighth Century). A prophecy in Christian Arabic where the Coptic saint Samuel of Qalamun uses the term Hijra for the Arab conquerors. (*Patrologia Orientalis*, vol 3; *L'Apocalypse de Samuel*,

superieur de Deir el Qalamoun, edited and translated by J. Ziadeh, in *Revue de l'Orient chrétien* 1915–17.)

12. Pseudo-Dionysius of Tell-Mahre (eighth century). Author of a Syriac *Chronicle* (once wrongly attributed to the ninth-century patriarch) that describes the conditions of the peasant in Mesopotamia. The chronicle ends in the year 774. (*Chronique de Denys de Tell Mahré* [Pseudo-Dionysius], edited and translated by Jean-Baptiste Chabot, Paris, 1895.)

13. The Hebrew Apocalypse, "Secrets of Rabbi Simon ben Yohay" (mid-eighth century). It has embedded in it an earlier apocalypse, contemporary with the Arab conquests. (*Bet ha-Midrasch*, A. Jellinek, Leipzig 1855; B. Lewis, "An Apocalyptic Vision of Islamic History," *BSOAS*, 1950.)

14. Ghevond (Levond) (late eighth century). Armenian historian, author of *History of the Wars and Conquests of the Arabs in Armenia. (Histoire des Guerres et des conquetes des Arabes en Armenie*, translated from Armenian by Garabed V. Chahnazarian, Paris 1856.)

15. Theophanes (d. 818). Byzantine (Greek) Historian whose work ultimately derives from the work of Theophilus of Edessa. (*Chronographia*, edited by K. de Boor, Leipzig, 1883–85). Important for our knowledge of the Arab conquests.

16. Dionysius of Tell-Mahre (d. 845). Patriarch of the Jacobites;[65] extracts of his *Chronicle* are preserved in Michael the Syrian's twelfth-century work. He travelled to Mosul, Baghdad, and Egypt.

17. Agapius (d. ca. 950). Syrian Melkite[66] wrote a history of the Arab conquests of Syria in Arabic, which is ultimately derived from the Syriac Historian Theophilus of Edessa (ca. 749–50). (*Kitab al-unwan*, edited by Louis Cheikho, Paris 1912; *CSCO 65, Scr.Arabici.*)

18. Thomas Artsruni (Ardzruni) (tenth century). An Armenian historian who names the Prophet's base as Midian, and identifies Mecca with Pharan located in Arabia Petraea. He considers the Koran as the work of Salman al-Farsi. (*Histoire des Ardzrounis*, in *Collections d'Historiens Arméniens*, edited and translated by M. F. Brosset, Paris, 1874.)

19. Severus b. al-Muqaffa (tenth century). A Coptic bishop of Ashmunein (Egypt) from 955–987, Severus is important for his observations about the direction in which the early Muslims prayed. (*History of the Patriarchs of the Egyptian Church, Known as the History of the Holy Church*, translated from Arabic by Yassa Abd al-Masih, O. H. E. Burmester, and A. Khater, 6 pts. in 3 vols., Cairo, 1943–70.)

20. Michael the Syrian (twelfth century). Jacobite patriarch of Antioch from 1166 to 1199. His *Chronicle* reproduces earlier sources, before describing con-

temporary events. (*Chronique de Michel le Syrien*, 4 vols., edited and translated by Jean-Baptiste Chabot, Paris 1899–1905.)

21. Chronicle of 1234 (*Chronicum ad annum Christi 1234 pertinens*, edited by J. B. Chabot, Paris, 1916–20; CSCO, Scr.Syri.)

22. Bar Hebraeus (Abu al-Faraj, d. 1286). Bar Hebraeus was born in Armenia of a Jewish convert to Christianity. He seems to have mastered Syriac, Greek, and Arabic, and was learned in theology, philosophy, and medicine. He was consecrated bishop in 1246, and eventually rose to a high post among the Eastern Jacobite (Monophysite) Christians. He wrote a universal history in Syriac, transmitting the learning of his predecessors. (*The Chronography of Gregory Abul-Faraj 1225–1286. The son of Aaron, the Hebrew physician commonly known as BAR HEBRAEUS, being the first part of his Political History of the World,* translated from Syriac by E. A. T. Wallis Budge, 2 vols., 1st ed., Amsterdam, 1932.)

E. Inscriptions: The Dome of the Rock, Jerusalem, 691

Strictly speaking, if not the oldest surviving building of Islamic architecture,[67] the Dome of the Rock is "in all probability the first Islamic monument that was meant to be a major aesthetic achievement."[68] It was built in 691 during the reign of Abd al-Malik (ruled 685–705). What is important for our purposes are the inscriptions in blue-and-gold mosaic that decorate the inner and outer faces of the octagonal arcade and are also on the hammered copper plaques installed on the exterior faces of the lintels over the inner doors in the eastern and northern entrances respectively.[69] They consist of passages from the Koran, but often diverging from the standard text of the Holy Book of the Muslims, particularly in the copper plaques. Many of the passages challenge Christian dogma, and the whole edifice can be seen as a symbol of the "emergence of the self-definition of Islam over and against Christianity."[70]

F. Coins

It is significant that until circa 70 A.H. no coins bear the name Muhammad or any specifically Islamic phrases (see Koren and Nevo's essay, "Methodological Approaches to Islamic Studies"). No seventh-century coin identifies the Arab era as that of the Hijra. Coins from Islamic lands have, of course, already taught us a great deal about political and administrative history, providing evidence about the reigns of rulers and the territorial extent of their influence, for instance.[71]

G. Archaeology

Koren and Nevo have interesting observations on the fact that there are no pagan inscriptions in Classical Arabic. Cook and Crone[72] point out the importance of K. A. C. Creswell's discovery while excavating the Great Mosque of Wasit: "the mosque [was] first discovered rest[ing] on another mosque which faced south-west, instead of being properly oriented towards Mekka, the difference being about 33."[73]

However, as Humphreys has remarked, Islamic archaeology has yet to make the contributions to historical studies which we might hope for. Until recently, very few trained archaeologists were interested in the Islamic period. That the situation has changed can be seen in the many archaeological journals being published in Islamic countries,[74] not only in Iraq, Iran, Syria, Egypt, Turkey, and Jordan, but also in Saudi Arabia. Koren and Nevo also point to very exciting finds in the Negev desert that could have far reaching consequences for our knowledge of the Rise of Islam.

H. Conclusions

While certain historians remain skeptical about the value of papyri, archaeology, and non-Muslim writings for reconstructing our knowledge of the beginnings of Islam—"An adequate and convincing reconstruction of Islam's first century from these materials alone is simply not possible"[75]—others like Alphonse Mingana, and in recent years Wansbrough, Cook, Crone, and Nevo and Koren have used the non-Muslims sources, including the archaeological, epigraphic, and numismatic evidence, to reconstruct a picture of the rise of Islam that is startlingly different from the traditional one familiar to us from the exclusively Muslim literary sources. Mingana was perhaps the first to look at the Syriac and Armenian Christian sources to show that "the Christian historians of the whole of the seventh century had no idea that the 'Hagarian' conquerors had any sacred book; similar is the case among historians and theologians of the beginning of the eighth century. It is only towards the end of the first quarter of this century that the Koran became the theme of conversation in Nestorian, Jacobite, and Melchite ecclesiastical circles."[76] Since Ibn Rawandi very ably discusses the work of Wansbrough, Cook, and Crone below, I shall not dwell upon it here, but their conclusions are, very generally speaking, that "Islam" did not somehow emerge fully developed as the traditional accounts would have us believe but slowly over a long period of time as the Arab conquerors came into contact with the far older cultures and civilizations, which pushed the Arabs to question and forge[77] their own religious and cultural identity. It is worth pointing out that this thesis is different from and far more radical than the commonly held opinion that not all the Arab tribes at the time of death of the Prophet had adopted Islam. For instance, Renan contends that apart from a few thousand men close to Muhammad there was only undisguised incredulity with the majority of tribesmen continuing their ancient ways. Sprenger held a similar view; and more recently, Humphreys has asked, "ought we to imagine that the mass of new Muslims— reluctant converts from Quraysh and the rebellious tribes of the Ridda wars—had more than an inkling of what the new revelation was or how it ought to affect their lives? Should we not assume that they continued to direct their conduct in large part according to the values and attitudes of the Jahiliyya?"[78] (Humphreys is, of course, relying on the traditional account, which is precisely the account Wansbrough is skeptical about.) Cook and Crone go further than that and argue that "Islam" simply did not exist at that time (632 C.E.) for anyone to convert to it, since there were *no* Muslims at all. The earliest evidence of the use of the word "Muslim" is the Dome of the Rock, 690 C.E.; early coins of the Arab conquerors do not bear any specific Islamic legends. The tribesmen did not know the Koran simply because it did not exist, for it was put together piecemeal at a much later date. In other words, all the traditional accounts are hopelessly wrong.

I. *Koran*

Michael Cook sums up what historical material we can glean from the Koran:

> Taken on its own, the Koran tells us very little about the events of Muhammad's career. It does not narrate these events, but merely refers to them; and in doing so, it has a tendency not to name names. Some do occur in contemporary contexts: four religious communities are named (Jews, Christians, Magians, and the mysterious Sabians), as are three Arabian deities (all female), three humans (of whom Muhammad is one), two ethnic groups (Quraysh and the Romans), and nine places. Of the places, four are mentioned in military connections (Badr, Mecca, Hunayn, Yathrib), and four are connected with the sanctuary (three of them we have already met in connection with the rites of pilgrimage, while the fourth is "Bakka," said to be an alternative name for Mecca). The final place is Mount Sinai, which seems to be associated with the growing of olives. Leaving aside the ubiquitous Christians and Jews, none of these names occurs very often: Muhammad is named[79] four or five times (once as "Ahmad"), the Sabians thrice, Mount Sinai twice, and the rest once each. Identifying what the Koran is talking about in a contemporary context is therefore usually impossible

without interpretation. . . . Without it we could probably infer that the protago-
nist of the Koran was Muhammad, that the scene of his life was in western
Arabia, and that he bitterly resented the frequent dismissal of his claims to
prophecy by his contemporaries. But we could not tell that the sanctuary was in
Mecca, or that Muhammad himself came from there, and we could only guess
that he established in Yathrib. We might indeed prefer a more northerly location
altogether, on the grounds that the site of God's destruction of Lot's people (i.e.,
Sodom) is said to be one which those addressed pass by morning and night
(Koran 37 verse 137–38).[80]

J. Hadith

The Hadith, or the books of tradition, are the records of what Muhammad did,
what he enjoined, what was done in his presence, and what he did not forbid.
They also include the authoritative sayings and doings of the Companions of the
Prophet. The doings and sayings of the Prophet are traced back to him through a
series of putatively trustworthy witnesses—any particular chain of transmitters is
called an *isnad*, while the text or the real substance of the report is called a *matn*.

There are said to be six correct or authentic collections of traditions accepted
by Sunni Muslims, namely, the compilations of al-Bukhari (d. 870), Muslim ibn
al-Hajjaj (d. 875), Ibn Maja (d. 887), Abu Dawud (d.889), al-Tirmidhi (d. 892),
and al-Nisai (d. 915). One usually adds to this list the name of Ahmad ibn Hanbal
(d. 855), whose great encyclopedia of traditions called the Musnad contains
nearly 29,000 traditions and has "been the subject of pious reading."

John Wansbrough raised doubts about the authenticity of all early Muslim
written sources in general, while Goldziher and Schacht questioned the authenticity of both the isnads and the *matns* of the Hadith literature specifically. Faced
with Goldziher's and Schacht's impeccably documented arguments, historians
began to panic and devised spurious ways of keeping skepticism at bay, by, for
instance, postulating ad hoc distinctions between legal and historical traditions.
But as Humphreys says, the Hadith and historical khabar (reports/anecdotes)
were very similar in their formal structure; furthermore, many eighth- and ninth-
century Muslim scholars had worked on both kinds of texts. "Altogether, if
hadith isnads were suspect, so then should be the isnads attached to historical
reports."[81] Similarly, the resemblance of the legal Hadiths in form and content
with exegetical Hadiths suggest that the same doubts apply to the latter also.[82]

K. The Nature of the Literary Evidence: A Dialogue on Methodology [83]

> *All we know is what we have been told. With neither artifact nor archive, the student of Islamic origins could easily become victim of a literary and linguistic conspiracy.*
> —John Wansbrough, *Res Ipsa Loquitur: History and Mimesis,*
> Albert Einstein Memorial Lecture, Jerusalem, 1986.

Ibn Cleanthes: My dear friend, we are indeed lucky in having so many details of the life of the Prophet; we can practically follow his daily movements, listen to his homilies, speeches, read his letters, and have his opinion on countless subjects of the utmost importance to regulate our humble lives. The Prophet has set us an example that we would all do well to emulate, a source of comfort in this profane and irreligious age. What say you, Philo, come let us hear your sentiments.

Ibn Philo: Without wishing to vex you or to disturb your piety, I venture to say that you seem unacquainted with science and profound enquiry, particularly into the evidence for our knowledge of the Prophet's life.

Cleanthes, Come, Philo, enough of your skeptical pleasantries. You do not deny that there are over seventy historians that have written about the Rise of Islam, the life of Muhammad, and so on. Surely we have more documentary evidence about Muhammad than Jesus Christ.

Philo: Yes, we do know the *names* of some seventy historians for the period up to 1000 C.E., but the writings of the earliest historians have not survived. They are quoted by later historians, writing over a hundred years after the events they purport to describe. Thus, there is scarcely a Sira text that dates back to the first century of Islam.

Cleanthes: What of our beloved *Sira* by Ibn Ishaq, a copy of which I have here next to my bed? What of all the details that he gives us?

Philo: Ibn Ishaq wrote over a hundred years after the Hijra. As to the putative details, dear Cleanthes, we do not have many for the early years of the Prophet's life, we know scarce little of his childhood, his early education and development, and we probably never shall. The details that he does give cannot be trusted, and we do not seem to have any objective way to verify them, no external source against which to compare or judge them. We are dealing with theocratic legend. Can we really call figures like Ibn Hisham, Ibn Ishaq, and Abu Mikhnaf "historians"? For, as you know full well, the Greek word for history, *historein*, simply means to enquire or investigate, which is what Herodotus set out to do, whereas the writers of the sira give us the impression that they did not set out with the same purpose; rather, they *bore witness;* an altogether different activity and aim.[84] They are indulging in what Collingwood calls "theocratic history," which "means not history proper, that is, scientific history, but a statement of known facts for the information of persons to whom they are not known, but who, as worshippers of the god in question, ought to know the deeds whereby he has made himself manifest."[85] Of course, Muslims do not worship Muhammad, and he is not a God, but mutatis mutandis, Collingwood's remarks apply equally to Muslim "historians" and their hagiographic attitude to the Prophet and his supposed deeds. They did not distinguish the "duty of reporting from the legitimacy of believing."[86]

Cleanthes: Yes, but Ibn Ishaq must have talked to many people who had known the Companions of the Prophet.

Philo: True, but we cannot rely upon a purely oral tradition to scientifically reconstruct the events at the dawn of Islam. The chances are that the material being transmitted will have undergone a considerable amount of change: people's memories may have failed them, and their prejudices, even fears of being accused of impiety, will have affected, distorted, or altered the contents of what was being transmitted. In any case, it is not at all certain that people living the events that are later seen to be of significance saw them as such, and highly improbable that anyone (assuming he was literate) thought of recording the details that he was living through. Tendency to exaggerate, or even to fabricate details will have been great. Furthermore, we do not even have Ibn Ishaq's book.

Cleanthes: Ah, Philo you indulge in raillery and artificial malice; otherwise, what can one say of your paradoxes? What, do you expect to be able to explain away the existence of this volume that I have perused nearly every day for the last twenty years? Although I do not hold the original book in my hand, it must, nonetheless, lie somewhere in some museum or library, with the paper slightly yellowed undoubtedly, but unmistakably bearing the handwriting of Ibn Ishaq himself, in short, a volume that has survived inviolate from the eighth century.

Philo: No, I trifle not, Cleanthes. First, it seems unlikely that Ibn Ishaq had access to paper, which was only just being manufactured in Baghdad in the late eighth century; the oldest paper with Arabic writing on it found in Egypt dates from between 796 and 815. Second, the original work of Ibn Ishaq has been lost, and we only possess the recension of Ibn Hisham, someone who died over two hundred years after the Hijra. Ibn Hisham got Ibn Ishaq's work from the latter's pupil al-Bakkai. So the work that you optimistically call Ibn Ishaq's is really Ibn Hisham's version, much abbreviated, edited, and even altered by Ibn Hisham, of al-Bakkai's copy. Thus, we depend entirely on Ibn Ishaq's transmitters, of which there are at least fifteen; in other words, his biography of the Prophet, that you keep by your side, dear Cleanthes, has not been preserved as a single work. We do not possess an autographed manuscript of his work, and we are entirely dependent for our knowledge of what he wrote on manuscripts well-removed from the original. And even the various versions of his text that we do possess are full of discrepancies and contradictions concerning both dates and the contents, reminding us that texts copied by hand are very quickly liable to corruption; it really is not so easy as you think to make an accurate copy. In any case, there seems to be no nonarbitrary way of deciding between the various versions.

Cleanthes: What of al-Tabari's use of Ibn Ishaq? Does he not frequently quote him? Can we not reconstruct Ibn Ishaq's original from al-Tabari, and perhaps from some of Ibn Ishaq's more reliable pupils?

Philo: Al-Tabari was as selective as Ibn Hisham, and as Conrad has argued, "here too personal criteria of selection and al-Tabari's explicitly stated intention of giving versions of events which enjoyed the general assent of the Community would lead us to expect from him not a verbatim transcription of the text, but a redaction which Muslims in the late third century A.H. would have found appropriate and useful."[87] In any event, it is probable that al-Tabari was often quoting from memory, in which case again it is unlikely that we would have verbatim transcriptions.

As for Ibn Ishaq's pupils, I perhaps gave the impression that it was all only a matter of correcting the errors of the scribes and copyists. But as Conrad has observed, "Ibn Ishaq's numerous students and their successors took what they received from the master and redacted and transmitted it in different ways. Witness, for example, the differences between Ibn Hisham, the quotations in al-Tabari, the recension of Yunus ibn Bukayr, and that of Muhammad ibn Salama al-Harrani. As different lines of transmission represent potentially different redactions, efforts to reconstruct the original form of a text cannot simply combine quotations from different lines of transmission, as if Ibn Ishaq's students and their successors were making no revisions or changes of their own. . . . Transmitters did not limit themselves to passing on what they had received from their teachers, but rather laid claim to the role of adapting and revising their materials as they saw fit, not just by the well-known means of the collective isnad, but also by rearranging, abbreviating, expanding, and recasting."[88]

Cleanthes: But, dear Philo, you do tire me. I must own, I never know if you are in earnest or in jest. But arguments in the hands of a man of ingenuity like yourself do acquire an air of probability. Did we not find in recent years papyri bearing the works of Wahb ibn Munabbih who was born in 654, hence, by the time he was twenty, must have met many people who were eyewitnesses to the events described in the sira?

Philo: Yes indeed. But one must distinguish between when the actual physical papyrus that we possess was written and when the text that it contains was first composed. In this case the papyrus dates back to only the ninth century, though a part of the text seems to go back to Wahb. So once again we cannot be sure that we have an unadulterated text, since too great a time gap exists between the composition of the text and the copying of the papyrus that we possess. But, my dear Cleanthes, you show yourself to be far too uncritical, nay, even credulous, when assuming that access to an eyewitness solves all our problems. Do not forget that a reliable witness should have been able to see and understand objectively what he saw, and not be so engrossed that his preconceptions would have shaped, altered, or distorted what he saw. Warriors in the midst of a battle see only a fraction of what is happening, and often through screens of sand and dust. Eyewitness accounts are as much filtered through personal experience and emotions as written ones, and are not infallible.[89] In any case, many rogues will pretend for various reasons (for example, to gain prestige) to have taken part in events when they had done no such thing.

Cleanthes: But, dear friend, you seem to wish to belittle our venerable ancestors. What of their prodigious memories? We know they were capable of the most astonishing feats of recollection. Come, do not deny that the Arabs of the first years of Islam were men of remarkable gifts.

Philo: Yes, indeed they were, but I do not denigrate them in particular; I only point to some common failings of all humans. Modern clinical psychologists have shown how "autobiographical memories are not accurate historical accounts of events as they happened at the time of encoding, but rather a reconstruction based on a number of affective and motivational factors. Memories are contaminated with information from similar events and so change over the years as we encounter new experiences. What we remember about an event depends on when and for what purpose we are remembering, reflecting our beliefs about ourselves and the world at present. Thus memory is continually reprocessed and reinterpreted with changing contexts and perceptions."[90]

Cleanthes: But how on earth can the Companions of the Prophet have failed to remember the momentous events they were living through? Surely their united testimony must be of some authority. They do furnish us with so many vivid details that it seems natural to assume the Companions were indeed overwhelmingly struck by their experiences.

Philo: As I have already remarked, Cleanthes, it is not certain they were aware at the time that they *were* living through momentous events; what is more important here is that, as David B. Pillemer shows,[91] "despite the vividness of our memory for such momentous events, our recall of the actual facts of the event and the circumstances we were in at the time are often incorrect. Neither the vividness of a memory nor the strength of our certainty in a memory can ensure its veracity. . . . As Jerome Bruner once said, 'a life is not "how it was" but how it is interpreted and reinterpreted, told and retold.' "[92]

Cleanthes: Ah, Philo, you do rank me in that class of fools you call "the credulous." So be it, but you do also shake me to the very foundations of my being. For you the sira is but a legendary history; for me, however, as John Milton put it in his *History of Britain*, "Yet those old and inborn names of successive kings, never any to have been real persons, or done in their lives at least some part of what so long hath been remembered, cannot be thought without too strict an incredulity."

Philo: That is indeed a feeble argument, Cleanthes, for all it amounts to is the claim that the tales in the sira are credible just because they have been "so long remembered," in other words, so often repeated. The rise of historical criticism should have destroyed faith in that sort of argument, but I see that it has not.[93] You are a conservative critic, Cleanthes, you are swayed by not reason but by your passions, and as Housman put it, the faintest of all passions is the love of truth. And in this matter at least, if you will forgive me Cleanthes, you are indeed the average man who "believes that the text of ancient authors is generally sound, not because he has acquainted himself with the elements of the problem, but because he would feel uncomfortable if he did not believe it."[94]

Cleanthes: It is indeed true, I do feel decidedly uncomfortable. Coming back to something more substantial and solid. There are, you must avow, well-attested traditions, with an impeccable chain of transmitters that take us back to the very days, nay, even into the very presence of the Prophet himself. We have the work of our intrepid Hadith collectors who sifted through thousands of traditions to arrive at an authentic core. You cannot dismiss the work of Bukhari, Muslim, Tirmidhi, Maja, Dawud, Nisai, and Ibn Hanbal so casually.

Philo: But these traditions were collected many years after the death of Muhammad; Bukhari died over two hundred years after 632 C.E., while al-Nisai died 280 years after. The traditions they gathered are tendentious in the extreme, a reflection of the society in which they were collected rather than any past historical reality. You will find that any change in social organization or practice is immediately accompanied by a corresponding proliferation of new traditions, which are often justifications for existing conditions or political situations. Though seventh-century Arabia was not uniquely an oral society; from what we can make out from our meager sources, it seems that written accounts were rare. So we have a predominantly oral society, and all oral societies, as Vansina reminds us, "tend to have a simpler notion of historical causality, one which negates gradual change altogether. They tend to view institutions and techniques as unitary phenomena that came into existence fully fledged as they are in the present."[95] But as Patricia Crone has argued, "new religions do not spring fully fledged from the heads of prophets, old civilizations are not conjured away."[96]

In any case these traditions were transmitted by storytellers, orally, that is. But not only did they transmit them, and colored them with their prejudices, but actually created them As Crone says, "the sound historical tradition to which they are supposed to have added their fables simply did not exist."[97] Theirs was very much a performance tailored to the moods, needs, and expectations of their audiences. Their function was very similar to the role that poets played in preliterate Ancient Greece. As Finley reminds us, "the audiences . . . had no more genuine knowledge of the 'once upon a time' world of the heroes than had the poets, but they too knew that it was in essentials unlike their own. Heroes fought in chariots and feasted in great palaces, and so on, and the wildly inaccurate ways in which the poets described these things seemed right. How could they possibly know that they were in fact wrong? *In a world wholly without writing, and therefore without records, disagreements could be resolved only by subjective judgements, by reference to the way it had been said before, by the superior auctoritas of one poet as against another, by anything other than reference to a document. Whatever dropped out of the poetic repertoire soon disappeared from 'memory' forever; whatever innovation proved 'successful' soon became accepted as part of the tradition ever since once upon a time.*"[98]

Cleanthes: Dear Philo, while I am full of admiration for your logical acumen, I am unable to approve of your doctrines, but I do not know how to confound your arguments; they seem but the cavils of atheists, libertines, and freethinkers. You seem unaware of how perturbing your conclusions are for a man of faith; you disturb a general harmony. You fail to place yourself in the mind of a believer. You start abstruse doubts and objections, and ask me countless questions. I know not, I care not. That concerns not me. I have found a deity and his apostle, and here I stop my inquiry. Let those go farther, who are wiser or more original.

Philo: I pretend to be neither. But it is true that I do not concern myself with actual Muslim practice and faith. I am not studying sociology, however worthy that discipline is; I am studying history; I am not straining for originality but striving for truth, objective truth. I am trying to establish what really happened. "Am I therefore become your enemy because I tell you the truth"?[99] It does seem to me a mistake, however, to base one's faith on putatively historical facts, which do not stand up to critical examination. For surely if there were a deity, He would approve of the search for truth.

THE PROBLEM OF SOURCES

*In our skeptical times there is very little that is above criticism, and one
day or other we may expect to hear that Muhammad never existed*
—Snouck Hurgronje

It was Gustav Weil in his *Mohammed der prophet, sein Leben und sein Lehre*
(1843) who first applied the historico-critical method to the writing of the life of
the Prophet. However, his access to the primary sources was very limited, though
he did manage to get hold of a manuscript of the oldest extant biography of the
Prophet by Ibn Hisham. However, it is only some years later with the discovery
and publication of the works of Ibn Sa'd, al-Tabari, and the edition of Ibn
Hisham in 1858 by G. Wustenfeld that scholars had the means for the first time
to critically examine the sources of the rise of Islam and the life of its putative
founder, Muhammad. Weil translated Ibn Hisham into German in 1864. Al-
Waqidi's *Kitab al-Maghazi* was edited in 1856 by Alfred von Kremer, and
printed at Calcutta. An abridged translation of the latter work by Julius Wellhausen appeared in Berlin in 1882. Parts 3 and 4 of al-Tabari were published in
the 1880s. The Tabaqat of Ibn Sa'd (vols. 1 and 2) was edited by a team of orientalists, Mittwoch, Scahau, Horovitz, and Schwally, at the beginning of the twentieth century.

The biography of the Prophet made great advances in the writings of Sir
William Muir, Aloys Sprenger, and Theodor Noldeke.

Muir's *Life of Mahomet* appeared in four volumes between 1856 and 1861.
It is worth examining Muir's methodological assumptions since they seem to
have been shared by many Islamologists to the present time. Muir brought a
highly critical mind to bear on the hitherto recalcitrant material on the life of the
Apostle of God. He recognized the purely legendary nature of much of the
details, he realized the utter worthlessness of the tales contributed by the storytellers, and he was equally skeptical of the absolute value of the Traditions.
"Even respectably derived traditions often contained much that was exaggerated
and fabulous." Muir then continues by quoting Weil approvingly: "Reliance
upon oral traditions, at a time when they were transmitted by memory alone, and
every day produced new divisions among the professors of Islam, opened up a
wide field for fabrication and distortion. There was nothing easier, when required
to defend any religious or political system, than to appeal to an oral tradition of
the Prophet. The nature of these so-called traditions, and the manner in which the
name of Muhammad was abused to support all possible lies and absurdities, may
be gathered most clearly from the fact that al-Bukhari, who travelled from land

to land to gather from the learned the traditions they had received, came to conclusion, after many years' sifting, that out of 600,000 traditions, ascertained by him to be then current, only 4,000 were authentic! And of this selected number, the European critic is compelled without hesitation to reject al least one-half."[100]

A little later, Muir passes an even more damning judgement on traditions, while written records would have fixed "the terms in which the evidence was given; whereas tradition purely oral is affected by the character and habits, the associations and the prejudices, of each witness in the chain of repetition. No precaution could hinder the commingling in oral tradition of mistaken or fabricated matter with what at the first may have been trustworthy evidence. The floodgates of error, exaggeration, and fiction were thrown open."[101]

Muir even takes Sprenger to task for being too optimistic about our ability to correct the bias of the sources, "It is, indeed, the opinion of Sprenger that 'although the nearest view of the Prophet which we can obtain is at a distance of one hundred years,' and although this long vista is formed of a medium exclusively Muhammadan, yet our knowledge of the bias of the narrators 'enables us to correct the media, and to make them almost achromatic.' The remark is true to some extent; but its full application would carry us beyond the truth."[102] One would have thought that these considerations would have induced extreme skepticism in Muir about our ability to construct a life of Muhammad out of such crooked timber. Not a bit of it! It was all a matter of "a comprehensive consideration of the subject, and careful discrimination of the several sources of error, we may reach at least a fair approximation to the truth."[103] Muir also accepted totally uncritically the absolute authenticity of the Koran as a contemporary record; and he had unbounded confidence in the accuracy of the early historians, particularly, Ibn Ishaq, Ibn Hisham, al-Waqidi, Ibn Sa'd, and al-Tabari. The result was the massive four volume *Life of Mahomet*. Even a cursory glance at Muir's labors makes one wonder just what he has discarded from the traditions, since he seems to have taken at face value and included in his biography of the Prophet countless details, uncritically garnered from al-Waqidi, that are of dubious historical value, from long speeches to the minutiae of Muhammad's appearance and dress.

Julius Wellhausen, in his pioneering work on the Old Testament, which he began publishing in 1876, showed that the Pentateuch was a composite work in which one could discern the hand of four different "writers," usually referred to by the four letters J, E, D, and P. A century later, his *Biblical Higher Criticism* is still considered valid and very influential. Wellhausen then turned his critical mind to the sources of early Islam. Toward the end of the nineteenth century, Wellhausen tried to disentangle an authentic tradition from the snares of a deliberately concocted artificial tradition; the latter being full of tendentious distortions. The authentic tradition was to be found in Abu Mikhnaf, al-Waqidi, and al-Madaini, while the false tradition was to be found in Sayf b. 'Umar. For Well-hausen the "value of the isnad depends on the value of the historian who deems it reliable. With bad historians one cannot put faith in good isnads, while good historians merit trust if they give no isnad at all, simply noting that 'I have this from someone whom I believe.' All this permits a great simplification of critical analysis."[104] As Patricia Crone says, "one might have expected his *Prolegomena zur altesten Geschichte des Islams* to have been as revolutionary a work as was his *Prolegomena zur altesten Geschichte Israels*. But it is not altogether surprising that it was not. The biblical redactors offer us sections of the Israelite tradition at different stages of crystallization, and their testimonies can accordingly be profitably compared and weighed against each other. But the Muslim tradition was the outcome, not of a slow crystallization, but of an explosion; the first compilers were not redactors, but collectors of debris whose works are strikingly devoid of overall unity; and no particular illuminations ensue from their comparison. The Syrian Medinese and Iraqi schools in which Wellhausen found his J, E, D and P, do not exist: where Engnell and other iconoclasts have vainly mustered all their energy and ingenuity in their effort to see the Pentateuch as a collection of uncoordinated Hadiths, Noth has effortlessly and conclusively demonstrated the fallacy of seeing the Muslim compilers as Pentateuchal redactors."[105]

The next great step in the critical examination of our sources for Muhammad and the rise of Islam was taken by the great scholar Ignaz Goldziher, who showed in his *Muhammedanische Studien* that a certain amount of careful sifting or tinkering was not enough, and that the vast number of hadiths were total forgeries from the late second and third Muslim centuries. This meant, of course, "that the meticulous isnads which supported them were utterly fictitious."[106] Faced with Goldziher's impeccably documented arguments, conservative historians began to panic and devised spurious ways of keeping skepticism at bay, by, for instance, postulating ad hoc distinctions between legal and historical traditions. But as Humphreys says, "in terms of their formal structures, the hadith and the historical khabar [pl. akhbar, discrete anecdotes and reports] were very similar indeed; more important, many second/eighth- and third/ninth-century scholars had devoted their efforts to both kinds of text equally. Altogether, if Hadith isnads were suspect, so then should be the isnads attached to historical reports."[107]

In 1905, Prince Caetani, in his introduction to his monumental ten folio volumes of *Annali dell' Islam* (1905 to 1926), came to "the pessimistic conclusion that we can find almost nothing true on Muhammad in the Traditions, we can discount as apocryphal all the traditional material that we possess."[108] Caetani had "compiled and arranged (year by year, and event by event) all the material which the sources, the Arab historians offered. The resultant conclusions based on the facts, which took into account the variant forms in which they were found in the sources, were accompanied by a critical analysis that reflected the methodological skepticism which Langlois and Seignobos[109] had just set forth as absolutely indispensible for the historian."[110] But like Muir, Weil, and Sprenger before him, Caetani failed to push to their logical conclusion the negative consequences of his methodology, and like his predecessors, he thought it was all a matter of critically sifting through the mass of Traditions until we arrived at some authentic core.

The methodological skepticism of Goldziher and the positivist Caetani was taken up with a vengeance by Henri Lammens, the Belgian Jesuit. Though born in Ghent in 1862, Lammens left for Beirut at the age of fifteen to join the Jesuit order there, and made Lebanon his home for the rest of his life. During the first eight years of his studies, Lammens "acquired an exceptional mastery of Arabic, as well as of Latin and Greek, and he appears also to have learned Syriac. In 1886 he was assigned to teach Arabic at the Beirut Jesuit College, and he was soon publishing his own textbooks for the purpose. His first work of Orientalist scholarship appeared in 1889: a dictionary of Arabic usage (*Kitab al-fra'id fi'l-furuq*), containing 1,639 items and based on the classical Arabic lexicographers."[111] He travelled for six years in Europe, and twice edited the Jesuit newspaper, *al-Bashir.* He taught Islamic history and geography at the College, and he later used his lectures notes when he came to publish his studies on Pre-Islamic Arabia, and the Umayyads. "With the establishment of the School of Oriental Studies at the Jesuit College in 1907, Lammens began his career as an Orientalist in earnest; and his appointment as professor at the newly founded school enabled him to devote his whole effort to study and research. His well-known works on the sira appeared during the first seven years following his appointment."[112]

Though he had what Rodinson calls a "holy contempt for Islam, for its 'delusive glory' and its works, for its 'dissembling' and 'lascivious' Prophet,"[113] and despite his other methodological shortcomings, to be discussed below, Lammens, according to F. E. Peters, "whatever his motives and style . . . has never been refuted."[114] Lawrence Conrad makes a similar point that despite Lammens's well-known hostility to Islam, he offers a "number of useful insights."[115] Rodinson also concedes Lammens's partiality, but once again realizes that Lammens's "colossal efforts at demolishing also had constructive results.[116] They have forced us to be much more highly demanding of our sources.With the traditional edifice of history definitively brought down, one could now proceed to the reconstruction."[117] Finally as Salibi summarizes, "although the Sira thesis of Lammens did not remain unquestioned, it continues to serve as a working principle.The modern reaction in favor of the authenticity of the sira, represented by A. Guillaume and W. Montgomery Watt, has modified this working principle in some details without seriously affecting its essence. Lammens certainly provided sira scholarship with an important clue to the riddle of Muhammad; and many of his own conclusions, as well as his technique, have been adopted and developed by later scholars."[118]

In the first of the three works translated here for the first time into English, Lammens, influenced both by Goldziher's analysis of Hadith, and Snouck-Hurgronje's emphasis on the importance of the Koran for the sira, "asserted that the traditional Arabic sira, like the modern Orientalist biographies of the Prophet, depended mainly on Hadith, whereas the Koran alone can serve as a valid historical basis for a knowledge of the Prophet's life and career. The historical and biographical Hadith, far from being the control of the sira or the source of supplementary information, is merely an apocryphal exegesis of the historical and biographical allusions of the Koran. The value of a Hadith regarding the Prophet's life or career, he argued, would lie in its independence from the Koran, where such independence can be clearly demonstrated. As a rule, he adds, a Hadith which is clearly exegetical of the Koran should be disregarded."[119]

Lammens is often criticized for accepting uncritically any material that disparaged the Prophet, and conversely, for applying rigorous criticism when the source material tended to praise the Prophet. In his defense, Lammens pleaded that "pious Traditionists and sira writers could not have invented information that reflected poorly on Muhammad; and therefore, any such information which may have slipped in must be true."[120] But at other times, Lammens adhered to the principle that we ought not to judge Muhammad from modern European standards of right and wrong, since traits in the Prophet's character, found to be unacceptable by Europeans, may have been highly thought of by the early Muslims.

In the third of his works in the present volume, *Fatima et les Filles de Mahomet (Fatima and the daughters of Muhammad)*, "Lammens set out to prove that Fatima was not the favorite daughter of Muhammad, and that the Prophet had never planned his succession through her progeny. All Hadith and sira material favorable to Fatima, 'Ali, and their sons, al-Hasan and al-Husayn, is subjected to a searching criticism, with interesting and often valid results."[121] But rather inconsistently, Lammens accepted uncritically all the anti-Ali material which showed that Muhammad cared neither for Fatima nor 'Ali. Given Lammens's hostility to Islam and the character of Muhammad, one is inclined to accept the argument that a biography of the Prophet completed by Lammens was never published by express orders from Rome; its publication would have caused considerable embarrassment to the Holy See. In any case, in this post-Rushdie world that we all inhabit now, there is probably only one publisher in the world who would risk it, and if it is ever published, it should be, as Jeffery puts it, "epoch-making."

The ideas of the Positivist Caetani and the Jesuit Lammens were taken up by a group of Soviet Islamologists, whose conclusions sometimes show a certain superficial similarity to the works of Wansbrough, Cook, and Crone. N. A. Morozov propounded the theory that until the Crusades Islam was indistinguishable from Judaism and that only then did Islam receive its independent character, while Muhammad and the first caliphs were mythical figures. Morozov's arguments, first developed in his *Christ* (1930), are summarized by Smirnov: "In the Middle Ages Islam was merely an offshoot of Arianism evoked by a meteorological event in the Red Sea near Mecca; it was akin to Byzantine iconoclasm. The Koran bears the traces of late composition, up to the eleventh century. The Arabian peninsula is incapable of giving birth to any religion—it is too far from the normal areas of civilization. The Arabian Islamites, who passed in the Middle Ages as Agars, Ishmaelites, and Saracens, were indistinguishable from the Jews until the impact of the Crusades made them assume a separate identity. All the lives of Muhammad and his immediate successors are as apocryphal as the accounts of Christ and the Apostles."[122]

Under the influence of Morozov, Klimovich published an article called "Did Muhammad Exist?" (1930), in which he makes the valid point that all the sources of our information on the life of Muhammad are late. Muhammad was a necessary fiction since it is always assumed that every religion must have a founder. Whereas another Soviet scholar, S. P. Tolstov, compares the myth of Muhammad with the "deified shamans" of the Yakuts, the Buryats, and the Altays. "The social purpose of this myth was to check the disintegration of the political block of traders, nomads, and peasants, which had brought to power the new, feudal aristocracy." Vinnikov also compares the myth of Muhammad to "shamanism," pointing to primitive magic aspects of rituals such as Muhammad having water poured over him. While E. A. Belyaev rejects the theories of Morozov, Klimovich, and Tolstov, which argued that Muhammad never existed, he does consider the Koran to have been concocted after the death of the Prophet.[123]

Ignaz Goldziher's arguments were followed up nearly sixty years later by another great Islamicist, Joseph Schacht, whose works on Islamic law are considered classics in their field. Schacht's conclusions were even more radical and perturbing, and their full implications have not yet sunk in.

Humphreys has summed up Schacht's theses as:

(1) That isnads going all the way back to the Prophet only began to be widely used around the time of the Abbasid Revolution—i.e., the mid-second/eighth

century; (2) that, ironically, the more elaborate and formally correct an isnad appeared to be, the more likely it was to be spurious. In general, he concluded, no existing Hadith could be reliably ascribed to the Prophet, though some might ultimately be rooted in his teaching. And though he devoted only a few pages to historical reports about the early Caliphate, he explicitly asserted that the same strictures should apply to them.[124]

Here is how Schacht sums up his own thesis:

> It is generally conceded that the criticism of traditions as practiced by the Muhammadan scholars is inadequate and that, however many forgeries may have been eliminated by it, even the classical corpus contains a great many traditions which cannot possibly be authentic. All efforts to extract from this often self-contradictory mass an authentic core by "historic intuition," as it has been called, have failed. Goldziher, in another of his fundamental works [Goldziher, *Muslim Studies*, pp. 1–274] has not only voiced his "skeptical reserve" with regard to the traditions contained even in the classical collections, but shown positively that the great majority of traditions from the Prophet are documents not of the time to which they claim to belong, but of the successive stages of development of doctrines during the first centuries of Islam. This brilliant discovery became the cornerstone of all serious investigation of early Muhammadan law and jurisprudence, even if some later authors, while accepting Goldziher's method in principle, in their natural desire for positive results were inclined to minimize it in practice. . . .
>
> This book [Schacht's own work, *The Origins of Muhammadan Jurisprudence*] will be found to confirm Goldziher's results, and to go beyond them in the following respects: a great many traditions in the classical and other collections were put into circulation only after Shafi'i's time [Shafi'i died 820 C.E.]; the first considerable body of legal traditions from the Prophet originated towards the middle of the second [Muslim] century, in opposition to the slightly earlier traditions from Companions and other authorities, and to the "living tradition" of the ancient schools of law; traditions from Companions and other authorities underwent the same process of growth, and are to be considered in the same light, as traditions from the Prophet; the study of isnads often enables us to date traditions; the isnads show a tendency to grow backwards and to claim higher and higher authority until they arrive at the Prophet; the evidence of legal traditions carries us back to about the year 100 A.H. [eighth century C.E.] only. . . .[125]

Schacht argues that, for example, a tradition did not exist at a particular time by showing that it was not used as a legal argument in a discussion which would have made reference to it imperative if it had existed. For Schacht every legal tradition from the Prophet must be taken as inauthentic and fictitious expression of a legal doctrine formulated at a later date: "We shall not meet any legal tradition from the Prophet which can positively be considered authentic."[126]

Traditions were formulated polemically in order to rebut a contrary doctrine or practice; Schacht calls these traditions "counter traditions." Isnads "were often put together very carelessly. Any typical representative of the group whose doctrine was to be projected back on to an ancient authority, could be chosen at random and put into an isnad. We find therefore a number of alternative names in otherwise identical isnads."[127] Another important discovery of Schacht's which has considerable consequences only appreciated recently by Wansbrough and his followers is that "Muhammadan [Islamic] law did not derive directly from the Koran but developed . . . out of popular and administrative practice under the Umayyads, and this practice often diverged from the intentions and even the explicit wording of the Koran. . . . Norms derived from the Koran were introduced into Muhammadan law almost invariably at a secondary stage."[128]

The distinguished French Arabist Régis Blachère, translator of the Koran and historian of Arabic Literature, undertook to write a critical biography of the Prophet taking fully into account the skeptical conclusions of Goldziher and Lammens. His short study appeared in 1952, two years after Schacht's pioneering work. Blachère takes a highly critical view of the sources, and he is particularly pessimistic about our ability to reconstruct the life of Muhammad prior to the Hijra in 622 C.E.[129] His preliminary reappraisal of the sources ends on this very negative note: "The conclusions to be drawn from this survey will appear disappointing only to those more smitten with illusion than truth. The sole contemporary source for Muhammad, the Koran, only gives us fragmentary hints, often sibylline, almost always subject to divergent interpretations. The biographical Tradition is certainly more rich and more workable but suspect by its very nature, it poses, in addition, a problem of method since for Muhammad's apostolate it originates from the Koran which it tries to explain and complete at the same time. In sum, we no longer have any sources that would allow us to write a detailed history of Muhammad with a rigorous and continuous chronology. To resign oneself to a partial or total ignorance is necessary, above all for everything that concerns the period prior to Muhammad's divine call [ca. 610 C.E.]. All that a truly scientific biography can achieve is to lay out the successive problems engendered by this preapostolate period, sketch out the general background atmosphere in which Muhammad received his divine call, to give in broad brushstrokes the development of his apostleship at Mecca, to try with a greater chance of success to put in order the known facts, and finally to put back into the penumbra all that remains uncertain. To want to go further is to fall into hagiography or romanticization."[130]

And yet, the biography that emerges despite Blachère's professed skepticism is dependent upon the very traditions that Goldziher, Lammens, and Schacht had cast into doubt. Blachère's account of the life of the Prophet is far less radical than one would have expected; it is full of the recognizable events and characters familiar from the Traditional Biography, though shorn of the details.

Some of the most-discussed works published in the 1950s were the three publications of Harris Birkeland, a Swedish Orientalist: *The Legend of the Opening of Muhammad's Breast, Old Muslim Opposition against Interpretation of the Koran*, and the third, *The Lord Guideth, Studies on Primitive Islam*, which examines five suras that he considers the earliest stratum of the Koran, and which express, so he contends, the early ideas of Muhammad. In *The Lord Guideth,* Birkeland argues that "Goldziher's method to evaluate traditions according to their contents is rather disappointing. We are not entitled to limit our study to the texts (the so-called matns). We have the imperative duty to scrutinize the Isnads too . . . and to consider the matns in their relation to the isnads. . . . For it is very often the age of the contents that we do not know and which we, consequently, wish to decide. The study of the isnads in many cases gives us valuable assistance to fulfill this wish, despite the fact that in principle they must be held to be spurious. However fictitious they are, they represent sociological facts."[131] However, Birkeland misses his own point when he treats the isnads also as historical facts.

Birkeland expends a vast amount of energy "in collecting, differentiating and thoroughly scrutinizing all traditions and comments concerning a certain passage of the Koran or some legend about the Prophet."[132] But the German scholar Rudi Paret, for one, finds the results "rather disappointing."[133] Birkeland maintains that "the Muslim interpretation of the Koran in the form it has been transmitted to us, namely in its oldest stage as Hadith, does not contain reliable information on the earliest period of Muhammad in Mecca." Nevertheless Birkeland continues: "The original tafsir of Ibn Abbas and possibly that of his first disciples must, however, have contained such information. . . . An exact, detailed and comparative analysis of all available materials, of isnads and matns and exegetical-theological tendencies, in many instances enables us to go behind the extant texts and reach the original interpretation of Ibn Abbas, or at least that of his time, thus obtaining a really authentic understanding of the Koranic passage."[134] Rudi Paret remains very skeptical: "to tell the truth I cannot make this optimistic outlook my own. Nor can I quite agree with Birkeland as to his evaluation of the so-called family isnads."[135]

Wellhausen's ideas were taken up by Albrecht Noth in 1968,[136] and then further developed in *Quellenkritische Studien zu Themen, Formen, und Tendenzen fruhislamischen Geschichtsuberlieferung. Teil I: Themen und Formen* (1973); the latter work was reissued, with the help of Dr. Lawrence I. Conrad, in a thoroughly revised English edition, which was published in 1994 under the auspices of the Late Antiquity and Early Islam project by the Darwin Press as *The Early Arabic Historical Tradition: A Source Critical Study* (translated by Michael Bonner).[137] According to Patricia Crone the result of Noth's approach was

> both enlightening and wholly negative. Form-criticism [*quellenkritische*] is like literary criticism, a method evolved for the study of the Pentateuch. Biblical form-critics treat Wellhausen's redactions rather as conglomerates in which each individual component has its own individual history, and in pursuing these they take us back in time. But just as the Islamic tradition is not the product of either slow crystallization or a gradual deposition of identifiable layers, so also it is not a conglomerate in which ancient materials have come together in a more recent setting. Hence, where Biblical form-critics take us back in time, Noth by contrast takes us forward. He demonstrates time and time again that the components of the Islamic tradition are secondary constructions, the history of which we are not invited to pursue: they simply have to be discarded. Where Biblical form-criticism takes us to the sources behind the sources, Noth exposes us to a gaping void behind the sources. And the practical outcome of his *Quellenkritik* is accordingly not the rewriting of Islamic history, but a warning to foolhardy Islamic historians.[138]

According to Noth and Conrad, "early Islamic historical tradition is typified by an abundance of formal elements."[139] By the latter term, they mean those recurring, transferable, and fixed elements, ranging from a simple motif to a complex plot, found in a number of situations and narrative settings which seem to be describing different and real historical events or facts, but which on closer inspection turn out to be stereotypes, of symbolic value perhaps, but often though not always totally devoid of any historical reality. For example:

> Traditions about sieges and the conquest of cities are not rare in the historical accounts of the period of the early caliphs. If we consider each of these traditions by itself, it seems plausible enough: things could have happened that way. This impression no longer holds, however, if we collect and compare reports on the conquest of different cities. For instance, Damascus and Caesarea in Syria, Babilyun/al-Fustat and Alexandria in Egypt, Tustar in Khuzistan, and Cordoba in Spain are all described as having fallen into the hands of the Muslims in precisely the same fashion. Certain motifs recur constantly in different combinations: the traitor who, with or without an *aman* (safe-conduct), points out a weak spot in the city's fortifications to the Muslim besiegers; a celebra-

tion in the city which diverts the attention of the besieged; then a few assault troops who scale the walls, often with a ladder; a shout of *Allahu akbar!*, "God is great!", from the assault troops as a sign that they have entered the town; the opening of one of the gates from inside, and the onslaught of the entire army. That these details are so readily transportable from accounts of one vent to those of another is in itself sufficient to indicate that they represent not the reporting of history, but rather the deployment of literary stereotypes.[140]

It is totally inadequate to appeal to the "kernel of truth" argument,[141] for often what we are left with after we have removed all the stereotypical elements is so general that it is useless to the historian. On their own certain traditions have an air of plausibility, but when looked at together and compared to other traditions we realize we are often dealing with stereotypes without factual reality. Noth and Conrad focus their attention on three formal elements that can be distinguished in early Islamic historical writing: literary forms, topoi, and schemata. Under literary forms they examine documents, letters, speeches, lists, and *awa'il* (works devoted to "who was first"), often with skeptical conclusions about their historical worth. Documents in the long process of largely oral transmission have been subjected to all sorts of changes, and cannot be taken at their face value; at best they only allow us a glimpse of the originals.[142] Similarly, "there can be no doubt that fictitious letters and correspondence entered into early Islamic tradition in large numbers."[143] As for speeches, "we must view them as fictions from beginning to end."[144] And "our lists are not documents of historical value for the period to which they refer, but rather fictions set into circulation by the tradents of later times."[145]

Under topoi, Noth and Conrad look at, amongst other things, topoi emphasizing feats of arms, glorifying former times, describing the summons to Islam, and so on.

> A topos is a narrative motif fact. Its scope is thus very narrow, and it is normally bound to description of a specific situation, definition of a brief moment, or characterization of a person. A topos may very well have a basis in fact, for it is often the case that a topos was once securely anchored to real historical referents. . . . Such references move from the domain of life to that of literature, however, when they become transferable. The key to the detection of topos is the way it drifts from one setting to another, reappearing again and again in situations to which it had never originally belonged, and indeed, never could have belonged. Topoi were sometimes used for mere embellishments or for literary effect, but also provided powerful means to promote certain distinct tendencies and biases.[146]

"A schema, on the other hand," North and Conrad tell us,

is a narrative motif which is, first and foremost, concerned with matters of form, with connecting, relating, and organizing matters of content. Thus, while a topos is rather narrow in scope, a schema is paradigmatic, and so tends to be very broad in scope. Further, while a topos may have an original basis in historical fact, a schema does not, for its starting point is a situation in which genuine interpretive connections and relations are not known. Its raison d'etre is to fill such voids, and since the point of departure is lack of knowledge, this process is a completely arbitrary one. If a schema has any relation at all to historical fact, this is purely a matter of coincidence.

[Topoi and schema] were tools which every historical writer had in his workshop, and which he used to craft reports and accounts which he considered would meet the expectations of his audience and stand in harmony with the mood of his times.[147]

Under schemata, Noth and Conrad discuss transitional formulae, pseudocauses, etiologies, systematization, undifferentiated reports. Again, in a rather similar fashion to Muir and others, despite their research, Noth and Conrad argue that the "tradition offers much material which, if in need of careful examination, is still of historical value for the early period."[148]

Independently of Noth, Eckart Stetter in his 1965 dissertation examines the topoi and schemata in Hadiths by taking a representative selection from Bukhari's Sahih, and in so doing raises questions about the authenticity and reliability of the Hadith material. Like Schacht, Stetter suggests plausible mechanisms for the creation of false Hadiths.[149]

A certain number of scholars built on the insights of Goldziher, Schacht, and Noth, and came to some very radical, even startling conclusions. We could with some justification date the rise of this revisionist school to July 1975, when the Near Eastern History Group of Oxford University organized its fifth colloquium on the theme of the formative period of Islamic history. As the organizers of the congress said in their statement of the aims of the colloquium: "The existing cultures of the Middle East, which provided most of the raw materials of the new civilization, are reasonably well known to us, and so is the end-product, the 'classical' Islamic civilization. But since the conquerors took some time to settle down, their own version of the process by which the new society and culture were created is a belated one and open to considerable doubt. If we rely on it alone, we shall form a picture of a discontinuity between the pre-Islamic and Islamic worlds which strains the imagination; if on the other hand we begin by assuming that there must have been some continuity, we need either to go beyond the Islamic sources or to reinterpret them."[150]

Rather surprisingly, Juynboll tells us in his introduction to the collection of papers presented at the colloquium that "for the first time in our lives many of us became acquainted with the outlook of non-Arab, non-Muslim historians on the conquests and its perpetrators"[151] on hearing S. P. Brock's "Syriac Views of Emergent Islam." This confession is surprising in that Juynboll must have been aware of the use made of Syriac sources, as early as 1916, by Alphonse Mingana in his original conclusions about the transmission of the Koran;[152] and the article by J. B. Segal, "Syriac Chronicles as Source Material for the History of Islamic Peoples,"[153] contained in the famous collection edited in 1962 by Lewis and Holt; or the works of Claude Cahen.[154] Nonetheless, it is true that Brock makes a number of original observations most important for our re-evaluation of the worth of the Muslim sources: "This confrontation with Syriac and Hellenistic source material for once pricked the balloons of such Islamic historians as swear exclusively by Arabic sources,"[155] observations whose implications are more fully explored by Koren and Nevo below.

The Oxford colloquium also saw the contributions of Michael Cook and Patricia Crone, later to be incorporated in their *Hagarism: The Formation of the Islamic World* (1977). Their papers at the colloquium were thought to lean too heavily and too exclusively on non-Arabic sources. Patricia Crone has since then argued very forcibly of the significance of these non-Muslim sources, pointing out the importance and luck of having the means to step outside the Islamic tradition:

All the while that Islamic historians have been struggling with their inert tradition, they have had available to them the Greek, Armenian, Hebrew, Aramaic, Syriac and Coptic literatures of non-Muslim neighbors and subjects of the Arab conquerors, to a large extent edited and translated at the end of the last century and the beginning of the present, and left to collect dust in the libraries ever since. It is a striking testimony to the suppression of the non-Islamic Middle East from the Muslim sources that not only have these literatures been ignored for questions other than the chronology of the conquests and the transmission of Greek philosophy and science, but they have also been felt to be *rightly* ignored. Of course these sources are hostile, and from a classical Islamic view they have simply got everything wrong; but unless we are willing entertain the notion of an all-pervading literary conspiracy between the non-Muslim peoples of the Middle East,[156] the crucial point remains that they have got things wrong on very much the same points. That might not, it is true, have impressed the medieval Muslims who held the Jews and Christians capable of having maliciously deleted from their scriptures precisely the same passages relating to the coming of Islam; but as the Jews and Christians retorted, given their wide geographical and social distribution, they could scarcely have vented their anti-Muslim feelings with such uniform results. It is because there is agreement between the independent and contemporary witnesses of the non-Muslim world that their testimony must be considered; and it can hardly be claimed that they do not help: whichever way one chooses to interpret them, they leave no doubt that Islam was like other religions the product of a religious *evolution.*[157]

It is worth noting that Wansbrough himself was very critical of Cook and Crone's *Hagarism*[158] and justly pointed out that the non-Muslims sources "also . . . exhibit polemical stereotypes (apocalyptic, 'dialogue devant le prince') and most, if not all, have been or can be challenged on suspicion of inauthenticity . . . [their] documentary value is here virtually unquestioned."[158] We must remain skeptical of the non-Muslim sources as well.

Since in chapter 2 Ibn Rawandi discusses the work of Crone and Cook, and John Wansbrough, which had a decisive influence on *Hagarism*, I shall not dwell on it here. In his own contribution on the origins of Arabic prose, Juynboll speculated "on authenticity and historical reliability and came to the conclusion that, on the whole, precious little historical evidence can be gleaned from isnads."[159] The contributions of Hawting at the congress are also reviewed by Ibn Rawandi below.

Schacht's theories inspired, among others, H. P. Raddatz,[160] Van Ess,[161] John Wansbrough,[162] John Burton,[163] and Cook.[164] There were also, of course, attempts to answer him, but though these critiques of Schacht may have in some way modified our views of his work, they come nowhere near in refuting it. Fuat Sezgin,[165] M. M. Azmi,[166] and Nabia Abbott[167] tried to argue that Schacht did not understand the processes of Hadith transmission in early Islam, while W. M. Watt[168] suggested that Schacht had taken a sound analysis too far. Again the work of Watt and his critics is discussed by Ibn Rawandi and I shall not refer to it further except to quote Crone's scathing survey of those who have either tried to answer Schacht or have simply ignored him:

Watt disposes of Schacht by casuistry. Gibb[169] defends the authenticity of a narrative relating to the mid-Umayyad period with reference to its superior isnad. Shaban[170] pretends never to have heard of Schacht, or for that matter any other critic of the sources. The reactions of the Arabists are very similar. R. Paret[171] takes Schacht seriously, but nonetheless ends by endorsing the soundness of the sira. A. Guillaume seems to be under the impression that the only attack ever made on the historicity of the sira is that by his own research students in respect of the sira's poetry.[172] Sellheim's innocence of Schacht has already been noted. [Sellheim[173] identified two strata in the sira consisting of miracle stories and Abbasid propaganda respectively: all the rest is labeled *Grundschicht* and characterized as *Felsbrocken* (p. 48). It is, however, this layer which is in need of analysis, and the assurance that it reflects the events of history more or less directly is hardly borne out by the soundings on pp. 73 ff.][174] Abbot and F. and U. Sezgin are of course anything but deaf, but their method consists in believing what the Muslims said about the formation of their own tradition while abstaining from too close an analysis of the character of this tradition which so flagrantly contradicts it: the conclusions of Schacht (and now also Noth) are denied, but not disproved. The only serious attempts to refute Schacht are those of N. J. Coulson[175] (who accepts the essentials of Schacht's conclusions), and Azmi[176] (who disagrees fundamentally with both Goldziher and Schacht).[177]

Azmi was effectively challenged by Michael Cook: "Azmi[178] . . . polemizes against Schacht along the following lines we often find that a tradition is transmitted by many different transmitters in a given generation that each of them should put about the same fabricated tradition presupposes a level of conspiratorial action which is historically quite implausible. One Companion might perhaps spuriously attribute a saying to the Prophet but how could five Companions, in different parts of the Muslim world do so independently? The only possible answer to this is that isnads spread. This indeed is the answer already indicated by Schacht.[179] . . . If we believe that isnads did spread on a significant scale, then Azmi's argument does not touch us. But if we do not, his position is irrefutable."[180] Cook gives some examples as to how the isnads could have spread, and we can look at one:

Suppose that you [B1] and I [B2] are contemporaries, and I learn something from you—an informal event which must be common enough in any scholarly culture. You had, or say you had it, from your teacher [A]. If I am scrupulously honest, I will transmit it from your teacher, leaving posterity with an isnad of the form

But as it happens, I say to myself that, even if I didn't actually hear it from your teacher, I could have—it goes against the grain to transmit from a mere contemporary. My behavior here is informed by one of the basic values of the system an elegant isnad is a short one. Ideally, one should have a saying direct from the mouth of the sayer and failing that, the fewer the intervening links the better. In the present case, provided your transmission survives independently of mine, posterity finds itself confronted instead with this:

Posterity then believes that it has two independent witnesses for the authenticity of the ascription to A, and thus thinks itself able to rule out fabrication in the generation following.[181]

Coulson's summary[182] of his views, however, is worth examining in detail since he shares with many Western, non-Muslim scholars an unease when confronted with the overwhelming evidence of the worthlessness of the Hadith, such that he is led to write in convoluted prose lest he offend Muslim sensibilities. Coulson points out that, although the Muslim scholars were aware of the possibility of Hadith forgeries, their test for authenticity was confined to a careful examination of the chain of transmitters who narrated the report. "Provided the chain was uninterrupted and its individual links deemed trustworthy persons, the Hadith was accepted as binding law. There could, by the terms of the religious faith itself, be no questioning of the content of the report; for this was the substance of divine revelation and therefore not susceptible of any form of legal or historical criticism. European and non-Muslim scholars, naturally enough, deemed the Muslim type of critique inadequate. The Hadith was to be tested by its content and by the place its terms occupied in the development of legal thought and institutions, ascertained objectively (from the non-Muslim standpoint) by reference to all the available literary sources."[183]

There are some strange assumptions that are not spelled out in this passage. First, why is it *natural* that European and non-Muslim scholars should find the Muslim approach unacceptable? Second, what are we to make of the phrase, "ascertained objectively (from the non-Muslim standpoint)"? Do we conclude that either Muslims are not capable of objectivity (which could be true), or that Europeans pretend that they are being objective, but "objective" simply *means* from the European point of view (in other words, there is no such thing as the truth of the matter, everything is relative, and there is no objective truth due to the intellectual baggage of post-modernism)?

Coulson continues a little later with this judgment: "There can be little doubt to the non-Muslim mind that Schacht's view of the origins of the legal Hadith and their role in the development of Islamic legal doctrine is essentially sound. Reservations must, however, be expressed as to the extent to which he drives his thesis. . . . The present writer regards Schacht's conclusion as too rigid, particularly because his arguments concerning the 'relative position' of a Hadith 'in the history of the problem with which it is concerned' are not always wholly convincing."[184]

Coulson ends his discussion with these observations:

> Schacht's approach, then, might be considered somewhat too narrow because he rigidly identifies the development of law with the growth of Hadith and fails to take proper account of intrinsically legal issues of this kind. In sum, he translates the negative proposition that the evidence of legal Hadith does not take us back beyond the second century of Islam into the positive statement that legal development began only in late Umayyad times. This creates an unacceptable void in the picture of law in the early Muslim community; for it is unrealistic to assume that legal problems created by the terms of the Koran itself were ignored for a century or more. Granted, therefore, that the formal isnad may be fictitious, it may well be argued, even from the secular standpoint of historical criticism, that the substance of the Hadith reflects an authentic decision of the Prophet.
>
>   In such cases, then, it may be that the truth lies somewhere between traditional Islamic legal theory and the rigorous historical approach of Schacht. At the same time it must, of course, be frankly recognized that the Muslim and the Western methods of Hadith criticism are irreconcilable because they rest upon totally different premises. Between the dictates of religious faith on the one hand and secular historical criticism on the other there can be no middle way of true objectivity.[185]

Coulson's conclusions evidently do not take into account those of John Wansbrough, who argued that the definitive text of the Koran had still not been achieved as late as the ninth century. There was indeed a legal void in the early Muslim community. As a conclusion let us note Coulson's qualifying clauses, "from the secular standpoint of historical criticism," which seems to amount to an apology, in the manner of Maxim Rodinson, to Muslims. Why do I consider it apologetic? Are we to use such a phrase *every* time we write about Islam, its rise, or the Koran and the Prophet, especially when we contradict the traditional accounts? If the answer is no, then its use can only be to soften the blow for Muslims, in other words, to apologize. Finally, what are we to make of Coulson's last sentence? Does it mean that there is no true objectivity, or that true objectivity only lies somewhere between the two approaches (the secular and the Muslim), or that we shall not arrive at true objectivity by pretending that the truth lies somewhere between the two?

Humphreys points to two other scholars who have tried to answer Schacht:

> Far more systematically, G. H. A. Juynboll[186] has tried to do justice both to medieval Islamic views and Schacht's critique. His cautious attitude toward his

data and his intricate logic tend to veil his conclusions on certain issues, but his work is surely the most sophisticated and wide-ranging assessment of the evidence we have yet had. Juynboll's tentative counter-revisionism seems to be supported by M. J. Kister's[187] close analysis of a number of particularly troublesome Hadiths. Kister is able to show that several of these Hadiths are extremely archaic in both language and content; whether or not they represent the teaching of the Prophet, they clearly reflect the ideas and problems of the first decades of Islam. But Juynboll's findings are explicitly provisional, and Kister deals with only a few odd cases. In the end, we may decide simply that Schacht is right and set out to explore the full implications of his thought.[188]

Humphreys is perhaps being rather optimistic when claims to know what "the ideas and problems of the first decades of Islam" are; we cannot assume what the first decades of Islam were like, since to decide what they were like is exactly what has proved to be so difficult given the very nature of our suspect sources. How can we possibly decide what language is archaic and what is not, without circularity and without some independent means of verification?

Generally speaking, those who defend the authenticity of Hadiths, like Abbot, Sezgin, and Azmi, argue that there was an early and continuous practice of writing Hadiths in Islam, and that reports about Muhammad were already being written during his lifetime. The problem is the obvious lack of of any early attempt to standardize all these reports and, of course, the lack of any extant manuscripts from this early period. Second, these authors presuppose the veracity of the isnads. They argue on the basis of isnads and the symbiotic biographical literature for an early practice of written Hadiths; these sources are not independent.Since it is isnads themselves and their authenticity that are at issue, writers like Abbot, Sezgin and Azmi, have simply developed circular arguments.[189]

A number of scholars have looked at particular incidents from the early history of Islam and, with patient scholarship, have shown the total confusion that reigns in the accounts, "the result not merely of falsifications or failures of recall but also of the conception which guided the Muslim scholars in their redaction of the material. The compilers, rather than their primary sources, are responsible for the confusion."[190] As Ella Landau-Tasseron argues, the fusion of several different accounts into one, for example, is the result of "the natural presuppositions and formulaic thinking of the Muslim thinkers, who apparently saw and presented things as they perhaps ought to have been, and not as they were."[191] Landau-Tasseron concludes her examination of the various accounts of the tribal delegation of the Tamim to the Prophet at Medina with these observations: "What has been said hitherto re-emphasizes the amount of caution needed when relying on Muslim sources. Some of the accounts of the Tamimite delegation are conspicuously the work of compilers, who assembled and redacted material from various sources indiscriminately. But this fact is not always obvious. The account of Waqidi, for instance, seems fairly coherent, and there is not much in it which makes it suspect. Only a careful analysis shows that it too is a complex structure which has deviated considerably from the original material. The historical material underwent considerable changes not only as a result of tendentious forgeries but also through the mere process of redaction, which was for the most part carried out in good faith."[192]

Even the most conservative scholars now accept the unreliability of the Muslim sources, but an increasing number also seem to confirm, however indirectly, the more radical conclusions of Wansbrough, Cook, and Crone. One of the most remarkable of the latter was Dr. Suliman Bashear, a leading scholar and administrator at the University of Nablus (West Bank). His generally radical and skeptical views about the life of the Prophet and the history of early Islam often got him into trouble not only with the University authorities but also with the students, who, on one occasion, threw him out of a second-story window (luckily he escaped with minor injuries). Bashear lost his post at the University after the publication of his *Introduction to the Other History* (in Arabic) in 1984, whereupon he took up a Fulbright fellowship in the United States and returned to Jerusalem to a position in the Hebrew University in 1987. He died of a heart attack in October 1991 just after completing his book, *Arabs and Others in Early Islam.*[193]

In one study, Bashear[194] examines verses 114 to 116 of sura 2 of the Koran and their exegesis by Shams al-Din Suyuti (d.880/) and others. Sura 2:114 reads: "Who is more wicked than the men who seek to destroy the mosques of God and forbid His name to be mentioned in them, when it behooves these men to enter them with fear in their hearts? They shall be held up to shame in this world and sternly punished in the hereafter." Sura 2:115 to 116 reads: "To God belongs the East and the West. Whichever way you turn there is the face of God. He is omnipresent and all-knowing. They say 'God has begotten a son.' Glory be to Him! His is what the heavens and earth contain all things are obedient to Him."

Bashear was intrigued by verse 114 and Suyuti's claim that it was revealed concerning the barring of Muslims by the Byzantines from the Jerusalem sanctuary. "Such a remarkable commentary in itself justifies further investigation. Moreover, 2:114 is followed by two verses (2:115–16) which could be taken as referring to the abrogation of the Jerusalem kiblah and the argument surrounding the nature of the relation between God and Christ."[195]

Bashear continues:

Two main questions are tackled here concerning the occasion of revelation of
the verse [2:114]: who are those it blames, and where and when was the act of
barring from, or destroying the mosques committed? The answers are split
between four notions current in exegetical traditions and commentaries:

   (i)   The Jerusalem-Christian/Byzantine context;

   (ii)   The Meccan-Qurashi context;

   (iii)   A general meaning without specific reference to any historical context;

   (iv)   It was the Jews who tried to destroy the Kaaba or the Prophet's mosque in Medina in reaction to his change of kiblah.[196]

Bashear, after a meticulous examination of the commentaries, concluded
that

> up to the mid second [Muslim] century a clear anti-Christian/Byzantine senti-
> ment prevailed in the exegesis of 2:114 which overwhelmingly presented it as
> referring to the Jerusalem sanctuary-temple. We have also seen that no trace of
> sira material could be detected in such exegesis and that the first authentic
> attempt to present the occasion of its revelation within the framework of
> Muhammad's sira in Mecca is primarily associated with the name of Ibn Zayd
> who circulated a tradition to that effect in the second half of the second
> [Muslim] century. Other attempts to produce earlier traditional authorities for
> this notion could easily be exposed as a later infiltration of sira material simply
> by conducting a cross-examination of sira sources on the occasions of both
> Quraysh's persecution of Muhammad before the Hijra and their barring of him
> at Hudaybiyya. . . . The notion of an early Meccan framework cannot be
> attested before the first half of the second [Muslim] century.
> *All in all, the case of verse 2:114 gives support to Wansbrough's main
> thesis since it shows that from the mid second [Muslim] century on Koranic exe-
> gesis underwent a consistent change, the main "impulse" behind which was to
> assert the Hijazi origins of Islam.*[197] In that process, the appearance and circu-
> lation of a tradition by the otherwise unimportant Ibn Zayd slowly gathered
> prominence. Simultaneously, other ingenuous attempts were made to find ear-
> lier authorities precisely bearing Ibn Abbas's name for the same notion while
> the more genuine core of the original tradition of Ibn Abbas was gradually
> watered down because it was no longer recognized after the "legend of Muham-
> mad" was established.[198]

Bashear also indirectly complements the work of G. Hawting[199] and M. J.
Kister[200] when he claims that "on yet another level, literary criticism of the traditional material on the position of Jerusalem in early Islam has clearly shown that

the stress on its priority was not necessarily a function of the attempt to undermine Mecca but rather was independent of the position of the latter since Islam seems not to have yet developed one firmly established cultic center."[201]

Toward the end of his analysis, Bashear remarks: "The present inquiry has shown how precisely around this period (mid second [Muslim] century) elements of a Hijazi orientation made their presence felt in the exegetical efforts to fit what became the canon of Muslim scripture into the new historical framework of Arabian Islam. From the literary scrutiny of the development of these efforts it becomes clear how such exegetical efforts affected the textual composition of 2:114–16 in a way that fitted the general orientation, attested from other literary fields, towards a Hijazi sira, sanctuary and, with them, scriptural revelation."[202]

In his study of the title "faruq" and its association with 'Umar I, Bashear confirms the findings of Crone and Cook[203] that "this title must be seen as an Islamic fossilization of a basically Jewish apocalyptic idea of the awaited messiah."[204] A little later Bashear says that certain traditions give "unique support to the rather bold suggestion forwarded by Cook and Crone that the rise of 'Umar as a redeemer was prophesized and awaited."[205] Again as in his discussion of sura 2:114 discussed above, Bashear thinks his analysis of the traditions about the conversion of 'Umar to Islam and sura 4:60 has broader implications for our understanding of early Islam. Bashear tentatively suggests that certain traditions were fabricated to give an Hijazi orientation to events that probably took place outside it.[206]

In "Abraham's Sacrifice of His Son and Related Issues,"[207] Bashear discusses the question as to which of the two sons was meant to be sacrificed by Abraham, Ishaq or Ismail. He concludes: "In itself, the impressively long list of mainly late scholars and commentators who favored Ismail confirms Goldziher's note that this view eventually emerged victorious. In view of the present study, however, one must immediately add that such victory was facilitated only as part of the general process of promoting the position of Mecca as the cultic center of Islam by connecting it with the Biblical heritage on the story of Abraham's trial or, to use Wansbrough's terminology, the reproduction of an Arabian-Hijazi version of Judaeo-Christian 'prophetology.'[208] Bashear once again brings his examination to a close with the observation that it was only later traditionists who consciously promoted Ismail and Mecca for nationalist purposes, that is, to give an Hijazi orientation to the emerging religious identity of the Muslims:

> For, our attempt to date the relevant traditional material confirms on the whole the conclusions which Schacht arrived at from another field, specifically the tendency of isnads to grow backwards.[209] Time and again it has been demon-

strated how serious doubts could easily be cast not only against traditions attributed to the Prophet and Companions but a great deal of those bearing the names
of successors too. We have actually seen how the acute struggle of clear national
motive to promote the positions of Ismail and Mecca did flare up before the turn
of the century, was at its height when the Abbasids assumed power and
remained so throughout the rest of the second [Muslim] century.

Though we did not initially aim at investigating the development of
Muslim hajj rituals in Mecca, let alone its religious position in early Islam in
general, our enquiry strongly leads to the conclusion that such issues were far
from settled during the first half of the second [Muslim] century. While few
scholars have lately arrived at similar conclusions from different directions,[210]
it is Goldziher who must be accredited with the initial note that Muslim consecration of certain locations in the Hijaz commenced with the rise of the
Abbasids to power.[211] Indeed we have seen how "the mosque of the ram" was
one of such locations.[212]

Bashear continues his research with his article "Riding Beasts on Divine
Missions: An Examination of the Ass and Camel Traditions,"[213] where he tentatively suggests that the "prominence of the image of the camel-rider was a function of the literary process of shaping the emergence of Arabian Islam."[214] Thus,
much of Bashear's work seems to confirm the Wansbrough/Cook/Crone line that
Islam, far from being born fully fledged with watertight creed, rites, rituals, holy
places, shrines, and a holy scripture, was a late literary creation as the early Arab
warriors spilled out of the Hijaz in such dramatic fashion and encountered
sophisticated civilizations, encounters that forced them to forge their own religious identity out of the already available materials, which were reworked to fit
into a mythical Hijazi framework. This is further underlined by Bashear's last
major work published posthumously in 1997, *Arabs and Others in Early Islam*.[215]
The core of the latter work was adumbrated earlier in chapter 8, "Al-Islam wa-l-
Arab," of his work published in Arabic in 1984, *Muqaddima Fi al-Tarikh al-
Akhar*. In *Arabs and Others in Early Islam*, Bashear questions the a priori acceptance of the notion that the rise of the Arab polity and Islam were one and the
same thing from the beginning.[216] Furthermore, he doubts the Hijazi origins of
classical Islam: "The proposition that Arabia could have constituted the source
of the vast material power required to effect such changes in world affairs within
so short a span of time is, to say the least, a thesis calling for proof and substan-
tiation rather than a secure foundation upon which one can build. One may
observe, for example, that in spite of all its twentieth-century oil wealth, Arabia
still does not possess such material and spiritual might. And at least as extraordinary is the disappearance of most past legacies in a wide area of the utmost

diversity in languages, ethnicities, cultures, and religions. One of the most important developments in contemporary scholarship is the mounting evidence that these were not simply and suddenly swallowed up by Arabian Islam in the early seventh century, but this is precisely the picture that the Arabic historical sources of the third [Muslim]/ninth [C.E.] century present."[217] A little later, Bashear explicitly endorses the revisionist thesis that "the first/seventh century witnessed two parallel, albeit initially separate processes: the rise of the Arab polity on the one hand, and the beginnings of a religious movement that eventually crystallized into Islam. It was only in the beginning of the second/eighth century and throughout it, and for reasons that have yet to be explained, that the two processes were fused, resulting in the birth of Arabian Islam as we know it, i.e. in the Islamization of the Arab polity and the Arabization of the new religion."[218] This Arabization of the new religion and the Islamization of the Arab polity is reflected in the attempts to stress the national Arabian identity of the prophet of Islam and of Arabic as the divine tool of revelation.[219]

Stefan Leder, in the important collection called *Studies in Late Antiquity and Early Islam*, examines the historical worth of writings that we refer to by the term *khabar* (pl. *akhbar*).[220] Often translated as discrete anecdotes or reports, these writings also include simple statements, utterances of authoritative scholars, saints, or statesmen, reports of events, and stories about historical events, all varying in length from one line to several pages. Leder shows that though *akhbar* give the impression that they are reports truthfully handed down from prior witnesses, they were, in truth, reshaped and gradually elaborated in the process of transmission. "Only when we encounter two or more irreconcilable accounts of the same event, possibly quoted from the same eyewitness, do we become aware that akhbar are fabricated."[221] Leder also shows that one cannot with any confidence always distinguish between *qisas,* the genre of tales and myth relating to the prophets of the Koran or the Old Testament, and folkloric stories, told by popular storytellers, *qussas* from akhbar. "Instead, it is expedient to accept that historiographical narratives quoted from the collectors of akhbar may include qisas material. . . . *Akhbar* narratives, just like qisas, have their roots in the oral tradition of social gatherings. Moreover, qisas may also contain authentic historical information, and anecdotal *akhbar* may of course be sheer inventions, or may have been modified or distorted in the interest of certain parties."[222] However, for Leder, even the presence of legendary elements in akhbar does not "necessarily invalidate them as historical sources."[223]

The same collection contains a contribution of Dr. Lawrence Conrad, one of its editors. In an essay of patient scholarship and analytical clarity and brilliance, Conrad examines and contrasts the non-Muslim sources with the Muslim ones

for the Arab conquest, in 29/650, of the island of Arwad, which lies two kilometers off the Syrian coast. Conrad first establishes that the extant Syriac material
as found in Michael the Syrian (d. 1199), Bar Hebraeus (d. 1286), and the Chronicle of 1234 derives ultimately from the now lost works of Theophilus of Edessa
(ca. 749–750). Since the taking of Arwad was a significant event for the Arabs,
we do "find the campaign fully described in the historical sources of the Arab-
Islamic tradition. We do in fact find several accounts, but the content of these
reports differs to an extraordinary extent from the versions given by Theophilus
of Edessa. In fact, the Arabic narratives are so utterly irreconcilable not only with
Theophilus, but also with traditional views on the transmission of Arab-Islamic
accounts pertaining to the conquests and early Islamic history, that they raise historiographical issues of no less importance than those that have emerged concerning the transmission of the chronicle of Theophilus of Edessa."[224]

In case after case, Conrad demonstrates that most of the details found in the
Arabic accounts are literary creations with no historical basis. Building on the work
of Noth, and his own collaboration with Noth, Conrad shows the stereotypic and
formulaic nature of Arabic historical writing, where standard topoi and schemata
are repeated through various accounts of different conquests. "In historical terms
this corpus of material tells us little that does not disintegrate upon closer historiographical inspection."[225] This obviously has profound implications for any investigation of early Arabic historiography, and indeed, for any attempt to reconstruct
events of early Islamic history. Conrad's findings clearly upset some of the most
entrenched views of modern scholarship on Arabic historiography:

> Since the beginnings of serious modern scholarship on the Arabic *futuh* [con-
> quest] tradition in the mid-nineteenth century, the explanation for the origins of
> this tradition has envisaged Arab warriors sitting at evening sessions devoted to
> narration of their exploits and great victories. For some cases this may well be
> an accurate characterization, but for the fall of Arwad it is absolutely false. The
> extant evidence for the tradition on this event allows for only three possible con-
> clusions. First, there were no old warriors sitting around their hearths telling the
> younger generation of their heroics at Arwad. Or second, if there were, what-
> ever they said was at a very early point almost entirely lost—*lost, that is, in the*
> *sense that no genuine old report survived to pass into the hands of the later*
> *Umayyad tradents to whom we can trace the extant accounts. Or third, the old*
> *warriors did tell their stories, these narratives did pass on to the Umayyad*
> *ruwat [transmitters], but then these transmitters ignored the old material and*
> *instead chose to circulate baseless accounts generated within their own circles.*
> *Each of these alternatives involves extraordinary implications: the first, that old*
> *warriors, in defiance of all we think we know about the ancient "battle-days"*

(ayyam) lore and the continuity of Arabian oral tradition, simply did not relate what must have been an engaging and eventful story; the second, that such stories were not of sufficient interest for later generations to preserve and transmit them; the third, that in Umayyad times there was a broad-ranging practice of discarding old narratives and inventing baseless new ones, and that Umayyad society either did not notice or care. . . . The Arab-Islamic material for the conquest of Arwad does not and cannot consist of accounts passed on from one generation to the next in a continuous tradition beginning with the generation of the Arab conquerors. Instead, the beginnings of the extant tradition for this event must be sought among Umayyad storytellers piecing together narratives with only the barest shreds of genuinely historical information to guide or restrain the process of reconstruction.[226]

Thus, despite the lack of genuine historical material, detailed narrative accounts could nonetheless develop. The Arabic Arwad tradition shows us exactly how "an account acquires new details and responds to current notions concerning the scope, themes, utility, and method of history, and what the archaic Islamic past 'must have been' or 'should have been.' Each successive stage thus involves new changes, at times tantamount to generating a new account, which may subsequently respond to the shifting views and conceptions of a later generation, and so forth."[227] The Arabic Arwad tradition was evidently shaped by the art of the storyteller whose "account had to be something his audience would find edifying and/or entertaining; it should be harmonious with that audience's conceptions of the origins of Islam and the early growth of the community and it had to meet prevailing expectations of what a historical report should be able to offer."[228] Transmitters also reshaped or elaborated the material passing through their hands. Despite the utter convincingness and consistency of many of the details, it is only when we step outside the Arabic literary sources, compare them with non-Muslim literary ones, and look at the archaeological, epigraphic, and geographical evidence that we can come to any firm conclusions about their historical truth. Conrad concludes that "access to 'what really happened' can be had only by sifting through the spurious material that conceals it."[229]

How can we characterize the situation in the year 2000? Even in the early 1980s, a certain skepticism of the sources was fairly widespread; M. J. Kister was able to round off his survey of the sira literature that first appeared in 1983, with the following words: "The narratives of the sira have to be carefully and meticulously sifted in order to get at the kernel of historically valid information, which is in fact meagre and scanty."[230] If we can consider the new edition of the *Encyclopedia of Islam* as some kind of a yardstick of the prevailing scholarly opinion on the reliability of our sources for the life of the Prophet and the rise of

Islam, then the situation is clearly negative. W. Raven, in the entry for "sira" (volume 9), written in the mid-1990s, comes to this conclusion in an excellent survey of the sira material:

> The sira materials as a whole are so heterogeneous that a coherent image of the Prophet cannot be obtained from it. Can any of them be used at all for a historically reliable biography of Muhammad, or for the historiography of early Islam? Several arguments plead against it:
> (1) Hardly any sira text can be dated back to the first century of Islam.
> (2) The various versions of a text often show discrepancies, both in chronology and in contents.
> (3) The later the sources are, the more they claim to know about the time of the Prophet.
> (4) Non-Islamic sources are often at variance with Islamic sources (see P. Crone and M. Cook, *Hagarism).*
> (5) Most sira fragments can be classed with one of the genres mentioned above. Pieces of salvation history and elaborations on Koranic texts are unfit as sources for scientific historiography.[231]

FOR AND AGAINST WANSBROUGH

Despite his meager output, John Wansbrough has, more than any other scholar, as Berg says, undermined all previous scholarship on the first three centuries of Islam. Many scholars continue as though nothing had changed, and carry on working along traditional lines by taking the historical reliability of the exclusively Islamic sources for granted. Others, sometimes known as the revisionists, find Wansbrough's methodology at least very fruitful. Thus, we are left with an ever-widening gap between the two camps, and this was nowhere more apparent than when several scholars opposed, or even hostile, to Wansbrough's work refused to contribute to a collection of essays devoted to the implications and achievements of his work.[232]

Space forbids us to devote too much time to those scholars who have extended or have been influenced by Wansbrough's work, such as Hawting, Calder, Rippin, Nevo, van Ess, Christopher Buck, and Claude Gilliot, among others, since their work is well represented in the present collection. It would be just as well to interject a word of caution here: the scholars who have been influenced by Wansbrough do not necessarily and uncritically endorse every aspect of his theories; for instance, not all would agree with Wansbrough's late date for the establishment of the canonical Koran. The so-called disciples of Wansbrough, far from being epigones, are formidable and original scholars in their own right and in true Popperian fashion would be prepared to abandon this or that aspect of the master's theories should contrary evidence materialize. Nor do the scholars who do not accept Wansbrough's conclusions necessarily blindly accept the traditional Muslim account of the sira, the rise of Islam, or the compilation of the Koran; John Burton, Gerd Puin, and Gunter Luling are some of the scholars in this latter category. But now perhaps I should say something about recent articles or books challenging Wansbrough's basic assumptions. One debate revolves around the person of Ibn Abbas, the cousin of the Prophet, and source of a great deal of exegetical material. Rippin sums up the arguments on both sides with admirable clarity:

> Wansbrough drew attention to a series of texts ascribed specifically to Ibn Abbas, all of them of a lexicographical nature. One of the roles of the figure of Ibn Abbas within the development of tafsir, according to Wansbrough's argument, was bringing the language of the Koran into alignment with the language of the "Arabs." . . . Identity of the people as solidified through language became a major ideological stance promulgated in such texts.
>
> Such an argument, however, depended upon a number of preceding factors, including the emergence of the Koran as authoritative, before it could be mounted. Such an argument could not have been contemporary with Ibn Abbas, who died in 687 C.E., but must stem from several centuries later. The ascription to Ibn Abbas was an appeal to authority in the past, to the family of the Prophet and to a name which was gathering an association with exegetical activity in general.
>
> Issa Boullata examines one such text attributed to Ibn Abbas, and argues "that the tradition which aligns Ibn Abbas with lexicographical matters related to the Koran is early, although it was clearly subject to elaboration as time went on." . . . But Boullata raises the crucial issue "J. Wansbrough believes that the reference of rare or unknown Koranic words to the great corpus of early Arabic poetry is an exegetical method which is considerably posterior to the activity of Ibn Abbas."[233] While the activity may have been limited, Boullata admits, "if there was anybody who could have dared to do it (or have such activity ascribed to him) it was Ibn Abbas, the Prophet's cousin and Companion, because of his family relationship and authoritative position."[234] "Oral tradition" would have been the means by which these traditions from Ibn Abbas were transmitted down to later exegetical writers. Just because poetical citations are not found in early texts (as Wansbrough had pointed out) does not mean, for Boullata, that such an exegetical practice did not exist. "One cannot determine what of these materials is authentic and what is not, but everything points to the possibility that there existed a smaller core of materials which was most likely preserved

in a tradition of oral transmission for several generations before it was put down in writing with enlargements."[235]

"Possibility" and "most likely" are the key methodological assumptions of this historical approach, and certainly all historical investigations proceed on the basis of analogy of processes which underlie these assumptions. But Boullata underestimates the overall significance of what Wansbrough has argued. The debate is not whether a core of the material is authentic or not. . . . By underemphasizing issues of the establishment of authority of scripture and bringing into comparison profane texts with scripture, Boullata avoids the central crux. Ultimately, the assertion is that it would have been "only natural" for the Arabs to have followed this procedure within exegesis. Boullata asserts that there is an "Arab proclivity to cite proverbs or poetic verses orally to corroborate ideas in certain circumstances. This is a very old Arab trait which Ibn Abbas . . . could possibly have had."[236] For Wansbrough, nothing is "natural" in the development of exegetical tools.The tools reflect ideological needs and have a history behind them.

Substantial evidence in favor of the overall point which Wansbrough makes in this regard stems from Claude Gilliot's[237] extensive analysis of the tafsir of al-Tabari (d. 923 C.E.).It is surely significant that al-Tabari would still be arguing in the tenth century about the role and value of the Arabic language in its relationship to the Koran, and that his own extensive tafsir work is founded upon an argument to make just that case for language. The relationship of the sacred to the profane in language was not an issue which allowed itself to be simply assumed within the culture. It was subject to vigorous debate and back-forth between scholars."[238]

Another scholar whose views and methodological assumptions differ radically from John Wansbrough's is C. H. M. Versteegh. Essentially, Versteegh has a vision of the rise of Islam that is no longer accepted by a number of historians. He is convinced that "after the death of the Prophet the main preoccupation of the believers was the text of the Koran. This determined all their efforts to get to grip on the phenomenon of language, and it is, therefore, in the earliest commentaries on the Koran that we shall have to start looking for the original form of language study in Islam."[239] However, by contrast, Wansbrough and others "have argued that 'Islam' as we know it took a number of centuries to come into being and did not spring from the desert as a mature, self-reflective, defined entity. The idea that Muhammad provided the community with its scripture and that after his death all focus immediately turned to coming to an understanding of that scripture and founding a society based upon it simply does not match the evidence which we have before us in Wansbrough's interpretation. Nor does it match the model by which we have come to understand the emergence of complex social systems, be they motivated by religion or other ideologies."[240]

Versteegh has a totally different conception of "interpretation"; where he sees it as "a process somewhat abstracted from society as a whole, an activity motivated by piety and a dispassionate . . . concern for the religious ethos and which took place right at the historical beginnings of Islam," Wansbrough sees it as "a far more interactive and active participant within the society in which it takes place. . . . The pressures of the time and the needs of the society provide the impetus and the desired results of the interpretative efforts."[241] However, as Rippin concludes, it is not simply a question of skepticism about texts, but also a question of our understanding of how religious and other movements in human history emerge and evolve, and finally of the "interpretative nature of human existence as mediated through language."[242]

Estelle Whelan in a recent article challenges Wansbrough's conclusions. She is perfectly aware of the rather devastating implications of Wansbrough's analysis, that is, "that the entire Muslim tradition about the early history of the text of the Koran is a pious forgery, a forgery so immediately effective and so all-pervasive in its acceptance that no trace of independent contemporary evidence has survived to betray it. An important related issue involves the dating of early manuscripts of the Koran. If Wansbrough is correct that approximately a century and a half elapsed before Muslim scripture was established in 'canonical' form, then none of the surviving manuscripts can be attributed to the Umayyad or even the very early Abbasid period; particularly, one controversial manuscript discovered in San'a in the 1970s . . . for which a date around the turn of the eighth century has been proposed, would have to have been copied at a much later period."

Ms. Whelan devotes considerable space to examining the inscriptions at the Dome of the Rock in Jerusalem since they represent the primary documents for the condition of the Koranic text in the first century of Islam, having been executed in the reign of Abd al-Malik in 72/691–92. Her main arguments are that these inscriptions "should not be viewed as evidence of a precise adherence to or deviation from the 'literary form' of the Koranic text; rather they are little sermons or parts of a single sermon addressed to an audience that could be expected to understand the allusions and abbreviated references by which Abd al-Malik's particular message was conveyed." Thus the apparent deviations from the Koranic text only show that there was conscious and creative modification of the text for rhetorical or polemical purposes, to declare the primacy of the new religion of Islam over Christianity. But in order for this device to work, the listener or reader must be able to recognize the text or references, which in itself is a strong indication, according to Whelan, that the Koran was already the common property of the community in the last decade of the seventh century. Ms. Whelan also argues that there is enough evidence for "the active production of copies of the Koran from the late seventh century, coinciding with and confirming the inscriptional evidence of the established text itself. In fact, from the time of Mu'awiya through the reign of al-Walid the Umayyad caliphs were actively engaged in codifying every aspect of Muslim religious practice. Mu'awiya turned Muhammad's minbar into a symbol of authority and ordered the construction of maqsurahs in the major congregational mosques. Abd al-Malik made sophisticated use of Koranic quotations, on coinage and public monuments, to announce the new Islamic world order. Al-Walid gave monumental form to the Muslim house of worship and the service conducted in it. It seems beyond the bounds of credibility that such efforts would have preceded interest in codifying the text itself."[243] Thus for Ms. Whelan the Muslim tradition is reliable in attributing the first codification of the Koranic text to 'Uthman and his appointed commission.

Whelan's arguments are by no means very convincing, and will certainly not appease the skeptics. First, one cannot argue from a part to a whole; the fact that there are *some* late seventh-century inscriptions at the Dome of the Rock which can be identified as being from the "Koran" as we know it today does not mean that the whole of the "Koran" already existed at the end of the seventh century. Because a part of the Koran exists, does not mean that the whole of it does. What we know as the Koran has a long history; it did not materialize out of nowhere, fully formed, but emerged slowly over time. We would expect the Koran to have some authority in the community, and there is no evidence that this is the case as early as the first Muslim century.

To assert that the deviations from the Koran which are apparent in the inscriptions at the Dome of the Rock are not really deviations but rather sermons seems a little ad hoc to say the least. One could just as easily argue that the inscriptions and the "sermons" are similar because they are drawing on the same not-yet canonical body of literature. In fact Wansbrough himself allows for the early existence of "Koranic logia," which precedes the canonized Koran, and which would account rather well or even better for the inscriptions at the Dome of the Rock.

Whelan also blithely sidesteps all the skepticism that has been directed against all the sources of our "knowledge" of early Islam, and in the section "The Copying of the Quran," takes for granted that these sources are totally reliable as history. We do not have independent sources for the biographical material that she uses, and she is reduced to using the very sources at which so much criticism has been leveled for over a century, from at least Goldziher onwards. The reliability of these sources is precisely the issue; the same forces that produced the literature about the formation of the canon are at work on these other materials used by Whelan, and which, hence, suffer from the same limitations (e.g., these sources are late, tendentious, they all contradict each other, and are literary fictions rather than history).

Fred Donner is another very distinguished scholar who takes issue with Wansbrough and the revisionists. In *The Early Islamic Conquests* (1981), Donner, though he is like so many historians in the past very cautious about the sources, is nonetheless very confident that a reliable account of the early Muslim conquests can be reconstructed.[244] However as Hawting points out in his review of Donner, "when contradictions between different accounts cannot be resolved, broad generalization is resorted to . . . and there is a tendency to accept information which is consistent with the thesis being argued while rejecting or even ignoring that which is inconsistent."[245] While Donner's account may be plausible, contradictory ones are no less so.[246]

More recently, Donner has argued that the language of the Koran and the language of Hadith are different, and that this suggests a chronological separation between the two, with the Koran preceding the Hadith.[247] He also argues for a Hijazi (Arabian) origin of the Koran. Again, skeptics find Donner's arguments less than compelling. Even the revisionists, on the whole, do not deny that there are differences between the two the language of the Koran is like nothing else, and obviously does not come from the same context as Hadith. The question is: What are the sources of those differences? We certainly cannot legitimately jump to the chronological conclusion in the way that Donner does; in any case, why make the Koran first? We need additional arguments whereas Donner has simply accepted the traditional Muslim account, which, as we have seen, is precisely what the skeptics are skeptical about. For a certain number of scholars the most plausible hypothesis is that much if not all of the Koranic material *predates* Muhammad, and that it is liturgical material used in some community of possibly Judeo-Christian, and certainly monotheist, Arabs.[248] That is why by the time the Muslims got around to writing their commentaries on the Koran, they did not have the faintest idea what large parts of this material meant.[249] They were forced to invent some absurd explanations for these obscurities, but it all eventually got collected together as the Arabian book of God, in order to forge a specifically Arabian religious identity. This scenario, of course, only makes sense if we accept the revisionists' thesis that "Islam" as such did not emerge fully fledged in the Hijaz as the Muslim traditions would have us believe. Even Luling and Puin's ideas make more sense if we do not try to fit these ideas into the Meccan/Medinan procrustean bed that the Muslim Traditions have prepared for us, but rather accept that the Arabs forged their religious identity only when they encountered the older religious communities *outside* the Hijaz, since the thought that Mecca in the late sixth and early seventh century was host to such a Judeo-Christian community seems highly improbable.

Juynboll once said that Wansbrough's theories were so hard to swallow because of the obvious disparity in style and contents of Meccan and Medinan suras.[250] There is indeed a difference in language, style, and even message between the so-called Meccan and Medinan suras. But all that shows is that there are two quite different styles in the Koran, and of course, Muslim exegetes solved this problem by assigning one set to Mecca and the other to Medina, with considerable tinkering (verses from the "Medinese" suras assigned to Mecca and vice versa). But why should we accept the Medinan and Meccan labels? What is the source or sources of this difference? To accept these labels is simply to accept the entire traditional Muslim account of the compilation of the Koran, the biography of the Prophet, and the rise of Islam. Again, this is precisely what is at stake—the reliability of the sources. The differences, if anything, point to a history far more extensive than the short life of Muhammad as found in the sira, and they do not have to be interpreted biographically through the history of the life of Muhammad in Mecca and Medina. There is nothing natural about the Meccan/Medinan separation. It is clear from Lammens, Becker, and others that large parts of the sira and Hadith were invented to account for the difficulties and obscurities encountered in the Koran, and these labels also proved to be convenient for the Muslim exegetes for the same reason. The theory of abrogation also gets the exegetes out of similar difficulties and obviates the need to explain the embarrassing contradictions that abound in the Koran.

THE QUEST OF THE HISTORICAL JESUS AND MUHAMMAD: A COMPARISON

As G. R. Hawting reminds us in his important article, one of Wansbrough's achievements was "to place Islam squarely within the development of Semitic or Middle Eastern monotheism. . . . By insisting that Islam developed and came to fruition in the Middle East outside Arabia following the Arab conquest of the region and that its account of its own origins has to be understood in the same context, Wansbrough has increased our understanding of the nature of Islam's own tradition and what can and cannot be done with it." The vast amount of work done since Reimarus's pioneering research on Christianity and the historical Jesus at the beginning of the eighteenth century, especially by German scholars well versed in many of the Semitic languages necessary for such a daunting task, throws a very illuminating light on the growth of religions and religious mythology, especially in the Semitic, Middle Eastern milieu (and thus can be of relevance for the study of Islam). Furthermore, the results of this research point to the striking similarities to the theories of Wansbrough and the revisionists on the rise of Islam and the Muhammad legend of the Muslim traditions.

Reimarus (1694–1768) was perhaps the first to undertake the criticism of the tradition from the historical and scientific point of view. For Reimarus the solution of the problem of the life of Jesus called for a combination of the methods of historical *and* literary criticism.[251] He concluded that the Baptism and the Lord's Supper, in the historical sense, were not instituted by Jesus but created by the early church on the basis of certain historical assumptions. We must ascribe to the miracles (the stories that turn on the fulfillment of Messianaic prophecy) the universalistic traits and the predictions of the passion and the resurrection to the creative element in the tradition.

For David Strauss, "even though the earthly life of the Lord falls within historic times, and even if only a generation be assumed to have elapsed between His death and the composition of the Gospels; such a period would be sufficient to allow the historical material to become intermixed with myth. No sooner is a great man dead than the legend is busy with his life. Then, too, the offense of the word myth disappears for anyone who has gained an insight into the essential character of religious myth. It is nothing else than the clothing in historic form of religious ideas, shaped by the unconsciously inventive power of legend, and embodied in a historic personality. Even on a priori grounds we are almost compelled to assume that the historic Jesus will meet us in the garb of Old Testament Messianic ideas and primitive Christian expectations."[252]

The Gospel narratives were woven on the pattern of Old Testament prototypes; the call of the first disciple is modeled upon the call of Elisha by Elijah.[253] Compare this to what Raven says of the sira: "As the Koran had done before, the sira aims at establishing the place of Muhammad among the prophets, and that of Islam among the other religions. The numerous stories which dwell upon the characteristics of prophethood react on the narrative repertoire of Judaism, Christianity and Manichaeism."[254]

Bruno Bauer suggested that a Gospel may have a purely literary origin; the histories of Jesus' childhood are not just literary versions of a tradition but literary inventions. "What if the whole thing should turn out to be nothing but a literary invention—not only the incidents and discourses, but even the Personality which is assumed as the starting point of the whole movement?"[255] Jesus Christ is a product of the imagination of the early Church, with traits, incidents in his life, and so on, all taken from or modeled on Old Testament figures like Moses. Contrast this with the theory that under the influence of the Pentateuch, the Arabs cast Muhammad in the role of Moses as the leader of an exodus (Hijra), as the bearer of a new revelation (Koran) received on an appropriate (Arabian) sacred mountain, Mt. Hira.

"According to Albert Kalthoff,[256] the fire lighted itself—Christianity arose—by spontaneous combustion, when the inflammable material, religious and social, which had collected together in the Roman Empire, came into contact with the Jewish Messinaic expectations. Jesus of Nazareth never existed and even supposing He had been one of the numerous Jewish Messiahs who were put to death by crucifixion, He certainly did not found Christianity. The story of Jesus which lies before us in the Gospels is in reality only the story of the way in which the picture of Christ arose, that is to say, the story of the growth of the Christian community."[257] "Christ" is in reality the sublimated religious expression of the sum of the social and ethical forces at work in that period.

Goldziher dismissed a vast amount of the Hadith about the life of the Prophet Muhammad as spurious, the greater part being the result of the religious, historical, and social development of Islam during the first two centuries. The Hadith was useless as a basis for any scientific history and could only serve as a reflection of the tendencies of the early Muslim community, exactly in the way that the early Christians attributed words and sayings to Jesus that only in reality reflected the experience, convictions, and hopes of the Christian community.

Just as we find that the early Christians fabricated details of the life of Jesus in order to explain doctrinal points, so we find that Arab storytellers invented biographical material about Muhammad in order to explain difficult passages in the Koran.

According to Schacht, in his *The Origins of Muhammadan Jurisprudence*, Muslim traditions were formulated polemically in order to rebut a contrary doctrine or practice; doctrines in this polemical atmosphere were frequently projected back to higher authorities: "Traditions from Successors [to the Prophet] become traditions from Companions [of the Prophet], and Traditions from Companions become Traditions from the Prophet." Details from the life of the Prophet were invented to support legal doctrines. For Wrede, the Messiahship of Jesus, as found in the Gospels, is a product of Early Christian theology's attempt to correct history according to its own conceptions. The gospel was simply a reading back into Jesus' life, the faith and hope of the early Church.[258]

Both religions in their early days, as they came into contact and conflict with a hostile community with a religious tradition of its own, developed and defended their doctrinal positions by inventing biographical details of their founders that they then projected back onto an invented Arabian or Palestinian point of origin. Where Christianity arose from a fusion of Judaic and Greco-Roman ideas, Islam finally emerged from Talmudic Judaic, Syriac Christian, and indirectly, Greco-Roman ideas. As for their respective holy scriptures, for the Christians, as Morton Smith put it, "the first century [Christian] churches had no fixed body of gospels, let alone a New Testament," whereas for the Muslims, it is now argued that the definitive text of the Koran still had not been achieved as late as the ninth century.[259]

BACK TO SCHOLARSHIP

Maxime Rodinson, commenting on the work of Father Y. Moubarac and Louis Massignon, remarked that their perspective represented "a necessary reaction against an understanding of a text in terms that were too often foreign to the text, and a tendency to isolate themes from the religious context to which they belong—tendencies which were characteristic of the nineteenth century. However, the historian must occasionally ask himself if the reaction has not gone too far. Some of the methods of this school of thought must be a matter of concern to historians. To study the internal logic of a faith and to show respect are very legitimate objectives. The scholar has a perfect right to attempt to re-experience within himself the 'fire' and the exigencies of the religious consciousness under study. However, the elements that comprise a coherent system could indeed have derived from a variety of very different sources and might well have played an entirely different role in other systems. *Respect for the faith of sincere believers cannot be allowed either to block or deflect the investigation of the historian. . . . One must defend the rights of elementary historical methodology.*"[260]

It is certainly disgraceful that, what Karl Binswanger called, the "dogmatic Islamophilia" of modern Islamicist scholars helped to deny Gunter Luling a fair hearing and destroyed his academic career.[261] German Islamicists are to quote Arabist Gotz Schregle wearing "spiritually in their mind a turban," practicing "Islamic scholarship" rather than scholarship *on* Islam. Equally reprehensible has been the imputing of various "suspect" motives to the work of Wansbrough and those influenced by him.[262] Western scholars need to unflinchingly, unapologetically defend their right to examine the Islam, to explain the rise and fall of Islam by the normal mechanisms of human history, according to the objective standards of historical methodology (which relies on conjectures and refutations, critical thought, rational arguments, presentation of evidence, and so on). The virtue of disinterested historical inquiry would be fatally undermined if we brought into it the Muslim or Christian faith. If we bring subjective religious faith with its dogmatic certainties into the "historical approximation process, it inevitably undermines what R. G. Collingwood argued was the fundamental attribute of the critical historian, skepticism regarding testimony about the past."[263]

NOTES

1. "In the full [or clear] light of history" is now a famous phrase but is often used without any acknowledgement to its rightful coiner, R. S. Humphreys, in *Islamic History—A Framework for Inquiry* (Princeton, 1991), p. 69; and A. Rippin, in *Muslims: Their Religious Beliefs and Practices*, vol. 1 (London, 1990), p. ix.

2. Interview with Salman Rushdie, *Critical Quarterly* 38, no. 2 (summer 1996): 59–60.

3. H. W. Wardman, *Ernest Renan: A Critical Biography* (London, 1964), p. 78.

4. Renan, *Histoire et Parole* (Laffont, Paris, 1984), p. 351.

5. Ibid., p. 263.

6. Those who see Renan as a racist would do well to read his celebrated lecture of 1882, "Qu'est-ce qu'une nation?" where he implicitly repudiates his earlier views on racial inequality put forward in the *Dialogues*; he explicitly rejects the attempt to rest the concept of nationhood on race, language, economics, geography, and religion. (See also Renan's *Islam and Science*, 1883.)

7. Wardman, *Ernest Renan*, p. 69.

8. David C. Lee, *Ernest Renan: In the Shadow of Faith* (London, 1996), p. 270.

9. Wardman, op. cit., p. 89.

10. Professor Montgomery Watt in his influential biography of Muhammad developed a Renan-like thesis that Islam responded to the deep spiritual needs of the people, and that Mecca, at the time was beset with a social malaise, even a spiritual crisis. W. M. Watt, *Muhammad at Mecca* (Oxford, 1953); *Muhammad at Medina* (Oxford, 1950).

11. P. Crone, *Meccan Trade and the Rise of Islam* (Oxford, 1987), p. 241.

12. Reprinted in *The Quran As Text*, ed. Stefan Wild (Brill, Leiden, 1996).

13. Mohammed Arkoun, review of *The Quran As Text,* in *Arabica* 45, no. 3 (July 1998): 274–75.

14. In *Why I Am Not A Muslim* (Amherst, N.Y.: Prometheus Books, 1995).

15. M. Rodinson, "The Western Image and Western Studies of Islam," in *The Legacy of Islam*, ed. J. Schacht and C. E. Bosworth (Oxford, 1974), p. 59.

16. M. Watt, *Muhammad at Mecca* (Oxford, 1953), p. x.

17. Sir William Muir, *Life of Mahomet*, 4 vols. (London, 1858–1861). This was a very scholarly but critical biography written from a Christian point of view. "The sword of Muhammad and the Koran are the most stubborn enemies of Civilization, Liberty, and Truth which the world has yet known." (*Life of Mahomet*, one vol.edn. 1894, p. 522.)

18. Hussein Amin, *La biographie muhammadienne entre Orient et Occident,* in *Le Livre du musulman désemparé*, ed. La Découverte (Paris, 1992), pp. 32f.

19. For example, M. Watt, *What Is Islam?* (New York, 1968), p. 21: "I am not a Muslim in the usual sense, though I hope I am a *muslim* as 'one surrendered to God.' "

20. Watt and Bell, *Introduction to the Quran,* Edinburgh, 1977, pvi.

21. M. Rodinson, "A Critical Survey of Modern Studies on Muhammad," in *Studies on Islam*, ed. M. Swartz (New York, 1981), p. 24.

22. Ibid., p. 61 n. 6.

23. Ibid., p. 63 n. 23. Cf. Ibn Hisham, *Sira, Das Legen Muhammeds*, ed. F. Wusten-feld (Gottingen, 1859–1860), p. 688; and al-Waqidi, *Muhammad in Medina*, trans. J. Wellhausen (Berlin, 1882), p. 215.

24. Ibid., p. 29.

25. Aqqad, *Abqariyat Muhammad* (The Genius of Muhammad) (Cairo, 1940). Emphasis added.

26. B. Jawzi, *Min Tarikh al-Harakat al-Fikriya fi'l-Islam* (Jerusalem, 1928).

27. Rodinson, "A Critical Surve," p. 29.

28. Rodinson, *Mohammed* (New York: Vintage Books, 1971); originally published as *Mohammed* (Paris, 1961).

29. Reported by Associated Press, Thursday May 14, 1998, 10.43 EDT.

30. Rodinson, *Mohammed*, pp. 217–18.

31. F. Sezgin, *Geschichte des arabischen Schrifttums* (Leiden, 1967), 1: 257–302.

32. Watt and McDonald, *The History of al-Tabari,* vol. 6 (Albany, 1988), p. xi.

33. W. Raven, "Sira," in *Encyclopedia of Islam*, 2d ed., vol. 9, pp. 660–63.

34. M. Hinds, *al-Magahzi*, in *Encyclopedia of Islam*, 2d ed., vol. 5, pp. 1161–64.

35. Ibid, p. 1161.

36. Stefan Leder, "The Literary Use of the *Khabar*," in *The Byzantine and Early Islamic Near East: Problems in the Literary Source Material*, ed. A. Cameron and L. I. Conrad (Princeton, 1992), pp. 277–78.

37. Stefan Leder, "The Literary Use of the *Khabar*," p. 311.

38. With, of course, no pretentions to completeness.

39. A. Guillaume, introduction to *The Life of Muhammad: A Translation of Ibn Ishaq's Sirat Rasul Allah* (London, 1955). Reprinted Karachi, 1987, pp. xiv ff.

40. J. Horovitz, "Wahb B. Munabbih," in *Encyclopedia of Islam*, 8: 1084–85.

41. J. Horovitz, "Al-Zuhri," in *Encyclopedia of Islam*, 8: 1239–41.

42. Guillaume, op. cit., pp. xvi–xvii.

43. Alternative dates for his death are 151, 153 and even 144 (768, 770, or 761). J. M. B. Jones, "Ibn Ishak," in *Encyclopedia of Islam*, 3: 810–11.

44. Ibid., p. 811.

45. A. Guillaume, *The Life of Muhammad*, p. xxx.

46. W. Raven, "Sira," in *Encyclopedia of Islam*, 9: 661.

47. R. Sellheim, "Prophet, Chalif und Geschichte-die Muhammad-Biographie des Ibn Ishaq," in *Oriens* 28, 29 (1965–66): 33–91.

48. Raven, "Sira," p. 661.

49. R. S. Humphreys, *Islamic History: A Framework for Inquiry* (Princeton, 1991), p. 82.

50. Raven, "Sira," p. 661.

51. W. M. Watt, "Ibn Hisham," in *Encyclopedia of Islam*, 3: 801.

52. A. Guillaume, op. cit, p. xvii.

53. Crone, *Meccan Trade and the Rise of Islam,* p. 223.

54. C. H. Becker, "Al-Baladhuri," in *Encyclopedia of Islam*, 2: 611–12.

55. R. Paret, "Al-Tabari," in *Encyclopedia of Islam*, 7: 578–79.

56. Raven, "Sira," p. 661.

57. C. H. Becker, "Matters of Principle Concerning Lammens' Sira Studies," in *Der Islam* 4 (1913): 263 ff.

58. J. Wansbrough, *The Sectarian Milieu: Content and Composition of Islamic Salvation History* (London, 1978).

59. Raven, "Sira," pp. 661–62.

60. Ibid., p. 662.

61. Ibid.

62. Again, this is not, needless to say, a complete list of all the manuscripts.

63. P. Crone and M. Cook, *Hagarism: The Making of the Islamic World* (Cambridge, 1977). My list of non-Muslim sources is, of course, nowhere near complete. For a thorough discussion of all the non-Muslim sources, see Robert G. Hoyland, *Seeing Islam As Others Saw It* (Princeton, 1997).

64. Ibid., p. 155 n. 27.

65. The Jacobites, taking their name from Jacob Baradaeus (ca. 500–78), were Syrian Monophysites rejecting the teaching of the Council of Chalcedon (451) on the Person of Christ.

66. Melchites or Melkites were Christians of Syria and Egypt who refused Monophysitism, accepted the Definition of Chalcedon (451 C.E.), and remained in communion with the see of Constantinople.

67. Geoffrey King and Ronald Lewcock in their survey of Islamic architecture in Saudi Arabia rather naively list for Medina, "Mosque of the Prophet, 622, with later enlargements." *Architecture of the Islamic World*, ed. Geroge Michell (London, 1978), p. 210. They seem to be relying entirely on very late and tendentious Muslim literary traditions rather than any hard archaeological evidence.

68. Oleg Grabar, *The Formation of Islamic Art* (1973, reprint, New Haven, 1978), p. 49.

69. E. Whelan, "Forgotten Witness: Evidence for the Early Codification of the Quran," in *The Journal of the American Oriental Society* (January–March 1998).

70. Rippin, *Muslims: Their Religious Beliefs and Practices,* vol. 1, p. 55.

71. Humphreys, *Islamic History: A Framework for Inquiry*, p. 53.

72. Cook and Crone, *Hagarism: The Making of the Islamic World*, p. 173 n. 26.

73. K. A. C. Creswell, *A Short Account of Early Muslim Architecture*, (Harmondsworth, 1958), p. 41.

74. R. S. Humphreys, op. cit., pp. 59 ff.

75. Ibid., p.69.

76. A. Mingana, "The Transmission of the Koran," in *The Origins of the Koran,* ed. Ibn Warraq (Amherst, N.Y.: Prometheus Books, 1998), p. 107. Mingana's article was originally published in 1916.

77. In all senses of the word.

78. R. S. Humphreys, op. cit., p. 89.

79. Though as H. Berg has pointed out to me, we should rather say, "the term Muhammad is found in the Koran," a subtle but useful distinction.

80. M. Cook, *Muhammad*, (Oxford, 1983), pp. 69–70.

81. Humphreys, *Islamic History*, p. 83.

82. I owe this point to H. Berg.

83. With apologies to David Hume, *Dialogues Concerning Natural Religion* (Harmondsworth, 1990). First published in 1779.

84. M. I. Finley, *Aspects of Antiquity* (Harmondsworth, 1978), p. 177.

85. R. G. Collingwood, *The Idea of History* (1946; reprint, Oxford, 1951), pp. 14–15; quoted by M. I. Finley, op. cit., p. 177.

86. Robin Lane Fox, *The Unauthorized Version: Truth and Fiction in the Bible* (Harmondsworth, 1991), p. 167. It is not clear who Mr. Fox is quoting in this instance, but probably Collingwood, though I have been unable to locate the phrase in *The Idea of History*.

87. Lawrence I. Conrad, "Recovering Lost Texts: Some Methodological Issues," *Journal of the American Oriental Society* 113, no. 2 (April–June 1993): 258–63. See chapter 10, in this volume.

88. Ibid.

89. Jan Vansina, *Oral Tradition as History* (London and Nairobi, 1985), p. 4.

90. Janet Feigenbaum, "How We Tell It and How it Was," *Times Literary Supplement* (October 30, 1998): 14–15.

91. David B. Pillemer, *Momentous Events, Vivid Memories* (Harvard, 1998).

92. Feigenbaum, "How We Tell It and How it Was."

93. Finley, *Aspects of Antiquity*, p. 35.

94. A. E. Housman, *Selected Prose* (Cambridge, 1961), p. 43.

95. Jan Vansina, op. cit., pp. 130–31.

96. P. Crone, *Slaves on Horses: The Evolution of the Islamic Polity* (London, 1980), p. 12.

97. Crone, *Meccan Trade and the Rise of Islam*.

98. M. I. Finley, *The World of Odysseus* (Harmondsworth, 1979), p. 149. Emphasis added.

99. Gal. 4:16.

100. Muir, *The Life of Mahomet*, pp. xli–xlii. Muir is referring to G. Weil, *Geschichte der Chalifen*, 3 vols. (Mannheim, 1846–1851), vol. 2, p. 290; *Historisch—Kritische Einleitung in der Koran* (Bielefeld, 1844), vol. 2, p. 595.

101. Ibid., p. xlvi.

102. Ibid., p. xlviii (quoting Sprenger's *Mohammad*, p. 68).

103. Ibid., p.xlviii.

104. J. Wellhausen, *Prolegomena, 4*, quoted by Humphreys, *Islamic History*, p. 83.

105. Crone, *Slaves on Horses*, p. 13.

106. Humphreys, *Islamic History*, p. 83.

107. Ibid., p. 83.

108. Quoted by R. Blachère, *Le Probleme de Mahomet* (Paris, 1952), p. 9.

109. C. V. Langlois and C. Seignobos, *Introduction aux études historiques* (Paris, 1898), English trans., *Introduction to the Study of History*, 5th. ed., London, 1898, and New York, 1932.

110. Rodinson, "A Critical Survey of Modern Studies on Muhammad," p. 24.

111. K. S. Salibi, "Islam and Syria in the writings of Henri Lammens," in *Historians of the Middle East*, ed. B. Lewis and P. M. Holt (Oxford, 1962), p. 331.

112. Ibid.

113. Rodinson, *A Critical Survey*.

114. F. E.Peters, "The Quest of the Historical Muhammad," *International Journal of Middle East Studies* 23 (1991): 291–315. See chapter 13, of this volume.

115. Lawrence I. Conrad, "Abraha and Muhammad Some Observations Apropos of Chronology and Literary Topoi in the Early Arabic Historical Tradition," *Bulletin of the School of Oriental African Studies* 1 (1987): 225. See chapter 13, of this volume.

116. Cf. A. Schweitzer, *The Quest of the Historical Jesus*, trans. W. Montgomery (London, 1945), pp. 4, 5: "For hate as well as love can write a Life of Jesus, and the greatest of them are written with hate that of Reimarus, the Wolfenbuttel Fragmentist, and that of D. F. Strauss. . . . And their hate sharpened their historical insight. They advanced the study of the subject more than all the others put together. But for the offense which they gave, the science of historical theology would not have stood where it does to-day."

117. Rodinson, op. cit, pp. 26–27.

118. Salibi, op. cit, p. 335.

119. Ibid.

120. Ibid.

121. Ibid., p. 336.

122. N. A. Smirnov, *Russia and Islam* (London, 1954).

123. E. A. Belyaev, *Arabs, Islam, and the Arab Caliphate in the Early Middle Ages* (New York, 1969).

124. Humphreys, op. cit., p. 83.

125. J. Schacht, *The Origins of Muhammadan Jurisprudence* (Oxford, 1950), pp. 4–5.

126. Ibid., p. 149.

127. Ibid., p. 163.

128. Ibid., p. 224.

129. R. Blachère, *Le Probleme de Mahomet Essai de Biographie Critique du fondateur de l'Islam* (Paris 1952), pp. 11, 15.

130. Ibid., pp. 17–18.

131. H. Birkeland, *The Lord Guides: Studies on Primitive Islam* (Oslo, 1956), pp. 6ff.

132. R. Paret, "Researches on the Life of the Prophet Muhammad," in *JPHS* (1958): 81–96.

133. Ibid., p. 89.

134. Birkeland, op. cit., pp. 133–35.

135. Paret, op. cit., p. 89.

136. A. Noth, "Isfahan-Nihavand. Eine quellenkritische Studie zur fruhislamischen Historiographie," *ZDMG* 118 (1968): 274–96.

137. All references are to this second edition, which shall be referred to as Noth and Conrad, at Albrecht Noth's own request in the preface, p. xi.

138. Crone, *Slaves on Horses*, p. 14.

139. A. Noth and Lawrence I. Conrad, *The Early Arabic Historical Tradition: A Source Critical Study,* trans. Michael Bonner (London, 1994), p. 62.

140. Ibid., p. 19.

141. Ibid., p. 22.

142. Ibid., p. 72

143. Ibid., p. 84.

144. Ibid., p. 87.

145. Ibid., p. 103.

146. Ibid., p. 109.

147. Ibid., p. 110.

148. Ibid., p. 24.

149. E. Stetter, *Topoi und Schemata im hadit*, 1965. I am indebted to H. Berg for referring me to Stetter's work.

150. G. H. A. Juynboll, ed., *Studies in the First Century of Islamic Society* (Illinois, 1982), pp. 1–2.

151. Ibid., p. 2.

152. Alphonse Mingana, "The Transmission of the Koran," in *The Origins of the Koran,* ed., Ibn Warraq (Amherst, N.Y.: Prometheus Books, 1998), pp. 97–113.

153. Bernard Lewis and P. M. Holt, eds., *Historians of the Middle East* (London, 1962).

154. C. Cahen, "Fiscalité, proprieté, antagonismes sociaux en Haute—Mésopotamie au temps des premiers Abbassides d'après Denys de Tell Mahré," in *Arabica*, vol. 1 (1954), and "Note sur l'accueil des Chrétiens d'Orient à l'Islam," *Revue de l'Histoire des Religions*, 1964.

155. Juynboll, op. cit., p. 3.

156. Though Crone's argument that Jews and Christians, given their wide geographical and social distribution, could scarcely have conspired to fabricate their uniform results, is a good one, we should be aware that scholars such as Azmi use the same arguments to defend Hadiths.

157. Crone, *Slaves on Horses,* pp. 15–16.

158. J. Wansbrough, review of *Hagarism: The Making of the Islamic World*, by M. Cook and P. Crone, *Bulletin of the School of Oriental and African Studies* 41, part 1 (1978): 155–56.

159. Juynboll, op. cit., p. 5.

160. H. P. Raddatz, *Die Stellung und Bedeutung des Sufyan at-Tauri* (Bonn, 1967). '*Fruhislamisches Erbrecht nach dem Kitab al-Fara 'id des Sufyan at-Tauri*, DWDI, 1971.

161. J. Van Ess, *Zwischen Hadit und Theologie* (Berlin, 1975).

162. J. Wansbrough, *Quranic Studies* (Oxford, 1977).

163. J. Burton, *The Collection of the Qu'ran* (Cambridge, 1977).

164. M. Cook, *Monotheists Sages: A Study in Muslim and Jewish Attitudes towards Oral Tradition in the Early Islamic Period,* unpublished typescript.

165. F. Sezgin, *Buhari'nin Kaynaklari hakkinda Arastirmalar* (Istanbul: Ibrahim Horoz, 1956).

166. M. M. Azmi, *Studies in Early Hadith Literature* (Beirut, 1968).

167. N. Abbott, *Studies in Arabic Literary Papyri*, vols. 1 and 2 (Chicago, 1957 and 1967).

168. W. M. Watt, *Muhammad at Mecca* (Oxford, 1953); "The Materials used by Ibn Ishaq," in *Historians of the Middle East*, ed. B. Lewis and P. M. Holt (London, 1962); introduction to *The History of al-Tabari*, trans. W. M. Watt and M. V. McDonald (Albany, N.Y., 1988).

169. H. A. R. Gibb, *Studies on the Civilization of Islam* (London, 1962), p. 53.

170. M. A. Shaban, *Islamic History: A New Interpretation* (Cambridge 1971–76), 1: 1.

171. R. Paret, "Die Lucke in der Uberlieferung uber den Islam," in *Westostliche Abhandlungen Rudolf Tschudi*, ed. F. Meier (Wiesbaden, 1954).

172. A. Guillaume, trans., introduction to *The Life of Muhammad* (Oxford, 1955); "The Biography of the Prophet in Recent Research," in *Islamic Quarterly Review* (1954): 5–11.

173. R. Sellheim, "Prophet, Chalif und Geschichte. Die Muhammed-Biographie des Ibn Ishaq," in *Oriens* (1967), pp. 33–91.

174. Crone, *Slaves on Horses*, p. 210 n. 78.

175. N. J. Coulson, *A History of Islamic Law* (Edinburgh, 1964), pp. 64 ff.

176. Azmi, *Studies in Early Hadith Literature*, pp. 222–47.

177. Crone, *Slaves on Horses*, p. 211, n. 88.

178. Azmi, *Studies in Early Hadith Literature*, pp. 222–47, especially pp. 230 ff.

179. Parallel with the improvement and backward growth of isnads goes their spread, that is the creation of additional authorities or transmitters for the same doctrine or tradition. J. Schacht, *Origins*, p. 166.

180. Cook, *Early Muslim Dogma: A Source Critical Study* (Cambridge, 1981), pp. 115–16.

181. Ibid., pp. 109–10.

182. N. J. Coulson, "European Criticism of Hadith Literature," in *Cambridge History of Arabic Literature: Arabic Literature to the End of the Umayyad Period*, ed. A. F. L. Beeston et al. (Cambridge, 1983).

183. Ibid., p. 317.

184. Ibid., p. 319.

185. Ibid., p. 321.

186. G. H. A. Juynboll, *Muslim Tradition Studies in Chronology, Provenance, and Authorship of Early Hadith* (Cambridge, 1983).

187. M. J. Kister, *Studies in Jahiliyya and Early Islam* (London, 1980).

188. Humphreys, *Islamic History*, p.84

189. I owe all these points to H. Berg.

190. Ella Landau-Tasseron, "Processes of Redaction The Case of the Tamimite Delegation to the Prophet Muhammad," *BSOAS* 49 (1986): 253–70.

191. Ibid., p. 263.

192. Ibid., p. 270.

193. S. Bashear, *Arabs and Others In Early Islam*, vol. 8 of *Studies in Late Antiquity and Early Islam* (Princeton, 1997).

194. S. Bashear, "Quran 2114 and Jerusalem," *BSOAS* (1989): 215–38.

195. Ibid., pp. 215–16.

196. Ibid., p. 217.

197. J. Wansbrough, *Quranic Studies* (Oxford, 1977), pp. 58, 179. Emphasis added.

198. Bashear, "Quran 2114 and Jerusalem," pp. 232–33.

199. G. Hawting, *The First Dynasty of Islam* (London, 1986), pp. 6–7; "The Origins of the Muslim Sanctuary at Mecca," in *Studies in the First Century of Islam*, ed. G. H. A. Juynboll (Illinois, 1982).

200. M. J. Kister, "On 'Concessions' and Conduct: A Study in Early Hadith," in *Studies in the First Century of Islam*, pp. 89–108.

201. Bashear, "Quran 2114 and Jerusalem," p. 237.

202. Ibid, p. 238.

203. Crone and Cook, *Hagarism*.

204. S. Bashear, "The Title 'Faruq' and Its Association with Umar 1," in *Studia Islamica* 72 (1990): 69.

205. Ibid.

206. Ibid., p. 70

207. S. Bashear, "Abraham's Sacrifice of His Son and Related Issues," in *Der Islam* 67 (1990): 243–77.

208. Wansbrough, *Quranic Studies*, pp. 58, 179.

209. Schacht, *The Origins of Muhammadan Jurisprudence*, pp. 107 and 156.

210. Bashear's note: "G. R. Hawting has lately argued that Islam does not seem to have one firmly established cultic center in the first [Muslim] century, *The First Dynasty of Islam*, London, 1986, pp. 6–7. Before that Kister has shown how the struggle between Mecca and Jerusalem over primacy in Islam goes to the first half of the second [Muslim] century. 'You Shall Only Set . . . ,' *Le Museon* 82 (1969): 178–84, 194."

211. Goldziher, *Muslim Studies* (New York, 1971), 2: 279–81.

212. Bashear, "Abraham's Sacrifice of His Son and Related Issues," p. 277.

213. S. Bashear, "Riding Beasts on Divine Missions: An Examination of the Ass and Camel Traditions," *Journal of Scientific Studies* 37, no. 1 (spring 1991): 37–75.

214. Ibid., p. 75.

215. Bashear, *Arabs and Others in Early Islam*.

216. Ibid., p. 3.

217. Ibid,p. 113.

218. Ibid., p. 116

219. Ibid p. 118.

220. Stefan Leder, "The Literary Use of the Khabar: A Basic Form of Historical Writing," in *The Byzantine and Early Islamic Near East*, no. 1, vol. 1 of *Problems in the Literary Source Material,* ed. Averil Cameron and Lawrence I. Conrad (Princeton, 1992), pp. 277–315.

221. Ibid., p. 308.

222. Ibid. pp. 311–12.

223. Ibid, p. 306.

224. Lawrence I. Conrad, "The Conquest of Arwad: A Source—Critical Study in the Historiography of the Early Medieval Near East," in *The Byzantine and Early Islamic Near East*, pp. 308–309.

225. Ibid., p. 386.

226. Ibid., pp. 387–88. Emphasis added.

227. Ibid. p. 391.

228. Ibid., p. 393.

229. Ibid., p. 401.

230. M. J. Kister, "The Sirah Literature," in *Arabic Literature to the End of the Umayyad Period*, ed. Johnstone Beeston et al. (Cambridge, 1983), p. 367.

231. Raven, "Sira," p. 662.

232. Which eventually appeared with only the contributions of the advocates of Wansbrough: "Islamic Origins Reconsidered: John Wansbrough and the Study of Early Islam, in *Method and Theory in the Study of Religion*, volume 9–1, ed. Herbert Berg (Berlin: Mouton de Gruyter, 1997), with articles by Herbert Berg, G. R. Hawting, Andrew Rippin, Norman Calder, and Charles J. Adams.

233. Issa Boullata, "Poetry Citation as Interpretive Illustration in Quran Exegesis: Masa'il Nafi' ibn al-Azraq," in *Islamic Studies Presented to Charles J. Adams*, ed. Wael B. Hallaq and Donald P. Little (Leiden: E. J. Brill, 1991), pp. 27–40.

234. Ibid., p. 38

235. Ibid., p. 40.

236. Ibid., p. 38

237. Claude Gilliot, *Exégèse, langue et theologie en Islam.Lexégèse coranique de Tabari (m. 311–923).* Paris:Vrin.

238. Andrew Rippin, "Quranic Studies, Part IV: Some Methodological Note," in *Islamic Origins Reconsidered John Wansbrough and the Study of Early Islam, in Method & Theory in the Study of Religion,* volume 9–1, ed. Herbert Berg (Berlin: Mouton de Gruyter, 1997), pp. 41–43.

239. C. H. M. Versteegh, *Arabic Grammar and Quranic Exegesis in Early Islam* (Leiden: E. J. Brill, 1993), p. 41.

240. Rippin, op. cit., p. 44.

241. Ibid., p. 44.

242. Ibid., p. 45.

243. E. Whelan, "Forgotten Witness: Evidence for the Early Codification of the Quran," in *JAOS* (January–March 1998).

244. F. Donner, *The Early Islamic Conquests*, Princeton, 1981.

245. G. R. Hawting, review of Donner, in *BSOAS* 47 (1984): 130–33.

246. Humphreys, *Islamic History*, p. 70.

247. F. Donner, *Narratives of Islamic Origins: The Beginnings of Islamic Historical Writing* (Princeton, 1998).

248. G. Luling asserts that a third of the Koran is of pre-Islamic Christian origins; see *Uber den Urkoran* (1973; reprint, Erlangen, 1993), p. 1.

249. Gerd Puin is quoted as saying, "The Koran claims for itself that it is *'mubeen'* or 'clear.' But if you look at it, you will notice that every fifth sentence or so simply doesn't make sense. . . . The fact is that a fifth of the Koranic text is *just incomprehensible. . . ."* *Atlantic Monthly* (January 1999).

250. G. H. A. Juynboll, review of *Quranic Studies by* John Wansbrough, in *JSS* 24 (1979): 293–96.

251. A. Schweitzer, *The Quest of the Historical Jesus*, trans. W. Montgomery (London, 1945), p. 24.

252. Schweitzer, *The Quest of the Historical Jesus*, p. 79.

253. Ibid., pp. 81, 82.

254. Raven, "Sira," p. 662.

255. Schweitzer, *The Quest of the Historical Jesus*, pp. 141, 145.

256. A. Kalthoff, *Das Christusproblem.Grundlinien zu einer Sozialtheologie* (Leipzig, 1902), pp. 87 ff.

257. Schweitzer, *The Quest of the Historical Jesus*, p. 313.

258. Ibid., p. 336.

259. R. Joseph Hoffmann and G. A. Larue, eds., *Jesus in History and Myth*, (Amherst, N.Y.: Prometheus Books, 1986), p. 48.

260. M. Rodinson, *A Critical Survey of Modern Studies on Muhammad*, p. 57. Emphasis added.

261. G. Luling, "Preconditions for the Scholarly Criticism of the Koran and Islam, with Some Autobiographical Remarks," in *The Journal of Higher Criticism* 3 (Spring 1996): 73–109.

262. See, for example, R. B. Serjeant's review of Wansbrough's *Quranic Studies*, *JRAS* (1978): 76–78.

263. Hoffmann and Larue, eds., *Jesus in History and Myth*, p. 199.

Chapter 2

Origins of Islam: A Critical Look at the Sources

Ibn al-Rawandi

The life story of Muhammad—his birth at Mecca 570 C.E., marriage to Khadija 595, first Koranic revelation 610, migration (Hijra) to Medina 622, conquest of Mecca 630, death 632—is a story that Muslims have told themselves for over 1,200 years. It is the story that is told to any potential convert and offered generally as a reliable account of the origin of Islam, but that story as usually presented is but the barest bones of what is supposed to be known to have happened.

The material on the life of Muhammad to be found in the works of Arab historians is of formidable proportions and incredible detail. Everything from the names and lineages of minor characters to the inner thoughts and motivations of the major protagonists, everything, in short, that anyone who enjoys a good story might want to know. Some idea of the detail available can be gathered from Martin Lings' book *Muhammad: His Life Based on the Earliest Sources*. Lings, as a pious Muslim, presents it all without the least hint of doubt or reservation, but a life of Muhammad "based on the earliest sources" is precisely the problem for the secular historian, since the sources are not early at all but late and tendentious.

The way that Muslims in general like to imagine the situation with regard to our knowledge of the life of Muhammad is well illustrated by a passage from a contemporary introduction to Islam aimed at young Muslims:

> The life of Muhammad is known as the *Sira* and was lived in the full light of history. Everything he did and said was recorded. Because he could not read and write himself, he was constantly served by a group of 45 scribes who wrote

down his sayings, instructions and his activities. Muhammad himself insisted on documenting his important decisions. Nearly three hundred of his documents have come down to us, including political treaties, military enlistments, assignments of officials and state correspondence written on tanned leather. We thus know his life to the minutest details: how he spoke, sat, sleeped (sic), dressed, walked; his behaviour as a husband, father, nephew; his attitudes toward women, children, animals; his business transactions and stance toward the poor and the oppressed; his engagement in camps and cantonments, his behaviour in battle; his exercise of political authority and stand on power; his personal habits, likes and dislikes—even his private dealings with his wives. Within a few decades of his death, accounts of the life of Muhammad were available to the Muslim community in written form. One of the earliest and the most-famous biographies of Muhammad, written less than (a) hundred years after his death, is *Sirat Rasul Allah* by Ibn Ishaq.[1]

In contrast, the following is the verdict of John Burton, Professor Emeritus of Islamic Studies at the University of St. Andrews, on the translation of a volume of al-Tabari's *History* dealing with the early life of Muhammad:

In this series of translations of the History of al-Tabari, four volumes on the life of Muhammad are projected, of which this, the first, covers the part from birth to early fifties. None will fail to be struck by the slimness of a volume purporting to cover more than half a century in the life of one of History's giants. Ignoring the pages tracing his lineage all the way back to Adam and disregarding the merely fabulous with which the author has padded out his book, is to realize how very meagre is the hard information available to the Muslims for the life of the man whose activities profoundly affected their own as well as the lives of countless millions. Of the childhood, the education of the boy and the influences on the youth, all of which set the pattern of the development of the man, we know virtually nothing. We simply have to adjust to the uncomfortable admission that, in the absence of contemporary documents, we just do not and never shall know what we most desire to learn. To admit that we do not know as much as we thought we did is the sign of maturity, and have we not been told that of that whereof we cannot speak, we must perforce be silent? Otherwise we speculate. There is nothing wrong with speculation, as long as it is not called History.[2]

The gulf between the mental attitudes represented by these two quotations forms the theme for the rest of this article.

The claim that Ibn Ishaq's life of Muhammad was "written less than a hundred years after his death," is disingenuous, not to say deliberately misleading.

When this kind of statement is found in books written by Muslims it is hard to know whether they are the result of ignorance, wishful thinking, or a conscious desire to deceive. It is indeed true that the earliest biography of Muhammad is the *Sirat Rasul Allah* by Ibn Ishaq, it is also true that he was born about 717 and died in 767. Ibn Ishaq was the oldest of the sources for the life of Muhammad relied upon by al-Tabari (d. 992), and as Burton says: "was himself a man who died as much as a century and a half after the time of the Prophet. Born some eighty-five years after Muhammad's arrival at Medina, Muhammad b. Ishaq would have reached his teens only as much as one hundred years after the events he affects to portray."[3]

The only way to ameliorate the effect of Ibn Ishaq's debilitating remoteness from the time of the purported events of Muhammad's life is to claim he had access to reliable sources who were themselves eyewitnesses or hearers of eyewitnesses. This amounts to a claim for the reliability of the chain of transmission (isnad) of the traditions of the Prophet (Hadith), a claim without foundation, as we shall see. In any case, as Burton goes on to say:

> To demonstrate the feasibility of the isnad is to say nothing about the authenticity of the matter being transmitted. . . . In judging the content, the only resort of the scholar is to the yardstick of probability, and on this basis, it must be repeated, virtually nothing of use to the historian emerges from the sparse record of the early life of the founder of the latest of the great world religions. . . . So, however far back in the Muslim tradition one now attempts to reach, one simply cannot recover a scrap of information of real use in constructing the human history of Muhammad, beyond the bare fact that he once existed— although even that has now been questioned.[4]

So much for the life "lived in the full light of history." In addition to these devastating caveats it has also to be borne in mind that we do not possess Ibn Ishaq's *Sira* in its original form, but in the redaction of Ibn Hisham (d. 833). who edited it so as to omit "things which it is disgraceful to discuss; matters which would distress certain people; and such reports as al-Bakka'i told me he could not accept as trustworthy."[5]

The Muslims' delusion that they have eyewitness reports for every aspect of Muhammad's life, is similar to the delusion of fundamentalist and evangelical Christians that in the gospels they have eyewitness reports of the life of Jesus. Likewise, Orthodox Jews are convinced they have a record of all that is worth knowing about the life of Moses in the Pentateuch and the Talmud. The motivation for all these fantasies is the same. Believers, of necessity, need something to believe, and if the information is not to hand there are always those ready to supply it. Not always or necessarily in a spirit of deliberate falsification and conscious deceit, but as a natural product of the hothouse that is the pious imagination—this is how it *must* have been—given their view of God, man, history, and the scraps of information about the past that they happened to have. In other words, not what actually happened but what certain people *believed* to have happened. What we have in such documents as the Pentateuch, the New Testament, and the *Sira*, is not history as understood by modern secular historians, but something that is best called salvation, or sacred history, the history of God's plan for mankind. That is, not history at all in the sense of a record of real events in the ordinary world, but an imaginative literary genre.

This view of the Muslim sources for the life of Muhammad and the origins of Islam has been advocated by John Wansbrough of the London School of Oriental and African Studies, in his two books *Quranic Studies* (1977), and *The Sectarian Milieu* (1978). Wansbrough's achievement was to bring to the Koran and to Islam the same healthy skepticism developed in modern biblical and historical studies. This was needed in order to counteract a certain overeagerness to attain positive results that had become predominant in Islamic Studies, an overeagerness which tended to ignore or dismiss the achievements of an older generation of scholars who had shown just how untrustworthy the Muslim sources are.

The first chapter of *The Sectarian Milieu* is devoted to a study of Muslim historiography, particularly the *Sira* of Ibn Ishaq and the *Maghazi* of Waqidi (d. 822). Wansbrough concludes that the primary components of salvation history to be found in these works were "largely derived from the discourse of interconfessional polemic" (p. 40), the sectarian milieu of the title. By means of narrative techniques that Wansbrough calls "historicization" and "exemplification," these components or topics (topoi) were introduced into the *Sira* as incidents in the life of the Arabian Prophet, thus giving them an apparently authentic life situation (*Sitz im Leben*). Most of these standard topics, twenty-three in all, appear in one passage of the *Sira* (1:544–72) summarizing Muhammad's purported encounter with the Jews in Medina.

The six most basic themes are adduced as anecdotes in the following forms:

(1) Prognosis of Muhammad in Jewish scripture.
(2) Jewish rejection of that prognosis.
(3) Jewish insistence upon miracles for prophets.
(4) Jewish rejection of Muhammad's revelation.
(5) Muslim charge of scriptural falsification.
(6) Muslim claim to supersede earlier dispensations.

The most important of these themes, which became a habitual and hackneyed topic in Muslim polemics against their Jewish and Christian opponents, was that of scriptural falsification. It was hardly original. The same thing had been alleged between Jews and Samaritans, Jews and Christians, Pharisees and Saducees, Karaites and Rabbinites, and the accusation that fabricated passages were introduced into scripture by Satanic intervention, as in the notorious "Satanic Verses," was an Ebionite accusation against the Pentateuch. In the Muslim case the last is to do with the doctrine of divine annulment of "false" revelation, that is to say, the necessity of superseding or abrogating previous prescriptions. As Wansbrough says: "It is not unlikely that what became the doctrine of abrogation (*naskh*) was originally a polemical *topos* employed to justify a new dispensation, and hence readily transferable within the sectarian milieu" (p. 41).

After hundreds of pages of this kind of analysis nothing is left of the *Sira-Maghazi* literature as evidence for what actually happened in early Islam.[6] Radical as this conclusion is, even more devastating for the traditional picture of Islamic origins is Wansbrough's view of what the underlying motive was for the production of all this polemical literature. It is mentioned in passing in *Quranic Studies* and might easily be overlooked. It is that "tafsir (Koranic exegesis) traditions, like traditions in every other field, reflect a single impulse: to demonstrate the Hijazi origins of Islam" (p. 179).

Why would the Hijazi origin of Islam need to be demonstrated if the traditional view of the origin of Islam is correct? The obvious answer is that it was a matter for dispute in the sectarian milieu of the eighth and ninth centuries. It was not generally known or believed at that time that Islam *had* originated in the Hijaz, because it was not yet entirely clear, either to Muslims or non-Muslims, exactly what Islam was. It was still in the process of definition, and that definition took the form of an extended and simultaneous literary exercise in the fields of history (*Sira*, tarikh), law (sharia, fiqh), and religion (Koran, Hadith). This alters the whole traditional picture of the origin of Islam and the purported life of its Prophet.

The views of John Wansbrough on the historical value of the Muslim sources and the likely geographical location for the self-definition of Islam had a profound effect on two scholars who have produced the most radical version of Islamic origins. Patricia Crone and Michael Cook first presented their views at a colloquium on the first century of Islamic society held at Oxford in 1975, later published as *Hagarism: The Making of the Islamic World* (1977). In the preface to this work the authors admit that without exposure to "the sceptical approach of Dr. John Wansbrough to the historicity of the Islamic tradition . . . the theory of Islamic origins set out in this book would never have occurred to us" (p. viii).

Recognition of this approach led to a theory which is "not one which any believing Muslim can accept: not because it in any way belittles the historical role of Muhammad, but because it presents him in a role quite different from that which he has taken on in the Islamic tradition. This is a book written by infidels for infidels, and it is based on what from any Muslim perspective must appear an inordinate regard for the testimony of infidel sources" (pp. vi–viii).

The "infidel sources" are the non-Muslim historians of the period of the Islamic conquests. The reasons for resorting to them are set out in the opening paragraph, which well summarizes the situation in Islamic studies that called for the book to be written:

> Virtually all accounts of the early development of Islam take it as axiomatic that it is possible to elicit at least the outlines of the process from the Islamic sources. It is however well known that these sources are not demonstrably early. There is no hard evidence for the existence of the Koran in any form before the last decade of the seventh century, and the tradition which places this rather opaque revelation in its historical context is not attested before the middle of the eighth. The historicity of the Islamic tradition is thus to some degree problematic: while there are no cogent internal grounds for rejecting it, there are equally no cogent external grounds for accepting it. In the circumstances it is not unreasonable to proceed in the usual fashion by presenting a sensibly edited version of the tradition as historical fact. But equally, it makes some sense to regard the tradition as without determinate historical content, and to insist that what purport to be accounts of religious events in the seventh century are utilizable only for the study of religious ideas in the eighth. The Islamic sources provide plenty of scope for the implementation of these different approaches, but offer little that can be used in any decisive way to arbitrate between them. The only way out of the dilemma is thus to step outside the Islamic tradition altogether and start again. (p. 3)

In other words the book represents a leap of unfaith, both in the Muslim sources and the scholarly establishment in Islamic studies.

The reconstruction which resulted from this alternative approach has Muhammad alive during the conquest of Palestine and acting as the herald of a coming Jewish Messiah, 'Umar al-Faruq. This Muhammad was the leader of a movement to retake Jerusalem and the Holy Land, the participants in which were known as *Magaritai* (Greek), *Mahgraye* (Syriac), or *muhajirun* (Arabic), indicating that they were associated with Hagar and that the original Hijra was to Jerusalem. With the Arabs' increasing success the need for a break with the Jews became pressing, and this was occasioned by a quarrel over building on the

Temple site at Jerusalem. After a flirtation with Christianity which precipitated a respect for Jesus as prophet and messiah and Mary as Virgin, Islamic identity finally asserted itself in identification with an Abrahamic monotheism independent of and ancestral to both Judaism and Christianity. This notion was filled out by borrowing from Samaritanism the idea of a scripture limited to the Pentateuch, a prophet like Moses, a holy book revealed like the Torah, a sacred city with nearby mountain and shrine of an appropriate patriarch, plus a caliphate modelled on an Aaronid priesthood. In short, up until about the time of the caliph 'Abd al-Malik (685–705), Hagarism was a Jewish messianic movement intent on reestablishing Judaism in the Promised Land, with little Arabic about it apart from the language.

As was surely anticipated, these ideas stirred up a hornets' nest, not so much amongst affronted Muslims, as amongst the old school of established authorities in the field, who had, for the most part, been content to go along with the traditional account. This is not to say that many, even among the skeptics, were convinced by Crone and Cook's reconstruction. Wansbrough, for one, could see no more reason to believe the Jewish and Christian version of events than the Muslim, since they were just as much a part of the sectarian milieu and involved in the production of polemical literature.[7] The great achievement of the book was to explode the academic consensus and demolish deference to the Muslim view of things, thus making it possible to propose radical alternative hypotheses for the origins of Islam.

Patricia Crone went on to write several more books challenging accepted views on early Islam. *Slaves on Horses* (1980), asked why it was that ninth century Muslim rulers in the Middle East chose to place military and political power in the hands of imported slaves. The conceptual framework was still that of *Hagarism*, and the book was regarded by its author as an overextended footnote to that work, even though it was based firmly on the Muslim sources. The historiographical introduction contains many astute observations on Islamic origins and the state of Islamic studies.

Of Ibn Ishaq's *Sira* Crone says:

> The work is late: written not by a grandchild, but a great grandchild of the Prophet's generation, it gives us the view for which classical Islam had settled. And written by a member of the *ulama*, the scholars who had by then emerged as the classical bearers of the Islamic tradition, the picture which it offers is also one sided: how the Umayyad caliphs remembered their Prophet we shall never know. That it is unhistorical is only what one would expect, but it has an extraordinary capacity to resist internal criticism . . . characteristic of the entire

> Islamic tradition, and most pronounced in the Koran: one can take the picture
> presented or one can leave it, but one cannot *work* with it. (p. 4)

As for the reputed fabulous memories of the bedouin: "the immediate disciples
of a man whose biography was for some two hundred years studied under the
title of *ilm al-maghazi*, the Prophet's campaigns, are unlikely to have devoted
their lives to the memorization of Hadith" (p. 5).

The Constitution of Medina preserved in the *Sira* "sticks out like a piece of
solid rock in an accumulation of rubble" (p. 7). The document itself "depicts a
society of Muhajirun, Arab tribes and Jewish allies preparing for war in the name
of a creed to which there is only the most cursory reference. The *Sira* nonetheless has Muhammad arrive as a peacemaker in Medina, where he spends a substantial part of his time expounding Islam to the Arab tribes and disputing with
Jewish rabbis" (nt. 15, p. 202).

The religious tradition of Islam is in fact "a monument to the destruction
rather than the preservation of the past," and it is "in the *Sira* of the Prophet that
this destruction is most thorough, but it affects the entire account of the religious
evolution of Islam until the second half of the Umayyad period" (p. 7). Furthermore, it is a tradition full of "contradictions, confusions, inconsistencies and
anomalies." For example:

> There is nothing, within the Islamic tradition, that one can do with Baladhuri's
> statement that the kiblah (direction of prayer) in the first Kufan mosque was to
> the west (opposite direction to Mecca): either it is false or else it is odd, but why
> it should be there and what it means God only knows. It is similarly odd that
> Umar (second caliph) is known as the Faruq (Redeemer), that there are so many
> Fatimas, that Ali (Muhammad's cousin) is sometimes Muhammad's brother,
> and that there is so much pointless information. . . . It is a tradition in which
> information means nothing and leads nowhere; it just happens to be there and
> lends itself to little but arrangement by majority and minority opinion. (p. 12)

This is evidenced by the work of modern historians with this material: "reinterpretations in which the order derives less from the sources than from our own
ideas of what life ought to be about—modern preoccupations graced with
Muslim facts and footnotes . . . maybe Muhammad was a Fabian socialist, or
maybe he merely wanted sons; maybe the Umayyad feuds were tribal or maybe
that was how Umayyad politicians chose to argue. What difference does it make?
We know as little as and understand no more than before" (p. 13).

In the end just about the only positive conclusion to be drawn is that "there
is of course no doubt that Muhammad lived in the 620s and 630s, that he fought

in wars, and that he had followers some of whose names are likely to have been preserved. But the precise when, what and who, on which our interpretations stand and fall, bear all the marks of having been through the mill of rabbinic arguments and subsequently tidied up" (p. 15).

In *God's Caliph* (1986), written with Martin Hinds, Crone examines the nature of religious authority in early Islam. The conventional view is that under Abu Bakr, Umar, and Uthman, all of whom were Companions of the Prophet, religious and political powers were united, but that under Ali this situation changed so that the caliph became a political figure only, and the transmission of Muhammad's religious and legal legacy was left in the hands of his remaining Companions and their successors. Crone and Hinds argue that this picture of early Islamic history was invented by the ulama (scholarly elite) two or three centuries later, to support their own position and power by claiming that things had always been that way.

The authors find the demonstration of this theory in the substitution of the title *khalifat rasul Allah*, deputy of the Prophet of God, for the title *khalifat Allah*, deputy of God. Whereas the latter implies the inheritance of power directly from God, the former implies that it comes via the Prophet, or the Prophet's latter day representatives, the ulama. If this is correct it would mean that the original conception of the caliphate was of political and religious authority concentrated in the single person of the caliph, not divided between secular and religious authorities. This in turn would mean that it is the Sunni, not the Shia, version of the caliphate which is the deviation from the original conception.

Once again, the book is full of evidence and argument that undermines the traditional picture of early Islam and the role of Muhammad in its formation. For instance: "It is a striking fact that such documentary evidence as survives from the Sufyanid period (661–684) makes no mention of the messenger of God at all. The papyri do not refer to him. The Arabic inscriptions of the Arab-Sassanian coins only invoke Allah, not his rasul" (p. 24). It also appears that early Hadith reflect a stage at which God's law was indeed formulated by God's caliph: "It is clear that the caliphs were free to make and unmake Sunna as they wished. 'We do not know of anyone who adjudicated on the basis of this rule before Abd al-Malik,' a transmitter remarks without in any way wishing to depreciate the validity of the rule in question; in other words, it was valid because a caliph had made it, not because it went back to the Prophet or a companion" (p. 52). The earliest form of Sunna was thus not the Sunna of the Prophet, let alone something documented in Hadith: "As for Sunna, it was good practice in general and that of prophets and caliphs in particular. Among the prophets David and Solomon have pride of place" (p. 54). In short, Sunna was originally simply ancestral custom or the established way of doing things, but with the advent of the ulama it became Muhammad's way of doing things, and against that there was no appeal, even by the caliphs.

This view of the development of Islamic law is confirmed in *Roman, Provincial and Islamic Law* (1987). Here Crone examines the cultural origins of the Sharia by comparing Sunni, Shia, and Ibadi law to Roman law and provincial law in Byzantine Syria and Egypt. She concludes that the Islamic institution of the Sharia is the result of a long process of adjustments by the ulama, who inherited its substance from the Umayyad caliphate in general and Mulawiya, in particular. What the Arab invaders reshaped into the Sharia was essentially provincial law as they found it: "substantially it was of ancient Near Eastern and Greek origin, or in other words it was the indigenous law of the Near East as it had developed after Alexander. The Muslims sifted and systematized this law in the name of God, imprinting it with their own image in the process" (p. 99).

Uncongenial as the conclusions of these four books may be to the way that Muslims like to imagine their past and the origin of their religion, they are merely incidental compared with the implications of Crone's innocuously titled *Meccan Trade and the Rise of Islam* (1987). We have already noted how John Wansbrough concluded that the underlying purpose of all Muslim traditions, whether historical, legal, or religious, was "to demonstrate the Hijazi origins of Islam". The implication of such a propaganda exercise is that in reality Islam did *not* originate in the Hijaz, and more specifically, did *not* originate at Mecca.

There has long been an undercurrent of unease among Western students of Islam about the part played by Mecca in the Muslim account of Islamic origins. In the Muslim sources Mecca is portrayed as a wealthy trading center, full of merchants exchanging goods by caravan with Yemen in the south and Syria and the Roman empire in the north. Yet there is no mention anywhere in the non-Muslim sources of a Mecca placed where the Mecca we know today is placed, that is to say in the southern Hijaz. Before the first world war D. S. Margoliouth noted that "The classical geographers, who devote considerable attention to Arabia, are apparently not acquainted with this settlement; for the Makoraba of Ptolemy (VI. vii. 32) is derived from a different root."[8] Yet such is the weight of the traditional Muslim account amongst Islamicists, and such the general inertia in Islamic studies, that we still find the following in a book published in 1988: "Mecca is known to the ancient geographers as Macoraba."[9] The identification of Macoraba with Mecca is demolished by Crone in *Meccan Trade*. After examining the various theories she says: "The plain truth is that the name of Macoraba has nothing to do with that of Mecca, and that the location indicated by Ptolemy for Macoraba in no way dictates identification of the two . . . if Ptolemy mentions Mecca at all, he calls it Moka, a town in Arabia Petraea" (p. 136). That is to say a town in the northern part of Arabia in the area of the city of Petra in present day Jordan.

Crone well describes the odd silence of the non-Muslim sources on Meccan trade:

> It is obvious that if the Meccans had been middlemen in a long-distance trade of the kind described in the secondary literature, there ought to have been some mention of them in the writings of their customers. Greek and Latin authors had, after all, written extensively about the south Arabians who supplied them with aromatics in the past, offering information about their cities, tribes, political organization, and caravan trade; and in the sixth century they similarly wrote about Ethiopia and Adulis. The political and ecclesiastical importance of Arabia in the sixth century was such that considerable attention was paid to Arabian affairs, too; but of Quraysh and their trading center there is no mention at all, be it in the Greek, Latin, Syriac, Aramaic, Coptic, or other literature composed outside Arabia before the conquests. This silence is striking and significant. (p. 134)

Furthermore:

> This silence cannot be attributed to the fact that sources have been lost, though some clearly have. The fact is that the sources written after the conquests display not the faintest sign of *recognition* in their accounts of the new rulers of the Middle East or the city from which they came. Nowhere is it stated that Quraysh, or the "Arab kings," were the people who used to supply such-and-such regions with such-and-such goods: it was only Muhammad himself who was known to have been a trader. And as for the city, it was long assumed to have been Yathrib. Of Mecca there is no mention for a long time; and the first sources to mention the sanctuary fail to give a name for it, whereas the first source to name it fails to locate it in Arabia. (The *Continuatio Arabica* gives Mecca an Abrahamic location between Ur and Harran, n. 21.) Jacob of Edessa knew of the Ka'ba toward which the Muslims prayed, locating it in a place considerably closer to Ptolemy's Moka than to modern Mecca or, in other words, too far north for orthodox accounts of the rise of Islam; but of the commercial significance of this place he would appear to have been completely ignorant. Whatever the implications of this evidence for the history of the Muslim sanctuary, it is plain that the Qurashi trading center was not a place with which the subjects of the Muslims were familiar. (p. 137)

Crone concludes that if Qurashi trade existed at all the silence of the classical sources must be due to its totally insignificant nature.

It was assumed by practically all Islamicists before Crone that Mecca must have been involved in the spice trade, presumably because spices are indelibly linked in the Western mind with the romance of Araby. By careful examination of the documentary evidence on the classical spice trade Crone shows that Mecca, even if it existed as a trading center, could not have been involved at all.

To begin with it is simply not true that Mecca, that is Mecca in the location that we know today, was situated at the crossroads of major Arabian trade routes. Neither was it a natural stopping-place on the so-called incense route from south Arabia to Syria: "as Bullier points out (*Camel and Wheel*, p. 105), these claims are quite wrong. Mecca is tucked away at the edge of the peninsula: 'only by the most tortured map reading can it be described as a natural crossroads between a north-south route and an east-west one.' And the fact that it is more or less equidistant from south Arabia and Syria does not suffice to make it a natural halt on the incense route" (p. 6). What is more: "Why should caravans have made a steep descent to the barren valley of Mecca when they could have stopped at Ta'if? Mecca did, of course, have both a well and a sanctuary, but so did Ta'if, which had food supplies, too" (pp. 6–7). In fact it would appear that Mecca was not on the incense route at all, since going from south Arabia to Syria via Mecca would have involved a substantial detour from the natural route. Indeed "the incense route must have bypassed Mecca by some one hundred miles. Mecca, in other words, was not just distant and barren; it was off the beaten track, as well" (p. 7).

If Mecca does not make sense as a trading center, for spices, incense, or any other conceivable commodity, what of its purported role as a sanctuary and place of pilgrimage? On examination of the sources Crone confirms the conclusion of Wellhausen, reached as long ago as 1887, that "the pre-Islamic Arabs *did* trade during the pilgrimage. But they did not go to Mecca during the pilgrimage, because the pilgrimage did not go to Mecca before the rise of Islam" (p. 173). Moreover, the Hubal-Allah sanctuary at Mecca, of which the Quraysh are supposed to have been the guardians, does not make any sense either, in fact "there would seem to be at least two sanctuaries behind the one depicted in the tradition, and Quraysh do not come across as guardians of either" (p. 195).

Taking all these factors into account Crone summarizes the problems surrounding Mecca and the rise of Islam as follows:

> We seem to have all the ingredients for Muhammad's career in northwest Arabia. Qurashi trade sounds perfectly viable, indeed more intelligible, without its south Arabian and Ethiopian extensions, and there is a case for a Qurashi trading center, or at least diaspora, in the north. One might locate it in Ptolemy's Moka. Somewhere in the north, too, there was a desert sanctuary of pan-Ara-

bian importance, according to Nonnosus . . . Jewish communities are well attested for northwest Arabia. Even Abrahamic monotheism is documented there, and the prophet who was to make a new religion of this belief was himself a trader in northwest Arabia. Yet everything is supposed to have happened much further south, in a place described as a sanctuary town inhabited since time immemorial, located, according to some, in an unusually fertile environment, associated with southern tribes such as Jurhum and Khuza'a, linked with Ethiopia and the Yemen, and endowed with a building accommodating Hubal and his priests. Why? What is the historical relationship between these places? (pp. 196–99)

Nobody knows. All we do know is "the sources on the rise of Islam are wrong in one or more fundamental respects" (p. 196).

In the process of examining these sources Crone has already had occasion to remark that "the tradition asserts both A and not A, and it does so with such regularity that one could, were one so inclined, rewrite most of Montgomery Watt's biography of Muhammad in reverse" (p. 111). In her penultimate chapter she subjects that tradition to a further withering analysis. Examining the contradictory traditional exegesis of the chapter of the Koran called "Quraysh," she concludes that the Islamic commentators had no more idea of what it means than we do today (pp. 204–14). The numerous purported historical events that are supposed to have occasioned a revelation (Badr, Uhud, Hudaybiyya, Hunayn, and so on) owe many of their features, and often their very existence to the Koran itself. That is to say, wherever the Koran mentions a name or an event, stories were invented to give the impression that somehow, somewhere, someone, knew what they were about. This means that "much of the classical Muslim understanding of the Koran rests on the work of popular storytellers, such storytellers being the first to propose particular historical contexts for particular verses" (p. 216). In short: "What the tradition offers is a mass of detailed information, none of which represents straightforward facts" (p. 222).

This manufacture of detail is well illustrated by the steady growth of apparent information: "It is obvious that if one storyteller should happen to mention a raid, the next storyteller would know the date of this raid, while the third would know everything that an audience might wish to hear about it. This process is graphically illustrated in the sheer contrast of size between the works of Ibn Ishaq (d. 767) and al-Waqidi (d. 823), that of al-Waqidi being much larger for all that it covers only Muhammad's period in Medina." This fact naturally leads to the thought that "if spurious information accumulated at this rate in the two generations between Ibn Ishaq and al-Waqidi . . . even more must have accumulated in the three generations between the Prophet and Ibn Ishaq" (pp. 223–24).

Now it might be suggested in mitigation of these negative conclusions that although the storytellers may have embroidered their stories somewhat, underneath it all there is a core of true memory of real events, a sound tradition. Crone totally rejects this idea: "it was the storytellers who created the tradition: the sound historical tradition to which they are supposed to have added their fables simply did not exist." Nobody remembered any of these events "but nobody remembered anything to the contrary either" (p. 225), so there was nobody to deny them. The only reason the sources are agreed on the historicity of certain characters and events is because there were well-known stories about them, not because there was an unbroken transmission of a sound historical tradition: "There was no continuous transmission. Ibn Ishaq, al-Waqidi, and others were cut off from the past: like the modern scholar, they could not get behind their sources" (pp. 225–26).

Finally, it has to be realized that the tradition as a whole, not just parts of it as some have thought, is tendentious, and that that tendentiousness arises from allegiance to Islam itself, "its aim being the elaboration of an Arabian Heilsgeschichte (salvation/sacred history)" (p. 230). It is this that has shaped the facts as we have them.

It should not be supposed from our dependence upon the analysis of Patricia Crone that she is alone in her views on the historical value of the Muslim sources and the factitious nature of Mecca in the southern Hijaz as the location for the origin of Islam; Crone's analysis is simply the most thorough, comprehensible, and courageous. At the same colloquium at Oxford in 1975 where Crone and Cook first presented the views published later in *Hagarism*, S. P. Brock delivered a lecture on "Syriac Views of Early Islam." In this lecture he noted that "for Muhammad the title 'prophet' is not very common, 'apostle' even less so. Normally he is simply described as the first of the Arab kings, and it would be generally true to say that the Syriac sources of this period see the conquests primarily as Arab, and not Muslim."[10] Also, in another lecture on "The Origins of the Muslim Sanctuary at Mecca," the historian G. R. Hawting expressed the view that "it appears that certain Muslim sanctuary ideas and certain names which Islam applies to its sanctuary at Mecca originated in a Jewish milieu, in the context of Jewish sanctuary ideas, and that they were then taken up by Islam and applied to the Meccan sanctuary."[11]

The complete unreliability of the Muslim tradition as far as dates are concerned has been demonstrated by Lawrence Conrad. After a close examination of the sources in an effort to find the most likely birth date for Muhammad, traditionally '*Am al-fil*, the Year of the Elephant, 570 C.E., he remarks that "well into the second century A.H. scholarly opinion on the birth date of the Prophet displayed a range of variance of eighty-five years. On the assumption that chronology is crucial to the stabilization of any tradition of historical narrative, whether transmitted orally or in writing, one can see in this state of affairs a clear indication that *sira* studies in the second century were still in a state of flux."[12] That is to put it politely and to say the least. If Muslim historians in the second century of the Hijra could be that vague about Muhammad's birth date, what could they possibly have known about the date of his death or any other event in his life? Indeed, it appears that the only secure date anywhere in the whole saga of the origins of Islam is 622 C.E., which has been confirmed from dated coinage as marking the beginning of a new era. But there is no seventh century source that identifies it as that of the Hijra, and the only clue to its nature comes from two Nestorian Christian documents of 676 and 680 that call it the year of "the rule of the Arabs."[13]

The uncertainty of the Muslim historians about Muhammad's dates is just one indication that it was some time before Muslims were much interested in him at all. As we have seen, the important Islamic concept of Sunna, the right or established way of doing things, began as a generalized idea. There was the Sunna of a region, the Sunna of a group of persons, or the Sunna of some particular distinguished person, such as David or Solomon or the Caliph, even the Sunna of Allah. It was not until the manufacture of Hadiths (Prophetic traditions) got under way in the second Islamic century that all these vague notions were absorbed and particularized in the detailed *sunnat an-nabi* (Sunna of the Prophet). Likewise, it was only with the gradual emergence of the legend of Muhammad that places that had for well nigh two centuries gone unmarked and unregarded became places of reverence and honor. As Goldziher long ago pointed out: "The fact that the Prophet's birthplace (at Mecca) was used as an ordinary dwelling house during Umayyad time and was made a house of prayer only by al-Khayzuran (d. 173), the mother of Harun al-Rashid, would suggest that the consecration of places associated with the legend of the Prophet did not date from the earliest period of Islam."[14]

It is likely that Muhammad, insofar as he was remembered at all, was remembered chiefly as a political and military leader who brought the Arab tribes together and urged them to conquer in the name of their ancestral deity. That is all that is needed to explain the Arab conquests and the so-called rise of Islam. In reality there was no Islam as we know it for another two or three hundred years, there was simply the barbarian conquest of civilized lands. Muhammad, as Prophet and mouthpiece for the universal deity Allah, is an invention of the ulama of the second and third centuries A.H. As Patricia Crone says: "In short, Muhammad had to conquer, his followers liked to conquer, and his deity told him to conquer: do we need any more?"[15]

It is important to realize that for a hundred to two hundred years the Arab conquerors were a minority ruling a majority and that majority was not Muslim. It has been estimated that by the middle of the eighth century only about 8 percent of the subject populations had become Muslim, whatever being Muslim involved at that time.[16] Christians, Jews, and Zoroastrians, in all their varieties, vastly outnumbered Muslims, and it was in that sectarian milieu diagnosed by Wansbrough that the forms of Islam, such as the source of its authority, the life of its Prophet, and the Koranic canon, were gradually worked out. As Gordon Newby says, confirming the above analysis: "The myth of an original orthodoxy from which later challengers fall away as heretics is most always the retrospective assertion of a politically dominant group whose aim is to establish their supremacy by appeal to divine sanction."[17]

Taking Crone and Cook's messianic *Hagarism* as the first stage of what later became Islam, the following scenario becomes plausible. Once the Arabs had acquired an empire a coherent religion was required in order to hold that empire together and legitimize their rule. In a process that involved a massive backreading of history, and in conformity to the available Jewish and Christian models, this meant they needed a revelation and a revealer (prophet) whose life could serve at once as a model for moral conduct and as a framework for the appearance of the revelation; hence the Koran, the Hadith, and the *Sira*, were contrived and conjoined over a period of a couple of centuries. Topographically, after a century or so of Judaeo-Muslim monotheism centered on Jerusalem, in order to make Islam distinctively Arab the need for an exclusively Hijazi origin became pressing. It is at this point that Islam as we recognize it today—with an inner Arabian biography of the Prophet, Mecca, Quraysh, Hijra, Medina, Badr, etc.—was really born, *as a purely literary artefact*. An artefact moreover, based not on faithful memories of real events, but on the fertile imaginations of Arab storytellers elaborating from allusive references in Koranic texts, the canonical text of the Koran not being fixed for nearly two centuries. This scenario makes at least as much sense of the sources as the traditional account and eliminates many anomalies.

From the vantage point of this skeptical analysis the narrative related in the *Sira*, that purports to be the life of the Prophet of Islam, appears as a baseless fiction. The first fifty-two years of that life, including the account of the first revelations of the Koran and all that is consequent upon that, are pictured as unfolding in a place that simply could not have existed in the way it is described in the Muslim sources. Mecca was not a wealthy trading center at the crossroads of Hijazi trade routes, the Quraysh were *not* wealthy merchants running caravans up and down the Arabian peninsula from Syria to the Yemen, and Muhammad, insofar as he was anything more than an Arab warlord of monotheist persuasion, did his trading far north of the Hijaz; furthermore, Mecca, as a sanctuary, if it was a sanctuary, was of no more importance than numerous others and was *not* a place of pilgrimage.

If we cannot believe the life of Muhammad at Mecca, we can no more believe his life at Medina either. That, too, is just as likely to be a fiction concocted for propaganda purposes, and perhaps after all that is just as well since, as Margoliouth long ago observed of the *Sira*: "The character which the narrator ascribes to his Prophet is, on the whole, exceedingly repulsive."[18]

If we cannot believe the traditional Muslim account of the origins of Islam, that raises the question of why so many have been so ready to believe it for so long. There is a sense in which Islam is like one of those endlessly repeating patterns typical of its art, or like a fractal that remains the same whatever the scale of magnification. Whether it be a pillar of the religion such as the daily prayer (salat), or a seemingly inconsequential element of correct behavior (Sunna) such as the right foot with which to cross the threshold of a mosque, the same atmosphere prevails and the same metaphysical principles can be discerned. Once the mind has succumbed to what Paul Kurtz has called "the transcendental temptation"[19] within the ambience of Islam, all its circular assertions become plausible and unbelief appears an incomprehensible perversion. Indeed, Islam becomes the veritable living proof that "with God all things are possible" (Matt. 19:26).

In one of his early works the traditionalist writer Frithjof Schuon gives an acute description of this Muslim mental world:

> The intellectual—and thereby the rational—foundation of Islam results in the average Muslim having a curious tendency to believe that non-Muslims either know that Islam is the truth and reject it out of pure obstinacy, or else are simply ignorant of it and can be converted by elementary explanations; that anyone should be able to oppose Islam with a good conscience quite exceeds the Muslim's imagination, precisely because Islam coincides in his mind with the irresistible logic of things.[20]

No explanation is necessary for the Muslim who has, quite literally, had the Koran whispered in his ear and pounded into his brain from birth. In a society in which the themes and phrases of God's book are all pervading, and where, until recently, a Muslim could live his whole life without meeting an alternative view, it is hardly surprising that Islam appears "the irresistible logic of things."

Not only is Islam for the Muslim born and bred the obvious explanation of life and the world, it is also his family and cultural heritage from which he can sever himself only with the utmost anguish and danger. For such a person in such a world rejecting Islam is not like failing to turn up in church on Sunday, it is like a traitorous act in time of war, a deliberate going over to an enemy for whom no good word can be said, an act for which the only appropriate penalty is death. That Muslims born in a Muslim culture think in these terms is understandable, that educated Westerners voluntarily adopt it and actively promote it is a phenomenon in need of explanation.

There has long been a kind of love affair between certain westerners and the Arabs in which a romantic view of "the East," of the desert and the bedouin, combines with an intellectual pursuit of Arabic language, literature, art, and architecture. This fascination with the Arabs and Islam does not always end in conversion, but when it does it usually combines vague aspirations towards "the spiritual," with the expression or adoption of thought processes and attitudes to life that could not be respectably maintained in any other contemporary context. Islam is in fact the last refuge for those conservative western intellectuals who wish it were true that the Renaissance, the Enlightenment, the Industrial Revolution, the French Revolution, in short "the modern world," had never come about. Islam is, indeed, the only remaining mental space in which these events have not yet happened.

The result is a world-view in which the existence of God and the revelation of his word and will in an inerrant and infallible text are absolutely unquestionable. To raise questions about these primary items of the religion is, in effect, to put oneself outside it, and if one is Muslim born or a convert, to become guilty of the ultimate crime of apostasy (*irtidad*), and deserving of death. In view of these facts it might seem that the conversion of any intelligent and educated westerners is unaccountable, but curiously enough it is precisely the uncompromising severity of Islam that is its most attractive feature for those with a psychological need for certainty in an uncertain world. In addition there is a seductive side to Islam that consists of its mysticism and its art, and it is these features that seem to have figured largely in the conversion of many intellectuals.

There are in fact two broadly opposed ways in which westerners approach Islam. The first, which might be described as rational-analytic, retains an overtly western point of view, be it religious—Jewish/Christian, or secular—rational/humanist/skeptical/atheist. The second, which might be described as mystical-romantic and often leads to conversion, adopts an antiwestern posture and styles itself traditionalist, a kind of universalist religiosity that regards Islam as the final and most complete of a host of divine revelations. Despite the pretensions of the traditionalists both approaches are indelibly western in that neither could have arisen within the Muslim world, which is subjectively self-enclosed and seamlessly self-confirming, affording no foothold for any kind of objective assessment. These two approaches have produced two separate literatures on Islam which barely acknowledge each other's existence.

Prominent representatives of the rational-analytic approach are: Ignaz Goldziher, Joseph Schacht, William Montgomery Watt, Kenneth Cragg, Patricia Crone, Michael Cook, John Wansbrough, John Burton, Andrew Rippin, Julian Baldick, and Gerald Hawting. Prominent representatives of the mystical-romantic approach are: René Guénon, Frithjof Schuon, Titus Burckhardt, Martin Lings, Toshihiko Izutsu, Michel Chodkiewicz, Annemarie Schimmel, William Chittick, Sachiko Murata, and Seyyed Hossein Nasr. Nasr is unique amongst this latter group in that he is an Iranian academic who has adopted as his mentors a group of western writers who purport to know better than Muslims themselves what is the real meaning of Islam. Nasr is now the senior proponent of traditionalism in the West.

The rational-analytic group study Islam from the outside and seek to know how it came to be the way it is. They look critically at the evidence, or lack of evidence, for the traditional account of Islamic origins, and as a result see Islam as a series of problems in need of solution. The solutions tend to be favorable or unfavorable to Islam in direct proportion to the sympathy for religion as such; Christians, such as Watt and Cragg, are most notably sympathetic, though this is little appreciated by Muslims. The mystical-romantic group study Islam from the inside and accept it at its own estimation; they refuse to consider anything which might undermine faith and treat the traditional explanations as divinely guided. Because of their universalist mysticism these too are looked at askance by most Muslims. These contrasting approaches to Islam emerge most starkly in their respective attitudes to the Koran and the Hadith.

The mystical-romantic attitude to the Koran is well described by Nasr:

> As viewed by Muslims, what is called higher criticism in the West does not at all apply to the text of the Koran. Elaborate sciences concerning conditions in which the verses were revealed (*sha'n al-nuzul*), how the Koran was compiled, how the verses were enumerated, as well as the science and art of the recitation of the Koran, have been developed by Muslim scholars over the centuries . . . these traditional sciences provide all the answers to questions posed by modern western orientalists about the structure and text of the Koran, except, of course, those questions that issue from the rejection of the Divine Origin of the Koran and its reduction to a work by the Prophet. Once the revealed nature of the Koran is rejected, then problems arise. But these are problems of orientalists that arise not from scholarship but from a certain theological and philosophical position that is usually hidden under the guise of rationality and objective schol-

arship. For Muslims, there has never been the need to address these "problems" because Muslims accept the revealed nature of the Koran, in the light of which these problems simply cease to exist.[21]

In other words, problems cease to be problems as long as you can delude yourself that they are not there. Unfortunately, like a toothache that refuses to go away no matter how hard you try to ignore it, the problems surrounding the Koran are not so easily dismissed. If the western scholar is prejudiced in refusing to accept that the Koran is divine revelation, and that is by no means true of them all, the Muslim scholar is even more prejudiced in accepting that it is without ever considering any alternative. But in Islam belief (Iman) is the greatest virtue that overwhelms all fault, and unbelief (kufr) is the greatest fault that can never be forgiven.

Another advocate of the mystical-romantic view of Islam tells us that:

> History as such has never held much interest for most Muslims. What is important about historical events is simply that God works through them. The significant events of the past are those that have a direct impact on people's present situation and their situation in the next world. From this point of view, the one event of overwhelming significance is God's revelation of the Koran. The actual historical and social circumstances in which it was revealed relate to an extremely specialized field of learning that few scholars ever bothered with. The fact that western historians have devoted a great deal of attention to this issue says something about modern perceptions of what is real and important, but it tells us nothing about Muslim perceptions of the Koran's significance.[22]

This is surely an oblique reference to the work done by scholars of the rational-analytic school, such as Wansbrough, Crone, Cook, and Hawting, on the historical origins of Islam. It is also a preemptive hedging of bets. If it turns out that the work of these scholars becomes undeniable and the traditional picture of the origin of Islam is gone forever, it can then be claimed that that does not really matter. All that matters is "Muslim perceptions of the Koran's significance." Rather like the liberal Christian acknowledgment that the gospel picture of Jesus may not be historically accurate, but "the Christian message" is still God's work and somehow wonderfully valuable and important.

Further, it is simply not true to say that the historical and social circumstances in which the Koran was revealed "relate to an extremely specialized field of learning that few scholars ever bothered with." The Muslim literature on the so-called "occasions of revelation" (*asbab all-lnuzul*) is substantial, precisely because Muslims liked to think they knew everything that could possibly be known about Muhammad and the circumstances surrounding the revelation of the Koran.[23] The fact that it is all fictitious and historically worthless tells us, in turn, something about Islamic "perceptions of what is real and important." Namely, that believing a fantasy is better than knowing the truth or admitting ignorance.

Andrew Rippin says of the *asbab* reports that they are cited

> out of a general desire to historicize the text of the Koran in order to be able to prove constantly that God really did reveal his book to humanity on earth; the material thereby acts as a witness to God's concern for His creation. . . . The *sabab* is the constant reminder of God and is the "rope"—that being one of the understood meanings of *sabab* in the Koran—by which human contemplation of the Koran may ascend to the highest levels even while dealing with mundane aspects of the text.
>
> The major literary exegetical role that the *asbab* plays, however, is what could be called a "haggadically exegetical" function; regardless of the genre of exegesis in which the sabab is found, its function is to provide a narrative account in which the basic exegesis of the verse may be embodied.[24]

The term "haggadically exegetical" derives from Wansbrough's *Quranic Studies*. Haggadah is a Hebrew word meaning "the telling," and in Judaism is a book containing passages dealing with the theme of the Exodus read at the Passover Seder. Generally speaking Haggadah refers to material of a homiletic or allegorical character, as opposed to Halakah, another Hebrew term that refers to all legal matter. The Haggadic character of the *asbab* reports is most crucially apparent in the hadiths purporting to relate the circumstances surrounding the initial Koran revelations. The historical insubstantiality of these reports is fully confirmed by the rational-analytic study of the sira-maghazi literature.

We have already seen the gulf that looms between the traditional and the critical accounts of the origins of Islam. The implications of this gulf are quite literally shattering. The *Sira* of the Prophet Muhammad contains, perhaps as its primary raison d'etre, an account of where, when, and how, the Koran came to be revealed. This event is depicted as taking place at or near a town called Mecca in the southern Hijaz. As shown above there are very good reasons for thinking that this Mecca is a late and tendentious literary fabrication. The event could not have occurred as related in the Muslim sources because the place in which it is depicted as happening simply did not exist, at least not in the way it is described in those sources.

Furthermore, Muslims like to think they know the exact circumstances of the revelation of the Koran because they have an account of the event from the Prophet himself as recorded in the Hadith. This, too, is a sad delusion. Despite the fact that the Hadiths reporting the circumstances of the initial Koran revelations are contained in the supposedly sound collections of Bukhari and others, it is quite obvious that these accounts are not independent reports originating from the Prophet or the Companions, but fictions based on the Koranic text.

The Hadith describing the first revelation[25] arises from the fact that the command "Recite" at the beginning of sura 96 seems appropriate as an opening for a first revelation, so the story was duly invented to satisfy the curious. Likewise, the hadith describing the second revelation[26] clearly arises from the odd words "O thou enwrapped in thy robes" or "O thou shrouded in thy mantle" (*muddathir/muzzamil*), that occur at the beginning of suras 73 and 74 respectively. Any of these texts could be plausibly construed as first revelations and Hadiths were accordingly invented to that effect, which led to the invention of further Hadiths in order to reconcile the differences.[27] The truth is that nobody knew anything about the circumstances of the first revelations, or any of the other revelations, and the same goes for the physical effects they are supposed to have had on the Prophet.[28] The description of Muhammad moving his lips during revelation obviously derives from the text of sura 75:16–17, just as the report put into the mouth of Zayd ibn Thabit concerning the weight of the Prophet's thigh is concocted from sura 75:5.[29] Such Hadiths do not explain the Koranic text; they are simply generated by it.

If the place where the first revelations are supposed to have occurred did not exist, and the precise circumstances surrounding them are fabrications based on Koranic texts, the Koran itself becomes detached from any fixed place in space and time. Its only remaining anchor is that it is somehow attached to the name Muhammad, "the richly praised one," a sobriquet that itself floats free and remains unattached to any plausible human biography. Like the early Muslim scholars who invented the historical circumstances of the birth of Islam all we have to go on is the text of the Koran.

At this point a crucial distinction has to be made between the Koran as source (*asl*), and the Koran as document (*mushaf*). This distinction was first made by John Burton in his study of the Muslim theories of abrogation (naskh).[30] In studying the sources on this topic it becomes clear that reference to the Koran is not necessarily reference to the canonical text since mention is made of verses and rulings that that text does not now contain. On the other hand the liturgical function of scripture convinced Burton that it must have had an early fixed form in addition to being an authoritative source. Since on close examination the Muslim accounts of how the Koran was collected appear to be fictive and designed to exclude the Prophet from the process Burton, somewhat perversely, concludes that "what we have in our hands today is the *mushaf* of Muhammad."[31] Which is at odds with both Muslim tradition, which regards the text as having been fixed in the time of the Caliph 'Uthman, and the rest of western scholarship. John Wansbrough, in his review of the book in which this conclusion "is reached, concedes the antiquity of much of the Koran's "paraenetic phraseology," but sees no reason why that should "include, or require the entire canon," and especially not those verses which seem to be "exegetical in character, namely, of fiqh and Sunna at a time when scriptural 'props' for community authority were being sought (i.e., by opponents of Shafi'i's prophetical Sunna)."'[32]

In his own study of the same materials Wansbrough concludes that:

> No element in either the style or the structure of halakhic (legal) exegesis points unmistakably to the necessity, or even to the existence, of the canon as ultimately preserved and transmitted. . . . The dichotomy of "Koran as document" and "Koran as source" proposed by Burton, while not without a certain methodological utility, is misleading if meant to postulate the historical existence of the canonical text before it became a source of law.
>
> Logically, it seems to me quite impossible that canonization should have preceded, not succeeded, recognition of the authority of scripture within the Muslim community. Chronologically, the data of Arabic literature cannot be said to attest to the existence of the canon before the beginning of the third/ninth century.[33]
>
> It was only after the articulation of law as divinely decreed that a scriptural canon was established, the result primarily of polemical pressure. Once stabilized, the document of revelation was no longer exclusively the "word of God" but also, and equally important, a monument of the national literature. In that capacity its service to the community, and to the cause of polemic, was unlimited.[34]

In short, the Koran as we have it is not the work of Muhammad or the 'Uthmanic redactors, much less the immaculate word of God, but a precipitate of the social and cultural pressures of the first two Islamic centuries.

As a piece of literature assembled over a couple of centuries by persons unknown the Koran exhibits "a variety of recognizable literary forms in no recognizable order."[35] From his extended analysis of the text Wansbrough concludes that the structure of Muslim scripture lends little support to the theory of a deliberate edition. Not only in the examples of salvation history characterized by variant traditions, that is, the repeated telling of the same story in different words, but also in passages of exclusively paraenetic or eschatological content "ellipsis and repetition are such as to suggest not the carefully executed product of one or many men, but rather the product of an organic development from originally independent traditions during a long period of transmission."[36]

These independent traditions appear in the canonical text in the form of the juxtaposition of independent pericopes unified by rhetorical phrases, this stylistic method accounting for the homogeneity of the text. The content of the pericopes consists of what Wansbrough calls "prophetical *logia*," in a number of recognizable literary forms, concerning the means of salvation. In the text of the Koran these sayings are expressed as the utterances of God, but outside the text they appear as reports about such utterances. The quality of reference, repetitious employment of rhetorical devices, and polemical tone of these pericopes of prophetical *logia*, all suggest "a strongly sectarian atmosphere, in which a corpus of familiar scripture was being pressed into the service of as yet unfamiliar doctrine."[37] A case in point here is the Islamizing of the figure of Abraham by associating him with an Arab sanctuary at Mecca.

The Arabs were Ishmaelites according to Jewish scripture (Gen. 17:20) and the belief that Abraham had bequeathed a monotheist religion to them, including descent from Ishmael and Hagar and prohibition of pork and other Jewish practises, is attested for northwest Arabia in a Greek source, *The Ecclesiastical History* of Sozomen, as early as the fifth century. Sozomen was a native of Gaza and his mother tongue was Arabic, so we have testimony from a reliable source that by the fifth century Arabs, at least in that area, were familiar with the idea that they were Abrahamic monotheists (hanifs) by origin; whether this was true of Arabs throughout the peninsula it is impossible to say.[38]

In the Koran Abraham is mentioned in 245 verses in 25 suras, only outnumbered by Moses, 502 verses in 36 suras.[39] The Koran categorizes Abraham as a Prophet (sura 19:42, cf. Gen. 20:7), equips him with an autonomous religion (*din Ibrahim*) (suras 16:124, 22:77) and scripture (*suhuf Ibrahim*) (suras 53:35, 87:18 f.), and credits him, in conjunction with Ishmael, with the foundation of what Muslim tradition identified as the sanctuary at Mecca. This association of Abraham with an exclusively Arab sanctuary in the southern Hijaz is the means, at once geographical and sacerdotal, of distancing Islam from its Jewish roots in the north.

The unmistakable Jewish foundations of Islam are usually explained in two ways. Either Muhammad "borrowed" these Jewish elements from his contacts with Judaism, or they are the result of the common ancestry of Jews and Arabs and their joint inheritance of a hypothetical original "Semitic religion." The Jewish elements in the Muslim sanctuary traditions, however, do not admit of either of these solutions.

In his studies of these traditions Gerald Hawting recognized that "there are certain names and terms which, with reference to the Muslim sanctuary at Mecca, have fixed and precise meanings but which sometimes occur in the traditions, in the Koran and in the poetry in a way which conflicts with their usual

meanings, or at least suggests that they are being used with a different sense."[40]
He concludes from this that these terms date from a time before the Muslim sanctuary was established in its classical form as we know it today, a time when Islam
was much more closely conjoined with Judaism than previously supposed:

> It seems that the Muslim sanctuary at Mecca is the result of a sort of compro-
> mise between a preexisting pagan sanctuary and sanctuary ideas which had
> developed first in a Jewish milieu. I envisage that Muslim sanctuary ideas orig-
> inated first in a Jewish matrix, as did Islam itself. At a certain stage in the devel-
> opment of the new religion the need arose to assert its independence, and one
> of the most obvious ways in which this could be done was by establishing a
> specifically Muslim sanctuary. The choice of sanctuary would have been gov-
> erned by already existing sanctuary ideas and when a suitable sanctuary was
> fixed upon these sanctuary ideas would themselves have been modified to take
> account of the facts of the sanctuary which had been chosen. It seems likely that
> the Meccan sanctuary was chosen only after the elimination of other possibili-
> ties—that in the early Islamic period a number of possible sanctuary sites
> gained adherents until finally Mecca became established as the Muslim sanc-
> tuary. And it also seems likely that one reason for the adoption of the Meccan
> sanctuary was that it did approximate to the sanctuary ideas which had already
> been formed—although they had to be reformulated, the physical facts of the
> Meccan sanctuary did not mean that already existing notions and terminology
> had to be abandoned.[41]

Hawting's analysis of sanctuary terms and names is too technical to detail here,
but confirms the conclusions of Crone, Cook, and Wansbrough, that the Hijazi
origin of Islam is a late literary fiction. Further confirmation of this conclusion
is to be found in the work of Reuven Firestone and Norman Calder on the evolution of the Abraham-Ishmael legends in Islamic exegesis.

The notoriously allusive nature of the Koran—its reference to characters and
stories without providing the relevant narrative in the text—is manifest in the tale
of Abraham and Ishmael. In sura 2:125–29, these characters are described as
building what Muslim tradition interpreted as the Kaaba at Mecca, without any
word as to how they arrived there from Syria, where the biblical version of the
Abraham legend is set. This lack of information was more than amply offset in the
exegetical literature (tafsir). Firestone traces at least three different legends of the
transfer of Abraham and Ishmael to Mecca from Syria, attributed to three different
traditionists: Ibn Abbas, Ali, and Mujahid.[42] Clearly, none of these tales are a record
of real events, any more than the original biblical stories that gave rise to them.

What emerges from a close examination of the Muslim sources is that in the

early days of Islam Koran, Hadith, tafsir, and sira, were fluid and interacting literary categories, not distinct entities. It is not the case that from early times there
was the canonical text of the Koran and that Hadith, tafsir, and sira, supplemented that bedrock as commentary and exemplification; the Koran is tafsir on
itself and on Sunna, the sira is tafsir of Koran and Sunna as well as a collection
of hadiths, and the Hadith is an alternative Koran. All these genres continually
interacted, each molding the others as generation followed generation, until
Islam finally defined itself in its classical form as reaction to its previous forms
and its non-Muslim environment. Far from it being true, as Muhammad is made
to say in his so-called "farewell sermon," that: "this day have I perfected for you
your religion" (sura 5:3), it was two or three centuries before Islam knew precisely what it was, beyond being not Judaism and not Christianity.

The fluid nature of Koran and tafsir appears in Norman Calder's study of the
sacrifice of Abraham in early Islamic tradition. He well describes the situation
that produced the interaction of these two genres:

> In the course of the seventh century when Arabic speaking peoples found them-
> selves ruling the ancient polyglot culture of the Near East, and came thereby to
> constitute a new market and a new demand for story, old cycles were new-trans-
> lated, amongst them the tales of the patriarchs and prophets of the Old Testa-
> ment. Something of that process of Arabization may be illustrated, for the Bib-
> lical tales, by reference to the extensive antiquarian activity of Muslim scholars
> in the nineth century, scholars who collected in the form of Traditions (*ahadith*)
> snippets and fragments of what the community recalled or ascribed or invented
> or preserved and deemed relevant to their understanding of religion. Many ver-
> sions may be found of the story of Abraham's sacrifice in collections whose pur-
> pose was avowedly scriptural (Koranic) exegesis, and whose context was there-
> fore academic.[43]

In studying the various versions of the Abrahamic sacrifice to be found in such
encyclopaedists as al-Tabari and al-Suyuti, Calder found that:

> The actual wording of the call to Abraham, where it occurs, is always Koranic
> but invariably introduced by the non-Koranic formula *nudiya* (there was a call).
> The assumption must be that a standard narrative formula indicating the irrup-
> tion of the supernatural has been edited and reformulated as *nadayna-hu* (we
> called him) for inclusion in a work ascribed to God. The Koranic version, if my
> argument is correct, is secondary to and dependent on the narratives. The sto-
> ries, it may be remarked, freely refer to God as subject of action. Had they been
> dependent on a preexisting Koranic text there would have been no reason to
> avoid mentioning the there explicitly identified caller.[44]

This confirms Wansbrough's conclusion that the Koran only achieved its canonical form in the eighth or early ninth century:

> I find the burden of his [Wansbrough's] argumentation perfectly satisfactory, and indeed consistent with what scholars working on the forms of prayer or scripture have come to expect. Such materials do not spring fully fledged into existence in their final form: they achieve a canonical form gradually over a period of time. Clearly the sacrifice narratives, if they do not actually *require* a late date for the canonical text of the Koran, are at least consistent with such a date, ca. 800.[45]

Finally, in confirmation of Hawting and Firestone, Calder concludes that "all early Arabic versions of the sacrifice narrative may, then, be analyzed as built primarily out of narrative materials derived ultimately from Rabbinic sources; and as exhibiting, secondarily, interference from Arabian (Meccan sanctuary) traditions."[46]

Beside the Koran the other source for classical Islam as we know it today is that vast body of literature known as the Hadith, and the Hadith has been subjected to an even more thorough critique by western scholarship than the Koran. The devastating nature of that critique has been fully recognized by the mystical-romantic school of Islam. Nasr has remarked that the criticisms that European orientalists have made of the Hadith is "one of the most diabolical attacks made against the whole structure of Islam."[47]

As Nasr sees it, the danger inherent in this criticism is that it leads Muslims who accept it to the fatally dangerous conclusion that the body of Hadith is not the sayings of the Prophet and therefore does not carry his authority: "In this way one of the foundations of Divine Law and a vital source of guidance for the spiritual life is destroyed. It is as if the whole foundation were pulled from underneath the structure of Islam."[48] This assessment is of course perfectly correct, and Nasr expresses the hope that Muslim scholars will come to the defense of the traditional view of the Hadith. This is vital because the western critical attitude, with which some western educated Muslims have become imbued, "hides an a priori presumption no Muslim can accept, namely the negation of the heavenly origin of the Koranic revelation and the actual prophetic power and function of the Prophet."[49] The same argument quoted above against Western scholarship and the Koran.

Nasr's plea for a defense of the Hadith from the traditional Muslim point of view was originally made over thirty years ago and in all that time has produced no response worthy of note. His own efforts in this direction are hardly inspiring and consist mostly of hysterical outbursts and circular assertions. The primary reply to criticism is, as always, that belief (Iman) cures all problems: "Were the critics of Hadith simply to admit that the Prophet was a prophet, there would be no scientifically valid argument whatsoever against the main body of Hadith." The "main body of Hadith" is a necessary caveat since even Nasr has to admit that "there is of course no doubt that there are many Hadiths which are spurious," but that is all taken care of within acceptable parameters by means of the Islamic sciences of Hadith authentication (*ilm al jarh/ilm al dirayah*).[50]

However, since those ancient methods would not satisfy modern western critics Nasr makes an effort of his own, which perfectly exemplifies the circular nature of Muslim reasoning:

> The Sunna of the Prophet and his sayings had left such a profound imprint upon the first generation and those that came immediately afterwards that a forging of new sayings, and therefore also new ways of action and procedure in religious questions that already possessed precedence, would have been immediately opposed by the community. It would have meant a break in the continuity of the whole religious life and pattern of Islam which, in fact, is not discernible. Moreover, the Imams, whose sayings are included in the Hadith corpus in Shi'ism and who themselves are the most reliable chain of transmission of prophetic sayings, survived after the third Islamic century, that is, ' after the very period of the collection of the well-known books of Hadith, so that they bridge the period to which the modern critics point as the "forgery" of Hadith.[51]

How does Nasr think he knows what the Prophetic Sunna was, and what the first generation of Muslims was like? His only possible way of knowing these things is by means of the Hadith. The Sunna cannot validate the Hadith any more than the Hadith can validate the Sunna. The Sunna is unknown apart from the Hadith and was invented along with the first generation of Muslims who are supposed to have witnessed and reported it. As we have seen, other literary genres such as Koran, tafsir, and sira are not sources of evidence independent of Hadith, which might give us a different perspective, they are all of the same fluid and insubstantial nature, primarily concerned with differentiating Islam from Judaism and giving it an origin in the Hijaz. The Shiite Imams are irrelevant since the Shias were just as cut off from authentic information about the origins of Islam as were the Sunnis, and had just as much of a vested interest in an idealized, fictional picture.

The credit for uncovering the spurious nature of the Hadith must go to the Hungarian scholar Ignaz Goldziher (1850–1921), in the second volume of his *Muslim Studies*, first published in German 1889–90. This work has never been translated into Arabic and is ignored in the Muslim world apart from a handful of scholars, such as Nasr, who happen to have had a western education. In its basic argument the book is unanswerable and does, indeed, remove the foundations from under Islam.

We have noted Patricia Crone's remark that the Muslim sources assert A and not A with such regularity that in the end it becomes impossible to believe anything, this is also the verdict of Goldziher on the Hadith. The undisguised disagreement of the Hadith on every conceivable matter, together with the vast increase in their number with every succeeding generation, led him to conclude that:

> In the absence of authentic evidence it would indeed be rash to attempt the most tentative opinion as to which parts of the Hadith are the oldest original material, or even as to which of them date back to the generations immediately following the Prophet's death. Closer acquaintance with the vast stock of Hadiths induces sceptical caution rather than optimistic trust regarding the material brought together in the carefully compiled collections. We are unlikely to have even as much confidence as Dozy regarding a large part of the Hadith, but will probably consider by far the greater part of it as the result of the religious, historical and social development of Islam during the first two centuries.
>
> The Hadith will not serve as a document for the history of the infancy of Islam, but rather as a reflection of the tendencies which appeared in the community during the maturer stages of its development. It contains invaluable evidence for the evolution of Islam during the years when it was forming itself into an organized whole from powerful mutually opposed forces.[52]

These forces were political: Umayyad, Shia, Khawarij; legal, with regional groups of scholars vying for predominance; and religious, with quarrels over such issues as freewill and predestination.

Particularly devastating is Goldziher's critique of the institution of the isnad, the chain of authorities that supposedly takes a Hadith back to its origin with a follower, companion, or the Prophet. The isnad is the only method available to Muslims for authenticating the Hadith and is wholly inadequate:

> Traditions are only investigated in respect of their outward form and judgement of the value of the contents depends on the judgement of the correctness of the isnad. If the isnad to which an impossible sentence full of inner and outer contradictions is appended withstands the scrutiny of this formal criticism, if the continuity of the entirely trustworthy authors cited in them is complete and if the possibility of their personal communication is established, the tradition is accepted as worthy of credit. . . . Muslim critics have no feeling for even the crudest anachronisms provided that the isnad is correct. Muhammad's prophetic gift is used as a factor to smooth over such difficulties.[53]

Precisely the method used by Nasr quoted above—all problems are solved if only it is admitted that Muhammad was a Prophet.

It turns out that not only are the isnad false, they are a late innovation which explains why they are false. In his study of Hadith G. H. A. Juynboll says:

> In my view, before the institution of the isnad came into existence roughly three quarters of a century after the prophet's death, the *ahadith* and the qisas (mostly legendary stories) were transmitted in a haphazard fashion if at all, and mostly anonymously. Since the isnad came into being, names of older authorities were supplied where the new isnad precepts required such. Often the names of well-known historical personalities were chosen but more often the names of fictitious persons were offered to fill the gaps in isnads which were as yet far from perfect. . . .[54]
>
> I contend that the beginning of standardization of hadith took place not earlier than towards the end of the first/seventh century. . . .[55]
>
> The overall majority of allegedly the most ancient traditions is likely to have originated at the earliest in the course of the last few decades of the first century (700s–720s), when for the first time the need for traditions became generally felt. The isnad as institution had just come into being and slowly but gradually the concept of sunnat an-nabi began to eclipse the Sunna of a region or of a (group of) person(s).[56]

On the period of the introduction of isnads Wansbrough is even more sceptical than Juynboll: "The supplying of isnads, whether traced to the prophet, to his companions, or to the successors, may be understood as an exclusively formal innovation and cannot be dated much before 200/815."[57] In any case, it must be true, as Kenneth Cragg has remarked of the collection of Hadith in general: "This science became so meticulous that it is fair (even if somewhat paradoxical) to suspect that the more complete and formally satisfactory the attestation claimed to be, the more likely it was that the tradition was of late and deliberate origin. The developed requirements of acceptability that the tradition boasted simply did not exist in the early, more haphazard and spontaneous days."[58]

Juynboll's mention of the fact that the Sunna of the Prophet (sunnat annabi) slowly came to replace the Sunna of a region, person, or group of persons, is an insight due to the other great pioneer of Hadith study after Goldziher, Joseph Schacht (1902–1969). Building on Goldziher's works, but concentrating on legal hadiths, Schacht recognized the significance of Shafi'i's insistence on the Sunna of the Prophet:

> Shafi'i insists time after time that nothing can override the authority of the Prophet, even if it be attested only by an isolated tradition, and that every well-

authenticated tradition going back to the Prophet has precedence over the opinions of his Companions, their Successors, and later authorities. This is a truism for the classical theory of Muhammadan law, but Shafi'i's continual insistence on this point shows that it could not yet have been so in his time.[59]

Before Shafi'i (d. 204/820) "Islamic" law was not only not necessarily connected with the Prophet, it was not even necessarily connected with the companions and their successors.

It was also Schacht's achievement to show how isnads not only grow vertically, that is to say, backwards in time to the earliest possible attestation, but also horizontally, that is to say, spread geographically from region to region. This last point is important in that it answers the objection of Muslims who hold that the bulk of the Hadith must be authentic because the same Hadith is often attested with the same isnad, in the same generation, in regions remote from each other.[60] Finally, Schacht showed that the study of Hadiths only takes us back to about the year 100/719, which forms a horizon or Hadith barrier, beyond which what went on must be surmised from material outside the Hadith.

Now, a point often made by Muslims, and which appears to be ceded by Burton, goes as follows: "If hypocrisy lies precisely in the adoption of the external demeanor of the pious and the counterfeit testifies to the existence of the genuine coin, pseudo-Hadith imitates real Hadith otherwise the exercise is pointless."[61] But this is not really so. All that is needed for the invention of false Hadiths is knowledge that Hadiths are the current means of gaining power and influencing people, *none of them need be true.* Because at some point a coinage appears that seems to be made of gold, to bear the king's head, and to come from the royal mint, it does not necessarily follow that any of that is the case. Especially when there is no means of assaying the metal, no one has seen the king, and the location of the royal mint is unknown. The coinage is accepted because it is a convenient means of exchange and for no other reason, the forgers can proceed from there.

The final nail in the coffin of the Hadith comes from consideration of the sheer number of traditions:

> Bukhari is said to have examined a total of 600,000 traditions attributed to the Prophet; he preserved some 7,000 (including repetitions), or in other words dismissed some 593,000 as inauthentic. If Ibn Hanbal examined a similar number of traditions, he must have rejected about 570,000, his collection containing some 30,000 (again including repetitions). Of Ibn Hanbal's traditions 1,710 (including repetitions) are transmitted by the Companion Ibn Abbas. Yet less than fifty years earlier one scholar had estimated that Ibn Abbas had only heard

nine traditions from the Prophet, while another thought that the correct figure might be ten. If Ibn Abbas had heard ten traditions from the Prophet in the years around 800, but over a thousand by about 850, how many had he heard in 700 or 632? Even if we accept that ten of Ibn Abbas' traditions are authentic, how do we identify them in the pool of 1,710? We do not even know whether they are to be found in this pool, as opposed to that of the 530,000 traditions dismissed on the ground that their chains of authorities were faulty. Under such circumstances it is scarcely justified to presume Hadith to be authentic until the contrary has been proved.[62]

In conclusion it can be said that if the Sharia is based on the Hadith it does not have even a semblance of divine sanction, and if it depends on the Koran its case is no better since the Koran's claim to divine origin rests on the Hadith.

Faced with all this argument and evidence Muslims have two options. They can avert their eyes, denounce it all as the work of Shaitan and the enemies of Islam and go on believing the traditional account as literally true (fundamentalism), or they can adopt the posture of the mystical-romantic school. These, too, will regard the critics as the agents of Shaitan, but will go on to say that even if the criticisms are correct, which of course they are not, this cannot affect the claims of Islam since those claims do not depend on historical origins but on an inner knowledge of God, the accompaniment and reward of piety. What make Islam true is the spiritual life of Muslims, not religious history but religious experience. This is the realm of Sufism or Islamic mysticism, the discussion of which must be left for another occasion.

REFERENCES

Ali, M. M. *A Manual of Hadith*, London, 1983.

Azmi, M. M. *Studies in Early Hadith Literature*. Indianapolis, 1978.

Bashear, S. *Arabs and Others in Early Islam*. New Jersey, 1997.

Brock, S. P. "Syriac Views of Early Islam." in G. H. A Juynboll, *Studies on the First Century of Islamic Society*, 1982, pp. 9–21.

Burton, J. "Those are the High-Flying Cranes." *Journal of Semitic Studies* 15, no. 2 (1970): 246-65.

———. *Collection of the Qur'an*. Cambridge, 1977.

———. Review of Watt and McDonald, *The History of al-lTabari*, vol. 6, *Muhammad at Mecca*. *BSOAS*, vol. 53, (1990): 328–31.

———. *An Introduction to the Hadith*. Edinburgh, 1994.

Calder, N. "From Midrash to Scripture: The Sacrifice of Abraham in Early Islamic Tradition." *Le Museon*, vol. 101 (1988): 375–402.

Chittick, W. C., and S. Murata. *The Vision of Islam*. New York, 1994.

Cook, M. *Early Muslim Dogma: A Source Critical Study*. Cambridge, 1981.

Conrad, L. "Abraha and Muhammad: Some Observations a propos of Chronology and Literary Topoi in the Early Arabic Historical Tradition." *BSOAS*, vol. 50, (1987): 225–40

Cragg, K. "Hadith, Traditions of the Prophet." *Encyclopedia Britannica*, vol. 22 (1974): 10–12.

Crone, P., and M. Cook. *Hagarism: The Making of the Muslim World*. Cambridge, 1977.

———. *Slaves on Horses: The Evolution of the Islamic Polity*. Cambridge, 1980.

Crone, P., M. Cook, and M. Hinds, *God's Caliph: Religious Authority in the First Centuries of Islam*. Cambridge, 1986.

———. *Meccan Trade and the Rise of Islam*. Oxford, 1987.

———. *Roman, Provincial and Islamic Law: The Origins of the Islamic Patronate*. Cambridge, 1987.

Firestone, R. *Journeys into Holy Lands: The Evolution of the Abraham-Ishmael Legends in Islamic Exegesis*. New York, 1990.

Goldziher, I. *Muslim Studies*. 2 vols. London,1966, 1971.

Guillaume, A. *The Life of Muhammad*. (translation of Ibn Ishaq's *Sirat Rasul Allah*) Oxford, 1955.

Hawting, G. R. "The Origins of the Muslim Sanctuary at Mecca." In Juynboll, *Studies on the First Century of Islamic Society*, 1982, pp. 23–47.

———. Review of Lecker *The Banu Sulaym. BSOAS* 50 (1991): 359–62.

Juynboll, G. H. A. *Studies on the First Century of Islamic Society*. Carbondale, 1982.

———. *Muslim Tradition*. Cambridge, 1983.

Kurtz, P. *The Transcendental Temptation: A Critique of Religion and the Paranormal*. Amherst, 1986.

Lecker, M. *Muslims, Jews, and Pagans: Studies on Early Islamic Medina*. Leiden, 1995.

Lings, M. *Muhammad: His Life Based on the Earliest Sources*. London, 1983.

Margoliouth, D. S. 1915. "Mecca," "Muhammad," "Qur'an." In J. Hastings, *Encyclopaedia of Religion and Ethics*, vols. 8 and 10 (1915).

Nasr, S. H. *Ideals and Realities of Islam*. London, 1966 Tr. Tabatabai, Shi'ite Islam. Houston.

———. *Islamic Spirituality*. 2 vols. London, 1989, 1991.

Newby, G. D. *A History of the Jews of Arabia: From Ancient Times to Their Eclipse Under Islam*. Columbia, S. Carolina, 1988.

———. *The Making of the Last Prophet: A Reconstruction of the Earliest Biography of Muhammad*. Columbia, S. Carolina, 1989.

Rippin, A. "The Exegetical Genre Asbab Al Nuzul: A Bibliographical and Terminological Survey." *BSOAS* 48 (1985): 1–15.

———. 1988. "The Function of Asbab Al Nuzul in Quranic Exegesis." *BSOAS* 51 (1988): 1-19.

Rubin, U. *The Eye of the Beholder: The Life of Muhammad as Viewed by the Early Muslims*. New Jersey, 1995.

———. "The Shrouded Messenger: On the Interpretation of al-Muzzammil and al-Mud-daththir." *Jerusalem Studies in Arabic and Islam* 16 (1993): 96–107.

Sardar, Z., and Z. A. Malik, *Muhammad for Beginners.* London, 1994.

Schuon, F. *Stations of Wisdom.* London, 1961.

Wansbrough, J. *Quranic Studies: Sources and Methods of Scriptural Interpretation.* Oxford, 1977.

———. *The Sectarian Milieu: Content and Composition of Islamic Salvation History.* Oxford, 1978.

———. Review of Burton's *The Collection of the Qur'an. BSOAS* 41 (1978): 370–71.

———. Review of Crone and Cook's *Hagarism: The Making of the Muslim World. BSOAS* 41 (1978): 155–56.

Whelan, E. "Forgotten Witness: Evidence for the Early Codification of the Qur'an." *The Journal of the American Oriental Society* (January–March 1998).

NOTES

1. Sardar and Malik, *Muhammad for Beginners*, p. 30.

2. Burton, *Bulletin of the Society of Oriental and Africn Studies* (Hereafter *BSOAS*) vol. 53 (1990): 328.

3. Ibid.

4. Ibid.

5. *Sira*, translated by Guillaume, p. 691.

6. Wansbrough's pioneering work on the *Sira* and the sectarian milieu has now been confirmed and broadened by examination of a wider range of sources. See Uri Rubin, *The Eye of the Beholder*, and Suliman Bashear, *Arabs and Others in Early Islam*. If Rubin and Bashear can be said to Follow in the footsteps of Wansbrough, Michael Lecker can be said to follow in the footsteps of W. M. Watt. In his *Muslims, Jews, and Pagans: Studies in Early Islamic Medina*, Lecker finds indubitable history in Samhudi, who lived nine hundred years after the Prophet. Samhudi is to be believed, apparently, because he quotes such "early" sources as lbn Zabala, who only lived two hundred years after the Prophet. Lecker's argument appears to be that because the material in these sources is incredibly detailed and does not contradict the *Sira* it ought to be trusted. In short, wilful naiveté driven by a lust for positive results. Cf. Hawting's review of Lecker's *The Banu Sulaym, BSOAS*, vol. 54, 359–62.

7. See *The Sectarian Milieu*, pp. 116–17, and his review of *Hagarism* in *BSOAS*, vol. 41, pp. 155–56.

8. See the article "Mecca," in Hastings, *Encyclopaedia of Religion and Ethics*, vol. 8, p. 511.

9. Newby, *A History of the Jews of Arabia*, p. 13.

10. Juynboll, *Studies in the First Century of Islamic Society*, p. 14.

11. Ibid. p. 25.

12. See the article "Abraha and Muhammad: Some Observations Apropos of Chronology and Literary topoi in the Early Arabic Historical Tradition," *BSOAS* 50 (1987): 239. Also Rubin, op. cit. chap. 12.

13. Crone and Cook, *Hagarism*, p. 160 n. 56.

14. Goldziher, *Muslim Studies*, 11, p. 279.

15. Crone, *Meccan Trade*, p. 244.

16. Newby, *The Making of the Last Prophet*, p. 1.

17. Ibid., pp. 1–2.

18. See the article "Muhammad," in Hastings, *Encyclopaedia of Religion and Ethics*, vol. 8, pp. 873, 877–78.

19. Kurtz, *The Transcendental Temptation: A Critique of Religion and the Paranormal*.

20. Schuon, *Stations of Wisdom*, p. 64 n.1.

21. Nasr, *Islamic Spirituality*, p. 9, 19 n.1.

22. Chittick and Murata, *The Vision of Islam*, pp. xiv–xv,

23. Rippin, "The Exegetical Genre *Asbab Al Nuzul*: A Bibliographical and Terminological Survey," *BSOAS* 28 (1985): 1–15.

24. Rippin, "The Function of *Asbab Al Nuzul* in Quranic Exegesis," *BSOAS* 51 (1988): 2–3.

25. Bukhari, 1:1. See Ali, *A Manual of Hadith*, pp. 3–9.

26. Ibid. Ali, pp. 9–10.

27. See Burton, *An Introduction to the Hadith*, pp. 30–32. Also Rubin, op. cit., chap. 6, and "The Shrouded Messenger," *JSAI*, 16, pp. 96–107.

28. Bukhari, op. cit. Ali, pp. 12–13.

29. Bukhari, 8:12. Ali, p. 13.

30. Burton, "Those are the High-Flying Cranes" *JSS* 15 (1970): 251–52, 259.

31. Burton, *The Collection of the Qur'an*, pp. 239–40.

32. Wansbrough, review of Burton's *The Collection of the Qur'an*, *BSOAS* 41 (1978): 370.

33. Wansbrough, *Quranic Studies*, pp. 201–202.

34. Ibid., p. 27. Cf. Whelan, "Forgotten witness: evidence for the early codification of the Quran," *JAOS* (January–March, 1998). Whelan seems to regard any appearance of a Koran text, no matter how brief, as evidence for the existence of the whole canonical Koran as we know it today. This trades on an ambiguity in the use of the term "Koran," since it can stand for a phrase, a verse, a sura, a group of suras, or the whole canonical text, as needed. If people are reported as copying "the Koran" in the seventh century it does not follow that they were copying the whole canonical text; even if the existence of the sequence of suras 91 to 114 were confirmed for the seventh century it would not warrant that assumption, since these suras represent less than a thirtieth of the whole text and in any case were mainly for liturgical use in prayer and thus likely to be early.

35. Ibid., p. 14.

36. Ibid., p. 47.

37. Ibid., p. 20.

38. Crone, *Meccan Trade*, pp. 190–91.

39. Wansbrough, op. cit., p. 49.

40. Hawting, "The Origins of the Muslim Sanctuary at Mecca,"in Juynboll, *Studies in the First Century of Islamic Society*, p. 24.

41. Ibid., pp. 27–28.

42. Firestone, *Journeys in Holy Lands*, chap. 8.

43. Calder, "From Midrash to Scripture: The Sacrifice of Abraham in Early Islamic Tradition," *Le Museon* 101 (1988): 376.

44. Ibid., pp. 388–89.

45. Ibid., p. 389.

46. Ibid., p. 395.

47. Nasr, *Shi'ite Islam*, translated by Tabatabai, p. 119 n.24.

48. Nasr, *Ideals and Realities of Islam*, p. 82.

49. Ibid., p. 82.

50. Ibid., p. 80.

51. Ibid., p. 81.

52. Goldziher, *Muslim Studies*, vol 2, pp. 18–19.

53. Ibid., pp. 140–41.

54. Juynboll, Muslim Tradition, p. 5.

55. Ibid., p. 10.

56. Ibid., pp. 72–73.

57. Wansbrough, *Quranic Studies*, p. 179.

58. Cragg, *Encyclopedia Britannica*, vol. 22, p. 11. However, this does not mean that the more complete isnads are necessarily later than those less complete. See Rubin, op. cit., chap. 15.

59. Schacht, *The Origins of Muhammadan Jurisprudence*, p. 11.

60. See Azmi, *Studies in Early Hadith Literature*, pp. 230f., and the reply of Michael Cook. Early Muslim Dogma, chap. 11, esp. pp. 115ff.

61. Burton, *An Introduction to the Hadith*, p. xii.

62. Crone, *Roman, Provincial, and Islamic Law*, p. 33.

PART TWO

RENAN

Chapter 3

Muhammad and the Origins of Islam

Ernest Renan

All origins are obscure, the origins of religions even more so than others. The product of the most spontaneous instincts of human nature, religions do not recall their infancy any more than an adult remembers the history of his childhood and the successive stages of development of his consciousness; mysterious chrysalides, they appear in broad daylight only in the perfect maturity of their forms. It is the same with the origin of religions as with the origin of humanity. Science shows that on one particular day, in virtue of the natural laws that, up to now, had governed the development of things without exception and without external interference, the thinking being emerged, in full possession of all his faculties and complete in his essential elements—and yet, to try to explain how man appeared on earth by laws which govern the phenomena of our globe since nature has ceased to create, would be to open the door to such extravagant fancy, that not a single serious thinker would wish to give it a moment's thought.

It is further true, beyond doubt, that on a certain day, by the natural and spontaneous expansion of his faculties, man improvised language, and yet

Originally published in *Revue des Deux-Mondes* (December 1851): 1023–60. Translated for this volume by Ibn Warraq. This article is a review of A. P. Caussin de Perceval, *Essai sur l'Histoire des Arabes avant l'islamisme* (3 vosl., 1848); H. G. Weil, *Mohammed der Prophet, sein Leben und sein Lehre* (Stuttgart, 1843), *Historisch-kritische Einleitung in den Koran* (Bielefeld, 1844), *Geschichte der Chalifen* (3 vols., Mannheim, 1846, 1848, 1851); Washington Irving, *Lives of Mahomet and his successors* (New York, 1850).

nothing in our current knowledge of the human mind can help us to understand this wondrous fact, whose comprehension is considered an impossibility in our intellectual circles. Likewise, one should abandon the idea of explaining by the ordinary processes available to our experience the primitive facts of religions, facts which no longer have any equivalents since mankind has lost its religious fecundity. Faced with the powerlessness of reflected reason to found and control belief, how can we fail to acknowledge the hidden force which at certain moments penetrates and enlivens the entrails of humanity? The supernatural hypothesis offers perhaps fewer difficulties than the superficial solutions of those who tackle these formidable problems without having fathomed the mysteries of spontaneous consciousness. If, to dismiss this hypothesis, it was necessary to reach a rational opinion on these truly divine facts, then very few men would have the right not to believe in the supernatural.

All the same, is it right that science should forego explaining how the earth was formed because the phenomena that are responsible for the state in which we find it are no longer apparent in our days on a grand scale? Should science renounce explaining the appearance of life and living species because the contemporary period has ceased to be creative, explaining the origin of language because languages are no longer being invented, the origin of religions because religions are no longer being created? No, certainly not. It is the infinitely delicate task of science and critical thought to divine the primitive by the faint traces it has left of itself. Thinking has not taken us away so far from the age of creation that we cannot, by dint of imagination, reproduce in ourselves the feelings of the spontaneous life. History, niggardly as she is for the nonconscious eras, is nevertheless not entirely silent; she allows us, if not to tackle the problem directly, at least to circumscribe it from the outside. Then, since there are no absolutes in human matters and there are no two events in the past which belong to the same category, we have intermediate nuances, closer to us, that enable us to describe the phenomena which are inaccessible by direct study. The geologist finds in the slow deterioration of the present state of the globe enough information to explain the past revolutions. The linguist, by observing the unceasing development of languages is led to infer the laws which have governed their formation. The historian, lacking the early evidence that would have indicated the appearence of religions, can study the degenerate and half-successful semireligions, if I may say so, that openly show, though on a smaller scale, the processes by which the great creations of unreflecting periods were formed.

The birth of Islam is, in this respect, a unique and invaluable fact. Islam was the last religious creation of humanity, and, in many respects, the least original. In place of the mystery under which the other religions have covered their origins, this one was born in the full light of history; its roots are on the surface. The life of its founder is as well known to us as that of any sixtheenth-century reformer. We can follow year by year the fluctuations of his thought, his contradictions, his weaknesses. Elsewhere, the origins of religions are lost in dreams; the effort of the sharpest criticism is hardly enough to distinguish the real from under the misleading appearance of myths and legends. Islam, by contrast, born in the midst of advanced reflection, entirely lacks the supernatural. Muhammad, 'Umar, and 'Ali are neither seers, visionaries, nor miracle workers. Each one knows very well what he is doing; none of them is fooling himself. Each one reveals himself naked and with all the weaknesses of humanity.

Thanks to the excellent works of Gustav Weil and A. P. Caussin de Perceval, we can say without exaggeration that the problem of the origins of Islam has in our day found a definitive solution, free from mystery. Caussin de Perceval, particularly, has introduced an important element into the question by the new points of view that he has brought to bear on the antecedents and precursors of Muhammad, a sensitive subject which had not been dealt with before. His excellent work will remain a paradigm of this robust and sober scholarship which could be called the French school, if good sense, accuracy, and solidity are enough to found a school. The finesse and penetration of Weil are worthy of a compatriot of Creuzer[1] and Strauss.[2] From the point of view of choice and the richness of sources, his work is, however, inferior to that of our learned fellow countryman, and one can reproach him for resting too much confidence in Turkish and Persian authorites who are on this question of little value. America and England have also taken a great interst in Muhammad. A well-known novelist, Washington Irving, has narrated his life with great interest, but without showing a highly critical mind. His book, however, is a real improvement in this respect when one thinks that in 1829 Charles Forster published two big volumes[3] much enjoyed by clerics, which established that Muhammad was nothing but "the little horn of the beast that appears in Daniel chapter 7, and that the pope was the big horn." On this ingenious parallel, Forster founded a whole philosophy of history: the pope represents the western corruption of Christianity, and Muhammad the eastern one, hence the striking resemblance between Muhammadanism and Papism!

If told, it would make a curious story—the ideas that Christian nations have held of Muhammad, from the accounts of the false Turpin of the golden idol *Muhom* worshipped at Cadiz (which Charlemagne dared not destroy for fear of the legion of demons that were shut up in it) up to the day when critical thought gave him his title of prophet, though with a multitude of meanings, but very real for all that. The pure faith of the first half of the Middle Ages, which had but the dimmest ideas of the religions foreign to Christianity, conceived of *Maphomet*, *Baphomet*, *Bafum*[4] as a false god to whom one offered human sacrifices. It was only in the twelfth century that Muhammad was perceived as a prophet, and that one seriously thought of unmasking his imposture. Later, in the sixteenth and seventeenth centuries, Bibliander, Hottinger, and Maracci ventured to study the Koran, only to refute it. Prideaux, Bayle, and Voltaire finally considered them as historians and no longer as polemicists, but the lack of authentic documents restricted them to the discussion of childish tales, which up until then had aroused the curiosity of the people and the wrath of the theologians. It was left to Gagnier to write the first biography of Muhammad based on Oriental sources. This scholar was led by his studies to seek information from Aboulfeda [Ismail Abu'l-Fida, 1273–1331], and this was fortunate, since it is doubtful whether his own critique would have been discerning enough to grasp the huge difference between the historical value of the chronicles of the Arab historians and the collection of legends spawned by the Persian imagination. This fundamental distinction that Caussin de Perceval alone has rigorously observed is, truly, at the heart of all the problems pertaining to the origins of Islam.

When based upon the Arab accounts of Ibn Hisham [d. 834] and Abu 'l-Fida, the biography of Muhammad is plain and unaffected, almost without miracles. When based upon Persian and Turkish authors, his legend appears like a ridiculous collection of absurd fables, and in the worst style. Although the traditions associated with Muhammad's life only began to be collected under the Abbasids, the historians of that period were already relying on written sources, whose authors themselves referred back, in citing their authorities, to the companions of the Prophet. Around the mosque adjoining the Prophet's house was a bench on which dwelled men without family or home, men who lived on his generosity and often ate with him. These men, called "men of the bench" (*ahl as suffa*) were thought to know a lot of details of the person of Muhammad, and their recollections became the origin of innumerable sayings or Hadith. The Muslim faith itself was alarmed by the mass of documents thus obtained; only six collections of Hadith were eventually considered lawful. The indefatigable Bukhari confessed that of the 20,000 hadith he had collected, only 7,225 seemed to him genuine beyond doubt. Without being accused of recklessness, European criticism could assuredly proceed to an even more strict selection. However, it cannot be denied that these early accounts show a lot of features of the true character of the Prophet, and are distinguished in a clear-cut manner from the collection of pious stories solely imagined for the edification of their readers. The veritable monument of the early history of Islam, the Koran, remains absolutely impregnable, and suffices in itself, independently of any historical accounts, to reveal to us Muhammad.

I do not know of any work of literature whose process of composition could accurately reflect how the Koran was written. It is neither a book carefully planned nor a vague and indeterminate text arriving little by little at a conclusive lesson. Nor is it the teachings of the master put in writing afterward, based on the recollections of his disciples. The Koran offers a peculiar instance of a nonwritten text, and yet very decided, even composed, with much reflection. It is a collection of preachings, and, if I may say so, of Muhammad's general orders, still showing the date and place where they were given and the circumstances that provoked them. Each one of these pieces was written, after its recitation[5] by the Prophet, on leather, the shoulder blades of sheep, camel bones, palm leaves, or preserved in the memory of the principal disciples who were called the *bearers of the Koran*. It was only under the caliphate of Abu Bakr [632–634], after the battle of Yamama, when a great many old Muslims perished, that someone thought of "putting the Koran between two covers," and to join end to end these loose and often contradictory fragments. It is beyond doubt that this compilation was carried out in the most perfect good faith. There was no attempt to coordinate or reconcile; the longest fragments were put first, and they gathered together at the end the shortest suras[6] containing only a few lines. Hafsa, 'Umar's daughter and one of Muhammad's widows, was entrusted with the care of the original. A second recension was compiled under 'Uthman's caliphate [644–656]. Since variant spellings and different dialects were introduced into the copies in the different provinces, 'Uthman appointed a commission of grammarians to establish a definitive text in the dialect of Mecca. Then by a procedure typical of eastern criticism, he had all the other copies collected and burnt to cut short all discussion. This is why the Koran has come down to us without any significant variants. True, such a method of composition is likely to inspire doubts. The integrity of a work committed to memory for a long time is unlikely to be well preserved. Could not interpolations and alterations have slipped in during the successive revisions? Weil was the first to raise doubts on these points, and he has maintained that the recension of 'Uthman was not purely grammatical, as the Arabs claim, but politics played its part, above all with a view to puncturing the pretensions of 'Ali. Nevertheless, the Koran comes to us with so little organization, in such complete disorder, with such flagrant contradictions, each piece bearing its own peculiarity, that nothing could attack the broad authenticity of this book. Thus, we hold the immense advantage of having for Islam the very pieces of her origins, undoubtedly very suspect pieces, which express not the truth of the events but the needs of the moment; for that very reason, they are precious in the eyes of the critic who knows how to interpret them. It is to this strange spectacle of a religion coming to life in full daylight, entirely conscious of itself, that I should like to draw the attention of thinkers for a moment.

I

Criticism, in general, must abandon the goal of knowing anything for certain about the character and biography of the founders of religion. For them, the tissue of legend has entirely covered the tissue of history. Were they handsome or ugly, vulgar or sublime? No one will know. The books that are attributed to them, the speeches they are credited with, are usually more modern compositions, and we learn far less of what they were like than the way their disciples conceived of the ideal. The very beauty of their character is not theirs; it belongs entirely to human nature, which creates them in its own image. Transformed by this incessantly creative force, the ugliest caterpillar could become the most beautiful butterfly.

It is not the same for Muhammad. Around him, the efforts of legend have remained feeble and unoriginal. Muhammad is really a historical person: we can touch him on all sides. The book that remains to us under his name gives us almost word for word the speeches that he delivered. His life has remained a biography like any other, without miracles, without exaggerations. Ibn Hisham, the earliest of his historians, and Abu 'l-Fida, his learned biographer, are sensible writers. It has almost the tone of "The Life of the Saints," written in a devout manner, but reasonable, something like Alban Butler or D. Lobineau. And moreover one could cite twenty legends of saints (that of St. Francis of Assisi, for example) which have become infinitely more mythic than that of the Prophet of Islam.

Muhammad did not want to be a miracle worker, he only wanted to be a prophet, and one without miracles. He unceasingly repeats that he is a man like any other, mortal like any other, subject to sin, and having need of God's mercy like any other. At death's approach, wishing to ease his conscience, he climbed the pulpit, saying,

"Fellow Muslims, if I have struck anyone amongst you, here is my back, let him strike me; if anyone has been offended by me let him return injury for injury. If I have taken someone's property, everything that I own is at his disposal."

A man stood up and claimed Muhammad owed him three dirhams. The Prophet said, "Better to suffer shame in this world than in the one to come." And he paid him back instantly. This extreme moderation, this good taste, totally exquisite, with which Muhammad understood his role as prophet, were imposed on him by the genius of his nation. Nothing is more inaccurate than to picture the pre-Islamic Arabs as a coarse, ignorant, and superstitious people. On the contrary, we should talk of a cultured, sceptical, and unbelieving nation. Here is a curious episode from the early days of Muhammad's mission, which shows very well, it seems to me, the icy scepticism that he encountered around him and the extreme reserve that he was forced to observe when having recourse to the miraculous. He was seated in the parvis of the Kaaba, not far from a circle formed by several Qurayshite chiefs, all opposed to his doctrines. One of them, 'Utba, the son of Rabia, approached and took his place next to Muhammad, and speaking on behalf of the others said to him:

"Son of my friend, you are a man distinguished by your qualities and your birth. Even though you have disrupted your country, sown discord in families, and have insulted our gods, though you accuse our ancestors and elders of impiety and error, we wish to treat you with consideration. Listen to the proposals that I am going to make to you and see if you cannot accept a few of them."

"Speak," said Muhammad, "I am listening."

"Son of my friend," continued 'Utba, "if the purpose of your behavior is to acquire riches, we will all club together to provide you a fortune considerably greater than that of any Qurayshite. If you have set your sight on honors, we shall appoint you our chief, we shall not make any resolutions without your advice. If the spirit that appears to you attaches itself to you and dominates you in such a manner that you cannot free yourself from its influence,we shall call the best doctors, we shall pay them to cure you."

"I am neither greedy for possessions, nor ambitious for honours, nor possessed by an evil spirit," replied Muhammad. "I have been sent by God, who revealed to me a book, and instructed me to announce the rewards and punishments that await you."

"Well, Muhammad," said the Qurayshites, "since you do not accept our proposals and you persist in pretending to be the messenger of God, give us clear proofs of your prophethood. Our valley is narrow and sterile, get God to widen it, get Him to move apart these mountain chains, which confine it, from one another; let Him make rivers flow like those in Syria or Iraq, or better still let Him make some of our ancestors rise from their tombs, and among them, Qusayy, son of Kilab, this man whose words had such authority; and let these illustrious dead resurrected acknowledge you as prophet, then we will also recognize you as such."

"God," replied Muhammad, "did not send me to you for that sort of thing, He only sent me to preach His law."

"At least," insisted the Qurayshites, "ask your Lord to make appear one of His angels as a witness to your truthfulness and to order us to believe you. Ask Him also to show unequivocally the choice that He has made of you in dispensing you from the need to look for your daily necessities from the markets, like the humblest of your fellow countrymen."

"No," said Muhammad, "I will not address Him these demands: my sole duty is to preach to you."

"Well, let your Lord make the sky fall on us, as you maintain that He is able to do, for we shall not believe you."

We can see that a buddha, a son of God, a thaumaturge of the highest class were above the temperament of this people. The extreme subtlety of the Arab mind, the frank and clear way with which it situates itself in the real world, the freethinking manners and beliefs which prevailed in the Islamic period, ruled out the Prophet giving himself airs. Arabia totally lacks the element which engenders mysticism[7] and mythology. The semitic nations have never understood God to mean variety, pluralism, and gender: the word goddess, in Hebrew, would be the most horrible barbarism. From there comes this trait, so characteristic, that they have never had a mythology or an epic. The direct and simple fashion with which they conceive of God as separated from the world, neither begetting nor begotten, having no equal, excludes these grand embroideries, these divine poems where India, Persia, and Greece have developed their imagination, and which were possible only in the minds of a people who leave the boundaries of God, humanity, and the universe floating indecisively. Mythology is pantheism in religion; the spirit furthest from pantheism is assuredly the semitic spirit. Arabia had, at least, lost or perhaps never had the gift of supernatural invention. One hardly finds in all the Moallakat[8] [al-Mu'allaqat] and the vast repertoire of pre-Islamic poetry a single religious thought. These people did not have the sense of the holy, but, on the other hand, it had a very lively feeling for the real and the human.

That is why Muslim legends have remained so meagre outside Persia, and why the mythic element in them has remained absolutely nil. Undoubtedly the life of Muhammad, like those of all great founders, is surrounded by fables, but these fables have gained some approval only with the Shiites, dominated by the colossus of the Persian imagination. Far from occupying the heart of Islam, they are only the inessential dross tolerated rather than consecrated, a bit like the inferior mythology of the books of the Apocrypha that the Church has never openly adopted, although she has been careful not to show herself too strict in this matter.

How could the popular imagination not have embellished such an extraordinary life with a few miracles? Above all, how could the childhood of the Prophet, a theme so conducive to legends, not have tempted the storytellers? The credulous historians will tell you, for example, that the night the Prophet was born, the palace of Chosroes was shaken by an earthquake, the sacred fire of the Magi went out, lake Sawa dried up, the Tigris overflowed, all the idols of the world fell flat on their faces. All this, nonetheless, never rises to the height of a supernatural and hallowed legend; in short, the stories of Muhammad's childhood, despite some patches, have remained a charming page of grace and naturalness. In order to make one better appreciate this sobriety, I shall here give a sample of the way that India knows how to celebrate the birth of its heroes.

When the creatures learn that the Buddha is going to be born, all the birds of the Himalayas rush to the palace of Kapila, and perch on the terraces, balustrades, vaults, galleries, and roofs of the palace, all the while singing and beating their wings; the ponds become covered with lotus; butter, oil, honey, and sugar, although used in abundance, seem always untouched; the drums, harps, theorbos, and cymbals give out melodious sounds without being touched. Gods and hermits rush from each of the ten horizons to be at the Buddha's side. The Buddha descends accompanied by hundreds of millions of divinities. At the very moment he descends, the three thousand regions of the world are lit up by an immeasurable brilliance, eclipsing that of the gods. Not a single being experiences any fear or pain. All are overcome by a feeling of infinite well-being, and have only tender and affectionate thoughts. Hundreds of millions of gods, with their hands, shoulders, and head, support and carry the Buddha's cart. A hundred thousand apsaras conduct the musical choirs in front, at the back, to the right, to the left, and sing the praise of the Buddha. At the very moment he is about to come out of his mother's womb, all the flowers open their calyx, the young trees rise up from the ground and burst into bloom, the perfumed waters flow everywhere; from the sides of the Himalayas, the young lions rush all joyous to the city of Kapila, and stop at the gates without harming anyone. Five hundred young white elephants come and touch the feet of the king, the father of Buddha, with their trunks. The children of the gods, adorned with belts, appear in the women's quarters, coming and going from one side to the other; the wives of the nagas, leaving half their body uncovered, are revealed fluttering in the air; ten thousand daughters of the gods, holding fans made of peacock tails in their hands, are seen motionless in the sky; ten thousand brimming urns come in sight, making a tour of the great city of Kapila; a hundred thousand daughters of gods, carrying conches, drums, and tambourines around their necks, present themselves to view motionless; all the winds hold their breath; all the rivers and streams stop flowing; the sun, moon, and the stars stop their movements. A light of a hundred thousand colors, creating a sense of well-being in body and mind, is diffused everywhere. Fire no longer burns. Precious stones and pearls suspended from galleries, palaces, terraces, and vaults of doors strike the eye.

The rooks, vultures, wolves, and jackals cease their cries; only soft and agreeable sounds are heard. All the gods of Salas wood, half protruding from the foliage, loom still and leaning. Large and small parasols unfurl themselves in the air on all sides. Meanwhile the Queen advances into the Lumbini gardens. A tree bows to her in hommage, the Queen seizes a branch of it, and looking up at the sky with gracefulness, yawns and remains motionless. The Buddha emerges from her right side without hurting her. A white lotus pierces the earth, and opens its petals to receive him; a parasol descends from the sky to protect him; a river of cold water and a river of hot water rush to bathe him; and so on.[9]

Now that is what I would call breaking recklessly into legends, and not skimping on the supernatural. Arabia had arrived at a too great an intellectual sophistication to be able to create a supernatural legend of this style. The only time Muhammad allowed himself to imitate the transcendental fantasies of other religions, in his nocturnal journey to Jerusalem on a fantastic animal, things turned out badly; this story was greeted with a storm of derision, many of his disciples retracted their allegiance, and the prophet hastened to withdraw his regrettable idea by declaring that this marvellous voyage, first given as something real, had only been a dream. The entire Arab legend of Muhammad such as we can read in Abu 'l-Fida, is limited to some stories very soberly conceived. One seeks to put him in touch with the illustrious men of his time, and the previous generation; another makes some venerable elders prophesy his mission. When he was wandering around the lonely spots near Mecca, he heard voices which said to him, "Good day, Apostle of God."

He turned round but only saw trees and rocks. On his flight from Mecca, he took refuge in a cave. His enemies were about to enter it when they noticed a nest in which a dove had laid her eggs and a spider's web which stood in the way. His she-camel was inspired, and when the chiefs of the tribes came to take the reins of his mount to offer him hospitality, he said, "Leave it alone, it is the hand of God which is guiding it." His sabre also performed some miracles. At the end of a battle, he was sitting apart at the foot of a tree, having on his knee this weapon whose handle was made of silver. An enemy bedouin saw him and approached making a long detour. Pretending to be attracted by simple curiosity, the bedouin said to him, "Would you allow me to examine your sabre?" Muhammad gave him the weapon without a hint of suspicion. The Arab took it, drew it from the scabbard, and was about to strike with it, but the sabre refused to obey.

All the miracles of his life are as transparent; he himself did not know how to invent anything new of this kind. The Angel Gabriel stood the cost of his miracles, for it seems that he did not know any other device. The Battle of Badr alone provides some examples of a great and marvellous invention improvised on the spot. A legion of angels fought on the side of the Muslims. An Arab who was assigned to the surrounding mountains saw a cloud approaching him, and from the heart of this cloud he heard the neighings of horses and a voice which said, "Forward Hayzoum!" (the name of Angel Gabriel's horse). A Muslim explained how, sword in hand, when pursuing a Meccan, he saw the head of the fugitive fall to the ground even though his own sword had not touched him. He concluded that the hand of a celestial warrior had anticipated his blow. Others confirmed having clearly distinguished the angels with their white turbans, one of whose ends waved over their shoulders, while Gabriel, their chief, had his forehead girded with a yellow turban.

When one knows the state of excitement that the Arabs get themselves into before and during the battle, and when one considers that this day was the first outburst of Muslim fervor, far from being astonished that these stories were believed, one is amazed that the imagination of the warriors at Badr had given birth only to such sober marvels. At a much more recent period and under the influence of Persian genius, so radically different from the Arab spirit, the legend of Muhammad became, I know, embellished with miraculous elements which brought it much closer to the great mythological legends of deepest Asia. Al, though subdued by Islam, Persia never bent to the Semitic spirit. Despite the language and the religion which were imposed on her, she was able to lay claim to her rights as an Indo-European nation by creating a philosophy, an epic, and a mythology. Open the Hyat-ul-Kulub, a collection of Shiite traditions: there you will see that the night the Prophet was born, seventy thousand palaces of rubies, and seventy thousand palaces of pearls were built in Paradise and were called the palaces of the birth. He was born wholly circumcised. Midwives of extraordinary beauty were present even though they had not been told beforehand. A light whose brilliance radiated over the whole of Arabia emerged alongside him from the breast of his mother. As soon as he was born, he fell to his knees, looked up to the heavens and cried: *There is only one God and I am His Prophet.* God clothed His apostle in the shirt of divine happiness and the robe of holiness attached by the belt of God's love. He wore the sandals of respectful terror and the crown of precedence, and took in hand the sceptre of religious authority. When he was three, two angels opened his side, removed his heart, squeeezing out from it the black drops of sin and replacing it with the prophetic light. Muhammad could see behind him as well as in front, his saliva made sea water fresh, and his beads of sweat were like pearls. His body did not cast a shadow either in sunlight or by the light of the moon; no insect approached his person.

There is nothing Arab in this insipid style, and those who have looked for Muhammad in these grotesque stories, impregnated with the Persian taste, have totally misunderstood the character of the legend of Muhammad. These ridiculous fantasies are no more harmful to the purity of the primitive Arab legend than the dreary exaggerations of the Apocrypha are prejudicial to the incomparable beauty of the canonical texts.

Thus, the legendary elements of the origins of Islam have always remained in the form of a sporadic tradition and without authority. Instead of a superhuman being suspended between heaven and earth, without a father or brother down here, we only have an Arab tarred with all the faults of character of his fellow countrymen. In place of this high and inaccessible rigor of the supernatural— "Woman, what is there between you and me? My mother and my brothers are those who listen to and act on the word of God"—we have all the likeable weaknesses of humanity.

At the battle of Autas, a woman captive that the Muslims were dragging along roughly cried out, "Respect me. I am close to your chief." They took her to Muhammad. She said to him, "Prophet of God, I am your foster sister, I am Schayma, the daughter of Halima, your wet-nurse, of the tribe of Banu-Sad."

"What proof can you give me of this?" asked Muhammad.

"You bit me on the shoulder one day when I was carrying you on my back," she said and showed him the scar. This sight, awakening in Muhammad memories of his early childhood and the care that he had received in a poor bedouin family, moved him to compassion. His eyes glistening with tears, Muhammad said to Schayma, "Yes, you are my sister," and taking off his cloak, he made her sit on it. Then he continued, "If you wish to stay from now on next to me, you will live peacefully and will be honored among my people; if you prefer to return to your tribe, I will make it possible for you to lead a life of ease." Schayma indicated that she preferred to stay in the desert, and Muhammad sent her off laden with gifts.

Nothing of his weaknesses or his humble side is concealed. He began by being a commercial traveller to Syria, where he was very successful. No special sign distinguished him. Like everyone else he had a nickname; they called him al-Amin, the dependable. In his early youth, he fought on the side of the Qurayshites against the Hawazin, and the Qurayshites were, nonetheless, cut to pieces. In a race, his she-camel was beaten by that of a bedouin, and he was deeply resentful of it. In order to exalt her prophet, Arabia did not feel obliged to raise him above humanity and to screen him from the affections of the tribe, the family, and others even more humble. Historians tell us that he loved his horse and she-camel, and that he used to wipe their sweat with his sleeve. When his cat was hungry or thirsty, he would get up to let her in. He took great care of an old cock, which he used to keep by his side to protect him from the evil eye. At home, he seemed to be the best of fathers. Often taking Hasan and Husayn, (born of the marriage between 'Ali and his daughter Fatima) by the hand, he would make them skip and dance while chanting nursery rhymes whose words have been recorded.[10] When he saw them, right in the middle of a sermon, he would go and kiss them, place them near him on the pulpit, and after some words of apology for their innocence, he would continue his speech. After the conversion of the Banu-Semin to Islam, one of their principal leaders, Qays, son of Asim, when in Medina, once went to Muhammad's house and found him holding a little girl in his lap and smothering her with kisses.

"What is this ewe you are sniffing?" he asked.

"It is my child," replied Muhammad.

"My God," continued Qays, "I have had many little girls like her, I have buried them all alive, without sniffing one."

"You wretch," cried out Muhammad, "God must have deprived your heart of all feelings of humanity. You have not experienced the sweetest pleasure that has been given to man to feel."

His biographers did not care to hide his ruling passion, any more than he did: "Two things in the world," he used to say, "attract me: women and perfume, but I find unadulterated joy only in prayer."

This was the only point on which he departed from his own laws, and claimed his privilege as a prophet. Contrary to all his regulations, he had fifteen wives, others say twenty-five. The most delicate situations could not fail to arise in such a household. Added to that, the acutest jealousy seems to have been one of the features of his character. One verse of the Koran expressly forbids his wives to remarry after his death. During his last illness, he said to Aisha:

"Wouldn't you be happy to die before me, knowing that it would be I who would wrap you up in the shroud, and who would pray for you, and would lay you down in your grave?"

"I would rather like that," replied Aisha, "if I were not convinced that right after my funeral you would come here to console yourself for my loss with one of your other wives."

This sally made the Prophet smile.

The episode of his marriage to Maria the Copt is one of the oddest. Though a Copt, a slave, and a Christian, she found herself preferred for several nights to the noble daughters of Abu Bakr and 'Umar, who were of the purest Qurayshite blood. This choice provoked a veritable rebellion in the harem, regarding which God revealed the following:

"O Apostle of God why, with a view to pleasing your wives, should you abstain from that which God has permitted you? The Lord is good and merciful, He revokes thoughtless oaths. He is your master, He has knowledge and wisdom."

Thus authorized to punish the rebels, the Prophet repudiated them for a month, which he dedicated to being entirely with Maria. It was only after the ardent entreaties of Abu Bakr and 'Umar that he consented to take back their daughters, after having admonished them with this further verse:

"If you oppose the Prophet, you must realize that God will take his side. God will insist that Muhammad repudiate you all, and God will give better wives than yourselves, good Muslims, pious, submissive, and devout."

There was an even greater scandal when Muhammad married Zaynab. She was already married to Zayd, the Prophet's adopted son. One day when the Prophet went to see Zayd, he found Zaynab alone and so scantily clad that none of her charms was concealed. His emotions were betrayed by these words: "Praise be to God who changes men's hearts!" Then he went away, but the meaning of this exclamation did not escape Zaynab, who repeated it to Zayd. The latter immediately ran to Muhammad and offered to divorce his wife. The Prophet at first fought against this proposal, but Zayd insisted. "Zaynab," he said, "proud of her noble descent, had adopted a haughty attitude towards him which was destroying their marital bliss."

Despite the custom that forbade Arabs to marry the wives of their adopted sons, some months later, Zaynab took her place among the wives of the Prophet. Some verses of the Koran silenced the whisperings of the puritanical Muslims, and the complaisant Zayd saw his name inscribed in the holy book.

On the whole, Muhammad seems to us like a gentleman, sensitive, faithful, free from rancor and hatred. His affections were sincere; his character in general was inclined to kindness. When someone shook him by the hand on addressing him, he would warmly return it never withdraw his hand first. He greeted children and revealed a great tenderness for women and the weak. "Paradise," he used to say, "is at the feet of mothers." Neither ambition nor religious rapture had dried up the personal feelings in him. Not at all akin to this ambitious, heartless, and machiavellian fanatic, he explained his projects to Zopire in rigid alexandrines:

> I must rule as a God this universe forewarned
> My empire is destroyed, if the man is exposed.[11]

On the contrary, with him, the man is always exposed. He had guarded all the soberness and simplicity of manners of the Arabs without any notion of majesty. His bed was a simple cloak and his pillow a skin stuffed with palm leaves. He could be seen milking his ewes himself, and he would sit on the ground to mend his clothes and repair his shoes. All his conduct contradicts the enterprising, audacious character that one is in the habit of attributing to him. He regularly shows himself to be weak, irresolute, and unsure of himself. Weil goes so far as to brand him a coward; it is certain that, in general, he advanced cautiously and almost always resisted being led astray by his companions. His precautions during the battles were unworthy of a prophet. He wore two coats of mail and a helmet with a vizor that covered his face. During the rout of Uhud, his behaviour could hardly be more unbecoming of a messenger of God: having been knocked down into a ditch, he owed his life only to the devotion of the Helpers, who shielded him with their bodies, and he got up again all covered in blood and mud. His extreme caution showed at each step. He willingly and with much deference listened to advice. Often, one could even see him giving in under pressure of public opinion, and led to take steps that his prudence disapproved of. His disciples, having a much higher conception than he of his prophetic gifts and believing in him much more than he did himself, understood nothing of these hesitations and these precautions.

All the energy that was deployed in founding the new religion came from 'Umar. 'Umar is really the St. Paul of Islam, the sword which cuts and decides. The indecisive character of Muhammad would undoubtedly have jeopardized his mission, without the addition of this impetuous disciple, always ready to draw his sword against all those who did not immediately acknowledge the religion that he had persecuted at first.

The conversion of 'Umar was the decisive moment in the progress of Islam. Up to then the Muslims had practised their religion in secret and had not dared to confess their faith in public. The audacity of 'Umar, his ostentatious way of declaring himself Muslim, and the terror which he inspired gave them the confidence to appear in broad daylight. It does not seem that Muhammad had envisaged anything beyond the confines of Arabia, nor had he thought that his religion could have been suitable for anyone other than Arabs. The conquering impulse of Islam, this notion that the world must become Muslim, was 'Umar's idea. After Muhammad's death, just at the moment when the Prophet's work, barely sketched, was about to collapse, it was 'Umar who governed in reality, in place of the ineffective Abu Bakr. 'Umar stopped the defection of the Arab tribes and gave to the new religion its final and fixed form. If the zeal of an imperious temperament clinging frantically to dogma, in order to be able to hate at his leisure, must be called faith, then 'Umar really was the most energetic of believers. No one has ever believed with more passion, no one has ever got more angry in the name of the unquestionable. The need to hate often leads loyal, crude, and unsubtle characters into faith, for absolute faith is the most powerful pretext for hatred, the one to which one can abandon oneself with the clearest conscience.

The role of the prophet always has its thorny aspects, and faced with compatriots always eager to find him at fault, Muhammad could not avoid going through difficult moments. He got out of them, in general, with much skill,

without overdoing his role, and always fearing to venture too far. It must seem
surprising that one sent by God could suffer defeat, see his prophecies thwarted,
and win half-victories. In the great supernatural legends things are very differently managed; there, all is clear-cut, absolute as it should be when God inter-
feres. It was too late to adopt such a high tone: this is why, in the life of this last
of the prophets, everything takes place by halves and approximately in a manner
entirely human and historical. He is defeated, he makes mistakes, he retreats, he
corrects himself, he contradicts himself. Muslims acknowledge up to two hundred and twenty-five contradictions in the Koran, that is to say two hundred and
twenty-five passages which were later abrogated, within the perspective of
another policy.

As to the features of the life of Muhammad which, to our eyes, would be
unpardonable blots on his morality, it would be unjust to criticize them too
harshly. It is obvious that his acts did not make the same impression on his contemporaries and Muslim historians as on us. Nonetheless, one cannot deny that
on several occasions he consciously did harm knowing perfectly well that he was
obeying his own will and not an inspiration from God. He allowed brigandage,
he ordered assassinations, he lied and permitted lying as a stratagem of war. One
could cite a host of circumstances where he compromised morality for political
ends. One of the most peculiar instances of that is assuredly when he promised
'Uthman, forgiveness in advance for all the sins that he might commit until his
death in return for a large financial sacrifice.

He was above all pitiless against mockers. The only woman that he dealt
harshly with at the capture of Mecca was the musician Fertena, who used to sing
satirical verses that were composed against him. His conduct toward his secretary was also infinitely typical. This man, who was writing the Koran under the
dictation of the Prophet, was a too intimate witness of Muhammad's inspiration
for there to be any deep mutual trust. Muhammad did not like him, and he
accused him of changing words and distorting the meaning of his dictations, so
that the secretary, filled with foreboding, fled and abjured Islam. After the capture of Mecca, he fell into the hands of the Muslims. It was only with great difficulty that a pardon was extracted from Muhammad, and once the apostate had
left, the Prophet petulantly expressed his displeasure to the Muslims because
they had not got rid of this man.

It would also be unjust to judge severely and with our own considered ideas
the acts of Muhammad, which in our days would be called swindles. One can
hardly imagine to what extent, among Muslims, conviction and even in a sense
nobleness of character can combine with a certain degree of imposture. The leads
of the Wahhabites, 'Abd al-Wahhab, a true deist and the Socinus[12] of Islam, did he

not inspire in his soldiers the blindest confidence by giving them, before the battle, a safe-conduct signed by his hand and addressed to the treasurer of heaven, so that he let them in without further ado and without preliminary questioning? All the founders of Khouan, or religious orders of Algeria,[13] combine the dual character of ascetics and audacious charlatans. Sidi-Aissa, the strangest of these modern prophets, Sidi-Aissa, whose legend has almost reached the proportions of Muhammad's legend, was but a juggler and an exhibitor of beasts who knew how to exploit his business cleverly, and none of those who have travelled to Algeria will believe that the Aissaoua are fooled by their own tricks. Certainly, it would be in bad taste to compare Muhammad to these second-rate impostors. However, one must admit that if the principal condition of a prophet is to deceive himself, then Muhammad does not deserve this title. His entire life betrays premeditation, schemes, and politics which hardly accord with the character of a fanatic obsessed with his divine visions. Never was a head so lucid as his; never did a man master his thoughts better. It would be a narrow and superficial way of asking a question to wonder if Muhammad believed in his own mission; for, in a sense, faith alone is capable of sustaining man in his struggle for the moral purpose that he has embraced; on the other hand, it is absolutely impossible to admit that a man with an awareness as clear as Muhammad's believed that he bore the seal of the prophets between his two shoulders and that it was from the Angel Gabriel that he received the inspiration for his passions and his premeditated designs. Weil and Washington Irving assume, not without possibility, that in the first phase of his life as a prophet a truly holy fervor uplifted him, and that the premeditated period only came later, when the struggle and the realization of the difficulties to be overcome had tarnished the early scrupulousness of his inspiration. The last suras of the Koran, so dazzling with poetry, are the expression of his naive conviction, while the earlier suras, full of politics, loaded with disputes, contradictions, and insults, are the work of his practical and meditated period. It is undeniable that the first manifestations of his prophetic genius are characterized by great holiness. One saw him praying alone in the deserted valleys in the vicinity of Mecca. 'Ali, son of Abu Talib, unknown to his father and his uncles, used to accompany him some-times and pray with him, copying his movements and postures. One day, Abu Talib surprised them in this activity.

"What are you doing?' he asked them, "and what religion do you follow?"

"The religion of God, of his angels, of his prophets," replied Muhammad, "the religion of Abraham."

How great is he also in the first ordeals of his apostolate! One evening, after having spent the day preaching, he returned home without having met a single person, man or woman, freeman or slave, who had not heaped abuse on him, and who had not rejected his exhortations with contempt. Humiliated and discouraged, he wrapped himself in his cloak, and threw himself on a straw mat. It was then that Gabriel revealed to him the beautiful sura: *O you who are wrapped in a cloak, rise and preach. . . .*

However, this fragrance of holiness only appeared at rare intervals during his period of activity. Perhaps he recognized that moral feelings and purity of soul were not enough in the struggle against passions and interests, and that religious thought, from the moment it aspires to proselytism, is obliged to adopt the demeanor of its less sensitive adversaries. At least, it seems that after having believed without ulterior motive in his prophethood, he then lost his spontaneous faith but nonetheless carried on, guided by reflection and his will, less great thenceforth—almost like Joan of Arc who became a woman as soon as she reflected on her mission and lost her naivety. Man is too weak to bear for long the divine mission; only those are blameless whom God has relieved of the burden of apostleship.

Perhaps a more strange question and one that a critic, however, cannot refuse to ask is: To what extent did the disciples of Muhammad believe in his prophetic mission? It might seem strange to put in doubt the perfect spontaneity and the absolute conviction of men, the eruption of whose faith carried them in one bound to the confines of the world. However, important distinctions are necessary here. In the circle of the original loyal supporters, among the Muhajir and the Ansari,[14] faith was, it must be confessed, almost absolute; but if we leave this group, which did not exceed a few thousand men, we find around Muhammad, in all the rest of Arabia, only undisguised incredulity. The antipathy of the Meccans for their compatriots was never fully subdued; the Epicureanism which reigned among the the rich Qurayshites and the relaxed and libertine manners of the fashionable poets did not leave room for any profound convictions.

As to the other tribes, it is certain that they embraced Islam as a matter of form, without inquiring about the dogmas they should believe and without attaching great importance to them. They could not see any great inconvenience in pronouncing the Islamic formula, except to forget it when the Prophet was no more. When Khalid appeared in front of the Jadhima calling on them to embrace the faith of the Prophet, this good people understood very little of what it was all about; they believed it concerned Sabeaism, and they laid down their arms crying, "We are Sabeans!" The proud tribe of the Thaqif thought up a strange compromise to save them from the shame of conversion: they agreed to submit to the new faith on condition that they could keep their idol Lat for another three years. This condition having been rejected, they asked to keep Lat for a year, for six months, and then for one month. Their pride required a concession. They ended up asking to be exempted from prayer. The conversion of the Tamimites was no less curious. Their ambassadors presented themselves proudly, and on approaching the Prophet's and his wives' quarters, cried out, "Come on out, Muhammad, we come to propose a glorious combat;[15] we have brought our poet and our orator."

Muhammad came out and they found him a place around the adversaries. The orator Utarid and the poet Zibrican [al-Husayn ibn Badr] exalted the superiority of their tribe, one in rhymed prose, the other in verse, Qays and Hassan, son of Thabit, responded with some improvised pieces with the same meter and the same rhyme, and established with such energy the superiority of Muslims that the Tamimites conceded defeat. "Muhammad is truly a man favored by the heavens," they proclaimed. "His orator and his poet have beaten ours." And they converted to Islam.

All the conversions were of this kind. One set one's conditions—one took it or one left it. Old Amir, son of Tufayl, having come to see Muhammad, said to him, "If I embrace Islam, what will be my rank?"

"That of other Muslims," replied Muhammad. "You will have the same rights and the same duties as everyone else."

"This equality is not enough for me. Proclaim me your successor in the ruling of the nation, then I shall adhere to your creed."

"It is not up to me to delegate authority after me; God will give it to whomever He pleases."

"Oh, well, let us share the power now, you rule over the towns, over the Arabs with fixed addresses, and I shall rule over the Bedouins."

With Muhammad unwilling to consent to these conditions, Amir gave up the idea of becoming a Muslim. It is, above all, after the death of Muhammad that one can see the extreme weakness of conviction which had rallied the different Arab tribes around him. This was apostasy on a huge scale. Some of them said that if Muhammad had really been God's messenger then he would not have died; others maintained that his religion would only to last during his lifetime. The news of his illness had hardly been broadcast when there appeared a host of prophets throughout Arabia. Each tribe wanted to have one of their own, like the Qurayshites; the model was infectious. Almost all these prophets were, moreover, second-rate intriguers, entirely without religious initiative. Addressing themselves to simple tribes, far less sophisticated than the Meccans, they had at their disposal magic tricks, which they presented as proof of their divine mission. One of them, Musaylima (Maslama), ran up and down the country, showing a flask with a narrow neck, in which he had inserted an egg by means of a method he had learnt from a Persian juggler. He also recited rhymed sentences that he passed off as verses of a second Koran. Who believed him? This vile impostor kept at bay all the Muslim forces grouped around Abu Bakr for several years, and held the destiny of Muhammad in the balance. He found a formidable rival in the prophetess Sajah, who had succeeded in rallying around her a powerful army of Tamimites. Musaylima, pressed in the Hadjr, saw no other way to disarm his beautiful rival than to propose a tete-a-tete which was eagerly accepted. The prophet and the prophetess came out of it married. After days given over to the wedding, Sajah returned to her camp, where her soldiers were eager to question her over the outcome of her interview with Musaylima.

"I recognized in him a true prophet, and I married him," she said.

"Did Musaylima give us a wedding gift?" asked the Tamimites.

"He didn't speak of that," replied Sajah.

"That would bring you and us shame if he married our prophetess without giving us anything," they replied. "Go back to him and demand a present for us."

Sajah went and appeared before the gate of Hadjr, and finding it barricaded, she had her husband called. He appeared on the wall. A herald explained to him the demands of the Tamimites.

"Very well," replied Musaylima, "you will be given satisfaction. I instruct you to proclaim publically the following: 'Musaylima, the prophet of God, grants the Banu-Tamim exemption from the first and the last of the five prayers that his colleague Muhammad has imposed on them.' "

The Tamimites took this dispensation seriously and it is claimed that since then they have not performed the dawn or the evening prayers.

One can judge from these stories how shallow the religious movement was among the Arabs. There was absolutely nothing dogmatic about this movement outside of a small, reduced group. It is told that, after a victory, 'Umar ordered that each person should have his part of the booty in proportion to the amount of the Koran that each knew by heart. However, when it came to the test, it turned out that the bravest of the bedouins were only barely able to recite the initial formula, "In the name of God, the Compassionate, and Merciful" (*Bismi 'illahi ar rahmani ar rahim*, in Arabic), which made the onlookers laugh a lot. These men of a robust and simple nature understood nothing of mysticism. On the other hand, the Muslim faith had found in the rich and proud families of Mecca a center of resistance which it was not able to entirely subjugate. Abu Sufyan, the leader of this opposition, never openly took on the colors of a true believer. At his first interview with Muhammad, after the capture of Mecca, Muhammad told him:

"Well, Abu Sufyan, do you now admit that there is no other god but Allah?"

"Yes," replied Abu Sufyan.

"Would you also not confess that I am the messenger of God?"

"Forgive my outspokenness," replied Abu Sufyan, "but on that point I still have some doubts."

A host of piquant anecdotes bear witness to the lightly sceptical and mocking tone that this figure maintained toward the new faith. However, a crowd of Meccans shared his sentiments. One could find in Mecca a whole party of total unbelievers—witty, rich, having grown up on ancient Arabic poetry. These men had too much good taste and finesse to offer any keen opposition to the nascent sect; they embraced Islam but all the while conserving their habits and their profane attitudes. It was the party of Munafiqun, or false Muslims, who played such a great role in the Koran. At the Battle of Hunayn, where the Muslims were put to rout, they did not hide their malicious joy.

"By my faith," said Calada, "I believe this time Muhammad has reached the end of his magic."

"Look at them," said Abu Sufyan. "They will run until the sea stops them."

Muhammad had no illusions about their real feelings but, being an astute politician, he accepted their external submission, and even saw to it that in the dividing of the booty they received a larger share than his loyal supporters.

The entire first century of Islam was but a struggle between two parties: on the one side, the faithful group of Muhajirs and Ansars, and on the other, the opposing party represented by the family of Umayyads or Abu Sufyan. The party of sincere Muslims drew all its strength from 'Umar, but after the latter's assassination, that is to say, twelve years after the death of the Prophet, the opposing party triumphed with the election of 'Uthman, the nephew of the most dangerous enemy of Muhammad, Abu Sufyan! All the caliphate of 'Uthman was a reaction against the friends of the Prophet, who were excluded from affairs of state and violently persecuted. From then on, they were never able to regain the upper hand. The provinces were unable to put up with the fact that the tiny aristocracy of Muhajir and Ansar, gathered in Mecca and Medina, accorded itself the sole right of electing the caliph. 'Ali, the real representative of the pristine tradition of Islam, was an impossible man all his life, and his election was never taken seriously in the provinces. On all sides, one held out one's hand to the Umayyad family and become Syrian out of habit and out of interest. Now, the orthodoxy of the Umayyad was always very suspect. They drank wine, performed pagan rites, and took no account at all of the tradition of the Prophet, the Muslim customs, and the sacred character of the friends of Muhammad. Hence the astonishing spectacle that the first century of the Hijra presents, all busy scrutinizing the original Muslims, the true founding fathers of Islam. 'Ali, the saintliest of men, the adopted son of the Prophet, 'Ali whom Muhammad had proclaimed as his vicar, had his throat cut mercilessly. Husayn and Hasan, his sons, whom

Muhammad had dandled on his knees and covered with kisses, had their throats cut. Ibn Zubayr, the first born of the Muhajir, who had received the saliva of the Prophet of God as his first nourishment, had his throat cut.[16]

The original faithful believers crowded around the Kaaba and continued the Arab life there, whiling way the time talking in the court and circumambulating the Black Stone. They had become totally powerless, and the Umayyads respected them only until the day they thought they could take them by force in their sanctuary. It was a strange scandal, that last siege of Mecca, where one saw Muslims of Syria setting alight the hangings of the Kaaba and destroying it with the stones fired from their ballistas. It is said that on the firing of the first stone against the holy house, thunder was heard; the Syrian soldiers were trembling.

"Continue," said their chief, "I know the climate of this country, thunderstorms are frequent at this time of year." At the same time, he took hold of the ropes of the ballista and himself set them in motion.

Everything thus leads to this strange conclusion: the Muslim movement came about almost without religious faith, and apart from the small number of early followers, Muhammad in fact inspired little conviction in Arabia; he never succeeded in defeating the opposition represented by the Umayyad party. It is this party which, at first curbed by the energy of 'Umar, definitively won the day after the death of this redoubtable opponent, and got 'Uthman elected; it is this party which put up invincible resistance to 'Ali and finished by immolating him in its hatred; it is this party which finally triumphed with the accession to power of the Umayyads, and went on to slaughter, right up to the Kaaba, all those who remained of the first and unsullied generation. To that we also owe this uncertainty in which all the dogmas of the Muslim creed floated right up until the twelfth century; from there we derive this robust philosophy that proclaims forthrightly the unlimited rights of reason; from that these countless sects, bordering on, by indiscernable nuances, the most avowed unbelief: Karmathians, Fatimites, Ismailis, dualists, Druses, assassins; Hernanites, zendiks, secret sects with double meanings, combining fanaticism with incredulity, licentiousness with religious fervor, the robustness of a freethinker with the superstition of an initiate.

It is really only in the twelfth century that Islam triumphed over the undisciplined elements seething within its bosom, with the accession of the Asharite theology and the violent extermination of philosophy. Since this epoch, not a single doubt has emerged, nor was any protest been raised. Perhaps Islam has never been as strong as today. Faith is the work of time; the cement of religious edifices hardens with aging.

II

Human nature, in its ensemble, being neither entirely good nor entirely bad, neither totally saintly nor totally profane, it is equally a sin against critical thought to pretend to explain the religious movements of mankind by passions and individual interests, or by the exclusive action of deep religious genius. It would be to lack totally a historical sense to suppose that a revolution as profound as Islam could be accomplished merely by some clever scheming, and Muhammad is no more explicable by imposture and trickery than by illuminism and religious fervor. In the eyes of the logician looking at things from an abstract point of view and opposing the one against the other like absolute distinct categories such the beautiful and the ugly or the true and the false, there is no middle term between impostor and prophet.

In the eyes of the critic, seeing the fugitive and unseizable aspects of life, nothing that originates from man is pure, everything carries its original ugliness with it alongside the marks of beauty. Who could distinguish in his own moral feelings the line that separates the loveable from the hateful, the foolish from the beautiful, the angelic from the satanic, and even to a certain degree the joy from the pain? If religions are the most perfect manifestations of human nature, then those who express it with the greatest unity take part in, more than anything else, the complexity of this nature, and exclude simple and absolute judgements.

To apply with firmness to these capricious apparitions the categories of the scholastic, or to judge them with the self-assurance of the logician tracing a deep line between wisdom and folly, is to distort their nature. Everything alternates as in a fantastic mirage in this great sabbath of all the passions and all the instincts, in these Walpurgis nights of human intelligence. The saint and the villain, the charming and the horrible, the apostle and the juggler, the virgin and the hangman, heaven and hell follow one another like visions during troubled sleep, where all the images hidden in the innermost recesses of human fantasy appear in turn.

I have lengthily testified to the inborn infirmity of Islam; it would be unjust not to add that nothing would stand up to the test that we could submit it to. What prophet could withstand criticism, if that criticism pursued him, as in this case, right up to his alcove? Happy are those who are covered in mystery and who fight criticism entrenched behind a cloud! Also, perhaps our century has overused the word spontaneity in explaining phenomena that neither experience nor history are able to penetrate. In reaction to a school which had exaggerated the creative power of the critical faculties, which had wanted to see in language, in religious beliefs, in morals, in primitive poetry only calculated inventions, we are perhaps too inclined to assume that any idea of composition ought to be excluded from primitive poems, and all ideas of imposture from the formation of great legends. Instead of saying that languages, religions, beliefs, and folk poetry were self-created, it would be more exact, it seems to me, to say that we do not see them being created. Spontaneity is only perhaps obscurity, for here is the only religion whose origins are clear and historic, and in its origins we find much reflection, deliberation, and scheming. God forbid that I should wish, in any way whatsoever, to damage the majesty of the past. When the critic applies himself for the first time to a fact or a book which had inspired the respect of a great many generations, one discovers almost always that the admiration was misplaced; one perceives a thousand tricks, a thousand alterations, a thousand approximations, which destroy the great impression of beauty or saintliness which had seduced uncritical centuries. What a fateful day for Homer when the unlucky scholia of Venice came to reveal to us the pencil strokes of Zenodotus and Aristarchus, and introduced us, in some sort of way, to the committee where the poem was elaborated, a poem which upto then had seemed to be the most direct expression, the clearest burst of individual genius. Does that mean criticism has destroyed Homer?[17] You might as well say that progress in philosophy and aesthetics has destroyed antiquity because they have demonstrated the worthlessness of certain works of beauty highly esteemed for a long time, and of which antiquity was perfectly innocent. You might as well say that exegesis has destroyed the Bible, because instead of the mistranslations of the Vulgate admired by Bossuet, in place of the solecisms in which Chateaubriand found sublime beauty, it has revealed to us surprising and original literature. Criticism displaces admiration but does not destroy it. Admiration is essentially a synthetic act; it is not by dissecting a beautiful body that one discovers its beauty, nor is it by examining the events of history and the works of the human mind with a magnifying glass that one will recognize their greatness. One can assert without hesitation that if we could see the origin of great things of the past as closely as the shabby tumults of the present, all its prestige would vanish and nothing would remain to adore; but isn't it also fitting that we search for beauty in this inferior region of the fluctuations and weaknesses of the individual?

Things are beautiful only because of what humanity sees in them, through the feelings it attaches to them, and through the symbols it draws from them. It is humanity that creates these absolute tones, which never exist in reality. Reality is a complex mixture of good and evil, admirable and open to criticism at the same time, worthy of both love and hatred. Whereas what invites mankind's praise is simple, blameless, entirely admirable.

Since he knows that his results do not penetrate into those regions where illusions are necessary, the critic, exclusively concerned with the truth and reassured besides about the consequences, has as his mission to correct these mistranslations about which humanity hardly bothers. He does not delude himself as to the importance of this mission. What does it matter that humanity commits historical errors in its admiration, that it makes out those men it has adopted to be more beautiful and more pure than they were in reality? Its hommage is nonetheless admirable since it is addressed to the beauty that humanity assumes in them and has vested in them. From the point of view of historical truth, only the scholar has the right to admire, but from the ethical point of view, the ideal belongs to everyone. Feelings have their own value independently of the reality of the object that excites them, and it is doubtful if humanity ever shares the scruples of the scholar who only wishes to admire when certain.

After having shown the founder of Islam's feet of clay, I should now show in what way his work was holy and legitimate, that is to say, how it fulfilled the deepest instincts of human nature, and in particular, how it answered the needs of seventh-century Arabia.

Islam appears, up to now in history, to be a perfectly original endeavor without precedent. It is almost a cliché to present Muhammad as the founder of Arab civilization, Arabic monotheism, and even (this serious mistake has been endlessly repeated) Arabic literature. Now, far from starting with Muhammad, we can say that the Arab genius found in him its ultimate expression. I do not know if there is in the entire history of civilization a spectacle more gracious, more attractive, and more lively than that offered by the Arab way of life before Islam, such as it is revealed to us in the Mullaqat, and above all in the admirable character of Antar: unlimited liberty of the individual, complete absence of law and power, an exalted sense of honor, a nomadic and chivalrous life, humor, gaiety, roguishness, light, impious poetry, and courtly love. This efflorescence of refinement of the Arab way of life ends precisely with the advent of Islam. The last poets of the great school disappear while vigorously opposing the nascent religion. Twenty years after Muhammad, Arabia is humiliated and overtaken by the conquered provinces. A hundred years after, the Arab genius is totally erased: Persia triumphs with the advent of the Abbasids, and while Arabia's language and religion are going to carry civilization from Malaysia to Morocco, from Timbuctoo to Samarkand, she disappears forever from the world scene; forgotten and driven back into the desert, she resumes her life as in the times of Ismail. It is so in the life of races: there is a first and sudden flash of consciousness, a divine moment when, prepared by a slow evolution, they emerge into the light, produce their masterpieces, and then fade away, as if this great effort had exhausted their fertility.

Muhammad was no more the founder of monotheism than of civilization and

literature among the Arabs. It follows from the numerous facts, pointed out for
the first time by Caussin de Perceval, that Muhammad only followed rather than
anticipated the religious movement of his time. Monotheism, the cult of the
supreme Allah (Allah taala), had always been the foundation of the Arab religion.
The Semitic race had never conceived of the government of the universe as anything other than an absolute monarchy. Its theodicy has not made any progress
since the Book of Job; the grandeur and aberrations of polytheism have remained
forever alien to it. Some superstitious embroideries, which varied from tribe to
tribe, had however corrupted the purity of the patriarchal religion among the
Arabs, and in face of more strongly organized religions, all the more enlightened
minds of Arabia were aspiring toward a better form of worship. A people can
hardly ever understand the inadequacy of its own religious system except
through its contacts with the foreign, and the periods of religious creation always
follow the periods of racial mixture. Now in the sixth century, after having
remained inaccessible until then, Arabia opened up on all sides: Greeks, Syrians,
Persians, and Abyssinians reached it at the same time. The Syrians brought with
them writing, the Abyssinians and the Persians reigned in turn in the Yemen and
Bahrain. Several tribes recognized the suzerainty of the Greek emperors and
received from them a toparch. Perhaps the oddest incident of pre-Islamic history
is that of the poet-prince, 'Imru'l-Qays, who came to Constantinople seeking
asylum. He formed a romantic alliance with Justinian's daughter, extoled her in
Arabic verse, and was poisoned by the secret orders of the Byzantine court.
Equally, the diversity of religions accommodated a remarkable movement of
ideas in Arabia. Entire tribes embraced Judaism while Christianity boasted large
churches in Najran and the kingdoms of Hira and Ghassan. On all sides one
argued over religion. A curious monument of these controversies has come down
to us in the dispute of Gregentius, Bishop of Zhefar, with the Jew Herban. A
vague sort of tolerance and syncretism of all the Semitic religions ended up by
being established: the ideas of a unique God, of paradise, of resurrection, of
prophets, and of sacred books insinuated themselves little by little, even among
the pagan tribes. The Kaaba became the pantheon of all the creeds; when
Muhammad drove out the pictures from the holy house, among the gods expelled
was a Byzantine Virgin painted on a column, holding her son in her arms.

This great religious activity betrayed itself externally by significant facts,
which betokened an approaching efflorescence. One saw a crowd of men
unhappy with the old religion setting off on a journey to look for a better one,
trying in turn the different existing creeds, and in desperation, creating a personal
religion in harmony with their moral needs. All sudden appearances of religion
are so preceded by a kind of anxiety and vague longing, which manifests itself

in some privileged souls by forebodings and desires. Islam had its own John the Baptist, and its old man Simeon.[18] Some years before Muhammad's preaching, while the Qurayshites were celebrating the festival of one of their idols, four men more enlightened than the rest of their people gathered together slightly apart from the crowd and exchanged views. "Our fellow countrymen," they said to each other, "are going down the wrong road. They have wandered far from the religion of Abraham. What is this putative divinity to whom they sacrifice victims and around whom they turn in solemn processions? Let us look for the truth, and to find it let us leave, if necessary, our country and scour foreign lands." The four people who formulated this plan were Waraqa, son of Naufal; 'Uthman, son of Huwayrith; Ubaydullah, son of Jahsh; and Zayd, son of Amr.

Waraqa had acquired, through his frequent relations with Christians and Jews, a learning superior to that of his fellow citizens. According to a rather widespread belief, he was persuaded that a messenger from heaven would soon appear on earth, and that this messenger ought to come from the Arab nation. He had acquired a knowledge of Hebrew writing and had read the holy books. Khadija, his cousin, having told him about the first vision of her husband, he proclaimed that Muhammad was the prophet of the Arabs, and prophesized the persecutions that he would endure. He died soon afterward, having only caught a glimpse of the dawn of Islam.

'Uthman, son of Huwayrith, took to travelling, questioning all those from whom he hoped to extract some enlightenment. Some Christian monks inspired in him a taste for the faith of Jesus Christ. He went to present himself at the court of the Emperor of Constantinople, where he was baptised.

After vain efforts to reach the religion of Abraham, Ubaydullah, son of Jahsh, lived in incertitude and doubt until the moment Muhammad began to preach. At first he thought he recognized in Islam the true religion that he was looking for; however, he soon renounced it to dedicate himself definitively to Christianity. As to Zayd, son of Amr, he went every day to the Kaaba and prayed to God to enlighten him. One could see him, his back pressed against against the wall of the temple, devoting himself to pious meditations, from which he emerged crying: "Lord! If I knew in which manner you wish to be served and worshipped, I would obey you your will, but I do not know." He would then prostrate himself, his face touching the earth. Adopting neither the ideas of the Jews nor those of the Christians, Zayd created for himself a religion apart, trying to conform to what he thought must have been the religion followed by Abraham. He rendered hommage to the unity of God, publicly attacked the false gods, and energetically denounced superstitious practices. Persecuted by his fellow citizens, he fled and wandered throughout Mesopotamia and Syria, everywhere consulting men devoted to religious studies in the hope of recovering the patriarchal religion. A learned Christian monk, with whom he had become intimate, apparently informed him of the sudden appearance of an Arab prophet who was preaching the religion of Abraham in Mecca. Zayd hastened to set out to go and hear the apostle, but he was stopped on the way by a band of thieves, robbed, and killed.

Thus, on all sides one had a presentiment of a great religious revival, and on all sides one said that the hour of Arabia had arrived. Prophetism is the form which all great revolutions assume among the semitic peoples, and prophetism is only, to tell the truth, the necessary consequence of the monotheist system. Primitive peoples, incessantly believing themselves to be in immediate contact with the deity, and regarding the great events of the physical world and of the moral order as the effects of the direct action of superior beings, had but two ways of conceiving this influence of God in the government of the universe: either the divine power is incarnated in human form, that is, the Indian avatar, or else God chooses as His instrument a privileged mortal, that is, the nabi or semitic prophet. The distance between God and man is so great in the Semitic system that they can only communicate with one another through an interpreter remaining perfectly apart from the One who inspires him. To claim that Arabia was about to enter an era of great events was to say, in consequence, that she was about to have her own prophet like the other members of the Semitic family. Several individuals, anticipating the fullness of time, believed themselves to be, or pretended to be, the expected apostle.

Muhammad grew up in the midst of this movement. His journeys to Syria, his contacts with Christian monks, and perhaps the personal influence of his uncle Waraqa, who was well versed in Jewish and Christian writings, would soon have introduced him to all the religious confusions of his century. He did not know how to read or write, but the biblical stories had penetrated through to him by way of the narratives which had deeply impressed him, and which, having stayed in his mind as hazy recollections, gave his imagination free rein. To reproach Muhammad for having corrupted the biblical stories is totally misguided. Muhammad took these narratives as they were given to him; the narrative of the Koran is but the reproduction of the Talmudic traditions and the Apocrypha, above all the Gospel of the Infancy. This Gospel, which was translated into Arabic early on, and which has only survived in this language, had acquired a considerable reputation among Christians of the remote parts of the East, and had almost eclipsed the canonical texts. It is certain that these narratives were one of the most powerful sources of Muhammad's actions. Nadr, son of Harith, who sometimes undertook to compete with him, had spent some time in Persia and knew the legends of the ancient kings of that country. When Muhammad, rallying around him a circle of listeners, was delineating the life of the patriarchs and prophets and giving examples of divine retribution that had fallen on impious nations, Nadr would speak after him and say:

"Listen now to things which are as good as those with which Muhammad has entertained you."

He would then relate the most astonishing facts of the heroic history of Persia, of the marvellous exploits of the heroes Rustam and Isfendiar; then he would add: "Are the stories of Muhammad more beautiful than mine? He is spouting ancient legends that he has gathered from the mouth of men more learned than he, just as I myself have collected, during my travels, and put into writing the tales that I am recounting to you."

Long before Islam, the Arabs had adopted Jewish and Christian traditions to explain their own origins. One has often considered the legend by which the Arabs attach themselves to Ismael as having historical validity and furnishing powerful confirmation of the Biblical stories. In the eyes of a more discriminating critic, that is inadmissible. There can be no doubt that the biblical reputations of Abraham, Job, David, and Solomon began among the Arabs around the fifth century. The Jews (the people of the book) had guarded, up to then, the records of the Semitic race, and the Arabs willingly acknowledged their superior learning. The Book of the Jews spoke of the Arabs, attributing a genealogy to them; that was enough for the latter to accept it with confidence: such is the prestige of books amongst naive peoples, and the eagerness with which they looked to be connected to the written origins of more civilized peoples.

It is said that at the period when Muhammad began to attract attention, the Meccans had the idea of sending delegates to Medina to consult the Rabbis of this town about what one should think of this new prophet. The delegates delineated Muhammad's character to the scholars, summarized his speeches, and added: "You are learned men who read books: what do you think of this man?"

The scholars replied: "Ask him: Who are the certain young men of past centuries whose adventure is a marvel? Who is the person who reached the limits of the earth in the East and the West? What is the soul? If he replies to these three questions in such and such a manner, then he is truly a prophet. If he replies otherwise, or he is unable to reply, then he is a charlatan."

Muhammad resolved the first enigma with the story of the Seven Sleepers, which was popular all over the Orient, and the second with Dhul-Qarnayn, the mythical conqueror who is none other than the legendary Alexander of Pseudo-Callisthenes. As to the third, he replied, alas! perhaps all that is permitted to be answered is: "The soul is something the knowledge of which is reserved for God. It is given to man to possess but an insignificant part of knowledge."

The dogmatic part of Islam assumes even less creation than the legendary part. Muhammad was totally devoid of inventiveness in this sense. The subtleties of mysticism being alien to him, he only knew how to found a simple religion, limited on all sides by common sense, cautious like everything that is born of reflection, narrow like everything that is dominated by a feeling for the real. The symbol of Islam, at least before the invasion of Persian subtleties, hardly goes beyond the simplest facts of natural religion. No theological pretentiousness, none of those bold paradoxes of supernaturalism where the imagination of races gifted for the infinite is deployed with such originality, no priesthood, no form of worship outside prayers. All the ceremonies of the Kaaba, the circumambulations, the pilgrimage, the Umra, the sacrifices in Mina valley, and the stampede from Mount Arafat had been organized in all their details long before Muhammad. The pilgrimage above all had been since time immemorial an essential element in Arab life, in the same way as the Olympic Games for Greece, or eulogies for the nation, all at once, religious, commercial, and poetic. The valley of Mecca had become the central point of Arabia, and despite the division and rivalry of the tribes, the hegemony of the family who guarded the Kaaba was tacitly acknowledged. It was a grave occasion, which almost marks an era in the history of the Arabs, the when they put a lock and key on the Sacred House.

Thenceforth authority was attached to the possession of the keys to the Kaaba. The Qurayshite Qusayy, so the legend goes, having made the Khuzaite Abu-Ghobschan, the guardian of the keys, drunk, bought the keys from him for a leather bottle of wine and thus established the primacy of his tribe. It is at this time that the great movement of the organization of the Arab nation began. Up to then, one had only dared to put up tents in the sacred valley; there Qusayy gathered together the Qurayshites, rebuilt the Kaaba, and was the real founder of the city of Mecca. All the most important institutions date from Qusayy: the nadwa, or the central council headquartered at Mecca; the liwa, or the flag; the rifada, or the alms intended to meet the expenses of the pilgrims; the sicaya, or the management of the waters, a primordial responsibility in a country like the Hijaz; the nasaa, or the insertion of supplementary days in the calendar; the hidjaba, or the guardianship of the keys of the Kaaba. These offices which summed up all the political and religious institutions of Arabia were exclusively reserved for the Qurayshites. Thus, from the middle of the fifth century, the seeds of the centralization of Arabia had already been planted, the point from which the religious and political organization of this country ought to take off had been selected in advance. Qusayy, in a sense, had founded far more than Muhammad. He was even regarded as a sort of prophet, and his will was taken for an article of religion.

Hashim, in the first half of the sixth century, completed the work of Qusayy, and extended in an astonishing way the commercial relations of his tribe: he established two caravans, one in the winter bound for the Yemen, the other in the summer bound for Syria. Abd al-Muttalib, son of Hashim and grandfather of Muhammad, continued the traditional work of the Qurayshite oligarchy through the discovery of the well of Zem Zem.[19] The well of Zem Zem, independently of the tradition which one associates with it, was in an arid valley and as frequented as the one in Mecca, a fact of fundamental importance, and guaranteed the pre-eminence of the family which had appropriated it for itself. The tribe of Qurayshites found itself thus elevated, like Juda among the Hebrews, to the rank of a privileged tribe, destined to accomplish the unity of the nation. Muhammad only crowned the work of his ancestors; in politics, as in religion, he invented nothing, but achieved with energy the aspirations of his century. It remains to discover what help he found in the eternal instincts of human nature, and how, in taking advantage of the weaknesses of the human heart, he knew how to give his work the most unshakeable foundation that ever was.

Independently of all dogmatic belief, there are in us religious needs that even incredulity is unable to remove. One is sometimes astonished that a religion can survive so long after the whole structure of its dogmas has been undermined by criticism; but in reality, a religion is neither founded nor overthrown by reasoning. It has its raison d'être in the most imperious needs of our nature: the need to love, the need to suffer, and the need to believe. Here is why woman is the essential element of all religious foundations. Christianity has been founded literally by women.[20] Islam, which is not precisely a holy religion but a natural religion, serious, liberal, in short, a religion of men, has nothing, I admit, to compare to these admirable examples of Madeleine, de Thecla, and yet this cold and reasonable religion held enough attractions to fascinate the devout sex.

Nothing could be further from the truth than the widespread ideas in the West of the status of women under Islam: the Arab woman, at the time of Muhammad, nowhere resembled the stupid creature that resides in the Ottoman harems. In general, it is true, the Arabs had a low opinion of the moral qualities of women, because the character of women is exactly opposite to that which the Arabs considered as the model of the perfect man. One reads in the *Kitab al Aghani*[21] that a young chief of the tribe of Jaschkor, called Moschamradj, had abducted a young girl of noble family during a raid against the Tamimites. The uncle of the young girl, Qays, son of Asim, went to Moschamradj to ask for her back, offering him a ransom. Moschamradj gave the captive the choice of staying with him or going back to her family. The young girl, who had fallen in love with her abductor, preferred him to her parents. Qays went back so stupefied and indignant at the weakness of a sex capable of such a choice that on arrival at his tribe, he had his two young daughters buried alive, and swore that he would treat in the same manner any daughters born to him in the future. These simple and loyal natures could not understand the passion which elevates a woman above the exclusive affections of the tribe, but they were far from considering her a lesser being without individuality. There were women mistresses of themselves, having the right of disposal of their belongings, who chose their husband and had the right to get rid of him whenever they wished. Several distinguished themselves by their poetical talents and their literary taste. Had one not seen a woman, the beautiful El Khansa, fight with glory against the most illustrious poets of the great century? Others turned their houses into meeting-places for men of letters, and men of wit.

Muhammad, in further raising the position of women, whose charms touched him so deeply, was not paid with ingratitude. The sympathy of women contributed to his consolation when he received insults in the early days of his mission: they saw him persecuted, and they loved him. The first century of Islam offers several women of really remarkable character. After 'Umar and 'Ali, the two principal figures in this great era are those of women, Aisha and Fatima. A delicious halo of sanctity glows around Khadija, and it is truly a honorable testimony in favor of Muhammad that, by a unique fact in the history of prophetism, his divine mission was first acknowledged by the one person who knew his weaknesses the most. When at the beginning of his mission, accused of imposture and subjected to much mockery, he went to confide in her his troubles, she consoled him with her words of tenderness and reaffirmed his shaken faith. Also, Khadija was never confounded in Muhammad's mind with the memories of his other wives. The story goes that one of those who succeeded her, jealous of this constancy, one day asked the Prophet if Allah had not given him something to make him forget old Khadija, and the Prophet replied: "No. When I was poor, she enriched me, when others accused me of lying, she believed in me, when I was anathematized by my people, she remained faithful to me, the more I suffered, the more she loved me." Since then, whenever one of his wives wanted to win his good graces, she would begin by praising Khadija.

The touchstone of a religion, after its women, is its martyrs. Persecution, in effect, is the first of the religious pleasures; it is so sweet to the heart of man to suffer for his faith, that this attraction suffices sometimes to make him believe. This is what Christian consciousness has wonderfully grasped in creating these admirable legends where so many conversions take place through the charm of torture. Although it has remained foreign to this depth of feeling, Islam has also sometimes arrived at, in its accounts of martyrs, some touches of subtle psychology. The slave Bilal would not be out of place among the touching heroes of the Golden Legend.[22] In the eyes of Muslims, the true martyrs are those who fell in fighting for the true faith. Although there is a confusion of ideas here to which we cannot subscribe, the death of a soldier and that of a martyr evoking totally different feelings in us, and the Muslim genius has managed to surround their deaths with quite high poetry. An example of a beautiful and great scene is that of the funerals that followed the battle of Uhud: "Bury them without washing their blood off," cried Muhammad, "they will appear on the day of resurrection with their bleeding wounds which will exhale the smell of musk, and I will testify they died martyrs to the faith." The standard bearer Jafar had his two hands cut off, and fell pierced with ninety wounds, all received from the front. Muhammad went to bear these tidings to his widow. He took on his knees the young son of the martyr, and carressed his head in a way that made the mother understand everything: "His two hands were cut off," he said, "but in exchange God has given him two wings of emerald with which he flies now wherever he wants amongst the angels of paradise."

The conversions are also, in general, arranged with a great deal of art. Almost all are conceived on the same theme as Saint Paul's. The persecutor becomes an apostle: the victim brought to the paroxysm of his anger, receives the supreme stroke which lays him out full length at the feet of victorious grace. The legend of the conversion of 'Umar is, in this respect, an incomparable page of religious psychology. 'Umar had been the most relentless enemy of the Muslims. His dreadful fits of temper had made him the bogy of the believers, still shy and forced into hiding. One day, in a moment of exaltation he went out with the firm intention of killing Muhammad. On the way, he met Nu'aym, one of his relatives, who, seeing 'Umar with a sword in his hand, asked him where he was going and what he intended to do. 'Umar explained his plan to Nu'aym. "Passion is carrying you away," Nu'aym told him. "Shouldn't you rather punish those members of your family who have abjured, without your knowledge, the religion of your fathers?"

"And these members of my family, who are they?" asked 'Umar.

"Your brother-in-law Said and your sister Fatima," replied Nu'aym.

'Umar flew to his sister's house. Said and Fatima were, at that moment, receiving secret lessons from a disciple, who was reading to them a chapter of the Koran written on a sheet of parchment. At the sound of 'Umar's step, the catechist hid himself in a dark recess and Fatima slipped the sheet under her clothes.

"What was it that I heard you chanting in a low voice?" asked 'Umar on entering.

"Nothing—you are mistaken."

"You were reading something, and I have learnt that you have joined Muhammad's sect."

On saying these words, 'Umar rushed towards his brother-in-law. Fatima wanted to shield him with her body, and both cried out: "Yes, we are Muslims. We believe in God and his prophet. Massacre us, if you wish."

'Umar, hitting out blindly, struck and seriously wounded his sister Fatima. At the sight of blood of a woman spilled by his hand, the impetuous young man suddenly softened.

"Show me the text you were reading," he said with obvious calm.

"I am afraid," replied Fatima, "that you will tear it up."

'Umar swore to return it intact. He had hardly read the first lines when he cried out, "How beautiful that is! How sublime! Show me where the Prophet is. I shall devote myself to him at once."

At that moment, Muhammad was in a house situated on the Hill of Safa with forty of his disciples, to whom he was explaining his doctrines. There was a knock on the door. One of the Muslims peered through the crack. "It's 'Umar, with a sword at his side," he said in terror. The consternation was general. Muhammad ordered them to open the door to him; he went toward 'Umar, took him by his coat, and, pulling him to the middle of the circle, said to him, "What brings you here, son of Khattab? Will you persist in your impiety until punishment from the heavens falls on you?"

"I come," replied 'Umar, "to confess that I believe in God and his Prophet."

The whole assembly thanked heaven for this unexpected conversion.

On taking leave of the faithful, 'Umar went straight to the house of Jamil, said to be the biggest gossip in Mecca. "Jamil," 'Umar said to him, "I have news for you. I am a Muslim. I have adopted the religion of Muhammad." Jamil hastened to run to the square in front of the Kaaba, where the Qurayshites used to spend the day chatting to one another. He arrived shouting at the top of his voice, "the son of Khattab's perverted!"

"You are lying," said 'Umar who was following close behind, "I am not perverted, I am a Muslim. I confess that there is no other god but Allah, and that Muhammad is his prophet."

His provocations ended by infuriating the idolaters, who threw themselves on him. 'Umar withstood the attack, and repelling the assaillants he cried out, "My God, if we were only three hundred Muslims, we would well see who would remain master of this temple."

This is the same man who later could not understand that they compromised with the infidels, the same man who, sword in hand, having left the house where he had just seen Muhammad die, declared that he would strike off the head of anyone who dared to say that the Prophet could have died.

Finally, by his marvellous understanding of Arab aesthetics, Muhammad created an all-powerful means of action over a people infinitely sensitive to the charm of beautiful language. The Koran was, in a sense, a literary revolution as much as a religious revolution; it signals, among the Arabs, the passage from verse to prose, from poetry to eloquence, a moment so important in the intellectual life of a people. At the beginning of the seventh century, the great poetic generation of Arabia was disappearing; signs of fatigue were apparent everywhere; the ideas of literary criticism appeared to be a threat to genius. Antar, this kind of Arab so open, so unspoilt, begins his Mu'allakat almost as a Latin poet of decadence would, with these words: "What subject have the poets not sung about?"

It made a great impression when Muhammad appeared in this dull environment with his lively and earnest recitations. The first time that Utba, son of Rabia, heard this energetic language, sonorous and full of rhythm even though not in verse form, he returned dumbfounded to his own people.

"What's the matter?" they asked him. "Well," he replied, "Muhammad spoke to me in a way that I had never heard. It is neither poetry nor prose nor the language of the magicians, but something penetrating." Muhammad did not like the complicated prosody of Arab poetry; when quoting verse he got the measures wrong, and God Himself undertook to excuse him for it: "We have not taught versification to our prophet" (sura 36: 68). He repeated on every occasion that he was neither a poet nor a magician;[23] the common herd, in fact, were unceasingly tempted to confuse him with these two classes of men, and it is true that his rhyming and sententious style had some resemblance to those of magicians. It is indeed impossible for us today, while reading the Koran, to understand the so powerful charm of that eloquence. This book seems to us declamatory, monotonous, and boring. An uninterrupted reading of it is almost unbearable, but one must remember that Arabia, never having had the slightest idea of the plastic arts nor of the great beauty of composition, made perfection consist of style only.

Language, in Muhammad's view, was something divine; the most precious gift that God had given to the Arabs, and an unequivocal sign of their preeminence, was Arabic itself, with its sophisticated grammar, its infinite richness, and its exquisite subtlety.[24] Muhammad undoubtedly owed his principal successes to the originality of his language, and to the new turn he gave to Arab eloquence. The most important conversions, that of the poet Labid, for example, took place on reading certain portions of the Koran, and to those who demanded a sign,[25] Muhammad offered no other response but the perfect purity of the Arabic that he spoke, and the charm of the new style whose secret he knew.

Thus, Islam sums up, with a unity of which it would be difficult to find another example, the ensemble of moral, religious, and aesthetic ideas, in a word, life according to the genius of one great family of mankind. One should not ask of it the heights of spirituality that India and Germany alone have known, nor that harmony or that sense of restraint and perfect beauty that Greece has bequeathed to the neo-Latin races, nor that gift of strange charm, mysterious and truly divine, which has united all civilized humanity, without distinction of race, in the veneration of the same ideal. It would be pushing beyond all bounds pantheism in aesthetics to put on an equal footing all the products of human nature, to place on the same scale of beauty the pagoda and the Greek temple because they are equally the result of an original and spontaneous conception. Human nature is always beautiful, it is true, but not equally beautiful. It is always the same motif, the same consonance and dissonance of terrestrial and divine instincts, but not the same fullness or the same sonority. Islam is obviously the result of an inferior, even mediocre, mixture of human elements. That is why it was triumphant only among mediocrities of human nature. The primitive races could not lift themselves up to its level; on the other hand, it did not suffice for the people who bore the germ of a more powerful civilization. Persia, the only Indo-European country where Islam achieved absolute domination, only adopted it by first submitting it to the most profound modifications in order to adapt it to her own mystical and mythological tendencies. The progress of Islam, moreover, ceased a while ago, and it has since lost all its converting capabilities.

If one wonders what its fate will be when faced with an essentially overwhelming civilization, and destined, it seems, to becoming universal, as far as the infinite diversity of the human race will allow, it must be confessed that nothing up to now can help us to have an exact idea of the way this immense revolution will be accomplished. On the one hand, it is certain that if Islam ever comes, I do not say to disappear, since religions never die, but to lose its high intellectual and moral eminence over a large part of the universe, it will succumb not to the efforts of another religion, but to the blows of modern science, which carry with them their habits of rationalism and criticism. On the other hand, one must remember that Islam, being different from those lofty towers that stiffen against the storm and fall all in one piece, has in its very flexibility hidden forces of resistance. To carry out their religious reform, the Christian nations were obliged to shatter violently their unity and to revolt openly against the central authority. Islam, which has no pope, no synods, no bishops divinely instituted, no well-determined clergy, Islam, which has never fathomed the bottomless pit of infallibility, has perhaps less to be frightened of by the rise of rationalism. As a matter of fact, what would the critic attack? The legend of Muhammad? This legend has scarcely more sanction than the pious beliefs that, at the heart of Catholicism, one could reject without being a heretic. Strauss obviously has no work to do here. Would one attack the dogma? Reduced to bare essentials, Islam adds to natural religion only the prophethood of Muhammad, and a certain idea of fatality which is less an article of faith than a general turn of mind, susceptible of being conveniently guided. Would one attack its ethics? One has the choice of four sects equally orthodox, in which a moral sense keeps a large part of liberty. As to rites, freed from some minor superstitions, they can be compared for simplicity only to the most purified Protestant sects. Did we not see at the beginning of this century, in Muhammad's own homeland, a sectarian stir up the vast political and religious movement of the Wahhabites, whose fates do not yet seem to be finished, in proclaiming that the true religious worship of God consisted in prostrating oneself in front of the idea of His existence, that the invocation of any intermediary or intercessor in His presence was an act of idolatry, and that the most meritorious act would be to raze the tomb of the prophet and the mausoleums of imans?

Symptoms of a more serious nature are appearing, I know, in Egypt and Turkey. There, contact with European science and customs has produced freethought, sometimes scarcely disguised. Sincere believers, who are aware of the danger, do not hide their disquiet, and they denounce the books of European science as containing deadly errors and subversive of all religious faith. I nevertheless persist in believing that if the East can surmount its apathy and go beyond the limits that up to now it has been unable to overcome as far as rational speculation was concerned, Islam will not pose a serious obstacle to the progress of the modern mind. The lack of theological centralization has always left a certain degree of religious liberty to Muslim nations. Despite what Foster says, the caliphate never resembled the papacy.

The Caliphate was strong only as long as it represented the first conquering idea of Islam. When the temporal power passed to the *emirs-al-omra*, and when the Caliphate was no more than a religious power, it fell into the most deplorable decadence. The idea of a power purely spiritual is too subtle for the East: all branches of Christianity themselves were unable to attain it. The Greco-Slav branch has never understood it; the Germanic family discarded it and went beyond. Only the Latin nations accepted it.

Now experience has shown that the simple faith of people is not enough to maintain a religion, if it is not safeguarded by an organized hierarchy and spiritual leader. Were the Anglo-Saxons lacking faith when the will of Henry VIII led them, without them perceiving it, one day into schism and the next into heresy? Muslim orthodoxy, not being defended by a permanent, autonomous, self-recruiting and self-governing body, is thus rather vulnerable. It is superfluous to add that if ever a reformist movement manifests itself in Islam, Europe should only participate in it by the influence of a most general kind. It would be ungracious of her to wish to settle the faith of others. While acitively pursuing the propagation of her dogma which is civilization, she ought to leave to the peoples themselves the infinitely delicate task of adjusting their own religious traditions to their new needs, and to respect that most inalienable right of nations as much as of individuals, the right to preside oneself, in the most perfect freedom, over the revolutions of one's conscience.

NOTES

1. [Georg Friedrich Creuzer (1771–1858), German historian and philologist, professor of Ancient History at Heidelberg; his first and greatest work was *Symbolik und Mythologie der alten Volker, besonders der Griechen* (4 vols., 1810–12).—Trans.]

2. [David Friedrich Strauss (1808–1874), German theologian. "His famous Leben Jesu applied the myth theory to the life of Christ. It denied the historical foundation of all supernatural elements in the Gospels, which were assigned to an unintentionally creative legend (the myth), developed between the death of Christ and the writing of the Gospels in the second century." *The Concise Oxford Dictionary of the Christian Church* (Oxford, 1980).—Trans.]

3. "Mahometism unveiled: an inquiry in which that arch heresy, its diffusion and continuance, are examined on a new principle, tending to confirm the evidences, and aid the propagation of the Christian Faith." It is the same Charles Forster who has just enlivened the pages of learned journals by such an amusing mystification of the Sinaitic inscriptions, where he purports to find the original scripts and language and the original text of Exodus, and so on.

4. From which we get *bafumerie, mahomerie, momerie,* to indicate all impure and superstitious religious practices.

5. The word *Koran* means recitation, and in no way does it evoke the analogous idea a book (*kitab*) of the Jews or Christians.

6. This is the name given to the chapters of the Koran.

7. If you confront me with the general tendency of Oriental philosophy to mysticism, I shall point out that it is only a misapplication to use the term Arab philosophy to a philosophy which never had roots in the Arabian peninsula, and whose appearance was a reaction of the Persian mind to the Arab spirit. This philosophy was written in Arabic, and that is all—it was entirely Persian in spirit.

8. *Mu'allaqat*: we call *Mu'allaqat* or the Suspended Ones those pieces of verse which had won the prize in the poetry competitions and were suspended with golden nails from the gate of the Kaaba. There remain seven to which we usually add two or three other poems of the same character.

9. We have taken these details from a thousand in the Lalitavistara or the legend of the Buddha, translated by M. Edouard Foucaux (Paris 1848).

10. Needless to say, I am far from attaching any historical importance to these stories; here I am only emphasizing the character that the Arabs have attributed to their prophet, and the general tenor of his legend.

11. [Voltaire, *Mahomet* 5.4. The last two lines of the play.—Trans.].

12. [Latinized name of Fausto Paolo Sozzini (1539–1604), who, in 1562, published a work denying the divinity of Christ. By 1563 he had rejected the natural immortality of man. He was responsible for the spread of moderate Unitarian views—Trans.]

13. See the curious work of Captain de Neveu on this subject, Paris 1846.

14. The Muhajirs were the Meccans who accompanied Muhammad during his flight (Hijra), and the Ansari were the Medinans who welcomed him and became his defenders against their fellow citizens.

15. Glorious combats (or in Arabic *mufakhara*) were the poetry tournaments where each tribe was represented by a poet who was given the task of presenting the rights of the tribe to preeminence. Victory went to the tribe whose poet had found the strongest and most felicitous expressions.

16. For a picture of this strange period, one could consult the elegant study of the life of Ibn Zubayr by Quatreniere

17. [As the *Encyclopedia Britannica* (11th ed.) puts it, "The real work of [Homeric] criticism became possible only when great collections of manuscripts began to be made. . . . In this way the great Alexandrian school of Homeric criticism began with Zenodotus, the first chief of the museum, and was continued by Aristophanes and Aristarchus. . . . Our knowledge of Alexandrian criticism is derived almost wholly from a single document, the famous Iliad of the Library of St. Mark in Venice."

The *Oxford Classical Dictionary* further explains, "It has been thought that the poems are collections of lays put together from different sources, or original poems much expanded and altered." *Oxford Classical Dictionary*, 2d ed. (London, Oxford, 1978), p. 524.—Trans.]

18. Buddhism also. In view of the marvellous apparitions which attended the birth of the Buddha, an anchorite from Himalaya, learned in the five transcendental sciences, came to Kapila across the skies, took the child in his arms, and recognized in him thirty-two signs of a great man and eighty signs of a Buddha.

19. It is the spring which, according to Arab legend, God made gush out in the desert to quench Ismael's thirst.

20. Consult the spritual insights of Saint-Marc Girardin on the role of women in the origin of Christianity, in his *Essais de Litterature et de Morale*, t.II.

21. [This was a great collection of songs, made by Abu'l Faradj (897–967), which were popular at the time. It is our most important authority for literary history, and also for the history of civilization.—Trans.]

22. [*The Golden Legend* was a "medieval manual of ecclesiastical lore: lives of saints, commentary on church services, homilies for saints' days, and so on." *Oxford Companion to English Literature*, ed. M. Drabble (Oxford: Oxford University Press, 1985), p. 400.—Trans.]

23. See suras 21:5; 36:68; 37:36; 52:29; 69:40–42.

24. The Arabs imagine that only their language has grammar, and that all other languages are but crude dialects. Sheikh Rifa, in the account of his voyage in France, took great pains to destroy this prejudice in his fellow countrymen, and to teach them that the French language also possesses rules, subtleties, and an academy.

25. The word "ayat," which designates the verses of the Koran means "sign" or "miracle."

PART THREE

LAMMENS AND BECKER

Chapter 4

The Koran and Tradition
How the Life of Muhammad Was Composed

Henri Lammens

W hat is meant by the title sira, which means "the life," is the collection of writings concerned with the deeds of Muhammad. This vast library, without parallel to anything in our Western literature, so far as quantity is concerned, derives primarily from the Hadith, or Muslim Tradition.

Since the critical researches of Professor Goldziher,[1] it is not possible to deny the highly tendentious character of this Tradition. Even so, Western students of Islam continue to treat it, as far as the sira is concerned, as of great importance. This becomes evident from a reading of the more recent biographies of Muhammad. Like those of old, they finally turn out to be derived from the Hadith. What has been the good of so much erudite and patient research? Even a Semitic scholar of such caliber as Noldeke declares that for his part he renounces any attempt to scrutinize the mystery which surrounds the personality of Muhammad.[2]

In order to make our view clear, and without ignoring the irregularity of the procedure, we shall state at once the conclusions which we would draw to the attention of future historians of the Prophet:

a. The Koran provides the only historical basis for the sira.
b. As to the assertions found in the sacred text of the Muslims, the Tradition [the Hadith] is neither a confirmation nor does it provide additional infor-

Originally published in *Recherches de Science Religieuse* 1 (1910): 25–51. Translated for this volume by Ibn Warraq.

mation as was thought until now. It is an apocryphal development. On the fabric of the Koranic text, the Hadith has embroidered its legends, being satisfied with inventing names of additional actors presented or with spinning out the original theme. Its work is limited to these embellishments, considerable and exceeding by far the invention of Christian apocryphal authors.

c. The value of a tradition depends upon its independence from the Koran. It is therefore necessary to enquire, above all, from the Koranic text how far it has served as an inspiration for the variations in the Hadith. This is the best way to determine the real meaning and the value of the information provided. Until the authenticating passage is discovered, the Hadith can be used provisionally before a cleverer researcher puts his finger on the join that links the Koran to the various traditions. This is a question of method and a matter of time!

d. We accept the fact that for the Medinan period of the life of Muhammad a vague oral tradition existed from the beginning of the Hijra. If this had been preserved in its integrity, it would be a valuable check to determine the soundness of the tradition. But from an early stage it was tampered with by being adjusted violently to the Koran, which had become the supreme rule of knowledge, both sacred and profane. When it came to establishing the traits of the historic figure of the Master, the very earliest traditionalists began by opening this compilation. When they were dealing with testimonies of the contemporaries of Muhammad, their rule was to harmonize them in order to make them fit with the assertions of the "Book of Allah." How could the memories of fallible mortals correct the incomparable testimony of God speaking in the Koran? The oral tradition of the first century of the Hijra was transformed on the Procrustean bed of the strict framework of the Koran. Even the eyewitnesses in the end only saw events through the eyes of Muhammad. They may have believed that they remembered, whereas they were the unconscious echoes of the suras, which by constant repetition had encrusted their contents upon their minds. Contemporary poets retained a measure of independence and for that reason were discredited by the Prophet. Unfortunately, we do not possess their complete works. Of these valuable witnesses of the past the sira preserves only those pieces where it believes it has found confirmation of its theories. The rest were not worth the trouble of conserving, or must be suppressed as blasphemy. The habits of Ibn Hisham[3] in his significant works serves to provide an example of this.

e. Since there has been no scientific exegesis of the Koran so far, the Tradition preserves a certain value of its own.

In the present state of our knowledge, the historical allusions in the Koran largely escape us. We still await a critical edition, and meanwhile the chronology of the text remains an open question.[4] In spite of its preconceptions—which are themselves very instructive—the ancient tradition, by its nearness to the events, could, to a certain extent, know the intentions of the Master and describe both persons and happenings, as seen by him. After spending some time in the study of this literature, one can, by proceeding cautiously, reach a point at which the primitive core can be recovered, and the traditional records stripped of their foreign accretions.

Thus, when the Muslim Tradition presents itself as an independent source of information, based upon extensive research provided by contemporaries on the life of the Arab Prophet, we do well to receive it with skepticism, the same skepticism shown by Muhammad's own friends vis-à-vis the inexhaustible fluency of the famous Abu Huraira; we can thus consider the Muslim Tradition as one of the greatest historical frauds, whose memory the annals of literature have preserved. If, within Islam as well as outside, the illusion has persisted so long, it can only be due to a false critical apparatus, the seeming naivité of the supporting authorities,[5] the ingenuity of their erudition, and the implacable logic in error which this enormous compilation demonstrates. In view of all this, we cannot praise enough the perseverance of the untold generations of scholars, from the second to the ninth century of the Hijra, bound to this sterile task. In the absence of true history—which must be reconstructed out of the testimonies that have escaped from them involuntarily—it is to Arab literature that their pious zeal has built a monument truly unique of its kind.[6] We shall later demonstrate the truth of this by several examples. For the present we shall be content with brief illustrations and summary references, reserving a fuller treatment on these points for a more complete work devoted to the life of Muhammad.

The preexistence of the soul of Muhammad is a favorite dogma of the Tradition, accepted as a belief by the sira,[7] but of Platonic and Gnostic origin.[8] Both[9] have taken the idea and read it into certain texts which they have badly understood, where Allah says to the faithful: "We have sent you a *light*."[10] This term was taken up later and applied to the living person of the Prophet. Hence his body emitted luminous waves, rendering him visible in the thickest darkness. One night this miraculous light enabled Aisha to find a needle she had lost. The person of Muhammad "produced no shadow. His radiance outshone the rays of the sun and dimmed the light of the blazing torch." As an intense source of light, he also saw behind his back. He saw by day as by night. Better still, he possessed a physical eye, planted in the middle of his back, or between his shoulders—one is not quite sure where—and his clothes did not prevent the light from passing through.[11] Such an example shows the fertility, the strange logic, and the legendary style of the Tradition, doggedly pursuing a word, although interpreted wrongly.

At his birth Muhammad had received the name Qutham,[12] but since the Book of Allah had given him the name Ahmad and Muhammad, the Tradition, with a slightly apologetic ulterior motive,[13] wishes to hear of no other. One needs only to be wakeful in one's pursuit and to research patiently into the remote corners of the Hadith to discover the real significance of what orthodoxy did not or would not understand.

What about Muhammad's age? He was not himself interested in his age, just as the Arabs of today cannot see what is so important about knowing exactly how old you are. But the Tradition was written at a time when dates were important, since a calendar was composed from the Hijra. This made it necessary to improvise a chronology for the sira. The age accepted was between sixty and sixty-five, with a preference for sixty-three or sixty-five, the former guaranteed by Aisha and the latter by Ibn Abbas. The favorite was nine years old when she married the Prophet; Ibn Abbas hardly knew him. The use of these two names has no significance whatsoever. They are simply attempts to tidy up the Hadith and give it a coherent form, in other words, to provide the last link in the isnad (the uninterrupted line of authority back to Muhammad). That forms a part of the pseudoscientific method, a veritable *trompe-l'oeil* style, still taken seriously by a number of Islamic scholars.

This then is how the Tradition came to form an opinion of the age of the Master. The duration of the Medinan period was sufficiently well known: about ten years. In a passage of the Koran, Muhammad says to the pagans of Mecca, "At first, I dwelt among you for the space of an 'umur" (sura 9:10). In the interest of their calculations, the editors of the sira decided that

1. "at first" meant the period before the revelation,
2. the term 'umur had the value of precisely forty years.

With the ten at Medina, that added up to fifty years. Forty years was a sacred number! In order to adopt this definitively, our chronologists were able to appeal to certain verses in the Koran (sura 46:15), one of which seemed to fix about forty years for the full development of the religious ideas. We have every right to suppose that all the subtleties were used in this masterpiece of ingenuity, which we call the sira. There remains to determine the duration of the stay at Mecca, after the *revelation*. In order to determine this, the sira detached the following verse from an apocryphal piece of a problematic poet, *Sirma Abu Qays*: "He sojourned among the Quraysh some ten years, preaching and trying to find one believer, one companion."

This vague expression, *"some* ten years"[14] fitted perfectly with the calculations of the sira; it could signify 10, 13, or even 15. And so, 10 + 40 + 10 (or 13 or 15). From that the figures 60, 63, and 65 years[15] are the most commonly adopted for the age of Muhammad.[16]

Conforming to the custom of the Arabs, always very proud to affirm fatherhood, Muhammad bore the cognomen, or *kunya*, of Abul Qasim, that is, father of Qasim, his eldest son. Among the names of the Prophet, Abul Qasim is one of the best attested. According to the Tradition he would have forbidden his followers to adopt for themselves this *kunya* and, to make matters worse, add it to the name Muhammad. Hence a Muslim of the name of Muhammad, father of a son named Qasim, would have to settle upon another *kunya*—a fact contradicted by history! Among his contemporaries and in the generation after the Prophet, we know of more than one Abul Qasim, who was also called Muhammad. What motive could have suggested this fictitious prohibition? And that other, where Muhammad forbids questions being asked of him?[17] To make it law, the Tradition drew its inspiration from the Koran: "Do not interrogate the Apostle as you interrogate one another." Allah intended to restrain the faithful from an improper familiarity with the Prophet. The literal exegesis, the intemperate zeal of the Tradition, has gone beyond the intention.

About the youth of Muhammad the writers of the sira remain totally ignorant. In Mecca, having failed to suspect the future greatness of this obscure Qurayshite, no one had bothered to observe him, still less preserve the impressions collected. But in sura 93, Allah said: "We found you poor, an orphan without a family." These words furnished the framework for a veritable "Gospel of the Infant Muhammad." We have no way of checking the truth of this romance, based upon inconsistent material sources, making him endure all the hardships of Arab orphan children. The imagination of the traditionalists supplied all that was needed.

The Meccan suras, the most numerous of the collection, furnish important points of reference for the preaching and the mission in Mecca. They affirm the fact of resistance to the Reformer. The Tradition, however, reads into it a veritable persecution.[18] In its eyes this period becomes the age of the Muslim catacombs. Throughout the whole Koran, Muhammad is careful to mention the names of only two men, and because of this, Abu Lahab[19] became the typical persecutor, the soul of all the conspiracies against burgeoning Islam. "Every prophet must have an ungodly person as an opponent."[20] Abu Lahab was quite naturally the butt of the Tradition's animosity. Was he more fierce than Khalid ibn al-Walid, the sword of God, or other great saints of Islam, converted late to that religion, like 'Abd ar-Rahman, son of the future caliph Abu Bakr, and the majority of Hashimites? Among these latter we would name Aqil, his cousin and brother of 'Ali; he had pushed his arrogance to the extent of confiscating the Prophet's own house. That did not prevent the orthodox from recording his Manaqib, that is, his eminent qualities.[21] But Muhammad had refrained from highlighting them, as he did for Abu Lahab. In the Hadith, Muhammad begins his preaching within the family. Again there is a text for this in the the Koran: "Convert your nearest relatives." For the visits to Taif and the markets in the area around Mecca there is the text: "Preach in the Mother of Cities (Mecca) and its surroundings." The Tradition knew in detail the objections made to Muhammad. They are developed from those the Koran addresses to the prophets, his predecessors, and to Muhammad himself. Very seriously the sira professes to inform us of the peculiarities of Qurayshite polytheism. We would gladly give credit in this case since the companions of Muhammad in Mecca must have known about their ancient cult. But how could our skepticism fail to be aroused when we see the sira limiting itself to paraphrasing the indications given by the Koran?[22] The loss of the *Kitab al-Asnam* by al-Kalbi continues to be regrettable. But was it so original, I mean independent, of the Koran? The fragments which have been preserved, with their mythology so largely Koranic,[23] do not encourage us to answer in the affirmative. This consideration may serve to temper our regrets.

What should we think of the infanticide practiced by the Arabs, and above all their custom of burying their daughters? The Tradition affirms it, but the examples cited are very few and mostly anonymous, except for the chiefs of Tamim. In times of famine, cruel fathers in harsh Arabia may have killed their own daughters. But was this general and did they go to the extreme of burying them alive?[24] We suspect once again that the Tradition has interpreted literally the question about the father who has been told of the birth of a daughter, taken from the Koran: "Is he going to let her live, or bury her underground?"[25] To the traditionalists the idea would not occur to be aware of hyperboles. It was too good a chance for the hotheaded polemicist to use this audacious affirmation to blacken his adversaries in order to flaunt his own good turns. As this barbarous custom did not exist in Arabia, its suppression cannot be accredited to Abul Qasim.

For Muhammad paternity brought little consolation. He had mostly daughters, not very attractive and difficult to place matrimonially, with the exception of Zaynab. Khadija gave him only one son as the *kunya* Abul Qasim seems to prove. Or to put it more exactly, it was from this *kunya* that the Tradition has assumed the existence of little Qasim, who otherwise remains completely unknown. For the sira this one son appeared insufficient, unworthy of the Master. The Koran indicated that the prophets, among their characteristics, should have a numerous progeny. Hence the efforts to give Qasim brothers. They went as far as splitting them into two, mistaking for real names the epithets *Tahir*, pure, and *Tayb*, good, accorded to the sons of Muhammad by the piety of posterity. He was even supposed to have had twin sons,[26] and that several times. These childish inventions resulted in twelve children, and of these eight were boys.[27] This is the triumph of sentimental logic. When reading the Koran, it is impossible not to be struck by the impression of sadness in Muhammad because of his unblessed paternity and his protests against the description *abtar*,[28] a man without male heirs, or by his tenderness towards boys especially, "the adornment of this earthly life," placed by him with wealth among the only things worthy of envy.[29] Hence the long series of anecdotes showing the Prophet occupied with and busy playing with his grandchildren, even in his prayers. The Tradition was happily inspired in this matter, although it was wrong to rely on apocryphal sources in order to create an effect, as usual.

As for the details preserved by the Tradition on the means and the circumstances by which Muhammad received the first revelations, there is room for caution, because they were transmitted under the authority of Aisha, a source suspect even to Muslims. In fact, it is in the Koran that the sira has, as always, found the principal outlines of its narration,[30] whose confusion however shows up clearly enough the clumsiness of the forger.

As for the wives of Muhammad, why does Tradition stop at nine? This figure was certainly exceeded and some passages of the sira speak of twenty-three wives.[31] The choice of nine by the Tradition was, we believe, influenced by a passage in the Koran: "Marry two, three, or four wives." The sum gives us precisely the figure nine. I am quite prepared to admit, with our esteemed Islamic scholar, Prince Caetani,[32] that in this verse the disjunctive style is the work of a later editor, and that, as with the concubines, it was not Muhammad's intention to restrict his followers to four wives. The great companions of the Prophet profited abundantly from this accorded license.[33]

"Obey the Prophet when he speaks," says the Koran. This text has given birth to a whole series of Hadith. This would encourage the obligation to interrupt whatever one were doing, even prayer, in order to listen to a word from Muhammad. The obligation was extended much further than this. A woman desired by him cannot refuse to marry him. If she is married, her husband must renounce her. The Apostle can marry her, willingly or by force, even against her will or that of her family. Has Allah not said,[34] "The believers must prefer the Prophet to themselves "?[35]

The *mo'ahat* or fraternity provides another example of literal exegesis. The Koran likes to insist on the fraternity uniting the Muhajir or emigrants to the Ansars or Muslims of Medina (suras 3:102; 8:72; 39:10; 59:9). In this call to harmony, which concerned certain effects of physical kinship, among others in matters of inheritance, the sira has wanted to discover the institution of a true religious affinity. The sira cites, in a moving way, the case of a man from Medina offering to share with the Qurayshite, 'Abd ar-Rahman ibn 'Auf, all he had, even his wives. It is difficult to find an authentic trace of this fraternity thus extended. It is acknowledged, however, that it could have been deleted later. Muhammad was intelligent, but with an intelligence more agile than extensive, he changed a great deal in the course of his career as a legislator. This mobility fed a whole special literature: that of Nasikh wa Mansukh, that is, the abrogations. To put an end to the divisions between the great factions separating the Muslim community, he multiplied his appeals for unity; but he never made the mistake of establishing a law like that dreamed up by Hadith under the influence of misunderstood Koranic texts.

Until quite recently, I had believed in the historicity of the traditional accounts of the great days of Islam: Badr, Tabuk, Hunayn. On the subject of the battle of Uhud, one had to rely upon the testimony of 'Abd ar-Rahman ibn 'Auf. When he was asked about these events, a long time afterwards, he was content to say of the battle: "Read sura 3, beginning at verse 120; you will imagine yourself to be there." In other words, the great companion of the Prophet neither knew nor was prepared to know any other version than that recorded in the Koran![36] Ibn Ishaq could not be more difficult. As for Badr, we have a good account, attributed to Urwa ibn Zubayr. It states quite clearly that the Muslims, led by Muhammad, ran into a battle without being aware of it, when all they were thinking of was pillaging a caravan! But this important detail is implicit in the Koranic account, relating to Badr, and one retains the right to ask to what extent it was independent from it. Nine hundred to a thousand Qurayshites beaten by three hundred Muslims, trembling with fear. The whole great miracle of Badr is held within this antithesis!

If the miracle leaves us cold, we must find the source of the figures given for the size of the enemy. As the Koran affirms (sura 8:43, 44), at Badr itself (and this miracle was "purely the result of divine compassion") the Muslims were unaware of the crushing superiority of the Qurayshites. It did not stare them in the face. Was the later Tradition better informed in this regard? We beg to differ. But wishing to highlight the miracle, hypnotized by the figure of "a thousand angelic horsemen," it deduced from it the number of the adversaries. The more heroic spirit of the Badrites is confirmed by Muhammad.[37] Under these conditions, the Meccans, better armed, mounted on horses, and fighting to save the fortunes and honor of their city, could not have been beaten by a band of brigands if they had the superior numbers deduced by the Hadith from a text of the Koran.[38] The whole traditional account of the day of Badr needs reexamination.[39]

As with Uhud, where he declaimed a funeral oration over his fallen companions, the Prophet must have devoted a complete sura to the Day of Badr, which is a real paean of victory. Only fragments of this dithyramb exist, bizarre and entangled, in the the eighth sura, with disparate developments. By the use of these fragments, awkwardly put together, the Tradition attempted, but without success, to compose an acceptable account of the battle of Badr, the *Tolbiac*[40] of Islam. One can only state the impossibility of reconstructing this military affair from such incoherent material.

The traditional account of *Hunayn* is no less confused. In contrast to Badr, the Muslims found themselves with twelve thousand warriors. Why were the fortunes of war at first against them? "To punish them for putting their faith in numbers"—a mystical reason, furnished by the Koran (sura 9:25, 26). With its usual prolixity the Hadith has developed this without adding anything essential to the brief allusions in the Book of Allah. It is impossible to understand why the Bedouins of Hawazin decided to take to flight after the spectacular success of their first attack, instead of pursuing the defeated. Was there not a need to explain the intervention of "the invisible troops" (sura 9:26)? As with Badr, this unexpected reinforcement determined the victory. To go by the Tradition—it names the witnesses—heads rolled, prisoners were led in chains, but one does not discover who the authors are of these feats. There we have the mythical developments[41] into which the Hadith strays. In fact, we learn the quality of Muhammad's adversaries. But after the surrender of Mecca, a move in the direction of Hunayn must have had as its objectives the town of Taif and the confederacy of Hawazin.

The tedious information of the Hadith about the preparations for the expedition to Tabuk is known. Planned for the hottest period of the year the expedition met with lively opposition. Many remained in Medina: these are the sedentary ones, "Qa 'idoun." The Hadith has an infinite variety of descriptions of their situation, attempting to dramatize the excommunication launched against these lukewarm Muslims. Here the fluency of the tradition could feed upon the many indications in sura 9.[42] True to its usual procedure, it has invented some proper names. This literary device gives life to the anonymous declamations of the Koran. Fictitious life, when one onsiders the lack of historic sense in the Tradition.

We know of the incident of the "masjid," a dissident mosque, first authorized by Muhammad, then destroyed by his orders. We do not know the precise date. If it is placed on the return from the expedition to Tabuk, it is apparently to make it fit the suggested chronology which the Koran seems to favor (sura 9:107), where it places the account of the episode at the end of the verses relating to Tabuk. If the conquest of Khaybar follows closely on the expedition to Hudaybiyya, it is again because of a suggestion in the Koran (sura 48:18–20), establishing a connection between these two events. Now, we know that it is well to avoid taking the Koran chronology too seriously. Not only do the suras follow one another pell-mell, without any order of date, but the verses form a disparate conglomerate, where the Meccan texts are side by side with the Medinan revelations. The Muslim exegesis does not hesitate to confess the fact,[43] and it even occasionally breaks up into very uneven sections the chronological sequences of the great suras.

We possess voluminous descriptions of the person of Muhammad. They promise to acquaint us with every detail of his physique, his moral character, his habits, his tastes. Nothing has been omitted by these authors, or wassaf.[44] They have even counted the number of hairs going grey on his temples: not quite twenty of them! These collections carry the generic names of *Shama'il*, or *Khalq an-Nabi*, more rarely of *Sifa* or of *Hilia*. After the work of Tirmidhi[45] became popular, the first name, that of Shama'il, was more generally used. What credence can we give to these compositions destined to become very popular among the Muslims? An observation first awakens our suspicion.

The early Christians found themselves divided on the question of the physical beauty of Christ. These Shama'il know nothing of such hesitations. Their general tendency is to present us with Muhammad as "the most beautiful of the children of men," as the ideal of human perfection.[46] To arrive at such a conviction, here is the course adopted by the authors of the *Shama'il*. They started by a systematic perusal of the early Arab poets to establish the canon of masculine aesthetics, as at least the ancient bards of the Peninsula saw it. This picture presented certain gaps, which were filled out by consulting the innumerable descriptions, the *nasib* [amatory prelude to the ode], devoted to feminine beauty by the authors of the *qasidas* [odes]. Using this research, all the traits are applied to the person of Muhammad. The traces of this process can easily be recovered by consulting the fine manuscript of Leiden, ND.437, *Khalq an-Nabi* of respectable antiquity, and sufficiently independent, as an edition, of *Tirmidhi*. The author is quite clearly dependent upon the poets, in spite of his efforts to disguise the source of his borrowing. In the fashion of the ancient Arab philologists, he is content at the end of each Hadith, which form his voluminous dossier, to cite the verse, as *sawahid* [quotation serving as textual evidence] or *teste di lingua*, whereas in reality the verse serves as the source of his material. He and his colleagues have applied the same procedure in dealing with the verses of the Koran, a point which interests us especially in this survey, where we intend to study the influence of this collection on the Tradition.

When we see the Tradition start by establishing its thesis—namely, the moral and physical perfections of Muhammad—and then go on to confirm the whole by citing the sacred text,[47] the real order of the premises in this syllogism may be invisible to an inexperienced reader. We must not forget that in the whole demonstration, the Koran forms the principal argument. "The morals of the Prophet?" Aisha cries, "but they are to be found the Koran."[48] One begins with the Koran while pretending to conclude with it. The traditionalists did not start with an attempt to discover the memories of the survivors of the heroic age, but rather by opening the Book of Allah to discover what they wanted to see there; then they proceeded to adapt to their preconceived ideas information, more or less authentic, or even invented by themselves.[49] The names of the great impostors: Aisha, Ibn Abbas, Abu Huraira; names most frequently cited in the Shama'il, do not weaken our conclusions.

Described as "a flaming torch of light,"[50] Muhammad was bound to possess characteristics corresponding to this description: thus he was pale of face; "shining like a mirror," his thighs themselves were diaphanous.[51] He had proclaimed himself the khatam (seal) of the prophets. This term has given rise to a profusion of interpretations and fantastic traditions. Certainly the author of the Koran intended to say that he was the last of the Prophets to arise, or even that he marked the end of a series of supernatural revelations. For the Arab the word "khatam" can also mean "seal"! This meaning was seized upon, and on the flesh of Muhammad, it was alleged, a place was marked by this prophetic seal, although its nature was not always certain—a knob, a fleshy growth, a tuft of hairs. Nor was it quite certain where it was on the body: between the shoulders or on the back?[52] Yet no traditionalist has ever doubted the physical existence of this miraculous mark.

The Koran applies to Muhammad the attribute of "ummi." The Koranic meaning of this term is far from firmly established. This did not prevent the Hadith from settling for "illiterate." This philological exegesis has resulted in a cycle of Hadith, showing Muhammad's inability to read or write. We learn without difficulty the apologetic implication of this argument: An illiterate author of an incomparable masterpiece, the Koran,[53] "surpassing the united efforts of men and jinns!"[54] The Hadith, however, has conserved anecdotes where we can see Muhammad reading and writing. For example, faced with 'Ali's refusal at Hudaybiyya, he decides to draw up and write the text of the agreement with the Meccans himself;[55] even in the Koran it is not impossible to discover traces of his literary knowledge.[56] Nevertheless, Muslim orthodoxy has plumped for the thesis of Muhammad's ignorance.[57]

And poetry? With indignation God rejects the epithet poet for his Messenger.[58] To give substance to this allegation, the Hadith ingeniously multiply the reports where Muhammad seems totally ignorant of poetic rhythm, incapable of reciting a verse without destroying the prosodic meter.[59] Deplorable inferiority at a time when the most ignorant Bedouin fancied himself as a rhymester! This situation betrays once more the servility of the Muslim Traditions vis-à-vis the Koran. "He is not one of us," this is how they speak of him, "who does not modulate the recitation of the Holy Book" (Darimi, *Mushad*, Leider Manuscript, p. 283b).

Very hostile to music in general, and to liturgical music above all,[60] if the Traditions seem to hesitate on the modulated recitation of the suras,[61] it is still under the influence of the sacred text.[62] This attitude gives us the following Hadith: "All prophets have a beautiful face and an agreeable voice." One is equally reminded of David, the Prophet-King Musician.[63] It is besides an axiom established by Tradition[64] that the "seal of the prophets ought to combine in his person the prerogatives of all his predecessors."[65] A compromise, therefore, intervened: Muhammad, enemy of music, would have made an exception in the case of the reading of the Koran.

The sira and the *Shama'il* expand endlessly on Muhammad's passion for honey.[66] We owe to this predilection one of the most curious incidents of his conjugal life: the collective repudiation of his entire harem, the day when he stopped too long at one of his wives to taste some honey. It was not the only case when Muhammad had recourse to the expedience of divorce; he even proposed it openly in the Koran[67] to quarrelsome widows, composing his interior household. Certain biographies of Muhammad, such as the voluminous *Imta*[68] of the celebrated Maqrizi, even contain a chapter entitled: "Of honey, recommended as a medicine by the Prophet." All this literature proceeds in the last analysis from an expression in the Koran (sura 16:69) praising the curative virtues of honey. As a corollary, they have deduced his pronounced taste for sweets and confectionery.

When running through the innumerable versions of the life of Muhammad, one is not moderately surprised to discover the considerable place given to feasts. We see him, with or without Aisha, running from invitations to invitations, without ever declining one—this detail figures sometimes in the sira as proof of his humility—eating there with an excellent appetite, meats, marrows, tarid (a sort of Qurayshite broth) and all the culinary art of Arabia is to be found there.[69] With the exception of roast lizards, the Prophet, the Traditions declare, was careful not to refuse anything at the table. He ate a lot of everything.

Obviously, we do not owe these indulgent descriptions to the desire to highlight the zuhd or asceticism of the Arab reformer, extolled in other contexts by Muslim orthodoxy. Here, above all, one must assume a Koranic inspiration. According to the book of God, the contemporaries of Muhammad appeared to be shocked by the vulgar habits of their fellow citizen. "Like them he took part in the festivities and one saw him visiting the bazaar" at Mecca.[70] In reply, God sent down this revelation: "All the predecessors of Muhammad, we created them mortal, having the need to eat."[71] In their zeal, the Hadith wanted to lean on this divine justification without asking if its realism did not go beyond the aim. They thought themselves encouraged on this path by the numerous invitations in the Koran to "drink and eat,"[72] to enjoy to the full the good things of life, in Arabic the "taiybat,"[73] by which one is to understand primarily food, and meats above all.[74] They thought of the outbursts of the Prophet against certain abstentions or food taboos observed by the pagans and the Jews of his time.[75] The sira, claiming to demonstrate this, began by giving an example: indirectly also protesting against the ideal of evangelical detachment; we have here one of the many tendencies which influenced the Hadith.

The Traditions applied the same procedure when they wished to form an opinion on the respective merits of the first Companions, the great saints of Islam. In the view of orthodox Islam, the most eminent of all was not 'Ali, the son-in-law and cousin of the Prophet, but Abu Bakr. Some excellent reasons could justify this decision, above all the notorious incompetence of Fatima's husband [i.e., 'Ali]. The determining reason was a certain verse of the Koran, commemorating the episode of the cave, where the Prophet, accompanied by Abu Bakr, took shelter during their flight from Mecca: "God will help him [Muhammad] as He helped him when he was driven out by the unbelievers with one other [Abu Bakr]; In the cave he said to his companion: 'Do not despair, God is with us.' "[76] Thus you have Abu Bakr associated with Muhammad, put so to speak on the same footing, the second of two, called his companion, his friend, for the Arabic term *sahib*[77] has the two meanings. No other Muslim has been the object of such a distinction, and so Abu Bakr had to be ahead of all others.[78] That is how the Hadith thought.

These examples will suffice,[79] we believe, to define the nature and worth of our propositions. They present in a new light the meaning of the sira. The composition of the latter is derived not from two sources, parallel and independent, mutually complementing and controlling each other, but from just one, the Koran, servilely interpreted and developed by the Traditions from preconceived ideas. Thus, the prolix information on the childhood and youth of Muhammad should be relegated to the domain of legend, with the exception of one trait: his being a poor orphan. For the future historians of Muhammad, this view of the subject, if it is well founded, suppresses with one stroke thousands of pages of fanciful documents; it reduces to one line the first thirty years of one of the most extraordinary men of the Orient. The beginning of his prophetic career leads us onto a surface less shifting but always confined to the information he was willing to divulge to us.

During the Medinan period above all, the Koran functions like a diary of his public and domestic life. This infinitely shabby journal records his prejudices, his hates, his political passions, the proof of his conjugal disgraces, his taste for romantic adventures, like the miserable intrigue[80] hatched with Zaynab, the wife of his adopted son, Zayd. Despite the obvious bias of the narrator, this kind of autobiography is of the highest value for us. If only we possessed the key to the enigmatic language[81] in which it finds itself enveloped with innumerable allusions undoubtedly understood only by its contemporaries. Too often, the Traditions, as we saw, were not (or refused to be) better informed than us. On the historical person of Muhammad, on so many points exciting our scientific curiosity to the highest pitch, their interest was only belatedly awakened. Orientalists accord too much honor to the uncouth companions of the Prophet in assuming the opposite. This lovely enthusiasm goes back to the great expansion of Arab imperialism under the Umayyads. Contemporary with the conception of Islam as a world religion,[82] it was principally the work of maulas or foreign neophytes, authors of the entire scientific movement at the heart of Muslim society. Absorbed by more realistic preoccupations, that is, the conservation and extension of the political state founded by Muhammad,[83] his Arab friends showed greater indifference to the science of history. The latter undoubtedly concerned the future of Islam. But we ascribe to them our own ideas when we imagine that they already had thenceforth an inkling of this fact. How do we explain the silence[84] of Abu Bakr, of 'Umar, of Sa'd, when the Hadith overwhelms us with accounts going back to Abu Huraira, to Ibn Abbas, to Ibn 'Umar, all children, or Muslims of recent date? The first companions of Muhammad would have noted the smallest details, encircled the Master with an idolatrous veneration to the extent of holding out a hand to collect his spit![85] But why do we see them showing, on the other hand, such a coldness for the Prophet's family? Apart from Zaynab, his daughters had difficulties in establishing themselves; several of his grandchildren[86] died in obscurity. After the surrender of Mecca, nobody dreamt of returning him his house, confiscated by Aqil.[87] Throughout the first century, his tomb was neglected, and they auctioned off the bier that had been used to carry him in to the earth. On his death, his most intimate friends, Abu Bakr and 'Umar, abandoned the corpse of the Master, and left it without a burial place, in a hurry to ensure his political succession. Neither Sa'd, Abd ar-Rahman, nor several other members of the incomparable group of Mobassara[88] have left any authentic accounts. The Hadith itself recognizes the fact. These people, the traditions, affirm were afraid of making a mistake; they felt a repugnance for writing.[89] These pathetic explanations cannot make us blindly accept the improbable assumption on which the whole system of Hadith pretends to rest, namely, the existence of intellectual curiosity, the existence of scientific method,[90] or foresight, such as we do not meet even at the cradle of societies infinitely better endowed. Our textbooks will continue—it is to be expected—to present Islam as a religion born in the clear light of history. The day when criticism will have dismantled piece by piece this enormous machine of Hadith, we will ask ourselves how its heavy mass could have forced acceptance of it for such a long time.

At the beginning of the second century of the Hijra, when the broad outlines of the sira were established, the editors grappled with the suras of the Koran, trying to get clear the meaning, to sprinkle dates and proper nouns everywhere, getting help, if necessary, from the context and from certain memories more or less accurate. The latter advantage is the only one they could appeal to us with, had they but known how to calm their prejudices. Product of this exegesis, proceeding at random, the sira remains to be written, just as the historical Muhammad remains to be discovered. Will we ever succeed in achieving this? I confess to sharing, on this issue, the doubts of the Nestor of our discipline, Noldeke.

Does that mean that henceforth we no longer need to draw upon the vast reservoir of the Hadith? Such is not our opinion. But on having recourse to this murky source, one should do it with the distrust demanded by the nature of these apocryphal documents. In their inspiration they are, incontestably, literary forgeries. On the other hand, this collection includes numerous portions of historical truth, without us yet possessing the secret of filtering out the suspect material. Let us continue, then, to use this contribution, but only to correct the partial conclusions in step with progress in Islamic studies. Instead of the solid portrait painted by Caussin de Perceval and Sprenger, and Muir, we must provisionally make do with a pale sketch. Artists may regret its loss. We shall repeat with the Koran: "Truth has come and Falsehood has been overthrown. Falsehood is ever bound to vanish" (sura 17:81). Tradition puts these words in the mouth of the Prophet at the very moment he had knocked over the picturesque pantheon of the Qurayshites. They will form the conclusion of this critique of the sources of the sira.

NOTES

1. I. Goldziher, *Muhammedanische Studien*, 2 vols. (Halle, 1889–90).

2. "Because in my riper years I no longer venture to enquire into the personality of Muhammad," as he expressed himself in *WZKM*, t.XXI, p. 298, no. 3.

3. The author of one of the oldest and most popular biographies of the Prophet.

4. We have every right to expect considerable research, so happily inaugurated among us, by the late K. Vollers and by Professor R. Geyer. [R. Geyer, "Zur Strophik des

Qurans," *WZKM* 22 (1908): 265–86; Geyer, Rezsension Uber: Karl Vollers, *Volkssprach un Schriftsprache in alten Arabian* (Strassborg, 1906).—Trans.]

5. Thus they give the impression of being reluctant to reproduce the words of Muhammad in their lists, where they confess artlessly to having forgotten the references. Muslim critics have been long since suspicious of these infantile ruses; Ibn Qutaiba, *Oyoun al akhbar*, p. 444. Orientalism has often shown itself more confident.

6. Cf. the excellent introduction of Professor E. sachau to volume 3 of Ibn Sa'd's *Tabaqat*, Leiden, in the course of being published.

7. Cf. Ibn al-Jawzi, *Wafa* (ms. Leiden), pp. 11a, 12a–b.

8. Professor Goldziher gave a paper on this subject at the last Orientalist Congress in Copenhagen (1908).

9. See the *Khasais*, a category of works giving details of the special privileges of Muhammad; e.g., Ibn Aqila (Asir effendi, Constantinople, no. 66), Pseudo-Waqidi (Berlin, ms. no. 9548), p. 1a, Maqrizi, *Imta* (ms. Kuprulu, Constantinople). The pages of the majority of the manuscripts are not numbered.

10. The word "light" is here synonymous with the Koran: "a light for the lost," or "on the right path" as Muhammad says. Cf. Koran, suras 3: 186; 5:15; 4:176; 35:24; 64:8

11. Cf. Ibn al-Jawzi, *Wafa,* pp. 83a, 94a. Suyuti, *Khasais al Kubra* (ms. Berlin) pp. 47a, 52a. Darimi (ms. Leiden) *Musnad*, p. 102b. An Nisai, *Sunan* (ms. Nouri Otmani, Constantinople).

12. Ibn al-Jawzi, *Wafa*, p. 32a; idem, *Talqih* (ms. Asir effendi, Constantinople), II, p. 3a; Anonymous, *Sira* (Berlin, no. 9602), p. 155a; al-Barizi (Berlin, no. 2569), p. 81b; Maqrizi, *Imta*, III; Sibt ibn al-Jawzi, *Mirat at az-zaman*, II (ms. Kuprulu, Constantinople), p. 149 b.

13. The similarity with the Paraclete announced by Christ.

14. Cf. sura 30:4. We are quoting the local lithographed edition.

15. This is how Mughlatay, *Isara* (ms. Omoumiya, Constantinople) argues to establish his figure for the age of the Prophet: "Each prophet attains half the age of his predecessor; now Isa (Christ) lived 125 years!" Conclusion: Muhammad would have attained 62 and half years!

16. The poetical borrowing is confessed to by Ibn Yosri, *Istiab* (ms. Nouri Otmani, Constantinople).

17. Cf. Ibn Hanbal, *Musnad*, III, pp. 143, 12, and the *Sahih*. Darimi, *Musnad*, p. 63a.

18. He was in danger of being killed. Once more a recollection of the sura 8:30: "They thought of killing you."

19. Sura 111:1. He was allied to the clan of Umayyads, for which the Tradition had little sympathy for having evicted the parents of Muhammad. The Tradition exploited this fact.

20. Sura 25:31.

21. Cf. *Jami al-Fawaid* (ms. Berlin) p. 146b.

22. Sura 8:35

23. E.g., the angels, daughters of God. Cf. suras 52:39, 53:11.

24. Cf. the author's *Etudes sur le règne du calife Mo'awia*, I, (Beyrouth, 1908). The references will be found there on p. 77.

25. Sura 16:59.

26. Ibn al-Jawzi, *Talqih*, II, pp. 5b, 6b.

27. Cf. Berlin, ms. no. 296b. Treatise on the children of Muhammad, Qudai, *Oyoun* (ms. Omoumiya, Constantinople).

28. Sura 108:3

29. Suras 9:55, 69, 85; 18:39, 46; 23:55; 26:88, 134, and so on.

30. E.g., suras 53:6, 7; 73:1, etc.; 74:1, etc.; 81:23.

31. Cf. Maqrizi, *Imta*, 3e part.

32. Cf. *Annali dell'Islam*; Tome III of which I have been able to read the proofs.

33. As confirmed by the anonymous Paris manuscript no 5094, p. 3b.

34. Sura 33:6, 36.

35. Cf. Maqrizi, op. cit.; Ibn al-Athir, *Jamaial al-Usul* (Paris, ms. no 728), p. 130a.

36. Waqidi, Wellhausen, p. 145.

37. Sura 8:42–44.

38. The episode of the rain, the mysterious sleep, that took place unexpectedly at the height of the battle, are all equally legends of Koranic origin (sura 8:11). God must "have sent the rain to strengthen the feet" of the faithful (Koran, loc. cit.), that is to say, encourage them. The Tradition, seeing only the material or literal sense, solemnly report how the sand was hardened under the feet of the Muslims but changed into mud for the Qurayshites.

39. Uhud being the Qurayshite revenge for Badr, the number of Muslims killed was seventy, against the seventy Meccans killed at Badr. Obviously arbitrary figures, and the parallel is suspect!

40. [Tolbiac (present day Zulpich, west of Bonn) was the site of a famous victory of the Franks of the Rhine over the Alamans in 496 C.E.—Trans.]

41. Transposed to Badr by the *Musnad* of Ibn Humaid (ms. Sainte Sophie, Constantinople).

42. Sura 9:41–46, 81, 83, 86–87, 91–94, 118. These texts betray the discontent of Muhammad.

43. Cf. Baghdadi, *Nasikh wa Mansukh*, Berlin ms., e.g., pp. 23a, 35a.

44. Literally, the describers; they formed the counterpart of the *nassaba* or secular genealogists.

45. Author of a *Shama'il*.

46. They thought here of sura 68:4. In fact this text is quoted in a *Shama'il* (Nouri Otmani, Constantinople, ms. no. 750).

47. Cf. *Khalq an-Nabi* (ms. Leiden) pp. 118, 385–86; here we find examples of this process.

48. Cf. *Shama'il*, ms. Nouri Otmani, quoted above.

49. E.g., this chapter of *Khalq*, p. 382: "How the ground opened to receive his excrement and how it retained the perfume of musk."

50. Suras 33:46, 17:52.

51. Cf. *Khalq*, pp. 312–13.

52. Cf. the *Sahih* or six authentic collections; this seal bore the inscription "Muhammad the apostle of God," *Khalq*, p. 324.

53. The tiny opening sura "*Fatiha*" would contain at least "10,000 mysteries." Cf. the commentary on the Koran by Ibn 'Umar Ar Razi. Paris ms. no 613.

54. Sura 6:12, cf. 2:21, 10:39.

55. Darimi, *Musnad*, ms. Leiden, p. 212b. Other evidence: placard in complicated calligraphy written out by Muhammad; ibid., p. 233a.

56. Cf. suras 25:5; 29:48.

57. Muslim orthodoxy is equally inspired by sura 26:48. This passage only affirms that Muhammad has not consulted a *kitab*, book, that is to say, a previous revelation. This same applies to sura 42:52: "you were unaware of the book or faith [you knew nothing of scripture or faith]."

58. Sura 36:69.

59. The putative evidence of these scenes carelessly recall the verses of the Koran, attesting to the poetical ignorance of the Master. Impossible to betray oneself with more ingenuity.

60. Cf. Lammens, *Mo'awia*, pp. 366–74.

61. Cf. Darimi, *Musnad*, pp.119b, 120a.

62. Sura 25:32.

63. Cf. sura38:18–19.

64. Utilized in the editing of *Khasa'is*.

65. Cf. Suyuti, Paris, ms. no. 659, p. 2b. The Hadith seriously discusses the relative superiority of Muhammad and Solomon, the latter having possessed an even larger harem.

66. Haidari, *Khasa'is*; ms. in the Khedive's Library. Al-Baladhuri, *Ansab*, ms. Paris, p. 274a

67. That is the obvious meaning of sura 33:28–29; he offers to them a choice between himself and the outside world, that is to say, freedom. In the latter case he will release them honorably (Arabic: *sirahan jamilan*). This exegesis is already to be found in Nisa'i, *Sunan* (ms. Nouri Otmani, Constantinople), The Book of Marriage.

68. Kuprulu Library, Constantinople.

69. Cf. Ibn Qayyim al-Jawziya, *Zad al-Mo'ad*, ms. Bayazid, Constantinople.

70. Sura 25:7, 20.

71. Sura 21:8

72. Suras 2:167, 171; 7:32, 33; 5:88, 93; 6:117, 118, 141; 57:15.

73. Sura 7:157; 10:91

74. Suras 2:171, 172; 7:160; 8:26; 20:54, 69, 81; 23:51, 81; 16:114; 40:65, etc. Having given up meat, he condemned certain of his companions. "Do like me," he told them. Cf. Nisa'i, *Sunan* (ms. Nouri 'Otmani).

75. Cf. sura 10:59.

76. Sura 9:40.

77. In the Hadith, in speaking of Muhammad, Abu Bakr tends to call him his friend. "If I had to choose a friend, I would take Abu Bakr" is how the Prophet would have put it. All the hadith derive from sura 9:40.

78. Cf. *Jami'al-Usul*, Paris, ms. no. 728, p. 112b sqq.; the *Sunan* of Ibn Maja (ms. Paris), p. 8b; in the *Kitab al Fada'il*, Abu Bakr always leads the way. Cf. *Khasa'is al-Asara* (Berlin, ms. no. 9656), he accords thirty privileges to Abu Bakr, twenty-four to 'Umar, twenty to 'Uthman; 'Ali had to make do with eighteen. This descending order reflects the orthodox point of view.

79. We have given another in *Mo'awia*, pp. 203–208 on the subject of minbar or pulpit. Let us briefly indicate other borrowings. The oath of allegiance of Aqaba is derived from sura 59:9; in verse 12, 60, we find the idea of the pledge of women. The entire episode of the Banu Nadir was taken from sura 59:1–11: their expulsion, the destruction of their houses, the trees chopped down, the promise of help from the Hypocrites. The incident raised by Ibn Ubaiy, during the expedition of Moraisi, comes from sura 58:7–8. The deputations were suggested by sura 60, one of the last of the collection.

80. Now the subject of a novel. Cf. ms. no. 457, p. 1b, Ste-Sophie, Constantinople.

81. I have always sincerely admired the heroism of the translators of the Koran. A good version assumes a profound knowledge of the sira. As the latter is derived in the last resort from the Koran, this is to turn in a vicious circle!

82. Cf. Lammens, *Mo'awia*, pp. 420–27.

83. We hope to show that once the paper presented at the Congress of Berlin (August, 1908) is published. *The Triumvirate of Abu Bakr, Umar, and Abu Ubaida*.

84. This silence embarrasses Tradition.

85. Ibn al-Athir, *Jami ' al-Usul*, no. 728, p. 29b.

86. We mean the children of Zaynab, that is to say, 'Ali and 'Umama.

87. Cf. Lammens, *Mo'awia*, pp. 112–113.

88. Ten Mulims to whom, while still alive, Muhammad had promised paradise. These are the "Evangelized" as d'Ohsson translates literally in his *Tableau général de l'Empire othoman*, I, 300. p. [See glossary.]

89. Cf. Darimi, *Musnad*, pp.50a ff.

90. As the Hadith attests elsewhere (cf. the Six Authentic collections), apart from Abu Huraira, the Meccans and Medinans had lost interest in it, too absorbed in their businesses. Here you have the truth.

Chapter 5

The Age of Muhammad and the Chronology of the Sira

Henri Lammens

I n its efforts to determine Muhammad's age, Muslim tradition has arrived at the following result: the Prophet is thought to have lived from sixty to sixty-five years. Between the minimum of sixty and the maximum of sixty-five years of age can be placed the different solutions adopted by the versions of the sira. With the aid of astronomical calculations, the Egyptian scholar Mahmoud-effendi sets the year of the Hijra as 571 C.E. and gives Muhammad "sixty-one solar years or about sixty-three lunar years."[1] "It is not worth the trouble!" So say some competent judges.[2] If, with Prince Caetani,[3] we accept a possible error of three years for the Prophet's chronology, according to Islamic tradition, astronomy and orientalism, we come back to the outside figures of sixty and sixty-five years of age[4] as barriers that it would be imprudent to cross.

In his very substantial study, *Het Mekkansche Feest* (The Meccan Festival, p. 66), Professor Snouck Hurgronje notes the prejudices that have distorted the chronology of the sira. According to him, "the question should be submitted to a detailed examination." Is it possible to find a definitive solution? I do not think so any more than he does. But it does seem worthwhile to show the inconsistency of the traditional opinion. More research must be done and in another direction from what has been done thus far.

Muhammad himself did not know his age and did not seem to worry about

Originally published in *Journal Asiatique* (March–April 1911): 208–50. Original translation of text by anonymous, notes translated by Ibn Warraq.

it.[5] This would be easy to prove, since calculation according to year was practically unknown to him as it was to the pre-Islamic Arabs and Companions of the Prophet, all indifferent to chronology.[6] Tradition thought it must attribute this concern to them and this, just when chronological discussions began to assume some importance in the young empire.[7] At that time, care was taken to date the principal facts of the sira with the same preoccupations that had strangely disfigured the legend of the Prophet. Just as proper names had been hastily added everywhere, there was a will to arrive at a variety of precise figures. This arithmetic is worth no more nor less than the whole of Muhammad's life.

Even if one admits the existence of direct testimonies in chronological matters, one must take into account the very different mentality of two generations, that is, the one that gave the testimonies and the one that collected and interpreted them. The former never thought of the importance of a chronology. But, not wanting to be outdone, when questioned by the tabi'is, these men gave any answer at random.

The tab'is and their successors took it upon themselves to elaborate into a real chronological system the vague details and *rudis indigestaque moles* (shapeless, uncoordinated mass)[8] provided by their elders.

Tradition has generally opted for "the year of the Elephant"[9] as the point of departure; it probably represented the year of Muhammad's birth. To what precise fact does this strange designation correspond? Might it not derive in the last analysis from the Koran (sura 101:1)? Given the dependence of the sira on the sacred text (Koran), one always has the right to suspect such a relation.

If this connection were to be positively excluded, then the date of the Elephant might answer to a concrete reality. Some ancient lines which are sufficiently authentic might lead us to accept that.[10] But, in any event, it becomes impossible[11] to line up the date with our era.

To add to the confusion, tradition hesitates when it dares to specify the exact relation between the date of the Elephant and the birth of Muhammad. An anonymous synopsis of the sira[12] sums up the diverse opinions thus: "The Prophet is supposed to have been born that very year, fifty days or two months after the departure of the Elephant, or even ten, fifteen, or even twenty years later." Fayumi[13] also mentions an opinion that admits of a ten-year interval between the two events.[14] That gives us considerable latitude.

All we need to excite our suspicion is to come up against the abuse of parallel and symmetrical numbers in the versions of the sira.[15] It is impossible to juggle more naively with figures.[16] Let us take a few examples. They will be chosen preferably among the persons in intimate contact with the Prophet.

Thus, Khadija is said to have given him four sons and as many daughters.[17]

At the death of Muhammad, Aisha's eighteen years are divided in this way: nine years before and nine years after her marriage.[18] According to certain biographers, the twenty years of the Prophet's career were divided in two equal sections: ten years at Mecca, ten years at Medina. Others, while they accept twenty-three years for this period, distinguish ten years at Mecca and ten years at Medina. During those twenty years, he remained under the influence of Gabriel;[19] during the three preceding years, Asrafil is said to have played this role.[20] This strange opinion, which is considered as such by many exegetes,[21] is indicative of the attraction exerted by parallel numbers. The two Qurayshite contemporaries of Muhammad, Hakim ibn Hizam and Huwaytib ibn Abdul'uzza,[22] as well as the Ansarian poet, Hassan ibn Thabit, are said to have lived, all three of them, sixty years before and after Islam.[23] The same particularity is reported of Adi ibn Matim, 'Abd Hayr ibn Yazid, and Salma ibn Naufal. It would be amusing to complete the series, if the game were worth playing.[24]

While accepting these 120 years on trust, some Muslim authors have admitted that it was impossible to come to the right number for Hassan.[25] If only they had taken their investigations further! Dahabi did so, concerning Salman al-Farisi, an even more wonderful specimen of longevity or of Mu'ammaroun, as these Arab Methusalehs are usually called. They would without doubt have arrived at the same result. Having noted the unanimity of the tradition that grants Salman a minimum of 150 years of age, Dahabi does not hesitate to confess: "When I wanted to control the results, I could not go beyond the figure 80."[26] Besides, we know to what end Hakim ibn Hizam and the poet Hassan have been made older. The former had to be made to narrate the scene in which 'Abd al-Muttalib realized he was about to sacrifice Abdullah, Muhammad's father.[27] Hassan had to be there to attest the appearance of the star of Ahmad, the counterpart of the star of the Magi.[28] They all had to be able to add: *wa ana a'qil*, "I had attained the age of reason." Another personage—he will be discussed later— Qabat ibn Asiam, had seen with his own eyes the greenish turd left in Mecca by the Abyssinian elephant.[29] Unfortunately, Hakim later used the excuse of his youth to explain why he had not embraced Islam sooner: "I had before me," he said, "the example of the old Qurayshites, all attached to their errors."[30] If, as has been asserted, he was born in the year 12 or 13 before the Elephant, at the time of the vocation, *mab'ath*, of Muhammad, he would have been over fifty. We can see the value of these calculations, as well as how little the Tradition cares about being consistent.

In the chronology of the Prophet, one can discover everywhere similar methods and the influence of symmetrical figures. For Muhammad's age, the number 60 was once accepted as a minimum,[31] and it was broken down as follows: 40 years before the vocation + 10 at Mecca + 10 at Medina.[32] If certain authors pronounce in favor of 13 years at Mecca, they bring in Asrafil and Gabriel to reestablish the symmetry between the 10 years in Mecca and those in Medina,[33] or else they assign—against the usual opinion—13 years to the period at Medina.[34]

Everywhere they take the utmost care to preserve symmetry.[35] That gives us for Badr seventy dead and seventy prisoners.[36] To the seventy Qurayshites killed at Badr will correspond the seventy Muslims who fell at Uhud,[37] the Meccan revenge for Badr. In seventies, too, the Ansars count their dead, as at Bir Ma'ouna, in the Islamic battles.[38] The sieges of the little Jewish settlements of the oasis of Medina last two weeks; those much greater of Khaybar and Taif about twice as much time, that is, a month! Such are the requirements of parallelism.[39]

It is generally supposed that Muhammad was about fifty years old at the time of the Hijra. When it wants to be precise about this figure the Tradition starts to hesitate between fifty-three and fifty-five, corresponding to the uncertainties about the Prophet's age at the moment of his death—sixty-three or sixty-five years.[40] As Grimme[41] observes, the latter figure has the weaker guarantee, if one can talk about guarantee in this matter.[42]

But this figure sixty-three rouses certain legitimate objections. It reappears in the annals of early Islam with the regularity of a cliché. One day in the pulpit the caliph Mu'awiya is supposed to have said: "I have just reached my sixty-third year, the age at which Muhammad and his first two successors died."[43] He could have added the names of his rival 'Ali[44] and the other great Companions, their contemporaries, aged "around sixty or seventy years"[45] at their death. On the other hand, in the style of the sira the first approximation is often calculated and laid down as sixty-three years.[46] All this shows the usual horror of accurate research. So the figure sixty-three years must be accepted with reservations.

The figure sixty-five years is perhaps no better founded. It was the age of Khadija and other wives of the Prophet;[47] in fact, it was a new transcription in figures of the traditional formula "sixty or seventy years," and a way of covering up the ignorance in which one found oneself over the chronology of the heroic age. That was what was done for Bilal, the freed slave and friend of Abu Bakr.[48] When one wants to get to the bottom of certain calculations registered by the sira, one often finds the combination sixty, sixty-three, and sixty-five.[49] According to an odd text cited by Ibn Sa'd, "a century amounted to one hundred and twenty years. The Prophet received his mission in the century whose last year saw the death of Yazid, son of Mu'awiya."[50] As this caliph died between sixty-three and sixty-five of the Hijra, our author must have thought of these numbers. Similarly, to verify his theory on the extent of a century, he seems to have limited himself to doubling the figure sixty. In his eyes the main importance of these numbers was to produce as many evaluations of the Prophet's age.

The only people who dare mention a figure for the life of Muhammad are not only suspect authorities, but they only knew him at the end of career. This is the case for Aisha and Ibn Abbas.[51] The witnesses of his first preaching generally avoided committing themselves definitely, or else they got out of it by playing on the double meaning of *kabir*: "Which of you or the Prophet was the elder?" they asked his son-in-law 'Uthman. He replied: "The Prophet was the greater, but I was the senior in years."[52] This reply must have seemed very witty because it was often repeated. According to the Tradition it was given to the same 'Uthman by a Sahabi[53] called Qabat ibn Asiam of the Banu Amru ibn Layt and later again by Qabat, to the caliph 'Abd al-Malik.[54] We are bound to make Muhammad younger or Qabat older beyond the limits of human life. Even if he placed this conversation in the first year of Abd al-Malik's caliphate, Qabat ought to arrive at one hundred and ten years. But hasn't one made the poet Nabigha al-Ja'di the contemporary of the great Nabigha al-Dhubyani and Akhtal?[55]

In the whole of the sira only one piece of information seems acceptable—the ten years that elapsed between the Hijra and the death of Muhammad. Even then, according to an opinion mentioned by Maqrizi,[56] these years should be reduced to eight, or reckoned as thirteen, to correspond with another recorded earlier.[57]

The Prophet is said to have died at Medina, on the 13 of Rabi 1, in the eleventh year of the Hijra, that is, 8 June 632.[58] That would fix the date of his arrival in that town at about 622 of our era. These are two dates, 622, 632, which deserve to inspire confidence of a relative kind. As for the earlier time, the Meccan period remains wrapped in the thickest obscurity. To disperse it one frequently has recourse to the line of a certain Sirma on the subject of Muhammad[59]: "He stayed among the Quraysh preaching for some ten years, trying to find a believer, a companion."

One could discourse at length on this disconcerting expression: *bida' 'ashara sana*. It would no doubt overvalue the expression. The examples quoted above[60] allow one to guess at the elasticity of the word *bida'*. This means in the style of the sira more than one and less than ten.[61] Did Sirma want to contain in it another meaning? A very improbable supposition where it is a question of figures in an Arabic poet. At this period and in the same company don't we see Hassan ibn Thabit substituting one proper name for another that did not go so well in the verse meter?[62] But in the shortage of solid information, the curiosity of the biographers has taken hold of the line of Sirma,[63] each one adapting it to his own chronological system.[64]

One tradition attributed to Ibn Abbas[65] speaks of the "fifteen years and more as the time taken by the revelation received at Mecca." Another[66] reduces this period to eight years.[67] With good reason, no doubt, the sira distinguishes between the beginning of this revelation and that of the public preaching. The poem of Sirma neglects this distinction.

It is impossible to ignore the inconsistency of the figures for the whole of the Meccan period. Only the length of time of the Medinan episode was well known enough: ten to eleven years or "around ten years" as it was perhaps reckoned.[68] According to the system of arithmetical parallelism,[69] it has been immediately applied to the earlier period. The Ansar poet, if he ever existed, probably had no other information.[70] The muhaddith used him as an authority.[71] According to their rather rough way of interpreting[72] "around ten years" they arrived, by adding the ten or eleven Medina years, at the figures of twenty, twenty-three, or twenty-five years. This led to the vocation of Muhammad. Forty years remained to be found. In their distress the traditionalists made use of the phrase in the Koran addressed by Muhammad to the Qurayshite in a Meccan sura:[73] "Earlier I stayed among you for the space of one *'umur* ('umuran)."[74] To back their calculation, they decided (a) that the word "earlier" covered the time between the birth and vocation of Muhammad, and (b) the term *'umur* corresponded exactly to forty years. They thus arrived at the total of sixty to sixty-five years, according to the particular interpretation given to the line of Sirma.[75] How can one remain unaware of the feebleness of all this argumentation? If the Koranic verse has any meaning, it must be the following: "I stayed among you a long time."

The term *'umur*, with or without the article, occurs again and again in the Koran, always with the meaning of human life, existence, or generation;[76] that is, it represents an indeterminate period, as understood by the Arabs of those days and of now, only moderately in favor of calculation by years. Years interested them less than seasons, those natural divisions of the civil or astronomical years. They had practically forgotten about the latter, and for them the term *sana* had become synonymous with famine and stress.[77]

The Koran frequently mentions years. It says they are determined by the progress of the sun and the moon.[78] But, apart from this indication, it prefers to leave an indefinite value to this measure of time. It likes to borrow from the Bible the expression "a thousand years,"[79] more rarely "a hundred years"[80] to indicate a vague period. From the same source it has borrowed the forty years spent in the desert by the Israelites.[81] Elsewhere it places at the end of the same lapse of time the full moral development of man when there arises in his soul the feeling of his responsibility and his religious needs.[82] The Tradition may have thought of this verse when, to give a precise timing for a similar phenomenon in the Prophet's life, it gave this numerical value to the word *'umur*. All hypotheses are allowed in this masterpiece of subtlety that is the hadith.[83] Add the seven years of abundance and famine in Egypt (sura 12:47), those years spent by the Seven Sleepers in their cave, where the Tradition manages to hesitate between the figures 103 and 112 years.[84] Noah spent "1000 years less 50" evangelizing his contemporaries (sura 29:13).

Apart from these cases, Muhammad, just as he always avoided mentioning proper names in his revelations, refused to supply figures. The vague words "years, a few years" were enough for his imprecise mind. It was the length of time given by him for Joseph's time in prison, and to that of Moses in the country of Madian and in Egypt.[85] The number of months, he declares, is twelve[86]—the object of this remark is to exclude the *nasi,* or intercalary month (sura 9:37), but in no place does he add that this total constitutes a year.[87] Why should he have done so? The Arabs undoubtedly observed the measures of time which we call days, months, and years. In their eyes the latter have kept a mainly theoretical value. They bring back to them periods[88] of ill fortune, or the return of the time of the annual pilgrimage. Hence came among their ancient poets the frequent use of the word *hijja* instead of year, a term that they had avoided.

On the other hand, they insist on the opposition of day to night. They like to mark this continuing alternation, and the regular, uninterrupted succession of the seasons. These alone had a practical significance for these realists, for this race of shepherds, caravaneers, and perpetual nomads before Allah: "From the movement of the stars they calculate an abstract time that is abstract and stagnant, whose movement displaces nothing on this motionless earth" (*Viconte de Vogué, Syrie, Palestine, Mont-Athos,* 1876.). The calendar loses its value for these men who are in permanent contact with the changeless desert. If they are interested in meteors in the sky, it is in connection with their livelihood, their own survival and that of the herds. These preoccupations made them indifferent to the exact measure of time. The latter does not represent money in their eyes. They do worry about leaving or arriving several days late. Only one delay seems to them relevant—that of the *rabi',* [spring, springtime, also the name of the third and fourth months of the Muslim year] on which their existence depends.[89]

One has only to open the Koran to be convinced of this. Many passages reveal a fervent but naive observation of nature. When listing the signs (Arabic = *aya*) of divine power, the Koran comments often with satisfaction on the way day follows night, on the sun and the moon obliged by Allah to follow their course and so distinguish time,[90] or, as the text puts it, to teach men "the number of years and their calculation."[91] The Prophet cannot wax enthusiastic enough on this rule of Providence, "effacing the vision of night to replace it by the brilliant vision of day, during which the faithful[92] must enjoy the generosity of their Lord" (sura 17:13). Like all artists of limited literary inventiveness,[93] he constantly returns to this theme. He shows God "folding day over night and night over day" (sura 39:7), forcing the sun and the moon to play their part.[94] He swears by these meteors just as he would swear by the Creator.[95] He shows far less interest in the months and the years, mere artificial divisions and chronological units that made too little impression on his intelligence to have made their mark.

The ancient poets[96] felt just the same. They expressed the same admiration before the double phenomenon of night and day, always ancient, always new, *al-jadidan* (meaning "the two new ones").[97] The bards of the desert liked to cast a melancholy glance on their past. This past they never saw as a procession of years. As their imagination did not react positively to this abstraction, they talked about the succession of days and nights. These had taken away their youth and devoured their strength.[98] And yet they found consolation for this. Did not day and night once triumph over the sage Luqman? Dhu 'l-Isba', one of the most ancient of these poets, declared unequivocally: Man succumbs to the combined assault of day and night.[99] Our whole mortal existence here below is reduced to two days—even less, to one day and one night! These two enemies, without growing older, see everything age and perish around them.[100] They have laid low the peoples of Ad and Thamud, Himyar [South Arabians], Tubba' [ancient kings of South Arabia], and Odaina [Odaenathus, d. 267 C.E.], the powerful lord of Palmyra. Against their attacks, the hero remains disarmed; the most powerful fortresses cannot hold out. Don't they possess the key of all the locks?[101]

So it seems hard to deny—the ancient Arabs were not familiar with calculation in years. In the division of time they mainly used the smallest unit. For them the usual time measures remained the day.[102] Except for this point of reference the passage of time seemed like the desert, a space without signposts or interruptions, which their intelligence did not trouble to fathom. Why did their poets not always show the same reserve? The value of years escaped them entirely. That is why they assert brazenly that they have lived for hundreds of years:[103] three hundred years, four hundred years have passed them by, and they are still waiting,[104] older than Alexander the Great and tired of dyeing their beards![105] At the same time, they fortunately admit to seeing double.[106] When it came to the notion of time, they ought to have said five times!

Nothing entitles us to count on the Koranic verse (sura 10:17)—'umur can mean twenty, twenty-five, or thirty-five or forty years, or more simply, a period of undetermined length. But at the time when the composition of the sira was getting settled, a need for definite solutions was being felt. The contact with the "possessors of the writings" had shown the existence of a firm chronology everywhere. One did not want to be left behind. This need gave *ahl*, one of the synonyms of *'umur*, the meaning of sixty years. After having composed the hemistich, *thalathat ahlin afnaytuhum* (I destroyed them for three *ahl*),[107] the poet Nabigha al-Ja'di was entitled to one hundred and eighty years. One of his colleagues was given one hundred and twenty years "for having worn out three turbans!"[108] All this lexicographical exegesis has the same value: whethas *'umur*, *ahl*, *'amama*, one always comes back to the parallel figures of forty or sixty years. This insistence on years contrasts with the practice of the ancient sira where they seem to be ignored,[109] and months are preferred. During the Medina period, instead of dating events by the second, third, or fourth years of the Hijra, they talk of the twentieth, twenty-seventh, thirty-third, forty-seventh, or fifty-ninth month since the *mahjar* (emigration) of Muhammad.[110]

So once again we catch the Tradition following its usual procedure. To form its opinion, it does not explore the memories of contemporaries but instead poetry and the Koran. To wish to confirm by these two sources the conventional indication of the sixty/sixty-five years is to upset the procedure. It is to imitate the authors of the sira. In their ignorance they were at pains to go through the Book of Allah and the collections of poetry,[111] when they were not giving the impression, with the help of Hadith manufactured ad hoc, of drawing directly on the stock of contemporary witnesses. To sum up, the line of Sirma, the verse in the Koran (sura 10:17), the period of ten years in Medina—with these three elements of unequal value the problem of Muhammad's age was solved. They managed to proceed in an even briefer way without giving up the system of geometrical numbers. The prophetic period was simply divided into two more or les equal sections. Then, for the whole time before the *mab'ath* or vocation, it was decided to double the twenty years obtained in the first calculation. The result gave sixty, sixty-three, or sixty-five, according to the more or less liberal interpretation of the term *bida'*, supplied by Siram Abu Qays.

What should one think of the poetic contribution of Sirma? First of all, the authorship is uncertain. The honor has also been accorded to Hassan ibn Thabit. Ibn Hisham[112] admits that some verses of the Taghlibite Afnun (real name Suraim ibn Ma'sar) may have been introduced into the qasida [ode] of Sirma. Suraim, Sirma, the confusion is easy. The existence of Sirma[113] is no more proven than the authenticity of his verses.[114]

In the sira there is nothing suspect like those stories of hanif with their inventions and boring developments. Now, Sirma happens to be one of those vague people, invented for the needs of the cause, and destined to act as precursors of Abul Qasim [Muhammad, the Prophet] and encourage belief in the existence of a Hanifite cult mentioned by the Koran. Neither his name nor his kunya nor those of his father are fixed.[115] Was he an Awsite (of the Aws tribe) or Khazrajite (of the Khazraj, one of the two chief non-Jewish Medinan tribes)? Does Sirma represent one or two inhabitants of Medina?[116] One does not know. The fact that they wanted to attach him to the Medinan clan of the Banu Najjar proves above all the well-known devotion of the latter to the cause of Islam. His curriculum vitae is no better elucidated, apart from the generalities attached to all the hanif.[117] He is generally said to have died in the first year of the Hijra.

More or less consciously Sirma has been mixed up with other hanif of Medina, like Abu Qays ibn al Aslat, all just as mythical,[118] and also authors of verses dedicated to Muhammad. The Tradition here betrays its dependence on poetry. When this is missing the Tradition does not hesitate to invent it.[119] The *Sira* of Ibn Hisham teems with apocryphal pieces. If one had to list in decreasing order of importance the elements that make up the *The Official Life of Muhammad*, I would give the following list: the Koran, poetry, and oral tradition. One can make an exception for the Medina period where tradition precedes poetry. In any case, Muslim critics have been happy to quote the precious *shawahid* [from Arabic *shahid*, pl. *shawahid*, piece of evidence, or quotation serving as textual evidence] of Sirma and to draw chronological conclusions from it. This preoccupation has prevented them from recognizing in it a disguised satire[120] of Ansarian origin, destined to blight the lack of faith of the Qurayshite rivals.[121] Certain authors of Traditions admit frankly the poetic borrowing. The time that elapsed between the revelation and the Hijra was under discussion. Ibn Abbas favored a period of thirteen years. But the objection was voiced: Urwa ibn Zubayr counts only "ten years." "That is true," said Ibn Abbas, "he was influenced by the opinion of the poet."[122] It is impossible to show more clearly how in its chronological calculations the sira depends on Sirma, even including Ibn Abbas.[123]

In our view a certain prejudice has enormously contributed to distort this calculation and that of the orientalists following in the steps of the Tradition. Without good reason about ten years have been added to the Prophet's existence.

When a man has passed his fiftieth birthday, he generally lacks the illusions or energy necessary to create a new existence. Leaving Mecca involved a last effort of this kind. This consideration did not worry the Tradition, and it bravely dated the Hijra in the fifty-third or fifty-sixth year of the Prophet. Study of the sira leaves a rather contrary impression. At his death Muhammad felt himself to be in the prime of life and was surprised by the event,[124] which was hastened on by his excesses.

One feels convinced of this when one examines the longevity attributed to certain contemporaries and men senior to the Prophet. Among them the number of those who survived him would make one believe that centenarians or near-centenarians were common in the Hijaz. As we have already seen, the Tradition is not frightened by this conclusion. Just like the Bible, it wanted to have its own pre-Islamic patriarchs. The Arab imagination and the boasting of the ancient poets provided material for these legends. They nourished the special literature of the Mu'ammarun (literally, the seniors or elders, that is, those who lived to an old age) to which Muslim apologetics paid an especial interest.[125] Without opening up here a debate on the subject, we ought to examine to what extent the extraordinary longevity of the Companions squares with the hypothesis of a Prophet who died at sixty, as was maintained by current opinion.

On the other hand, there has been a strange bringing together of Muhammad's birth and that of his uncles[126]—Hamza, presented as his foster-brother, and Abbas, destined to survive him by many years. To reduce the distance of age between the two, the Tradition decided to have Abbas born only three years before his nephew.[127] Subtle combinations abound in this masterpiece of ingeniousness called the sira.[128] One is never justified in supposing that any research is disinterested, even when one is not in a position to assign the why and the wherefore of certain assertions, such as the forty years generously accorded to 'Abd al-Muttalib.[129] The Tradition has never operated blindly, but always with a fixed aim in view. It is the task of the critic to uncover gradually these particular aims or tendencies.

We now know what series of calculations led to the prolonging of Muhammad's career up to his sixties. This conclusion, erected into historical dogma, is the source of all our troubles. It has given rise to the most frightful chronological muddle. Furthermore, for the needs of the cause, the sira decided to push forward the birth of several Companions. Their evidence was indispensable to support the reality of some miraculous deeds. Also, as these people survived the Master by many years, one sees how the considerable number of nonagenarians and centenarians came into being in the early annals of Islam. An error in history never stands alone. The sira did not see, or refused to see, this complication.

Among these witnesses, thus made older, let us name—'Ammar ibn Yasir, born the same year[130] as the Prophet; Sulayman ibn Surad, the head of the penitents (or tawwabun in Arabic), who was killed under the caliphate of Marwan I;[131] and Abu Sufyan, one of the accepted chiefs in Mecca, when the Reformer started to appear there, the real shaikh of Quraysh, not only by his influence but by his mature age. Authority was so prized in Arab circles where young saiyd were mistrusted. When mentioning Muhammad, Abu Sufyan gave him the description of nephew,[132] which was a manner of speaking, showing a notable difference in age. There is, moreover, general agreement that he was born in year 10 before the Elephant.[133]

According to one Tradition quoted above, the future caliph 'Uthman was presented as being older than Abul Qasim. Another Tradition, however, makes him born in year 6 of the Elephant.[134] Whatever we may think, there cannot have been a sizeable difference in age between 'Uthman and his father-in-law. A proof of this is the extreme deference shown by the latter for that Umayyad, who was twice his son-in-law. Hakim ibn Hizam was born thirteen years before the Elephant.[135] One can say as much of the freewoman of Umm Ayman, if we want to keep for her the title of governess (*hazina*), of the little Muhammad.[136] Safwan ibn Umaiya and Huwaytib ibn 'Abd al 'Uzza, the two Qurayshite bankers; Qays ibn 'Asim,[137] the well-known saiyd of Tamim;[138] Amru, the future conqueror of Egypt; and the poet Hassan ibn Thabit were either older than Muhammad or his equal in age at the moment they made contact with Islam. Now all these people—some of them were probably born thirteen to fifteen years earlier—survived Muhammad by twenty to forty years, if one believes the Hadith. Some of them, such as 'Adi ibn Hatim, Sulayman ibn Surad, and Qabat ibn Asiam survived him by sixty years.[139]

Hence, it was necessary for the Tradition to make them older. Thus Ammar, Abu Sufyan, Abbas, and 'Uthman were said to have died at over ninety.[140] This assertion does not correspond with the vigor shown by them to the very end of their lives, for example, Abbas at the day of Hunayn, Abu Sufyan at the battle of the Yarmuk, by Ammar ibn Yasir, 'Adi ibn Hatim, and Amru ibn al-Asi al-Siffin. This last one must have carried out the conquest of Egypt[141] on behalf of Mu'awiya at the age of ninety-five. These are a mass of impossibilities. One would reduce them considerably if one made the Prophet younger,[142] as we must in view of other considerations.

When, in the fourth year of the Hijra,[143] perhaps even later, Muhammad proposed marriage to Umm Salama, this widow gave her age as a pretext for turning down the honour. Now the Makhzumite had not reached forty or, more exactly, "some thirty years" according to the hallowed formula. Muhammad replied to her: "I am in the very same boat."[144] In other words, we are more or less of the same age. A mass of indications confirms this interpretation. Thus, her favored position with Muhammad counterbalanced at first that of the seductive Aisha.[145]

At his death, according to the Hadith, Muhammad was corpulent and in all the vigour of his youth, like the youngest of men and the most corpulent.[146] A year before the Bedouin chief Amir ibn at-Tufayl called him "the young Qurayshite *fata min Quraysh*."[147] When he arrived in Medina, according to the Tradition, Abu Bakr[148] was the only old man among all his followers. The youth of Muhammad at the time prevented the Ansars from distinguishing him from his companion. He had no different judgment of himself. At Medina he saw himself one night transported to Paradise. Stopping in front of a palace reserved, he was told, for a young Qurayshite, he thought "it must be for me," when in fact it was an eternal dwelling prepared for his faithful 'Umar.[149]

On the death of the Prophet one could not see more than twenty hairs on his head or his beard.[150] All information agrees on this point. Although the use of dye was recommended by Muhammad himself, he did not live long enough to have recourse to it, since he had not reached that point.[151] To the question, "did the Prophet reach old age?" (*akana shaykhan*) a Sahabi replied, "He was too young to merit this description (*kana ashabb min dalika*)."[152] Unlike other prophets before him, such as Noah and Abraham, he was not counted among the old men.[153] His appearance would have militated against such inclusion. He had just seen the birth of his last son Ibrahim, and had not given up hope of a numerous progeny, that characteristic of the Prophets according to the Koran.[154] Only death prevented him from contracting several new marriages, the fiancées having arrived too late. The end of his career coincided exactly with numerous matrimonial arrangements.

In front of his corpse Abu Bakr, having assured his election to the caliphate, would cry out "Oh my son!" (*wa abnayah*),[155] which does not fit in with the hypothesis of a Prophet over sixty. At the moment of his first arrival at Median after the Hijra, his juvenile appearance would prevent him from being recognized both by the Ansars and the Bedouins,[156] met on the road from Mecca to Medina. To his friend Abu Bakr, mounted tandem behind him, the nomads would invariably ask the same question: "Who, then, is this young man seated in front of you?" In Mecca, at the beginning of his public ministry, the Qurayshites also treated him as *ghulam*[157] (Arabic, youth, boy, but also slave, servant). The Arabs, challenged by him at fairs near Mecca, warned each other, mutually crying out: "Beware of the young Qurayshite!"[158] One can, it is true, interpret the expression *ghulam* as slave. But the orthodox Tradition would hesitate to follow us. Did it not know of the hadith in which Muhammad is supposed to promise to his followers a period of sixty to seventy years[159] as the limits of a normal life? This can explain why, when it is a question of fixing the length of life of the Master, it keeps an equal distance from the two figures. It also explains its efforts to give this deduction the less dubious support of so-called contemporary witnesses.

Let us conclude. Among the traditional figures, the lower ones for the life of Muhammad are the least removed from reality. They should probably be lowered further by about ten years, or even twenty. A curious tradition makes him say: "For each prophet the date of his mission corresponds to half the age of his predecessor. At the beginning of his public life, Isa (Jesus) was forty years old.[160] I was sent at the age of twenty."[161] This is an embarrassing Hadith for the traditional chronology of the sira, so an attempt was made to adapt it by force. It was the aim of the following variant of the same Hadith, quoted from the Iklil: "Every prophet reaches half the age of his predecessor, so Christ lived 125 years (sic)."[162] In describing the farewell pilgrimage, there is the question of determining the number of victims sacrificed by Muhammad. The Tradition hesitates between the following figures: seven, thirty, sixty, sixty-four, and sixty-three. The last "is related to the number of years that the Prophet was supposed to have reached that day. It is symbolic. The other figures show how, after the death of Muhammad, arbitrary decisions were taken on events of which one had no knowledge."[163] With his absence of all historical sense, one was bound to arrive at the answer desired— the average of sixty-three years! But why wouldn't Allah have answered the prayer of his envoy who dreaded above all the humiliation of old age?[164]

In reducing the age of Muhammad by ten years, we finally approach the date indicated by Barhebraeus[165] for his birth—the year 892 of the Seleucids, corresponding to the year 580 of Jesus Christ.[166] So he would not have gone past the age of fifty-two. Primitive Muslim Tradition admitted its inability to fix the exact date of Muhammad's birth. When sixteen or seventeen years after the death of the Master the caliph 'Umar thought of establishing the Muslim era, like us he came up against the same difficulty. As with the Christians his first thought was to fix dates starting from the birth of the religion's founder. If in fact he preferred the departure from Mecca, it was to find a less shaky basis in a more recent event that was observed by many contemporaries.[167]

It remains to throw a rapid glance on the chronology of the sira itself, that is, on the sequence of main events as laid down in the official account of the Life of the Prophet. There is no question of giving each event an exact date. This would involve considering the whole sira in detail. We only want to show by a few examples how in this matter decisions were taken by a priori calculations.

Here again we must regard the Koran[168] as the main inspiration admitting a distinction between the two great periods, that of Mecca and that Medina. In the latter case, even if we regard it as rash to exclude all oral tradition, we must equally guard against exaggerating its importance!

The Meccan period is less easy to tackle.[169] In giving itself the task of filling in the gaps of these years, the sira has consulted the Meccan suras in large quantities, but also the most laconic and poetic of the collection. Their impersonal inspiration makes one regret the drier, more precise revelations of the Medinan writings where fragments of the Prophet's autobiography find a place. The Tradition has exploited the Meccan suras to introduce into this long section of the Master's career some movement and life, a life that is in fact fictitious. We owe a lot of events to this intervention, to this untimely zeal where lack of genuine, direct witnesses is cruelly felt. We have acquired a sort of Gospel of Muhammad's Childhood.

Unlike modern biographers, the most ancient ones like Ibn Ishaq and Ibn Hisham provide few chronological indications for the Meccan period. Usually they are content with general information,[170] such as before or after Muhammad's vocation, or the emigration to Abyssinia. This reserve shows how uncertain they found the material. Their successors wanted absolute precision. At fifty years and three months, Muhammad received the visit of the Nisibe jinn. At fifty-one years and nine months, he did the night journey or Isra.[171] Such precison cannot inspire confidence.

The marriage with Khadija and the long-winded legend came out of the same workshop. This Qurayshite woman could have been the grandmother of Muhammad in a country where there were grandmothers at twenty-two years of age. Why does no Koranic verse, no poem of the period or of the Umayyad era come to vouch for the existence of this great businesswoman (Arabic, *tajira*), as the sira called her? The latter conveniently hesitates when there is a question of deciding the date of this marriage and the respective ages of the couple. The difference between the figures given go from twenty to twenty-eight years.

There is the same uncertainty for the years of birth of the Prophet's children and the order of their coming into the world. Let us leave aside Qasim, whose personality is based above all on the Abul Qasim kunya of the Prophet. Thus from the name of Abu Talib, uncle of Muhammad, we have deduced the existence of a son called Talib, whom we can find nowhere. For the daughters we are luckier. The most widespread view among the orthodox consists of presenting Zaynab as the eldest. Fatima must have been the youngest. The greatest difference of view reigns on the subject of Ruqayya and Umm Kulthum. Why was it agreed to regard Zaynab[172] as the oldest daughter? Because she appears to have been the first to find a husband. Muhammad (so the Tradition makes out) no doubt started by marrying off his eldest daughter. In the case of Fatima, a similar argument caused her to be declared the younger daughter of Abul Qasim. This child, who was not very gifted, had to wait until after Uhud before finding a mate. This gave her more than twenty years at the time of her marriage with 'Ali. The conclusion could not satisfy the Shia. The Sunna, less enthusiastic about the 'Alids, were up in arms out of respect for the Master's person. Could it show 'Ali's indifference to the honor of becoming his son-in-law and the father of his grandchildren? Therefore, efforts have been made to make Fatima younger, and for that reason she was placed last in order of daughters. On no account could the fiancée of 'Ali be more than fifteen years old[173]—an enormous age in a country where a daughter should be married between nine and twelve.[174] We shall come back to the children of Muhammad. These indications will be enough to judge the value of traditional information on the respective ages of Muhammad's posterity and on this part of Meccan chronology.

We will leave aside the retreat in the house of Arqam, and the long quarrels of the Qurayshites with Hashimites on the subject of Muhammad. Before examining the chronology of these events, one must establish their historical value. And the emigration into Abyssinia?[175] The sira even talks of a double African emigration. The critics have fortunately simplified this duplication. But the event itself demands further study to allow for criticism of the traditional date, which is in any case very vague, like all the dates of this period.[176]

We are not on more solid ground for the date of the first Muslim conversions: Zayd, 'Ali, Abu Bakr, Sa'd, Ibn Aqi Waqqas. This abundant literary material has been nurtured and perverted by tendentiousness.[177] 'Umar was said to be the fortieth Muslim. One more doubtful figure. With the conversion of Hamza a few days before, it discreetly veils the tardy rallying of these distinguished persons. Every family, every party wanted to have their representatives in the early Islamic church. As no one's title was free from criticism, there was a tacit agreement to let all these pretensions pass without comment. They indirectly protested against the religious indifference of the Qurayshites, a theme exploited by their Ansarian rivals. This whole literature, which was enough to decide the Tradition, explains the success of these chronological combinations and accordingly diminishes their historical value.

Why were the voyage to Taif, the visits to fairs (Arabic, *mawasim*) near Mecca, supposing they occurred, placed a short time before the Hijra? Because it was desirable to leave the Prophet time to carry out a commandment of Allah: "Preach to the mother of cities and her surroundings," before making him take the road to Yathrib (Medina). At the mawasim he was going to meet his future assistants at Medina for the first time. As in a well-organized play this episode had to be brought to the right moment, the natural beginning of the Medinan period.[178]

Eight or ten years? As we have seen, the Tradition decided on the latter figure when the length of the period had to be defined. For the Prophet, who until then had had only one wife, it was the signal for great matrimonial activity. One marriage follows another at short intervals: Aisha, Hafsa, the two Zaynabs. Must one regard it as a simple coincidence if the first marriages tighten his personal links with his two immediate successors? One of the constant preoccupations of the Tradition was to multiply the relations of the "two 'Umars" with the Master. Umm Salama's husband, we know, had been wounded at Uhud. So his widow was married to the Prophet after this battle. Maymuna generally comes last[179] in the series of official wives, "the mothers of the believers," perhaps to give Abbas, who had remarried at Mecca, the chance of playing a part in this event. One wonders whether one ought to reserve the last position to Umm Habiba.[180] Her marriage would have made up the first act in the comedy, performed about the surrender of Mecca, when Abu Sufyan was to figure as one of the main actors. But the sira did not notice the gradual coming together of Abul Qasim and shaikh of Quraysh after the treaty of Hudaybiyya.

The series of great Islamic days usually reads as follows: Badr opens the series, then come Uhud, the siege of Medina and Muta, and the surrender of Medina, Mecca, Hunayn, Taif, and Tabuk. This list can, I think, be kept. Only two names, Badr and Hunayn, are mentioned in the Koran.[181] This text seems also to allude to Uhud and the Khandaq. Uhud having been, as we know, the Qurayshite revenge for Badr, this last battle must have come first. Furthermore, the Koran suggests that this was so. Hunayn and Taif, which can only have happened after the surrender of Mecca, must have followed this event. The incident of the "dissident masjid" must have happened at Tabuk, in order to make it square with the chronology suggested by the Koran where the episode is described at the end of the verses relating to Tabuk.[182] If the conquest of Khaybar follows close on the Hudaybiyya expedition, it is again in virtue of suggestion in the Koran establishing a connection between these two events.

We are no more certain about the times of year or seasons in which these military events took place. Thus, for the siege of Medina by the Qurayshites the Hadith, interpreting the Koran, talks of cold, stormy nights when in other ways it looks as if the harvests had just been gathered in. At Hunayn the temperature seems to have been exceptionally high. Other authorities however indicate rainy weather.[183]

The Muslim scholars, like us, do not know when Muhammad suppressed the *nasi*, or intercalary month. This lack of certainty did not prevent the authors of the sira from adopting a fixed chronology. The months which elapsed before this suppression were denominated as if the suppression had already occurred,[184] and so introduced a new cause for confusion.

The *wufd*, or deputations, of Arabs must have belonged to the last year of the Medinan period. The Koran appears to allude to them in a sura (110) placed at the end of the collection.[185] The Koran, the Tradition, and the critics are all in agreement on this point. This harmony is too rare not to be noticed. If elsewhere it is lacking, this is due to the origin of the sira.

This sira owes its birth not to historical curiosity—a sentiment alien to the Arabs—but to Koranic exegesis. This occupied the attention of the first Muslims. They were keen to lay down the sense of the verses in the book, which had become the code of their political and religious life. The mass of allusions contained in the sacred text gave rise to a crop of anecdotes, all the more exuberant as the generation of the revelations became remote. In the Koran, Allah says to Muhammad: "You have a great character." To this expression we owe the vast library of the Shamail,[186] just to take one example.

Once this critical work was over, one found oneself with a mass of facts relating to the person or deeds of Muhammad. A massive collection indeed, but of a doubtful authenticity because of the prejudices that decided its origin. The idea then arose to collect the narrative sections separately and arrange them under certain headings so as to obtain a consecutive story. The result was the *Kitab al-Maghazi*, or account of Muhammad's campaigns. Since Islam was a fighting religion, this was of capital interest. In the Koran there were many allusions and the reminiscences were relatively recent. The influence of the Gospels encouraged another new move. Muhammad and his first Companions saw the New Testament as a collection of laws, like the Torah, or perhaps like the suras, recalling those of the Koran. By absorbing the Gospels at close quarters, their successors, the Tabiun, found an account of facts and a real life of Christ. They, too, wanted their own biography of Muhammad. To achieve this end, they widened the scope of the *Maghazi*. They enriched the sira with endless anecdotes gathered together by the scholars on the Meccan and Medinan periods that had not yet been used in the *Maghazi*. That is how the sira was put together—as an inspirational work of exegesis instead of a history in the true sense of the word. It was a compilation drawn from the Koranic tafsir and not based on documents gathered for the purpose.

Signs of this origin remain. Often ordinary careful attention is enough to discover the instructional thread, joining these isolated Hadith to the Book of Allah. We have tried to show this elsewhere.[187]

The chronology was bound to show signs of this original fault—it derived mostly from the Koran. Hence its lack of certainty. If proper names, except for two, are lacking in the Book of Allah, the historic events are even more unreliably dated, apart from certain battles and some events of home life. The whole work belongs to the Medinan period.

The Arabs followed the same procedure for secular history. In the numerous *riwayat* (recensions) of the *Kitab al-Aghani* ("The Book of Songs," a vast compilation by the tenth-century Abul Faraj al-Isfahani), the only serious historic nucleus is made up of the ancient verses saved from the wreckage of pre-Islamic literature. They form the only archives of the Arabs (*Diwan al-Arab*), as 'Umar would have called them. The professed oral tradition of the tribes is mixed in with those poetical archives that were entrusted to the memory of the *rawia* (transmitters). Around this solid nucleus there has clustered a mixture of notes and commentaries gathered by the *nassaba*, or genealogists, by the authors of *ayyam an-ans,* or general history (*Days of the Arabs*), and *ayyam al-arab*, or national history (*Days of the pre-Islamic Battle Days*). The orientalists, since Caussin de Perceval, have no allusions about the value of this so-called historical erudition.

Sometimes the poetic quotation serves as a point of departure, but one also finds it mixed into the middle or the end of the narrative, as a confirmation of its authenticity.

Let us not protest at the boldness of this comparison with secular history, as if the Muslims could not treat the life of their Prophet in such an offhand manner! It would be to forget the mentality of the Companions and to give them our conception of history. In their eyes Muhammad was the greatest and the last of the prophets, and his book was the "word of Allah." The whole being reflected in the whole, wasn't the Koran, first of all, required to give information on the life of the author, as the Torah did for the ancient prophets and the Gospels for Christ? When questioned on the battle of Badr, 'Abd ar-Rahman ibn 'Auf sent his questioners back to the Koran. "Read it," he said, "you'll imagine that you were there."[188] The favorite Aisha, when asked to describe her husband's character, was astonished at this unreasonable curiosity: "Aren't you Arabs?" she replied to the group of *tabi'un*. "Open the Koran and you'll find there the portrait of Abul Qasim."[189] Whether they are historical or not, these Hadith are a simple illustration of the procedure followed and of the narrow dependence of the sira on the Koran.

When it is a question of fixing the traits of the historic Master, the oldest traditionalists began by opening this compilation. When they were concerned with the accounts of contemporaries, it was to bring them into line and make them square with the assertions of the book of Allah. When God speaks in the Koran, how can one dare to check this supreme witness with the memories of fallible mortals? As far as the oral tradition of the first-century Hijra is concerned, the narrow limits of the Koran turned into a bed of Procrustes. Even eyewitnesses only saw things through the eyes of Muhammad.[190]

We think that we have made our point on the question of chronology discussed in the previous pages. Truth to tell, we have above all raised some questions and demonstrated the artificial character and absence of critical sense of the systems adopted by the sira. A negative result! May it shake the confidence of criticism in general and rally the scholars to seek the solution in another direction! There can be no question of rejecting the whole en bloc. It would mean sacrificing as well the important nuggets of truth which are mixed in with the rest. Instead of upsetting the massive edifice erected by Tradition, let us be content to dismantle it stone by stone and examine the value of the materials employed. A boring task, but indispensable! Would there be enough left to build a modest monument to the memory of one of the most extraordinary men of the medieval Orient? The material to be examined is so considerable; on the other hand, the work of revision is still too little advanced to allow a definite reply to be given.

NOTES

1. Cf. *Mémoire sur le calendrier arabe avant l'islamisme et sur la naissance et l'age du Prophète Mahomet*, in Académie royale de Belgique, *Mémoires des savants étrangers*, I, XXX, pp.1–45

2. Noldeke-Schwally, *Geschichte des Qorans*, I, 68, n. 2.

3. Caetani, *Annali dell'Islam*, I, 267.

4. "He who says sixty means by tens upto sixty, and he who says sixty-three means all the years together," Ibn al-Jawzi, *Safwat as-Safwa* (ms. Bibliotheque khédiviale), I, 80.

5. Cf. Noldeke-Schwally, loc. sup. cit., WZKM, XIII, 282.

6. In the historical narratives of contemporary Bedouins,dates are always missing. Cf. al-Musil, *Arabia Petraea*, III, 27. For the first century of Islam, compare Wellhausen's remark, "Tageszeiten werden ofters angegeben, Kalenderaten nicht." *Religios-oppositionsparteien*, p. 59 n. 2 [*Die religio-politischen Opposition Sparteien in alten Islam, in Abhandlungen de Koniglichen Gesellschaft der Wissenschaften zu Gottinger 5*, no. 5 (1901). Translated by R. C. Ostle and S. M. Walzes as The Relio-Political Factions of Early Islam (Amsterdam, 1975).—Trans.]

7. See author's article: "Koran and Tradition" [chapter 4 of present volume—Trans.] (originally published in *Recherches de science religieuse*, I, 1910, Jan–Feb., pp. 25–51)

8. [Ovid, Metamorphosis, I, 7.—Trans.]

9. The "*day* of Fil (Elephant)" is also mentioned. Ibn Sa'd, *Tabaq*, I i, 62–63. According to Ibrahim ibn al-Mundir, the master (*saih*) of the famous Bukhari, "no one doubts the date of the elephant." Fayumi, *Al Akhbar al-Mardiya* (ms. 'Asir eff., Constantinople); Tab., *Annales*, I, 966–967.

10. Jahiz, *Haiawan*, VII, 59–60, quotations from poetry.

11. Compare the synchronisms given by Masudi, *Tanbih* (ed. de Goeje), pp. 228–29, 230. Moreover, the Koran presents the fact like a charming fable, as if it were a feature belonging to ancient history.

12. Anon ms. No. 5051, Paris, Bibl.nat., p. 17b.

13. Op. et loc. cit.; Ibn Sa'd, *Tabaq.*, I i, 62, puts "25 nights" between Muhammad and the Elephant, "65 days" more or less after this event; Masudi, *Tanbih*, 228–29.

14. In pre-Islamic history of Mecca there is an attempt to link everything to the date of the Elephant. Maqdisi, *Ansab al-Qorasiyn* (ms. 'Asir eff.) also speaks of a "ten year interval" between the two facts.

15. Cf. Caetani, *Annali*, III, 87, n. 2.

16. Hakim ibn Hazm frees 100 slaves before and after Islam; he takes 100 victims on pilgrimage, uses 100 camels in holy war, etc.

17. Tabari, *Annales*, I, 1767; Qudai, *Oyoun al-Ma'arif* (ms. Omoumiya, Constantinople).

18. Bukhari, *Sahih*, III, 210, 5.

19. Tab., *Annales*, I, 1245–46, 1248–49; Ibn Sa'd, *Tabaq.*, I i, 126–27. The line from Sirma—see below—seems to substantiate this opinion.

20. Same parallelism in the names. Abu Bakr was called Atiq; he had two brothers: Mutaq and Utaiq; Tab., *Annales*, I, 2133–34. The sons of Abu Lahab, said to have repudiated the daughters of Muhammad, were called Utba and Muattib.

21. Cf. loc. cit.

22. Ibn Abdalbarr, *Istiab* (ms. Bibl. kh.), t.I; Maqdisi, *Ansab al-Qorasiyn* (ms. Asir eff., Constantinople); Muslim, *Sahih*, I, 447; *Usd al-ghaba*, II, 40–41, 75; Ibn al-Jawzi, *Montazam*, II, 77b (ms. Asir eff.); *Tab.*, III, 2419, 2324, 2325. In the year 2 A.H. (Muslim), Huwaytib—then 80, according to traditional calculations—accompanies the caravans; Ibn Sa'd, *Tabaq.*, II i, 25, 1.

23. Another poet, the famous 'Umar ibn A.Raba: 40 years of debauchery, 40 years of asceticism; *Aghani*, I, 36, bottom; cf. Noldeke, *WZKM*, XIII, 182–283.

24. Nawawi, *Tahdib*, 416; Tab., III, 2319, 2325, 2351, 2361; Ibn al-Jawzi, *Montazam* (ms. Asir eff) sub anno 68. The Jew Afak, assassinated by Muhammad, is also said to have been 120 years old; Sibt ibn al-Jawzi, *Mirat* (ms. Kuprulu), II, 213. According to the Montazam, sub anno 50 (ms. Omoumiya), Hassan ibn Thabit is said to have lived 104 years, the exact age of his father, grandfather, and great grandfather. It is not known whether he died in 40 or 54 A.H., but the age of 120 years is generally maintained *Istiab*, t.I, entry for Hassan.

25. Ibn al-Athir, *Usd al-ghaba*, II, 41–42 Ibn Sa'd, *Tabaq.*, V, 335 d. 1. Compare the calculations of *Aghani*, IV, 3. Hassan, who died in 40 or 50/54 A.H., is said to have known Nabigha Dhubyani, but cannot have lived 60 years in Islam, as Maqdisi, after many others, assures us, *Ansab al-Ansar* (ms. Omoumiya). At the time of the Hijra, he was in the prime of life. Hasim and Abdul al-muttalib are also said to have reached the age of 130; Baladhuri, *Ansab* (ms. Paris), 37, 45.

26. "I have reconsidered, and it appears that he was not more than eighty years old," Ibn Aqila, *Anwan as sa'ada* (ms 'Asir eff.).

27. Ibn al-Jawzi, *Montazam*, II (ms. 'Asir eff.) 74b, 76a.

28. *Aghani*, IV, loc. cit. Ibn al-Jawzi, *Montazam*, loc. cit.

29. Tab., *Annales*, I, 967; *Usd al-ghaba.*, IV, 189–90.

30. Ibn al-Jawzi, *Montazam* (ms. Omoumiya, Constantinople), sub anno 54. The 60 years spent under Islam are counted "since its appearance (Islam) and propagation," Nawawi, *Tahdib*, 215–216. Hakim ibn Hazim only embraced Islam at the time of the surrender of Mecca.

31. For the significance of this number for the Semites, cf. Vigouroux, *Dict. de la Bible*, s.v. number.

32. Bukhari, *Sahih*, IV, 13 Muslim, *Sahih*, II, 219.

33. Cf. Tab., I, 1248–49. See above.

34. Baladhuri, *Ansab* (ms. Paris), 68–69; Tirmidhi, *Shama'il*, ms. Bibl.khed. Ibn Abdulbarr, *Istiab*, 8a, ms. Bibl.khed.

35. In the sira, the principal events occur on a Monday, the first of Rabi', birth,

death, calling, departure from Mecca, arrival in Medina, etc. Tab., *Annales*, I, 1255; Hanbal, *Musnad,* V, 299; Ibn Sa'd, *Tabaq.*, I i, 62; Qutaiba, *Ma'arif,* 55; Masudi, *Tanbih,* 229, 231.

36. At Uhud, seven Qurayshites and seven Ansars resisted there is absolute equality in praise. Waqidi (Kremer), 287.

37. Yaqubi, II, 46; at Hunayn 70 dead are counted; Ibn Sa'd, *Tabaq.*, II i, 111, d.l., 112, 1.

38. Cf. Waqidi (Wellh.) 153; Ibn Sa'd, *Tabaq.*, II i, 30.

39. For the Pre-Islamic period, 40 years is the length of long wars as distinct from ordinary raids, like the battle of Bakr—Taghlib, that of Ghatafan.

40. Choice of Hadith in Tirmidhi, *Shama'il,* ms. B.Khéd.

41. H. Grimme, *Mohammed,* I, 47, n. 2.

42. Compare al-Biruni, *Chronologie* (ed. Sachau), 30, 7–15.

43. Hanbal, *Musnad,* IV, 96 Tab., *Annales*, I, 2129.

44. Ibn Sa'd, *Tabaq.,* VI, 6 Muslim, *Sahih,* II, 219. However, at the time of the Hijra they gave Muhammad the same age as Abu Bakr. I. Hisham, *Sira,* 334, 7. We shall return to this.

45. Ibn Sa'd, *Tabaq.*, VI, 7: three examples quoted in one page. According to Noldeke-Schwally, op. cit., 122 n.7, 'Ali was only 58 years old. In reality we do not know the year of his birth. The Great Sahabis (Companions of the Prophet), involved with the history of Kufa, were "about 60 or 70 years old" or just simply "70 years old," for variation. Thus Sad ibn Abi Waqqas, Ibn Masud, Mughira ibn Suba. When they venture to give a figure, those are the ones. Cf. Ibn Sa'd, *Tabaq.,* V, 7, lines 3, 21 8; lines 9 9, 5 12, 13, etc. To 'Umar, in addition to 63 they give him 61 and even "some 63 years of age," Ibn Sa'd, *Tabaq.,* III i, 265–266; to Abu Bakr "60, 63, or 65 years of age," Ibn Askir, VIII (ms. Damascus), entry for Abu Bakr. The celebrated maula Suhaib, the friend of Aisha, Safwan ibn al-Muattil died at "about 60" or "about 70 years of age." See their entries in *Istiab,* ms. B.Khed.

46. Tab., III, 2310, 3, 19; 2313, 4, 21; 2322, 8; 2323, 3.

47. Tab., III, 2296, 2451, Ibn Sa'd, *Tabaq.,* VIII, I 1, 86 Masudi, *Tanbih.*

48. Ibn Sa'd, *Tabaq.*, III 1, 170. Others say he was the same age (Arabic = *tirb*) as Abu Bakr. Bilal is one of the Companions belonging, like 'Umar, to the circle of Abu Bakr.

49. To vary it, the authors assign 66 years to Aisha, 60 to Hafsa. Safiya should be 60 to 65 years of age. For the inner circle of Muhammad, they rarely deviate from these figures; cf. Ibn Sa'd, *Tabaq.,* VIII, 54, 60, 92. They made an exception for Maymuna, who had survived for too long. At the time of their marriage with Muhammad, the "mothers of the believers" were some 30 years of age "or 35"; thus Umm Habiba, Umm Salama, Zaynab bint Jahsh, et al. Ibn Sa'd, *Tabaq.,* VIII, 70, 10; 81, 9. When they got married, both Muhammad and his father Abdallah were 25 years old. For the figures 60 and 70 in the Hadith, cf. Bahaqi, *Adab* (ms. B.Khed.), I a, and Goldziher, *Literaturgeschichte der Sia,* p. 9. For the 65 years of Aisha, see Baladhuri, *Ansab,* 285, 271.

50. I adopt the correction of the editor Mittwoch, Ibn Sa'd, *Tabaq.,* I 1 137.

51. Cf. "Koran and Tradition" [chapter 4 of present volume.—Trans.]. Ibn Abbas must have been born 3 years before the Hijra and must have been 13 at the time of Muhammad's death. Ibn Abdalbarr, *Istiab* (ms. B.khed.), I, 8a. They have done the impossible to advance the birth of this father of the written Tradition.

52. "al nabi akbar minni wa ana aqdam minhu fi-l-milad jami' al nuwa'id" (ms. Berlin), 22a. Reply, attributed, with variants, to several Companions. The Hadith thrives on certain clichés. Some Tabi'un have appropriated these replies for themselves; "I am greater in years, he is greater in intelligence," Ibn Sa'd, *Tabaq.,* VI, 65, 12 130, 20. They had 'Uthman being born the year 6 of the Elephant; Maqdisi, *Ansab al Qorasiyn* (ms. Asir eff.). Would this be new evidence that Muhammad was born after this date?

53. Several years older than the Prophet, since he had seen the dung of the Elephant. See above. Cf. Tab, *Annales,* I, 967, 1, etc.

54. *Usd al-ghaba,* IV, 189–190 Tab., *Annales,* I, 967, 17 *Iqd²,* I, 273.

55. Tab., III, 2397 cf. The author's *Chantre des Omiades,* 175.

56. Imta, I (ms. Kuprulu, Constantinople). This is how according to this opinion they sort out the chronology of the Sira the Calling (Vocation = *mab'ath*) at 45 + 10 years at Mecca, finally 8 years at Medina.

57. Baladhuri, *Ansab* (ms. Paris), 68–69.

58. Cf. Wustenfeld, *Vergleichungs-Tabellen.*

59. Ibn Hisham, *Sira,* 350 Tab., *Annales,* I, 1247 Azraqi (ed. Wustenfeld), 377.

60. Others follow below.

61. [Cf. the author's "Koran and Tradition," chapter 4 of present volume.—Trans.]

62. Waqidi (Wellh.), 231; Ibn Sa'd, *Tabaq.,* II 1, 59, 2–5.

63. As our sources agree on this by adding after the principal authority: "he took as an example this line."

64. Ibn al-Athir, *Kamil,* II, 44, plumps for 13, Ibn Abbas for 15, Tab., *Annales,* I, 1248. They followed the same procedure for the other facts of the sira (on the meaning and use of *bida',* cf. Tab., *Tafsir,* XII, 124). Compare Ibn Sa'd, *Tabaq.,* II 1, 71, 19 "some ten days," but they add "and they say twenty" at Hudaybiyya "few 1,000," when the minimum number of participants was 1,400; Ibn Sa'd, *Tabaq.,* II, 71–73, 75, 1. Muhammad had chosen this elastic expression in the only prophecy risked by him, sura 30:1–3. The siege of Khaybar had lasted "some ten days," Qutaiba, *Ma'arif,* 53, i.e., a month, as they say generally. At Quba, Muhammad passed "some ten days," understand more than 15 days, certain hadith agree on this, but the Tradition is looking to hide this break; Safwat as-Safwa (ms. B.Khed.) I, 49 b. Cf. Ibn Sa'd, *Tabaq.,* II 1 91, 1; 114, 23, further examples of this formula, above all Masudi, *Tanbih,* 237.

65. Ibn Sa'd, *Tabaq.,* I 1, 151, 18, etc., Tab., *Annales,* I, 1248.

66. Ibn Sa'd, *Tabaq.,* I 1, 152, 23-25.

67. Thus almost by a half.

68. As Sirma had done for the Meccan period.

69. Yet another example: 'Ali had four brothers, all separated by ten year intervals,

"and that is not convenient in a phratry," adds the *Jami' al-musanid* of Ibn Kathir, vol. III, ms. B.Khed.

70. See the ingenious calculations of Grimme, op. cit., I, 47, n.2.

71. "They counted," says Ibn al-Jawzi (*Safwat as-Safwa*, I, 40 a-b) "10, 13, or 15 years." He himself plumps for 13 years 3 years of private preaching and 10 years of public ministry.

72. [Cf. "Koran and Tradition," chapter 4 of present volume.—Trans.] Ibn Abdalbarr, *Istiab* (ms. B.Khed.), 8a, gives 48 years to Muhammad towards the period of his Calling. According to this opinion he would have died in his seventies.

73. Entirely Meccan, cf. Noldeke-Schwally, op. cit., 158.

74. Cf. Tab., *Tafsir*, XI, 60–61.

75. Or Sorma, we find the two vocalizations in the manuscripts. Cf. *Lisan al-Arab*, XV, s.v. Srm, 227–231. For the figure 40 among the Semites, cf. Noldeke-Schwally, op. cit., p. 68. The conversion of Umar brought the number of Muslims to 40 *Khasais al-Asara* (msBerlin), 8b.

76. Suras 16:72; 21:45; 22:5; 26:17; 27:27, 45; 28:45; 35:12.

77. *Aghani*, XIX, 5, bottom; Buhturi *Hamasa*, no. 422. See the dictionaries; compare the Hadith: "Send to Mudar the years of famine, like the years of Joseph," the seven lean years; Ibn Sa 'd, *Tabaq.*, II 1, 37, 23; cf. the Sahih, the expression musnitun, tested: "the ordeals by the sana, i.e., the famine"; Ibn al-Jawzi, *Safwat as-Safwa*, I, 47b, 49a. Cf. "Famine due to sterility," *Aghani*, XI, 83; Darimi, *Musnad* (ed. litho.), p. 262. We find 'am sana, meaning the year of famine, and simply 'am; Labid, *Mu'allaqa*, verse 88, Tab., *Annales,* III, 2395, 10. In the Koran, it is difficult to determine the synonymy of 'am and of sana, cf. Suras 2:261, 9:127, 12:49, etc.

78. Suras 10:5, 12:13.

79. Suras 2:90, 22:46, 29:13, 32:4, 70:4.

80. Sura, 2:261.

81. Sura 5:24.

82. Sura 46:14. Cf. Ibn Sa'd, *Tabaq.*, VI, 70, 24, putting at 40 years "the perfection of youth," or *takamil shababi*.

83. Cf. "Koran and Tradition," p. 10. For the use of months and years in the Koran, cf. Opitz, *Die Medizin im Koran*, pp.15-17.

84. Sura 18:10, 24.

85. Suras 20:42, 26:17, 30:3.

86. Sura 9:36; hijja = year; sura 28:27.

87. He insinuates this conclusion, Sura 9:37. Ibn Sa'd, *Tabaq.*, II 1, 133, 20, makes him express it. Cf. Snouck Hurgronje, *Het Mekkaansche Feest*, 66.

88. Cf. "It was a year when men were stricken by the famine;" Abu Ubaid, *Gharib al-hadith* (ms. Kuprulu), 227b.

89. Cf. the author's study on *Badia et la Hira*, in *Mélanges de la Faculté orientale de Beyrouth*, IV, 91–112.

90. Suras, 6:13, 96–97; 36:37–40; 41:37; 55:6–8.

91. Suras 10:6, 17:13.

92. That is to say, to work to guarantee their existence. Cf. St. John, IX.4 D. Nielsen, *Die altarabische Mondreligion*, 83 ff.

93. When he thinks he has found a neat turn of phrase, he reuses it to death. According to Hirschfeld, *New Researches into the Exegesis of the Qoran*, 60, 72, this insistence on the signs, physical miracles (*ayat*) wished to prove the uselessness of other miracles to establish his mission.

94. Suras, 39:7; 45:3-5, 6 and passim.

95. Suras 74:36–38; 84:16–18; 89:1–6 and passim.

96. On certain poets, subsequent to Islam, one can admit the influence of the Koran. From the Marwanids onwards (Kurdish dynasty 983–1085 C.E.) this influence gathered force and diminished in equal measure their worth from the historical and social point of view.

97. Buhturi, *Hamasa* (ed. Cheikho), nos. 412, 424, 427, 429.

98. Ibid., nos. 413, 415, 416, 418.

99. Ibid., nos. 417, 420.

100. Ibid., nos. 422, 423, 424, 430.

101. Buhturi, *Hamasa,* nos. 425, 428.

102. Ibid., nos. 414, 424; mentions however the months and the years (*hawl, 'am*), but in their vaguest denomination; no. 422 contains *sana* but with the addition of *jamad*, thus in the sense of famine. It is less a chronological measure than a succession of unhappy seasons, in reality one year where the *rabi* (spring) is lacking! Cf. Tab. III, 2395, 10, *'am sana*, the year of famine.

103. *Hamasa*, nos. 460, 461, 465, 468.

104. Ibid., no. 1068.

105. Ibid., no. 981.

106. Ibid., nos. 1062—1064. Manzur ibn Zabban, called Manzur, (Arabic, meaning expected, anticipated) because they waited four years for his birth; Aghani, XI, 54, 10 d.l. From there the Arabs derived their theories on long gestations they calculate their years badly! Cf. Qutaiba, *Maarif,* 198; Ibn Sa'd, *Tabaq.,* VI, 210; Jahiz, *Haiawan,* VII, 40.

107. Goldziher, *Kitab al-Mu'ammirin* 72, 11, with the annotations of the author; Aghani, IV, 130.

108. Sijistani, *Kitab al-Mu'ammirin*. 92, with the remark, the turban could be worn for 40 years. The turban was a sign of the great saiyyids, for that often qualified as *mu'ammam* (turbanned). Cf. Ibn Sa'd, *Tabaq.,* II 1, 64, 2 122, 11: the Prophet confers the 'amama (turban) on the leaders of the great expeditions; cf. Lammens, *Califat de Yazid,* I, 219, etc.

109. For the importance of months for Arabs, cf. D. Nielsen, *Die altarabische Mondreligion*, p. 50.

110. Cf. Ibn Sa'd, *Tabaq.,* II 1, 21, 24, 25, 43, 56, etc. Cf. Koran 46:14 From the year 6 of the Hijra, the Sira takes up generally calculation by year.

111. See the texts cited above. For the poetic borrowings compare a confession in Ibn

Sa'd, *Tabaq.*, II 1, 59, 2–5, on the subject of a sariya; a verse of Hassan ibn Thabit he wrongly attributed to Miqdad.

112. Sira, p. 350, d.l. 351.The author cites a quantity of apocryphal verses. He sometimes has the honesty to then add an unfavorable note as when he introduces modifications. cf. 462, 463, 516, 518, 530, etc. We can see how much they have striven to make the poetry contribute to the making of the Sira.

113. Yaqut, *Mu'jam*, III, 567 only knows him as Sirma al Ansari. On its occasion would have been revealed the Koranic verse: I have rendered legal for you to be daring. Cf. the *Asbab al Nuzul al Kuran*, such as no. 111, ms. Nouri Otmani, p. 4b; there they call him *Abu Qays Sirma*.

114. Cf. *Istiab* (ms. B.Khed.), 7b. We have narrated these lines according to Safyan ibn 'Ayyina, according to Yahya, according to Sa'd al-Ansari, and this the most perfect of narrations. Elsewhere they cite them without the isnad. One sees here the Ansarian source and how the antiquity of the transmission or the isnad—assuming it is authentic—does not go beyond without doubt Sufyan.

115. *Abu Qays Sirma b. Qays al-Ansari;* Ibn Abdulbarr, *Istiab* (ms. Nouri Otmani, Constantinople): Abu Qays Sirma b. Abi Anas Akhi bani 'Ady b. al-Najjar Tab., I, 1247: *Sirma Abi Anas* or *Sirma ibn Abi Anas Abu Qays;* Sibt ibn al-Jawzi, *Mirat*, II, 123b, 193b (ms. Kuprulu) or *Abu Qays Sirma ibn Abi Anas Qays b. Sirma b. Malik b. 'Ady*, they add *kunya Aba Qays;* Maqdisi, *Ansab al-Ansar* (ms. Omoumiya) or simply *Abu Sirma* (Aghani, VIII, 105).

116. Cf. Usd al-ghaba., III, 17–19 Istiab, in places cited. They cite a stand–in of Sorma Abu Sirma al-Mazini. They say on the contrary that he was of the Banu al Najjar. Then they enumerate all the variants possible of this nasab (genealogy), where the kunya Abu Qays constantly recurs. Finally a note in the margin declares that it must be the same as the first Sorma, because this name is not to be found among the Banu Mazin *Istiab*, ms.cited.

117. Sibt Ibn al-Jawzi, *Maqdisi*, loc. cit. Sirma is the Medinan counterpart of the Meccan hanif, Zayd ibn Amru ibn Nufail, whom they quote willingly. Cf. Sibt ibn al-Jawzi, loc.cit., *Hizanat al Adab*, II, 543–44 *Aghani*, VIII, 105 Tab., *Annales,* I, 1247 –1248 Masudi, *Prairies*, IV, 141. Maqdisi, *Ansab*, loc.cit., gives other hanif verses from him, though they have an apocryphal air. Abu Darr, *Sarh as-Sira* (ms. Berlin) le ms. no. 349, *Tarikh*, B.Khed. Al–istibsar fi ansab al-Ansar. The *Istiab*, ms. cited, note on Sorma, the so-called son of Abu Anas the named Abi Anas Qays b.Sirma b. Malik . . . his kunya was Aba Qays but his kunya had taken over, and perhaps some people said Sirma b. Malik. Volume III mentions Abu Qays. According to Qatada, he would be Abu Qays Malik ibn Sirma it is besides the same person, the details given being identical.

118. They make of them mu'ammarin, (men of great age) another suspicious circumstance, Ibn Hajar, *Isaba*, II, 486–87 Usd al-ghaba., III, 17–18 they are of the number of "orakelnden Su'ara' " Goldziher, *Abhandlungen*, II, p. XIV, n. 4.

119. Ibn Sa'd, *Tabaq.*, IV², 94–95 Wellhausen, *Skizzen*, IV, 16 Goldziher, *Abhandlungen*, loc. cit., and in the journal *Der Islam*, II, 103.

120. Goldziher, *M.S.*, I, 96. Schwally, op. cit., p. 68 consider the poetry of Sirma to be authentic. Hassan ibn Thabit boasted of replying to the satires of the Quraysh; see his Diwan (ms. B.Khed., no 29), I st. qasida. The apocrypha of Sirma betrays itself by the style of the poetry which is posterior to the Umayyads. Cf. Hassan ibn Thabit (ed. Hirschfeld), XIX, XXII, XXV, LXXIX, 11.

121. See the same theme in Hassan ibn Thabit, X, loc. cit. The forger could have got his inspiration from it, Tab., III, 2410, 2413–14. The *diwan* (collection), attributed to Sirma, celebrates the glories of the Ansars, *Aghani,* VIII, 105.

122. "Innama akhadahu min qawl al-sha'ir," Ibn Abdalbarr, *Istiab*, ms. cit.

123. Muslim (cf. Schwally, op. cit., 69) equally criticizes those who prefer the poetry of Sirma to the Tradition. We can see the influence he has exercised. A Hadith shows Ibn Abbas paying visits to Sirma to learn the poetry: "he stayed with the Quraysh." Cf. Al istibsar fi ansab al-Ansar, ms. B.Khed., p. 2. It is an anachronism at the death of Sirma, Ibn Abbas was still out at nurse. He only came to Medina after the conquest, that is seven years after the death of Sirma. It is odd to note how everything ends up in him. Under the caliph Mahdi, there circulated a diwan attributed to Sirma, cf. *Aghani,* VIII, 105.

124 We do not see him sorting out any of the serious questions left unanswered, his succession, etc. Cf, the author's Triumvirat, in M.F.O., IV, 113 ff.

125. Cf. the introduction of Goldziher to his edition of *Kitab al–Mu'ammarin.*

126. Thus Abu Talib would have died at the age of 48 Masudi, *Prairies,* IV, 46; cf. Wellhausen, *Skizzen*,IV, 27.

127. Waqidi (Wellh.), 54; Ibn Sa'd, *Tabaq.,* IV 1, p. 3; Tab., III, 2311 adds delicately: "according to what say."

128. [Cf. "Koran and Tradition," Chapter 4 of the present volume—Trans.]

129. Fayumi, *Akhbar* (ms. Asir eff.), p. 3r. In his *Tanbih*, 232, Masudi attributes to Abu Talib "some 80 years." Cf. *Istiab* (ms. cit.) p. 8a.

130. Or even earlier, Tab., III, 2317, 8. Arqam the owner of *dar* of this name, so famous in the annals of early Islam, died in 54/55 A.H. The date of birth is nowhere indicated, but he was one of the earliest Muslims; Ibn Sa'd, *Tabaq.*, III 1, 173–74. Later we shall draw attention to the obituary date 54/55 A.H. According to Tab., III, 2328, Arqam died in 54; in the Index, the editor de Goeje puts the date 55.

131. Yaqubi, II, 19. Ibn Surad, while Muhammad was alive, was already "very old," he died in battle at the head of the penitents, thus in full vigor. His title of Companion seems to me debatable; he owes it to his Shiite fervor. Ibn Sa'd, *Tabaq.,* IV², 30, 5; Ibn Hajar, *Isaba*, II, 253–54, he died when 93 years old, according to Nawawi, *Tahdib*, 302 *Usd al-ghaba.*, II, 352, Tab., III, 2334.

132. Yaqubi, II, 57, 5, etc.

133. Maqrizi, *Imta,* III (ms. Kuprulu) All these dates have been calculated later and were unknown to contemporaries.

134. Maqdisi, *Ansab al-Qorasiyn* (ms. Assir eff.).

135. Ibn Sa'd, *Tabaq.*, VIII, 10.

136. Died during the caliphate of 'Uthman, Ibn Sa'd, *Tabaq.*, VIII, 164; cf. Lammens, *Mo'awia*, 413 n.7.

137. Tab., III, 2324, 2325, 2351, 2419. Hassan, Hakim, Huwaytib, Makhrama ibn Naufal, etc., the celebrated centenarians of the sira, died in 54 A.H.; cf. Tab., III, 2323–27. Where does this coincidence come from? Did the authors make them die then because they were centenarians or did they declare them centenarians because they died at this date? Their biographical sketches in the *Istiab* (ms. cit.) agree that they did not know the exact year but they were inclined toward 54! Baladhuri, *Ansab*, 59.

138. See his biographical sketch in *Aghani*, XIII, 149, etc.; their long wars before Islam, 154; they affirm of him *sada fihima*, he was sayyid before and after Islam, 149, 7 d.l. all are compelled to attribute to him a mature age when he knew the Prophet.

139. For Qabat ibn Asiam, see above. Born before Muhammad, he replied to the questioning of caliph Abd al-Malik, Tab. *Annales*, I, 967. At Yarmuk he would have commanded "one of the two sides." Cf. *Usd al-ghaba.*, IV, 189–90. Adi ibn Hatim died in 68 A.H. Cf. Ibn Sa'd, *Tabaq.*, V, 13; Tab., III, 2361. At Yarmuk, in accordance with Tradition, he must have been 90 years old! Other Companion dead at 104, Tab., III, 2326, 11. Jabir ibn Abdallah died at 94. He had been aged in view of the traditions which they wanted him to confirm, like Ibn Jafar, the son of Taiyar, by the Shiites, to give him time to have known the Prophet personally; Tab., III, 2339, 13; 2340, 1.

140. Maqdisi, *Ansab al-Qorasiyn* (Asir eff.); Ibn al-Jawzi, *Talqih*, 19b. Ammar ibn Yasir would have ben 93 or 94 years old. Nawawi, *Tahdib*, 486 *Tabaq.*, III 1, 189.

141. As Bayasi, *I'lam* (ms. B.Khed.), I, 49a, would have it. At Khandaq one of the most valiant Qurayshite warriors was 90 years old Ibn Sa'd, *Tabaq*, II 1, 49, 6. Safwan ibn Umayya was at least the same age as the Prophet he died in 42 A.H. Maqdisi, *Ansab al-Qorasiyn* (ms. Asir eff.) Huwaytib ibn Abd al-Uzza fought valiantly at Hunayn (cf. Ibn Sa'd, *Tabaq.*, II 1, 97, 6), he must have been however in his eighties; Tab., 2317–18, 2357, 2361.

142. By "some ten years" to use the hallowed expression.

143. Waqidi (Wellh.), 152. The date nor the order of Muhammad's marriages are not yet fixed. See below.

144. Hanbal, *Musnad*, IV, 28, 4 V, 120. Elsewhere they make him say, "I am older than you." Ibid., V, 121; Ibn Sa'd, *Tabaq.*, VIII, 61, 63, 64, 67; died in 59 A.H., aged 84; Ibn al-Jawzi, *Montazam*, II (Asir eff.), 87a.

145. A situation at variance with the hypothesis of an advanced age.

146. One could also translate it as like the youngest of men. Umm Salama was a beauty, fresh evidence of her youth; Ibn Sa'd, *Tabaq.*, VIII, 66, 17, etc.

147. Ibn al-Jawzi, *Wafa* (ms. Leiden), 157b; I. Hisham, *Sira,* 937, 7 d.l. Cf Ibn Sa'd, *Tabaq.*, VIII, 10, 1. 19–23; described as *Shab* (youth), several years after his Calling (*mab'ath*), as *ghulam* (youth, boy, lad) at Medina see above.

148. Sibt ibn al-Jawzi, *Mir'at* (Kuprulu): There was no greying among the Companions, if it is not Abu Bakr. Cf. Maqdisi, Ansab al-Qorasiyn The oldest of the Prophet's Companions were Abu Bakr and Suhayl b. Bayda' . . . , Ibn Aqila, 'Unwan al-sa'ada . . . (Asir eff.) makes Abu Bakr to be older than Muhammad: the former having heard trees prophesying his coming. Do not forget, however, of the posthumous child born to Abu Bakr..

149. Hanbal, *Musnad*, III, 102, 107, 179, 263. 'Umar must have been his junior by 13 years; Caetani, *Annali*, I, 163. The Tradition again exaggerates here. At the time of his conversion, 'Umar seems in all the impetuousity of first youth.

150. Hanbal, *Musnad*, III, 100 *Khalq al Nabi* (ms. Leiden), 289–91; Tab., *Annales,* I, 1792–93.

151. He had not acquired white hairs, Hanbal, *Musnad*, II, 216, 251, 262; *Khalq al Nabi*, loc. cit.

152. Hanbal, *Musnad*, IV, 187, 190; Tab., *Annales*, I, 1792–1793.

153. He was not included in the group of old men like Noah and Abraham, *Khalq al Nabi*, p. 299.

154. [Cf. "Koran and Tradition," chapter 4 of present volume.—Trans.]

155. Cf. Lammens, *Triumvirat,* 135, n.2.

156. The references will be given later, when we recount the arrival at Medina. The Hadith reveals itself here busy with proving the physical vigor of the Prophet until the last moment. Is it more believable for 60–65 years, especially after the contradictions revealed above?

157. *Ghulam* or *shab*. For the synonym for *shab*, cf. *Aghani*, XII, 156, 19.

158. Ihadaru ghulam quraysh . . . Ibn Sa'd, *Tabaq.*, VI, 27, 13; Ibn al-Jawzi, *Wafa* (ms. Leiden), 50b.

159. Quoted by Goldziher, *Abhandlungen*, II, pp.xxx–xxxi. In the sira the persons described as ghulam are about 20 years old. Cf. Ibn Sa'd, *Tabaq.,* II 1, 136, 9; Ibn al-Jawzi, *Wafa* (ms. Leiden), 158b. Muhammad described as ghulam in a Hadith belonging to the Medinan period, Darimi, *Musnad* (ed. litho.) 88, 1.

160. Is this an allusion to St. John, VII, 57: "You are not yet fifty years old. How can you have seen Abraham?" However the celebrated Ansar Mu'ad ibn Jabal died at 33, "the age of Jesus," Ibn Sa'd, *Tabaq.,* III 2, 125.

161. Tab., *Annales*, I, 1140: "lam yu'bat nabi illa bu'ita al-ladi ba'dahu bi-nisfin min 'umrihi wa bu'ita 'ina li-arba'an, wa bu'ittu li-'ishrin."

162. Mughlatay, *Isara* (ms. Omoumiya, Constantinople).

163. Al-Haram, Hanbal, *Musnad*, III, 232, d.l.; Nasai, *Sunan* (ms. Nouri Otmani): Kitab al istimana; Jahiz, *Haiawan,* IV, 54.

164. Snouck, op. cit., 163.

165. Unfortunately this author forgot to tell us how he arrived at his figure. For the maulid (the birthday), the Tradition usually indicates the year 882 of Alexander, Masudi, *Tanbih*, 228-229. Barhebraeus's estimate comes close to those who put "ten years between the birthday and the Elephant." See above.

166. *Dynasties,* éd. Salhani, 160.

167. Cf. Al Biruni, *Chronologie* (ed. Sachau) p.30. Was the Hijra established in the year 16–17, by 'Umar, like all the great institutions? Let us accept that for the moment. It remains to decide when Muhammad suppressed the *nasi* or the intercalary month. The exact date of sura 9:36–37 is unknown. Cf. Noldeke-Schwally, op. cit, 223.

168. [Cf. "Koran and Tradition," chapter 4 of present volume.—Trans.]

169. Cf. Noldeke-Schwally, *Gesch des Qorans*, 66–67 comp. 58.

170. Cf. Schwally op. cit, 69, 145.

171. Ibn al-Jawzi, *Safwat as-Safwa*, I, 37a.

172. If nevertheless she is not the Sunni counterpart, opposed to the idolatrous veneration of the Shia for Fatima. Only the the existence of the latter is solidly established thanks to her descendants.Zaynab would have been born when her father was 30 years old *Tarikh*, ms. 349, B.Khed.

173. On condition of giving her a mother in her sixties. Our authors struggle between the 65 years of Khadija and the 15 which they did not want to go beyond for the fiancée of 'Ali.

174. In our days still, even among the sedentary tribes of Petra, a girl is married at ten years of age, Musil, *Arabia Petraea*, III, 184.

175. Highly convenient hypothesis to explain the absence of Jafar, 'Ali's brother, and so many other illustrious people!

176. Cf. Schwally, op. cit. p. 70.

177. Cf Noldeke, *ZDMG*, 1898, p. 18 etc. The favorite Zayd has been, I suspect, glorified by the Sunna, as a counterweight to 'Ali. To his son Usama, the Prophet shows no less affection than for the children of Fatima. In the two cases they repeat the same traits they did as much for the children of Zaynab. We are here confronted with a maneuver of orthodox Tradition.

178. Schwally, op cit., 58, for this period allows "some indubitably exegetical traditions," for example "sura 48 is connected to the peace of Hudaybiyya." Despite the mention of the "tree and of the bai'a" (oath of allegiance), in this sura 48:18, I confess to still having doubts on this point.

179. She is also the last one to die.

180. She received 400 dinars as a dowry, and not 400 dihram, like the preceding wives. That indicates a period when Muhammad had become rich, and also the importance attached to this union.

181. Suras 3:9, 9:25. These are, as it was to be expected, two victories. Because of the Qurayshites, Muhammad had avoided mentioning the conquest of Mecca and perhaps also Hudaybiyya.

182. Cf. Waqidi (Kremer), 160, 2; the fact is put into relation with the battle of Badr.

183. Cf. Ibn Sa'd, *Tabaq,* II 1, 112, 113; perhaps because certain transmitters had calculated the year without taking into account the *nasi* (intercalary month).

184. Snouck, op.cit., 65.

185. For the age of this part, cf. Noldeke-Schwally, op. cit., 219.

186. [Cf. "Koran and Tradition," chapter 4 of present volume.—Trans.]

187. Ibid.

188. Ibid.

189. Cf. Ibn Sa'd, *Tabaq.*, vol. 1 ms. of Top Kapou or Old Sérail, Constantinople: Are you not an Arab? Read the Koran. Nuwairi, *Nihaia*, II, 16 section (ms. Kuprulu, Constantinople), numerous hadith with this meaning, as in the majority of Shamail.

190. [Cf. "Koran and Tradition," chapter 4 of present volume.—Trans.]

Chapter 6

Fatima and the
Daughters of Muhammad

Henri Lammens

INTRODUCTION

This monograph opens a series of detailed studies which we propose to devote, God willing (Inshallah), to the sira and the beginnings of Islam. They are the follow-up of articles previously published between 1910 and 1911 in the *Journal Asiatique,* the *Recherches de science religieuse* of Paris, and the *Bulletin de l'institut égyptien* of Cairo. As in the present study where the main questions concerning the sira are raised, they will make it possible to judge the documentary value of early Muslim literature.

In these monographs we will not lose sight of the fact that, just as in the corpus of Muslim Tradition, the sira is, first of all, intended to be an exegesis. Inspired directly from the text of the Koran, the sira is intended to be used as an active commentary for it. It must translate into precise and picturesque anecdotes the most obscure allusions and the most unintelligible verses, and hunt down what is anonymous or impersonal, which is so disconcerting when one reads the suras. In other words, it sets up commemorative notices and multiplies the mention of dates and proper names, all of which are prudently avoided by Abul Qasim [the Prophet Muhammad].

Henri Lammens, *Fatima and the Daughters of Muhammad* (Rome and Paris: Scripta Pontificii Instituti Biblici, 1912). Original translation of text by anonymous, notes and abbreviations translated by Ibn Warraq.

By its exegetical nature, the sira becomes doctrinal, but with greater abandon and a less obvious form of affectation than in the Tradition. The exegesis and the doctrine, that is, a comprehension of the Book of Allah, as well as the setting-up of religious law, dogma, morality, and liturgy (so neglected by the Prophet), became the multiple task which entirely occupied the early generations of Islamists. The historical interest developed much later, at the same time as the worship of Abul Qasim's personality. It was a question of finding a base for this veneration, starting with a closer knowledge of the Master's deeds and actions, and of gathering together the recollections and traces of his passage through life. What also contributed to this evolution were the contacts with those who possessed religious records, the political discussions raised by the organization of the Arab empire, and questions concerning the Caliphate, entitlement to pensions, and so on.

This declaration of principles leaves intact the objective value attributed to the special tradition of the Medinan period. However, in the case of these Hadith, recognized as authentic (sahihs), after having examined them one finds that their historical interest takes second place to the exegesis and the establishment and teaching of the doctrine. The present study will help to understand this. In subsequent monographs we will attempt to complete and, if possible, conclude this demonstration, God willing (Inshallah).

I. Fatima's Sister

First among the regrets that tortured Muhammad to the end of his life was his desire to have children. For him it was one of the distinctive signs of his predecessors in the path of prophetism. "We gave them wives and descendants," said Allah.[1] He had allowed himself wives beyond the measure granted to his followers. None had given him a male descendant destined to survive him. Like all Semites he attached the greatest importance to this mark of divine blessing. The former orphan, never having known his parents or shared his games with a brother, aspired to survive in heirs of his own blood.

These preoccupations may have inspired his polemics against infanticide. Everywhere in the Koran we note a love of children, particularly of boys. He gracefully calls them "the ornaments of this earthly life."[2] They appear beside wealth and amongst the riches of a world truly worthy of desire. They can be summarized in the stereotyped formula of the Koran[3] and later adopted by the Tradition: *al amwal wa-l-banun*, possessions and sons. God alone decides among his followers the division between boys and girls, favoring according to his whim or condemning them to sterility. These children are a true temptation for the hearts of the faithful.[4] Here we have much attention developed in the Koran and later adopted by the Tradition.

Abtar, deprived of male descendants! Again and again Muhammad thinks he hears this insult, when it is not the image of the *sonbour*, an isolated palm tree with a miserable trunk and little foliage. "Such is Muhammad," said the Qurayshites, "having no son or brother, his memory is condemned to disappear."[5] How can one remain untouched by such malevolent insinuations? They made him lose his self-control and led him, contrary to his habit of cursing en bloc, to curse outright and by name the principal author of these invectives. This was fully realized by Muslim Tradition. In the efforts of this Tradition to multiply the number of Muhammad's children, one cannot fail to recognize a posthumous consolation granted to this great misfortune.

In the end these efforts were unfortunate. The cause was ill served by the exaggeration used to defend it. Islamic orthodoxy is not entirely unanimous in believing in the existence of Tahir, Motahhar, Tayb, Mutaib, Abdul 'Uzza, and Abdul Manaf. If little Qasim is entitled to exist, it can only be by virtue of the *kunya* of Abul Qasim.[6] Was the existence of Ibrahim [the putative son of Muhammad] more solidly attested? At the time when they were dealing with the setting up of the main lines of the sira, they showed in Medina a belvedere known as "the Belvedere of Umm Ibrahim." Umm Ibrahim was probably a Jewess! Muhammad' s contemporaries in the Hijaz did not usually bear biblical names.[7] In Medina, a vague local tradition later thought that it recognized in her the Copt concubine of the Prophet and her second son in Ibrahim, who died very young, and who was, moreover, as elusive as little Qasim.

The sira never questioned the existence of his four daughters: Zaynab, Fatima, Ruqayya, and Umm Kulthum. The two last mentioned disappeared without leaving any descendants. Their names figure among the most common female names of that period. As to Umm Kulthum, outside this *kunya* she is not known by any other names.[8] Nor was any trouble taken to vary the biographies of the two sisters. It is impossible not to be aware of clichés common to them both. Married to sons of Abu Lahab[9] and then repudiated by them, they both ended up in 'Uthman's harem. He was the providential character responsible for extricating Abul Qasim from his political and financial problems at Hudaybiyya, Tabuk, and elsewhere when Abu Bakr and 'Umar backed out as they did in the case of Umm Kulthum.[10] But before she saw the obliging Umayyad finding her a status, this daughter of Muhammad had to kick her heels in interminable widowhood[11] and wait for her sister's death before being offered asylum by Ibn Affan. How can we reconcile this attitude with the enthusiasm shown toward Fatima, and with the blind devotion that we are assured the Companions felt for her? They fought over Muhammed's hair and his spittle. Why, then, hesitate to give shelter to his daughter? Those who drafted the sira do not appear to have noticed this discrepancy in the version they preferred.

This must be laid down to the origin of this strange compilation which consists of successive contributions. As in the Koran, beside the *nasikh* and the *mansukh* [*nasikh* is the term used for a verse or sentence of the Koran or Hadith which abrogates a previous one, called *mansukh*] there remain the most shocking discrepancies. Should they have attempted to weed them out and make them consistent? The attempt would have failed, faced with the belief—*still* shared by many contemporary orientalists—in the authenticity of these discordant fragments. Early on the sira removes Ruqayya by sending her to Abyssinia. We see her reappear for a moment; on his return from Badr Muhammad arrives too late to attend her funeral,[12] as did 'Ali at Fatima's last moments. Her only son, Abdullah, died in infancy. It looks as if all embarrassing witnesses were removed. Umm Kulthum is mentioned only once in the oldest version which has reached us.[13] Like ephemeral ghosts the two sisters pass by without ever revealing their presence on the screen of history.

The question remains of the nickname of their common husband, 'Uthman, *dou'n nourain*, owner of the two lights. What does this really mean? How ancient is this name? Why is it not mentioned in the long note which Ibn Sa'd devoted to the third caliph?[14]

Tufayl ad-Dausi, a very obscure Companion, bore the nickname of *dou'n-nour*.[15] In the "two lights" the Tradition hastens to recognize the Prophet's two daughters.[16] This explanation does not, however, impose itself. Surnames of this kind were frequent among both male and female contemporaries. One of Abu Bakr's daughters was called *dhat al-nitaqayn*, the woman with two belts. Among the Sahabis, one knows the Dou' Asabi, Yadain, and the Dou's-Simalain.[17] For all of them the Hadith collections were able to find appropriate explanations, which infallibly honored the people concerned even when it was a question of surnames as compromising as *dhat al nitaqayn* (woman with two belts) and *dhu-l-shahadatayn* (the man with two professions of faith, or *shahadah*. Today what man or woman would consider taking pride in these names? All this proves, in particular, the vivid imagination of our authors. In the case of 'Uthman, the commentary could promise success because it favored both the dynastic pretentions of the Umayyads, their veneration for 'Uthman and the tendencies of the sira which was keen to assure the Prophet the honor of a wider paternity.[18]

What must one think of Zaynab, who also died before her father? It is difficult to understand why her descendants died amid the indifference of Muslim opinion.[19] Why did Zaynab not emigrate, following her father? At the moment of the Hijra she is said to have been on holiday in Taif with a Taqafite.[20] An awkward explanation! In fact, she did not bother to leave Mecca or her rich Umayyad husband, Abul Asi.[21] A text which fortunately has not been revised clearly states that "Abul Asi stayed with her in partnership until just before the conquest of Mecca."[22]

With the object of arranging everything, the authors invented her husband's captivity and his second rescue by Zaynab, who had taken refuge in Mecca. In a distich, which is moreover apocryphal, he certifies both his status as Zaynab's husband and the latter's sojourn in Mecca, al-haram (the Sacred). Since she is called the daughter of the amin in that text, the sira hastens to attribute this honorable quality to Abul Qasim[23] without worrying about the fact that it was a denial of its Zaynab legend. There is also the question of an accident which occurred at the moment when she tried to escape from Mecca.[24] If her marriage to Abul Asi was never broken off,[25] as the Tradition says, then Zaynab did not agree to separate her fate from his. It was decided to have her die before her father, so as not to complicate even further the situation created by Fatima's survival. The authors had acted in this way for their sisters.

When Abul Asi was to follow her into the grave in the year 12 A.H., he acted as if he had no heirs and made 'Zubayr ibn al-Aw'wam, his uncle's son, his sole legatee. This was a most disconcerting attitude! We are assured that his son 'Ali had died, but his daughter Umama survived him by nearly forty years and bore her successive husbands sons, all of whom died as she did in obscurity.[26] Why deprive these descendants of the Prophet of their share of the inheritance? Why did their contemporaries not protest against this denial of justice? If Zaynab ever existed, why did she voluntarily class herself with her husband among those who had "rallied" (al-mu'allifa qulubahum) and were spurned by the Alid tradition? Let sleeping dogs lie! When critics pay no heed to this axiom, they see the house of cards so laboriously built up by our authors collapse under their eyes. Giving way to discouragement, they decided to make the daughters of the Prophet disappear prematurely. By multiplying their number,[27] they had only thought of the advantage of granting him some sort of posterity. Their prolonged coexistence would pointlessly compromise the unity and coherence of the different parts of that historical romance, the sira.

In the case of Fatima we are on more solid ground. Her existence can neither be denied nor put in doubt. This is the main significance of this daughter, born of Muhammad's first marriage with old Khadija. To tell the truth, we find it difficult to make out the indistinct outlines of this vague figure, who has remained in a sort of mysterious twilight. On the other hand, the ambition of her descendants has earned the mother a noisy celebrity. An advantage denied to her sisters, her name appears in the poetry of a relatively late period.[28] Fatima has her own biography; however, it is inadequate as far as historical reality is concerned. This is yet another advantage she has over Muhammad's other daughters, mainly Ruqayya and Umm Kulthum, both fraternally associated and mistaken for one another in life's most ordinary events.

Among Muhammad's four successors, the order in which power was transmitted was to correspond to the degree of Muslim saintliness of these characters. This conviction seems to have established itself very early within the core of orthodoxy. The thesis, however, came up against one difficulty—how could 'Uthman have preceded Fatima's husband? The first caliphs had all been related to the Prophet, and 'Ali was his son-in-law. For 'Uthman to have obtained precedence over him, they assumed the existence of even closer links between Muhammad and his third successor. In order for 'Uthman to have supplanted 'Ali, it was decided to grant him the title of son-in-law of the Prophet. These subtleties—and they are numerous in this masterpiece of ingenuity which we call the sira—offer the advantage of giving Abul Qasim [Muhammad] two other daughters, who have in fact disappeared without leaving any trace. 'Uthman was to vouch for their existence. The authors even discovered his surname of "owner of the *two* lights"—not a very ancient discovery, but enough to remove the last hesitations and to make acceptable conclusions on which all parties wished to agree, since they were believed to honor the Prophet.

To return to Fatima and the date of her birth, this question begs another one which has remained unsolved—the rank occupied by Fatima among the Prophet's daughters. Of the four of them, which one was the eldest? This advantage has been claimed for all of them, except perhaps Umm Kulthum,[29] the least interesting in the eyes of Tradition. There she is used to increase by one the number of Muhammad's posterity and make less enigmatic the description "owner of two lights" given to 'Uthman. One could not decently claim primogeniture for this daughter married only after Badr. This would only have renewed unnecessarily the embarrassment caused by Fatima's late marriage. In multiplying the number of the Prophet's daughters, those who wrote the sira did not worry about problems of chronology. These fluctuations are due to the system adopted by each of our authors. Especially struck by the contradictions observed in the sira, they hoped to eliminate them by making use of a more precise method of numbering the Prophet's family. Above all it was necessary to take into account Khadija's advanced age. In spite of the privilege claimed for the wives of Quraysh to be able to give birth at the age of sixty,[30] it was judged prudent not to underline this claim. On the other hand, it was desirable to avoid too advanced an age for Fatima at the time of her marriage with 'Ali. According to the importance attached to each of these difficulties, her date of birth was at different times advanced and at others held back. She was even presented as the eldest of the group.[31] This is the opinion that is most rarely maintained, and we must add, the most compromising if one wishes to maintain the multiplicity of Muhammad's daughters.

In the absence of any direct information, the authors relied on some a priori principles. "As the good father of a family," they reasoned, "the Prophet must have started by getting the oldest daughter married."[32] That is why Zaynab[33] and Ruqayya, settled in marriage, we think, before Fatima, are considered to have been older than her, and Ruqayya even older than Zaynab. The latter view seems to have been in fashion, and the sira decided to ship Ruqayya off to Abyssinia in the company of her husband 'Uthman after her divorce from Abu Lahab's son. Because of this divorce they decided that she had been married before the "revelation."[34] It should not be said that Muhammad had married his daughters off to polytheists, who were as worked up against Islam as the Lahabids were thought to be. For the same reason Zaynab, married to an infidel Umayyad, could claim the right of primogeniture over Ruqayya. It is rather surprising that Muhammad, so fierce in his monotheism, should have shown preference for his pagan sons-in-law. When the latter consented to keep them, Abul Qasim's daughters made no attempt to leave. In the Prophet's family social conventions exercised a decisive influence.

According to Ibn al-Kalbi,[35] Ruqayya was the youngest and Fatima came immediately before her. One wonders how one can justify her entering Abu Lahab's pagan family, her emigration to Abyssinia, and her marriage to 'Uthman, much to the disadvantage of her elder sister Umm Kulthum. We can see among what contradictions our genealogists flounder and how their evident goodwill must end with the discouraging solution: "We do not know the exact order of Muhammad's daughters." The well-known Zuhri, "the main authority in this matter,"[36] and Zubayr ibn Bakkar, another specialist,[37] did not prove to be any better informed. According to them, Fatima was certainly not the eldest. That is, all the rest remains uncertain.[38] To sum up, Zaynab was never presented as the youngest nor Umm Kulthum as the eldest of the four sisters. All the other combinations were imagined. All were based exclusively on reasons of convenience and we can accept none of them, as none won the unanimity of the Islamic *nassaba* (genealogists).

These hesitations could not satisfy later tradition, particularly among the Shiites, who were fervent admirers of the "members of the family." Ibn Abdulbarr claimed that Zaynab was the eldest and Fatima the youngest: "The contrary view does not deserve any attention." If at times Fatima was refused this final qualification, "it was the fault of Musab and of Zubayr ibn Bakkar."[39] In fact, these two Zubairids mainly labored to glorify the families of Abu Bakr and Zubayr. [40] Musab's father was even known for his animosity against the Alides.[41] Abdulbarr seems, on the other hand, to have ignored the affirmations of the very serious Zuhri, which concorded with that of the Zubairid genealogists.

Be that as it may, one can understand the indignation of the author of the *Istiab*. Anyone can see how embarrassing are the consequences of this affirmation that he attempts to impose: the indifference shown by Muhammad toward his eldest, little enthusiasm shown by the Companions for becoming members of the Prophet's family, and finally the personal insignificance of Fatima,[42] who sees the trial of celibacy prolonged for her. How is it possible to reconcile all this with the system so laboriously built up by the sira? The Zubairite theory brutally marked its collapse.

In his life of Muhammad, Sprenger has not succeeded in finding his way about the chronological discussions which took place around Fatima. He thought "they had calculated the date of her birth according to traditions which we no longer possess."[43] As we can see, it is always the fundamental error, the gratuitous assumption of direct information, the illusion of the isnad and the pseudo-erudition of the Hadith. In the present case our authors did not got as far in seeking out their documentation.

The point of departure was provided by Fatima's death, placed in year 11 of the Hijra. This retroactive argumentation is the usual procedure when it is a question of estimating the age of witnesses of that period.[44] The chroniclers grope their way downward rather than upward where careers are concerned. If this method appears to us to be empirical, we would be wrong to criticize it. The date of birth was generally unknown, but that of death, more contemporary and better observed, provided a more solid base even though it was not absolutely certain. To the eleven years thus obtained were added three more[45] that separated the Hijra from Khadija's death. Beyond these indications provided by the sira, our authors no longer agree, the apple of discord being Khadija's age.

Will we ever discover why the *Vulgate* accepted the Prophet's marriage to a woman who could have been his grandmother?[46] But once the fact admitted, it had to be taken into account when drafting Fatima's legend, unless one skilfully manipulated the details so as to reject the hypothesis of a mother aged sixty. That is why it was generally decided to situate her birth before the "prophecy." This decision did not appear to compromise anything, and left the door open to the most ingenious combinations. In fact, we do not know the number of years which went by between the first revelation and the emigration to Medina. Was it fifteen, ten, or seven years?[47]

If some of the authors tried to see in Fatima the eldest or one of the older sisters, it was because they feared the objection arising from the advanced age of the mother. Other authors, on the contrary, plainly preoccupied with the date of her marriage to 'Ali, hesitated to adopt this solution. They contented themselves with situating Fatima's birth four or five years before the "prophecy"[48] Muhammad would then have been between thirty-five and forty-one;[49] one does not know exactly. She would have been born the same year as Mu'awiya and Abu Huraira,[50] two Companions who were not very favorable to the claims made later by the Alids. The Hadith does not scorn to resort to the effect of contrasts. This artifice makes it possible to divert the attention by giving the appearance of chronological erudition, thanks to invented synchronisms. Other biographers, always with the intention of reducing the distance separating Fatima's birth from her marriage, place the first event "a Year before the Prophecy." In this line one must expect to see authors known for their affection, for the Alids distinguish themselves by their zeal. Thus, according to Yaqubi, she was born after the "prophetic vocation." The vision of the lively Aisha haunts them and they are loth to admit a real disproportion between her and Fatima.

Some authors manage to do away with it by deciding that Hasan's mother was eleven years old at the birth of her first son.[51] Others, more moderate or more skilful, accept that there is a difference of five years[52] between the two women. According to Masudi,[53] Fatima was born "eight years before the Hijra." As he has them both married a year after that last date, the tendency is obvious—to put in the same line 'Ali's wife and the favorite married at the age of nine. One detail,[54] however, escaped the author of the *Golden Prairies*—eight years before the Hijra, Khadija[55] was well over sixty! It was no doubt thought that the problem was solved by extending for the wives of the Quraysh the limit of maternity to about sixty.[56]

II. FATIMA'S MARRIAGE

In order to obtain a precise image of Fatima's fleeting personality, we must start by removing the halo which later historians placed on her head. During her lifetime she was treated as an ordinary woman by her contemporaries, including her father, her husband, and the most eminent Sahabis [Companions of the Prophet] such as Abu Bakr and 'Umar. Nowhere do we see her enjoying special privileges or greater consideration than that paid to the ordinary Bedouin women of that period. In the Prophet's circle she occupies a very restricted place, disappearing behind the Aishas, the Hafsas, the Zaynabs, and other "mothers of believers." To be convinced of this, it is only necessary to measure the space alloted to her by the oldest chroniclers, such as Ibn Hisham's *Sira*. She is only mentioned twice in this work,[57] which is so favorable to 'Ali.

In composing his notes on the latter, Ibn Sa'd in his *Tabaqat* manages to not even mention his wife's name. One has only to compare the 230 pages[58] devoted to the *musnad* of Aisha in Ibn Hanbal's work. The systematic veneration for "the people of the family" began in the second century. As it was not a question of history but of creating a war machine, no trouble was taken to bring out Fatima's unattractive personality. Her husband and her sons were the main object of attention in the elaboration of this dynastic theory. That is why 'Ali finds favor to the advantage of his pale companion. She hardly appears in the collection of the Aghani, a significant reserve on the part of an author whose tendencies were so distinctly pro-Alid. All these authors belong to diverse schools and regions. As to the specifically Fatimite flowering of the Alid legend, we find certain examples in Masudi and Yaqubi. Their successors took on the task of developing it. We know how the caliphs of Baghdad made use first of the popularity of the Alids and then drowned them in rivers of blood, as can be seen in the *Maqatil at-Talibiyn* martyrology, a significant title where Fatima's name is replaced by her husband's patronymic.[59]

So we have no right to be astonished if we know practically nothing about Fatima's childhood prior to the Hijra. The name seems to have been a common one in Abu Talib's family.[60] Because of the importance accorded in the Arab world to the Kunya theory, so appreciated by the sira,[61] they also wished to transmit her *kunya*, Umm Abiha.[62] Its very archaic style was probably intended to produce a favorable impression of authenticity. In later notes[63] she is presented as much adored by her father. We will avoid going into details here on this question. Well informed as usual, our authors do not know the exact date of Fatima's birth within ten years. This does not prevent them from describing minutely her wonderful antecedents, her father's visit to Paradise, and the fruit received from Gabriel. Fatima was said to have been born nine months after the *isra* [the night journey of Muhammad to Jerusalem]. Yaqubi[64] describes her sorrow on the death of her mother Khadija. From then on it became usual to decribe as one of her characteristic features the shedding of tears. 'Ali, when necessary, will be ready enough to produce more tears.

Among the personalities of the sira none cried as much as Fatima, unless it was Abu Bakr, but the tears of this rough tradesman were due to religions fervor. He possessed *charisma* or the gift of tears! Fatima was the Niobe of the Sira.

A sad creature, perpetually in mourning! The Alid family were not ignorant of this. The sparkling and frivolous Sukaina, Husayn's daughter, congratulated herself on not including Fatima among her maternal ancestors, and gave this as an explanation of her playful character.[65] Physically Fatima had no particular advantages. Her weak constitution, her thinness,[66] her anaemic coloring and her frequent infirmities made her unsuitable for the hard work[67] which at that time was the lot of Arab women. Like all Muhammad's real or imaginary children, she died young and expressed her discouragement in a final lament. Unless one sees her as does the Shia, one wonders how they attempted to make this ghost of a wailing woman interesting. One guesses at her unhappiness and that of her descendants, one understands Muhammad's indifference toward her, and one practically excuses 'Ali's harshness toward his unfortunate companion.

Even among the authors who were on the side of the Alids, rarely did anyone vaunt Fatima's beauty, unlike her sister, Ruqayya. A whole cycle of tales describes the charms of that daughter of Muhammad.[68] They probably moved 'Uthman, one of the handsomest of the Qurayshites,[69] to adopt the new faith in order to obtain her hand. In Abyssinia, people stopped in their tracks to gaze at her. In the end she was obsessed by this, and would burst forth in imprecations against her indisceet admirers.[70] Nowhere does Fatima enjoy the praise Zaynab[71] garnered from Muhammad, who described her as being "the most capable of his daughters" (afdal banati). Whenever Urwa ibn Zubayr told this Hadith, the peaceful 'Ali ibn Husayn became furious: "In this way you hope to diminish Fatima."[72] This suspicion was in part well founded. It did not fall on Urwa (a Zubairid name cleverly chosen) to close the gaps in the isnad, but on the orthodox tradition, which wished to counterbalance the exaggerations of the Shia. To exalt was not dangerous since there were no descendants to take advantage, as in the case of Fatima. If her beauty is rarely mentioned, there is even less praise for her intelligence. Given these conditions, she could not fight successfully against a rival as well endowed as Aisha, nor thwart the intrigues hatched by the favorite to the advantage of the Abu Bakr and 'Umar group.[73] Thus, in the least altered Tradition, Fatima appears to us as "the embodiment of all that is divine in womanhood, the noblest ideal of human conception," if one is to believe the enthusiasm of a modern Indian writer, Ameer 'Ali.[74]

Under these circumstances it is obvious that in the eyes of her contemporaries she could hardly be considered a desirable wife. The fact that she was the Prophet' s daughter[75] would no doubt have made up[76] for all these disadvantages,[77] that is, if the worship and devotion to the figure of Abul Qasim had reached the pitch imagined by the sira, and also if one had known the words that 'Umar attributed to him: "On the day of the resurrection all family relationships will disappear excepting mine." The second caliph used this as an authority to marry a daughter of 'Ali who was not yet of marriageable age. It is not impossible that our chroniclers invented this tale in order to conceal this act of senile sensuality!

An Arab is never immune to calculating his own interests. Fatima was going to bring no dowry to her future husband. Personally without means, Muhammad inherited nothing from his first wife. During the entire Meccan period, Allah refused to allow his representative to combine supernatural gifts with earthly riches. At Medina, the skilful policy of the Reformer was to compensate for this poverty. One must be sceptical about the descriptions of the *musnad* of Aisha,[78] and also about the penury of the Prophet's family, where two months were spent without lighting a fire,[79] and where "the two blacks," (*al-aswadan*), dates and water, made up the daily menu. These were legendary details intended to produce a superior idea of Muhammad's *zuhd* (asceticism). We are entitled to ask ourselves what had happened to Khadija's possessions, since she was the opulent widow all the Qurayshites coveted. They should have constituted the dowries of the daughters of the rich *tajira* (merchant). Had by any chance the banking partnership[80] run by the enterprising lady of Mecca gone bankrupt,[81] or did it exist only in the fertile imaginations of our chroniclers? Here we see the inconsistencies of the tales which make up the plot of our Vulgate. One must not press too hard if one wants to avoid tearing it apart or causing the whole tale is not to collapse. Later Muhammad was to express his regret that Usama, the son of his favorite Zayd ibn Haritha, was not a young girl, as he would have liked to cover her with jewels so as to make her the most desirable match in Medina.[82] Why do we not hear him express this wish in the case of Fatima?

Our authors do not allow these questions to worry them. Eventually we will have to try to calculate the length of time it took to find a husband for Fatima. These delays should not be laid to the door of absence, but to the number and quality of the suitors. Among them we must mention Abu Bakr and 'Umar without forgetting the principal Companions who all fought for such an honor.[83] The first two caliphs courted 'Ali's future wife! This is no ordinary picture. In composing it the Shiite artists probably remembered the humiliations the duumvirs inflicted on the Prophet's daughter the day after her father's death. They enjoyed this hidden vengeance.[84] In Islamizing itself and passing from poetry to the Tradition, the former Arab satire became more polished. It learnt how to dissimulate its venom by wrapping it in a Hadith less offensive in its expression, which was received in a religions manner by our *sahihs* and *musnads*. In the *Rawias* of profane divans or religious Hadith, we note the same passion and the same absence of scruples. In changing their style they in no way raised their level of honesty. Why did our Islamists not realize this earlier?

In the midst of all this competition, 'Ali also thought of joining the ranks.

But he let himself be discouraged by the imposing titles of his rivals. Why did Muhammad refuse to comply with their wishes? All of them already owned large harems. Was he reluctant to get the inexperienced Fatima involved in these turbulent circles? He began, in order to soften his refusal, by invoking the tender age of his child.[85] Coming from Aisha's husband, who had married her when she was nine years old, this amounted to a pityful defeat. Even if we forget that her mother was sixty-five and make Fatima younger, well beyond the limits of credulity, she must have reached around the date of the Hijra the age of Aisha at the time of her marriage or even more. We will furnish proof later on. In fact we are looking at a fiction imagined in order to conceal the abandonment and lengthy spinsterhood of our heroine. It was essential, at all costs by imagining the most improbable situations, to save her face as well as that of her father, both compromised by this indifference.

Why, having finally changed his mind, did Muhammad suddenly give her to 'Ali?[86] He is said to have replied to the remarks of various evicted suitors: "It has nothing to do with me. This marriage was decided by Allah."[87] The intervention of heaven in the domestic affairs of the Prophet seemed in no way improbable. His contemporaries were prepared to accept this. In this connection we must remember the great number of regulations in the Koran, and the romance of Zaynab, married by Allah to his Envoy,[88] or as this rival of Aisha's liked to boast, "by a decree proclaimed in the highest of the seven heavens."

Even when the name of Yaqubi is not sufficient to raise our suspicions, it seems difficult not to recognize the contentious nature of these numerous incidents. 'Ali was preferred by Allah and and his Prophet over the two 'Umars, his future rivals! To these imaginary hesitations we must oppose the ease with which Muhammad gave away his two other daughters to pagan but wealthy sons-in-law. In order to excuse these marriages they are made out to have taken place prior to the "revelation."[89] This was a clumsy justification. What, then, becomes of the excuse that Fatima was extremely young? Before the "vocation" none of her sisters can have been more than ten years old. If, however, this must be taken into consideration, we are then obliged to admit in the case of Umm Kulthum that she must have been a widow for the fifteen to eighteen years[90] which separated her divorce from Abu Lahab and her marriage to 'Uthman. This brings us back to a fact already noted—the indifference shown by the Companions to the honor of becoming the son-in-law of the Prophet. There is nothing as instructive as the enumeration of these contradictions. They justify our scepticism as to the historical importance of the sira. Prior to the Hijra we know nothing of 'Ali's activities apart from his name and that of his family. This ignorance could not satisfy Islamic historiography. To supplement their knowledge, the historians manufactured an *evangelium infantiae* for 'Ali. Noldeke was one of the first, in fact probably the first, to raise certain doubts as to the value of the composition.[91] The ancient chronicles took as their objective to forge very early on the relationship between the Prophet and his four successors, *al-khulafa al-rashidun*, the Rightly Guided Caliphs. In these relationships, women play the principal role. We must call to mind the names of Aisha, Hafsa, and the Prophet's daughters. Regarding 'Ali, this zeal was not an entirely happy one. Among his contemporaries, 'Ali was considered to have a rather limited mind (*mahdud*).[92] This was certainly Abu Talib's opinion, if we are to accept the legend of 'Ali as established in the sira. The ease with which this father got rid of his children, 'Ali in particular, seems most odd. He handed them over to Abbas, to Hamza and to Muhammad,[93] only remaining in charge of Aqil, who, it is true, was the most capable of them. One wonders how this strange idea managed to impose itself.

In fact the idea had the advantage of satisfying everyone. If it glorified the Alids, it made them the grateful protégés and debtors of the Abbasids prior to the Hijra. This was a stroke of genius! It summarized the policy of the caliphs of Baghdad. Before them Mu'awiya and his Umayyad successors[94] had proposed to make the Alids renounce their ambitious dreams by gorging them with gold. Taking this astute policy even further, the Abbasids wanted to appear as having protected the sons of Abu Talib even before the emergence of Islam. This bold invention veiled the odious role played by Abbas and his sons in the history of the Prophet's family—that of traitors, as the Ansarian Qays ibn Sa'd was later to tell. This consideration could not have been sufficient to remove the support of 'Ali's friends. But the Abbasid explanation provided the best means of assuring him a title so dear to the Shia,[95] that of the First Believer, this to the disadvantage of Abu Bakr. To achieve this with greater certainty, they backdated the latter's conversion so as to situate it after that of Abu Darr, an obscure name but one that was dear to the Shiite school.[96] A final consideration assured the success of this historical arrangement—it closed the distressing gap of the Meccan period and hid the incredulity of the mass of Hashimites. That is how the legend of 'Ali became an integral part of the official sira, where Muhammad figures as presiding over the education of his young cousin.

We must not allow this agreement to be imposed on us. 'Ali was the member of a family which, up to the Fath, remained indifferent or hostile towards Islam. As everyone admitted, Abu Talib, Muhammad's protector, and his wife, too, insisted on dying as unbelievers. The name of Talibyun willingly given by the Abbasids[97] to Fatima's descendants underlined this deplorable trait. Amid the hostility of his family, 'Ali seems to have been the first exception. Here we see his true priority. He was the first not of the believers but of the Hashimites to embrace Islam. Nevertheless, he waited to declare himself until the departure of Muhammad for Medina. Abbas[98] and Aqil[99] decided to follow the same path around the period of the Meccan Fath.[100] Both of them, with Talib (if he ever existed), were to swell the contingent of Badr's Qurayshites. The Koran and the Tradition mention a ferocious enemy of Islam, a personal enemy of the Prophet, and this was Abu Lahab, yet another Hashimite. To weaken the impact of this objection, orthodoxy at 'Ali's side wanted to find a place for Khamza, "the lion, the sword of God and of his Messenger." But why before Badr are we unable to state with certainty the presence of Khamza in Medina, whereas his wife and his daughter remained in Mecca? As to Jafar, another of 'Ali's brothers, he is skilfully removed to Abyssinia. Why did he wait for Khaybar's conquest before deserving the glorious epithet of *taiyar*? This neglect is difficult to justify. Among all his relations why should 'Ali, the least determined, the least intelligent of them, have separated himself from them to share the fate of a reformer who preached in the desert? This is not a satisfactory conclusion.

And that is not all. When the time came to emigrate, Muhammad's followers preceded him to Medina. On the list of these *muhajir* one cannot find 'Ali's name. All the chroniclers agree about this.[101] If we are to believe them, 'Ali remained at Mecca by devotion. He wanted to help the escape and wind up the affairs of Muhammad, and finally protect and accompany Fatima's exodus.[102]. This is the first time we find these two names mentioned together.

This last mission must be attributed to the Shiites. In the other versions 'Ali arrives alone at Medina, on foot and in a pitiful state.[103] On the part of the Prophet we refuse to admit such a lack of regard for a cousin, if he had just shown him such heroic proof of his devotion.

Zayd ibn Haritha, Muhammad's *maula*[104] [freed slave], replaces 'Ali as the person in charge of bringing Fatima to Medina. He is one of the favorites of the orthodox school. The Sunna sometimes lacks the courage to attack directly the ridiculous exaggerations of the Shia, being frightened of indirectly attacking the Prophet and thus toppling over the fragile monument erected in his honor. It prefers parallel movements and a complicated series of maneuvers to frontal attacks. Disqualified by its own gullibility and incapable of handling the art of criticism, it limits itself to mining the ground under its enemy in an underhand way. By seizing on Zayd it has made out its statement to be the orthodox reply to the Shiite legend. These subtleties do not, however, make it any more believable. When the Shi'a presents 'Ali as the first Muslim, orthodoxy merely mentions what entitled Zayd to this qualification.[105] According to Noldeke, "it was to no one's interest to invent such merits for a person whose descendants played no role in the future. At most one could make out that they may have been underlined by the anti-Shiite reaction."[106] There can be no doubt about this reaction, as the entire history of this *maula* proves.

Nothing is as formidable as the insidious candor of the Hadith.[107] The progress achieved by the comparative studies of this branch of Islamic history, due largely to Goldziher's erudition, makes it possible to take it into account. We discover mysteries in what appear to be the most inoffensive variations. It is enough to be alert, so as not to be led astray by these childish stratagems[108] and the apparent objectivity[109] of these tales. The choice of Zayd as the first of the believers will provide another example of this. One had to possess a devious mind to suspect that this was a case of ulterior motives. This obscure Kalbite could be glorified without compromising anything, without provoking dangerous ambitions, without annoying the powerful of the period or provoking the Abbasid censorship. By using Zayd's name one could indulge in polemics while preserving an air of impartiality. 'Ali's followers liked him to have been granted the title of brother by his father-in-law. Zayd is equally favored. By the vividness of the terms[110] used by the Prophet to grant him this privilege, it is difficult not to recognize a controversial intention. Zayd not only brought Fatima to Medina, he also accomplished the same mission for Zaynab.[111] Here we have 'Ali outstripped!

This zeal is finally suspect. To the exaggerations of the Shia, orthodoxy opposed its own. To the obscurity in which Muhammad left his son-in-law, it opposed Zayd's military commands. Never, they observe, does he appear in a junior position, and that was when he had the college of Mubassara with him. To crown this tendency, Muhammad, had he survived, had thought of leaving him his inheritance. [112] Here, if I am not mistaken, is a direct assault[113] against 'Ali's followers, to whom 'Ali is par excellence the "emir of the believers." Why do we owe these important revelations to an authority as suspect as that of Aisha?[114] And what about the Prophet's affection which was transferred to Usama, Zayd's son? After having noted, as we have done, the paternal affection shown by Muhammad in the Koran, the authors of our canonical volumes like to show him amusing himself with Fatima's children, seating them on his knees. But opposite them, on the other thigh we are sure to see Usama appear. This picture is one of the most ingenious inventions of orthodoxy. The idea was that this perfect balance achieved between the Sunna and the Shia would neutralize the extremist theories. This is a point to which we will return.[115] But it was necessary at once to point out these praiseworthy efforts, so as to be able to gauge the value of the legend intended to glorify the 'Ali-Fatima relationship.

With Suhayb ibn Sinan, 'Ali found himself the last person to join Muhammad in Medina.[116] We do not know what time elapsed[117] between the

Hijra and his departure from Mecca. His presence at Badr is duly noted and he does not then appear as a newcomer among the Muslims. Our documents, duly interpreted, do not allow us to be more affirmative. We do not see him taking part in any of the earlier adventures. At Badr he is said to have shown a super-human activity and courage. The sira, in which 'Ali plays one of the principal roles from this point onward, does its best to help him make up for lost time. *Nemo fit repente summus* (no one reaches the summit in one go). No attention was paid to this axiom and not least by the enthusiastic Shiite al-Waqidi[118] in his *Kitab al-Maghazi*. The number of Qurayshites sacrificed by 'Ali[119] at Badr was enormous. As if these feats were not enough to show a beginner, the historians did their utmost to associate him with the prowesses of the other heroes at Badr.[120] Was not this going a bit too far? Now that 'Ali was caliph, many of his contemporaries contested his knowledge of military science.[121] His personal valor seems to have been real. But how could this young acolyte of the Prophet, brought up until then in Muhammad's bourgeois home,[122] and having never handled a sword, show on the first occasion such ardent courage and such an experience of combat?[123] For my part, I cannot attempt to explain this phenomenon. Life in the bazaaar and stalls of Mecca was not likely to develop military qualities to such a point.

Up to the end of his life, 'Ali remained on bad terms with his brother Aqil. After the Badr disaster he refused to intervene to soften his imprisonment.[124] These disagreements and his personal poverty may have prodded him to go and seek his fortune in Muhammad's circle. His beginnings in Mecca were difficult. He had to put himself at the disposal of a Jew and water the palm groves.[125] This would explain the delay in his marriage to Fatima. The Shia complicates the situation by asserting that they were already engaged prior to the Hijra. Yakubi dates the marriage at two months after their arrival in Medina. Other writers, in order to make things agree, resort to a hypothesis already used in the legend of Aisha. In both cases one has to admit to a double marriage. The final one should be situated after Badr, most likely after Uhud. As everyone presumes, there was an interval of one year between the two acts of this matrimonial scheme; the conclusion seems to have been somewhat laborious.[126]

For Arab women[127] the normal age of marriage was between nine and twelve. We can see parents worrying about the future of their daughters when there were no suitors around the age of ten.[128] Although not frequent, grandmothers of twenty-two were not exceptional in Arabia.[129] Amru ibn al-'Asi was married at the age of twelve, and there is mention of a divorce at the age of fourteen in the case of Usama ibn Zayd.[130] Consequently, we must expect our authors to try to insist that Fatima was younger at this important period of her life.[131] The great number of chronological combinations enumerated above that bring the date of her birth nearer the Hijra are not disinterested in intention.

The question of the marriage makes it necessary for our authors to quote figures and temporarily give up the method of elastic coincidences, as they did for Fatima's date of birth. A figure frequently given is that of fifteen or fifteen and a half[132] with a discreet clause (*aw akthar*, meaning "or more"), giving one to understand that there may be an addition. There are indeed authors, especially among the most ancient ones,[133] who speak of the age of eighteen. This last estimation is closer to the truth without being really true. If we accept an average of thirty for her total life span, Fatima must have been over twenty at the Badr period, possibly even the age when she could in Arabia[134] assume the title of grandmother. The acceptance of this fact makes clear the meaning of certain Hadith where she claims to be older than her husband,[135] a claim which cannot be accepted in the case of an engaged girl of fifteen.

'Ali would then have been about twenty-five.[136] This is yet another improbability if, with the entire Tradition, we have to consider 'Ali as having remained a bachelor up to that time. His poverty explains nothing. In the peninsula the old matrimonial code accepted a whole variety of cheap unions—the *muta*,[137] for example. Marriage was early for both sexes. What about the precedent established by Muhammad, marrying his first wife at twenty-five? Certain authors have, however, felt a need to make both the Prophet and 'Ali appear younger at that moment of their careers. The serious implications of this hypothesis did, however, make them hesitate. Even during Fatima's lifetime 'Ali forgets himself to the extent of speaking of "his wives" in connection with a coat received from the Prophet.[138]

Could they have not known the Master's teaching? He is supposed to have said, "I tremble for a young man who is not married." In his eyes bachelors were not only damned but were all firebrands of hell. In spite of the vigor of these expressions, and the more demonstrative eloquence of his behavior, he appeared to fear the contagion of the example of John the Baptist described as "hasur," a bachelor in the Koran. But the Prophet hastened to add that he did not wish to see his own people imitating the sons of Zacharia. He never ceased to develop these principles, resorting to the most expressive comparisons. "Two prostrations of a married Muslim are worth more than seventy by a bachelor." "Even if a bachelor possesses millions, he is poor, twice as poor." "One obtains more merit by spending a dinar on one's wife than on the poor or a holy war." "When a married couple hold each other by the hand, their sins disappear through the space dividing their fingers." "Is not the worth of a Muslim measured by the number of his wives?"[139]

One of Muhammad's last maxims seemed aimed at 'Ali' s physical infirmi-ties: "To gaze at greenery and a woman's face, there is nothing which strengthens sight as much as this."[140] Here we have a plea *pro matrimonio* attributed to Muhammad, and we have merely contented ourselves with a superficial selection from this rich anthology. How many of these maxims go back as far as Abul Qasim is not up to us to determine. But in attributing them to him, the Tradition was not too presumptuous in thinking that they were faithfully recording the thought of the Master and that of his contemporaries.

The conclusion that the Prophet[141] was not yet married by the age of twenty-five, and that this was also the case with 'Ali and Fatima, seems most probable; they were all frightened, as were the most devoted disciples of the Master, of dying as bachelors ("they were afraid of meeting God as bachelors"). On the other hand, the composition of the sira implies so many other problems that we must resign ourselves to taking note of that one as well. Sensual by nature, as was all his family, 'Ali did not wait for Fatima's death to show how heavily monogamy weighed on him. After her death he hastened to fill the void left by her absence by forming a large harem for himself.

As to the date of the marriage, apart from the Shiite authors and those with Alid tendencies,[142] no one dared to date it before the battle of Badr.[143] Those who claim that it was after Uhud must no doubt have excellent reasons for doing so.[144] It is not easy to understand the tendency which inspired them here. If, to estab-lish his daughters, Abul Qasim followed the order of primogeniture, Fatima, sup-posed to be the youngest, could not have preceded Umm Kulthum. The latter was married to 'Uthman in the interval between the battles. This conclusion is in agreement with the least uncertain deductions provided by comparative study of the sources.[145] In spite of their contradictions and the intentional lack of order, our documents do not succeed in hiding a certain painful discovery affecting Muhammad's self-respect—the difficulty in finding a son-in-law. Arabia does not recognize the status of spinsters—the demand seems always to exceed the supply.[146] This must particularly have been the case if we admit as widespread the custom of burying very young girls according to the idea recommended by the Koran. How poorly endowed must a girl have been to remain a spinster beyond the age of twenty! According to contemporary opinion, our portrait of Fatima must be a good likeness. 'Ali seems to have resigned himself to this with the pas-sivity which formed one of the features of his character.

Yet he apparently began by refusing any dowry, giving as an excuse that he was too poor. The Prophet had to insist, reminding him of the fine armor he had collected on the battlefield of Badr.[147] This fact, in the absence of any other direct information, determined many authors to date the marriage after the second year of the Hijra. The Prophet was, as we know, a great lover of scents and, according to Aisha's authorized testimony, accepted only the most exquisite of these.[148] So he recommended 'Ali to use two-thirds of his modest dowry—four hundred dirhems—on perfumes, the remainder being sufficient for the establishment of the new couple.[149] That is how our authors thought they could explain the young couple's poverty. At the same time they thought of a lesson in detachment, whereas they showed in Muhammad a deplorable example of improvidence, which very much conforms with the Arab character.

"When the Prophet thought of marrying off one of his daughters, he sat down close to her apartment, saying out loud—'So-and-so has pronounced your name.' If the fiancée said nothing, the affair was concluded. If she shook the curtain, negotiations were broken off."[150] This Hadith attempts, by putting forward Muhammad's example, to guarantee a precarious freedom to future brides—a freedom recognized by the ancient *jahiliya* [pagan, pre-Islamic Arabia]. Unfortunately, this concession was restricted by the insistence with which they have the Prophet saying that the young fiancée's[151] silence was equivalent to consent.

Consulted by her father about her future marriage to 'Ali, Fatima began by remaining silent.[152] A *silence* of surprise and bewilderment! The unfortunate child does not seem to have expected such a proposal. She immediately exploded[153] and noisily manifested her discontent. "You are marrying me off to a beggar,"[154] she screamed. Muhammad had to silence her.[155] Then, to calm her down, he started to enumerate 'Ali's qualities. "The oldest Muslim of his family the most intelligent, the best educated."[156] "God himself had destined him to be her husband." In this panegyric, the least questionable assertion, the ancientness of 'Ali in Islam, if it was of importance to Muhammad, could well leave his daughter indifferent. If her future husband and cousin had really been brought up with her in her father's house, and if through a thousand dangers he had brought her to Mecca, we must ask ourselves why Fatima refused to take all this shared past into account.

The heart has its reasons. Was it wrong for Fatima[157] to revolt? Why resist her father's eloquence? If the Prophet's daughter was not beautiful, 'Ali was far from being a model of male good looks. Among their heroes, Arab attach importance to height.[158] This would have been the case with the Hashimites, especially with Abbas.[159] Fatima's fiancé was very much lacking in this respect. From a bust that was too short[160] hung ridiculously thin arms above an exceedingly protuberant stomach.[161] In the middle of an enormous head were small, dim, and rheumy eyes and a snub nose.[162] This feature distinguished him from the Hashimites, whose noses were long enough to drink with before using the lips.[163] On seeing 'Ali for the first time, a woman had exclaimed, "What a strange

person! He looks as if the pieces had been fitted together haphazardly."[164] So
much for the physical appearance of Fatima's fiancé. To this must be added a
complete lack of intelligence—this was to weigh heavily during his entire
career—and finally extreme poverty, a feature common to all the members of
Abu Talib's family. Greedy Abbas had taken advantage of this to obtain the privilege of the *siqaia* [office of water supplier] at the Kaaba in exchange for a loan
of money that Abu Talib was unable to pay back to a money-lender.[165] We can see
that among the Abbasids spoliation of the Alids was a family tradition.

'Ali used the excuse of his poverty to refuse Fatima's dowry at first.
Muhammad was always to resent this as well as the misfortunes of their married
life. He openly contrasted 'Ali's attitude with that of his Umayyad sons-in-law,
the husband of Zaynab and 'Uthman, "the owners of the two lights" Ruqayya and
Umm Kulthum.[166] They at least knew how to appreciate the honor of an alliance
with the Prophet's family.[167]

III. THE FIRST YEARS OF MARRIAGE

In the story of this marriage we find self-esteem often wounded. The Prophet
must have been deeply mortified. His daughter had been his responsibility up to
around the age of twenty, more than double the age of Aisha and of the normal
Arab fiancée at the peiod of their marriage. On top of this, the marriage was not
a brilliant one. If Muhammad accepted it, it was undoubtedly to extricate himself
from a tricky situation. On the other hand, he was able to insert into the matrimonial contract the clause of monogamy, which was the position in which he had
found himself in relation to Khadija. We will later on be able to convince ourselves of this. All these small unpleasant incidents help us to understand the lack
of enthusiasm shown by the principal actors in this mysterious affair, where
nothing gives us the impression of a love match.

The Muslim authors prefer to fix their attention on the marriage ceremony,
very carefully organized by the Prophet.[168] But in their long descriptions they did
not mistrust enough their chronological knowledge. In their desire to glorify the
Hashimite family, they describe as present at the ceremony people who were
sojourning in Abyssinia or remaining with the non-believers in Mecca. In their
eagerness to flatter the Baghdad court these authors rather overdo things.

The marriage of Fatima and 'Ali, concluded under these auspices, could not
have been a happy one. In the new home, beside poverty,[169] discord soon
appeared. If Muhammad did not attempt to remedy the first problem, Tradition
attributes it to his detachment from worldly things; elsewhere, however, he is

shown covering Umama, the daughter of Zaynab, and Usama ibn Zayd with jewels. Fatima called this indifference and did not hesitate to tell him so straight out.[170] The following year, the battle of Uhud coincided with developments which took place in Muhammad's harem. The prophet was not short of resources, having become wealthy through the spoils taken from Qurayshite caravans, the plundering of the Jews and commercial speculation. For the latter he was associated with clever traders called *kalbites*,[171] and others who had a wonderful knowledge of the Syrian market from which Muhammad in Mecca attempted to evince his rivals. His favorite, Zayd ibn Haritha, combined the talents of a captain with those of a crafty commercial agent, and operated with skill for the account of his associate and master. They shared everything, and at times Zayd did not hesitate to lend his wife Zaynab to Muhammad.

The disagreement between 'Ali and Fatima, on the other hand, caused him serious worries. The Prophet felt constantly obliged to intervene, without managing to reestablish peace.[172] The births of Hasan and Husayn produced no improvement. The delicate Fatima did not feel strong enough to feed her children.[173] Traditionalist courtiers made Umm al Fadl, Abbas' wife,[174] carry out this task. Always the same system! They multiplied the obligations of the Fatimites toward the caliphs of Baghdad so as to make less odious the obscure and inferior position in which their suspicious policy aimed to maintain them. This dynastic zeal failed to take into consideration the religions indifference of Abbas who had remained in Mecca up to the period of the *fath*.[175] Under these circumstances one wonders how his wife was able to take over the inferior role of wet nurse in Fatima's home.[176] But all means were acceptable if they succeeded in making people forget the duplicity of Abbas and his family toward the Alids,[177] and made less improbable the conversion *in petto* of the Hashimite family. The success of this maneuver was helped by the credulousness of Muslim opinion and the complicity of the authors of the sira, who wished to remove from their path this obstacle and to protect themselves from the severity of official censorship.

On the birth of her eldest child, Fatima wished to carry out the customary sacrifice, the *Aqiqa*,[178] to celebrate the birth of a boy. Muhammad advised another custom—to cut the infant's hair,[179] calculate its weight in silver, and give it to the poor, preferably the *muhajir* beggars, known as *ahl as-suffa*. This same custom was observed on Husayn's birth.[180] A few minutes after Fatima had given birth, the Prophet hastened to whisper into his grandson's ear the Muslim profesion of faith[181] and then give him his saliva to taste. This was the *tahnik*,[182] a usual practice with Abul Qasim when newborn infants were brought to him. In the case of Husayn he arrived too late, for Fatima hastened to suckle him. "That is why," the narrator adds, "Hasan was the more intelligent of the two brothers."[183] It is impossible to trace in advance a more bloody caricature of the lamentable hero of Kar-bala.[184] They finished him off by having 'Ali declare that "among my children none resembles me more than Husayn."[185]

Besides Hasan and Husayn, documents grant Fatima a third son—Muhassin.[186] His problematic existence—it was useful to have him disappear early on—was mainly affirmed by the Shiites or by the partisans of the Alids, who wished to multiply for Fatima the honors of motherhood.[187] His head filled with warlike ideas, 'Ali, as he was later to say, had imposed on all his sons the warrior name of *Harb* [war]. This move was not approved of by his father-in-law. For Harb he substituted the names which the sons of Harun[188] had borne in the past. Thus the connection between 'Ali and Harun so dear to the Shia was strengthened by the Prophet's testimony. At the same time, they intended this to be a demonstration[189] against a name honored by the Umayyads.[190] The Alid legend did not hesitate to resort to petty suggestions.

If one can rely on these tales, the young couple was not short of money. Around this period Fatima was even able to relieve the poverty of Abul Qasim and give him a slice of bread, "the first he had eaten for three days." Hunger sometimes obliged him "to fix a stone on his stomach." The same story was told about 'Ali,[191] and one wonders how Fatima managed under these painful circum-stances, and why a Hadith describes the Prophet as "corpulent, youthful and full of physical vigor."[192]

Nor can we explain any better the attitude of the Ansars, who left the Master reduced to such extremities. Also, the *musnad* of the inhabitants of Medina[193] pro-vides us with a completely different version. I suspect their patriotic narrators exaggerated the generous Ansarian hospitality when they made such a point of his robust appetite. He went from banquet to banquet where he was gorged with meat, and he generally did justice to it. At one of these feasts he had eaten his favorite dishes—the national *tarida* of Quraysh, meats, and pumpkin. Back home he discovered a large basket of dates, a present from a Medina family. He was fond of them and ate the entire contents of the basket.[194] In Medina everyone wanted to entertain the Prophet to a meal. When he received an invitation to a meal, he often made it a condition that Aisha[195] should accompany him. But never do we hear him making the condition in favor of Fatima or 'Ali.[196]

Early on the chroniclers felt a need to embroider on the debacle of Uhud. Two groups contributed especially to this—the Medina school, happy to exalt the merits of the Ansar, at times at the expense of the *muhajirs*,[197] and later 'Ali's circle of friends and "the people of the house." Among the legendary develop-ments this latter group tried to introduce the intervention of Fatima in this mili-tary event of primitive Islam. It is not part of the oldest texts, and neither Ibn

Hisham or al-Tabari take the trouble to mention Fatima here. This could not be an omission among writers who were well disposed toward the Alids.[198] During this disorderly retreat, from which Muhammad withdrew with difficulty, it is hard for us to explain the presence of a woman, and particularly such a woman as 'Ali's feeble wife. The legitimist zeal of al-Waqidi did not allow this to worry him. His story shows Fatima proceeding in the courtyard of the mosque to dress Muhammad's wounds on his return from Uhud. A few lines later, without the introduction of a *new isnad,* we can see the same Fatima in the middle of the battlefield nursing her father's wound, assisted by 'Ali.[199] It remains to be determined how they managed to link up the two versions. Unfortunately, the extreme defectiveness of the text edited by von Kremer makes it impossible to check on this.

Hamza's death caused Fatima's tears to start flowing again. From then onward she apparently adopted the habit of going every other day to Uhud to weep on the tomb of the "lion of Allah."[200] It was a hard journey on foot for this sickly mother of numerous children, when, to visit the village of Qoba close to Medina, Muhammad always rode on Yafur, his legendary donkey.[201] Was it not necessary to legitimize the cult of saints and tombs[202] in Islam making use of such an authorized example? Fatima's contemporaries hastened to forget where her remains rested, as well as those of 'Ali. Primitive Islam took no interest in the dead.

After the death of Jafar, whom she hardly knew, Fatima resumed her role as weeper.[203] None suited her better. Her lack of experience made her less succeseful in more delicate missions, such as when she allowed herself to be persuaded to intervene in the quarrels within her father's harem. This daughter of the great politician that was Muhammad lacked the finesse necessary to succeed in diplomatic negotiations. In Abul Qasim's home there existed, as we have noted elsewhere,[204] two parties, that of the triumvirs formed by Aisha and Hafsa, who were two formidable intriguers and worthy daughters of Abu Bakr and 'Umar as the Tradition candidly observes, and that of their opponents, consisting of the other wives who were divided among themselves; all of them were in league against the scandalous favoritism shown towards Aisha. Tired of seeing the uselessness of their protesting to the Master, they resolved to use his daughter as a go-between. It was an unfortunate choice. Fatima accepted, as both she and her husband were on bad terms with the favorite, and they had strong hopes of regaining part of the influence removed from Abu Bakr's wilful daughter.

Fatima, dressed in Aisha's skirt, "martuha," met her father with other people present. "Your wives," she said "have sent me to you to claim equality of treatment[205] with Abu Quhafa's daughter."[206] "All right, my child (*bunayya*)," Muhammad replied, "is not my pleasure yours?" "Of course, Prophet!" "Then you must approve of my behavior toward Aisha."[207] After this rejoinder, Fatima withdrew and went to give an account of her mission to the other spouses. They all cried out, "Your mission has failed. You must start again!" "Never will I bring up the subject again," replied Fatima.[208] Az-Zuhri added this thought: "Fatima truly was the daughter of Allah's Envoy." He was happy to conclude by this flattering sentence such a discreditable tale.[209]

Fatima's relationship with Aisha, who was already on extremely bad terms with 'Ali, did not subsequently improve. Once, as night was falling, Muhammad had just returned to Aisha's apartment where Umm Salama, another of his wives, was present. He did not notice the presence of the Makhzumite despite Aisha's signs attempting to draw his attention in that direction. In the end Umm Salama, no longer able to control herself,[210] said, "I see perfectly well that your other wives do not count in your eyes." Addressing herself directly to Aisha, she began to abuse her. The Prophet tried in vain to calm her down. Unable to succeed, he said to Aisha, "Go on, reply to these insults," which the favorite was not reluctant to do. With her well-known talent[211] she soon reduced Umm Salama to silence, slandering[212] Fatima and her husband in the course of the outburst. Furious, Umm Salama went to see them: "Aisha," she told them, "has insulted you and said outrageous things about you!" 'Ali addressed his wife and said, "Go and see your father to protest against Aisha's attitude toward us." Fatima proceeded to do this, but after listening to her, Muhammad merely replied, "By the Master of the Kaaba she is your father's favorite (*hubba*)." When 'Ali heard the results of the interview, he went to see his father-in-law and said to him, "Was it not enough to be insulted by Aisha? Was it necessary in front of Fatima to add the words 'She is my favorite?'"[213] To put an end to these quarrels, Abul Qasim felt obliged to block the door[214] which led from his house to Fatima's.[215]

These incidents did not increase 'Ali's consideration for her, nor did they reestablish peaceful relations between the couple. Intellectually they were both too limited to understand the necessity of reciprocal concessions. Their relationship with the Prophet and the members of his harem strengthens this impression. According to our documents,[216] Ali resigned himself to monogamy during Fatima's lifetime.[217] I must admit that I am not convinced. In the custom of the period, monogamous marriages were the exception, and only when the wife was in a position to dictate her conditions, as "the great Khadija"[218] had done to Muhammad.

'Ali's poverty has been exaggerated. It was an attempt to ensure his aura of *zuhd* [asceticism] on which his legend insisted.[219] Was his son Muhammad ibn Hanafiya younger than the two Hasans? He was called Muhammad al-Akbar, the elder, to distinguish him, we are assured, from another brother, Muhammad, who was younger. But we have learnt to be wary of this traditional erudition where there is an explanation for everything. In the battles of the Camel and of Siffin he appears in full vigor and compares favorably with Hasan and Husayn, thanks to his courage.[220]

After Karbala, 'Ali was the hope of the Shia, although to the detriment of the descendants left by Hasan and Husayn. Regardless, in addition to Fatima's difficult character and Muhammad's indifference, monogamy soon weighed on 'Ali, and he showed his intention of abandoning it. Once more we can put our finger on the lack of judgment[221] which characterized the Prophet's son-in-law.[222]

Among the Qurayshite clans one distinguished the Banu Makhzum. In Medina, Umm Salama, Muhammad's future wife, was accused of lying, when she stated that she was a member of that family.[223] Along with the Umayyads, the Makhzumites were in the first rank of the financial aristocracy of Mecca. The rout of Badr hit them badly—"a punishment for their infidelity," 'Ali is supposed to have said.[224] This unkind judgment did not prevent him from lending a sympathetic ear to the matrimonial propositions coming from the Makhzumite party. He did not refuse them since he allowed the Banu Mujira to sound out Muhammad on the subject. It might have been a maneuver intended to goad his father-in-law. The son-in-law accused him of showing coldness toward him. Almost at the same time (at least if the historians have not confused two of Muhammad's enemies, Abu Jahl and Abu Lahab), 'Ali is said to have asked for the hand of the latter's daughter.[225] Had not Zayd, Muhammad's favorite, also married Abu Lahab's daughter, whom he later repudiated?[226] On 'Ali's side this step[227] was particularly unfortunate, given the well-known hostility of the Lahabids.

Our chroniclers felt this and did their best to discover a way of toning down this error. 'Ali, they insisted, did not think to sadden Fatima. In his case such thoughtlessness does not seem to be a way of toning down *a priori*, the improbable. The Lahabid fiancée was said to belong to an early[228] Muslim family.[229] This suggestion is as plausible as is the secret Islamism of Abbas and his family. On the other hand, the Prophet is said to have uttered these affectionate words to Abu Lahab's daughter: "You are one of mine and I am one of yours" (*anti minni wa ana minki*)[230] in defense against the unkindly allusions of the Surat—"Woe to Abu Lahab!" (*tabbat yaddan Abi Lahab*).[231]

"Very jealous of his daughters, Muhammad did not wish them to have rivals."[232] Here we have a statement which is contradicted by the history of the Prophet's daughters- and sons-in-law. The excellent 'Uthman had a large harem which corresponded to the size of his fortune. Abul Qasim seems to have accepted this and, according to the testimony of the *Sahih* he continued to show him the greatest regard. He never received him wearing a dressing-gown, as he allowed himself to do with Abu Bakr and 'Umar. [233] Undoubtedly 'Ali, a soldier of fortune, could not compare with the opulent and generous Umayyad. Having become a head of state, Muhammad was only too pleased to forget his previous ranting against financiers.[234]Abul Asi was chosen by the sira to become Zaynab's husband. We know very little about this other Umayyad, but we would be misleading ourselves to imagine this Qurayshite banker as monogamous. This did not prevent Muhammad from praising him highly.

Muhammad carried this debate to the pulpit in Medina, where he was in the habit of dealing with his family affairs. He protested with vigour against 'Ali's attitude, "claiming to shelter under the same roof the daughter of the enemy of God and that of his Envoy." Moreover, he allowed him the possibility of divorce![235] This clearly showed how little his son-in-law meant to him. The Hadith did not foresee this conclusion, being mainly concerned with preparing the final eulogy for Fatima pronounced by her father under these circumstances: "She is part of my flesh and blood" (*Innaha bad'a minni*).[236]

Obviously during this whole affair 'Ali was tactless. He had just given a new proof of his incurable thoughtlessness by neglecting to take into account his wife's legitimate annoyance. To the reproaches of his father-in-law he could have opposed his grievances, all of which were not imaginary. Muhammad persisted in taking no notice of him. This astonished the Qurayshites, as 'Ali one day remarked to Fatima's father.[237] This coldness brings a discordant note to the closeness imagined by the Shiite legend[238] between the Prophet and the fortunate mortal chosen by Allah and his Envoy to perpetuate the descendance of the "seal of the prophets."

On her side Fatima never stopped complaining. "You do not side with your daughters (*la taghzibu li-banatika*)," she said to her father. In these recriminations she continually harped on her poverty. If one literally accepts the tales of our authors, this must have been heartbreaking. At times even bread was lacking. Under the weight of this demoralizing atmosphere, Fatima did not feel inclined to give alms. At times she criticized her husband for his indiscreet acts of charity.[239] This theme was developed with satisfaction by the Shiite *musnad*.

Bilal arrived late one day to announce the morning prayer. The Prophet reproached him for this. "I was passing by your daughter's house and she was busy grinding wheat, while Hasan was crying in his cot," replied the Abyssinian. "I hastened to offer her my services either for grinding wheat or for looking after her son. She refused. 'My son,' she said, 'touches me even more than you do.'[240] Here you have the reason for my lateness. Poor woman! God take pity on her, and you too!"[241] To these tiring tasks were added the weight of her illness. Her father came one day to enquire after her health. "I feel weighed down by sadness and misery," she replied. "I cannot see an end to my miseries and disabilities."[242]

To this moaning she probably added recriminations against 'Ali. The Prophet took this opportunity to exalt the merits of his son-in-law and his seniority in Islam. 'Ali's unfortunate wife seems to have expected less illusory consolation and less theoretical comfort.

When, in the interval between her ailments, she was able to explain in detail to her father the inconvenience of her position, exposed to the torture of hunger;[243] when she showed him the roughness of her hands worn down by grinding wheat or kneading bread,[244] and begged him to provide her with some form of help,[245] the Prophet would teach her a prayer to recite on going to bed.[246] Around that period on the return of the victorious *maghazi,* prisoners of war flooded into Medina. Fatima wanted to find a servant among them to help her with domestic tasks. Muhammad again refused to comply with his daughter's wishes. He seemed worn out and bored by her incessant complaints.[247] 'Ali then asked his mother to help Fatima "by fetching water from outside the house, in exchange for which Fatima would take her mother-in-law's place in the baking of bread."[248] Unfortunately for this version, 'Ali's mother never left Medina prior to the *fath,* and from that time on there was no lack of servants in 'Ali's house.

Because of her weak constitution, Fatima lacked the energy required to combat the pernicious effects of Medina's feverish climate. It continued to affect Muhammad's Qurayshite companions[249] to the extent of preventing them from standing up, perhaps the essential part of the primitive *salat.*[250] Fatima's difficult life, her domestic problems, and her moral sufferings finally diminished her resistance. She soon became frighteningly thin and her body seemed to be wasting away.[251] Rejected by her father,[252] she should have had the support of her husband. If she had ever had any illusions about him, these soon disappeared. As head of the family, 'Ali showed the same incapacity that was later to ruin the caliph of Iraq.

Poor when they arrived at Medina, most of the Meccan Companions managed to find resources. They provided no recruits for the "veranda corporation" (*ahl al-suffa*), poor devils living off public charity. Several rapidly enriched themselves by taking part in profitable raids against the Qurayshite caravans or by resuming their former trades. They soon managed to obtain the comforts of life (*al-tayyibat*) as is asserted by Allah, or rather Muhammad, happy to remind his followers of their obligations toward himself. Abu Bakr, 'Uthman, Zubayr, Talha, and Abdurrahman ibn Auf, to name but a few,[253] had acted thus. They spent their time in the bazaar (*al-safq bi-l-aswaq*) waiting for the opportunity to embark on profitable speculation. 'Umar was soon able to acquire property taken from the Jews. This prosperity, this cupidity, occasionally worried Muhammad. He feared they would be less easy to control. "You are becoming too rich," he said one day to Abu Bakr. His friend 'Umar was later to agree with this. His passion for commerce had often prevented him from regularly attending the Prophet and acquiring the historical erudition of a Abu Huraira. From the second year of the Hijra we see these people surrounded by slaves and *maulas*.[254] The victory of Badr was above all a commercial success for Medina, to which Muhammad had at first dreamt of transporting the economic prosperity of Mecca.

The sira did not exaggerate when it showed the privileged position acquired by the Abu Bakr and 'Umar group.[255] If Abul Qasim trusted them, it was because he found in them the intelligent initiative and the boldness which characterized the true Qurayshites. [256] Here lies the secret of the prodigious wealth of these self-made men operating within Young Islam. This became obvious after the *fath*. The political eclecticism of the Prophet would not have waited for this date to grant the same distinction to the capable Umayyads if from the beginning he had found them at his side. One must also no doubt take into account the intrigues of the harem, where Aisha and Hafsa were in charge and operated freely without fearing the intervention of poor Fatima.[257] But it would be grossly exaggerating the importance of these maneuvers if one did not attribute to 'Ali's incapacity the main reason for the isolation in which his father-in-law allowed him to moulder. In spite of his sensuality (*quwwa shawatihi*, meaning the force of his desire) complacently noted by the Tradition[258] at critical moments or when the interests of the state were involved, the very positive Abul Qasim knew how to pull himself together. Henri de Bornier noted that side of his character when he had him saying:

> The woman is the pleasure for a day
> But the man who lets her usurp in his soul
> The place of his austere duties, God blames!
> The wiseman must also be sometimes astonished,
> I share my heart[259] so as to not give it!
> I perform, even in that, the duty of the Apostle;
> Aisha, they said? She not more than another.[260]

If he made use of 'Ali's courage in the *mashahid* (the meetings), he never thought of highlighting it in any other way, even by giving him a military command or entrusting him with certain missions, as, for example the *sadaqa* (the alms). Muhammad disliked the idea of handing over to the grasping Hashimites the administration of these funds. He even openly refused to do so, as he had done previously for 'Ali.[261] "The Prophet was not fond of the company of his son-in-law (*kariha sahbatahu*, meaning he detested his company)," said the Companions.

During his numerous absences from Medina, he preferred to be replaced if necessary by a blind man, Ibn Umm Maktum. He had so little confidence in the capabilities of his son-in-law. "A mountain can change places, but not a man of character" is what they have Muhammad saying.[262] Entirely involved in his political plans, he hoped for nothing from 'Ali.

This situation could not bring Fatima back to him. Out of consideration for the Prophet's daughter, 'Ali seems not to have reacted to her recriminations,[263] without, however, taking the trouble to mend his ways. In the interval between the principal events of military history during the Medina period, it is impossible to reconstruct 'Ali's time-table.

One is led to believe that he remained lying down[264] (*idtaja'a*) as the Hadith shows us, particularly after the frequent disputes with his wife. He, did, however sometimes bring home a handful of dates, a meager salary earned by drawing water for a Jewish proprietor. "Eat," he said to Fatima, "and feed the little ones."[265] On other occasions, pressed by hunger, he had to run to Awali, an hour's distance from Medina, to look for work. But after these intermittent efforts, his natural indolence again took possession of this "great sleeper," as he called himself.[266]

Muhammad did not disdain the help of poets to reply to the attacks of the Qurayshites. It was suggested that he use 'Ali. "He is incapable," he replied (*laysa 'indahu dalika*.)[267] Yet he was the brother of the witty Aqil, a fact which very much astonished his contemporaries.[268] A century later Kumait,[269] the minstrel of the Shia, was to celebrate him as "the glorious model of unselfishness and virtue, capable of solving difficulties and restoring shattered situations" ("*kana ahl al 'afafi wa-l-majdi wa-l-khayri wa-l-naqdi al-umuri wa-l-ibrami*").

For the moment he showed none of these heroic qualities. Instead of squarely tackling the problems caused by his domestic situation, he adopted the habit of deserting his home. He frequently preferred to spend the night under the veranda of his father-in-law's *dar*, which served as a mosque. In this way he must have acquired the nickname of Abu Torab.[270] The Muslim authors did not manage to provide a plausible explanation for this curious nickname. It might be an allusion, as Sarasin suspects,[271] to Fatima's husband's fatness. It certainly does not celebrate a heroic action, as we can guess by the desperate efforts of the Alid writers to transform it into an honorific *kunya*.

The great Sahabis showed no tenderness toward their female companions.[272] These unfortunate women hesitated to complain to Muhammad in order to avoid increased violence. Such a case had occurred and the Tradition hastened to put the blame on an Umayyad, Walid ibn Uqba. When a deplorable action took place in the Master's neighborhood, in the exemplary community of Medina, the *Sahih* managed to put the blame on a member of that family. Only the Ansarian women showed sufficient independence to resist the least justifiable whims of their

Qurayshite husbands. Should we consider this as the reason why there was not a single woman from Medina in Abul Qasim's harem?[273]

More than once the Prophet is said to have protested against these brutalities. "Among the faithful," he said, "the most perfect man should distinguish himself by showing civility toward his wife."[274] 'Ali did not understand this lesson. The volumes of the Hadith mention violent scenes between the couple. They show 'Ali's hard attitude to the mother of his children. He forgot himself to the point of ill-treating this ailing woman, forcing her to take refuge in her father's house.[275]

We know the Prophet's attitude when faced with these delicate situations. Whether 'Ali or 'Uthman, Fatima or Ruqayya[276] were concerned, he ordered his daughters "to comply with their husbands' moods." "If a mortal," he also said, "had the right to bow down before an equal, I would order a woman to do the same in front of her husband."[277] It would be difficult to find someone who was less of a feminist! In the very middle of the day he found Fatima lying down. Was it indolence or illness? In the case of 'Ali's anaemic wife, both explanations are possible. Muhammad kicked her brutally with his foot, one of his familiar gestures to waken sleepers.[278] If he met her alone in the streets of Medina, he rudely challenged her: "What has pushed you out of your house?"[279] There is no doubt that our authors intended here to have the Prophet instil the obligation of cloistering women. They did not ask themselves if these customs did not give the impression of a family where there was a lack of unity. The only important point in their eyes was to establish a doctrine. They did not concern themselves with other logical conclusions.[280] No matter if such a discrepancy threatened the coherence of the whole of the sira.

IV. HEAD OF STATE, MUHAMMAD NEGLECTS FATIMA

The moment has come to examine more closely the reasons why Muhammad abandoned 'Ali and Fatima in a state of near-destitution. Are we entitled to put forward the personal poverty of the Prophet and his spirit of detachment toward his family? Should we agree with the explanations produced or insinuated by the Hadith?

Mainly since the conquest of the Khaybar, one notes in his case signs of an important evolution. The Prophet transformed himself imperceptibly into a head of state. This change in Abul Qasim's personality did not escape the notice of the Bedouins, who were astute observers. "That man aspires to dominate the Arabs," said the Taiyite chief Zarr ibn Sadus. "I see a man who possesses the napes of Arabs."[281] The shrewd politician Abu Sufyan was to make the same observation: "Prophetism is finished, the empire is beginning."[282] It is impossible to be more perspicacious. By protesting against this opposition, the banker Abbas, Muhammad's uncle, with the enthusiasm of a convert, flattered Abul Qasim's pride. In the secret depths of Muhammad's conscience there surged more and more precise aspirations toward domination and sovereignty, or *al-mulk* as the Arabs say. [283] He felt he had been born[284] to govern his contemporaries, and in this he was not mistaken.

In a the past, he had enumerated in the Koran (sura 3:12, in Fluegel's rescension) the series of temptations which could enslave human beings: "The passion for women,[285] the desire for male children, the thirst for gold and silver, spirited horses, and the possession of cattle and land, in fact all the pleasures of life on earth." Now the Prophet wanted to possess them. In Mecca he had continually stated the purity of his intentions and his unselfishness. This claim he put, for his own account, into the mouths of the prophets, his predecessors.[286] Why was all this not said in good faith? These statements had been made at the start of his career. Where was it to lead him? Did this misunderstood innovator himself fail to recognize where his ambition was to bring him, and how he was to be seduced by riches, "the greatest that any leader in Central Arabia had ever possessed" (Caetani)? After a painful period of tentative efforts, success had come. This was a difficult test! Was it to leave him with the strength to resist? To persevere in his first role of a reformer, and this without mental reservations?

From then onward his main preoccupation consisted in surrounding himself with luxury and the attributes of supreme power, of *mulk* as it appeared to an Arab of the Hijaz in the first half of the seventh century. He had become a sovereign,[287] not only in his own estimation but also that of his contemporaries.[288] In the midst of the splitting-up of tribes and since the ruin of the Himyarite state, no one could remember such power in the hands of one man. The oases of the northwest belonged to him, and he had imposed his authority on the three great cities of the Hijaz. In spite of their intelligence, the superiority of their culture, and their wealth, the People of the Book had been unable to resist him. If he had consented to tolerate certain establishments of theirs, it was only by reducing them to the condition of dependants or tenants. In various respects, the Bedouins underwent his influence. They filled the gaps in the ranks of his officers and served as spies and pirates in the desert. At the eastern borders of the Hijaz, the large tribes of the Najd, the Solaim, the Catafan, and the Tamim remained neutral or offered their services in exchange for subsidies provided by the *talif* funds.[289] In the midst of their internal divisions, the minorities and the conquered parties came to solicit his intervention, asking as a favor to be assimilated into the Medina confederation. After such demonstrations, how could he doubt his power?

How could they not have considered him as the "king and arbiter of the Arabs"? The great poet Asa[290] proclaimed him thus, after having contemplated the glory of the Lahmids and the Jafnids. He appeared to them as the successor and heir to the power of these emirs.[291] The court poets Hassan ibn Thabit, Abdallah ibn Rawaha, and Kas'b ibn Malik sang his praises as Asa and the Prophet in no way protested against their profane language. After years of humiliation, he privately revelled in his triumph. "Have we not made your chest swell? Relieved you of the burden under which you bowed?—After your ordeals came success![292] Soon the munificence of your Lord will fulfil your wishes—Having found you as an orphan, did he not protect you? Finding you wandering he showed you the way, finding you naked he made you rich? As to the favor of the Lord, you can proclaim it!"[293] Thus Allah tried to support his Envoy.

This encouragement was in fact superfluous. He was never able to understand the humiliated and crucified figure of Christ. He has all the prophets present at the crushing of their enemies. His Islam is a restoration of Semitism in its most acute and down-to-earth form. Earthly possessions, the joys of life (at-taiybat), are the rewards of Allah's envoyas. "Live richly and in affluence"![294]

He asked no better than to preach the realization of divine promises, the fulfilment of his triumph. He considered it prudent to hide this development from the eyes of his followers and to humor their revolutionary instincts of independence.[295] Did he not attempt to present the mulk as the natural complement of the prophecy? Certain Koranic verses[296] allow us to suppose this.[297] To a poor Bedouin impressed by the display surrounding the Prophet, he consented to say, "I am not a king, but the son of a woman from Qurays."[298] When members of deputations addressed him by the title of "master of Saiyd," he coyly told them not to exaggerate.[299] But by the lack of emphasis of the recommendation one can guess how much he really enjoyed these trappings of royalty. Why, in a scene no doubt improbable, does the Hadith forget to have him protest when the Companions, shattered by his fatalistic sermons, fall down on their knees (jathu 'ala-l-rikab) to ask for mercy.[300]

To their most influential saiyds, to Adi son of the great Hatim, the Bedouin contested the right to sit down on a carpet during the nadi, the council of their tribe. To obtain this privilege, 'Ali was to invoke his great age and his infirmities.[301] Up to that day Muhammad had modestly presided over the Friday meetings in his masjid, crouching on a leather cushion,[302] his back leaning against the trunk of a palm tree.[303] The victor of the Azhab or Confederates, the conqueror of the Khaybar and of Mecca could not be satisfied by this democratic display.

So on the day of general prayers[304] for the solemn reception of the *wufuds*[305] he would give orders to have the mosque scented. The rarest essences were burnt in large urns, *mijmar*, at times decorated with figures in relief,[306] brought from Syria or the Yemen by his commercial agents. In Arabia, "the homeland of perfumes, *Arabia odorifera*," more than any other country in the Orient, perfumes were one of the chief luxuries.[307] Abul Qasim and his disciples remembered at the right moment that in Abyssinia and Syria they had seen the important officials seated on thrones placed on platforms.[308] This dominating position was to seduce their primitive minds: it symbolized the power of the ruler! The excuse for it was that it would allow the assembly to follow the movements of Muhammad's prayer,[309] undoubtedly in order to calm their democratic prejudices. Muhammad hastened to adopt this custom which was the origin of the *minbar*, so famous in the history of Islam.[310] He soon owned a whole collection of pulpits, more or less luxurious, according to the degree of solemnity in which they were to appear. On ordinary Fridays, certain accounts show him installed on a seat resting on iron legs.[311] The philological explanation of these *Hadith* worried the commentators and authors of the *Gharib* [rare and isolated tradition].[312] At the beginning, they were satisfied with a simple wooden stepladder counting three or four rungs, the work of a carpenter, the slave of an Ansarian woman, and probably a native of Syria.[313]

From this height, from what was both a throne[314] and a platform, he would lecture the crowds, not standing up[315] as the old-fashioned Tradition claimed, but sitting in the fulness of his authority as a legislator and of his prestige as a King-Prophet. In his hand he held a sort of scepter (*'asa, qadib*); a stick (*mihjan*) made of precious wood, encrusted with gold and ivory; and a short spear or javelin[316] (*'anaza*) like the command batons artistically fashioned that the Byzantine government gave to the barbarian chieftains who rallied to the Empire.[317] If he had to move his attendants carried this insignia in front of him, when it pleased him to hand it to them.[318] Once installed in his pulpit, he took it back and used it to emphasize parts of his speech.[319]

Also in imitation of the imperial governors, he had chamberlains[320] and heralds known as *mo'addin* or *monadi*.[321] The latter were attached to his public relations department, the most active agents of the local chancellery in Medina, responsible for issuing proclamations and summoning people to meetings, assemblies, and prayers. The negro Bilal combined the functions of attendant and town-crier. He was Abu Bakr's man (*maula*), the latter being interested in finding out about the incidents of his son-in-law's daily existence. His stentorian voice made him a suitable candidate for this position. He was not the only one, as a certain Tradition would have one believe,[322] but the best known among those who formed the Prophet's entourage. He has remained the typical *monadi-mo'addin*.

On important days Bilal would precede the Prophet, unfolding a sort of canopy[323] above his head. The Abyssinian negro had poor sight, and his pronunciation was defective.[324] Another colleague, Ibn Umm Maktum, Muhammad's usual representative during his absences from Medina, was totally blind. This infirmity would have been unfortunate if at that time the system of the five prayers had been established, since they took place at fixed hours. But we know what reservations we must have about this!

When Muhammad presided in the minbar, Bilal would stand at the foot of the throne, an unsheathed sword in his hand,[325] the very sword which belonged to Muhammad. It was a sumptuous weapon with its artistically engraved hilt, a ceremonial sword which had never been used in action. We see where the Umayyads and their governors[326] got the idea of surrounding themselves with soldiers when in mosques. Crimson and red were the signs of power.[327] Muhammad had proclaimed in the past that Satan's favorite color was red. [328] Early on, however, we see him wearing a scarlet tunic and in this garment attending the fairs, *mawasim,* in the Hijaz.[329] As a sovereign, Abul Qasim reserved for himself the right to abandon the prejudices of the old reformer. In the *Imta,* Maqrizi shows him continually changing his clothes,[330] absolutely refusing to wear woollen materials.[331] His delicate sense[332] of smell could not stand the characteristic odor caused by his abundant perspiration, although according to the sira he was always perfumed.

Liking simplicity in everyday life, Muhammad had nothing against display. He knew how to be a sovereign. For solemn occasions he would put on a large red *chlamys* [short cloak].[333] It cost him fifty dinars,[334] fifty of those brilliant *aurei* [gold coins of the Roman Empire] of Heraclius, so lovingly cherished by the *sarraf* of Mecca.[335] Or he would wear silk tunics,[336] crimson robes,[337] or the beautiful coat, richly trimmed in gold, brought back by Kalid ibn al-Walid from Dumat al-Jandal [on the borders of Syria]; or other ceremonial tunics, gifts from the monks who lived in the neighboring deserts[338] or Christians from Najran,[339] or purchased by his agents in Syria, Egypt,[340] Aden, Sohar, Qatar, the Hadramaut, and in other manufacturing centers[341] such as Manbig in Syria. The garments made in that city were called *anbijaniya*[342]—that is, at any rate, the slightly deformed[343] version kept by our *sahih* and our *musnad,* instead of the correct spelling *manbijaniya.*

The red tunic in particular suited him perfectly. When he dressed[344] his fine and abundant hair (*mutarajjil,* meaning very masculine), all eyes were riveted on him. Everyone agreed on this point.[345] What a varied wardrobe the Prophet possessed! For him nothing was too precious when it was a question of dazzling the Bedouin of the region. The simple faithful were on this earth to abstain from wearing silk, crimson robes, or brocade, and from all other worldly luxuries.[346] Otherwise, they would not enjoy these advantages in the next world. But the sovereign of Medina, "the good example for his followers," understood what his new dignity demanded. More especially on days of combat, he would remember to don a precious silk tunic.[347] For official parades such as the farewell pilgrimage, he would shelter under a brocade parasol.

Moreover, he allowed the members of his close circle, the great Sahabis, such as Zubayr, Talba, and Abd ar-Rahman ibn 'Auf, to wear silk to protect themselves from vermin or as a cure for skin complaints! This is a banal exegesis intended to satisfy the alleged asceticism of early Islam. The readers of the *sahih* and the *musnad* were willing to accept this distinction.[348] Nothing obliges one to imitate their discretion.[349] We see Muhammad distributing rich silk tunics, not only to the women of his circle and his relations to Hashimites and the mothers of believers, but also to Usama, 'Ali, and 'Umar,[350] three carefully selected names to prove the impartiality of the donor and to warn off any interpretation by the extremist schools. The austere son of al-Khattab hastened to sell his so as not to have to sacrifice the silk tunics reserved for the blessed inhabitants of Paradise. The Tradition asserts this, and may well be right. These merchants from Qurays were never able to resist the lure of profitable transactions! But elsewhere we see the Master on feast days, surrounded by a veritable court, and in the first row the college of the *Mubassara*[351] or, as the texts say, the most distinguished of his companions [see glossary under *asharah mubashsharah*]. Moreover, if among the Companions there existed an aristocracy, it was above all composed of the Mubassars. Following his orders, they appeared dazzling in their brilliant uniforms.[352] By attempting to pour the *imago primi saeculi* into the mold of Christian asceticism, the rearrangement in the Tradition neglected to efface these characteriatics, thus disturbing the harmony of the whole. Even when travelling, these great friends of Muhammad, directly trained in his school, took with them precious garments from the Yemen or from Sephoris in Galilee.[353]

Apart from the Friday *khutbas* for the reception of deputations, sometimes set up in the vast courtyard of the mosque was a spacious scarlet leather tent[354] like those which the Jafnids and Lakhmid emirs[355] had owned. Muhammad took it with him on his journeys.[356] Among the ancient Arabs, the most ostentatious of races[357] (*afkhar al-umam*), this showy color was meant to strike their guests. It was a symbol of grandeur and power. By placing Muhammad in his background we are getting closer to the truth. In the large pavilion, in the Prophet's *majlis*, were spreadout Persian hangings, damask materials from Syria, and carpets from the East.[358] Everywhere, on the divans, on the heavy door curtains, there was a glittering vision of scarlet and gold colors with figures of men and representations of animals and fantastic creatures, all surrounded by crosses (*tasalib*),[359] interlacing designs, and geometrical shapes in profusion. According to the Hadith, Muhammad disliked seeing them in his apartments. Not because of icon- oclastic prejudices! Among the Arabs, who were great admirers of Byzantine images,[360] Islam would later develop these sentiments. But as a pious interlocutor of Allah, the Prophet found them distracting during his conversations with heaven.[361] He resented them for coming[362] between him and the kiblah, and, finally, because they reminded him inopportunely of the vanity of temporary things.[363] The themes of Christian *zuhd* [asceticism] were always shame- lessly exploited by the *Sahih*! Gabriel, as Muhammad knew, avoided homes dec- orated with profane figures as much as those where one saw a dog or a small bell. This last detail sufficiently betrayed the tendency. Figures? There are plenty of them in Muhammad's home—in his living rooms, on the carpets,[364] on the door curtains of the women's quarters, on the clothes worn by his wives, on the gems of their rings,[365] on the utensils in use, even on the dolls intended to amuse the capricious Aisha.[366]

The presence of these objects—and the list is not an exhaustive one—sug- gests the economic dependence of the Peninsula on its neighbors. The old Islam—the liberal Hanifism as Muhammad liked to call it—found nothing shocking in these forced borrowings. Without attempting to alter things, he meanwhile happily enjoyed the progress provided by these more advanced civi- lizations.[367] Here we are touching on the origins of Muslim art, a problem which Abul Qasim and his contemporaries with their mercantile mentalities did not comprehend. The Tradition commits yet another anachronism by attributing to these naive pleasure seekers its own lack of tolerance and its iconoclastic protests.[368]

Among the Sahabis, the wealthiest imitated "the fine model" (*la rahbaniyya fi-l-islam*, meaning no monkery/monasticism in Islam). None of them adopted the austere conception of life which they observed among the great representa- tives of oriental monasticism.[369] After the hardships of the primitive Hijra, the idea of refusing the pleasures of life, the Tayyibat celebrated by the Koran[370] did not occur to this realistic generation. The profits of the former Jewish estates, the contributions of the cities of the Syrian limes, of Najran and the shores of Eritrea, and their own speculations were enough to provide them with luxuries. By mul- tiplying the protests of the Prophet against this indecent exhibition (*makruh*) of representations with figures, orthodoxy merely pointed out how frequent they were. And not only the carpets but also the covers, bedside rugs, and the edging of women's dresses[371] were all concessions obtained with much difficulty from the condescending Master.

By protesting as he did, he obviously forgot to look at himself. When he dressed, he preferred, as we already know, fine materials from Syria, Egypt, and the Yemen, to the rough fabrics manufactured by Jewish industry at Khaibar and Fadak.[372] On these fabrics,[373] geometrical patterns framing fantastic animals and human figures predominated. It was the triumph of what came to be known as the arabesque: a network of squares, circles, crosses, lozenges, zigzags, and leafy tendrils [374]—all this announcing and preparing the way for late Arab art.

Later on, the influence of Jewish neophytes was to contribute to the triumph of a violent iconoclastic reaction. One cannot hold the Prophet responsible for this. It would be slandering the liberalism of this intelligent opportunist to make him responsible for miserable polemics of the following kind: "On the Day of Judgment Allah will oblige the authors to communicate life to the work of their hands."[375] To display his princely way of life, the sensual Abul Qasim did not forego any of the means within his grasp, and thanks to the very wide commercial connections of the Hijaz[376] with the neighboring countries, these means were less restricted than is generally imagined. This subject deserves a monograph of its own. We will limit ourselves to the remarks which escaped the orthodox revision, and are recorded in the great canonical volumes, including those of Bukhari,[377] "that sultan of the armies of the faith"[378] and of Muslim, his brilliant second-in-command.

This is not all. When the Arab conquests put the Companions in the presence of foreign civilization, providing at the same time the means of satisfying their taste for luxury, one meets painters who were authentic disciples of the Prophet.[379] The aristocracy of Medina would have them decorate with frescoes their town palaces[380] and their luxurious villas, lost in the greenery of the Aqiq.[381] A century later the Abbasids imitated them, or rather they maintained the old tradition in Baghdad and Samarra. The connoisseurs in Medina could only be the Umayyads, that "handful of nobodies from whom stem all that is evil." The Tradition pretends to mention here only the names of Said and Marwan;[382] but we can no longer be taken in by this. The phenomenon was not an isolated one, since in the provinces we can see icons of the Virgin[383] in the homes of the *sahabis* and the *tabi'is* [*sahabis* are people who had lived in the society of the Prophet and were the best authority for a knowledge of the sunna of Muhammad Tabi'un, or "successors," people of the first generation after Muhammad].

During the period of the *jahiliya*, the sanctuaries, the important Saiyds[384] had their *hima*—wells, land for grazing, hunting, and agriculture, removed from the common land. These were timid attempts at private property within anarchic Arabia. Muhammad saw the advantages he could obtain from this institution. He claimed it as a right for Allah and his Envoy.[385] In this way he was able to establish a *haram* similar to the sacred territory at Mecca.[386] The school of Medina is unanimous about this. While we can admit the probable tendency of this Hadith—the desire to confer on the city of the Ansars a holiness comparable to that of the Qurayshite metropolis—in Muhammad's case there is nothing improbable in the attempt. He wished to raise the prestige of himself and his capital, particularly prior to the period when he foresaw the possibility of conquering Mecca. Like the great Bedouin chiefs, he owned enclosures and grazing for his herds and his horses.[387] "Not for his own horses," Ibn Umar hastened to add pointing out this particularity, "but for the horses of the Muslims."[388] This correction is in the spirit of primitive Islam, entirely impregnated with the democratic instinct of the Arab race. Above all, it was necessary to remove from Muhammad any suspicion of profane royalty, following the severe condemnation he had pronounced himself concerning the institution of the *hima*.[389]

But the Master knew how to get around this difficulty. As a misunderstood reformer longing for popularity in Mecca, he had, in spite of his aristocratic preferences, flattered the masses. The sovereign of the Hijaz had a very different *weltanschauung* (worldview). From now on he was to praise the monarchic force of human power. The older he became, the more he would pose as a partisan of unity concerning religion, the family, and the state, and at the same time an enemy of polytheism, matriarchy, and anarchy. A single God, a single Prophet-King! That was in the future to be his motto. The Koran no longer separated the three personages—Allah, his Envoy, and the King. The faithful in their submission must combine them: "Love them more than themselves, their families, their fortunes and all of humanity."[390] If he happened to point out the *hima*, one of the phenomena which accompanied the appearance of idolatry, as an infraction of Ishmael's *din*,[391] he hastened to add this correction, *la hima illa li-llah wa li-rasulihi*, "the *hima* remains reserved for Allah[392] and his Envoy."[393]

Consequently he possessed studs.[394] He would devote the money of the Banu Quraysh to the acquisition of horses, sold on the markets of the Najd. While encouraging among his followers the breeding of horses, indispensable for his later plans of conquest, he did not hesitate to establish racing.[395] He seems rarely to have taken advantage for himself of this means of transport, which was at first a luxury in Medina.[396] He is generally seen on a camel or a donkey.[397]So certain Muslim apologists apply to him the RKB GML (in Hebrew letters: riding camels) of the Prophet Isaiah.[398] Later he also used Doldol, the mule bought for him in Egypt.[399] He rode round the villages scattered around the oasis of Yathrib[400] on a donkey. Should he arrive on foot, he was taken back on a donkey, which was given to him as a present.[401] During one of these expeditions, while visiting the Ansarian chief Ibn Ubaiy as-Szalouli, his donkey nearly started a row between an inhabitant of Medina and one of Mecca, Hazrag and Aus. Ibn Ubaiy, upset by the stench of the Prophet's mount, asked the Prophet to get rid of Yafor. "But," shouted the impatient Ibn Rawaha, the future martyr of Mouta, "he smells better than you do." This reply gave rise to a general scuffle between Muhammad's followers and Ibn Ubaiy's family. We can also see him on his donkey riding to the siege of Khaybar. Buraq, the fantastic mount of the *isra'* [Muhammad's night journey to Jerusalem], was a cross between a donkey and a mule.[402]

One day, however, he was seen on horseback in the Wadi'l Qora,[403] and later during one of those panics, *faza'*, which periodically disturbed the peace of Medina,[404] even after the police regulations decreed by Muhammad.[405] This was undoubtedly an exceptional event because the authors of the sira constantly mention it in order to prove the courage of their hero.[406] So highly prized was the prestige of the horseman in the country of the camel![407] During another of his cavalcades he was thrown against a palm tree and sprained his foot.[408] The accident may have discouraged him from trying again.

In spite of his limited equestrian experience,[409] he nonetheless claimed to have a good knowledge of horses, even better than that of Oyaina ibn Hisn, the Fazara chief,[410] one of those fickle sayyid Bedouin, who were in turn Muhammad's allies or his enemies according to what was to their advantage. He claimed that nothing pleased him so much as horses.[411] As a commentary[412] the Hadith records at length the Prophet's sayings[413] in honor of the equine race. To encourage its development, he is said to have forbidden the breeding of mules, and during the races he went as far as to allow betting.[414] He was apparently keen to acquire "the token of nobility that a horse transmits to those who live with horses and devote their time to them."[415] The rarity of horses in the Arabia of that period made it a preeminently "noble animal."[416] *Faris*, the rider, was synonymous with the sayyid.[417] The Lord of Medina could not decently show a lack of interest in such a distinguished sport,[418] particularly after the painful experience of Uhud, where he was able to note the military superiority of the Qurayshites' cavalry.[419] He got the Almighty to tell him that he should give the order "to prepare a strong cavalry so as to dominate the enemies of Allah."

V. MUHAMMAD AND FATIMA'S CHILDREN: THE PROPHET AT HOME

In pre-Islamic history, enterprising leaders appeared from time to time and tried to group around themselves the thinly spread tribes of the Peninsula. They were inspired by narrowly personal ambitions badly coordinated, and their efforts achieved nothing beyond the formation of temporary confederations. Before the Hijra, classical Arabia, that is, central and north, knew no permanent states and no politically viable setups. Force by itself was not enough to ensure continuity and neutralize the disruptive action of bedouin anarchy. A moral lever was needed, a religious program. Muhammad brought this lever and this program with Islam. He managed them with an incomparable dexterity. And yet he did not neglect the more common means at his disposal. We think we have shown this in preceding pages, always supposing that we have understood the traditional documents quoted by us. In spite of their reticences and incoherence, which were more or less intentional, these writings show the Prophet's understanding of the situation and wonderful political activity. Just as if he had a premonition of his approaching end, he was feverishly active in order to win back lost time. And this activity coincided precisely with the years of Fatima's marriage.[420]

Unfortunate coincidence for the Prophet's daughter! Her personal influence on her father had never been considerable. It further declined as the bustle of politics invaded the soul of Abul Qasim. How could the pale, plaintive[421] figure of Fatima succeed in catching his attention[422] while he was preparing to change the power balance in Arabia[423] to the advantage of his political fief? For this she lacked the graces or the redoubtable capacity for intrigue of the very intelligent Aisha. Even if 'Ali had always walked in step with her, if he had shown her the consideration due to a daughter of the Prophet—the position of his daughter, as he wrongly boasted[424]—the assistance of her unforeseeing spouse would have been of little help in fighting against the shrewd Abu Bakr. The domestic quarrels of this disunited couple had eventually worn down the patience of Abul Qasim, who was already obsessed by incessant appeals to his generosity. Ever since he planned the conquest of Mecca, the help of competent men like Aisha's father had been indispensable to him. At the beginning, the Prophet could count on the collaboration of 'Ali. After putting him to the test he found him to be a brave soldier, but clumsy. So he had to turn to Abu Bakr's group. As this party tended to be hostile to 'Ali, it ended by ruining Fatima's influence to the advantage of the Aisha-Hafsa group.

With the object of destroying this harmful impression, our authors show us her father, before and after his travels, making a visit to her.[425] On his rising[426] he could not stay still[427] before announcing the time of prayers at Fatima's door. But above all, the authors spare us no details to show the affection of Abul Qasim for his grandsons Hasan and Husayn.

In this family anthology not everything is pure invention. As was their way, our authors lacked moderation and gave excessively free play to their imaginations. But these long-winded developments must contain a kernel of historical truth. Toward the end of his time at Medina, when the Prophet happened to cast an eye on his stormy career as opposed to his political successes, he was bound to admit the disappointments of his domestic life.

In spite of the idyllic picture painted by the sira, his marriage to the elderly Khadija had not reconciled him to monogamy. Free to control the composition of his harem, he did not have a happy touch in his choice of the believers' mothers. Their quarrels and intrigues troubled the last years of his life. Just as he was pondering the conquest of western Arabia, he succeeded with difficulty in establishing control of his turbulent womenfolk. "When the Prophet falls ill," observed Umar, "his women rub their eyes, red with tears. When he gets better, they take him by the throat."[428] "Womankind is fatal!"[429] Abul Qasim repeated sententiouely. He called it "the toughest trial of the strong sex." "Beware of women," (*attaqu al-nisa'*) he often said to his Companions. "Hell is full of them."[430]

One after another, the daughters of Khadija, and finally little Ibrahim, had died. The grass had grown over their remains buried in the damp depths of the Baqi, just near his dar. The children of Fatima offered him the last hope of perpetuating his name, and a Semite[431] is always moved by that possibility! Impossible now to keep his illusions. Would he have many descendants? Allah had refused him that distinction of the prophets. " 'Ali will take my place," he said to himself sadly.[432] This feeling, as we have seen, did not make him any more tender toward the father of his grandchildren. If he had wanted to show tenderness, he would have been very embarrassed. When he tried to move nearer 'Ali, he provoked the loud protests of the irascible Aisha. "You don't love me," she would shout, so as to be heard outside, "you sacrifice me for 'Ali, me and my father Abu Bakr." Only the intervention of the latter managed to bring her back to reason.[433]

"I love women, scent, and good meals," the Prophet had said.[434] As we have already mentioned, he was equally fond of children. One day as he was carrying one of his daughter's children in his arms, he was heard to cry, "Dear little ones, because of you man becomes cowardly and mean. You are the perfumes of Allah!"[435] According to the Tradition, the likeness between him and Hasan was striking.[436] He seems to have concerned himself much with that grandson, and later Husayn. On this subject, the *sahih* and the *musnad* abound in affecting touches and picturesque details, which cannot always be translated literally. As well as producing a favorable view of the Prophet's humility and family tenderness, they aim to lay down certain practical rules on ablutions[437] and on the correct attitude to adopt during prayers.[438] To bring out these traits, our authors with their love of human detail needed children, and they selected them by preference from the Prophet's immediate circle. But in the absence of a concrete link between these figments of pure imagination and historical personages, the child actors involved sometimes varied. It depended on the schools and tendencies represented by the authors.

So one often sees the prophet amusing himself with "the two Hasans," letting them for instance pass between his legs. During prayers he allowed them to climb on his back. In that position, he prolonged his prostration so as not to disturb the pleasure of his dear little ones. Finding this trait charming, the fiery Shiite Said al-Himyari put the scene into verse—mediocre poetry, but at least it helps to fix the *terminus a quo* [the starting point] of the Hadith.[439] Once prayers were over, Muhammad took the children on his knees and in his arms. He placed their feet on his chest in order to lift them to his lips [440] and suck their tongues greedily.

This age is without pity. One day the angel of rain (*malak al-matar*[441]) asked Allah's permission to interview Abul Qasim. Once arranged, the latter instructed his wife Umm Salama to keep an eye on the door[442] so as to stop intruders. Then Husayn came along. He overcame the instructions and resistance of Umm Salama. Without letting himself be intimidated by the presence of the celestial visitor, the little fellow climbed onto the back and shoulders of his grandfather. "Do you love him?" asked the angel. "Most certainly," Muhammad replied. "And yet," continued the angel, "your people will put him to death. If you like, I can indicate to you the place where he will perish." Then, slapping it in his hand, he produced a lump of red earth. Umm Salama hastened to preserve this bit of evidence. The narrator concluded that the conversation alluded to Karbala.[443] As for the tale, it belongs to the wonderful cycle, destined to embellish the end of this expedition's inglorious hero. At the time of this last event, the lump of earth and Umm Salama[444] are again produced. The only thing forgotten is that this Mother of the believers had been buried three years at the time of Karbala. Chronology—that is one of the numerous snags that often disturbs the finer points of our muhaddith!

Once the angel had disappeared, Muhammad came back to his grandchildren. He kissed them on the stomach,[445] he started to sniff them,[446] to suck their lips and their tongue, and to bestow on them all the signs of a rather primitive tenderness usual among Arabs. So the caliph 'Uthman sniffed his newborn babies at length[447] "in order to keep a sentiment of affection if he came to lose them" (literally, "I should like, if something were to happen to him, that something should take place in my heart, called love").

A detail no less significant which shows Muhammad's laxness at this period is the fact that he takes the children with him into the minbar.[448] The pulpit—the central point and most important feature of a mosque's furniture, which showed a shy attempt to fill the desperate void—was reserved for the imam of the gama'a. He appeared in it to prononce the *khutba*, to receive the *baia*, or in times of calamity to proceed to the *du'a* [supplication as distinguished from *salat*, or the liturgical form of prayer] or the ceremony of the *istisqa* [prayers for rain, consisting of two *rakah* prayers].[449] If one wanted to emphasise the importance of an affirmation of the Prophet, one said that it was declared from the pulpit.[450] In their fervor on 'Ali's behalf, our authors remembered all these prerogatives of the minbar. That is why they were keen on showing Fatima's children beside the Prophet-King![451] This is a significant gesture, suggesting a long series of conclusions, all to the greater glory of the mediocre idols of the Shiite legend. In depicting them, the Master seemed, as it were, to link them closely to himself and attract toward them, as on eventual successors, the attention of his followers. This showed up[452] sometimes blatantly when he presented Hasan to the audience and gave him the title of *Sayyid*.[453]

One day, seeing Hasan and his brother Husayn advancing to the middle of the mosque in their brilliant red livery, and stumbling at each step Abul Qasim suddenly interrupted his address. Coming down from the pulpit, he picked them up in his arms, carried them to the dais and cried out: "Allah and his Envoy were right in saying, 'Your children are a temptation for you.' "[454] "When I saw these two little ones advancing with tottering steps, I could not help stopping my address to take them with me."[455] The object of the anecdote was, above all, to secure for the children of 'Ali the title of children of the Prophet. One understands the irritation of someone like Hajjaj witnessing these maneuvers that were dangerous for public peace. One ought to call them, he affirmed, the sons of 'Ali, to conform with the terminology laid down by the Koran since Zaynab's romance.

These family scenes sometimes had an unexpected epilogue.[456] Cherished, kissed, snuggling in the Prophet's lap, bestriding his shoulders, the innocent infants sometimes forgot themselves to the point that they wet his clothes. This sort of accident must have been frequent among the kids of that time,[457] judging by the importance given to such episodes by the literature. The most-venerated *sahih*, the *musnad*, and the very ancient Sunna like to devote a special paragraph to them, and never fail to come back to them in various connections. They cleverly vary the social condition and the sex of the little actors, so as to establish the *sunna*, the specific treatment to be applied in the circumstances.[458] Sometimes they bring in a member of the Abbasid family or the Ansar clan. No occasion is lost to show these privileged people in the Prophet's circle. With the latter, the most vulgar operations acquire an inestimable value. Thence, in the ancient annals, there arose a category of modest incumbents,[459] the *ashab al-wodou*, who were appointed to watch over the ablutions of the Master. For lack of more distinguished tasks, they had to be content with this job. Not everyone could be his standard-bearer. But everyone strove for his sandals, his prayer mat, or the dish used for purification.

VI. THE PEOPLE OF THE HOUSE

In the middle of his absorbing preoccupations as prophet and head of state, Abul Qasim, the former merchant, continued to interest himself in commercial questions. We know this from his relations with the Kalbites Zayd ibn Haritha and Dahia ibn Khalifa. Hence his frequent visits to Ukaz to the market of Banu Qaynuqa and the bazaar of Medina.[460] He liked to follow the fluctuations of local trade. These secular concerns had caused scandal among the pagans of Mecca. "Not only did he eat and drink like ordinary mortals, but he haunted the bazaars!" "He completed one of his usual strolls in the company of Abu Huraira, examining the goods and turning over the heaps of wheat on sale,[461] until he headed back to Fatima' s house. Stopping on the doorstep, he began to call Hasan— 'Come, little good-for-nothing, luka.' He repeated the call three times without getting a reply. He had just sat down in Aisha's apartment when Hasan arrived. Probably, thought the narrator Abu Huraira, his mother had detained him in order to put on his necklace (sakhab). On seeing him the Prophet hastened to press him to his breast while the boy threw his arms around him. 'My God,' he cried, 'how I love him. Love him as I do, and love all his friends with him!' "[462] He repeated these words three times (Hanbal 2:331).

Soon after the birth of Hasan, Umm al-Fadl (one does not know how she found herself in Mecca) had brought him to the Prophet. Sitting on his knees the baby, with the lack of awareness appropriate to his age, forgot himself. The wife of Abbas pounced on him and struck him between the shoulders. "Gently," cried the grandfather, "don't cause pain to my son." In these circumstances,[463] he contented himself with repairing the accident with a few drops of water, and then asked for his children again. Affecting scene! Down to the most intimate details Abul Qasim remained for posterity "the fine model" (uswa hasana). In the most convinced way the Tradition continued to give him full conscience of his role and made him, as it were, pose before an objective.[464] This curious fact benefited 'Ali's family and gave him importance in the eyes of posterity. When her children were brought back home, Fatima, as Bedouin mothers often did, amused herself by making them dance, and she sang: "They resemble the Prophet and not 'Ali." A naive Tarqis (dance) and hardly agreeable for her husband, who decided to laugh, no doubt out of respect for his father-in-law[465] (for the situation of his daughter).

Born of parents of mediocre gifts, the children were slow to awaken to the life of the spirit. Hasan took a long time to be able to utter a phrase. Muhammad had just gone out in his company when the opportunity occurred to cry the *takbir*. Immediately this shout was repeated up to five times by the child, to the Prophet's great joy. So the first phrase of Hasan is supposed to have been "Allah is great." Hence the custom of the five takbirs at the annual feast (*wa tilka sunnat al-'id*, meaning it is the tradition of the feast). It is not difficult to guess the inspiration of this edifying story where an effort is made to sanctify the beginnings in life of the very sensual son of 'Ali. One day Fatima brought her two elder boys to pay a visit to their grandfather. "Give them a present," requested the mother. "To Hasan," replied the Prophet, "I give intelligence and discretion;[466] to Husayn, generosity and consideration." Then, in a paternal manner he placed a child on each knee.[467] Discretion to Hasan, the man "of a thousand women"! Let us be grateful to our storytellers that they did not keep intelligence for his brother, the inconsiderate hero of Karbala.

An incident ably exploited by the Shia was the interview of Muhammad with the Christian representatives of Najran. It seems to have resulted in the *mobahala* (treaty with the Christians). Like a new Balaam, Abul Qasim wanted to try on the Najranites the effect of his imprecations. It must have been one of the rare occasions when Fatima saw herself brought to the fore with her family by her father.[468] This scene[469] inspired another one that was much more famous in the 'Ali literature—the scene of the *privileged* of the coat.

Among the lessons addressed by Muhammad to his restless harem, one must count this verse in the Koran: "Allah wants to remove from you, people of the house, all defilement and purify you." The whole context shows that the Prophet here upbraids his wives! His jealousy wanted to create for them a special situation, the benefit of a special sanctity. They had to be removed from the temptations and obsessions of his disciples after his death. These earnest requests did not wait for the final hour to make themselves felt. Sahabis and some of the most qualified of them—Hawari Talh was mentioned—announced their intention of marrying Aisha. Abul Qasim arranged to forestall such an eventuality, so much in keeping with Arab behavior, but disastrous, he thought, for his personal prestige.[470] It inspired the meticulous rules of the Koran, he conferred on his womenfolk the title of "mothers of the believers."[471] On the other hand he announced a double punishment for their faults.[472] Wasn't it necessary to reaffirm their precarious virtue, and foresee the renewal of the Aisha-Safwan romance? He was not afraid to have them addressed by Allah with pressing admonishments in the right direction—reserve, modesty, the practice of prayer, confinement, above all continence after his death! He wanted to inculcate all these virtues in "the people of the house."[473] There is nothing of this in the direction of the Alids. The Koran does not even allude to their existence—a silence that is difficult to reconcile with the exaggerations of the Shia.

But the privilege was so great and the opportunity too good to miss. The expression "people of the house" remained sufficiently vague to be claimed by the Alids and their partisans. In the Koran Muhammad had confined himself to designate the people gathered under his roof, his household, that is, his wives,[474] man's real *ahl*, as the Arab language understands it.[475] He had not thought of 'Ali, or Fatima[476] who lived elsewhere. As this restriction worried the Shia, it preferred to adopt a wider definition of the family. In its view the *ahl al-bayt* ought to mean Ali and his family to the exclusion of all others. So one day, sheltering them all under his cloak, Muhammad is supposed to have declared: "These are the people of my house!" Ever afterward the four characters carried in the Shi-ite tradition the title of "people of the cloak." One sees the tendency[477] to claim for the Alids[478] the privilege of a special purity declared by the Koran.

While accepting the story, the great orthodox compilations insist on making it inoffensive.[479] Thus, Umm Salama is made to attend the interview and be included by her husband among the "people of the house."[480] They throw in equally the Jafarids, the descendants of the miscreant Aqil, brother of 'Ali, and finally the Abbasids. This last extension was inspired by political motives.[481]

The Shia continued to push in favor of the Alids. One knows the Hadith where, among his contemporaries, Muhammad says he prefers Aisha, and then Abu Bakr among men. To this declaration the Shia has opposed the following: "Fatima is my favourite, then 'Ali."[482] When the latter came back to the question, curious to know if he was not first in the favor of his father-in-law, Muhammad is supposed to have replied: "Fatima is the most loved and you are the dearest" (*Fatima ahabb ilayya minta wa anta a'azz 'alayya minha*). This affection was shown on all occasions. One day he found the parents asleep. Hasan asked for a drink. Instead of waking the parents the Prophet milked an ewe to quench the child's thirst.[483] One sees how the authors sought to fill the gaps in the sira where in the first version Fatima occupies hardly more space than in the Koran.[484]

VII. MUHAMMAD, THE CHILDREN OF ZAYNAB, AND USAMA: THE LAST YEARS OF THE PROPHET

On the orthodox side the Prophet is shown as lavishing the same tenderness on the children of his daughter Zaynab. One day he excited the envy of his whole harem by giving her a precious necklace to admire. "I am going to give it," he declared gravely, "to the dearest member of my family, *'ahli.'* "[485] "In that case," cried out his wives in unison, "the daughter of Abu Quhafa is bound to carry it off." Without stopping to challenge this jealous insinuation of his known partiality for Aisha, the Prophet hung the jewel round the neck of Umama, the daughter of Zaynab.[486] Sometimes one sees him concerned to maintain an equal balance between his own people. He seems to want, by the correctness of his attitude, to repel the exaggerated conclusions of the extreme parties, and forestall the fierce fighting that might result from future divisions. For with the Islamic Tradition, we have to credit the Prophet with full conscience of his role and of the importance of the slightest gesture for the future of his community. This role attributed to Abul Qasim never failed to inspire the zest of Medina's sceptics, that is, Jews and others. "Happy mortals," they said to the believers, "your master has forgotten nothing, even the way to accomplish natural needs!" Should we again suspect our authors of introducing clichés already used? It is the repetition of moves and gestures already familiar, where only the names differ.

Fatima had two sons.[487] Zaynab probably had a son and a daughter. So just as he behaved with the "two Hasans," Muhammad takes Zaynab's children to the pulpit with him. He completed prayers keeping them in his arms, or perched on his back. As if he wanted to show his absolute impartiality,[488] he takes up with Zaynab's offspring all the attitudes of the ritual *salat*. This apparent bonhomie, this patriarchal free-and-easiness, are part of the traditional tactics. Not only do they speak in favor of the truth of such naive stories,[489] but they are mainly destined to deflect the attention of the reader. In the present case it is a question of masking the real designs of orthodoxy. By a few Hadith of an inoffensive nature the authors want to eliminate the divergences at the heart of the Muhammadan *jamaa* (community), or at least take the edge off the weapons in the hands of the Shiite opponents. Everything has been foreseen, even to remote conclusions. This departure from the seriousness and self-communion of prayer, we are assured, was one of the *Khasais* [privileges] of Abul Qasim.[490] On the day of his entry into Mecca he *had* 'Ali, the brother of Umana,[491] on his horse behind him. All these details were left out by the historians in the Shiite camp. We owe their survival to the orthodox zeal[492] of the Sunnite or Abbasid collectors of tales.[493] There is everywhere the same disdain for historic truth.

The father of Fatima showed himself, if possible, even more demonstrative on behalf of Usama, the son of Zayd. This meant that the uncommon title *hubb ibn hubb rasul Allah* ("love child of the love of Allah's apostle") was granted to the offspring of his favorite Zayd and the negress Umm Aiman. Usama, a monster of physical ugliness, potbellied, with a flat nose, and swarthy like his mother, the old housekeeper of the Prophet! Nothing prevents us from suspecting that the Tradition exaggerated the colors of this portrait to make its doctrinal demonstration even more conclusive—the justice of the Prophet in his affections and the impossibility of finding in it an argument for Shiite pretensions. When the little Usama fell and hurt his forehead, the imperious Aisha, in spite of the urgent request of her husband, did not deign to take care of the little black boy. Seeing this, Muhammad hastened to kiss the child's wound.[494] "Ah!" he cried out, "if Usama were a girl, I would cover her in silk and jewels from head to foot."[495] At the farewell pilgrimage, Usama had to draw aside to relieve himself. Muhammad suspended the ceremony and stopped the procession to wait for his favorite. This partiality provoked protests from the Yemenite pilgrims. According to the passionate Urwa ibn Zubayr, their discontent would even have incited them to revolt after the death of Abul Qasim.[496] It was assigning a pretty futile motive to the national movement of the Arab *ridda*!

In a moment of irritation, Muhammad had ordained that robbers should have their hands cut off. He had every intention of stopping at the threat, not wanting to have to mutilate the countless thieves of Arabia.[497] Same for the stoning laid down for adulterers. In adopting it, he mainlly wanted an opportunity to be disagreeable to his Jewish neighbors. On the return from his raids there were countless cases of misconduct brought before his tribunal. The laggards, or *qa' idoun*, left behind at Medina, had every opportunity to test the fragile virtue of the Muslim women in their husbands' absence.[498] So he advised the latter not to come home at nighttime, so as not to expose themselves to humiliating surprises.[499] While he described the *qa'idoun* as he-goats, he avoided being hard on these libertines.[500] Their number and their quality would have exposed his prestige as a legislator to too hard a trial. This consideration may have moved him to cut out the stoning verse from his writings, where the caliph 'Umar claimed to have read it.[501]

One day, however, he would think it necessary to make an example. He sentenced a Makhzumite woman thief to have her hand cut off. The indignation caused by the sentence was intense, touching as it did one of the most respected clans of Mecca. The Qurayshites addressed themselves to Usama: "Only he enjoyed enough influence on the Prophet. He would not refuse such an intercession!" The next day Abul Qasim mounted the pulpit and gravely declared: "If Fatima, daughter of Muhammad, had been found guilty of robbery, I would still order her hand to be cut off."[502] In fact, he was satisfied with the result produced. The application of the frightful penalty proved impossible in practice. The Koran had neglected to fix the value of the object stolen—a quarter of a dinar, three dirhems, or still less?[503] If the author of the *Kitab Allah* has done without this specification, one must apparently doubt his firm resolution to insist on the punishment. Orthodoxy has used the incident to bring fresh publicity to Usama and Fatima, but publicity cleverly worded so as not to disturb the balance between the pretentions of the Sunna and the Shia, the former represented here by the son of Zayd, the latter by the wife of 'Ali.

Having become the owner of the rich oases of the northern Hijaz, Muhammad awarded Fatima an annual dowry of eighty-five loads of barley.[504] On the eve of Mecca's surrender, Abu Sofian had arrived at Mecca with a view to coming to an agreement with the Prophet. It was in fact a question of organizing the action that would allow the latter to penetrate the city of the Qurayshites without striking a blow. His daughter Umm Habiba, married to Abul Qasim, had the job of smoothing the way for the negotiation, which then started. Yazid, son of Abu Sufyan, also may have been involved if he had already embraced the new faith, as certain documents seem to insinuate.[505]

Since they liked unforeseen situations, the compilers of the sira found it amusing to show the father of Mu'awiya in Fatima's house, begging her to intercede in his favor.[506] The description of the interview gives a rather grotesque role to the great Umayyad diplomat. We see the little Hasan crawling on the ground at his mother's feet,[507] a detail that does not fit in with his presumed *age* if, as certain people assert, he was born in the second year of the Hijra. In the eyes of the Shia it is of infinite importance to ante-date his birth in order to claim for Fatima's eldest son effective involvement with the Prophet.

Following her father and her husband, the mother of Hasan probably attended the surrender of Mecca. We then see her appearing at the ablutions of Muhammad.[508] The zeal of the authors of musnad and Sunna did not succeed in finding an activity or initiatives of a higher order. When they were rendered to the Prophet, the most lowly services acquired an infinite value!

Then came the Prophet's final illness. We have described elsewhere[509] the intrigues hatched during this long agony. Aisha mounted a strong guard round the dying man. Yet the Tradition was bound to arrange for him a final interview with Fatima, the only survivor among his children. Muhammad is said to have sent her to his women to obtain exemption from the *tawaf* or daily circumambulation (of Kaaba).[510] Here again the imagination of our authors could have found a more glorious mission,[511] that is, to avoid making her intervene to entrust her sick father to Aisha.[512] On his deathbed he is supposed to have prophesied to her that she would be the first of her family to follow him to another world. This prophecy was made likely by the total exhaustion of the unhappy wife of 'Ali. The grief of Fatima spilled out in verse, thus conforming to the ancient Arab custom. She is said to have gone to recite them on her father's grave. When Anas ibn Malik, the faithful servant of the Master, returned from the burial, she greeted him with the following reproach: "How had you the heart to entrust the remains of the Apostle to the earth?"[513]

VIII. THE LAST DAYS OF FATIMA

Fresh trials were going to mark the last days of the Prophet's daughter. While by a daring stroke the triumvirate Abu Bakr, 'Umar, and Abu Ubaida removed the califate from the *saqifa* of the Banu Saida,[514] their opponents, together with the main friends of 'Ali, had assembled in Fatima's house. This became the center of the opposition to Abu Bakr's power. Led on by 'Umar, the followers of the triumvirate hastened to besiege them. Among the Arabs the tent[515] and the private house were considered inviolable. All pursuits had to stop on the household threshold. This consideration did not hold back 'Umar,[516] and even less the mourning and prestige of Fatima. He came to blows with 'Ali, while the unfortunate daughter of the Prophet, leaving the house, threatened to reveal her head of hair in public,[517] the ultimate sign of distress among Arab women.[518] A real siege was organized around the house where 'Ali had retired with his supporters. Umar, the terrible wrestler, dreaded in the fairgrounds of Ukaz, came to measure his strength against the Prophet's son-in-law, against Zubair and the other adversaries of the Triumvirate.[519]

The Koran, then later the Tradition,[520] impose on the faithful the obligation of making a will.[521] Muhammad was a practical type, and wanted to anticipate useless disputes. Did he really neglect this precaution for himself? The Shiites refuse to admit it and their argument, let us face it, did not lack force. A mystery hangs over the death of Muhammad, insufficiently obscured by the intentional disorder of contradictory versions.[522] During his long death-agony of fifteen days, did not Abul Qasim find a lucid moment to announce his last wishes? Did the Triumvirate succeed in suppressing any proof of this event? Not that Muhammad had seriously thought of 'Ali for the succession seeing that in his lifetime he had affected to keep him apart from public affairs. In the eyes of the Shia, 'Ali was the *wasiy*, the Prophet's legatee *par excellence*, and his son, the sensual and frivolous Hasan, the *wasy al-wasy*, was the legatee of the legatee.[523]

If one understands the word *wasiy* in the sense of testamentary executor—and this often happened—the honor is pretty important. Among the contemporaries of Muhammad we often find Arabs, who were without male posterity or leaving children who were minors, choosing a *wasiy*. The choice always fell on influential persons, in a position to insist on respect for the rights of orphans "deposited in their bosom," as they used to say. Let us mention the first two caliphs and the very rich and violent Zubayr. Thus 'Ali would have been charged to keep watch on the family of Abul Qasim, that is, on his wives and his daughter and also on the newborn community. On him was bestowed the mission of warming them in his bosom. None of these considerations escaped the supporters of Fatima's husband when they claimed for him the title of *wasiy.* "How," cried Kumait, upbraiding the Prophet. "All men, apart from you, would leave a legatee, and we are blamed because with good reason we refuse to accept it."[524]

The Sunna on its side opposed this sort of argument vigorously. The titles of *waly al-amr* (legal guardian) *wasy,* successor, and legatee accorded to 'Ali,[525] it opposed a long series of Hadith, showing the Prophet as being laid low by the violence and suddenness of his last illness—in agony, unable to speak, and finally dying intestate. The obligation to write a will vanishes and becomes pointless once the dying man has nothing to leave. So the Prophet seems to have died in extreme poverty, and, even more serious, the debtor of a Jew in Medina! Why should he have thought of a document of this sort? Wasn't he leaving the Koran, the depository of his choicest thoughts?[526] Aisha found herself the natural recipient for those syllogisms and narratives with controversial tendencies. "The Prophet expired on my bosom and before I was aware of it."[527] This assertion was presented by the favorite in all its forms.[528] He died in her house, and she never left him for a moment. How could he have drawn up or dictated a will?

The obstinate politics of Muhammad and his struggles with the Jews had made him the biggest real estate owner of the Hijaz.[529] He possessed vast domains in Medina, Khaybar, Fadak, and Wadi Qora. Fatima was determined to claim her part in her father's heritage, especially the oasis of Fadak. She had already demanded possession of it in his lifetime. So if she is shown to have denied it, then it was no doubt to justify Abu Bakr's conduct in advance. The intervention of the widows of Abul Qasim, also demanding their share of Fadak, must have been part of the same preoccupation.[530] Whether they were historical or not, these challenges weakened the rights of the Alids. In the unfolding of this incident we come up everywhere against party prejudices. Faithful to its principles: "The Prophet left no will." The Sunna comes down on the side of Abu Bakr and Umar, pretending to consider the territorial fortune of Abul Qasim as state property.

The Prophet had received Allah's order not to hurry in the editing of the Koran as a separate work. This precaution was wise, having regard to the inconsistent character of certain revelations. He wanted to keep the freedom to revise them. Faithful to this instruction from on High, he avoided leaving behind written orders, even in a matter as important as the transmission of power at the heart of the infant community. With good reason he feared to see his last requests being ignored.

In bringing the case before the tribunal of Muhammad's immediate successor, Fatima went about things clumsily, as one might have expected. In the absence of a document supporting the authenticity of her father's donation, she quoted as witnesses 'Ali and his two sons Hasan and Husayn,[531] the latter being under six years old! One sees why the Shia tries to put forward the dates of their births and the marriage of their parents. To the claims of Fatima, Abu Bakr limited himself to advancing this hypocritical refusal—"Prophets do not leave heirs!" The distinction could not be difficult to find, and the historians, favorable to the Alids, gave credit to Fatima. She began by a quotation from the Koran: "Solomon acquired the heritage of David." Then she added the obvious distinction: "The power of prophecy and the important privileges attached to this dignity are not transmitted. Agreed. But the heritage remains!"[532]

Another version *(I.S.Tabaq* 2:86) prefers the intervention of Fatima's husband. To the example of Solomon, quoted by his wife, he seems to have added that of Zacharias, father of John the Baptist (sura 19:6).

If 'Ali and Fatima had earlier shown as much decision and intelligence, the triumvirate would probably have failed in its efforts to get hold of the caliphate. It would have been to the misfortune of the Arab empire as the sequel will show. But in the time of Ibn Sa'd and even of Kumait, the Shia must have already possessed its arsenal of arms for the fray. We see 'Umar later cancelling the decision of Abu Bakr and giving 'Ali and Abbas joint ownership in the Prophet's real estate in Medina, but on condition that the income should be applied to works of public utility. Apart from this onerous duty, the cunning Ibn al-Khattab gambled on their disagreement. This occurred before long. In the presence of the caliph, Abbas called his nephew 'Ali "a liar, a crook, a disloyal traitor" (*hada al kadib al-atim al ghadir al kha'in*), "exactly the same descriptions that the two Hashimites had addressed ten years before to Umar's predecessor. Sahih of Bukhari's version was eager to suppress these discordant comments.[533]

IX. THE DEATH OF FATIMA— HER FUNERAL, HER TOMB

Mourning among the Ancient Arabs and in Islam

There is general agreement in placing Fatima's end in the year 11 A.H.—one, two, three, four, six, or eight months after the death of her father.[534] This divergence is enough to show that we have no direct information on an event that passed unnoticed in the midst of internal struggles for the conquest of the caliphate and the bloody suppression of the *ridda*. Just as she had lived, the only surviving daughter of the Prophet passed away amid the general indifference of her contemporaries, who were anxious to share out among themselves the political heritage of the dead Master rather than to collect memories connected with this great figure. Even if they had glimpsed the usefulness of this historical learning, they lacked the intellectual freedom to carry it out.

The date of year 11 has been deduced from the prophecy attributed to her father on the imminent death of his daughter.[535] One can equally well imagine the process reversed. It is impossible to prove the existence of Fatima after her quarrel with Abu Bakr. She had sworn never to speak to the latter again.[536] As one sees 'Ali, soon after the death of Muhammad, coming to an agreement with the first caliph and building up a complete harem, one assumes that his wife was dead. That is how agreement has been reached on year 11. After that date the personality of Fatima had no further function. Her continued existence would have involved confessions painful for the reputations of Islamic heroes. So they hastened to suppress this unattractive character. Ali had acted thus in the new organization of his private life.

Fatima remained obsessed to the end by a persecution mania. To the widows of Muhammad around her deathbed she complained of the vexations of which she had been a victim throughout her life. She declared that she was happy to have to leave their company and this world of iniquity, where people had ridden roughshod over her rights and privileges, and violated justice in her case. "They had cancelled her father's will," gravely affirmed Yaqoubi, "and she died at the age of twenty-three." At this supreme moment 'Ali was absent from home,[537] surprised, they said, at the suddenness of the catastrophe.

At Medina 'Ali seems to have been the only one to have had no premonition. As far as one can judge from the length of Fatima's speeches to the wives of the Ansars and Quraysh who had come to visit her in her last illness,[538] this death was anything but sudden. But one had to lessen the shocking side of 'Ali's absence. So he is described as returning[539] to preside over the laying-out of the dead woman. When he lost one of his daughters, Muhammad, the Sahih maintained, wished the most minute attention to be lavished on her, multiplying lotions for the corpse mixed with expensive oils.[540] Fatima's preparation was rather summary, carried out with the inevitable assistance of Abbas and his son. The funeral took place on the night of her death[541] and with the greatest haste. Abu Bakr heard about it too late.

When Umm Salama, the future mother of the believers, lost her first husband, she proposed "to compose for him a lamentation that would be sensational" (literally, "I shall cry for him such tears that people will talk of them").[542] Though unemotional by nature, the Arab often yields to his vanity. If this sentiment was absent, respect for the Prophet had not yet struck deep enough roots to the point where his last child was entitled to these supreme marks of deference.

One must no doubt take account of the disarray then reigning at Medina, which was riven with internal dissension and menaced by the rising of the *ridda*, if one wants to understand this lack of intelligence of 'Ali and the triumvirs.

As for the age of Fatima, we have already heard Yaqubi talking of twenty-three years. Others give her twenty-seven or twenty-nine years "or there-abouts."[543] This final limit left a sufficient margin. Certain historians have taken advantage of it to give her thirty or even thirty-five years.[544] We think it useless to rake up these evaluations after having earlier discussed the reason for these divergences. If we have not gone astray in our presentation of this chronological imbroglio, the reader will have to make his choice among the highest figures.

The *jahiliya* knew nothing of the worship of the dead. Rather, one notes the haste shown in getting rid of mortal remains, and the frequency of nocturnal and hurried burials, all practices observed in the first years of Islam,[545] and even for the most venerated characters. We can mention the Prophet, his favorite Aisha, his father-in-law Abu Bakr and the first caliphs. Muhammad's religion struck its deepest roots in *Arabism*.[546] The author of the Koran did not understand the opportuneness of a reform of this sort. This positive Qurayshite, who knew nothing of psychology, limited himself to legislating for a male collectivity, for the rough comrades of his agitated career, often to the detriment of the most delicate sentiments of the human heart. Making up for his silence, the most ancient tradition advocates a stoicism in the presence of death that goes against nature. It insists that the Prophet excuse himself for the tears he shed on the death of his children. He severely forbade the most innocent manifestations of mourning.[547] Everywhere this severity affects to nose out a menace for his narrow conception of monotheism, when in fact he simply adds to the toughness of ancient Arab society.

For many Semites, observes Professor Sellin—for instance the Palmyre-nians, the Arameans, the Nabateans, and among Jews the monument of Absalom—"the stele appears to be the most important part of tombs."[548] Let us recall the well-known Quss ibn Saida placing among the tombs of his brothers a masjid, perhaps a stele. In its narrow zeal orthodoxy may have feared confusion with the *nasals* which were forbidden by *the* Koran. From this came the banning, as decreed by the hadith, of transforming tombs into masjid.

Before the Hijra, however, the tribes allowed an exception in favor of an ancestor, a paladin or a hero, immortalized by their courage or their generosity. A pile of boulders[549] or a circle of stones were enough to indicate the position of such tombs, and in honor of these glorious shades people came to pour out a glass of wine or the blood of victims.[550] "No tombs projecting, all at ground level!"[551] as the Tradition decreed. And to make a greater impression, it shows

Umm Habiba[552] putting on makeup and scent three days after the death of her father Abu Sufyan "in order to obey the instructions of the Prophet." One of the favourite characters of the Tradition Ibn 'Umar presided over horse racing[553] on his way back from the funeral of one of his children. Amru ibn al-Asi, the conqueror of Egypt, dies as a real believer. Here are his last instructions to his entourage: "When you have committed me to earth, linger long enough around my tomb to sacrifice a camel and eat its flesh. Your presence will console me." (Muslim, *Sahih*, 1:60).

The Bedouin prides himself on his calm in the face of the greatest disasters. He avoids weeping over his dearest affections.[554] A poet writing of a wife who has been removed by death is a rare event in Arab literature. Why torture oneself? A woman disappears, another takes her place. It was their way of consoling themselves, as the witty Aisha reminded her august spouse. On the tomb of his wife, Jarir had pronounced an elegy[555] where the truth of the emotion was allied to the naturalness of the expression, two characteristics uncommon in the abondance of elegiac poetry of the desert. But the unfortunate poet seems to be asking for mercy and wanting to disarm in advance the structures of opinion. Listen to the beginning:

> If it was not for a sense of dignity I would abandon myself again to tears, and visit your tomb as one visits a person dear to one.
>
> I would contemplate—and why look elsewhere?—a grave where the spade had penetrated!
>
> Your death has torn my heart at the evening of my life.[556]

We are at the dawn of the second century after the Hijra. In a hundred years Islam had had the time, it seems, to modify the nomad mentality and open it up to feelings of pity. The *naqida* or reply of Farazdaq will show us how the fears of Jarir were well founded. His macabre enthusiasm likes to belabor an unhappy husband or a rival poet:

> Visits can be made in a lifetime, but I cannot accept a visit to a dead person lying in his tomb, You had this shameful idea; you carried it out in front of a sepulchre where the spade had penetrated.[557]
>
> Your dead woman trembled with fright in her sight of two hyenas from Bolaiya,[558] as she found herself alone in the desert plain.[559]

In this day and age you feel pity for her over her bones, where the vertebrae shine among the joints. So you weep tears when the hyenas have devoured her ribs? May the All-Powerful confound you! Your lament dishonours her in her tomb. This is not the attitude of a man of honor![560]

One also comes across the echo of more human sentiments. Nature never loses its rights even at the heart of primitive Islam, which is so imbued with Arab prejudices. We have already seen how by the example of Fatima the authors have wanted to protest against the severity of ancient morals, a deplorable heritage of Bedouin barbarism (*jafa*). But these protests belong to a more advanced stage of Muslim evolution, and one may ask oneself if the author of the Koran would have approved of them. The Sahih felt bound to attribute them to him but their cliam does not amount to a proof. Thus, by insisting, the Prophet obtains from Allah permission to go and pray on his mother's tomb. He recommends hasty funerals. "If he is an upright man, it will speed on the hour of recompense. If not, there is every advantage in getting rid of the remains." On the other hand, he praises the merits acquired in following funeral processions. These discords above all serve to nourish the sagacity of commentators.

So we can hardly be surprised if the exact position of Fatima's tomb became forgotten.[561] The same thing happened to her husband's tomb. One day when Aisha complained of a headache, Abul Qasim said to her, "What a fine funeral I would arrange for you if you happened to die before me!" "Yes," replied the daughter of Abu Bakr sharply, "On your return from the funeral you would forget your grief in the company of one of your wives, and that in my house!"[562] According to Masudi, Fatima's disappearance brought deep despair to 'Ali.[563] Her death took away his main entitlement to the attention of Muslims.[564] He does not seem to have woken up to the fact.[565] Hence his indifference during the last illness of his wife[566] and his indecent haste in shortening the time of his widowerhood, and in yielding to numerous strangers the place left vacant by the daughter of the Prophet, in order to get nearer the triumvirate.[567]

X. THE DESCENDANTS OF FATIMA AND THE OTHER DAUGHTERS OF THE PROPHET

The fate of the sons of Fatima is well known enough. Their father was responsible for rivers of blood, *mauriq al-dima' fi l-fitna* (a pourer of blood in the ordeal) to take up the expression of his own nephew Ibn Jafar.[568] The ambition of his sons was no less disastrous for the peace of the Arab empire. They have been made the *rawias* of their mother, Fatima.[569] Yet another reason to advance the date of their birth! In this sphere it was not the daughter of Muhammad—they hardly saw her[570]—but an Iraqi of poor repute who would take over the completion of their education, more than a quarter of a century after Fatima's death,[571] that is, toward the time when the Shia would want to form a party at the heart of the Islamic *jama'a*.

Zaynab, sister of Hasan and Husayn, married Ibn Jafar, and then divorced from that courtier of the Umayyads. Umm Kulthum, the youngest daughter of Fatima, after her marriage to the caliph 'Umar I, passed in succession to the harem of Aun, of Muhammad and of Abdulla, all three sons of Jafar, the martyr of Mouta.[572]

After the death of their mother, the children of Fatima just managed to get on with their father, 'Ali,[573] much as he had got on with the daughter of the Prophet. One often saw them out on their own in the midst of 'Ali's numerous family and joining together, boys and girls, against their father and against the children of his new spouses. A very ordinary spectacle in Muslim households! But the descendants of Fatima had a right to show themselves shocked at his haste to forget his departed spouse, and remember how little effort he had made to make their mother happy. If Ibn al-Hanafiya was really the eldest,[574] this fact would help to explain their disagreements and also the success of his candidature among the numerous Shi-ites, who thought they recognized him as the Mahdi. This success would be a new proof of the mediocre prestige attached to the name of Fatima during the first century of the Hijra.

As for Zaynab, sister of Fatima and daughter of the Prophet, as we already know, she left a daughter called Umama. First of all the wife of 'Ali,[575] the husband of her aunt Fatima, Umama rejected the propositions of the caliph Mu'awya and, on the advice of the dying 'Ali, married the Hashimite Mugira ibn Naufal, grandson of Abd al-Muttalib.[576] The Umayyad king was said to have offered the enormous dowry of one hundred thousand dinars, that is, several million francs! There is no need of great perspicacity to guess the drift of this romance, which was ignored by the earliest annalists. Better informed than their predecessors, some later historians have put a matrimonial failure to the discredit of 'Ali's conqueror and shown the price attached by him to an alliance with the Prophet's family. But this zeal did not take account of the advanced age and the character of Mu'awiya. Opposed to unnecessary expense, he only became reconciled to it in exchange for considerable political advantage and for reasons of state. Besides, he had nothing to gain from opening his harem to a niece of Fatima, who was neglected by the most fervent Shiites. Did Umama even survive her mother? More than one Muslim encyclopedist refuses to admit this.[577]

According to other writers, Umama is said to have presented 'Ali, her first husband, with a son called Muhammad,[578] then another son Yahya. She then married the Hashimite Mugira ibn Naufal[579] and probably died at his house in the year 50. In Islamic records contemporary with the reign of Mu'awiya, the obituary lists have three chronological notations: the *beginning*, the *middle,* and the *end* of the caliphate. Some authors prefer to substitute figures for these summary headings. This precision is too often misleading,[580] especially when it is a question of such an elusive personality as Umama. It is believed that she had resisted the advances of Mo'awia, and then lived long enough to have a second son. These considerations are sufficient to place the date of her death in the year 50.

Her successors were quick to die out, if we can believe Zubayr ibn Bakkar.[581] With the exception of Fatima's descent, one notices a conspiracy of silence around the offspring of the "holy" family. It was really the most sensible attitude. The neglect of these offspring, the indifference of their contemporaries toward them—just a lot of embarrassing detail! Up to the death of 'Ali no one seems to have worried about the Prophet's descendants. From that event onward interest starts to awaken, but only in political form. The Shia confined itself in principle to being a dynastic opposition, a provincial party.[582] It represented the aspirations of Iraq[583] and the ambitions of the Arab aristocracy established beyond the Tigris against the hegemony of the Umayyads supported by Syria. It was against the monopoly of this province, which held the best posts of the empire.[584] In their eyes the principal achievement of 'Ali was establishing Iraq as the capital of the caliphate. Hence the interest shown in Hasan and Husayn, who continued their father's politics and eventually restored the primitive splendor of Iraq. As for orthodoxy, sobered down by experience and knowing the divisions caused by the intrigues of Fatima's sons, it had not the slightest desire to excite the ambition of collateral branches of the Prophet's family. This tendency was perpetuated in the numberless evenhanded Hadith, of which we have made use.

This attitude of prudent reserve was adopted toward the descendants of the daughters of Fatima, the sisters of the two Hasans. With complete correctness they could in the same way claim the privilege of perpetuating Muhammad's family. The eldest, Zaynab was, they said, remarkably intelligent, *'aqila jazila*.[585] She owed this reputation to her attitude during the Karbala escapade in which she alone showed some decision.[586] It would be hard to explain how this wife[587] of Ibn Jafar was mixed up in the affair if we did not know that she was divorced from her husband, who was very hostile to this pitiful adventure. Our authors insisted on including her in order to cover up the lamentable collapse of her brother Husayn. She presented Ibn Jafar with four sons and a daughter, who was later married to Hajjaj.

Her sister, Umm Kulthum,[588] was given in marriage when barely seven years old to the caliph 'Umar.[589] One thinks one is dreaming as one reads this story described at great length by the annalists.[590] 'Ali had at first refused his consent. It was all a sordid affair of rape. It was transformed after the event into marriage to put all in order, or else we have here a proof of the idea primitive Islam had of marriage, as understood by men of the calibre of 'Umar. Umm Kulthum presented the old caliph with a son called Zayd,[591] who died and was buried the same day as his mother. She was married after the death of 'Umar[592] to three sons of Jafar, but we do not know if she had other children.[593] As with the descendants of her aunt Zaynab, and her sister of the same name, the Tradition does not condescend to give any information.

The following tables will help readers to understand the immediate descent of Muhammad. Without claiming to be complete, they will give some guidance in the matter:[594]

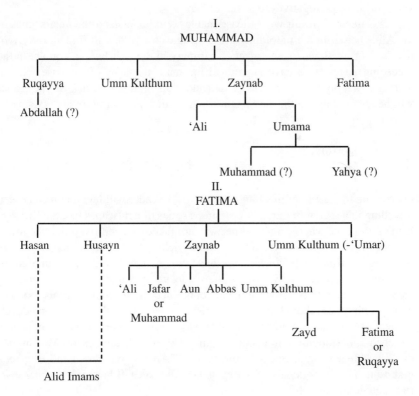

Even at the heart of orthodoxy, Fatima was regarded as "queen of the women of Paradise, after Mariam,[595] daughter of Imran."[596] The more one goes down the series of traditional accounts, the longer grows the list of *Fada'il*[597] or prerogatives attributed to this daughter of Muhammad, who was so little favored in her lifetime. The misfortunes of her family and married life, the gross unfairness to which she was victim after the death of her father, would almost excite our pity, were it not that 'Ali's wife is such an insignificant personality. On the day of the Resurrection she will find herself on the same level and in the same group as the Prophet. As she advances, an angel will cry out: "Lower your eyes, ye mortals!" The Mahdi, the Islamic Messiah, will be born of her posterity.[598] These details will be enough to give an idea of the Fatimite literature engendered by orthodox writers. A whole monograph would be needed if one wanted to sum up the Shia's rantings on this theme. The true importance of Fatima lies in this fact—by her the descent of the Prophet was perpetuated.[599] We have searched, but always in vain, for other prerogatives to attach to her.

This negative result will at least enable us to understand the misfortunes of the Alids better. In the unfolding of their tragic story. We wlll find all the frivolity, lack of intelligence, and want of harmony in the 'Ali-Fatima couple. In the preceding pages[600] we have assembled the main passages of the case without fearing to supply the references or indicate the slightest variants. So the reader will be able to take up the case again if our verdict seems to him unduly severe.

CONCLUSION:
THE POSTHUMOUS GLORY OF FATIMA

On coming to the end of this long marathon, the reader will feel that he has been travelling in a region of mirages, crossing a series of landscapes like the Switzerland of Tartarine where "not a corner was not faked and contrived like the lower regions of the Opera." Every time we have yielded to the temptation to explore the solidity of the route covered, we have everywhere found the ground crumbling under our feet. Every blow of the spade, every sounding showed the presence of a mine or trap, always clumsily concealed. In the course of this monotonous enquiry, even though it was valuable for the study of the origins and development of the Islamic tradition, in what way can we flatter ourselves on having enriched the store of our historical knowledge? A daughter of Muhammad existed, called Fatima. She was the wife of 'Ali and mother of the Prophet's grandson. The other details of her existence, the dates of her birth and her marriage, elude our researches.

"Islam is a religion, born in the full light of history!" So many authorities have repeated this claim that, when we go back to the origins of the movement and we come across "fiddling" everywhere, we cannot help but be disconcerted. Disappointment is followed by a vague annoyance as we start to examine the pseudoscientific apparatus, all the ironmongery of the isnad, and the variants and the editorial tricks destined to conceal this primitive machinery. How, in the case of Fatima, does one explain this lamentable poverty?

Her legend is part of the sira. The sources of the sira are, by order of importance, the Koran, the *Corpus* of contemporary poetry, and finally a limited number of local traditions and personal observations, going back to the witnesses of the heroic age.[601] They were memories written down long after the death of the first observers.[602] As we have already seen, the Koran says not a word on the subject of Fatima. This silence was imitated by the poets during all the first century of the Hijra. Absent from the Koran, ignored by ancient poetry, the mother of the "two Hasans" at first escaped the attention of the chroniclers and *muhaddit*. As for primitive tradition, we have seen how limited is the status and modest the role given to the daughter of the Prophet.

This is how Fatima was reduced to being just a name, belonging to a real person, but remaining enigmatic—a ghost fading away before all efforts to get near her. Around this insubstantial figure the Shiites and the Sunnites started to fight each other. It was a struggle consisting of underhand intrigues, secret moves, and parallel maneuvers where a mass of detail prevented a general view of the whole, and where the agitation of the parties failed to hide the emptiness of the action.[603] This petty, insincere squabbling, this war rich in surprises, ends by confusing the scrutiny of the historian wanting to fix the fleeting image of the pale heroine, who was the cause and stake of these mean struggles. To this war of the two main components of the Muslim army were added the quarrels of historical schools, special tendencies, and political parties, each claiming authority from the example of this daughter of the Prophet to impose a doctrine,[604] a rule of conduct,[605] or to conceal high ambitions under that venerated name. Posterity felt it had to take seriously this gaudy anthology, where the personality of Fatima was used as a pretext or a theme or a pious *trompe-l'oeil* destined to facilitate the agreement of the faithful by assuring the dictates of the heart.

The veneration for Fatima resulted from the worship of the Prophet. Its beginnings date from the first century of the Hijra. Before that time no one had suspected the significance or the possible supportive value of this Qurayshite woman. The number of devotees increased as Islam felt the need to possess its own religious writings, and then its own models for members of the weaker sex to imitate.

To strengthen the virtue of women, to beat them, to refuse them clothes, to condemn them to perpetual confinement, as was recommended by the dictatorial caliph Umar[606]—"beat them all naked"—all these remedies must have seemed inadequate. The authors thought they had provided everything required in proposing the example of Umm ad Darda,[607] as erudite as she was pious, of Mo'ada al-Adawiya, of Rabi'a al-Qaisiya and many other paragons of feminine perfection.[608] But could one decently, without showing disrespect for the Prophet, pass over his daughter's name in silence? Her vague legend lent itself better for edifying expansion than the noisy stories of the tiresome Aisha, who was too often distracted from the teachings of Muhammad (said the eccentric Abu Huraira) by her mirror and her eye lotion. It was better, too, than the romance of Abul Qasim and of Zaynab, which that same Aisha regretted to see perpetuated by the Koran.

The *musnad* of the other "mothers of the believers" did not make a more favorable impression than Aisha's.[609] However, the ancient orthodox school, that of Medina, entirely devoted to Abu Bakr, the founder of the Medina caliphate, gave total preeminence to Aisha. The compilers of the sira, the first historians, had patiently collected the materials to be used in the voluminous *musnad* of the favorite. This predilection is easily explained. The Koran had dealt with Aisha, a signal honor refused to Fatima! Derived from the commentary on the Koran, the sira concentrated most of its attention on the personalities named or indicated in the Book of Allah. It is enough to quote the case of Zayd ibn Haritha. If this obscure Kalbite exerted an extraordinary fascination on the most ancient Tradition, it is for having been the only person, with Abu Lahab, to see his name inscribed in the compilation of Abul Qasim.

Under pressure from the Shia, the rival of Medina (that is, the school of Kufa, which was grateful to 'Ali for having fixed the center of the Arab empire in Iraq) joined the others in the glorification of this woman. This reaction even aroused the fears of orthodoxy, which was keen to contain the movement and make it harmless. We had the chance above of becoming convinced of this. Just as 'Ali's record often gives the answer to the Medinan legend of Abu Bakr,[610] the traditional picture of Fatima is on more than one point the Shiite reply to the invading personality of Aisha. In many places one comes across contours traced from the *musnad* of the insolent favorite.[611] The reshaping has skilfully used the personalities of the two Hasans—a graceful element that one seeks in vain in the legend of Aisha, the proud wife without children, "flowers of life on this earth," to use the picturesque expression of Abul Qasim.

Orthodoxy ended by taking Fatima's side. Confident in the precautions it had taken to protect itself and in the effectiveness of its balancing act, it quieted its last scruples and forgot the ambition of the Alids, so dangerous for the unity of the Islamic *jama'a*. It also thought of the honor that the new policy would bring to the person and family of the master. As well as contributing to fill an important gap in the Sira, this reasonable reaction would remove from him the reproach of being indifferent to his own family.

No one profited from the alterations and the successive developments of the Prophet's legend as much as the Abbasids. This ambitious family had, so to speak, monopolized the person of Abul Qasim for its own profit. It had received payment with interest for admission into the Hashimite clan of the "orphan of Mecca," the son of Abdullah. The caliph Hisam, who witnessed their intrigues, had no illusions on that score. "Those folk," he used to say, "exploit the Envoy of Allah as if he were an article of trade."[612] This clever and persevering policy brought them a throne.

Reassured from that moment onward, and keeping the descendants of 'Ali under lock and key with the threat of punishment, the caliphs of Baghdad[613] thought it was the moment to cease the hostile neutrality that they had shown toward the Fatima legend.[614] It was a rallying with an advantage in view, and in every detail it showed their crafty policy.

Among the writers under their supervision, they would now tolerate the glorification of the 'Ali-Fatima group. But they imposed a condition that they put the obligations of the Alids to their powerful Hashimite cousins in a clear light, and show the family of Abu Talib as having always lived under their protection and fed on the crumbs of their wealth. Abbas and Khamza would find themselves responsible for the education of 'Ali's brothers. The former would buy Aqil[615] in Badr, and his wife would feed the children of Fatima. If, after the Hijra, Abbas continued to live at Mecca, "it was to keep an eye on the privilege of the Banul Muttalib of supplying water and hospitality to the pilgrims. Wasn't it necessary at all costs for them to retain this right?"[616]

These writers describe 'Ali kissing the hands and feet of Abbas and crying out: "For heaven's sake[617] give me back your goodwill!"[618] And to leave no doubt as to the intentions of all this anecdotal literature, one should record this confession of the same 'Ali to the same Abbas—"In your family rests the role of prophet and caliph."[619] It was as good as to accept in advance the usurpation of the Abbasids and their inhumanity toward the Fatimids. Eventually, that traitor Ibn Abbas would get hold of a collection of *Fada-'il,* as tedious and almost as exaggerated as those of his father.[620] After that, the caliphs of Baghdad could listen calmly to the glorification of the "people of the house." Their Macchiavellianism had rendered it inoffensive.

From this collaboration, or rather this conflict of opinions and prejudices, there emerged the too-detailed biography of Fatima. It is a heterogeneous com-position made up of elements that are for the most part apocryphal and often con-tradictory. This type of literature can shock us, and why not? The Muslim student is not worried by historical synthesis. His intellectuel effort does not rise above analysis, which is always purely external! He does not let himself question its intrinsic credibility. In his view the Hadith has, above all, theological value, invoked to support isolated doctrines.

The same methods and related principals were at work in the long-drawn elaboration of the sira. Around the kernel provided by the interpretation of the Koran were wrapped layers of information that had no consistency. There was a strange accumulation of Christian and Judaic accretions jumbled up with polit-ical theories and theocratic dreams. There were opinions of theological schools mixed up with the tendencies of ascetic schools and the aspirations of Sufism. "It is not the historical picture," remarks the author of *Vorlesungen uber Islam* [Lec-tures on Islam by I. Goldhizer] "that influences the believers. In its place there was early on substituted the pious legend of Muhammad, model of all the heroic virtues" (p. 20). In an infinitely more restricted field, the biography of Fatima has enabled us to come across the activity of this underground workshop. There remains the task of a detailed test applied to other parts of the sira. When this enquiry has been brought to completion, we shall no doubt be able to give an opinion on the value of the official life of the Prophet.

Fatima was not the ideal woman glimpsed by the Alid writers. Yet perhaps she did not play such a self-effacing role. As a person, she may have been less insignificant than was suggested by the clumsy editors of her orthodox *musnad*. Unfortunately, this unfavorable impression emerges from the impartial compar-ison with very balanced ancient documents, less burdened with imaginary addi-tions. One can imagine why the piety of later ages wanted to improve the image of the Prophet's daughter.[621] It is hard to understand why that piety sought con-sciously to reshape that image, if it had not felt justified in reacting against ten-dentious falsifications.

NOTES

Principal Abbreviations
Used by Henri Lammens

Aghani = Al-Isfahani, Abu al-Faraj *Kitab al-Aghani*, 1st. ed. 20 vols. Cairo and Bulaq, 1867–1869.

Baladhuri, *Futuh* = *Futuh al-buldan*, ed. M. J. de Goeje. Leiden: E. J. Brill, 1866.
Ansab = *Ansab al-Ashraf*, manuscript of Paris.
Bukhari, *Sahih* = *Le recueil des traditions musulmanes*, ed. L. Krehl and T. W. Juynboll. 4 vols. Leiden, 1862–1908.
Caetani, *Annali* = Leone Caetani, *Annali dell'Islam*, 10 vols. Milan, 1905–1926.
Studi = Leone Caetani, *Studi di storia orientale*, 3 vols. 1911.
Chantre = H. Lammens, *Le chantre des Omiades: notes biographiques et lit-téraires sur le poète arabe chrétien Akhtal*. Paris 1985. (Extract from *Journal Asiatique*, 1895.)
Chroniken (Wust.) = F. Wustenfeld, *Die Chroniken der Stadt Mekka*. 3 vols.
Fihrist = Al-Nadim, *Kitab al-Fihrist*, ed. G. Flugel. 2 vols. Leipzig, 1871–1872.
Al-Jahiz, *Bayan* = *Al-Bayan wa'l-tabyin*. 2 vols. Cairo, 1893–1895.
Haiawan = *Kitab al-Haiawan*. 7 vols. Cairo, 1905–1907.
Tria opuscula = ed. G. Van Vloten. Leiden: E. J. Brill, 1903.
Avares = *Kitab al-bukhala* (Le Livre des Avares), ed. G. Van Vloten. Leiden, 1900.
Mahasin = *Kitab al-Mahasin*, attributed to al-Jahiz, ed. G. Van Vloten. Leiden, 1898.
Goldziher, *M.S.* = *Muhammedanische Studien*, 2 vols. Halle: Max Niemeyer, 1889–1890.
Abhandlungen = *Abhandlungen zur arabischen Philologie*. 2 vols. Leiden, 1896–1899.
Hassan ibn Thabit, *Divan* = The Diwan of Hassan ibn Thabit, ed. Hartwig Hirschfeld.
Khamis = al-Diyarbakri, *Tarikh al-Khamis fi ahwal anfasi nafis*. Cairo, 1884.
Ibn Abdalbarr or I. Abdalbarr = *Ibn 'Abd al-Barr, al-Isti'ab fi ma'rifat al-ashab*. Cairo, 1910.
Ibn al-Athir, *Kamil* = *al-Kamil fi al-turikh,*, ed. C. J. Tornberg. 14 vols. Leiden: E. J. Brill, 1851–1876.
Ibn Duraid, *Istiqaq* = *Kitab al-Istiqaq*, ed. F. Wustenfeld, Gottingen, 1854.
Ibn Hanbal or Hanbal = Ahmad ibn Hanbal, *Musnad*. 6 vols. Cairo, 1893.
Ibn Hisham, *Sira* = *Sirat ar-rasul*, ed. F. Wustenfeld. Gottingen, 1854.
Iqd = Ibn 'Abd Rabbih, *al'Iqd al-Farid*. 3 vols. Bulaq and Cairo, 1876 (the figures as exponents refer to the editions of the *Iqd* used)
Ibn Hajar, *Isaba* = Ibn Hajar al-'Asqalani Abu'l-Fadl Ahmad ibn Ali, *al-Isaba fi tamyiz as-sahaba* (A Biographical Dictionary of Persons Who Knew Muhammad), ed. Aloys Springer et al. 4 vols. Calcutta, 1856–1888.
I.S. *Tabaq.*, = Ibn Sa'd, *Kitab al-tabaqat al-kabir,* ed. Eduard Sachau et al. 9 vols. 1904–1940.

Masudi, *Prairies* = al-Nasudi, Abu'l-Hasan 'Ali ibn al-Husayn, *Muruj al-dhahab (Les Prairies d'or)*, ed. Barbier de Meynard and Pavet de Courtelle. 9 vols. Paris, 1861–1877.

Moawia = H. Lammens, *Etudes sur le règne du calife omaiyade Moawia Ier.* Beirut, 1908. Also in *MFO*, vol. 1 (1906), pp. 1ff.; vol. 2 (1907), pp. 1 ff.; vol. 3 (1908), pp. 45ff.

Margoliouth, *Mohammed = Mohammed and the rise of Islam.* London, 3d ed. [1905 1st ed.]

Montakhab Kanz = Montakhab Kanz al-ommal. 6 vols., in the margin of Ibn Hanbal's Musnad.

Muslim, *Sahih* = Edition of Cairo. The superscript two refers to the edition of 1909.

Naqaid Jarir = Naqa'id Jarir wa'l-Farazdaq, ed. A. A. Bevan. 3 vols. Leiden, 1905–1912.

Nawawi, *Tahdib* = al-Nawawi, Abu Zakariya Yahya ibn Sharaf, *Tahdib al-asma* (Biographical Dictionary), ed. F. Wustenfeld. Gottingen, 1842–1847.

Noldeke-Schwally, *Geschichte* = Theodor Noldeke, *Geschichte des Qorans,* 1st ed. Gottinger, 1860. 2d ed. F. Schwally, G. Bergstrasser. and O. Pretzel. 3 vols. Leipzig, 1909–1938.

Qutaiba, *Maarif* = Ibn Qutayba, Abu Muhammad 'Abdallah ibn Muslim, *Kitab al-ma'arif,* ed. F. Wustenfeld. Gottingen, 1850.

   Oyoun = Ibn Qutaiba, *'Uyun al-akhbar,* ed. Carl Brockelmann. 4 pts. Berlin, 1900–1908.

   Poesis = Ibn Qutayba, *Liber poesis et poetarum,* ed. M. J. de Goeje. Lugd. Bat., 1904.

Qoran (Koran) = Fluegel, Gustav Lebrecht, *Corani Textus Arabicus.* Leipzig: E. Bredtil, 1834, 2d. ed. 1881.

République marchande = H. Lammens, *La république marchande de la Mecque vers l'an 600 de notre ere.* Taken from *Bulletin de l'Institut égyptien,* (1910): 23–54.

Sprenger, *Mohammad = Das Leben und die Lehre des Mohammad.* 2d ed. 3 vols. Berlin, 1869.

Tab., *Tafsir* = Tabari, *Tafsir al Qoran.* 30 vols. Cairo, 1905–1911.

Tab. = al-Tabari, *Tarikh al-rusul wa'l muluk (Annales)*, ed. M. J. de Goeje et al. 15 vols. Leiden, 1899–1901.

Triumvirat = H. Lammens, *Le Triumvirat Abu Bakr, 'Umar et Abu Ubaida.* Taken from *Mélanges de la Fac. Orient.* De Beyrouth, IV–V. 1909.

Usd = Ibn al-Athir, 'Izz al-Din, Abu'l-Hasan 'Ali ibn Muhammad, *Usd al-ghaba fi ma'rifat al-Sahaba.* 5 vols. Cairo, 1868–1869.

Yaqubi, *Hist.* = Al-Yaqubi *Historiae*, ed. M. Th. Houtsma. 2 vols. Leiden, 1883.

Yazid = H. Lammens, *Le califat de Yazid Ier.* Taken from *Mélanges de la Fac. Orient. de Beyrouth*, IV-V. Beirut, 1910–1919.

Waqidi (Kremer) = *Kitab al-Magazi*, ed. Von Kremer. Calcutta, 1856.

Waqidi (Well.) = *Al-Vakidi's Kitab Maghazi*, trans. Wellhausen. Berlin: G. Reimer, 1882.

Wellhausen, *Reste* = J. Wellhausen, *Reste arabischen Heidentums.* 2d ed. Berlin, 1897.

Ziad ibn Abihi = H. Lammens, *Ziad ibn Abihi, vice-roi de l'Iraq, lieutenant de Moawia.* Vol. 1, pp. 1–139, from *Rivista degli studi orientali*, IV. 1912.

WZKM = Wiener Zeitschrift fur die Kunde des Morgenlandes.

ZDMG = Zeitschrift des deutschen morgenlandische Gesellschaft.

MFO = Melanges de la Faculte orientale of Beyrouth.

The letter E refers to the Egyptian editions of the works used. The Arab geographers like Istakhri, Ibn Hauqal, Maqdisi, Ibn al-Faqih, Ibn Rusteh, Masudi, *Tanbih (= Kitab at-tanbih wal israf)* are quoted from the editions in the collection *Bibliotheca geogr.arabicorum* (ed. M. J. de Goeje, 8 vols. Leiden: E. J. Brill, 1879–1939) and Hamdani, *Gazirat al-Arab*, in the edition of D. H. Muller.

For the manuscripts we only refer to the place where they are to be located Leiden, Berlin, Paris, Damascus, Cairo (Khedive's Library), and so on. It is a matter of the Arabic archives of these repositories. Since the immense majority of the manuscripts in Constantinople have unnumbered pages, we had to confine ourselves to indicating the specific libraries of the Turkish capital. As in our previous publications we have followed the system of transcription adopted by the Catholic Printing Press of Beyrouth.

1. Sura 13:38. [Cf. the author's "Koran and Tradition," chapter 4 of present volume—Trans.]

2. Sura 18:44, *zaynat al-hayat al dunya.*

3. Sura 3:8, 112; 57:19, 20; 63:9; 64:15; 68:14; 71:12, 21; 74:12, 13.

4. Sura 2:48, 50, et *loc. supr. cit.* Cf. Ibn Hanbal, *Musnad,* VI, 118, 2; the eulogy of Khadija, introduced principally to confirm that she had provided him with posterity; cf. ibid. VI, 97 112, NB: *wulida lahu.* Notice how they excuse Husayn the son of Fatima of having left few children: *'Iqd* 4, II, 255, top; Yaqubi, *Histoire* (ed. Houtsma), II, 293.

5. Sura 108:3; *Muhammad abtar la ya'esh lahu walad dhakar:* Muhammad is *abtar*, he has no living male child; Baladhuri, *Ansab al asraf* (ms. Paris) 261a; *laysa lahu wa la akh fa-ida mata inqata'a dhikruh:* he has neither a son nor a brother and if he dies his memory will disappear; Abu Ubaid, *Gharib al hadit* (ms. Kuprulu, Constantinople) 3a.

6. In Interpreting the theory of Kunya wrongly and in attributing to him a necessary relation with a son. [Cf. "Koran and Tradition," chapter 4 of present volume.

—Trans.] Muhammad confers the kunya to the Companions without children; Waqidi (Kremer) 257, 4 d.l.; Hanbal, VI, 16 to Aisha, ibid., VI, 107, 151. At Medina "they call the descendants of Muhammad bin Sayfi Banu al-Tahira; they concluded they were descended from a daughter, who remained anonymous however, of the great Khadija; Baladhuri, *Ansab*, 261b, 262a.

7. Except the Jews; Ibn Hanbal, *Musnad*, VI, 6, 1.16. The Hawari Talha would have made a sensation in giving biblical names to his children; I.S. *Tabaq.*, III 1 70, 23.

8. *la yu'arif laha ism*, we do not know him by name, *Tarikh al-Khamis* (ed. 1302) I, 307.

9. *Ag.*, XV, 2; the marriage really took place; the Muslim annalists maintain the contrary; but in that case what became of Umm Kulthum during the period between her divorce and the death of Ruqayya; why did no Companion take the trouble to create a position for her?

10. One would be tempted to suppose this to be a Shiite accusation: of this animosity there have remained traces upto the Orthodox tradition, but subtle enough to conceal them from the attention of the Sunnis.

11. Since married *bikr*: virgin by 'Uthman (I.S. *Tabaq.*, VIII, 25). Like her sister, she had stayed a long time at Abu Lahab's; ibid., 24–25.

12. I.S. *Tabaq.*, III 1, 37; Ibn Hisham, *Sira*, 208, 241, 457.

13. Ibn Hisham, *Sira*, 121; *Usd*, V, 400

14. I.S. *Tabaq.*, III 1, 36–58. Frequency of names, formed with *dhu* possessor, owner, provided with); Waqidi, (Kremer) 108 d.l. *dhu-l-anyab*, "the man with teeth"; Hanbal, III, 117: dhu-l-uddhunayn the man with two ears. The index of Tabari sub verb (under the word) *dhu*. Neither Ibn Hisham, Ibn Qutaiba, nor Masudi mention the title *Dhu al Nurain*. According to Hanbal, II, 271, top, the nicknames Dhu'l Yadain and Dhus-Simalan indicate the same person. Let us compare it to Dhu 'l Waghain, obviously unfavorable, (Bukhari, IV, 126,) just as the Hadith does; Hanbal, 307; *dhat nitaq* the woman with a girdle or belt, that is, a woman. Ibid., VI; 358, 10; *dhu-l-bajadayn,* man with two garments made of striped material. Ibid. IV, 159. In his numerous elegies on 'Uthman, Hassan ibn Thabit does not mention this title of honor, all the while calling him the Prophet's son-in-law; see his *Divan* (ed. Hirschfeld) CLVII, 3, where it becomes difficult to determine the authentic parts; we must use it with infinite caution.

15. Ibn Rusta, *Kitab al-al'aq al-nafisa*, ed. M. J. de Goeje. 1892, p. 214. I.S. *Tabaq.*, IV 1, 176.

16. Nawawi, *Tahdib*, 409.

17. Ibn Rusta, loc. cit.; Ibn Hanbal, *Musnad*, IV, 67, 77; Goldziher, *Uber Dualtiteln, WZKM,* XIII, 324-25; Qutaiba, *Ma'arif* (Wust.), 164, 165.

18. Ibn Hazm al-Fasi (Berlin, ms. no. 9510) p. 11a; Tab., III, 2303; *Usd*, V, 400; *Isti'ab* (of Ibn 'Abdalbarr) 727; I.S. *Tabaq.*, VIII, 182.

19. Enemies and partisans of 'Uthman had need of Ruqayya; the former to attest to his absence from Badr, the latter to justify this absence; cf. Waqidi (Kremer) 96. Cf. anonymous ms., *Tarikh Khulufa* (History of Caliphs) (no. 1595, Paris), 7b, after having

mentioned the traditional explanation for Doun-Nourain, adds: "it is said that when he entered Paradise there were for him two flashes of lightning, and it said it is because he had memorized the Koran by heart and could recite it in one go, for the Koran is one light, to get up at night is one light, and one said even more that." In other words, the nickname was no longer understood. The slanderer is called "the man with two faces"; Bukhari, *Sahih* (Krehl), IV, 126, 3 d.l.

20. Yaqubi, *History,* II, 42.

21. Ibn al-Jawzi, *Talqih* (ms. Asir effendi, Constantinople), 6a; idem, *Mir'at* (ms. Kuprulu, Constantinople), II, 192 a "Abu-l-Asi lived with Zaynab next to him"; they claim that she converted six years before her husband; Hanbal, I, 261.

22. Tab., *Annales*, III, 2303.

23. I.S. *Tabaq.,* VIII, 21; this epithet does not have another origin.

24. Tab., *Annales*, III, 2296.

25. Cf. Hanbal, II, 208, top; I.S. *Tabaq.,* VIII, 22., Baladhuri, *Ansab* (ms. cited) 254b. Imaginative story of how Zayd ibn Haritha (see further on) succeeded in facilitating Zaynab's escape from Mecca.; *Tarikh al Khamis*, I, 309.

26. Baladhuri, *Ansab*, loc. cit. We shall mention it again at the end of the present monograph, as of the quality of legatee, accorded to Zubayr ibn al-'Awwam.

27. Sura 33:59: "qul . . . Tell your wives and daughters . . ." assumes the plurality of Muhammad's daughters. Starting from this inspired text, the authors wanted to find at the every least three sisters for Fatima.

28 Perhaps in *Aghani*, VII, 10 (with justifucation the index puts a question mark here) Abu Dahbal al-Gomahi, *Divan* (ed. Krenkow), XXI, 3 names them Bani Muhammad wa Bani 'Ali (the descendants of Muhammad and the descendants of 'Ali), without pronouncing the name of Fatima. It appears in some apocryphal verses (notice the *za'amu,* meaning they think that!); same applies to Masudi, *Prairies*, IV, 161. Not named in the *Hasimiyat* of Kumait (see the excellent ed. of Horovitz), beginning with the Second Muslim century. For the Shia, a political party, the personality of 'Ali absorbs all the interest; the dynastic idea takes precedence over religious considerations.Fatima is found named in the apocryphal elegies, dedicated to Muhammad; I.S. *Tabaq.*II², 93, 19; 95, 6; 97, 4, 9, 19. For their authenticity, see the introduction of the editor F. Schwally, p. VI. Composition relatively ancient, done with forms and pseudo-archaic turns of phrases, such as milbuka' = min al-buka' (98, 8). There they introduce the name of Amina, the mother of the Prophet, not to be found anywhere else, like that of Fatima; the nobleness of Muhammad is there found exalted (96, 2 d.l., 97, 1 etc.). In short, of the apocryphal writings, interesting for the date and formation of the sira.

29. I do not recall any text in her favor.

30. Cf. the author's *Califat de Yazid I,* p.43

31. Qazwini, *Nasab an-nabi* (ms. Berlin), 3a. Likewise if Zaynab, Ruqayya have been presented as the eldest, it is to prevent the scandal of their marriage to pagans, they thus declared it as taking place before the "prophecy." In order avoid the objection of the old age of Khadija, one opinion is that she married at the age of 28; see later.

32. "It is clear that the eldest married first, even if they have said the opposite." Ali ibn Soltan (Berlin, ms. no 9645) p. 297a; *Usd,* V, 519, 612; *Tarikh al Khamis,* I, 307.

33. Declared the eldest; I.S. *Tabaq.*, VIII, 20; Ibn Abdalbarr, *Istiab,* 753; Maqrizi, *Imta* (ms. Kuprulu) III, section consecrated to the children of Muhammad.

34. Tab., III, 2430; *Khamis,* I, 310; Ibn Hisham, *Sira,* 121, 208; Pseudo-Balkhi (ed. Huart) IV 1, 139; Masudi, *Prairies,* IV, 162, the third of the daughters of Muhammad. I.S. *Tabaq.*, VIII, 24.

35. Maqrizi, *Imta,* III, loc. cit; Ibn al-Jawzi, *Talqih* (ms. 'Asir effendi) p. 6a; *Khamis,* I, 308; Umm Kulthum, older than Fatima and Ruqayya, *Usd,* V, 612; Ruqayya, the eldest of them all; I.Hisham, *Sira,* 121.

36. "He is the most knowledgeable in this affair," Suhaili, *Sarh as Sira* (ms. Berlin) attributes to him a sira: "It was the first Sira that was written in Islam"; who has seen it?

37. "He is one of the imams in this affair," Kalai, *Iklifa* (ms. Berlin), 42 b.

38. Fatima would be the one before last, Umm Kulthum the youngest; I.S. *Tabaq.* I 1, 85; Maqdisi, *Khalsat al-sira* (ms. B.Khed.) 36 a; Ibn Qayym al-Jawziya, *Zad al-Moad* (ms. Bayazid) I vol.; According to *Khamis,* I, 310, Zubayr ibn Bakkar would have declared Ruqayya as the eldest. The fragment of his *Nasab Quraysh* [Genealogy of the Quraysh], conserved at Kuprulu, does not speak of the Prophet's family; Maqrizi, ms. cit.; Nuwairi, *Nihaia,* II (ms. Kuprulu) section 16. *'Iqd,* II, 202, in naming her in the first rank, seems to present her as the eldest of the girls.

39. *Istiab,* 753, 770 (ed. of Hyderabad).

40. Cf. the author's *Triumvirate,* p. 114, and his *Califat de Yazid* I (henceforth *Yazid*), p. 74

41. *Fihrist* (Fluegel) 110, 16. For the *musnad* of Aisha in vol. 6 of Ibn Hanbal, the prinicipal authority is Urwa Ibn Zubayr.

42. Declared the youngest of her sisters, but "greatest in power," Majmoua, no. 349 (ms. B. Khed.), I b; Yaqubi, *Histoire,* II, 19; Nawawi, *Tahdib,* 850.

43. Sprenger, *Mohammad, I,* 203.

44. Cf. the author's article, "The Age of Muhammad and the Chronology of the Sira" [chapter 5 of the present volume.—Trans.]

45. Or two years, as the *musnad* of Aisha says, in Ibn Hanbal, VI, or "five years" according to the Basra school; "that is an error," adds Baladhuri, *Ansab,* 261a; Urwa ibn Hisham talks of "two years or thereabouts." ibid.

46. "One of the old women of the Quraysh whose corners of the mouth are red," as Aisha describes her; Hanbal, VI, 150.

47. Cf. "The Age of Muhammad and the Chronology of the Sira" [chapter 5 of the present volume.—Trans.]

48. Tab., II, 2434; Ibn al-Jawzi, *Safwat as-Sawfa* (ms. Bib.Khed.), 51b; I.S. *Tabaq.* I 1, 85. According to one isolated version, Khadija was only 28 years old at her marriage; I.S. *Tabaq.*, VIII, 10, 2.

49. Tab., III, 2434; they quote Waqidi in favor of this opinion in Ibn Khajar, *Isaba,* IV, 725; Ibn Abdulbarr, *Istiab,* 771; *Khamis,* I, 213, Baladhuri, *Ansab,* 259 a talks of 35 years or even less; I.S. *Tabaq.*, VIII, 17, 15, of "35 years."

50. Caetani, *Annali*, I, 173–174.

51. *Khamis, I*, 313; Yaqubi, *Hist.*, II, 19.

52. Ibn Khajar, *Isaba*, IV, 725.

53. With addition of "it is said that." *Prairies, IV*, 157.

54. See the synchronism indicated, Hanbal, *Musnad*, VI, 118; to Aisha they grant 6 years at the burial of Khadija. Fatima must have been a certain age at the time, when "Warn your tribe" was revealed (sura 26:214), if one can compare it to Hanbal, *Musnad*, VI, 136, 9. According to the same account Muhammad behaved as if he did not have any other daughter and she must have been nubile! The antiquity of the sura 26:214 cannot be challenged; cf. Noldeke-Schwally, *Geschichte des Qorans*, 126; cf. Hanbal, II, 449.

55. According to everyone, dead at 65; see p. ex. *Maqatil at-talibiyn*, 19.

56. Cf. the author's *Yazid*, 43. In addition to the legend of Khadija, that of the mother of 'Ali, the mother of numerous boys, each one born at ten year intervals, must have contributed to the credibility of this tale.

57. Cf. Ibn Hisham, *Sira*, 121, 776; Sarazin, *Das Bild Alis*.

58. Cf. Ibn Hanbal, *Musnad*, VI, 29-282 see in the following pages the *musnad* of Fatima and of the husbands.

59. It concerns, moreover, equally the descendants of the other sons of 'Ali (but not born of Fatima).

60. Cf. in Baladhuri, *Ansab*, 349, etc., and the chapter "Recollection of Fatima and Atika."

61. It has there discovered the existence of Qasim, the son of the Prophet. This question of *kunya* deserves a special study because of its historical significance. It would allow us the get rid of all the Qasims, the Talibs, and so many other fictive characters from the stage of primitive Islam. Fatima received this name "for God on High saved her and those He loved from the fire," *Montakhab Kanz al-Ommal*, V, 97, 8 (= henceforth, *Montakhab Kanz*).

62. Tab., III, 2302–03; Dahabi, *Tarikh* (ms. Paris), 112b; *Usd*, V, 520; *Maqatil at-talibiyn*, 18 Nawawi, *Tahdib*, 850, gives her the Kunya Umm al-Had. Among the Shafaite names, one meets "Bou Abihi" father of his father, R. Dussaud, *Arabes de Syrie*, 100.

63. *Usd*, V, 520; Khamis, I, 313; I.Abdulbarr, *Istiab*, 772.

64. *Hist.*, II, 35, 4; they treat as fiction the history of the Safar *jala* (quince, meaning fruit)., *Montakhab Kanz*, V, 97.

65. Cf. *Aghani*, XI, 164, bottom; XVIII, 204, 8 Wellhausen, *Reste*, 198.

66. Cf. Tab., III 2436; other testimonies further down. Fatima weeps for the death of her sister Ruqayya (I.S. *Tabaq.*, VIII, 24, bottom) and when she learns that the Quraysh plotted the fall of her father Hanbal, I, 303 she curses her persecutors; Bukhari, *Sahih* (Krehl), II, 300.

67. Listed in Hanbal, VI, 347, 3–8; cf. I.S. *Tabaq.*, VIII, 182 bottom.

68. Accepted by M. Marcais, biography of Muhammad, in *Grande Encyclopédie* Reckendorf, *Muhammed und die Seinen*.

69. "Among the handsomest of men," despite marks of smallpox; Hanbal, I, 72, 8, 73; 'Iqd, II 214; Ibn Batriq (ed.Cheikho), II, 33.

70. *Khamis*, I, 310; she is "the best partner that a man has seen"; Majmoua no. 349 (Tarikh, ms. Bib.Khed.), p.1b; comes to complain to her father about her domestic problems; he sends her back: "I do not like to hear a woman complaining about her husband." Qazwini, *Nasb an-Nabi* (ms. Berlin, 9570), 3a.

71. Or take this other example the superiority of Aisha over women is like the superiority of soup (*tarid*) over other food," Hanbal, *Musnad*, VI, 159 for the beauty of Ruqayya, see further Maqdisi, *Ansab al-Qorasiyn* (ms. Asir eff., Constantinople) pages unnumbered; the daughter of Hamza was the most beautiful Qurayshite; *Montakhab Kanz* . . . II, 484, d.l. "the most beautiful girl of the Quraysh," notwithstanding she could not marry until after Khaybar; Hanbal, I, 98, 132.

72. *Khamis*, I, 309.

73. Cf. the author's *Triumvirat*, 122, etc. (in *MFO, IV*).

74. *Life of Mohammed*, 325.

75. A shopkeeper of Medina goes as far as to suspect her of wishing to buy without paying Hanbal, *Musnad*, VI, 147: "Muhammad wanted to leave with my tunic thjat is to say without giving me my money."

76. The same conclusion for her sister Umm Kulthum. Repudiated early on by her first husband, she waited 10 to 15 years before meeting a new partner.

77. Physical beauty is not an insignificant question among the descendents of the Prophet. A propos of a handsome and eloquent Alid, they write "these are people illuminated by the light of the caliphate and who pronounce the language of prophecy," *Iqd 4*,II, 35, 4–5.

78. Ibn Hanbal, *Musnad*, VI, 156, 158, 182, 187.

79. Cf. Waqidi (Kremer) 338, I, each morning they "cut the wood for Muhammad" at Medina. However, oatmeal bread remains a rarety there. *Ibid.*, 113, 6.

80. Cf. the author's *République marchande de la Mecque;* I.S. *Tabaq.*, VIII, 91.10

81. A common occurrence in Mecca, cf. *République marchande de la Mecque* 18 Hanbal, II, 7 d.l.

82. "Until his worth is recognized." I.S.*Tabaq.*, IV 1, 43.

83. Yaqubi, *Hist.*, II, 42; Baladhuri, *Ansab*, 258a; I.S. *Tabaq.*, VIII, 11–12; *Montakhab Kanz*, V, 98, 99.

84. The same inspiration, for the attitude of Aisha towards the Caliph 'Uthman Hanbal, *Musnad*, VI, 149, 15 etc. A. Bakr and 'Umar equally fought over the hand of Umm Salama, Muhammad's wife; ibid., II, 313, 317; it is the same proceeding for Fatima.

85. Nasai, *Sunan* (ms. Nouri Otmani, Constantinople), book of marriage, under the title "The marriage of women of an age comparable to hers."

86. Nasai, loc. cit.

87. Yaqubi, *Hist.*, numerous quotes in *Montakhab Kanz*, . . . V, 30. On the insistance of A. 'Bakr and 'Umar, Muhammad replied, "I am waiting for her the decree," Baladhuri, *Ansab*, 258b. I.S.*Tabaq.*, VIII, II at page 12, Muhammad, without beating about the bush, gives preference to his cousin over A. Bakr and 'Umar.

88. Sura 33:37.

89. Tab., III, 2303; *Aghani*, XV, 2.

90. Here is the reason why certain chroniclers present her as the youngest of the sisters. But then why married before Fatima how can they not make the latter older? All the same, the pious A. Bakr had first got Aisha engaged to the son of a rich pagan Motim ibn Adi (cf. Hanbal, VI, 211), the protector of Muhammad, after Abu Talib. This withdrawal puts the Prophet and his future father-in-law in a bad light.

91. *ZDMG*, LII, 28–31; in Ibn Hisham, *Sira*, 158–59, the account of 'Ali's childhood does not have an isnad.

92. Cf. the author's, *Moawia*, v. index; and his *Califat de Yazid I*, 132–33.

93. Cf. *Maqatil*, p. 9, bottom.

94. Cf. *Moawia*, 154, etc.; for the judgment of the Ansar Qais ibn Sa'd, see *Maqatil*, 25 bottom.

95. "The Words of the People of the House and their Supporters," Masudi, *Tanbih* (de Goeje), 231

96. Yaqubi, *Hist*. II, 22 bottom; he attended the funeral of Fatima; ibid., II, 128.

97. Noldeke's observation, *ZDMG*, loc. cit.

98. On his subject a Lahabid would say to the Caliph Harun ar-Rashid: "You do not know the story of your grandfather and what became of him. Listen to him each time he hates something"; Fihrist, 209, 13; a writer flagellated by the Abbasids for having talked freely about Abbas; ibid., 111, 28.

99. He sold the houses of Muhammad and those of his own brothers, 'Ali and Jafar Baladhuri, *Ansab*, 415a; "you are my father's slaves," cried Hamza to 'Ali and Muhammad; Hanbal, I, 142.

100. In Hassan ibn Thabit, *Divan* (ed. Hirschfeld), XXI, in the verses (elegy on the defeat of Mouta) there figure the names of Abbas and Aqil. Either the entire portion or just this verse are apocryphal. Certain biographers used this as a pretext to affirm thenceforth the conversion of Aqil; cf. *Khamis*, I, 184; Talib the eldest "died an unbeliever in the expedition of Badr." Jafar, "the man with two wings" is mentioned by Ibn Qays ar-Roqaiyat, *Divan*, (ed. Rhodokanachi), 174; likewise 'Ali, qualified as wasiy, legatee, the more so surprising because it concerns the panegyric of the Zubairite Mosab. If these verses are authentic, the legend of Mouta would have been fixed as soon as the second half of the first Muslim century.

101. Yaqubi, *Hist.,* II, 42, 3.

102. In Ibn Hisham, *Sira*, 819, it is Abbas who takes Fatima to Medina; cf. Noldeke, *ZDMG*, LII, 24.

103 Ibn al Athir, *Kamil*, II, 44, top "until his feet were oozing"; Maqrizi, *Imta* (ms. Kuprulu) 1 st part.

104. [Freed slave] Tab., III, 2440; I.S. *Tabaq.*, VIII, 42–43; cf.Caetani, *Annali*, II, 137; the substitution of Abbas for 'Ali or Zayd is a part of these attempts, where they make every effort to give back to the Alids those under an obligation to the Abbasids, like also multiplying the probabilities surrounding the conversion inwardly of Abbas.

105. I.S.*Tabaq*. III 1, 30 10; cf. Masudi, *Prairies,* IV, 137.

106. *ZDMG,* LII,19

107. In the question of "the acceptation of the one fasting," they give the impression of pitting Aisha with Umm Salama to affirm that the Prophet "could not love her more"; Hanbal, VI, 296.

108. They pretend to note the most insignificant variants *bihi* and *fihi, nazala* or *anzala, an yashuqqa* or *an ashaqqa, sadiqa* or *saliha;* "forty days" or "forty nights" the word *ridwan* placed before *maghfara* and vice versa; *marru* or *mararna* (it concerns women); *yashtaddu aw yashri'a shakka* etc., Hanbal, *Musnad,* VI, 133; 150, 153, 158, 171, 298, 300. Cf. ibid., 306, *saliha* and *hasana;* 309; *tarabat yaminuki or taribu jabinuka;* 326, *bana Allah lahu aw bana lahu;* 337, a name of a totally unknown woman, they hesitate between *shumaysa* or *sumaya* or *samayna;* 465, "he had profited from healthy food" or "he desired healthy food." Sufyan said, "It is my doubt and his doubt."

109. Thus in a list, notice the final: "and moreover two other details that I have forgotten." This ruse of editing is very common; see Muslim, *Sahih 2,* I, 392, II II, 71, 12; 98, 12; 399, 7d.l.; 462, 15; Maqrizi, *Khitat* (ed. G. Wiet), 213, N2.

110. "You are from me . . . and for me. And you are the most precious of men for me." I.S. *Tabaq.,* III 1, 29, 25; 30.

111. *Khamis,* I, 309, fictional development, inviting a smile.

112. Hanbal, *Musnad,* VI, 227, top 254, d.l. Cf. the Merits of 'Ali in *Montakhab Kanz. . . ,* V, 29, etc., there one will find the legend of 'Ali, to which that of Zayd corresponds; they are the same clichés. When in a Hadith, 'Ali finds himself in the Prophet's company, it is rare not to see Zayd spring up; Bukhari, *Sahih (*Krehl) II, 74, n.7.

113. Thus at the preparations of the funeral of Muhammad, the Hashimites appear alone, but orthodoxy took care to add to them Usama, the son of Zayd; Baladhuri, *Ansab,* 373a, 374b, 378. On the way to Badr, Muhammad shared the same camel with 'Ali and Zayd (ibid., 181a) thus harmony was reestablished.

114. In Hanbal, *Musnad,* VI, the *musnad* of Umm Salama proves to be more favorable to 'Ali than Aisha's.

115. Other proofs of affection for Usama; Hanbal, *Musnad,* VI, 82, 156–57; at the *fath* (conquest of Mecca) Muhammad got on Usama's camel, ibid., VI, 15. We will come back to this point later; cf. I.S. *Tabaq.,* IV 1, 43.

116. Baladhuri, *Ansab* (ms. cited) 112a.

117. The orthodox version limits it to a few days a longer absence would seem to be suspect.

118. Cf. *Fihrist* (Flugel), 98, 20–21; they call him Shiite but with *taqiya* (dissimulation).

119. Cf. Waqidi (Kremer), 146, etc.

120. *Sharika fihi,* meaning he took part in it, above all; p. 151, 7 d.l. where the the Shiite title Amir al-Mu'minin (Commander or Prince of the Believers) appears. A. Hunain, Abu Talha is the Ansarian answer to 'Ali.

121. Cf. *Moawia,* 144; *Maqatil,* 10, 4; *Aghani,* XV, 45, 7 d.l.

122. According to the data in the sira, the Ansarian legend claimed for the Medinans

certain feats, attributed to 'Ali. Thus it is Muhammad ibn Maslama who killed Marhab at Khaybar; Hanbal, III, 385. At Badr, Hassan ibn Thabit, *Divan* (ed. Hirschfeld), LXXVI, claims as their own the exploits attributed to the Hashimites. Unfortunately half of this divan is apocryphal. See the remark of Goldziher, in *Der Islam*, II, 103.

123. See the notes of Horovitz on Kumait, *Hasimiyat*, II, 95–96; the Alid Hadith took its inspiration from this Shiite poet.

124. Cf. *Moawia*, index s.v. 'Aqil the author's *Califat de Yazid I*, 135–36.

125. *Montakhab Kanz . . .,* V, 56; I.S. *Tabaq.*, VIII, 12–13; 16, 3; etc.

126. Suyuti (ms. Asir eff. Constantinople, Majmoua, no.115). Al thaghur al basima fi asma' Fatima, p. 161a; Sibt ibn al-Jawzi, *Mirat* (ms. Kuprulu), II, 195, 213b; *Maqatil,* 19; Qutaiba, *Ma'arif* (Wustenfeld) 70; anon ms. Ste Sophie, Constantinople, no. 457, pp. 13a–b; Hamza called upon Muhammad to find him the wherewithal to live on (Hanbal, II, 175, bottom). Poverty had also taken him to Medina; with the exception of the banker Abbas, all these Hashimites found themselves reduced to a wretched state.

127. It is still the case for the Arabs of Syria, cf. A. Musil, *Arabia Petraea*, III, 184.

128. Cf. *Aghani*, IX, 82, 4, etc.

129. Qutaiba, *Ma'arif* (ed. of Egypt), 97, 10; Qutaiba, *'Oyoun* (Brockelmann), 454, 16; Bukhari, *Sahih* (Krehl), II, 158, 3.

130. Cf. Moawia, 308 I.S. *Tabaq.*, IV 1, 50, bottom. A grand son of Ibn Abbas was "14 years younger than his father they distinguished them from the color of their beards, they did not use the same dye." Baladhuri, *Ansab*, 741, b.

131. At Medina, they made her play with the daughters of the Ansars; Muslim, *Sahih* II, 171; once again a cliché borrowed from the musnad of Aisha; Bukhari, IV, 142.

132. I.Abdulbarr, *Istiab*, 771; Dahabi, *Tarikh* (ms. Paris) 112 b.

133. Suyuti, Al thaghur al basima, ms. cited, 161a; *Maqatil*, 19; I.S. *Tabaq.*, VIII, 13; Tab., III 2435; Ibn al-Jawzi, *Shadharat al-shudhur* (ms. Kuprulu) pages unnumbered.

134. Caetani, *Annali*, I. 460.

135. I.S. *Tabaq.*, VIII, 17, 4; Baladhuri, *Ansab*, ms.cited, 259; Tab., III, 2434–35.

136. *Maqatil*, 9-10; I.'Abdulbarr, *Istiab*, 771.

137. [A marriage contracted for a limited period, for a certain sum of money.— Trans.] Maintained by the Shiites. According to the list of children of 'Ali, Ibn Sa'd, *Tabaq.* III 1, 12, l. 20 adds, "We are not sure if 'Ali had children other than these." but there may have existed others, born of marriages prior to the one with Fatima; we can notice the notable differences between the lists of children of 'Ali. See later on for Ibn al-Hanafiya.

138. "I shared it among my wives," with attempts at softening the situation Hanbal, I, 91, 2; 92; 6 d.l. 137; we shall come back to this point. Bukhari, *Sahih* (Krehl), IV, 85, 4.

139. Hanbal, *Musnad*, I, 243; Bukhari, op.cit., III, 412.

140. Cf. *Montakhab Kanz . . .* , VI, 389–392; the author's Moawia, 306. Hanbal, *Musnad*, III, "my monasticism (*rahbaniya*) is the jihad"; ibid., III, 266 "No one is single in Paradise," no one will remain single there, ibid., II, 247; IV, 58; *fahl,* meaning stallion, honorific description; Hassan ibn Thabit (ed. Hirschfeld) CII, 6. The ideal Muslim is the

pious *qadi* of Egypt (first half of the first Muslim century); "he washes four times a night, and recites the Koran four times a night," Kindi, Egyptian Qadis (ed. Gottheil), 8, bottom.

141. His father Abdullah had another wife, besides Amina; I.Hisham, *Sira,* 101.

142. Such as Yaqubi, cited above; cf.Tab., II, 2435.

143. Even Masudi, *Prairies,* IV, 146, 156; I.S. *Tabaq.,* VIII, 13 bottom.

144. *Khamis,* I, 462; I.Abdulbarr, *Istiab,* 771. Baladhuri, Maqdisi, *Ansab al-Qorasiyin* (Asir eff.) Ansab, 258a, names the year 2, without being explicit.

145. At Medina, Muhammad spent an entire year living at Abu Aiyub's, the Ansarian (I.S. *Tabaq.,* VIII, 14, 2). The marriage must have been after this date.

146. Among the Quraysh, the boys seem to have been specially numerous; cf. *Moawia,* index, s.v. *prolifiques.*

147. Hanbal, *Musnad,* I, 80; Ibn Hajjar, *Isaba,* IV, 725, according to Ibn Ishaq, "fi-l-maghazi al kubra. "

148. Hanbal, *Musnad,* VI, 207, 236; *Moawia,* 366–67.

149. Sibt ibn al-Jawzi, *Mir'at,* ms. cited, II, 213b; Hanbal, I, 93, 8; I.S. *Tabaq.,* VIII, 13, 7; *Montakhab Kanz,* V, 99, 8, d.l. where "fa-innaha imra'a min al-nisa'" ought to mean "for Fatima is but a woman." Apocryphal scene of the wedding night, they made the wife of Jafar, the Flyer, then in Abyssinia, attend! *Aghani,* XI, 67. Without rhyme or reason the Hashimites were supposed to intervene and oblige the Alids.

150. Hanbal, *Musnad,* VI, 78, bottom.

151. Hanbal, VI, 45, 165; cf. II, 259, bottom.

152. *Khamis,* I, 407; I.S. *Tabaq.,* VIII, 12.

153. *Ar'adat,* meaning she scolded.

154. *Montakhab Kanz . . . ,* V, 38–39; Baladhuri, *Ansab,* 431b.

155. "Shut up," *Montakhab Kanz,* loc. cit., Muhammad sometimes imposed a husband. Cf. Hanbal, VI, 412: "she made a sign with her hand, Usama is like this," i.e., "he was not acceptable to her." As we saw, Fatima's stupified silence was even more eloquent. See the detail in Baladhuri, loc. cit.

156. A lord in this world, and one of the honorable ones in the other"; Baladhuri, *Ansab,* 431b, "he who has the most knowledge among them, and is the most calm, and the oldest in Islam"; *Montakhab Kanz,* loc. cit. *Usd,* V, 520 they sought to ward off the reproach of unintelligence; *salaman = islaman,* to maintain the *saja'* rhyme. Hanbal, V, 26, bottom.

157. Margoliouth, *Mohammed,* 282, the marriage would not have displeased her; her gloomy character, ibid., 236.

158. Mobarrad, *Kamil,* 54–55; 298; Qutaiba, *Ma'arif,* E, 198; Ibn Rusta, *A'laq* (ed. de Goeje) 215; Qalqasandi, *Sobh.*I, 266, bottom, where one should read "qays bn sa'd"; Adam was 60 cubits Muslim, *Sahih,* II, 352, top. The *Musnad* of the Ansars demanded the same privilege for their heroes Hanbal, III, 121, bottom.

159. After Badr, it was impossible to find in Medina a tunic big enough for Abbas I.S. *Tabaq.,* IV.7, 1.19 he reached the top of a white tent; Ibn Rusta, *Alaq,* (ed. de Goeje) 225, d.l.; *Iqd,* III, 302, 11. The comparison has a double purpose: whiteness of complexion

and his height. Cf. *Maqatil,* p. 38; Kumait, *Hasimiyat* (ed. Horovitz), I, 31; I.S. *Tabaq.,* IV 1, 20.

160. A detail remarked by all the authors, e.g., Waqidi (Kremer), 87, 273. Abbas, his grandson 'Ali, tall like lances (*mu'tadil al-qanat*) Baladhuri, *Ansab,* 711a.

161. M. Friedlander (*JAOS* 30:78) wrongly believes that the allusions to this particularity are rare; cf. Ibn Batriq (ed. Cheikho), II, 33; *Mo'awia,* 144; *Yazid,* 132; *Maqatil,* 10, 6, *Iqd,* II, 225; Tab. I.; 3970; Abu' 1 Fida, *Histoire* (ed. Constantinople), I, 190; Qutaiba, *Ma'arif* (Wustenfeld), 106; I.S. *Tabaq.,* III1, 16, 17. Later, however, 'Ali will place among the signs of his party "empty stomachs." *Montakhab Kanz,* V, 440; the longest necks, meaning the most famous; Hanbal, III, 169, 7, d.l. 'Ali described as "Sheikh Belly" by the Bedouin poets; Baladhuri, *Ansab,* 427b; 433b. "the man with a belly . . . with a fat belly"; apocryphal verses cited by Yaqubi, *Hist.,* II, 143, d.l.: they contain a clumsy allusion to 'Ali's corpulence.

162. Qutaiba, *Ma'arif* (Wustenfeld), 106, "he was corpulent, snub-nosed, with slender arms."

163. See the references in *Mo'awia,* 98.n.9

164. Qutaiba, *Ma'arif,* loc. cit "like someone who is broken then stuck together again."

165. Baladhuri, *Ansab,* 707, a.

166. *Majmoua,* n.349, ms. Bibl.Khed. Muslim, *Sahih,* II, 248. *Fihrist,* I, 185, 13 quotes a book on the marriage of Fatima by Ibn Abi'd-Donia. On 'Ali's intellectual sluggishness, see an example in I.S. *Tabaq.,* VIII, 13, top; "With gummed up eyes he saw almost nothing"; Hanbal, *Musnad,* I, 99, 331. For his Islamic learning, see the anthology put together by I.S.*Tabaq.,*II², 100–02.

167. I.S. *Tabaq.,* VIII, 7. Casanova is astonished to see me point out "the naivety of 'Ali, who is eternally duped by the Umayyads"; *Mahomet et la fin du monde,* p. 58. But doesn't this antithesis explain the history of the first century? Didn't the Abassids continue the same game with their Alid cousins? The fact that 'Ali appears at the right time to guide the decisions of 'Umar (e.g., I.S. *Tabaq.,* II², 102, 13–14), shows that they felt the need to react against the contrary opinion.

168. He pronounces the Khutbah al-Nikkah, or marriage sermon (sic), *Khamis,* I, 408; Hanbal, I, 142, 7; *Aghani,* XI, 67, *Montakhab Kanz,* V, 99; I.S. *Tabaq.,* VIII, 13, 14–15.

169. No bed for the newly married (*Montakhab Kanz,* V, 56). I.S. *Tabaq,* loc. cit.; Baladhuri, *Ansab,* 439ab, they are looking to introduce the declaration of the Prophet that 'Ali is "his brother and the best person in the family"; he assimilated to "Haroun"; Hanbal, III, 32; Muhammad sprinkles the couple with water; I.S. *Tabaq.,* VIII, 14–15; cf. Goldziher, *Wasser als Daemonen abwehrendes Mittel,* in *Arch.f.Religionswis.,* XIII, 20 etc., Wellhausen, *Reste arabis. Heidentums²,* 155.

170. Hanbal, IV, 326 cf. ibid., I, 79, 80.

171. Like the mysterious Dahia ibn Khalifa.We shall develop this point of view elsewhere. "Allah gave me all his good things, his horses, his sheep, his slaves." (Muhammad); Hanbal, IV, 137, 7. Why, then, rebuff Fatima?

172. I.S. *Tabaq.*, VIII, 16–18; 23–25; intimate scene between the newly married couple and the father-in-law; the latter inserted his feet under their blanket and they "smelt the freshness on their chest"; *Khamis*, I, 463; Hanbal, *Musnad*, I, 96. This "freshness of hands and feet" of Muhammad is a cliché frequently used by the Hadith. It is said elsewhere "big hands and big feet"; instead of *dakhan* we find also *shathn*; Bukhari, *Sahih*, (Krehl), IV, 97, 98.

173. *Montakhab Kanz*, V, 92; Husayn would have had a wet-nurse from the Banu Kinana; *Aghani*, VIII, 112, 30, or Lobaba; cf. Baladhuri, op. cit., I.S. *Tabaq.*, VIII, 204.

174. *Khamis*, I, 471 Lobaba, the name of Abbas' wife; Baladhuri, *Ansab*, 737b.

175. Sura 33:49 mentions simply that "the daughters of thy paternal uncle and the daughters of thy maternal aunts who fled with thee," without asserting anywhere that their parents imitated them.

176. Hanbal, VI, 33, barring the postponement of the birth of Hasan after the *fath* the entire *musnad* of Umm Fadl (ibid.) is apocryphal, p. 340, they show her at Medina before the *fath*, carrying the children of Fatima; cf. Baladhuri, loc. cit.

177. Cf. *Maqatil*, 25, bottom.

178. [The custom observed on the birth of a child by Arabs, namely, leaving the hair on the infant's head until the seventh day, when it is shaved, and animals are sacrificed: two sheep for a boy and one for a girl.—Trans.] Cf. Hanbal, II, 182–83, 185, 194; Baladhuri, ms. cit. 259b. Muhammad carried out exorcisms (*yu' awwizu*, meaning in invoking God) on the two new born infants; ibid., I, 270; Bukhari, *Sahih*, II, 347. Husayn was born three months prematurely; Ibn Rosta, *A'laq* (ed. de Goeje), 227, 7.

179. Cf. Goldziher, *Le sacrifice de la chevelure chez les anciens Arabes*, in *Rev.hist.Relig.*, XIV, 49–51. On the *aqiqa* see Jahiz, *Avares*, 235.

180. Hanbal, VI, 390–91, 392; Muhammad "gave in alms the weight of their hair in silver"; Baladhuri, ms. cit., 259b.

181. He said the *azan* in Husayn's ears (*azana fi udan al-Husayn*), Hanbal, VI, 391.

182. Bukhari, *Sahih*, II, 81, 2; III, 512, IV, 115; Hanbal, III, 106, 171, 175, 188 (with addition of *takbir*), 254, 290; spit in the mouth of Ibn Abbas (read *tafala* in place of *naqala*) Baladhuri, *Ansab*, 720b.

183. *Montakhab Kanz*, V, 99; Baladhuri, *Ansab*, 592a.

184. *Montakhab Kanz*, V, 103; cf. *Yazid*, 149–66.

185. Baladhuri, *Ansab*, 448 a.

186. Yaqubi, *Hist.*, II, 252 Baladhuri, *Ansab*, 258a for him they also gave in alms the weight of the hair; Baladhuri, ms cit. 455b. According to al-Mofid ibn al-Moallim, *Kitab al-irshad fi ma'rifa hujaj allah 'ala-l-'ibad* (Leiden, ms. no.1647) p.132, after the death of Muhammad, Fatima *isaqatat* (a monster or abortion) called Mohsin (sic); Muhassin is not named in the *Hasimiyat* of Kumait, but Hanbal, 198 knows him. At Karbala for one of his newly born sons, Husayn, he performed the *tahnik* and the *adan;* Yaqubi, *Hist.*, II, 291, I; Muslim, *Sahih* 2, II, 232–34.

187. Masudi, *Prairies*, V, 148; Abul Fida, Hist., I, 190; Majmoua, n.349, ms. B.Khed., p. 2a adds wisely: Mohassin is only known to us through the Hadith.

188. Goldziher, *ZDMG*, L, 119, Majmoua, loc. cit. the names of Harun's sons are Shibr, Shabayr, and Muthabbir; Hanbal, I, 98.

189. Elsewhere, they make him say: the names most hateful to God are Harb and Morra; cf. Yazid, 228, n.10; Baladhuri, *Ansab*, 259–60.

190. For the daughters of Fatima, cf. Tab. I, 2029, 2733.

191. Sibt ibn al-Jawzi, *Mirat* (ms. cit.) III, 43; *Montakhab Kanz* V, 56 Hanbal, III, 44, 213, 300, d.l., 301; cf. ibid., II, 515. Oatmeal bread was at that time rare in Medina; Hanbal, II, 99, 13. Abu Huraira indicates to us the point of the operation: "He takes a stone and ties it to the middle of his stomach, then he tightens it with his dress so that it holds him upright," Hanbal, II, 324, 15; cf. ibid, VI, 18 bottom; it concerns the ahl as Suffa [see glossary]; it is said of them that during the prayer, "some men collapsed from all their height during the prayer such was their starvation." In their sight the Bedouins cry out: they are "majnun," one of the rare explicit texts, where *majnun* means epileptic. Cf. Bukhari, *Sahih*, IV, 124, 12. For the stone on the stomach, cf. Bukhari, Sahih (Krehl) II, 436, 11, above all Jahiz, *Avares*, 240, 241, 242.

192 E.g., that of Anas ibn Malik, in Ibn Hanbal, III, 184, bottom, 188, 218, 225, bottom, 203, 279, 289–90; Bukhari, *Sahih*, II, 12; 14.

193. Hanbal, III, 151. Like the youngest of men, the best, the most handsome, the most charming.

194 "Until he had reached the end"; Hanbal, III, 108. On the *tarida* or *tarid*, see the poetical anthology gathered together by Jahiz, *Avares*, 254, 255–56. At Medina, dates formed the basis of the diet, excluding the oatmeal. The poets reproached the Medinese of being eaters of dates; Jahiz, op. cit., 258. However, eaters of dates were taken to be less intelligent. See the author's *Taif, cité alpestre*, 3–4. At Medina the Jews had the monopoly of cereals until the end of his life, Muhammad had to have recourse to them; Bukhari, *Sahih* (Krehl), II, 9–10, 16.

195. Hanbal, III, 123, bottom; 177, 180; he licked his fingers at the end and requested to do the same for the dishes. VI, 410, 7, he burned himself when wishing to get hold of a choice piece from a boiling pot. Ibid.VI, 392 bottom, ate two shoulders of mutton, and recited a small part of a prayer, "then he found some cold meat and ate"; liked the deposit left by a stew or soup, ibid, III, 220, 13; has a special manager, in charge of keeping watch over his reserves of dates, *sahib al-tamar* (in charge of dates); ibid III, 3 n 1.9; 10, bottom. Fat and asthmatic, his "chest boiled like a pot"; ibid, IV, 26.

196. Muhammad forced to borrow from Medina; a Christian Medinese merchant refused to give him credit; Hanbal, III, 244, I; IV, 204. Accounts intended to show the Prophet's detachment, or perhaps to refer to his difficult beginnings among the Ansars. When they were rich, he had a mind to draw everyone's attention to the gifts of God (ibid., IV, 137), forbids one from abstaining from the good things in life: "Forbid not the good things which Allah has made lawful for you" (sura 5:89.)

197. The Ansarian A. Talha killed 21 enemies; Hanbal, III, 198, 5. This school affirms the flight of 'Uthman, and hints at that of Abu Bakr and of 'Umar; the Ansars saved Muhammad. One of the innumerable details of the rivalry between the Ansars and

the Quraysh, with which the Hadith seeth; cf. Yazid, ch. XIV, Ansars and Quraysh, 200–10.

198. Cf. Sarazin, op. cit.

199. Waqidi (Kremer), 245–46; Ibn al-Athir, *Kamil* (Tornb.) II, 122; Bukhari, *Sahih* (Krehl), II, 58.

200. Waqidi (Kremer), 283; 303, 10. Eight years after Uhud, Muhammad visited the graves there; I.S. *Tabaq.*, II², 10. If this datum possesses any value whatever, the date of this battle would belong to the beginning of the year 3 A.H.

201. Baladhuri, *Ansab*, 333b; see later for details about the Prophet's mounts. He spoke out against the breeding of mules; was not grateful when they gave him it for the first time as a present; Hanbal, *Musnad*, I, 77, 98; on a donkey and riding pillion Usama ibn Zayd (notice the vigor of the donkeys of Medina); Bukhari, *Sahih*, (Krehl) II, 45, 5, d.l.; baghl, Ethiopian loan word; Noldeke, *Neue Beit.z.sem.Sprachwiss.*, 58.

202. We shall come back to this at the end of this monograph. I.S. *Tabaq.*, III 1, 11, restricts himself to attributing him with the upkeep of the grave of Hamza faithful 'Uthman visiting the grave of Ruqayya; Baladhuri, *Ansab*, 258a.

203. Yaqubi, *Hist.*, II, 67; Baladhuri, *Ansab*, 399b.

204. Cf. the author's *Triumvirat*, 120 etc.

205. Cf. sura 4:128 You will not be able to deal equally between your wives, however much you wish to do so.

206. "Yas'alunnaka al-'adl fi ibnat Abi Quhafa"; Abu Quhafa, father of Abu Bakr.

207. *Ahibbi hadihi li-'Aisha*, or approve of these things (my preferences) in Aisha's favor. Other quarrels, scenes of insults in the harem of Abul Qasim; I.S. *Tabaq.*, VIII, 56, 71, 73, 90, 91. The Hadith of Alid origins substitute the name of Khadija in this saying of Muhammad the best of women is Aisha. Bukhari (Krehl) II, 366, 7, more frequently that of Fatima see the end of this monograph.

208. Hanbal, *Musnad*, VI, 88.

209. Hanbal, VI 150. Like the following extracts from the *Musnad* of Aisha, it tends to glorify the favorite.

210. Before her marriage with Muhammad, she would have put her jealousy forward to repulse the Prophet's propositions. The Tradition exploits this datum and strives not without success to keep the unity of character.

211. In the war of words between the "mothers of the believers," Aisha always had the last word Afhamtuha, the Hadith had her say.

212. As the account insinuates. Later on we never hear Aisha take the defense of 'Ali, as she sometimes did for other friends of 'Ali-'Ammar ibn Yasir etc., Hanbal, VI, 113, 6.

213. Hanbal, *Musnad*, VI, 130 Muslim, *Sahih 2*, II, 335.

214. Samhoudi (ms. Beyrouth), 114 b.

215. She was the house neighbor of her father; Ibn Hajar, *Isaba*, IV, 730; I.S.*Tabaq.*, VIII, 14.

216. E.g., Tab., *Annales*, I, 3470.

217. When the Qurayshite Muhajirs arrived in Medina, they used their first earnings to get married, e.g., Abdarrahman ibn 'Auf; Hanbal, III, 204–205. According to Hanbal, II, 26: "close the doors with the exception of Ali's in the mosque," as the same privilege is affirmed of Abu Bakr, one can guess the implications of these Hadiths and the impossibility of reconciling them; but one must reestablish the balance between the Sunna and the Shia, represented by A. Bakr and 'Ali. A. Bakr lived at Sonh; I.S. *Tabaq.*, II², 22; 53; 56; III 1, 132. We shall specify elsewhere the meaning of masjid in this Hadith, when we discuss the primitive concept of the word masjid (paper presented at the 16th Congress of the Athenian Orientalists, April, 1912).

218. Khadijat al-Kubra (the great Khadija).

219. Cf. Sarasin, op. cit., 28, 35, etc.

220. The Tradition tried to anticipate the objection that one could make of it; cf. Banning, *Muhammad ibn al Hanafiya*, 14–15. Besides this, Muhammad al-Akbar, two other sons named Muhammad, al-Asghar (the smallest), and al-Awsat (the middle one); I.S. *Tabaq.*, III 1, 11–12; Tab., I3473.

Silk robe, given by Muhammad to 'Ali. The latter shares it "between the women" or as he said, "my wives" (Baladhuri, *Ansab*, 397b). Thus 'Ali must have had several wives. Useless to speculate about the meaning of "the women of his family"; they all lived in Mecca.

221. The Hadith likes to connect it to his corpulence; Muslim, *Sahih 2*, II, 371, 11, 20.

222. M. Casanova, *Mahomet et la fin du monde, Fifty-eight,* in my evaluations of "the naivety of the eternally duped 'Ali" by the Umayyads sees "the condemnation in fact of the Umayyads from the Muslim point of view." And if the latter turned out to be in contradiction with history?

223. See her *Musnad* in Hanbal, VI, 288, etc.

224. *Montakhab Kanz,* V, 454.

225. Baladhuri, *Ansab* (ms. cit.), 259 b, names her Al-'Aura (sic).

226. I.S. *Tabaq.*, III²,30, 26.

227. See the variants of this move in Hanbal, IV, 326: "I do not ban the legal and do not declare legal the illegal," that is, I do not wish to ban monogamy which is legal. Fatima had denounced her husband's step. Muhammad took the occasion to sing the praises from the pulpit of Zaynab's husband's loyalty. From this affair, some authors have deduced that monogamy was one of the Khasa'is [privileges] of Fatima (Suyuti, al-thaghur al-basima, ms. cit. 162b), the other Muslim women would not have the right to it.

228. In that case, why did the Prophet express fears for the faith of his daughter; Sibt ibn al-Jawzi, *Mirat* (ms. cit) III, 230a; Hanbal, IV, 326.

229. They probably had in mind Dorra, the daughter of Abu Lahab, a legendary figure and deliberately confused with other Dorras; she married Dahia ibn Khalifa (another mythic figure), then Zayd ibn Haritha; *Usd,* V, 449; Ibn Hajjar, *Isaba,* IV, 568–70 I.S. *Tabaq.*, III 1, 30.

230. Hanbal, VI, 432, I. Orthodoxy used this formula of Muhammad very freely and

frequently to weaken the Shiite theory of the Ahl al Bayt, the people of the Prophet's household/family; cf. Hanbal, IV, 164, top. A daughter of Abu Lahab is a true sportswoman; she appears "carrying a bow and having the gait of a man"; Hanbal, II, 200, 2–3; Muhammad attended Abu Lahab's daughter's wedding; ibid. IV. 67.

231. A'mas read the variant *wa qad tabba* in this verse; Muslim, *Sahih 2*, I, 102, d.l.

232. *Usd.*, V, 521.

233. Cf. *Mo'awia*, 144, n.8, and index s.v. ' Otman.

234. Cf. the author's article, *Mahomet fut-il sincère?* p. 23 taken from *Recherche de science religieuse*, 1911, nos. 1 and 2.

235. Baladhuri, *Ansab*, 259 b, cf. *Usd*, loc. cit. On the night of Umm Kulthum's death, 'Uthman "approached his wives" (Hanbal, III, 229, 30); therefore he had a harem. These Qurayshites did not have our ideas of mourning (I.S. *Tabaq.*, VIII, 26, 4) and even less our ideas of monogamy, even out of respect for the Prophet! Why does he not include 'Uthman in his praise when talking of his matrimonial alliance with the Umayyads? Bukhari, *Sahih* (Krehl) II, 440, 7.

236. *Usd*, loc. cit.; Hanbal, IV, 326; *Khamis*, I, 464; Bukhari, *Sahih* (K) II, 440.

237. *Montakhab Kanz,* V, 55, top. Hanbal, loc. cit.

238. According to this legend, 'Ali received the last gift of the Prophet (pieces of silver distributed just before his death; I.S. *Tabaq.*, II², 34) and that from Aisha's hand. 'Ali received the last bits of advice from his father-in-law, but they were inoffensive, there was no question of the caliphate (I.S. *Tabaq.*, II², 37, top). Thus orthodoxy made every use of its wits to reconcile everything: the honor of 'Ali and the unity of the jama'a. And this Hadith is placed on the lips of 'Ali.

239. Masudi, *Prairies*, IV, 150, to the poverty of Fatima, contrast the tapestries, hangings, decorating Aisha's apartment Hanbal, VI, 246, 247; even at the Prophet's house they found "statues of men" to the great scandal of Gabriel, ibid., II 305, 14, 308. Fatima however soothes the distress of Abu Huraira (Baladhuri, *Ansab,* 441a); they have deliberately chosen this friend of the Umayyads. This kind of malice abounds in the Hadith; above all they contrast this charity (as in our account) to the hardness of the A. Bakr-'Umar group, who refuse to help the Dausite.

240. Maternal tenderness of the Qurayshites, confirmed by Muhammad; Hanbal, II, 275, 3.

241. "Farahamtuha rahimaka Allah," Hanbal, III, 150–51.

242. "Ishtadda huzni wa ishtaddat faqati wa tala suqmi," Hanbal, V, 26, bottom.

243. Ibn Abdulbarr, *Isti'ab*, 771.

244. Hanbal, III, 150; Sibt ibn al-Jawzi (ms. cit.) II, 214.

245. According to a scholium to the *Divan* of Hassan ibn Thabit (ed. Hirschfeld) he would have let her have the leader of the Fazarites, Masada ibn Hakama, later freed by Fatima. The Medinese school invented this tale to avenge themselves on the father of one of the Syrian Captains at Harra and at the siege of Mecca. Aisha had the means to buy several slaves (Hanbal, II, 100, b); the treasures of the Prophet remained open to her.

246. They should have preferred what was permanent, "that which lasts is the dearest to him," Hanbal, I, 79 II, 166; VI.298; Baladhuri, *Ansab,* 442b.

247. Ibn Hajar, *Isaba*, IV, 729–30; Bukhari, *Sahih* (Krehl), IV, 114, d.l.

248. "ma kana kharijan min al saqa wa ghayrihi wa takifiki ma kana dakhalan min al 'ajn wa-l-tahn "Baladhuri, *Ansab*, 397b.

249. "The city is full of fever and the people are feverish," Hanbal, III, 136; 214; cf. *Mo'awia*, 240–41 and the author's article, *La Badia sous les Omaiyades*, 94, etc. (MFO, IV).

250. To lengthen it they held themselves up by a rope, between two columns of the mosque; Hanbal, III, 101; 184, 6 d.l. 256; by dint of prolonging it Muhammad and his companions had swollen legs; God made this obligation optional; Hanbal, VI, 54, 6; 115, 8 d. l.; 349, 50; 351, bottom; the prayer sitting down has half the value of the one standing up; ibid., II, 193. Cf. *Yazid*, 188–89; *Ziad ibn Abihi*, 81–82; I.S. *Tabaq.*, II², 13, 9; prayer near a column; Muslim, *Sahih 2*, I, 194.

251. Kanat tadhuba; Tab., III, 2436; 'Ali enumerates the work imposed on Fatima; Hanbal, I, 153.

252. Of the latter it is said that "he used his own size as a criterion of measure," did he find her too long, too wide? Cf. Hanbal, VI, 299, 3; of the numerous protests against the lavishness of women.

253. Zayd ibn Haritha travelled on their behalf; I.S. *Tabaq.*, II², 65, 17; Muslim, *Sahih 2*, II, 235 bottom. They went to Basra and Syria; soon Ibn Auf would be back at the head of a caravan of 700 camels; Hanbal, VI, 115 316, 7; even Aisha had a business mind, ibid., II, 222, 11 d.l.: VI, 246, bottom; II, 125, 240. Abu Bakr, the other Muhajir in the market, I.S. *Tabaq.*, III 1, 132; Muslim, *Sahih²*, II, 357, 358.

254. Cf. Hassan ibn Thabit, Divan (Hirschfeld), VI, 41, where I found this allusion to the situation; cf. (CLXI. 8). We helped out, our neighbor is no longer afraid of adversity and he has found success in our homes and has become a *mawla* (client, non-Arab Muslim).

255. Cf. the author's *Triumvirat*, 117, 127, 129. The Muhajirs acquired large properties in Medina, and put them to good use. Hanbal, VI, 420, 13; they profited from the sale of slaves, Zubayr ibn al-Awwam was an owner, ibid., IV, 5, 6.

256. They were afraid of irritating A. Bakr, "that would be to annoy the Prophet, and then God," Hanbal, IV, 59, I.

257. Cf. *Triumvirat*, 122.

258. See for example Suyuti, Al numudhaj al-labib (ms. 'Asir effendi, Constantinople) p. 146b; Sira anonymous (Paris, nos. 5094), 2b, 3b.

259. Between numerous wives. The Koran invites, moreover, "Muslim women to give themselves to the Prophet" (sura 33:49). Aisha was jealous toward those women who had offered their person to God's Messenger; Muslim, *Sahih²*, II 567.3 d.l. The plural form is to be remarked and also the affirmation that the invitation was heard by numerous candidates. Bukhari, IV, 140.

260. *Mahomet*, pp. 42–43.

261. Cf. the variants of the Hadith cited, Hanbal, IV, 166; *Ana Abu l Hasan, al-qaram, la abrahu hatta anziru ma*, "should mean "I, Abu'l Hasan (i.e., 'Ali) the hero, al-

qaram, [not al-qawm as you find in some editions] will only move [he was in bed] when I will have seen." Muslim, *Sahih 2*, I. 399, 15; 400, 2.

262. Hanbal, *Musnad,* VI, 443. If he was not there, Muhammad advised them to speak to A. Bakr; certainly not 'Ali; Hanbal, IV, 82.

263. Cf. *Yazid,* 132.

264. Hanbal, IV, 166; Muslim[2], op.cit. I, 399, 400; this is his usual position, they said.

265. Kuli wa it'ami subyanaki, Baladhuri, *Ansab,* 441 b.

266. Kuntu rajulan nawman, Hanbal, I, 111, 3 d.l. 135. As to answer to this Hadith they affirmed that 'Ali, "he was not such a sleeper as the Prophet"; Iqd 4 II, 226, 3 it is possible to find there an antithesis to the Hadith, where 'Umar confesses that business distracted him from the company of the Prophet; Bukhari, *Sahih* (K.) II, 8.

267. *Aghani,* IV, 4, 1.11; Hanbal, IV, 166.

268. Jahiz, *Bayan*, I, 35, 8; they got the suspicious Ibn Abbas, who insisted on 'Ali's knowledge of poetry, to praise his intelligence; Aghani, I, 35, 8; they had to act and make the existence of a collection of 'Ali's poetry credible, used by the sira and by the Shia. They declared him the best poet of the first four caliphs; Baladhuri, *Ansab*, 430a. At Hudaybiyya, the agreement between Muhammad and the Quraysh would have been drawn up by a public letter writer (Bukhari, *Sahih*, Krehl, II, 180, 5) and not by 'Ali. The Shiites made the last version prevail, more favorable to the intellectual capacity of their heroes. Much other writing, documents, etc., attributed to 'Ali are also apocryphal, e.g., that addressed to the inhabitants of Maqna; Baladhuri, *Futuh*, 60; cf. Leszynsky, *Die Juden in Arabien*, 103, etc.

269. *Hasimiyat* (ed. Horovitz), I. 61.

270. Cf. *Moawia* 316. *Abu Torab* means the man of dust, the man lying down

271. *Das Bild Alis*, 34.

272. Cf. *Maqatil*, p. 9 *Moawia*, 145, 184; Bukhari, *Sahih* (Krehl), IV, 180.

273. Bukhari, *Sahih* (Krehl), II, 81, no.23. Numerous examples Hanbal, VI, 272, 411–14; Moawia, 314–34; 'Umar beat his wife, Hanbal, III, 328; Hassan ibn Thabit, *Divan*, 108 (scholium).

274. Hanbal, VI, 47, 10 d.l.; women "whipped like slaves," ibid., IV, 17, 33.

275. *Kana fi Ali shidda ala Fatima*, meaning 'Ali was violent toward Fatima; I.S. *Tabaq.*, VIII 16, l.19; Ibn Hajjar, *Isaba*, 730. *Turabi*, epithet used by the adversaries that emerge from Kumait, Hasimiyat, II, 25 at the same time, date for the appearance of the nickname, at the very least a point of reference.

276. The authors of these Hadith must have been very unhappy in their marriages, having frequent altercations (*kalam*) with their wives, in the way 'Ali had with Fatima; I.S. *Tabaq.*, VIII, 16. Zubayr treated his wife Asma, daughter of Abu Bakr, in the same way; ibid., 182–83. "Beat rather the stallion or the slave," Muhammad told them; Bukhari, *Sahih* (Krehl), IV, 123.

277. Hanbal, *Musnad,* III, 159; I.S. *Tabaq.*, VIII, 16, l. 21.

278. Modiri, Targib (ms. Berlin), 64a; Waqidi (Kremer), 366, 14; Hanbal, VI, 457; cf. I, 83 d.l.; cf. Jahiz, Mahasin, 349, 17; cf. 286, 15.

279. Hanbal, II, 269, top. Nasai, *Sunan*, book of marriage (ms. Nouri Otmani, Constantinople). A Medinan threatens to kill his wife for having, on his return, found her sitting at the entrance of the door. Hanbal, III, 41, 15.

280. Bukhari, *Sahih* (Krehl), I, 122 II, 435, where the quarrels between 'Ali and Fatima are reduced; IV, 180, no. 40 uses them in the Alid sense to explain the nickname of A. Turab.

281. *Aghani*, XVI, 49, bottom. According to Abdulmasih al-Kindi, *Risala*, 42, bottom, right from his marriage to Khadija, he claimed the power and title of chief of her tribe. That is going back too far. We believe he was sincere at the beginning; cf. *Mahomet fut-il sincère?* Elias de Nisibe (CSO, coll. Chabot), 126 calls him "the Prophet of the Muslims and the first of their kings. "

282. Yaqubi, *Hist.*, II, 60. "King or Prophet." To verify that the Jews used poison against him; I.S. *Tabaq.*, II², 7,4.

283. Cf. *Moawia,* chap. 10, Le *molk* des Umayyads, 189, etc.

284. Some contemporary elegies only partially authentic celebrate him as the sayyd I.S. *Tabaq.*, II², 93, 2; 95, 7; 98, 5.

285. With Muhammad the first symptom of the disease is pointed out thus he found himself separated from wives; his health having returned, the Prophet threw himself on his wives. I.S. *Tabaq.*, II², 5, 1. 23; 6, 5. At this sign the Companions began to hope.

286. Suras 6:25, 57, 90; 26:109, 127, 145, 164, 180; 34:46; 36:20; 38:86; 42:22, etc. Cf. *Mahomet fut-il sincère?* 46 (taken from *Recherches de science religieuse*, 1911 nos. 1, 2.)

287. On this evolution, cf. Caetani, *Studi di storia orientale*, I, 354, 360, 390 the author's *Mahomet fut-il sincère?* 48, etc. Cf. Omaiya ibn Abi's-Salt, *Diwan* (ed. Schulthess), XXIII, 3 an apocryphal tale besides, and belatedly attested to. The wise Ibn Hisham, who has an eye for the rather obvious apocryphal stories, was unaware of it or paid no heed to it. For the inauthentic poetry in I. Hisham, see Goldziher, *Abhandlungen*, I, 60, n.2; Wellhausen, *Reste,* 250.

288. Bukhari, *Sahih* (Krehl), IV, 92, no. 53; he had gold rings made, but would have refused to use them this a subsequent explanation. He only used the most precious perfumes; ibid., IV, 100.

289. Cf. *Moawia,* see this word in the index. Waqidi (Kremer), spies of Muhammad, 139, 206, 207, 345.

290. Ibn Hisham, *Sira*, 201, d.l. They also compared Muhammad to the "good shepherd." I.S. *Tabaq.*, II², 53, d.l.

291. From there we get the political character of the majority of *wafd* [*wafd* is a party coming to a king to receive honors—Trans.]. Many tribes made treaties with, not the Prophet, but with the Master of Medina. God "left him the choice of being Prophet-King," al-Babi, *Nozhat an Nazirin* (ms. Inst.bibl.), 27, b.

292. Sura 94:1, etc.

293. Sura 93:5, etc. For the age of these suras, cf. Noldeke-Schwally, op. cit., p. 94. The style of sura 94 seems too triumphant to belong to the Meccan period, where the tone remains more submissive or resigned.

294. *'Asha ghaniyan wa lan yuhtadam*, Umayya ibn Abi s-Salt, *Diwan* (ed. Schulthess), XXIII.3 see above for the author's remark on this verse.

295. As in sura 89:22; cf. Tabari, *Tafsir*, XXX, 91.

296. E.g., sura 4:56, 57. "You have enriched us, and made us be served by slaves," an elegy of doubtful authenticity tells him. I.S. *Tabaq.*, II², 97, 5. Koranic exegesis (see Tab., *Tafsir,* loc. cit.) has recourse here to [the doctrine of abrogation—Trans.] *nasikh wa mansukh* to affirm the sovereign power of the Prophet the Hadith argues in the same way Muslim, *Sahih 2*, II, 117, bas 118.

297. Cf. sura 4:67: "All prophets should be obeyed." Sura 81:19, 21; Rasul . . . muta'un amin; Mota, epithet of the great sayyds, cf. *Moawia*, 75, 79, 85.

298. Ibn al-Jawzi, *Wafa* (ms. Leiden), 101, b.

299. Hanbal, IV, 24, 25.

300. Hanbal, II, 412, 12 d.l. baraku 'ala-l-rikab; Muslim *Sahih 2*, I, 61, d.l.

301. Sigistani, Kitab al-Mo'ammarin (ed. Goldziher), 37–38 (arabic text) 'Adi would have been more than a hundred years old cf. Lammens, "L'age de Mahomet et la chronologie de la Sira," in *JA* 1 (1911): 213 [see chapter 5 of the present volume—Trans.]

302. That is how Adi ibn Hatim found him; Ibn al-Jawzi, *Montazam* (ms. cited) sub anno 68.

303 Hanbal, V, 137.

304. Frequently convoked unexpectedly; Hanbal, VI, 413, 1–2.

305. It was necessary to inspire in them an exalted idea of the new power.

306. Cf. Ibn Majja (ms. B.Khed. section Hadith), I vol.; *Moawia,* 367, n.8; Ibn an-Najjar, Al durrat al-thamina (ms. Paris), 26b, other references given below.

307. Cf. *Moawia*, 366–67.

308. Becker, Die Kanzel, in Orient. Stud., I, 335, 345, 346–68; Moawia, 204–208; a strange suggestion from a Rumi, according to what they assure us; Hanbal, V, 330; Darimi, Musnad (ms. Leiden), 7b, Waqidi (Kremer), 184; the author's *Ziad ibn Abihi*, 33.

309. Li-ta'lamu salati (so that you learn my prayer). Nasa'i, *Sunan* (ms. Nouri Otmani).

310. Hanbal, V, 137 Samhoudi, (ms. Beyrouth), 107 etc.

311. Kursi khalab (sic) *qawa' 'imuhu hadid*, meaning a seat in the form of a claw (sic) whose feet were of iron; Maqrizi, *Imta* III (ms. cited) and in the majority of the great Sahih Traditions.

312. Numerous variants and interpretations in Maqrizi, op. cit. They had read Khulb (vocalized thus) and explained by *lif* (palm tree fiber). Other explanation: "I saw him claiming it to be black wood that he thought was iron," of ebony then. According to Ibn al-Gauzi: It was more convenient that its feet were in palm tree fiber, coming from the palm branches of *ra*, or from the palm branches of *sa'f*. A variant would resolve all the difficulties it should read *kursi khiltu qawaimuhu hadidan*, "a chair whose feet seemed to me [the narrator of the Hadith] in iron."

Cf. *Moawia,* 204–208, 273, 342. A chair made of branches of palm trees can seem very fragile! Also Ibn al-Jawzi, *Wafa* (ms. cited), 124b does not dare to reject the first reading, so well attested. Nasai, *Sunan* (ms. cited) section *kitab al zina*, read *khiltu*. Possesses a small minbar; Muslim, *Sahih 2*, I, 376, 9 d.l.

313. Like most of the artisans in Medina, hence their epithet rumi [Roman/Byzantine]; cf. *Ziad ibn Abihi*, 20–21.

314. Abbas advised him to adopt an *'arsh* (throne); I.S. *Tabaq.*, II², 1.11.

315. Cf. *Moawia*, 206; Abu Dawud, *Sunan* (ms. Paris), 187a; Ibn al-Jawzi (ms. cited), 105b; Tirmidhi, *Sahih*, I, 321, bottom 324, 18; Muslim, *Sahih*, I, 239; II, 157, 230, 380; Qastallani, *Irsad as-sari*, III, 53; Osd, II, 280; Bukhari, *Sahih*, II, 411, 9; Hanbal, V, 198; VI, 373. 14; Samhoudi, (ms. cited), 17b, 69; Darimi, *Musnad*, 126b: you sit above as though you were standing; cf. ibid., p. 9a. Nasai, loc. cit. (this version tries to reconcile the two positions: standing up and sitting!).

316. Cf. Becker, op. sup. cit. Jahiz, *Bayan*, I, 51, 52, 60, bottom; *Aghani* XIII, 166, bottom; Bukhari, *Sahih*, I, 406, no. 58; 166, 7; Ibn al-Jawzi, *Wafa*, 144b; Muslim, *Sahih* 2, I, 191, 192.

317. Cf. Diehl, *Justinien*, 371; this stick would be a gift from the Negus; Ibn al-Jawzi, *Wafa*, 118b; it was a *anaza;* cf. Caetani, *Studi*, I, 341.

318 Bukhari, *Sahih*, II, 395, top. Muhammad called *sahib hirawa*, man with a club; Iqd, I, 134; Qastallani, op. cit., I, 278, 279; Ibn al-Jawzi, op. cit.; Paris, p. 231a; anon ms. no. 2007; Yaqubi, *Histoire*, II, 97, 3.

319. Muslim, *Sahih*, II, 380; Maqrizi, *op. cit.*; Waqidi (Kremer) 80.

320. Like Rabia ibn Ka'b; see his musnad; Hanbal, IV, 57–59; *musnad* of Anas ibn Malik; Hanbal, III, 98, etc.; Ibn Masud also exercised this function; Abu Ubaid, *Gharib*, 11a.

321. Ibn Hisham, *Sira*, 588; Sohaim, muezzin of Muhammad; Hanbal, III, 349, 12; I.S. *Tabaq.*, IV 1, 21, 17: a moaddin is sent to Qoba to announce the death of Abbas.

322. Nasai, *Sunan* (ms. cited) kitab al-sala; sa'd al-qarz, the maula (freed slave) of Ammar ibn Yasir is mu'addin (muezzin) in Qoba, little later we see him, he carried the goat of the day of the festival to Abu Bakr, to 'Umar, and to 'Ali; Ibn al-Jawzi, *Montazam*, (ms. Constantinople) numerous moaddin of Muhammad, cited in Maqrizi, *Imta*, III; Hanbal, IV, 47, 48, 51.

323. A frame carrying material, at the last pilgrimage; Hanbal, V, 268; I.S. *Tabaq.*, II 1, 127, d.l. Like kings, Muhammad had eunuchs; Jahiz, *Haiawan*, I, 75, feels obliged to excuse him for it, they were presents! He also had official interpreters for his foreign correspondence; I.S. *Tabaq.*, II², 115, 9.

324. He confused "s" and "sh," a Hadith rejected by Suyuti, Al durar al-muntathiru fi-l-ahadith al mushtahira (ms. Asir effendi), 173b.

325. Hanbal, III, 481, bottom Tab., *Tafsir*, VIII, 144; I.S. *Tabaq.*, VI, 22 bottom. Bilal goes before him carrying the *anaza* or the short lance; Baladhuri, *Ansab*, 115.

326. Cf. *Ziad ibn Abihi*, 101–102, in *RDSO*, 1911.

327. Red silk, reserved for sayyids; Bukhari, *Hamasa* (Cheikho) no. 1105; Ibn Qaiym al-Gauziya, Zad al-Moad (ms. Bayazid, Constantinople), 1 vol.

328. Qutaiba, *Mokhtalif al hadith*, 422, 423; Ibn Qayym al-Jawziya, op. cit.

329. Yaqubi, *Hist.*, II, 23, 2 d.l.; they depict him from that moment "between two red cloaks." Hanbal, IV, 63, bottom. Aisha will take out later the woollen clothes worn by the Prophet but her sister Asma has kept his gala dress in reserve. Muslim, *Sahih²*, II, 207, 210. All the shades of opinion can avail themselves of the Hadith.

330. *Montakhab Kanz,* IV, 198; Hanbal, IV, 281, 308; Bukhari, *Sahih*, I, 406, no. 58 cf. 166, 7; Muslim, *Sahih²*, II, 207.

331. Maqrizi, *Imta* III, section: Clothes of the Prophet; Hanbal, VI, 144, d.l., the same subject in Baladhuri, *Ansab*, 332, etc.

332. Cf. *Moawia,* 306–307.

333. Hanbal, III, 477, bottom IV, 295, 303; Baladhuri, *Ansab*, 253b; Dahabi, *Tarikh al Islam*, ms. Paris, 71–72; Muslim, *Sahih,* II, 217; Tirmidhi, *Sahih,* II, 133; *Khalq an-nabi* (ms. Leiden), 313, 337.

334. I.S. *Tabaq,* IV 1, 45, 14. Cf. *Naqaid Jarir* (ed. Bevan) 756, 5: pack-saddles for camels, sculpted, ornate, like dinars."

335. *Aghani,* XXI, 39, 4; cf. the author's *République marchande*, p. 14. On the occasion of *wufuds*, he put on his most beautiful clothes; Ibn al-Jawzi, *Wafa,* 158a. They knew the *wazzan*, responsible for weighing and calculating the money and precious metals. I.S. *Tabaq.,* III 1, 152, 6.

336. Ibn al-Jawzi, op. cit., 126, Bukhari, *Sahih*, IV, 27; Muslim, *Sahih*, II, 151 I.S. *Tabaq.,* IV², 58 Yaqubi, II, 98. Ibn Qaiym al-Jawziya has problems in proving that the Prophet only put on clothes with red bands or borders; Hanbal, III, 229, 7 d.l.

337. Arjwan, with silk trimmings, on top a red tunic he wore a cloak of the same hue. Maqrizi (ms. cited); Ibn al-Jawzi (ms. cited), 126b; wearing silk clothes during prayers; Hanbal, IV, 143, bottom.

338. Nasai, *Sunan* (ms. cited) Kitab al-Zina; Tirmidhi, *Sahih*, I, 331; Muslim, *Sahih*, II, 152; Hanbal, III, 317; 337, 7; 347.

339. Bukhari, Sahih (Krehl) IV, 78, no. 18. Hanbal, III, 121: annually thay had to provide 2,000 *hulla* (Christian vestments).

340. Ibn Qaiym al-Jawziya, *Zad*, I (ms. cited) in flax woven by Copts. These are the qubati, qubtiya, Dahia ibn Khalifa gave it to him as a present; cf. scholiast of Kumait, *Hasimiyat*, p. 69.

341. Like the *hulla seforia* (attire/vestments of Safur) of Sephoris (Galilee); Hanbal, III, 441, 12 d.l.; the *qissiya* (priests vestments) of Egyptian make had silk in it; I.S. *Tabaq.,* II², 124, Hanbal, I, 134, 12; 154, 6; Abu Ubaid, *Gharib* (ms. cited) p. 48a. The Syrian tunics were frequently called Rumiya; Hanbal, IV, 222, 223, 244, 255 bottom, 289; Masudi, *Prairies*, IV, 150; Ibn al-Jawzi, *Wafa,* 126a–b. Abu Dawud, *Sunan* (ms. cit.), 104a; Syrian clothes with 'alam, borders, Hanbal, VI 177, 6 d.l.; *Montakhab Kanz*, VI, 204; white clothes, qissiya material (etymology); Bukhari (Krehl) IV, 82, no. 24; 84, no. 28; 85; I.S. *Tabaq.,* II², 38, I.

342. Or even *fanbijaniyya* (for *manbijaniyya = manbijaniyya*); Nasai, *Sunan* (ms. cit). Dozy saw there a "biscuit, prepared with oil and sprinkled with water," *Vetements des Arabes*, 172. According to Baihaqi, *Adab* (ms. B.Kh) *l'inbijaniya* is a dress which has no

border and is coarse (it is an explanation derived from the Hadiths where this term is to be found). Ibn Qutayba said that it is *manbijaniyya*, whose origins are Manbij. Cf. *Taj al-Arous* s.v. Nabj; Yaquti, *Mojam*, IV, 655; Abu' l-Fida, *Taqwin*, 171; Hanbal, VI, 37, 8; 46, 10; 208; the Arabic review *Al Masriq*, 1911, 80, 240. Muslim, *Sahih* II, 463; cf. Karabacek, *Mittheil aus der Samlung Erzh. Reinier*, III, 131–32; C. H. Becker, *Papyri Schott-Reinhardt, Fifty-four*.

343. Bakri, *Mojam*, 543 indicates the correction and the connection with Manbij. The *nisba* [the derivative form, ending in "i," of a name] "Manbijani" from "Manbij "is rather strange, contrary to the toponyms in iya, like *Iskandarani* from *Iskandariya*, *Ladiqani* from *Ladiqiya*, *Salihani* from *Salihiya*, *Tabarani* from *Tabariya*, *Matarani* from *Matariya*, *Qirqisani* from *Qirqisiya* and not *Qirqisan*, as M. I. Friedlander proposes a propos of the Karaite Qirqisani, in *Zeits. F. Assyr.* XXVI, 93. In the Lebanon we find the *nisba* formed on the Manbijani paradigm let us cite *Mismisani* from *Mismis*; in Syria, *Magdalani* from *Magdal, Dairani* from *Dair, Gorgomani* from *Gorgom* (see the index in Tabari and Baladhuri, e.g., qurqusani, Tab., *Annales*, I, 2754, 4).

344. The care of which was confided to Aisha normally; Hanbal, IV, 163, VI, 50; cf. Bukhari, *Sahih,* IV, 96, bottom, 97, 100; Muslim[2], I, 82.

345. It concerned the "festive days"; Ibn al-Jawzi, *Wafa,* 94a, 126b.

346. Aisha all in red; I.S. *Tabaq.*, VI, 189, bottom; for the *two Hasans* see below; cf. Moawia, 166, 373; Muslim, *Sahih*[2], II, 203–209.

347. Hanbal, VI, 355, bottom. Compare it to the behavior of Husain and of Ibn al Gasil; cf. *Yazid*, 248; Muhammad wearing silk, but before the defense; Hanbal, III, 234; forbade the wearing of red. Ibid., IV, 141, bottom; Bukhari, IV, 87.

348. Qutaiba, *Oyoun* (Brockelmann); 25, 15; Abu Ubaid, *Gharib* (ms. cit.), 48a. He distributed to the Sahabis "cloaks of silk, gold broaches," Bukhari, *Sahih* (Krehl), II 280, no.11. Abu Huraira would say, "I don't wear silk" (like the other Companions); Bukhari, op. cit., II, 436, 10; against silk, ibid., IV, 82–83. Muhammad wears red but forbids it for others (that amounts to reserving it for himself); all a category of clothes forbidden; putting on gold brocade; ibid., 87, 89, 5 d.l.

349. Decidedly the words of Muhammad to 'Ali: "Share these dresses between your wives" indicate 'Ali's polygamy. This is the conclusion suggested by comparing numerous parallel Hadiths: even the invitation to Usama, who was a polygamist and had already divorced several women. Finally the extenuating phrases "between the Fatimas, between the women," end up by edifying us; Muslim, *Sahih*[2], II, 205, 5; cf. 208, 209.

350. A. Jafar; Hanbal, III, 229, 7 d.l. Cf. Bukhari, *Sahih* (Krehl), IV, 82–85, and ibid., whole of the *Kitab al-libas*, IV that of the prayer, I, 10, 3, etc. Muslim, *Sahih*[2], II, 206, 208.

351. I.S. *Tabaq.*, IV[2], 67, 24; *Sirat as Sami* (ms. Paris), I, 3b. To 'Umar the sale of the holla, received from Muhammad, brought in 2,000 dirhams; Muslim, *Sahih*[2], II, 206.

352. *Montakhab Kanz*, IV, 198; I.S. *Tabaq.*, IV[2], loc. cit. 'Umar, 'Ali, Usama wearing silk; Muslim, *Sahih*[2], II, 206.

353. Hanbal, IV, 75, 17. 'Umar's clothes entering Jerusalem: it is the image popu-

larized by Tradition; *Conférences de Sainte-Etienne* (Jerusalem), 1911, p. 132. See vol. 4 and 5 of Caetani's *Annali* where the asceticism of 'Umar is put in perspective. He gives his wives dowers of 10,000 dinars; Yaqubi, *Hist.*, II, 171, 10. He and other Companions pushed the Prophet on the path of luxury; Muslim, *Sahih 2*, II, 205. Sephoris, probably tunics of flax for its culture and manufacture in Galilee, cf. S. Krauss, *Talmudische Archaeologie*, I, 139.

354. Hanbal, I, 401, 445; it could hold 40 people, the entire delegation of Taqif Maqrizi, *Imta*, III, ms. cit.; Hanbal, IV, 7–8; Bukhari, E, *Sahih*, IV, 29; Baladhuri, *Ansab*, 117; Muslim, *Sahih 2*, I, 191, 192. Possession of the *qubba*, indication of power; cf. Bakri, Mojam, 34, 14, etc.

355. And the great sayyids; *Naqaid Jarir* (Bevan) 140, 8; Qutaiba, *Poesis*, 37, 11; Bukhari, *Sahih* (Kr.), I, 107, no. 17; II, 289, 2; 297, 1; *Aghani*, VIII, 65 X, 53, 3; XIV, 138, 1; Yaqubi, *Histoire*, I, 281, 6; *Chroniken* (Wust.), II, 135, 6; 141 the author's *Chantre*, 155; Goldziher, *ZDMG*, 1893, pp. 74–75.

356. Maqrizi, loc. cit. Abu Dawud, *Sunan* (ms. cit), p. 104 a Nasai, *Sunan* (ms. cit) *Kitab al zina*.

357. Cf. *Yazid*, 192–93. Jahiz, *Tria opuscula*, 45, 13: they are of all the nations the most ostentatious

358 Cf. Muslim, *Sahih²*, II, 218–23.

359. Bukhari, E, *Sahih²*, IV, 37, 11 d.l.; Darimi, *Musnad* (ms. Leiden), 226b. When he sees "a dress with a cross on top, according to al Asma'i, he would cut off the place where the cross was," thus of true crosses the insistance here becomes significant. Abu Ubaid, *Gharib*, 9a–b. After Muhammad they continued wearing materials of "musallaba"; Hanbal, VI, 140, bottom. Cf. VI, 52 d.l. For more than a century the cross continued to be represented on the back of official dispatches, sent by the Arab governors of Egypt. The latter refrained from making any remarks on this subject to the Christian scribes. Cf. Bell, *Aphrodito Papyri*, Introduction XXXVII. The fashion could not have shocked anyone. One more reason for putting into circulation Hadith reproving this latitudinarian attitude. Cf. Muslim, *Sahih 2*, II, 218–23; "angels avoided houses containing a dog or an image." The juxtaposition is significant.

360. As the collections of poetry confirm.

361. He had carpets made of them—a bias found later—Bukhari, *Sahih* (Krehl), I, 107, top. E IV, 24. Hanbal, III, 151, 486; Darimi, Nasai, loc. cit. He also protested against the extravagance of tapestries—illustrated with living creatures—along the walls Muslim, *Sahih 2*, II, 220, 11.

362. Comp. "If you are praying, do not cover the walls with hangings, "it concerned hangings with representations of living things *Sira* of 'Umar II, ms. Beyrouth, 11a, Hazimi, *Nasikh wa Mansukh* (ms. Berlin) 27 b, 119².

363. "Yadkuruni fi-l-dunya," Muslim, *Sahih*, II, 132, 163; Tirmidi, *Sahih*, II, 76, d.l.; Bukhari, *Sahih*, loc. sup. cit.

364. Hanbal, III, 151, 5 d.l.; Muslim, *Sahih*, II, 161, 4 d.l.

365. Like the one given by him to Aqil, and bearing *tamathil* (figures /representa-

tions); I.S. *Tabaq.*, IV 1, 30, 7; Bukhari, E, IV, 37–38; Tirmidhi, *Sahih*, I, 325; *khayl awlat ajniha*, winged horses; Hanbal, VI, 208, 5 d.l.; Nasai, loc. cit. We shall be content to just adumbrate the subject in order not to prolong this parenthesis beyond measure.

366. Muslim, *Sahih²*, II, 218–23. Cf. Hanbal, VI, 57, 6; they make her play "with the servants with dolls, and if they saw the Prophet they would hide, i.e., they stayed indoors, the meaning of this Hadith is permission. As to 'binat' = girls, they explain it in this way: These are effigies/images which are the game of boys, if they were for the grown ups it would be detestable because of the interdiction on all effigies/images and games." Abu Ubaid, *Gharib* (ms. cit.), 329b.

367. Like the baths, dimas (the foreign term itself was adopted) here new protests of the Prophet, and that against an institution still unknown in Medina; Hanbal, II, 282, 2 VI, 362, I Muslim, *Sahih²*, I, 81, bottom. For the presence of frescoes on the inner walls of the baths (see note 377 below) must have contributed to giving rise to these protestations. Cf. S. Krauss, Talmud. Archaeol. I, 218, 224, 232–33, where they refer to, in Hebrew dymvsyn or dymvsyvt, the demas = Greek demosia.

368. *Yazhar fi-him al-samn*, or they would get fat, a sign of the last days! They make the Prophet talk in this way; Hanbal, IV, 426, 427. Ibn Abbas had a small stove (*kanoun*) with figures in relief; Hanbal, I, 320. Ibn 'Umar went on pilgrimage with a cumbersome retinue of tents and pavillions; Bukhari, I, 386, no. 5.

369. Cf. Wellhausen, *Reste*, 232, etc., which confirms (p. 241) that the beginnings of Islam were ascetic the vigils, etc., commended by the Koran are an oratorical variant, an ideal, remaining as such. This distinction is important for the understanding of this book.

370. Concordance of the Koran, *sub.verb* [under the word or heading.—Trans.].

371. Cf. Bukhari, E, IV, 37–38; Hanbal III, 486 IV, 302, 303 and the preceding references. Paintings in a house under construction in Medina, belonging to Marwan ibn al-Hakam (anti-umayyad tendency), Hanbal, II 232, 5; cf. Bukhari (Krehl), IV, 104: "A house in town where there is a painting on the ceiling," of frescoes?

372. Hanbal, V, 205; Waqidi (Wellhausen), 170, 171, 242.

373. Qastallani, *Irsad*, I, 453, 463, 464; Muslim, *Sahih*, II, 158, 4 d.l.; velvet from Fadak; Bukhari, *Sahih*, IV, 45, 5 d.l. it serves as a pack-saddle for her donkey. When Abu Huraira saw the paintings in the houses of Medina, "he washed his arms upto the elbow" (*hatta balagha abtahu*); Bukhari, op. cit. IV, 104, 6 d.l. Is this the act of Pilate? The Prophet uses for prayers fabrics woven by the infidels and because of that the insistance of the sahih on the clothes of Najran, of Syria, etc.; see e.g. Buhkari I, 103, n. 7.

374. Cf. Gayet, *Art copte*, 215–16; 230, 236.

375. The *Sahih* in the places cited Bukhari (Krehl), IV, 104, 105–06.

376. Cf. the author's *République marchande*, p.4-7 24 etc.

377. Anon. ms. no. 750 (Nouri 'Otmani, Constantinople), Dr. E. Herzfeld wrote to me from Samarra on 23 December 1911 that he had found in the ruins of this locality numerous fresco fragments, representing people, many faces of women, etc. With reason he points to the importance of the find that "such wall paintings were nothing extraordi-

nary in the private houses of Samarra and were the norm in the baths, as at Qusair 'Amra."
No need to insist on the discovery, due to our gallant archaeologist.

378. *Ahad salatin 'asakir al-din.* On the merit of Bukhari, see *Sarh Sahih Muslim* by
Nawawi (with a, in our ms. *Institut biblique*), p. 9b.

379. It concerns a Muslim since he consults (istafta = consult) Ibn Abbas; Muslim,
Sahih², II 223, 1–8. An infidel would not feel any scruples on this subject or consult a
scholar of Islam.

380. Muslim op. cit., II, 223.

381. See this word in the index of *Moawia*.

382. From there the act attributed to Abu Huraira, friend and table companion of the
Umayyads, lieutenant of Marwan, as governor of Medina. See the reference of Bukhari,
cited above.

383. Muslim, op. cit., II, 222, 4 d.l. He also cites eagles, winged horses, and even
images in the appartments of the Prophet; 220; 221, 7.

384. Wellhausen, *Reste arabis. Heidentums²* 105–08; *Moawia*, 202, 225; *Aghani*,
XI, 26, hima of the Lakhmids; VIII. 159, the head reserved for himself the wells. Do not
graze in the domain of kings even if they give you permission, Sigistani, *Moammaroun*
(ed. Goldziher) 21, 6; (Muhammad) for each king a source of water; Darimi, *Musnad* (ms.
cit) 214b; Maqrizi, *Imta*, IV; paragraph on the hima of the Prophet Muslim, *Sahih*, I, 469,
9 d.l *Naqaid Jarir* (Bevan), 539, 3, 9; the institution still exists; Doughty, *Travels*, II, 245,
285; Jaussen, *Pays de Moab*, 136, *ard himiya*, read *himaya*; cf. *Ziad ibn Abihi*, 91, 92.

385. Hanbal, IV, 38, 1; hima of the tribes: Hassan ibn Thabit, *Divan*, CXIX, 2.

386. Hanbal, V, 309.

387. They are stolen by the Bedouins, all his wives possess numerous camels;
Hanbal, II, 100; IV, 52; VI, 337, 338.

388. Hanbal, II, 115; IV, 71, 13.

389. Listed among the damnable inventions of paganism; cf. Sura 5:102, the only
passage where it is mentioned.

390. Muslim, *Sahih²*, I, 37; "Obey God and His Messenger," "the booty belongs to
God and the Apostle," passim in the Koran. He would say, "the best of things is the commandment," Qutaiba, *Oyoun*, 17, 6.

391. He is the first to have navigated the sea . . . and having defended the hima;
Sigistani, *Moammaroun* (Goldziher) 36; Ibn Abdalbarr, *Kitab al-qasd wa-l-umam* (ms.
Asir eff.) Goldziher, *M.S.*, I, 236–37. All the petty kings of Kinda have their hima. Yaqubi,
Hist., 149, 2.

392. Hanbal, IV, 38, 71 Baladhuri, *Futuh,* 9. It is the application of the "*Ikhlas ad
din,*" [*ikhlas*, literally meaning, "sincerity," but "al-Ikhlas" is also the title of sura 112 and
probably means "clearing oneself," i.e., of belief in any but one God.—Trans.] recommended in the Koran. In getting God to intervene, he unprofaned a host of institutions the
Kaaba, the masair, the polytheist masjids. We shall come back to this in a work on the
primitive concept of masjid, the masjida of the Nabateans.

393. Besides the strictness of the Tradition is not difficult to explain hima is syn-

onymous with haram, and the existence of a haram leads naturally to polytheism. Muhammad wanted equally, I suspect, to keep for himself the use of the *kunya*; cf. Muslim, *Sahih²*, II, 229, 8; very explicit indeed on this subject. It was a mark of honor— with the exception however of nicknames—very rare at the time of the Hijra. No longer understanding this situation, the Hadith has limited the ban to the *kunya* Abu l' Qasim, which, besides, has not been observed; cf. Muslim, loc. cit., II, 228. It would have acted here as for the interdiction of the hima, red clothes, etc.

394. All the biographies of the Prophet, the siras, have a special chapter on this subject: Tab., I, 1782.

395. Darimi, *Musnad,* 205a; *Fawaid Jami al-Usul* (ms. Berlin), II, 19b; Baladhuri, *Ansab,* 334b.

396. He himself reminded the Ansars of it Hanbal, III, 89, 9.

397. Likewise the Ansarian sayyids, like the two Sads, Ibn Moad and Ibn Ubada, on a camel (*nadih*) or a donkey; the corpse of the former carried on a donkey; Muslim, *Sahih* 2, II, 364; I.S. *Tabaq.*, III², 5 d.l. At Khaybar Muhammad forbade their flesh, fearing not to have any more mounts for his return; see above all I.S. *Tabaq.*, II², 82, 13; Muslim, *Sahih* 2, 151–53. In Koran, II. 258, the ass seems the usual mount.

398. *21,* 6–9; cf. *Zeits.f.alttestam. Wissenschaft,* XV, 140, 340; the ms. Ar. no. 9602 (Berlin), 137b. Maqrizi, *Khitat* (ed. G. Wiet) 139 n. 4. Cavalcade in the Wadi 'l Qura Tab., *Tafsir,* I, 61.

399. Hanbal, IV, 407 V, 43; mule or donkey (the Tradition is uncertain). Ibid., III, 46, 175, 219.

400. Proof of humility, according to Ibn al-Jawzi, *Wafa,* 101b Hanbal, IV, 430 V, 59, 71, 149, 202, 2, 228; Yaqubi, *Hist.,* II, 42; at the seat of the B. Qurayza; Waqidi (Well.) 112, 211; praying on "a female or male donkey" (the variant is indicated) Hanbal, II, 75 rarely on foot, circumstance noted, ibid., III, 307; 12. Muslim, *Sahih²*, II, 2–3; "Male or female donkey" passed between him and the kiblah, "it cut our prayers" (Muhammad) on his donkey; Yafor, cf. ibid, IV, 149, 188; VI, 92. They also write it as "Yafour"; at Hunayn, uneasy on his mule, he gets down from it; Muslim, *Sahih,* I, 82–83.

401. Hanbal, VI, 7, 1–2. The multiplicity of donkeys in Medina raised the question, much debated in this school, as to if they could eat their flesh. In the Koran (sura 3:13) the possession of horses is listed as one of the most serious temptations that can assail mortals. It was an object of luxury in the Hijaz. Each Bedouin dreamed of his son becoming a horseman, owner of a horse; Bukhari, *Sahih²* (Krehl), II, 375, 4d. Elias Nisibenus, ed. Brooks (*CSO*, coll. Chabot), 128, incorrectly mentions, we believe, the horses of the Jews of Banu Nadir (and not B. Nusair as the editor has read it). The owner of a horse (it concerns a Medinese Sahabi) treats it like an object of value: on the road he mounts and walks alternatively; Bukhari, *Sahih,* I, 456, 3-6.

402. Hanbal, III, 495; Bukhari, *Sahih* (Krehl), II, 165. Muslim, *Sahih²*, I, 76, bottom.

403. Tab., *Tafsir,* I, 61; V, 91, 1.

404. Hanbal, IV, 204; V, 77; on horseback following a burial 215, buys horse from a Bedouin; ibid., IV, 67–68, refuses another (a shaft directed against the father of Samir

ibn Di'l Gausan, murderer of Husayn, cf. *Yazid,* 157 etc.). I.S.*Tabaq.,* IV², 90; Qutaiba, *Maarif,* E, 49. Muslim, *Sahih²,* I, 353, 356.

405. We possess a document of the edicts in its great *'ahd* (pact with the population of Medina).

406. Bukhari, *Sahih* (Krehl), IV, 121. He would ride then bareback, 'uri, *Khalq an Nabi* (ms. cit.), 355; Abu Dawud, *Sunan* (ms. cit.), 116; a *Montakhab musnad Abd ibn Humaid* (ms. Berlin), 106 b.

407. Where the pedestrians surpassed the horses; Hanbal, IV, 51, 2.

408. Hanbal, III, 300; Bukhari, *Sahih,* I, 476; he is carried off by his horse, Balad-huri, *Ansab,* 334b.

409. Cf. Caetani, *Studi di storia orientale*, I, 349, 350. He declares pride as a normal temptation for possessors of horses—because the horse is an animal of luxury—Muslim, *Sahih²,* I, 40.

410. They proclaim him, more competent in mounts than . . . , or, more competent in horses than . . .; Hanbal, IV, 387.

411. Hanbal, V, 27; cf. ibid., IV, 103, 104, 183, 184.

412. Cf. the variant "I love women . . . and horses," *Moawia,* 306–307. Bukhari, *Sahih,* II, 213, 214, 215; 216.

413. Cf. Qutaiba, *Oyoun,* 189; Muslim, *Sahih²,* II, 127–29; Tirmidi, *Sahih,* I, 316–17; Bukhari, *Sahih,* II, 213, etc., a real *musnad* of a horse!

414. Hanbal, I, 225 II, 3; III, 160; Tirmidi, *Sahih,* I, 316–17; Muslim², II, 127.

415. G. d'Avenel, *Les Français de mon temps*, 156. Here is why the caliph 'Umar must have been a horseman without comparison Qutaiba, *Oyoun*, 165, 8–10. To the Tabii, Urwa ibn abi'l Jad, a horse fanatic, we owe the saying, "Horses wear goodness on their foreheads"; I.S. *Tabaq.*, VI, 21; Bukhari, *Sahih,* II, 414–15.

416. It is the horse which gives the name to the horseman *kana yu 'rafu bihi*, scholium in *Naqaid Jarir*, 454, 5; cf. 247, 13; *Aghani,* XX, 165, 11–12; the term "al" = family, used for breeds of horses; *Naqaid Jarir*, 303, 4; Hanbal, I, 225. There were few horses at the Banu Hashim's Hashimites, a poor clan.

417. Or at least an indispensable epithet for a sayyid *Aghani,* XII, 148, 8 d.l.; XIV, 66 XIX, 139, d.l. *Usd.*, III 39, 11; 40, 7; IV, 227, 9; Ibn Duraid, *Istiqaq*, 124, 11; 138, 15; 180, 13230, 12; cf.*Moawia,* index, s.v. cheval; many Arab philologists have composed a kitab al khayl; Flugel, Grammatische Schulen, passim, Faris ibn Faris horseman, son of horseman; Hanbal, II, 170, 2.

418. Muhammad called the race horse the mount of the devil without doubt because of the gambling encouraged by the races (Hanbal, I, 395).

419. The mounts of Muhammad preserved their youth, "more he rode them, less old they got," Maqrizi, *Imta*, III, ms. cit. The traditional details on mules were found to serve as a commentary on sura 16:8. Their eternal youth is equally affirmed by al-Babi (from Bab, North Syria) Nuzhat al nazirin, (ms. Institut biblique de Rome), p. 14b. The donkey Yafour possesses the gift of speech al-Babi, ms. cit., 21b. The mule Doldol survived until the reign of Mu'awiya; Baladhuri, *Ansab,* 335, a.

420. Marriage, in all probability after the battle of Uhud. It is above all since the failure of "Ahzab" ["Confederates," title of of sura 33, said to have been written when Medina was besieged by a confederation of the Jewish tribes with the Arabs of Mecca, 5 A.H.] that Muhammad spread out his activity as a man of state.

421. She asked him for servants to ease her household burdens Muslim, *Sahih²*, II, 434–35; she showed him her calloused hands a frequent theme.

422. The histories of the Christian Arabs never forget to underline that Muhammad was a king. We can add Agapius Mabbugensis, ed. Cheikho, in *CSO*, 334, to the previous examples. The Koran, sura 88:22, forbids him from taking on the airs of a head of state (*musaytir*). But this verse—observe the commentators—would have been abrogated by other texts. The latter are in fact more numerous and more expressive; cf. Tab., *Tafsir*, XXX, 91.

423. Western. Nothing has shown that he looked beyond the Najd, the limitrophe of the Hijaz. For Muhammad and his contemporaries the extension of Arabia could not be notably different from that indicated in Bakri, op. cit., I, 5, 8–I d.l.

424. Muslim, *Sahih²*, I, 129, bottom.

425. The last person visited was Fatima, Sibt ibn al-Jawzi, *Mirat*, III, 37a. Ibn Abdalbarr, *Istiab*, 771; Hanbal, II, 21, III, 285; however refusing to enter because he saw a tapestry with figures (a new iconoclastic Hadith), ibid., II, 21 bottom.

426. Baladhuri, *Ansab*, 427, b; Hanbal, I, 77, 91, wakes them at night for prayers.

427. He granted her the privilege of a train (dress) (dayl) a cubit long (Hanbal II, 263) Cf. the polemic of the Hadith against this detail of feminine dress. To destroy the impression left by 'Ali's stupidity, the Shiite chroniclers like to show him indicating to 'Umar the appropriate solutions to problems of law, politics, etc. (Yaqubi, *Hist.*, II, 166, I 173–74) they make of him a great *faqih* (expert in Islamic jurisprudence) under the first three caliphs. I.S. *Tabaq.*, II², 100–102. In the affair of Aisha's romance, Muhammad consults him, but it is in company with Zayd ibn Haritha (the balance!); Muslim, *Sahih²*, II, 457, 2. They made the dying 'Umar pay a hommage to the intelligence and knowledge (*al fiqh wa-l-'ilm*) of 'Ali; I.S. *Tabaq.*, III 1, 247, 18. With the same intention they invented a book containing the sentences of 'Ali (*qada 'Ali*). On the worth of this compilation see Muslim, *Sahih²*, I, 8. They show us Aisha referring to 'Ali for a consultation, Muslim, op. cit., I, 122 when otherwise she suppresses the mention of 'Ali in the Hadith in her honor.

428. *Idha sahha akhadtunna bi-'unqihi*; I.S. *Tabaq.*, II², 37, 16.

429. "The bad omen is in women," Bukhari (Krehl), III, 418. Cf. the scene between Aisha and Zaynab: "They quarreled until they were exhausted"; Abu Bakr had to intervene, crying to the Prophet, "Go to prayers and put some earth in their mouths," Muslim, *Sahih²*, I, 567; II, 260–61; 261, 13, where woman is replaced by "khadim."

430. Muslim, *Sahih²*, II, 437–38. Jahiz, *Mahasin*, 272, d.l. To these Hadith and those affirming that the passing by of a woman broke the prayers, Aisha replied sneeringly" "Assuredly women are evil animals," (*inna-l-mar'a la—dabbat su'*) Muslim, op. cit., I, 195, 5.

431. Cf. Old Testament 2 Kings 17:18 the reflection of Absalon.

432. *Montakhab Kanz*, V, 30, bottom; God has so arranged that the descendants of each prophet was in his loins, and He has placed my descendants in the loins of 'Ali. Cf. Al badr al-munir (Asir effendi), 29b. His tears at the death of little Ibrahim; Hanbal, III, 112: I have never seen anyone who was more indulgent toward children than the Messenger of God: he describes the two Hasans, "my two myrtles in this world," ibid, II, 85. When Muhammad is angry, only 'Ali would dare to speak to him; Baladhuri, *Ansab, 428,* b. They insist on the resemblance between Muhammad and the sons of 'Ali, Hasan "from his face to his navel," Husayn, *min sarratihi ila qudumihi*; Baladhuri, *Ansab,* 632a; Hanbal, I, 99 II, 342; Bukhari, *Sahih* (Krehl), II, 446, 6; like Fatima, Abu Bakr observed that Hasan did not resemble 'Ali.

433. Hanbal, IV, 275.

434. Cf. *Moawia*, 307; Hanbal, VI, 409.

435. I read, *innakum la-tujbinun wa tubkhilun*; Hanbal, VI, 409.

436. Hanbal, III, 164 numerous variants, contrived to allow Husayn to participate in this privilege Fatima at Muhammad's initiative; Hanbal, VI, 282.

437. Muslim, *Sahih²*, I, 125.

438. And also to protest against the hardness, *jafa*, of the Bedouins; Hanbal, II, 241. Abu Huraira kisses Hasan on "the navel, there where he had seen Muhammad kiss it"; ibid., II, 255; he lifted up his shirt from his navel and kissed it. Baladhuri, *Ansab*, 588, b. The Shia tend to, in these circumstances, to make A. Huraira, the eccentric *muhaddith*, friend of the Umayyads, to intervene. We will never exhaust enumerating the hidden allusions of the Hadith.

439. He played with him between his feet until he escaped from the other side, Baladhuri, *Ansab*, 588 b; *Aghani*, VII, 16.

440. Maqdisi, *Ansab al-Qorasiyin* (ms. Asir eff.); *Usd,* V, 400, 12; Hanbal, II, 228, 440, V, 44; his prayer to God "love them just as I love them"; Hanbal, II, 249; "to love them is to love oneself"; ibid., II, 288.

441. In place of *malak al matar*, Goldziher (*ZDMG,* L, 485) reads "the angel Matran," taken from Talmudic angelology; cf. Hess in the *Recueil de travaux*, XXXIII, 157, notes Matir, name of a Bedouin born at the period of rain, those of his two brothers *Mutar* and *Mteran*. Al-Babi (ms. cit.), 27a, mentions the angel of the mountains. We also find it in the *Sahih,* like Muslim², II, 92.

442. Keep the door well-closed on us; we see him running after little Husayn, the boy rushed hither and thither and the Prophet laughed with him to catch him; ibid., IV, 172; on the same page, Hasan and Husayn try to get to their grandfather the first. "During Muhammad's prostration, a glass of water placed on his back was not spilled," (*law wudi'a qadah min ma' 'ala zahrihi lam yuhraq*); Hanbal, I, 123.

443. Hanbal, III, 242, 265.

444. Cf. the author's *Yazid,* 178; Hanbal, VI, 298; Gabriel gave it to him to smell, ibid., I, 85; Yaqubi, *Hist.*, II, 292. They equally got Umm Salama to intervene, the year after, a propos of the revolt of Ibn Zubayr and the Yazid's expedition against the holy cities of the Hijaz Muslim, *Sahih²*, II, 493, 16, cf. 494, 5.

445. Hanbal, II, 241, 393 488, 5; IV, 132; Maqdisi, *Ansab al-Qorasiyn*, ms. cit. Ibn al-Jawzi, *Wafa* (ms. Leiden), 14; a Suyuti, *Al Khasais al Kubra* (ms. Berlin) 48, a Balad-huri, *Ansab*, 588, b. *Khamis*, II, 331 makes Umm Salama die under Yazid I, to get rid of the contradiction.

446. On this mark of tenderness, cf. *Moawia*, 78, n.1; Hanbal, II, 305, 1; VI, 570; they recognize children by their scent (cf. Isaac and Jacob) sniffing and kissing, distinct terms (cf. Jahiz, *Haiawan*, II, 20), I.S. *Tabaq.*, IV 1, 123, 7; Tirmidhi, *Sahih*, II, 85, 6 d.l.; *Usd*, I, 289; Bukhari, *Sahih*, I, 328, 13; Nawawi, *Tahdib*, 263, 10; *Aghani*, V, 132, 10 d.l.; VIII, 90, 11; XVIII, 158, 4; XIX, 7, 1.8 *shamm*, to kiss, is the ordinary term in Baghdad and Muscat (communication of A. Goguyer of Muscat [Oman]). Cf. the scene between the Prophet and his son Ibrahim; Bukhari, *Sahih*, IV, 114, 1: "he kissed him and sniffed him," and then between Muhammad and Hasan, "he put out his tongue and if the boy saw the redness of his tongue, he was delighted, delighted in the sense that if we see something that pleases, one desires it, one holds it, one runs towards it and takes pleasure in it"; Abu Ubaid, ms. cit., 182b. Cf. Hanbal, IV, 93 bottom (notice the eulogy accorded to Hasan); we find it piquant to attribute this hadith to Mu'awiya. Jacob in Palestine smelled the odor of his son, Joseph; sura 12:96. The Hebrew *nshq*, to kiss, should have meant on the whole to sniff, as the comparison with Arabic *nashiqa* hints; Taj al'Arus, VII, 76; see Aug. Wun-sche, *Der Kuss in Bibel, Talmud und Midrasch, 1-2*.

447. We sniffed the women and children, Hanbal, *Musnad*, II, 228; 305 IV, 172; VI, 123.7 I.S.*Tabaq.*, III 1, 40.16.

448. *Usd*, II, 12, 4; Hanbal, V, 37–38; Bukhari, *Sahih* (Krehl), II, 443.

449. Hanbal, III, 261; cf. the author's *Ziad ibn Abihi*, 37 (from *Rivista*).

450. Cf. *Moawia*, 204–208; Bukhari, *Sahih*, II, 134, 2 d.l.; Muslim, *Sahih*, I, 236. I.S. *Tabaq.*, VI, 106, 6; Hanbal, III, 7, l. 8; 18; 62; II, 32, IV, 70.

451. Bukhari, *Sahih*, II, 169.

452. They helped themselves deliberately to Abu Bakr, known for his luke warm sympathies for the Alids; cf. the author's *Yazid*, 141, 133. Near the minbar, a false sermon, "and if he refreshes other than you, he deserves the fire" Hanbal, II, 329.

453. And son, "ibni hada"; Bukhari, *Sahih*, II, 169; Hanbal, V, 38, I.

454. Allusion to the Koran passages cited at the beginning of this study. Even in pre-siding over the public prayers, he performed the prostrations, having on his back and shoulders his granddaughter Umama; Muslim, *Sahih*, I, 205.

455. Hanbal, V, 354 Bukhari, *Sahih* (Krehl), II, 134, 2 d.l; Muslim, *Sahih*, I, 236.

456. Their saliva dribbled on him while he carried them on his shoulders; Hanbal, II, 467, 6: scene prepared to get attributed to them the privileges reserved for the Al Muhammad (the people/family of Muhammad), ibid. One day he heard them crying, "he got up frightened and said to the people I got up without thinking,"; a variant text adds the reflection, "children are a trial"; Baladhuri, *Ansab*, 588b; 632.6 (all according to Madaini). The latter annalist had composed a *kitab al Fatimiyat* (the book of Fatima), another one on the speeches of 'Ali; *Fihrist* (Flugel) 102, 8, 22. Baladhuri relied greatly on Madaini for his information on the Alids.

457. Bukhari, *Sahih,* III, 512; IV, 115.

458. Hanbal, *Musnad,* VI, 46 and passim.

459. Like the future caliphs Mu'awiya, Mugira ibn Suba, Abu Huraira, Ibn Abbas, Abu Musa al-Asari—he also works as a door-keeper; *Iqd* 4, II, 4; *Aghani*, XVI, 54, 2; I.S. *Tabaq.*, VIII, 139; Hanbal, *Musnad*, II, 311; IV, 101 Muslim, *Sahih²*, II, 322, 351, 542, 543. Ibn Masud is called the man with two sandals, at the pillow and at the ablutions fountain; Tab., *Tafsir,* XXX, 120, 9 d. l.; cf. Muslim, op. cit., I, 34, 119, above all 120–21, 168–69.

460. Tab., *Tafsir,* XXIX, 56. Hanbal, *Musnad,* I, 268, 9; II, 448, 17; IV, 6, 1.12; 45, 46; Muslim, *Sahih²*, I, 53, 176; II, 70, 330–31, 525. At Mecca he regularly visited the neighbouring *mawasim* (fairs) to preach monotheism according to the sira; at Medina he purchased at an enormous profit the cargo of a caravan; Hanbal, I, 235.

461. Bukhari, *Sahih* (Krehl), II, 21 IV, 94, no. 60.

462. However, having refused to visit him because of the presence of a dog serving to amuse his grandsons, he ordered the the animal killed; Hanbal, II, 305. On this order to kill the dogs, see the reflections of the sceptical; Jahiz, *Haiawan*, I, 141, etc.

463. Baladhuri, *Ansab*, 737, b. Hanbal, IV, 348; VI, 339; I.S. *Tabaq.*, VIII, 204, Umm al Fadl, from her name Lobaba, would be the "first convert to Islam after Khadija" (sic) she "emigrated to Medina after Abbas' conversion"; I.S. *Tabaq.*, VIII, 203–204. All that is affirmed without any isnad it is the official Abbasid doctrine. For the date they do not seem to be able to agree period of Khandaq, of Khaybar (suspect isnad); I.S. *Tabaq.*, IV1, 10; significant confessions; ibid., Abbas and his wife, converted before Badr, ibid., 20, d.l.

464. They made him choose the easiest of routines he was constantly afraid of "creating a sunna"; Hanbal, VI, 34, 51, 61, 86, 169, 170, 182, 183, 233; he is observed in the most intimate circumstances: 'Ali . . . ibid., 12, 13; Muslim, *Sahih²*, I, 118.

465. Yaqubi, *Hist.,* II, 130; *Iqd*, I, 277; Hanbal, *Musnad*, VI, 283; *Montakhab Kanz,* . . . V, 102; Baladhuri, *Ansab*, 354.

466. *Al hilm wa-l-haya'.* Cf. these words of 'Ali "the manifold divorces of Hasan have created for me numerous enmities"; Baladhuri, *Ansab*, 591, b.

467. Baladhuri, *Ansab*, 591b; 592, a. For Husayn's attitude at Karbala see *Yazid,* chap. X and XI.

468. Yaqubi, *Hist.*, II, 91; Baladhuri, *Futuh*, 64; *Aghani*, X, 164; Hanbal, IV, 107 (interesting variants). See in Yazid chapter 21, devoted to Najran.

469. Whose framework was provided by the Koran, sura 3:54 as in the preceding verse the Messiah is named, they thought of the Christians, finally of the Najranites. This is the usual procedure of the sira: it makes every effort to flesh out every obscure allusion in the Koran. [Cf. the author's "Koran and Tradition," chap. 4 , of the present volume.—Trans.]

470. Formally confirmed by Maqrizi, *Imta*, III, voluminous sira but the pages unnumbered (ms. Kuprulu).

471. Sura 33:6: this title of "mothers" meant that the faithful did not have the right

to marry them (cf. Maqrizi, op. cit.) by creating a family realtionship. Addressing Muslims, Aisha would invoke her right to motherhood *haqq al umuma*; Muslim, *Sahih*, I, 143.

472. Sura 33:30.

473. Sura 33:31, etc., 53. That they look after the backs of their carpets (*zuhur al hasar*) (Hanbal, II, 446, d.l.), that is to say, do not leave your houses! Hassan ibn Thabit, *Divan*, CXXXIV, 8 presents the widows of Muhammad like the nuns they wore the *masuh* (monastic garb). The Hadith, however, show us (text cited earlier) Aisha dressed in red! Muhkhannath frequent their houses while Muhammad was alive; Bukhari, *Sahih* (Krehl), IV, 94, no. 62. On the subjcet of sura 33:6, let us note the strange style of Jahiz, *Tria opuscula*, 19, 12: In certain texts his wives are their mothers. At the time of Jahiz, the passage relating to the motherhood of the wives of Muhammad, was it not to be found yet in the *textus receptus?* He points it out as a variant (certain readings of the Koran).

474. In Muslim, *Sahih²*, II, 325, above all 326, where they make every effort to prove the contrary the reasoning is specious.

475. Cf. *Moawia*, 320, 417. The expressions *al Muhammad* = the wives of Muhammad, *ahl al bayt* = the people of the house, in fact gathered together under the same roof [Muhammd's household]. Hanbal, *Musnad,* III, 208, 232, 14; 246, 11 d.l.

476. The purpose of the Prophet was to transform into taboo the "people of the house," as it is apparent from the context. However this interdiction could not please Fatima's family.

477. Muslim, *Sahih²*, II, 324. And also that of reserving for the Alids the expression *Ahl al bayt* numerous examples where they apply it to other families: Umayyad Makhzumites, Ansar, etc., I.S. *Tabaq.*, V, 88, 16; Tab.II, 425, 13; 1787, I; *Aghani*, IX, 79, 13 d.l.; Hanbal, I, 161; IV, 150, 7,d.l.; VI, 421; Waqidi (Kremer), 268, 4; Jahiz, *Mahasin*, 349, 6.

478. This tendancy fails in the smallest details; Muhammad snatches away from Hasan a date meant for alms, "the prophet's family do not eat the produce of the alms," Hanbal, II,409, d.l. "I leave you my family" (unclear passages), ibid., III, 14, 1.10; 17; the Mahdi would issue from the Prophet's family, III, 36.

479. I believe I found the same intention in a Hadith, instructing, in place of 'Ali, Abu Huraira to proclaim the truce (*bara'a*) at the pilgrimage presided over by Abu Bakr Muslim, *Sahih,* I, 517, 10 d.l.

480. Hanbal, VI, 292, bottom, 296, bottom, 298, 304, 305; the mantle is first from Fadak, then from Khaybar. In the Hijaz, as we know, the Jews were in possession of industry; from there we get the topographical hesitation.

481. Cf. Goldziher, *ZDMG*, L, 114, etc. Muslim, *Sahih²*,II, 332.

482. Cf. *Triumvirat,* 121; *Usd*, V, 522; Hanbal, III, 156.

483. *Usd*, V, 522; Hanbal, I, 101; VI, 391–92: the Banu Hashim belong to the family of Muhammad. "The al Muhammad would include all those who do not eat from the alms, that is the al-'Ali ['Ali's family], Abbas, Jafar, and Aqil." Baladhuri, *Ansab*, 442, b. The Hashimites formed "the family of Abul Qasim"; Komait, *Hashimiyat*, I, 45. All the themes are used to introduce them there surrepticiously. At the pilgrimage, Ibn Abbas declares having been sent in advance by the Prophet, to welcome his family, i.e., the women and

children; Bukhari, *Sahih* (Krehl), I, 423, I. During his last illness, Muhammad obliged everyone of the "people of his family "to take some medicine, except his uncle Abbas"; Muslim, *Sahih²*, II 253; 332, where Ibn Jafar is declared to be of the family.

484. Why put oneself out? When it does not concern the Prophet, 'Ali used to say, I take liberties with the Hadith, for war is a stratagem, Hanbal, I, 131. Precious confession! The Hadith is thus an arm in the hand of the parties they compare it to a strategem of war!

485. Term chosen intentionally: its worth constitutes the basis of the debate.

486. Ibn al-Jawzi, *Talqih* (ms. Constantinople), p. 6a Qudai, *'uyun al-ma'arif*, (ms. Omoumiya, Constantinople); Maqrizi, *Imta,* ms. cit; Hanbal, V, 295, 296; VI, 101, 119; *Fawaid Jami al-Usul* (ms. Berlin), II, 148 a; I.S. *Tabaq.,* VIII, 168–69.

487. The daughters of Fatima are not mentioned. The youngest Umm Kulthum would be born before the Prophet's death her sister Zaynab would have immediately preceded her; Fatima not having had children before the death of her father; *Usd.,* V, 469. If the marriage of their parents had taken place after Uhud, if the birth of the two Hasans preceded theirs, then these little girls would have been very small while Muhammad was alive: here is why they do not figure either in the sira or in the Hadith.

488. Nasai, *Sunan* (ms Nouri Otmani, Constantinople) paragra., *Fi hamal al sabaya fi-l-salat,* Ibn al-Jawzi, ms. cit., Maqdisi, *Ansab al Qorasiyn* (ms. Asir effendi); I.S. *Tabaq.,* VIII, 26; 168–69. Thus the Prophet takes on his camel Ibn Zubayr and neglects Ibn Jafar; Hanbal, IV, 5, bottom.

489. Another example in Muslim, *Sahih²*, I, 97, 98. Muhammad was in a good mood when he was eating meat, above all, the leg of mutton, that is; what he liked the most of mutton. After a vigorous bite, he cried out, "I shall be the lord of men on the day of the resurrection." Silence . . . again a bite; the Prophet repeated his first remark. When the Companions were having a conversation with Muhammad, they found themselves close enough to the apartments of Aisha to "hear the the sound of her toothpick"; Muslim, op. cit., I, 483.

490. Suyuti, *al numudaj fi khasa'is al habib* (ms. Asir eff.), 146b.

491. Maqrizi, *Imta,* ms. cit., Ibn al-Jawzi, *Talqih,* 6a.

492. E.g., Hanbal, III, 33 bottom. The Prophet predicted that they would fight for the exposition of the subject matter of the Koran. "Abu Bakr and 'Umar got up [wishing to know if they were designated]. Non, said the Prophet, but only he who sews up again the sole of his shoe. However 'Ali was sewing the sole of his shoe."Allusion to the allegoric interpretation practiced by the Shia.

493. Muhammad amused himself equally with the children of Abbas; racing with them, "they ran toward him and threw themslves against his chest and his back. He kissed them and kept them near him" (Hadith Abbasid). Baladhuri is full of such tales. Cf. *Ansab,* 699, 701b, 720a; Hanbal, I, 214. This theme was widely developed: Muhammad took on his back Ibn Jafar and Ibn Abbas and neglected Ibn Zubayr sometimes he adds the son of 'Ali to them. Fadl ibn Abbas is thus distinguished, simultaneously with little Usama; Hanbal, *Musnad,* I, 203, 204, 205, 210–211, 212, 216, 226; I.S. *Tabaq.,* IV 1, I, other Hashimites are taken by the Prophet while mounted, and placed in front or behind him;

ibid., 250 bottom. The Zubairides have succeeded in introducing the same privilege for Ibn Zubayr (Ibn Abbas undertook to confirm it in the isnad), ibid., 240. One of the artifices of the Hadith is—as here—to get an adversary to play the role of a guarantor.

494. Ibn al-Jawzi, *Montazam* (ms. cit), II, 61b; I.S. *Tabaq.*, IV 1, 43.

495. I.S. *Tabaq.*, IV 1, 43, *law kana Usama jariya la-kaswatuhu wa haliatuhu* . . . .; Ibn al Gauzi, *Montazam*; Muhammad penetrates the Kaaba, followed by Usama, Hanbal, II, 3; leaves leaning on him, II, 281, 8; the Makhzumite thief appealed to him to intercede on her behalf with Muhammad, IV, 386. Other Hadith relative to him, ibid., II, 20; Muhammad enters Mecca on a camel of Usama's, ibid., II, 32; Muhammad declares Usama the person he loves the most, but a variant adds, excepting Fatima; II, 106, d.l., 107, I; raised by Muhammad like someone of his family (the term ahl or family returns once again); receives a tunic of 50 dinars, worn by Muhammad first in the pulpit; I.S. *Tabaq.*, IV 1, 43, I; 45; Hanbal, II, 40; he galdly proposes Usama as husband to Muslim women coming to consult him (Hanbal, VI, 411–14).

496. I.S. *Tabaq.*, IV 1, 44; Bukhari, *Tarih*, I, (ms. Kuprulu, unnumbered pages), biographical sketch of Usama.

497. Cf. *Ziad ibn Abihi*, 42–43. These later compilations cite other cases the oldest Sahih know only the case of the Makhzoumite; Ibn Rusta (ed. de Goeje), 193–94; cf. Hanbal, I, 419; 'Ali cuts hands; Yaqubi, *Hist.*, II, 251.

498. *Mughiab* = women whose husbands are absent; they did not feel very safe in Medina; Hanbal, I, 245.

499. Muslim, *Sahih* 1, II, 146.

500. Muslim *Sahih*[2], II, 44–46, 136. He always intervened reluctantly, except in the case of Jews. As for wine, the regulation was hit upon under the first caliphs naturally they point out 'Umar here.

501. Noldeke-Schwally, *Geschichte*, I, 248, etc.

502. Muslim, *Sahih*[2], II, 42.

503. Muslim, *Sahih*[2], II, 41, 42. One Hadith prescribes cutting off the fist of someone stealing an egg or a rope. To get out of this, the commentators interpret *baida* as a helmet and *habl* as the huge cable of a ship. See the discussion in Nawawi, *Sarh Muslim*, I, 107–108 (ms. Instit.biblique, Rome).

504. Baladhuri, *Futuh*, 30; Yaqubi, *Hist.*, II, 142; Ibn Hisham, *Sira*, 776; I.S. *Tabaq.*, VIII, 17.

505. Cf. *Moawia*, index, s.v. Yazid ibn Abi Sofian.

506. Baladhuri, *Futuh*, 37, 7. The whole of this account is without an isnad in Ibn Hisham's *Sira*, 805, etc. There we discover the obvious intention of humiliating the Umayyads in the person of Abu Sufyan, and also to glorify the sons of Fatima; cf. I. Hisham, *Sira*, 807, 2 d.l. In reality, Abul Qasim was proud of his relations with the Umayyads, and the Tradition was equally proud. The Tradition insists on assigning him two Umayyad sons-in-law and puts their eulogy in the mouth of the Prophet. With Abu Bakr and 'Umar, he does not put himself out, he receives them dressed carelessly. But soon as they announce the visit of 'Uthman, he prepares his clothes. Muslim, *Sahih*[2], II,

321. These details betray the modest origins of Abul Qasim. By way of consolation, they show the most illustrious of the Companions carrying out the humblest of chores for him, seeing to his ablutions (see above), acting as door-keepers, like Abu Musa al-Ashari; Muslim, *Sahih*[2], II, 322 and Ibn Abbas, ibid., II, 351. If the *Sahih* compilations have so easily accepted the history of 'Ali's engagement with the daughter of Abu Lahab (ibid., II, 339), the desire to raise up the status of the poor husband of Fatima could have contributed to it, since the B. Makhzum were seeking him for a son-in-law.

507. *Yadabbu bayna yadayha*, he climbs between his hands. Tab., I, 1123–24.

508. Muslim, *Sahih*[2], I, 140; Hanbal, VI, 423, 424. Certain Muslims are there guaranteed Paradise, Muslim, *Sahih*[2], I, 188, 191.

509. Cf. the author's *Triumvirat*, 130, etc. On Fatima's (?) advice, they would have transported Muhammad from Maymuna's house to Aisha's; cf. Ibn Sa'd, *Tabaqat* (ms. Bib.Khed), 118a; unlikely event, given what we know about relations between Fatima and the favorite (Aisha).

510. Baladhuri, *Ansab*, (ms. cit.), 267b.

511. Let us mention her presence at the Farewell Pilgrimage; Hanbal, III, 320, 6 d.l. 'Ali associated with the offerings for Muhammad; 63 victims in keeping with the supposed age of Muhammad; ibid., cf. "The Age of Muhammad" and the chronology of the sira [chap. 5 of the present volume—Trans.] Everything was contrived here to highlight the couple 'Ali-Fatima Tab., I, 1750–51; I. Hisham, *Sira*, 967; Muslim, *Sahih*, I, 469, 3.

512. I.S. *Tabaq.*, II 2, 29, 2.

513. Tab. I., 1140; and all the collections of the Hadith. I.S. *Tabaq.*(ms. cit.) 126–27, II 2, 83, 24; 84, 7 Hanbal, III, 204; the last audience of 'Ali with Muhammad; ibid., VI, 300.

514. Cf. *Triumvirat*, 133, etc.; elegy of Fatima on her father; *Iqd* 4, II, 6.

515. Cf. *Yazid,* 158–59, 163; *Ziad ibn Abihi*, 91–92.

516. "Fatima said, O Ibn al-Khattab, you wear yourself out for me because of my father. He said, yes, it is even stronger than what your father brought" (i.e., his prophethood). According to Madaini; Baladhuri, *Ansab*, 384a. Should we translate the reply of Umar: "I can do it in virtue of the religion founded by your father"?—" You seem hardly concerned about the death of the Prophet," 'Ali had told Abu Bakr (I.S. *Tabaq.*, II 2,84, 13). A well-founded accusation, when we compare the eagerness of the latter to keep for himself the caliphate. See *Triumvirat*, 133–34. For thirty-six hours the corpse of the Prophet remained forgotten and horribly swollen up (I.S. *Tabaq.*, II[2], 57, 2; 58; d.l., 59, 1–3). To excuse indirectly this neglect, the Tradition tried at length to have us believe that they could not get used to the idea of Muhammad's death. This is the theory used by M. Casanova in *Mahomet et la fin du monde*. During the preparations of the corpse, a mysterious sleep took hold of the helpers (here you have the counterpart to the drowsiness that unexpectedly overtook them at Badr and Uhud). They finished their work with their eyes covered for fear of blindness lest they see the pudendum of Abul Qasim; Ibid., II[2], 60; 61, 16, etc. They also had their ears blocked up since they did not become aware of the coup d'état carried out by the triumvirate.

517. Yaqubi, *Hist.*, II, 191; house of Fatima searched, ibid, II, 155.

518. *Aghani*, XV, 71; 99, 18; XVIII, 137, 10; 202, 27; to turn away when a woman undoes her hair. Ibn Hisham, *Sira*, 809, 2 d.l.; Wellhausen, *Reste* 2, 199, cf. 195–96. At the conquest of Mecca, the Qurayshite women threw themselves in front of the horses with their hair uncovered; Baladhuri, *Ansab*, 226, a.

519. Tab., *Annales*, I, 1818, 1820; cf. I.S. *Tabaq.*, III 2, 223, 14. With a punch, 'Umar knocked over Abu Huraira, 'Umar had struck out with his hand at my chest and I collapsed immediately; Muslim, *Sahih²*, I, 34. This extraordinary physical vigor is the Sunni rejoinder to the person of 'Ali, reproducing the acts of Samson at Khaybar.

520. Never go to sleep without having made your will; Hanbal, II, 4 34; cf. *République marchande de la Mecque*, 20 Muslim, *Sahih²*, II, 10.

521. Sura 2:176, 5:105.

522. Cf. *Triumvirat*, 130–32; I.S. *Tabaq.* (ms. cit.), 123b, etc. 151b, etc.

523. Kumait, *Hasimiyat*, I, 60, 62, 72 (ed. J. Horovitz). Here is why at the pilgrimage 'Ali made it known that he was ready to pay off the debts left by Muhammad; I.S. *Tabaq.*, II², 89 (see below). One is inclined to associate the mothers of the believers to Fatima in their claims on the inheritance from Abul Qasim; Muslim, *Sahih*, II, 72. This claim is meant to reduce the rights of Fatima, and also to make a contrast. Abbas sometimes found himself backing the claims of Fatima; Muslim, *Sahih* II, 73. This detail, inspired by the Abbasids, should have proved that after Fatima they were the heirs closest to the Prophet. A dynastic thesis! In this version, note the absence of 'Ali. 'Ali would have defrauded Abbas of his share; Muslim, op. cit., II, 73, 3 d.l. One can see what arms the two parties had recourse to! On the nature and juridical effects of alms-giving—kind of inalienable domanial properties—see an interesting passage in I.S. *Tabaq.²*, 260, 5. The families of the caliphs 'Umar and 'Uthman were equally masters of their alms-giving; ibid., loc. cit.; Muslim, *Sahih²*, II, 13, 9, etc.; these are the *waqf* (endowments, dedication of property to charitable uses), as the marginal notes of Muslim indicate, loc. cit.; I.S. *Tabaq.*, III², 53, bottom.

524. Kumait, *Hasimiyat*, II, 44. I adopt the reading: *tastakhalafa*.

525. Kumait, *Hasimiyat*, II, 94.

526. Muslim, *Sahih²*, II, 13, 4 d.l.; 14, 10.

527. I.S. *Tabaq.*, II², 49 etc. Hanbal, VI, 274; cf. *Triumvirat*, loc. cit. *Yazid*, 73, 75.

528. Like the following: just before dying the Prophet left some dinars and urged Aisha to get rid of them. Some trivial advice, here is what the totality of the recommendations of the Prophet of God is reduced to. Hanbal, VI, 315, bottom Muslim, *Sahih²*, II, 14; I.S.*Tabaq.*, II², 44, etc.; Muslim, *Sahih*, I, 523–24. The Abbasid school had already realized that; see the reply attributed to Ibn Abbas on this subject. I.S. *Tabaq.*, II², 51, 21. They also counter the Hadith of Aisha with their own (ibid., 50–51). 'Ali had collected the last sigh of the Prophet. The Abbasid tradition protested against the brutal intervention of 'Umar on this occasion; Muslim, *Sahih²*, II, 13–14.

529. From the Jew Muhairiq he would have inherited the vast domain which formed the *sadaqa* of the Prophet at Medina; Waqidi (Kremer), 259, 7. Cf. the thesis of R. Leszynsky, *Die Juden in Arabien zur Zeit Mohammeds*.

530. Bukhari, *Sahih* (Krehl), II, 437; Baladhuri, *Futuh* 30–31; Yaqubi, *Hist.*, II, 142; Hanbal, I, 3, 6; VI, 44, 145 (with the suspect isnad Urwa—Aisha).

531. At his death, Husayn would have been 58. It was, we should add, the age of his father 'Ali, of his son 'Ali, then of Muhammad son of 'Ali ibn Husayn; *Khamis*, II, 334. It is the system of symmetrical figures; cf. "The Age of Muhammad," 212, [chapter 3 in the present volume.—Trans.]. According to Ibn al Batriq (ed. Cheikho), II, 38, 19. Husayn would have been 63; he must in that case have been born 2 years before the Hijra! Line 17 is to be read Maysum, daughter of Bahdal. For the meaning of sura 75:16, 17, cf. Tab., *Tafsir*, XXIX, 101. Muhammad changed suras during the last year of his life; I.S. *Tabaq.*, II², 104, 6.

532. *Inna al nubuwwa lam turath wa lam yabqa illa al-tawaruth*, Masudi, *Prairies,* IV, 55–56; cf. Tab., III, 14, 6 (an Alid source as the isnad insinuates). Muhammad had declared unacceptable the testimony of an intimate friend or a member of the family in favor of the family, the "testimony" of a "tributary" of the family of the Prophet is not legal . . . a "tributary" is someone who depends on the family of the Prophet, Hanbal, II, 204; Hadith aimed directly at the pretentions of Fatima (Abu Huraira); ibid., II, 242, 7–6 d.l.

533. Bukhari (Krehl), II, 272–74; Muslim, *Sahih²*, II, 71; Caetani, *Annali*, II, 687–89; cf. I.S. *Tabaq.*, II², 85–87.

534. Tab. I, 1869; Ibn Abdalbarr, *Istiab*, 771; Yaqubi, *Histoire*, II, 120.

535. Hanbal, VI, 283.

536. Muslim, *Sahih*, II, 72; Tab., II, 1825. Because, affirms Ibn Forat (ms. 1595, Paris), 7b, she would have recognized the justice of her decision; Ibn al-Jawzi, *Maudouat* (ms. B.Khed.) prefers to deny the quarrel. Here is the résumé of the dialogue (according to Baladhuri, *Ansab*, 340–41) between A. Bakr and Fatima:

"Who is your heir?" — "My family—Why do you hold my father's inheritance?"— "I have gathered neither gold nor silver."— And her land at Fadak (*sadaqathu ba'dak*, which should read *bi-fadak*)? Another version reconciles her with A. Bakr and shows the latter praying at her funeral. I.S. *Tabaq.*, VIII, 17, 19. Abandoned by his followers after the death of of Fatima, 'Ali made peace with Abu Bakr; Muslim, *Sahih*, II, 72, 'Ali had prestige among Fatima's living relatives. Personally his prestige must have been slim and even then he owed it to his being the son-in-law

537. I.S. *Tabaq.,* VIII, 17–18; Hanbal, VI, 461, 462; Ibn Hajar, *Isaba*, IV, 729.

538. Yaqubi, *Hist.*, II, 128–29.

539. Tab., III, 2435; Baladhuri, *Ansab,* (ms. cit) 260b; Muslim, *Sahih,* II, 54, 5. Fatima must have died of consumption, like her elder son Hasan (*Asall,* consumption) he died in coughing up his lungs; Baladhuri, *Ansab*, 602a. No need to bring in poison, as they pretended to; cf.*Moawia*, 149–54. Instead of the daughter of Asat, they nominated the daughter of Amru ibn Suhail, as Hasan's wife; she would have received 100,000 dinars from Mu'awiya for the turn. Baladhuri, *Ansab,* 603b.

540. Muslim, *Sahih²*, I, 345–47.

541. Numerous Hadith; 'Ali buries her without even having looked at her; I.S. *Tabaq.*, VIII, 18 top; Muslim, *Sahih²*, II, 72.

542. Muslim, *Sahih²*, I, 340, 13. For Fatima's will, cf. Hanbal, VI, 283: "There was in his will the curtain which people claim she made herself, and that the Prophet, in entering her house and seeing it went back." What is this *satr* (curtain hanging, drape) introduced by Fatima and matched with the door-curtain or tapestry covered with images, to which we referred earlier? 'Ali would have pronounced the elegy on his wife's grave; *Iqd* 4, II, 7, bottom.

543. Tab.I, 1825, 1869 III, 2302–03, 2435; Yaqubi, loc. cit. Ibn al-Athir, *Kamil* (Tornb), II, 259. She is *juwayriya* (unmarriageable) at the beginning of Muhammad's mission (Muslim, *Sahih*, II, 91). Which gives us a total at least of 30 years.

544. *Usd*, V, 524; I. Abdalbarr, *Istiab*, 773; Nawawi, *Tahdib*, 850–51; "31 years and several months"; Baladhuri, *Ansab*, 258 a.

545. Cf. *Triumvirat*, 133–34; Hanbal, II, 240, 388, 474. Wellhausen, *Reste* 2, 112. I.S. *Tabaq.*, III 1, 143, 146, 147, 148; VI, 64, 19; 73; Tirmidhi, *Sahih,* I, 189, 200; Muslim, *Sahih*, I, 258–59; at funerals, the pace must be rapid, but *dun al khabab* (without trotting); Hanbal, I, 432; Arabs hardly rebury the corpses frequently dug up by the hyaenas; Jahiz, *Haiawan*, VI, 154–55; at burials forbidden to "be long-drawn out like the Jews" said Muhammad, Hanbal, II, 344, I; besides Muhammad protested against the nocturnal burials, ibid., III, 295.

546. Cf. *Iqd* 4, II, 4, 9, d.l.; the last advice of Amru ibn al-Asi; Goldziher, *Abhandlungen*, II, 41; also by Goldziher, "le culte des morts dans le paganisme et dans l 'islam," M.S., I, 229–63; Wellhausen, *Reste* 2, 177–86. The majority of accounts where they discuss the worship of the dead among the pre-Islamic Arabs were made up, the ancient verses were reworked at the [Islamic] Imperialist period, when the conquerors felt the need to make their ancestors more presentable. As to those accounts attributing to the first Muslims indifference toward nature, one cannot help suspecting polemical tendencies against ancient customs, judged to be tarnished with polytheism (cf. Goldziher, *M.S.*, I, 258, etc.). The essence of Hadith is not historical but doctrinal. This characteristic makes the study of the rise of Islam particularly thorny. The life of Fatima provides the best proof of that. Aisha did not hesitate in making her bed near the spot in her room where the remains of the Prophet were resting I.S. *Tabaq.*, II², 85, 15. The latter Hadith perhaps contains an implicit protest against the worship of tombs.

547. *Divan* of 'Umaiya ibn Abi s-Salt (ed. Schultess), XXXV, 6. Cf. Hanbal, II, 134, 135, tears forbidden at funerals; numerous Hadith on this theme; 169, top; VI, 66; Muslim, *Sahih²*, I, 340.

548. Sellin, *Zu der ursprungl. Bedeutung der Mazzeben.*, in *Orientalist Litteraturz* (1912): 120. We shall come back to this in another study being prepared on the Arab mosque.

549. Cf. *Aghani*, II, 160, 17–18.

550. Cf. *Moawia*, 105, 106, 340–42, 446; Goldziher, *M.S.*, I. 230–34.

551. Tirmidhi, *Sahih*, I, 195; Muslim, *Sahih,* I, 264–65; Hanbal, I, 96; VI,18.

552. See the Sahihs: Muhammad forbids Fatima to take part in the public expression of mourning, otherwise, he adds: You will not see Paradise before the grandfather of your father, i.e., Abd al-Muttalib; Hanbal, II, 169; the family reunion of the Prophet and the

preparation of dishes after the burial of the dead (Hanbal, II, 244) was frowned upon; cf. *Ziad ibn Abihi*, 59. On the graves of the martyrs of Uhud the authors have Muhammad praying "eight years after" this battle (Hanbal, IV, 154, 13). At this period the Prophet was no longer alive, if we were to stick to the chronology of the sira; see "The Age of Muhammad" [chapter 5 of the present volume.—Trans.]. They realized the difficulty and they place this prayer during the last days of the Prophet; Muslim, *Sahih²*, II, 285. He apologizes for crying at the death of one of his children; ibid., I, 273, d.l. Aisha said to him "on your return from my funeral, until your last day you will not cease act like a newly married man with certain of your wives, Bukhari, *Sahih* (Kr.), IV, 46. For the form of the tombs, see the commentary of Fr. Schwally, I.S. *Tabaq.*, II², 38. We must take into account the practice of the Arabs to disguise their tombs to prevent posthumous acts of vengeance. Thus, during the occupation of Rhodes under Mu'awiya, Fadala ibn Ubaid had the tombs of the dead soldiers levelled to the ground; Muslim, *Sahih²*, I, 357, 5. Cf. *Moawia*, loc. sup. cit. For the stone tombs, cf. R. Hartmann in *Archiv f.Religionswiss.* XV, 148-49.

553. Another example of the ascetic Mutarrif ibn Abd allah; Sharani, *Lawaqih al-anwar* (ms. Institut biblique), 29a; Baladhuri, *Futuh*, 135; I.S. *Tabaq.*, V, 150; VIII, 70.

554 Cf. *Yazid*, 191.

555. Quoted for its beauty in Ibn Qutaiba, *Poesis*, 280, 308.

556. *Naqaid Jarir* (ed. Bevan), p. 847; *Aghani*, VII, 62, 2; Hadith favorable to the public expression of mourning the soul is extinguished, the eye cries, time is recent, Hanbal, II, 273, 10. To protest against this heartlessness and to establish the worship of tombs, they showed the mothers of the believers, the great Companions, the caliph Mu'awiya, loyally visiting the martyrs of Uhud; Waqidi (Kremer) 303–304 Muhammad qualifies as *kufr*—unbelief / blasphemy—lamentations of mourning explanation of this Hadith in Nawawi, *Sarh Muslim*, (ms. cit., Institut biblique de Rome), 152a. However, they insisted in making him visit cemeteries to pray "for the dead"; I.S. *Tabaq.*, II², 9–10. The Arabs frequently buried their dead inside the house, a custom found among many peoples of classical antiquity, cf. C. Pascal, *Il significato della formola Sit tibi terra levis* in *Symbolae litterariae in honorem Iulii de Petra*, p. 230.

557. The *naqida* (polemical poem, flyting poem, one of a pair in which two poets seek to outdo each other) pretends to take up the expressions of the targeted *qasida* (ode), as it uses the same rhyme.

558. Site of Jarir's wife's sepulture; cf. *Naqaid Jarir*, loc. cit.

559. As the text (cited above) of Jarir insinuates, the deed was frequent. Farazdaq exploits it here, literally, "the dead woman and the two hyaenas were three in desert plain (and the land was deserted except for the three)." Cf. Akhtal, *Divan* (ed. Griffini) 17, 11. Yaqubi, *Hist.*, II, 200 bottom.

560. *Naqaid Jarir*, 871. Cf. *Aghani*, VII, 66, 2–10. At Medina, Jarir is equally afraid of reciting this elegy, he stops himself after having started it. Medina however guarded the purest spirit of Islam.

561. Tab., III, 2436 I.S. *Tabaq.*, VIII, 19–20; Maqdisi, *Geographie* (de Goeje), 46, 12–13; the same thing happened for the tombs of Uhud; Waqidi (Kremer), 302–303.

562. Cf. I.S. Tabaq., II 2, 24, 1.24, 1.25; 'Uthman *qarafa ahalahu*, went unto his wives when Umm Kulthum died.

563. Masudi, *Prairies, IV*, 161.

564. At once he ran to make the *baia* (the oath of allegiance taken on the hand of the caliph on his ascending the throne) to Abu Bakr; *As-sawaiq al-mohriqa* (ms. B.Kh., p. 14a). On his piteous attitude in this situation, see Tab, *Annales, I*, 1825–26.

565. Except perhaps when he sees himself abandoned by all his followers. Cf. Tab., *loc. cit.*

566. Perhaps he left it to Abbas to pray for Fatima (Tab., *Annales, I*, 1869). We can also suspect the Abbasids of having put their ancestor in front.

567. He was hoping for a reconciliation with Abu Bakr, according to Madaini; Baladhuri, *Ansab*, 384b, Ibn al-Athir, *Kamil* (Tornb.), II, 251.

568. Baladhuri, *Ansab* (ms. cit.), 404b.

569. Ibn Hajar, *Isaba, IV*, 724.

570. Same remark for Fatima, the daughter of Husayn, although born after the death of her grandmother, the daughter of the Prophet; Hanbal, VI, 282 bottom.

571. Cf. *Yazid*, 131; *Ziad ibn Abihi*, 84 and passim.

572. Nawawi, *Tahdib*, 851; Baladhuri, *Ansab*, 258a; only Yaqubi, *Hist.*, II, 253, 7 assigns *three* daughters to Fatima.

573. *Fima anta wa daka* ("how does that concern you?") is how Hasan spoke to 'Ali; Hanbal, I, 144 d.l.; Cf. Muslim, *Sahih²*, II, 52, 4, which should read *walla haraha man tawalla qarraha* ("he who takes pleasure in his privacy takes pleasure in his lands").

574. He is nicknamed the Greatest (cf. Hanbal, I, 158); they say he was born after the death of Muhammad; ibid., I, 95. We rarely see him as in *Iqd 4*, II, 212, appearing in the company of the two Hasans.

575. Tab., *Annales, I*, 2077, 9–10. His father had bequeathed his assets to Zubayr ibn al-Awwam as though he was not leaving behind any descendants. Cf. above. Meaning perhaps equally that he was appointing him his testamentory executor as Ibn Masud seems to have done for the same Zubayr; I.S. *Tabaq.*, III 1, 112–13.

576. See the review in I.S. *Tabaq., V*, 14. Umama is not named there but they speak of a *homonym*, a daughter of this Mugira (should one admit a confusion?); they claim that Mugira belonged to the *al Muhammad*, Muhammad's family; I.S. *Tabaq., VIII*, 26, 168–69. Ibn Abdalbarr, *Istiab*, 258, in fact a Companion; cf. Majmoua (Bib. Khed, ms. no. 349).

577. *Usd, V*, 400. According to the same compilation (loc. cit), apart from Fatima, none of Muhammad's daughter's left any descendants an infinitely probable statement!

578. Tab., I, 3473, nicknamed *Muhammad al awsat*, the middle Muhammad, *Khamis, I*, 310.

579. Cf. *Istiab*, 727. Not named in *Tabaq., V*, 14; *Aghani, XI*, 70 is about the son of this Mugira, but anonymous; Baladhuri, *Ansab*, 594a. Married to 'Ali, Umama, she did not give him any children; I.S. *Tabaq., VIII*, 169. Infertility, the general characteristic of the family, true or supposed! They wanted to dilute this conclusion in multiplying for better or for worse the ephemeral representatives of his lineage.

580. For the chronology of this period, see *Ziad ibn Abihi*, 75, 126–27.

581. Cf. *Osd*, V, 520; *Khamis*, I, 310.

582. Cf. *Yazid,* 139. Goldziher does not allow "the exclusion of the theocratic points of view of the early opponents of the Umayyad dynasty. It is not only the flight of the state funds that stimulate the supporters of Husayn. The enthusiasm for the *ahl al-bayt*, the Prophet's family, is not a secondary factor in the development of Islamic politics" (Letter of 4 June 1911). We should perhaps allow a distinction between the Sufyanid and the Marwanid periods. While they were alive the two Hasans did not excite much enthusiasm around them.

583. Cf. *Ziad ibn Abihi*, 48.

584. Tab., *Annales* II, 194, 14.

585. *Usd*, V, 469.

586. Cf. *Yazid*, 173.

587. Divorced (*banat minhu*), Baladhuri, *Ansab,* 258a, 413. She and her sister Zaynab acquired the epithet *kubra,* great, to distinguish them from other homonymous children of 'Ali; Tab., I, 3470.

588. It is a girl who has not arrived at puberty.

589. The sensual character of the old caliph 'Umar; he does not pay any heed to the prescribed daytime continence during Ramadan, to the point of scandalizing his circle, normally so liberal in these matters; Baladhuri, *Ansab,* 452a. I.S. *Tabaq.,* VIII, 339–40 avoids insisting on it; Tab., *Annales*, I, 2734 tries to play it down and invents a story to explain this unlikely marriage. 'Umar makes Umm Kulthum get used to a more modest style. Always the *zuhd* (asceticism) of the austere caliph Tab., *Annales*, I, 2717, 2720.

590. Cf. *Moawia*, 307–308; I. Abdalbarr, *Istiab*, 795; Tab., *Annales*, I, 2733.

591. And a daughter called Fatima or Ruqayya; I.S. *Tabaq.*, III 1, 190; VIII, 339–40.

592. Killed by a cock; cf. Jahiz, *Haiawan*, I, 189.

593. *Usd*, V, 613–15; she married Ibn Jafar ba'd Zaynab, after Zaynab, i.e., after the divorce of his sister Zaynab; Baladhuri, *Ansab*, 258a, 456a. Generally they deny (I.S. *Tabaq.*, loc. cit.) that after 'Umar she had any children; dead before 50 A.H. since her brother Hasan attended her funeral. After her divorce, obviously anterior to the latter date, her sister Zaynab did not remarry, since we see her again at Karbala. Among her husbands only Ibn Jafar is mentioned; I.S. *Tabaq.,* VIII, 341.

594. Muslim, *Sahih²*, II, 6, I cites a "Muhammad son of Fatima, daughter of the Prophet." The parallel Hadith (*Ibid.*, II, 5, 2 penultimate line) tells us that it concerns not the son of Fatima but a great grandson, Muhammad ibn 'Ali ibn Husayn, the latter the hero of Karbala.

595. Suggestive comparison. We should add the term *batul*, virgin, accorded to Fatima. That they were thinking of the Virgin Mary it would be foolish to deny; cf. Margoliouth, *Mohammed*, 451.

596. Bukhari, *Sahih* (Krehl), II, 446–47; *Istiab*, 171; *Usd*, V, 519; Hanbal, III, 135; VI, 282.

597. Cf. Istiab, 727, 728; Hanbal, I, 293, bottom.

598. *Usd,* V, 523; Ibn Hajar, *Isaba,* IV, 727–28 *Montakhab Kanz,* V, 96. Muhammad classes among the Mahdis the husband of Umm Salama, one of his wives; Hanbal, VI, 297, 6. One can detect in this Hadith an attempt to render less dangerous the theory of the Mahdi, by stretching the title. In Bukhari, *Sahih* (Kr.), II, 446, the Manaqib (virtues, outstanding traits) of Fatima are contained in four lines as opposed to the two pages accorded to those of Aisha.

599. The Prophet's line was broken except by Fatima. Ibn Hajar, *Isaba,* IV, 725; cf. Tab., I, 3347, 3.

600. The pious Ibn Sirin declared the great majority of the Hadith concerning 'Ali to be apocryphal: Everything they have said of 'Ali is a lie; Bukhari, *Sahih* (Krehl), II, 436, 4. For Fatima the situation is even more serious. How can one reconcile this fact with the tenderness for children, the intensity of family feelings, attested to in the Prophet by the Tradition? See, e.g., Muslim, *Sahih²,* II, 291–92. The same author (I, 8) severely judges the Hadith attributed to 'Ali; he agrees to allow one exception, for those transmitted by Ibn Masud, himself a lightweight authority! Ibn Masud is the grand man of Kufa (see vol. 6, *Tabaqat,* Ibn Sa'd); the school of this town used his name, and from there we get the importance that the school attaches to *halaqat ibn Masud,* the Ibn Masud Circle, the circle of which he would have formed the center (See *Ziad ibn Abihi,* 84). Just as for Umm Salama whose existence is prolonged after Karbala (see above), they make every effort to have him participate at the battle of Siffin (Muslim, *Sahih²,* I, 15 d.1., 16, I). A famous Shiite muhaddith, Jabir al Jufi—he was waiting for the apparition of 'Ali in the clouds—possessed 50 or even 70 thousand unpublished Hadiths. From this number he must have succeeded in subtracting 30 thousand. One can see on which murky sources the legend of 'Ali-Fatima fed itself; Muslim, op. cit., I, 12–30. Read the introduction of Muslim, I, 9–17 on the fabrication of false Hadith. A Zindiq (sceptic, infidel, dualist), condemned to death by the caliph Mahdi, said to him, "I fabricated 4,000 Hadith in favor of the Hashimites" (I declared the forbidden permissible, and I declared the permissible forbidden. The Prophet did not say a word of that); 'Ali ibn Sultan al-Qari, *Maudouat* (msc. Université de Beyrouth, pages unnumbered). In his *Maudouat* (ms. B.Khed., section Hadith, no. 488), Ibn al-Jawzi rises up against the Hadith "of the amulets of Hasan and Husayn, cooked up with the pens of the Angel Gabriel."

601. Cf. "Koran and Tradition," [chapter 4 of the present volume.—Trans.] where this thesis is developed.

602. The vagueness of these recollections leave a margin for interpretation. Thus the family of Banu-t-tahira was considered as issuing from a previous marriage of Khadija; I.S. *Tabaq.,* VIII, 8. Tahira obviously ought to apply to the first wife of the Prophet, as they had given the name Tahir, Mutahhar to several of his sons (see above).

603. Thus Sauda, the wife sent away by Muhammad for reasons of old age, accepted in order to get back into favor the job of maid for the children of Fatima; Qudai, *'Uyun al ma'arif* (ms. Omoumiya, Constantinople). "She was the nurse of the child of Fatima, peace be upon her. One can see the insinuation!

604. Thus they make the Prophet say, "If Fatima stole, I would have her hand cut

off"; Bukhari, *Sahih* (Krehl), II, 378.

605. During the period of pilgrimage, Fatima is used to establish the ritual situation of husbands; Muslim, *Sahih,* I, 469, 3, etc. 'Ali boasts of practicing the *muta* (temporary marriage for sex); Muslim, op. cit., I, 473, I. As the Prophet only accomplished one pilgrimage, that would be despite the presence of Fatima. They are looking to establish a confusion between the two *muta, mut'a al-nisa',* and *mut'a al-hajj*. Ibid., loc. cit.

606. Jahiz, *Haiawan,* I, 78.

607. See the index of *Moawia* under this name.

608. Jahiz, op. cit. I, 78. Cf. Goldziher, *M.S.* II, 295–305.

609. Margoliouth, *Mohammed,* 450, places her between the Agrippinas [1] wife of Emperor Tiberius, [2] wife of Germanicus, and [3] daughter of Germanicus) and the Elizabeths of history.

610. Thus they have it said to 'Ali that he was the true *Siddiq* (honest, righteous [saint], *Al Siddiq* being the epithet of Abu Bakr) they show him elevated by Muhammad to take away from Abu Bakr the privilege of being the first believer (Muslim), etc. As an example see the speech that Yaqubi attributes to him (*Hist,* II, 251); 'Ali there proclaims himself the gate of the depot; he is the Cavern, "the Noah's Arc," and outside him there was no salvation.

611. Analogous remark for 'Ali. "Did Muhammad die with his head on Aisha's or 'Ali's breast?" Two chapters of I.S. *Tabaq.,* II², 49–51, discuss the question important for the Alid wasiya. They made 'Ali pay the debts left by Muhammad, to make us understand that he was the *wasiy* (executor), accepting the assets and the liabilities of the inheritance; I.S. *Tabaq.,* II 2, 89, 7; his sons continued the same maneuver; ibid.

612. Baladhuri, *Ansab,* 749; a *"hu'ula' qawm ja'alu rasul Allah . . . suqan."*

613. They would tolerate even the Hadith where the caliph 'Umar insists on the jealousy and treachery of the Abbasids, because there they affirmed their belonging to the family of the Prophet, "whose hearts God has purified"; Tab., *Annales,* I, 2771. Our compilations are full of these accounts with a double meaning. Cf. Muslim, *Sahih²,* II, 71, 5, where Abbas throws back at 'Ali the epithet of traitor (al ghadir al-kha'in). Abbas refuses to pay the alms (*sadaqa*) in order to give the Prophet the opportunity to pay for him, and in this way attest his quality as a member of the family Muslim²,I, 363, 9.

614. The love of 'Ali, characteristic of faith; Muslim, *Sahih²,* I, 46. Numerous Hadith insist heavily on the presence of Abu Talib, the father of 'Ali, in hell: all go back to Abbas and his son Muslim, *Sahih²,* I, 103. The anecdotic commentary to the Koranic verses ("warn your near relatives") is used to affirm that after Fatima the Hashimites were the closest relatives of the Prophet; ibid., I, 101. Distrusting their greed, Abul Qasim forbade them to collect the alms (*sadaqa*). This refusal is presented as a consequence of their kinship with Muhammad; Muslim, *Sahih²,* I, 399.

615. While 'Ali would refuse to speak in his favor.

616. He defended the privileges of the Banu Mutallib in matters of watering and canals, and they were afraid that these two things would slip away from them, Baladhuri, *Ansab,* 699a.

617. "O, Uncle be happy with me." Baladhuri, *Ansab*, 701b; cf. *Fragmenta histor.arab.*, ed. de Goeje, "Hashim fathered 'Ali twice and Abd al-Muttalib twice fathered Hasan" (i.e., they were very attached to them). In Bukhari (Krehl), IV, 282, no. 3, it is Abbas who supports the complaints of Fatima addressed to Abu Bakr; both of them asked for their land at Fadak (*ardi hima*): the aim of the dual is to surreptitiously introduce the Abbasids into the *Ahl al-Bayt*, the Prophet's family and their share at Khaybar. The latter was not denied them, at least for the income. Under the Abbasids, the watchword is to glorify the Hashimites. Cf. Tab., *Annales*, I, 1825. Thus the bit quoted in Ibn Hisham, *Sira*, 88–89, nothing proves that in the context it relates to them. The verse 89, 4 (*gazzat*) has given birth to the legend of the sepulture of Hashim in Gazza; cf. 90, 1, where the tomb is placed in the desert (*bayna gazzat*). Cf. again Ibn Hisham, *Sira*, 55, 3–4; family of allied-priests, disputed ownership by the Hashimites to the descendants of Abu Talib. According to the testimony of Ibn Abbas, the contemporaries, above all the Qurayshites, questioned the right of their own next of kin to be included among the relatives of the Prophet, *dhu al-qurba*, Muslim, *Sahih*, II, 104, 6d. "We claimed that it was them but our people refused us that." This Hadith seemed too dangerous; they strove to give it another meaning and to limit the denials of the contemporaries to one-fifth of the booty; see loc. cit., II, 103–104.Muhammad took onto his camel Ibn Jafar and Hasan, but the Jafarid found himself in front, Muslim, op. cit., II, 332. All these Hadith are to the honor of the Hashimites. They made 'Ali repeat these words of Muhammad: "The hope of this nation is at the end of a hundred years," i.e., to announce the coming of the Abbasids; Hanbal, I, 93, 6.

618. It concerns perhaps the violent scenes like those narrated, Muslim, *Sahih* 2, II, 71.

619. Baladhuri, ms. cit. 669, 701, b; cf. I.S. *Tabaq.*, II 2, 39, 6 (with an entirely Abbasid *isnad*).

620. Cf. Baladhuri, ms. cit. 720, b., etc.

621. Here is why in the Hadith affirming that Usama ibn Zayd was the favorite of Muhammad, we often find this correction: "with the exception of Fatima"; I.S. *Tabaq.*, II 2, 42, 6.

Chapter 7

Matters of Fundamental Importance for Research into the Life of Muhammad

C. H. Becker

I n recent years Henri Lammens has pursued his research into the life of Muhammad with admirable acumen and has shown that current historiography has been too much beholden to the supposedly historical source material of the sira. He has the great merit of having once again alerted us to the defective historical basis of our apparently so detailed knowledge of the genesis of Islam. I have made brief comments on his work in the *Archiv fur Religionswissenschaft* [Journal of Religious Studies] (15:540ff);[1] meanwhile, a new comprehensive study has come from his indefatigable pen: "Fatima et les filles de Mahomet, Notes Critiques pour l'étude de la Sira" [Fatima and the Daughters of Mahomet: Critical Notes for a Study of the Sira] (Rome, 1912). This brilliantly written work gives me occasion to renew my earlier reservations (loc. cit.) about his evaluation of source material and to justify them in somewhat more detail.

The sira, with its often extensive depictions of detail, is not an independent historical source, but no more than Hadith-material put together biographically. The individual Hadith are either exegetical elaborations of hints in the Koran, or tendentious dogmatic—legalistic inventions of later times. The exegetical and dogmatic interest is older than the historical. This latter does not arise until historical sources, analogous to the Christian ones which authenticate the miraculous powers and divinity of Jesus, seem desirable also for the founder of Islam.

First published in *Der Islam*, Band 4 (1913): 263–69, under the title, "Matters of Principle Concerning Lammens' Sira Studies." Translated for this volume by G. A. Wells.

Traditions which are really historical are sparse in the extreme. And so recourse is made to hints in the Koran which are spun out. Above all, the already available dogmatic and legalistic Hadith are collected and put into chronological order. From all this there results the sira.

This is, in brief, Lammens's theory of the sira, and in these general terms it is acceptable. Tafsir, Hadith, and sira all contain one and the same source material, but arranged under different aspects in each case. So much is obvious and generally accepted. New, however, is above all Lammens's recognition that the sira resulted only as a product of tafsir and Hadith and did not constitute their source. Although I accept this thesis, I must point out that it tell us nothing about the real historical tradition. For even if the historical interest which led to the development of the Sira as a literary form arose only late, there is nevertheless a great deal of historical tradition preserved in the tafsir and in the Hadith-tradition which must (or at any rate can) be ancient. And so the question of the historical foundation of the origin of Islam amounts to the question of the historical value of the Hadith and the tafsir. In the case of the tafsir, a distinction must be made between:

(1) The items which are dogmatic in tendency and which intrude[2] interpretations. These are unhistorical.

(2) The items which are purely exegetical. When, for instance, allusions to the battles of Badr, Uhud, and so on, are found in certain passages, this surely shows that, beside the wording of the Koran, there was a historical tradition that tried to illustrate it. So there must have been some tradition free from all tendentiousness—although it was an oriental tradition which, like all ancient historical traditions, combined the real with the figurative.

The situation is the same in the Hadith. Admittedly, the greater part of the Hadith is tendentious invention, colored by the later image of Islam's golden period, and so historically useless. But there are also very numerous Hadith which exploit ancient items of news in dealing with later problems. They form the basis for a truly historical picture of the origins of Islam, and only historical instinct can sort them out from the whole. In consequence, the results achieved can always only be subjective. When the sceptic Lammens reaches very considerable positive results, we are in danger of taking this outcome of his scepticism for objective truth. But in the account that here follows, I am concerned to show that Lammens's results are purely subjective. Above all, it seems to me that his scepticism is insufficiently consistent, and is in abeyance whenever the sources seem to support his own postive theory. Great as Lammens is in his scepticism, I am unable to follow him in his positive historical construction. Let me give some illustrations from his latest book.

I preface the result of Lammens's research, namely: all that we know for certain of Fatima is that she was the Prophet's daughter, was married to 'Ali, and was the mother of the Prophet's grandchildren. The Medina tradition, grouped around Abu Bakr and 'Umar, completely minimizes Fatima in favor of Aisha. Not until the Iraqi school, with its admiration of 'Ali, is there any idealized portrait of Fatima, too, and she then becomes the model Islamic woman, whereas in the non-Shiite tradition she has few appealing features. Not until the time of the Abbasids does orthodoxy take up the idealized picture of 'Ali and Fatima with Abbas always appearing as their patron. While the glorification of Fatima is clearly traceable to Shiite circles and is thereby unhistorical, there is conversely no ground for regarding the disagreeable portrait of Fatima in the orthodox Hadith as unhistorical, unless it represents a reaction against exaggerations in the reverse direction (pp. 133–40) ["Fatima and the Daughters of Muhammad," pp. 378–82 of this volume]. I assent in the main to these contentions, and it would be nice if the whole book reflected the sober historical sense of its final chapter. But in the detailed sections, all the unfavorable features are accepted without more ado as historical, and one is somewhat astounded to hear from the book's final sentence that things were perhaps not quite like that. Unfavorable traits in the life of a holy person have admittedly some presumption of historicity. This is so, for example, with the prophets, although even here some reservations are appropriate. Those who are aware what a shibboleth the attitude to the battle of Siffin was throughout the whole Umayyad period, and those who have learned from Lammens about the forgeries of 'Ali's admirers, are those people who are going to believe without more ado that the opponents of 'Ali's party (who were after all the dominant groups) went about matters with complete historical objectivity when they made Fatima's role appear as slight as possible and endowed her with gracious features. The Arabs fought each other by insulting the mothers. As the daughter of the Prophet, Fatima was spared the worst; but what was more natural than the fact that her influence on him and her standing with him should be represented as minimal, her outward appearance as unimpressive, her marriage with the arch enemy 'Ali as unhappy, indeed as dishonorable. With these Hadith one could hit out at the Alids without denigrating the Prophet, who had always been concerned to preserve a tolerable relationship between the wayward daughter and the nonentity of a son-in-law. It should not be forgotten that 'Ali was being cursed from the pulpits at the time when most of the Hadith originated. How sensitive the Alids were to such often inoffensive seeming anecdotes is illustrated by Lammens himself (p. 18) with a signal example, from which he fails to draw the necessary conclusions. In this regard I am much more sceptical than the great sceptic Lammens. With all Hadith connected with 'Ali and his family, it is only the tendency they represent, not their content, that is historically valuable.

Lammens's point of departure is the undeniable fact that tradition has multiplied the number of the Prophet's children by taking supplementary names for proper names of other persons. Thus Ruqayya and Umm Kulthum are perhaps one and the same person (p. 3). Perhaps, too, the Prophet's sons are inventions; for from sura 108:3 it could not be allowed that Muhammad was abtar[3]—rather, it was the case that an abundance of children was a token of prophetic dignity. But whether the whole life-history, chronology, and endless details of the daughters who really existed—indeed the way they followed each other—are tendentious constructions seems to me more than doubtful. Lammens sees here cleverly constructed compositions. Certainly there is a good deal that is glossed over, but the contradictions are due in the main part to gaps in the knowledge which were filled out in different ways by different persons once interest in even the most insignificant members of the Prophet's family had been aroused. The historiography that followed later was lacking in critical sense. It took the information recorded by tradition and harmonized it.

With hostile traditions about Fatima's physical charms as his basis, Lammens draws a repulsive picture of this "wretched person" (A moins d'avoir, p. 17) ["Fatima and the Daughters of Muhammad," p. 228 of this volume]. Well, tears in plenty form a feature characteristic for a saintly life; and her slimness—as a contrast with the fullness of ideal beauty—is as likely to have been malicious invention rather than historical truth. Naturally Muhammad can find no husband for this attractive old maid and has to be satisfied with the fat-bellied, insignificant poor relative 'Ali. After the shibboleth of Siffin, one does not need to question Lammens further about this sketch.

In portraying this marriage, Lammens follows the method of an Ibn Ishaq or a Waqidi. He takes traditions that are quite typically tendentious and manufactures a historical portrait from them. It is really the same method as that employed by Islamic historiography—just read page 34 and following and compare the quotations and their context. The only difference is that the Islamic writers have an ideal picture, for which they collect evidence, whereas Lammens appears to take pleasure in portraying both the Prophet and those closest to him as contemptible as possible. Tradition supplies material enough for 'Ali-Fatima, but this material is even more terrible in its effects in the merciless way in which Lammens's masterly technique has grouped the individual items. Here the apparently objective historian has unconsciously become a dogmatic polemicist.

I say unconsciously, for Lammens wants to be objective, but chance had it that his natural and justified Christian feelings of opposition to Islam have found marvellous support from his scientific hypothesis. And who does not gladly take his own theory for historical truth, quite apart from subconscious religious influences? Lammens shows occasional awareness that hostile feelings are at work, but does not turn this awareness to account in his literary portaiture.

For Lammens all unfavorable features in the harem-life of the Prophet or of 'Ali constitutes history. But is it not strange that on the one hand all the most important facts in the life of the Prophet's family are shown up as inventions and distortions, while on the other hand the most intimate details from the Prophet's dealings with his women and from the lives of 'Ali and Fatima are taken as historical? I have the greatest doubts about the historicity of all these harem stories. If Lammens calls in question the reliability of the rafsir in regard to the major events of Islam, would not the innumerable events where no witnesses were present deserve greater scepticism? Aisha was undoubtedly a dangerous girl, but the sum total of indiscretions ascribed to her by the Hadith exceeds what is human. Here everything is tendentious. But tendentiousness is not all; it seems to me that the hints in the Koran have been amply supplemented with ordinary, common gossip from Medina. Arabs like erotic narrative. The Prophet will surely have taken care not to display the details of his marital life. There were upheavals— the Koran bears witness to them, but how decent and dark is the Koran here! Contemporaries may well have elaborated the rumors, and later writers the Koran's hints. In this way there originated the Hadith-al-ifk and similar narratives, which show clearly that what prompted them was in part delight in piquant tales and above all folk-tale humor, rather than religious tendentiousness, and certainly not conscientous historiography. All that does not amount to history.

Unfortunately, it is only historical acumen that can decide these instances, and to my sense Lammens confuses, on practically every page, the historical and the unhistorical Hadith, which we have initially sifted out. That was already apparent in the main thesis of his book, and is all the more discernible in the numerous individual accounts he includes in order attractively to illustrate the life of Muhammad and his fellows. Lammens paints Muhammad with the features familiar from the court life of the later Umayyads (pp. 63ff., especially 68ff.): on his throne like a king, around him a horde of chamberlains and guards. He himself dressed in purple, with the royal sceptre and so forth. Much of this is, in simplified forms, undoubtedly historical. But many of these traditions surely have merely the function of justifying the later practices of the Umayyads against the postulates of orthodox apostles of simplicity. I also regard the questions of toiletry as later problems, mostly freely invented. But as I have said, now and then a really historical report may be included, and my thesis is just as subjective as that of Lammens. I am concerned only to record that his is subjective. The difference in principle between the way the two of us evaluate the Hadith appears most strikingly if one compares Lammens's discussion of the garments and materials, depicting living creatures (pp. 74ff.), with what I have said in the Festschrift for Goldziher (*Zeitschr. f. Assyr.* 26:191 ff.).[4] To me all these Traditions appear to have been invented so as to serve, under pressure from Christian questioning in the later Umayyad period, as documentation for or against images. For Lammens they are historical documents showing that in the Prophet's household these precious materials were commonplace. I regard this as quite impossible. The later period wanted to know whether such materials might be utilized as carpets, as clothes, and how altogether they might be used—it follows that they must have been used in this way and not otherwise already in Medina, and the Hadith supplies the answer to all the questions. But all this tells us nothing about the real situation in the Prophet's house. The whole construct built on this is false.

Where Lammens builds up, our ways part in principle, and I think I have not overstated when I accuse him of a certain amount of inconsistency in applying his method. He sees tendentiousness and construction everywhere; only where all those who know the *fiqh* see palpable tendentiousness does he find valuable building stones for a positive construction. Although we must in this way repudiate his positive results, his negative criticism wins our unqualified assent. He has shaken our complacency and put the whole sira problem on a new basis.

Addendum as this volume goes to print: I envisage the origin of the Sira to have been as follows:

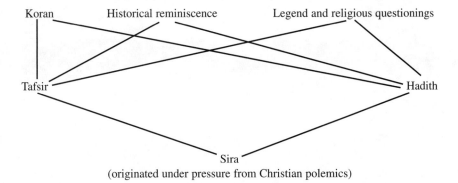

(originated under pressure from Christian polemics)

NOTES

1. The essay, "Qoran et Tradition, comment fut composee la vie de Mahomet," in Recherches de Science religieuse, Nr. 1 (1910) gives the best overview of his theory [chapter 4 in present volume.—Trans.].

2. [The original indeed says "intrude" and *not* "include."—Trans.]

3. [*Abtar* (from *batr*, meaning the cutting off of a thing) here means one from whom all good or prosperity is cut off, having no offspring or progeny.—Trans.]

4. Above [C. H. Becker, *Islam Studien* (Leipzig, 1924)], pp. 445ff.

PART FOUR

MODERN PERIOD

Chapter 8

The Quest of the Historical Muhammad

Arthur Jeffrey

I n 1906 there appeared in Germany an epoch-marking work on the life of Christ, entitled "Von Reimarus zu Wrede," by a young and till then almost unknown scholar, Albert Schweitzer, which in 1910 was translated into English by Montgomery under the title "The Quest of the Historical Jesus." Schweitzer's book was a very brilliant survey of the various types of "Lives of Christ," which had been produced by various schools of theological thought in Europe, ranging from the pious, orthodox, uncritical type, to the wildest excesses of eschatological and even mythical interpretation. His aim was to survey the various attempts that had been made to interpret the life of our Lord, and, if one may use the phrase, make an actuarial investigation of the position of scholarship on this question, and assess the value of the years of patient, critical research that had been devoted to its problems.

Quite recently it was suggested that the time was ripe for a similar survey on the life of the Arabian Prophet, that we may take stock of the work that has been done, gather up the assured results that have been won, and note the trends of critical scholarship indicating the lines of investigation that the future will have to follow. We may have long to wait for the rise of an Islamic scholar with the genius and scholarly preparation of a Schweitzer, to undertake this task, but we may endeavor with more or less success to briefly sketch the outlines of such an investigation.

Reprinted with the permission of *The Muslim World*, vol. 16: 327–48, copyright Harford Seminary, 1926.

SOURCES

Our first consideration is that of sources, and naturally we look to the Muslim literature, for Muslims themselves are likely to have been the first to write lives of their own Prophet. Here at first glance the student's heart might almost fail him before the bewildering array of Muslim lives of the Prophet, for there are literally hundreds of them in Arabic, Persian, Turkish, Urdu, Malay, and even in Chinese and lesser Eastern languages. The briefest investigation, however, suffices to reveal that the problem of sources is relatively simple, for all these hundreds of volumes represent but workings over with fabulous and irrelevant additions and modifications of perhaps half a dozen Arabic texts of primary importance.

The earliest Life of Muhammad of which we have any trace was written by Muhammad Ibn Ishaq, who died in 768 C.E., i.e., one hundred and thirty years after the death of the Prophet. The book of Ibn Ishaq, however, has perished, and all we know of it is what is quoted from it (and these quotations are fortunately considerable) in the works of later writers, particularly Ibn Hisham and al-Tabari. This work of Ibn Ishaq, in addition to being the earliest known attempt at biography, has a further importance in that, whether because the writer was somewhat of a free thinker, or because he had not come under the influence of later idealizing tendencies, his work contains very much information of a character that is distinctly unfavorable to the Prophet. To quote Dr. Margoliouth:

> The character attributed to Muhammad in the biography of Ibn Ishaq is exceedingly unfavorable. In order to gain his ends he recoils from no expedient, and he approves of similar unscrupulousness on the part of his adherents, when exercised in his interest. He profits to the utmost from the chivalry of the Meccans, but rarely requites it with the like. He organizes assassinations and wholesale massacres. His career as tyrant of Medina is that of a robber chief, whose political economy consists in securing and dividing plunder, the distribution of the latter being at times carried out on principles which fail to satisfy his followers's ideas of justice. He is himself an unbridled libertine and encourages the same passion in his followers. For whatever he does he is prepared to plead the express authorization of the deity. It is, however, impossible to find any doctrine which he is not prepared to abandon in order to secure a political end. At different points in his career he abandons the unity of God and his claim to the title of Prophet. This is a disagreeable picture for the founder of a religion, and it cannot be pleaded that it is a picture drawn by an enemy: and though Ibn Ishaq's name was for some reason held in low esteem by the classical traditionalists of

the third Islamic century, they make no attempt to discredit those portions of the biography which bear hardest on the character of their Prophet. (*Enyclopedia of Religion and Ethics*, volume 8, p. 878.)

Margoliouth also makes it a point in favor of this biography that it rarely has recourse to the supernatural, and even when the supernatural is introduced it does not appear to affect the causation.

The first important source that has actually come down to us, therefore, is Waqidi's *Kitab al-maghazi*, or *Book of the Wars*. Al-Waqidi died 822 C.E., and his book may best be consulted in the translation of the important parts of it given in Wellhausen's *Muhammed in Medina* (Berlin, 1882). Al-Waqidi's work, however, has the serious limitation that it deals only with Muhammad's campaigns. A little later are Ibn Hisham's *Sirat un-Nabi* (ed. Wüstenfeld, Göttingen, 1859, and trans-lated into crabbed German by Weil, *Das Leben Mohammeds*, 2 vols., Stuttgart, 1864), and Ibn Sa'd's *Kitab ul-Tabaqat ul-Kabir* (ed. by Edward Sachau, with the assistance of numerous other scholars, in nine volumes published between 1904–1921 at Leiden). Ibn Hisham died in 833 C.E., and Ibn Sa'd in 844 C.E. Later Arabic lives are of very secondary value as compared with these.

These works, however, are not primary sources, and are themselves based on two sources, Tradition and the Koran. The most important collections of Tradi-tion are those of Bukhari (who died in 870 C.E.), and Muslim (who died in 874 C.E.). What value can be placed on Tradition will be seen later; the important thing now to note is the dates of the collections, which are even later than those of the lives. The Koran, which was written down in approximately the form in which we have it within a generation of the death of Muhammad, will thus be seen to be our only primary source for the life of the Prophet. It will, of course, be evident to any one who has read the Koran, how very meager is the material it contains of a biographical nature. The importance of the evidence from this source was first worked out by Nöldeke in the first edition (1860) of his "Geschichte des Qorans," and may be studied in simple form in the summary made of it by Canon Sell in his *Historical Development of the Koran* (Madras, 1909) from a manuscript translation of Nöldeke's book made for him in India.

An excellent summary on the question of sources will be found in an article by Sachau given as Introduction to the third volume of the Leiden edition of Ibn Sa'd, or the older summary in the Introduction to Sir William Muir's *Life of Mahomet*.

EARLY CHRISTIAN ACCOUNTS

The earliest reference to Muhammad in Christian literature is apparently that in the Armenian "Chronicle of Sebeos," written in the seventh century, and which says little more than that he was an Ishmaelite, who claimed to be a Prophet and taught his fellow countrymen to return to the religion of Abraham. In the Byzantine writers we have little of any value, though it must be admitted that this source has not been thoroughly examined by Islamic scholars. Nicetas, of Byzantium, wrote a "Refutatio Mohammadis" (Migne *P. G.* cv), and Bartholomew, of Edessa, a treatise "Contra Mohammadem" (Migne *P. G.* civ), which may be taken as samples of this work, which grew out of the contact with Islamic power in the wars that robbed the Byzantine Empire of one after another of its fair Eastern Provinces.

The Latin writers of the Middle Ages got their information from two sources, from the Byzantine accounts and from the personal contact with Islam during the Crusades. It would be an interesting study to follow the development of the wild fables that spread abroad in Europe during this period, in which Muhammad comes to be one of the three great idols, Apollin, Tergavan, and Mahon, popularly supposed to be worshipped by Muslims. These legends crossed to England, and in the language of our forefathers the name Muhammad, in its corrupt form "mawmet," became the regular word for "idol." Thus in the "Legend of St. Andrew," we read:

> Wharto cums thou unto me
> Bot thou wald trow in Jesu fre,
> And leve thi *mawmetes* more and les
> And pray to Jesu of forgifnes.

And again in the "Life of Saint Juliana," written about 1200 C.E., we are told of the Emperor Maximinius of Rome that he was—"heinde and heriende hedhene mawmets with unmedh muchel hird and unduhti duhedhe." Among the ecclesiastical writers of the period, however, Muhammad was looked on as the arch heretic, a second Arius, worse than the first; and his legend was molded on that of the great legendary heretics, Simon Magus and the Deacon Nicholas. Renan points to the reason in his article in the *Atti della Academia dei Lincei*, for 1889, where he writes: "Dans les écrits populaires, il s'y joint d'atroces calomnies, destinées à couvrir d'ignominie l'auteur du grand mal que la chrétienté voulait a' tout prix supprimer" ["In popular writings, there have been added atrocious calumies designed to cover with ignominy the author of the great evil that Christianity wished to suppress at all

price"]. That there were noble exceptions, however, to this almost universal ignorance and misrepresentation can be seen from the cases of such men as Petrus Ven-
erabilis, who died in 1157, and the fragments of whose polemic have been published
by Thoma ("Zwei Bücher gegen den Muhammedanismus" [Two Books Against
Muhammadanism], Leipzig, 1896), and the Dominican monk Ricoldus, who died in
1320, and whose "Confutatio Alcorani," which so impressed Martin Luther, shows
an unusually accurate acquaintance with the subject.

PRE-CRITICAL PERIOD

After the Renaissance we find the question again attracting attention. Such works
as Raleigh's "Life and Death of Mohamet" (London, 1637), and Prideaux's "Vie
de Mahomet, ou l'on découvre amplement la verité de l'imposture" [The Life of
Mahomet, or Where One Abundantly Discovers the Truth of the Imposture]
(Amsterdam, 1698), are based on the Arabic material now being made available
in Latin translation but Hottinger's account of Muhammad's teaching in his "His-
toria Orientalis" (Zurich, 1651), and Marraccio's strictures which run through his
"Refutatio" (Padua, 1698) commence the tradition of relying on the original
sources themselves. Most of this early work is bitterly hostile and prejudiced,
though Hottinger had endeavored to give an impartial judgment. It is with the
Dutch scholar Reyland, however, that we enter on a new treatment of the subject.
In his "de Religione Mahommedica" (Utrecht, 1704), he seeks to break away
from the hostile attitude to Muhammad, and strive for a just appreciation of his
historical significance. His work, however, had the misfortune to be followed by
H. de Boulainvilliers' "Vie de Mahomed" (London, 1739), which was a bom-
bastic laudation of Muhammad in the interests of belittling Christianity. Hurgronje calls it "an anticlerical romance, the material of which was supplied by a
superficial knowledge of Islam drawn from secondary sources." A little of the tar
from Boulainvilliers' brush can be detected in Gibbon's account of Muhammad
in his "Decline and Fall" (London, 1776). It was in order to combat the distinctly
wrong impression produced by Boulainvilliers' work that Gagnier wrote his "Vie
de Mahomet" (Amsterdam, 1748), which strove to take the middle course
between Boulainvilliers on the one hand and Prideaux on the other. It was not
possible, however, to make further progress until more work was done at the
Arabic sources.

BEGINNINGS OF CRITICISM

It was the awakening of interest in Oriental studies at the beginning of the nine-teenth century that made possible a new departure in an attempt to do justice to the problem. The new period may be said to have begun with the work of Gustav Weil, whose "Muhammad der Prophet, sein Leben und seine Lehre" (Stuttgart, 1843) first applied in any real sense the historico-critical method to the problem of the life of Muhammad. Weil may not have got very far in this investigation, for his resources were still limited, but he found and applied the method, and in his translation of Ibn Hisham, in 1864, made yet a further great advance. Caussin de Perceval's "Essai sur l'Histoire des Arabes," 71 (3 vols., Paris, 1847), was apparently written quite independently of Weil, and contains an account of the life and work of Muhammad, which while not of any great value in itself, yet is of real importance for the mass of material from Arabic sources that it brings together. Wüstenfeld is another scholar in this period whose great contribution was not in his "Das Leben Muhammad's" (3 vols., Göttingen, 1857–1859), but in his excellent editions of early Arabic texts, and his masterly studies, such as his "Genealogische Tabellen der Arabischen Stamme und Familien" (Göttingen, 1852–1853), "Chroniken der Stadt Mekka" (4 vols., Leipzig, 1861), "Das Gebiet von Medina" (Göttingen, 1873), "Die Geschichtschreiber der Araber und Ihre Werke" (Göttingen, 1882), which have illumined so much of the early history. Much more important, however, is the work of Sprenger, Nöldeke, and Muir.

Sprenger's work will come under consideration in another section; we need only mention here that in addition to his very important "Leben Muhammads," he also, like Wüstenfeld, made important contributions to the study of the back-ground of the Prophet's life in his two studies "Die Post und Reiserouten des Ori-ents" (Leipzig, 1864), and "Die Alte Geographie Arabiens" (Bern, 1875). Nöldeke's great contribution was his essay "Geschichte des Qorans" (Göttingen, 1860), which really falls outside the scope of this essay, but which was the first critical attempt to evaluate the most important source for our reconstruction of the life of Muhammad. Nöldeke is by far the keenest and most cautious critic of this early period, and in general is very careful in his historical judgment. His "Das Leben Muhammads nach den Quellen popular dargestellt" (Hanover, 1863), is a much slighter and more popular work, which has now become almost forgotten. Muir's *Life of Mahomet*, which appeared in London in four volumes, between the years 1856–1861, is the crowning work of this first period of criti-cism. Sir William Muir had been long in the civil service in India, had an exten-sive acquaintance with Muhammadan literature in Arabic, Persian, and Urdu, and possessed a magnificent Oriental library. His work is based on a careful study of the best material available at the time, and is a very full and lucidly written account, remarkably free from prejudice on either side. In his introduction he gives a statement of the principles of criticism of the sources, which still repays reading, a subject which he again elaborates in an essay on "The Value of Early Mahometan Historical Sources," printed in his book *The Mohammedan Controversy* (London, 1897). Muir's work has been through many editions, the latest and most convenient being the one volume edition, edited by T. H. Weir (Edinburgh, 1912).

A number of smaller, popular works are largely based on the work of this period of the beginnings of criticism. Best known among such are Johnstone, "Muhammad and His Power" (Edinburgh, 1901); Sell, "Life of Mohammed" (Madras 1913); Wollaston, "Mohammed, His Life and Doctrines" (London, 1904); St. Hilaire, "Mohamet et le Coran" (Paris, 1865); Scholl, "L'Islam et son Fondateur: étude morale" (Paris, 1874); Delaporte, "Vie de Mahomet" (Paris, 1874); Albert Fua, "La Vie et la Morale de Mahomet" (Paris, 1912); Reiner, "Muhammad und der Islam" (Leipzig, 1905); Reckendorf, "Mohammed und die Seinen" (Leipzig, 1907); Krehl, "Das Leben des Muhammad" (Leipzig, 1884).

THE PATHOLOGICAL LIVES

European investigators could not fail to be struck with the statements found in the sources about the strange fits to which Muhammad was subject, especially at the time of his revelations.

> The notion . . . that he was subject to epilepsy finds curious confirmation in the notices recorded of his experiences during the proem of revelation—the importance of which is not lessened by the probability that the symptoms were often artificially produced. That process was attended by a fit of unconsciousness, accompanied (or preceded) at times by the sound of bells in the ears or the belief that someone was present: by a sense of fright, such as to make the patient burst out into perspiration: by the turning of the head to one side: by foaming at the mouth: by the reddening or whitening of the face: by a sense of headache. (Margoliouth, *Mohammed*, p. 46)

Not much has been made of these facts by Oriental writers, but Sprenger, who was a Doctor of Medicine of sorts, fastened on these evidences of epilepsy as the key to the solution of Muhammad's personality. He worked at this first in his

Indian book, "Life of Muhammad from Original Sources" (Allahabad, 1851), which is a meager sketch, stopping short at the Flight from Mecca, later in his monumental treatise, "Das Leben und die Lehre des Muhammads" (3 vols., Berlin, 1861–1865), and finally in "Mohammed und der Koran: eine Psychologische Studie" (Hamburg, 1889).

Sprenger's work in this direction is interesting rather than convincing, and has come in for much sharp criticism. Sir William Muir in an essay in the *Calcutta Review* for 1868 characterizes his work as "marked by a love of paradox and a tendency to strike out theories based on but slender grounds." Hirschfeld remarks, "he is surely mistaken in attributing a larger share in the creation of Islam to the state of his [Muhammad's] nerves than was really due to them. Hallucinations and hysterical frenzy are not factors strong enough to produce so general an upheaval as was caused by this new faith" ("New Researches," p. 20), and Hurgronje characterizes it as "an exaggerated display of certainty based upon his former medical studies" ("Mohammadenism," p. 42). He found followers, however, chief among whom is the veteran Semitic scholar of Copenhagen, Dr. Franz Buhl, who in his "Muhammed's Liv" (Copenhagen, 1903) puts forward a modified form of the same theory. Buhl makes much of the fact that it has been observed that hysterical natures find unusual difficulty and often complete inability to distinguish the false from the true. Such people, governed by compelling ideas, find it impossible to view things in their true light, and this he thinks is the safest way to interpret the strange inconsistencies in the life of the Prophet. A curious statement of this pathological view may also be found in the second essay "On the Hallucination of Mohammed," in a little work by one William Ireland, "The Clot on the Brain: Studies in History and Psychology" (New York, 1886).

A further development of this particular viewpoint is the psychoanalytic theory advocated by Dr. Macdonald, of Hartford, in his "Aspects of Islam" (New York, 1911), where he tells us that he looks for the future fruitful investigation of the Prophet's life to proceed upon the assumption that he was fundamentally a pathological case, and that "how he passed over at at last into that turpitude is a problem again for those who have made a study of how the most honest trance-mediums may at any time begin to cheat" (op. cit., p. 74)

A word further, before leaving this section, should be said about Sprenger's main work, the "Leben Mohammeds." Impatience with the theory should not lead the student to neglect this work, for it is one of the most stimulating of all the works we have on the life of Muhammad, and is a mine of material, gathered with great diligence and excellency set forth.

THE POLITICAL AND ECONOMIC LIVES

Quite a different starting point has been suggested to other scholars by the political and social conditions of Arabia in Muhammad's day. The social and political conditions of Arabia at the time of Muhammad's early manhood were bad. Arabia is none too fertile at the best of times, and just at this period practically all its fertile fringe was under domination of foreign powers—Byzantine, Persian, and Abyssinian—who were ever driving the Arab tribes further into their deserts. The contact with the civilization of these more progressive peoples had not been without its effect in making the needy Arabs turn longing eyes to the better things they had hitherto hardly dreamed of. The tribes themselves were restless and discontented, economic conditions were bad, and they were ready to rally round any banner that would give them the hope of national deliverance. It was Muhammad who held out the banner, and labored to weld them into a mighty national force that would secure Arabia for the Arabs.

Dr. Margoliouth's *Mohammed and the Rise of Islam* (London, 1905), probably the most brilliant study of the life of Muhammad that has yet appeared, is representative of this view, which may also be seen in the same author's articles on "Mohammed" in the *Encyclopedia Britannica* (11th ed.) and the *Encyclopedia of Religion and Ethics*, volume 8. According to this interpretation, Muhammad was a patriot, keenly alive to the opportunities of the time, who evolved a method of uniting the Arabs to face the common danger and utilize the golden opportunities of the age.

> A man who can organize an armed force and lead it to victory may rise from obscurity to autocracy anywhere. Probably every century of Islam had its tale of such personages. The 'Abbasid, Fatimid, Buwaihid, Seljuk, and Ottoman dynasties all arose in this way: and in most of these the religious appeal played an important part. The success of the founders was dearly due not to the objective truth of the doctrines with which they were associated, but to their skill as organizers and military leaders. . . . His (Muhammad's) ability to gauge the capacities of others was abnormal: hence in the choice of subordinates be seems to have made no mistakes. In the second place, he was thoroughly familiar with the foibles of the Arabs, and utilized them to the utmost advantage. The stories of his successes, as told by Ibn Ishaq, indicate a complete absence of moral scruple; but they also show a combination of patience, courage and caution; ability to seize opportunities, and distrust of loyalty when not backed by interest, which fully explain the certainty with which results were won. (*Encyclopedia of Religion and Ethics*, vol. 7, p. 873.)

At Medina, he was what one might justly call a robber chief, just as David, King of Israel, was in his early days. When he entered Mecca he entered it as a political leader rather than as a religious prophet, and was recognized by the Meccans as such. His dealings with Jews and Christians were largely dictated by political considerations: he dealt with the pagan tribes as a sovereign, and his whole attitude to the surrounding empires was that of a statesman. "The fact of primary importance in the rise of Islam is that the movement became considerable only when its originator was able to draw the sword and handle it successfully." So in endeavoring to estimate the significance of Muhammad, we must not judge him as a mystic or religious reformer, though he may have had elements of both, but rather as a statesman faced with peculiar pressing political problems among a somewhat barbarous people and at a critical moment in history.

A similar view is held by the Italian scholar Leone Caetani, though we are unfortunate in not having in our hands his complete picture of the Prophet. In the first and second volumes of his monumental "Annali dell' Islam" (Milan, 1905–1907), and in the third volume of his "Studi di Storia Orientale" (Milan, 1914), we have, however, the outlines of his treatment. Caetani holds that the great outburst, which sent Arab armies out in conquest of the surrounding fertile lands, is only the latest of a series of similar outbursts of Semitic peoples which in historical times have been disgorged by Arabia, due to the economic stress consequent on the gradual desiccation of Arabia. Muhammad thus becomes the leader of this movement, religious, if you will, according to the ideas of religion in Arabia at that time, but above all a politician and an opportunist.

> Si fatto carattere impulsivo associato con esimie qualita politiche di uomo di stato e di pastore di popoli rese Maometto uomo eminentemente opportunista, il quale animato da una cieca, immensa fiducia in se, si getto alla cieca nelle piu ardite imprese e si trascino appresso tutti i seguaci, inebbriati e sedotti dalla superiorita morale del Maestro. ("Annali," I. 205)

> [His impulsive character, combined with a rare political quality of a man of state and a guide of people, had made of Muhammad a supreme opportunist, animated by enormous self-confidence, enabling him to throw himself blindly and with rashness into an adventure in which he embroiled those who followed him, intoxicated and seduced by the superior morality of the Master.]

This view is also that of another great scholar, Dr. C. H. Becker, sometime editor of *Der Islam*, who writes in his "Islam and Christianity" (London, 1909, p. 29):

The Muhammadan fanatics of the wars of conquest, whose reputation was famous among later generations, felt but a very scanty interest in religion, and occasionally displayed an ignorance of its fundamental tenets which we can hardly exaggerate. The fact is fully consistent with the impulses to which the Arab migrations were due. These impulses were economic, and the new religion was nothing more than a party cry of unifying power, though there is no reason to suppose that it was not a real moral force in the life of Muhammad and his immediate contemporaries.

A curious development under this section is the economic theory of Professor Hubert Grimme. This writer has produced two interesting works on Muhammad. The first is his "Mohammed" (Munster, 1892), in which he seeks to explain the development of Islam as a socialistic phenomenon. After considering and rejecting Sprenger's theory that Hanifism was the original source of Islam, he points out that Islam can be more simply explained as a socialistic than as a religious system.

> The conditions under which we are accustomed, in history, to see socialistic movements appear, were existent in Mecca at the time of Muhammad. Conditions of opposition in the social organism had matured to that point where a rupture was imminent. A wealthy class, who had all the power in their hands, stood over against a numerous propertyless class who were suffering the pressure of a merciless usurious administration. Against the former class the Koran hurls its richly deserved accusations of the unhealthiness of their great possessions, their deceit, use of false weights and measures, foolish waste of their substance on the one hand, and continuous niggardly accumulation on the other, and lastly their discontent even in the face of their abundance. On the other hand, it is painfully evident how the needy hunger, the beggar is refused alms, orphans are kept out of their inheritance, and slaves strive in vain for liberty and manumission. It was in order to put an end to such adverse conditions that, under the aspect of compensatory justice, Muhammad, who in his youth had himself tasted the bitter loss of poor orphans (though later be became one of the propertied class), laid down strict legislation that every man should pay a settled assessment for the support of the needy. In this way an equality would be established in a peaceful way, wholly different from all other socialistic endeavors of antiquity, which always manifested a strong tendency to forcible alterations of social relationships.

Such a venturesome thesis was hardly likely to find acceptation, and on its appearance was keenly criticized, particularly by Prof. Snouck Hurgronje in *Revue de l'Historie des Religions*, volume 30, pp. 48 ff. who remarks both on the inaccuracy of Grimme's work, showing the limitations of his scholarship, and also on the uncertainty of the foundations on which his theory is built. Professor Grimme, unfortunately, has a reputation for wild theories, as witness his recent identification of certain weather markings (as Petrie calls them) on some stones from Sinai, as the very handwriting of Moses; and even if his theory had a sounder basis, it is hardly likely that the socialistic motive could be an explanation of all the facts to be considered.

ADVANCED CRITICISM

We have already had occasion to notice that besides the Koran and the early "Lives" of Ibn Ishaq and Ibn Hisham, etc., an important source for the life of Muhammad is Tradition. In fact we find that the early "Lives" are themselves largely based on Tradition, and in the period from Weil to Muir European writers went on the assumption that if a certain amount of careful sifting were done, a considerable body of reliable Tradition could be found on which reliance could be placed for biographical purposes. It was Ignaz Goldziher in his "Muhammedanische Studien" (Halle, 1889, 1890), especially the second volume, who gave the first rude shock to this assumption. Even after the most careful sifting we find that the oldest traditions only take us back to the first century after Muhammad, and very much of this oldest tradition is of very uncertain character, having been colored by theological bias, mixed with legendary material, and warped to favor the interests of certain families and political parties.

It might have been thought that careful criticism could still manage to find some sure basis, but the development of Goldziher's work at the hands of Caetani, and Henri Lammens would seem to force us to the conclusion that:

> Even the data which had been pretty generally regarded as objective, rest chiefly upon tendentious fiction. The generations that worked at the biography of the Prophet were too far removed from his time to have true data or notions; and, moreover, it was not their aim to know the past as it was, but to construct a picture of it as it ought to have been, according to their opinion. Upon the bare canvas of verses of the Koran that need explanation, the traditionists have embroidered with great boldness scenes suitable to the desires or ideals of their particular group: or to use a favorite metaphor of Lammens, they fill the empty spaces by a process of stereotyping which permits the critical observer to recognize the origin of each picture. (Hurgronje, "Muhammadanism," pp. 23, 24)

Caetani's work we have already referred to. Lammens has not yet given us his "Life," which should be epoch-making when it appears. He has contented himself so far with publishing a number of preliminary studies, which he calls "Sira-studies," working out his method, sifting his material, and as one might say, clearing the ground on which he is to build. "Notre procédé," he writes, "sera donc plus monographique que biographique. L'ensemble—si nous devons en voir la fin—formera une nouvelle Vie de Mahomet" ["Our method will be more monographic than biographic. The whole—if we ever see the end of it—will form a new life of Muhammad"] ("Le Berceau de l'Islam," p. vi). Perhaps the best introduction to his work is his essay "Koran et Tradition: comment fut composée la vie de Mahomet" [Koran and Tradition: How the Life of Muhammad was Composed] (Paris, 1910), where he shows how over and over again the traditions are simply elaborations of some phrase or word in the Koran and have no independent authority, and, of course, cannot be used as independent sources for biographical purposes. In 1911 appeared a further study, "L'Age de Mahomet et la Chronologie de la Sira" [The Age of Muhammad and the Chronology of the Sira], in the *Journal Asiatique*, and the following year the very important study, "Fatima et les Filles de Mahomet" (Rome, 1912). In this work he takes up the legend of Fatima in the Muslim writings, and shows in detail how out of the family conflicts and jealousies and the conflicting movements of opinion in early Islam there gradually evolved this detailed biography of Fatima, which is a conglomeration of heterogeneous elements mostly apocryphal and frequently contradictory. But this is only the stepping stone to a further conclusion:

> The same method and analogous principles governed the secular elaboration of the Sira. Around a nucleus, provided by interpretation of the Koran, have come to be superimposed inconsistent political theories with theocratic dreams, opinions of schools of theology and law, with the tendencies of ascetic circles and the aspirations of Sufiism.

So that as Goldziher observed ("Vorlesungen," p. 20): "It is not the historical picture whose influence the Faithful feel. In its place was early substituted pious legend, with its ideal Muhammad."

Further important studies of Lammens are "Mahomet fut il sincère?" [Was Muhammad sincere?] (Paris, 1914): "La République marchandise de la Mecque vers l'an 600 de notre ère" [The Merchant Republic of Mecca around the Year 600 C. E.] (Alexandria, 1910); "Le Triumvirat Abou Bakr, Omar et Abou 'Obaida" [The Triumvirate of Abu Bakr, 'Umar, and Abu Ubayda] (Beirut, 1909); "Le Califat de Yezid I" [The Caliphate of Yazid I] (Beirut, 1921); and "La cité arabe de Taif" [The Arab City of Taif] (Beirut, 1922). The student should also consult an article by Dr. Becker in *Der Islam*, vol. 4, 263–69 on "Prinzipielles zu Lammens' Sirastudien."

The dominant note in this advanced criticism is "back to the Koran." As a basis for critical biography the Traditions are practically worthless (Hurgronje, op cit, pp. 25, 26; Goldziher in "Kultur der Gegenwart" I. iiii, p. 100 seq; and *ZDMG*, 1907; Caetani, I, 197; Lammens, "Berceau, 17 p. vi; "Fatima, 97 p. 139; Nöldeke, *ZDMG*, vol. lii, *WZKM*, xxi, p. 298); in the Koran alone can we be said to have firm ground under our feet. As Snouck Hurgronje, who takes his stand with these advanced critics, puts it ("Mohammedanism," p. 24):

> While it may be true that the latest judges have here and there examined the Muhammadan traditions too skeptically and too suspiciously: nevertheless it remains certain that in the light of their research, the method of examination cannot remain unchanged. We must endeavor to make our explanations of the Koran independent of tradition, and in respect to portions where this is impossible, we must be suspicious of explanations, however plausible.

If the Koran is to be our primary foundation, the next question is to ascertain how firm ground it provides. It has usually been assumed that we were safe here at least, but recent work, such as that of Casanova and Mingana, has raised serious doubts as to the trustworthiness of even this source, but that is too big a question to enter upon at present.

MYTHOLOGY

It has already been noticed how soon the picture of the historical Muhammad was replaced by an ideal and legendary picture. Samples of such exalted pictures of Muhammad can be seen in the "Hyat ul-Qulub" (tr. Merrick, Boston, 1850), and in the "Borda du Cheikh el Bousiri, poème en l'honneur du Mahomet" (tr. by Basset, with Commentary. Paris, 1894). It is curious to note that Christian influence was apparently at the root of this legendary development (Becker "Christianity and Islam," p. 62), and it was natural that scholars should seek to trace the process of the development of this picture, which is the only one known to the vast majority of Muslims at the present day. Koelle, in the second part of his "Mohammed and Mohammedanism" (London, 1889), gave a popular account of the main lines of legendary development, but for a critical study of the problem the student needs to commence with an essay by Mez on "Die

Geschichte der Wunder Muhammeds" in the *Verhandlungen* of the second Congress on the History of Religion (Basle, 1905), and one by Horovitz "Zur Muhammadlegende," in *Der Islam*, vol. iv. The great work on this phase of the subject, however, is that of Tor Andrae, "Die Person Muhammads in Lehre und Glauben Seines Gemeinde" (Stockholm, 1918). An outline of his method was given in his essay "Die Legenden von der Berufung Muhammads," in *Le Monde Orientale*, vol. vi, but in the larger book he works out in detail the development and ramifications of the Prophet-legend, and shows its parallels in the divine-man conceptions of Zoroastrian and Hellenistic religious thought.

ESCHATOLOGICAL LIVES

It has frequently been pointed out that eschatology forms perhaps the dominating interest in the Koran. One cannot read many pages without coming upon something referring to the future joys of believers in Paradise or the sufferings of unbelievers in Hell, or threats of the awful judgment of God to be meted out to unbelievers. The thing seems to have been an obsession with Muhammad. Dr. Macdonald points out:

> The conception haunted Muhammad, that there was coming a Day of Doom when all must be judged, and that at that Day of Doom there would rule and judge—Allah. Few would be saved then.
>
> For Muhammad, then, this sense of evil was overwhelming. The invisible world, the awful thing lying behind this world that we look out upon, which conditions it and works in and through it, was dreadfully near. At every, turn he felt what has been so well put as "a sense of the wrath to come." (*Aspects*, pp. 70, 62)

Certain modern writers, e. g., Casanova and Horovitz, have seen in this the key to the problem of Muhammad's personality. No actual Life of Muhammad has been written from this point of view, but it has been used to attack many individual problems, particularly those arising in attempts at Koranic exegesis. The position is set forth by Casanova in his study "Mohammed et la Fin du Monde" (Paris, 1911–1921). The secret of Muhammad's mission he claims is found in the fact that his fundamental doctrine was that "the times announced by Daniel and Jesus had arrived: Muhammad was the last Prophet chosen by God to preside, conjointly with the Messiah who was to return to earth for this purpose, at the end of the world and the final judgment" (op. cit., p. 8). He firmly believed and taught that his coming, and the end of the world were causally connected and he must see the final dissolution before he died. When death overtook him, and he felt himself passing away, he was in dreadful distress, and it is well known that his more immediate followers refused at first to believe the news of his death. Casanova thinks that some of the curious phenomena of the Koran can be explained by the fact that the revelations had to be re-edited to square with the fact that he had died, and that many things in early Islamic development theologically and otherwise go back to this same point.

APOLOGETIC LIVES

We have already noticed that quite early in the revival of interest in Oriental studies, Boulainvilliers wrote a laudatory account of Muhammad, which was later used by Gibbon. His work was not based on any accurate firsthand study of the sources, and the same is true of two other famous apologies, namely, those of Carlyle, in his essay, "The Hero as Prophet," in "Heroes and HeroWorship," and Bosworth Smith, "Mohammed and Mohammedanism" (London, 1873, 3d ed. revised and enlarged, 1889). Carlyle's essay is reprinted and widely circulated by the modern Muslim school in India, as representing England's best thought on Muhammad, but they forget to mention that Carlyle takes back practically all his fine words in the essay on "The Hero as Poet."

It was to be expected that the leaders of the English-educated modernist school in Islam would be diligent in producing such apologies. Both leaders of the Aligarh school in India have written apologetic lives from their peculiar point of view. Syed Ahmad Khan in his "Essays on the Life of Muhammad and Subjects Subsidiary Thereto" (Aligarh, 1870), and Syed Ameer Ali in his "Life and Teachings of Muhammad," which was first issued in 1873, and later as the first part of his "Spirit of Islam" (last edition, London, 1923). Dr. Margoliouth's judgment on this school applies with particular aptness to Ameer Ali's work:

> These apologists endeavor to discredit the biography of Ibn Ishaq where it shocks the European reader, and where this cannot easily be done, they suggest honorable motives, or suppose the course followed by the Prophet to have been the least objectionable of those that were open to him at the time. Thus his toleration of polygamy is declared to have been a limitation with the view of ultimate suppression, and his attitude toward slavery is regarded as similarly intended to lead to its abolition. He has even been made to set an example of monogamy, but the ingenuity required for this is so great that the result is unconvincing. (*Encyclopedia of Religion and Ethics*, volume 8, p. 878)

An example of an attempt emanating from a different school will be found in M. H. Kidwai's "The Miracle of Mohammed, preceded by an Outline of Mohammed's Life" (London, 1906); but far more interesting is a more recent work from yet another modernist group, in the sumptuous volume produced by the Paris Book Club, limited to one thousand sets, 125 on Imperial Japanese Vellum at £18 per copy, and 875 on handmade paper at £8 per copy. This work is in large quarto with thirty-five magnificent colored plates and numerous ornamental decorations, and is entitled "The Life of Mohammed, the Prophet of Allah" (Paris, 1920). It is the joint production of the French artist, E. Dinet, and one Sliman ben Ibrahim, and is intended as a "counterblast to the many slanderous, vituperative lives of Muhammad that have appeared in European lands during the course of centuries." The same authors have produced also a little brochure "L'Orient vu de l'Occident" (Paris, 1921), indulging in vigorous but quite harmless criticism of the work of Lammens, Casanova, Hurgronje, and other scholars of the advanced critical school.

Mysticism

A more recent attempt to work out a new principle of interpretation for the life of Muhammad is that of Professor J. C. Archer in a monograph published in the Yale Oriental Series, and entitled, "Mystical Elements in Muhammad" (New Haven, 1924). This writer commences by a vigorous criticism of the pathological theory, and while admitting that there may have been pathological elements in his life, insists that the essential thing in his experience was that he was a mystic, so his book is to prove that "Muhammad the mystic is a greater figure than we had dreamed." "Muhammad," he claims, "was a mystic in the technical sense, and that, too, not merely in mental attitude, but in habitual practice." But when we look for his evidence for this amazing statement, all we find is a very strained interpretation of a very few Koranic texts, most of which are unfortunately suspect, and a very precarious theory of the influence of Christian ascetics on the early life of the Prophet. The theory is based almost entirely on the Koran, and modern research ought surely to have made clear that the Koran can hardly be taken at face value for attempts at psychological interpretation. Moreover, as Massignon has pointed out (*R. M. M.* lix, 337)— "on peut affirmer que plusieurs des versets qui ont une portée mystique pour certains lecteurs, ont pu n'avoir pour Muhammad que l'academisme d'une citation" ["We can assert that several verses which have a mystical connotation for certain readers can only have had the banality of a quotation for Muhammad"].

The most recent attempt at providing us with a point of view for the interpretation of Muhammad's life and teaching is that in Richard Bell's Gunning Lectures before the University of Edinburgh, "The Origin of Islam in its Christian Environment" (London, 1926). Bell's work is only a preliminary study; he bases himself entirely on the Koran, taking no account of Tradition or Sira, and he thinks that from the Koran itself we can find the main principles which will later guide us through the maze of Tradition. Bell thinks the clue to the problem is in the fact that a little before the coming of Muhammad Arabia had become permeated with new ideas of religion, partly from Jewish, but mostly from Christian sources, working into Arabia from three directions, downward from Syria to the northwest from Mesopotamia to the northeast and upwards from Abyssinia through South Arabia. One proof of this is that almost all his religious vocabulary is borrowed from either Ethiopic or Syriac, even Jewish terms and practically all Persian religious terms coming through the Syriac. Thus Allah, Koran, Furqan, Salawat, Jahannam, Janna, Firdaus, Zakat, Din, etc., are all words of this origin, and the great figures that move through the Koran—Ibrahim, Junus, Musa, 'Isa, Idris are all of Syriac origin.

Muhammad was in contact with this new world of religious ideas, at first only in so far as it had become Arabicised before his time, but later with Jewish and Christian sources themselves, and Bell claims that in the Koran itself we can see him gradually acquiring more and more information about these religions, particularly about Christianity, and developing his own teaching *pari passu* with his increasing knowledge. Thus in the early Suras we find his religious vocabulary confined to that which can be illustrated from the early poets; words, i.e., that had been naturalized in Arabic before he came. In this early period we find very little about the Prophets or the cult of the great religions. Later he learns and uses new religious terms borrowed from Christian and Jewish sources, and begins to talk about the Prophets. At this time he apparently did not know that Jews and Christians were not one people. Later he does find this out and his language changes immediately. So Bell would interpret him not as a mystic, nor an apoplectic, nor a pathological case of any kind. A politician, yes, but of a religious nature, who was grieved at the lack of religion among his people, and conceived his mission to be to give to the Arabs such a message as the Prophets had given to the great nations surrounding them.

This certainly provides us with a promising starting point, one that seems better than any so far suggested to fit the facts that appear from the Koran, and it may be that the application of Bell's suggestion may provide us with the clue for getting back, at least as far as we can expect, in our quest for the historical Muhammad.

The conclusion from this brief survey would seem to be that we have perhaps yet to wait for further research to be done among the early sources and for further discussion to allow a certain crystallizing of opinion as to where sound foundations can be laid, before anything much can be attempted further at biographical reconstruction. It is worthy of note, however, that the scholars who are most familiar with Arabic sources and have got closest to an understanding of the life of the period, scholars such as Margoliouth, Hurgronje, Lammens, Caetani, are the most decisive against the prophetic claims of Muhammad; and one must confess that the further one goes in one's own study of the sources the more difficult it becomes in one's own thinking to escape the conclusions of these scholars.

Chapter 9

A Revaluation of Islamic Traditions[1]

Joseph Schacht

I should like to present some ideas on what, I think, is a necessary revaluation of Islamic traditions in the light of our present knowledge; but am at a loss whether to call my conclusions something new and unprecedented, or something old and well known. No one could have been more surprised than I was by the results which the evidence of the texts has forced upon me during the last ten years or so; but looking back I cannot see what other result could possibly be consistent with the very foundations of our historical and critical study of the first two or three centuries of Islam. One of these foundations, I may take it for granted, is Goldziher's discovery that the traditions from the Prophet and from his Companions do not contain more or less authentic information on the earliest period of Islam to which they claim to belong, but reflect opinions held during the first two and a half centuries after the Hijra.

This fundamental discovery, as I scarcely need emphasize, put our study of early Islam for the first time on a sound basis, and I know of no serious contribution to the history of early Islam in any of its aspects, which does not take this character of Islamic traditions into account. But whilst general homage has continued to be paid to the work of Goldziher,[2] his results have gradually been whittled down and their implications neglected in the sixty years since they were first published. Historical intuition, as it was sometimes called, began to take the

Originally published in the *Journal of the Royal Asiatic Society* (1949): 143–54. Reprinted by permission of the Royal Asiatic Society.

place of sound historical criticism.[3] This lowering of standards need not surprise us. It is only natural for a historian to wish to arrive at positive conclusions, and I agree whole heartedly that it is not satisfactory to regard the collections of Islamic traditions as a mass of contradictory views formulated at uncertain times by unknown persons.[4] This, however, is a caricature rather than a definition of what follows from Goldziher's discovery, and I propose to show a workable and, I think, a successful alternative to the counsel of despair which, finding no guiding thread through the mass of traditions, tries by arbitrary guesswork to build a seemingly historical picture of certain aspects of early Islam.

I elaborated my method while studying the origins of Muhammadan jurisprudence.[5] Law is a particularly good subject on which to develop and test a method which claims to provide objective criteria for a critical approach to Islamic traditions, and that for two reasons. Firstly, our literary sources carry us back in law farther than, say, in history, and for the crucial second century they are much more abundant on law than on any other subject. Secondly, our judgment on the formal and abstract problems of law and legal science is less likely to be distorted by preconceived ideas (those expressed in our sources as well as our own), than if we had to judge directly on issues of political and religious history of Islam.

For instance, the analysis of technical legal problems shows that the doctrine of the Medinese often lags behind and is dependent on that of the Iraqians; our sources show that the term "Sunna of the Prophet" is early Iraqian and not Medinese; and the whole concept of Medina as the true home of the Sunna turns out to be a fiction of the early third century and as yet unknown at the end of the second. This direct evidence of our sources enables us to draw conclusions which we could not draw with anything like the same certainty if we had to apply our historical intuition or personal prejudice to the historical tradition which is notoriously weighted in favor of Medina and against the Umayyads. I shall later have occasion to mention another group of examples, in which the evidence of legal traditions is of even greater material importance for the correct appreciation of the Umayyad period.

Let us consider the broad outlines of the reasoning by which we can arrive at the new approach to Islamic traditions which I have in mind. Volume VII of the printed edition of Shafi'i's *Kitab al-Umm*[6] contains several treatises in which Shafi'i discusses the doctrines of his predecessors: Iraqians, Medinese, and Syrians. Widely as these ancient schools of law differ amongst themselves, they are agreed on one essential point, which divides them sharply from Shafi'i. According to the ancient schools, traditions from the Prophet as such do not as yet possess an overriding authority; only Shafi'i, obviously under the influence of the pressure group of traditionists, upholds consistently the doctrine that when there exists a tradition from the Prophet, no other argument is valid. Shaf'i's work is full of monotonous repetitions of this essential doctrine of his, and it is clear that this doctrine was a startling innovation in his time.

It is certain, too, that the great mass of legal traditions which invoke the authority of the Prophet, originated in the time of Shafi'i and later; we can observe this directly by following the successive stages of legal discussion and the ever-increasing number of relevant traditions incorporating gradual refinements. It can further be shown that legal traditions from the Prophet began to appear, approximately, in the second quarter of the second century A.H. This explains why the doctrine of Medina as established by Malik in his *Muwatta'*, disagrees often with traditions from the Prophet with Medinese isnads, related by Malik himself. These traditions sometimes express Iraqian doctrines and for this reason alone cannot represent the old Arab customary law of Medina as has been pretended.[7] They had gained currency in Medina immediately before Malik and are the result of the activity of a pressure group of traditionists, whose alms were the same as those of a corresponding group in Iraq, each group in sometimes successful and sometimes unsuccessful opposition to its local school of law.

This is the first consideration; the second is as follows. In the course of his polemics against the ancient schools of law, Shafi'i continuously reproaches them for relying on traditions from persons other than the Prophet, from his Companions and their Successors, rather than on traditions from the Prophet himself. This is borne out by the evidence of the texts. Malik's *Muwatta'* contains 822 traditions from the Prophet as against 898 from others, that is 613 from Companions and 285 from Successors. Shaibani's edition of the *Muwatta'* contains 429 traditions from the Prophet as against 750 from others, that is 628 from Companions, 112 from Successors, and 10 from later authorities. The *Kitab al-Athar* of Abu Yusuf[8] contains 189 traditions from the Prophet, 372 from Companions, 549 from Successors. In the incomplete text of the *Kitab al-Athar* of Shaibani[9] We find 131 traditions from the Prophet, 284 from Companions, 550 from Successors, and 6 from later authorities. It cannot be doubted that the stage of referring to the teaching and the example of the Prophet was preceded by, and grew out of, an earlier stage in which reference was made to Companions (and Successors) only. It is not the case, is has often been supposed a priori, that it was the most natural thing, from the first generation after the Prophet onward, to refer to his real or alleged rulings in all doubtful cases.[10]

The reference to Companions, as customary in the ancient schools of law, was not even of the same kind as the later reference to traditions from the Prophet, when a separate precedent was demanded for every individual decision.

Instead of relying on individual traditions from Companions, the several schools adopted rather one or the other Companion as their eponym, or I might say patron saint, putting their doctrine as a whole under his aegis and referring to him as their authority in general terms. In the case of the Kufians, for whom Ibn Masʿud fills this role, we can still see clearly that the general reference to Ibn Masʿud himself grew out of a similar reference to the Companions of Ibn Masʿud as the alleged founders of the Kufian doctrine, and most of the members of this group who are mentioned by name, turn out to be relatives of the Kufian Successor, Ibrahim Nakhaʿi, who died in A.H. 95 or 96, and to whom most of the earliest Kufian doctrine was attributed in the first place. In other words: even the general reference to Companions (or to Successors), a stage which preceded the technical and formal reference to individual traditions from the Prophet, dates only from about the year A.H. 100.

We must therefore abandon the gratuitous assumptions that there existed originally an authentic core of information going back to the time of the Prophet, that spurious and tendentious additions were made to it in every succeeding generation, that many of these were eliminated by the criticism of isnads as practised by the Muhammadan scholars, that other spurious traditions escaped rejection, but that the genuine core was not completely overlaid by later accretions. If we shed these prejudices we become free to consider the Islamic traditions objectively in their historical context, within the framework of the development of the problems to which they refer, and this enables us to find a number of criteria for establishing the relative and even the absolute chronology of a great many traditions. We find these criteria both in the text and in the isnad of traditions, and I should like to mention some of the more obvious conclusions.

One of these is that isnads have a tendency to grow backwards, that after going back to, say, a Successor to begin with, they are subsequently often carried back to a Companion and finally to the Prophet himself;[11] in general we can say: the more perfect the isnad, the later the tradition. Whenever traditions claim an additional guarantee by presenting themselves as transmitted amongst members of one family, e.g., from father to son and grandson, from aunt to nephew, or from master to freedman, it can be positively shown that these family isnads are not a primary indication of authenticity, but only a device for securing its appearance.[12] In other words: the existence of a family isnad, contrary to what it pretends, is a positive indication that the tradition in question is not authentic. This applies, for instance, to the legal and historical traditions related, according to their isnads, on the authority of ʿUrwa b. Zubayr by his son Hisham, and on the authority of Ibn ʿUmar either by his son Salim or by his freedman Nafiʿ. I do not deny, of course, that ʿUrwa was the father of Hisham, or Ibn ʿUmar the father of

Salim, or that a person called Nafi' was a freedman of Ibn 'Umar. But it is certain that neither 'Urwa nor Ibn 'Umar had anything do to with the traditions in question, and it can even be positively shown that the references to Hisham, Salim, and Nafi' themselves are spurious.

Our new approach to traditions disposes of the fictitious reputation as forgers acquired by some Companions of the Prophet. I mentioned how the natural desire to push back the frontiers of the unknown, caused some scholars after Goldziher to presume the authenticity of more and more traditions until they found themselves back in the generation of the Companions, in the thirty years after the death of the Prophet. From making the last step into the time of the Prophet himself, they were prevented by the influence of Goldziher's achievement and by their own critical sense. But then they had to credit the Companions of the Prophet, during the first thirty years or so after the death of their master, with the large-scale fabrication of spurious and contradictory information about him. This opinion seemed to gain credence from the fact that some groups of traditions which go under the name of individual Companions, show indeed common features, and from these features the alleged characteristics and tendencies of the personalities and doctrines of particular Companions were deduced.[13] The common characteristics and tendencies, however, are not those of the Companions themselves but of schools of thought in the second century, which put themselves under the aegis of the Companions in question in the way I have described before, and it is unwarranted to consider the Companions of the Prophet personally responsible for the large-scale creation of spurious traditions.

All this can be proved in detail with regard to legal traditions, and I should now like to say a few words on the application of the same method of research to traditions concerning other subjects. We ought, of course, not to overlook the possibility of different developments in different fields. Goldziher has pointed out that those traditions that were current in the Umayyad period, were hardly concerned with law but rather with ethics, asceticism, eschatology, and politics.[14] This is confirmed by additional evidence and by the modest remains of Umayyad literature which have come to light since.[15] "As early as the year 128 we read of an official appointing a committee of pious men to make a collection of *sunan* or approved practices and *siyar* rules of conduct, which were then to be written out by his scribe";[16] but this refers to the recording of a political program of government, and not to legal matters or traditions.

A. J. Wensinck, in studying the traditions concerning points of dogma, came to the conclusion that they reflected the development of dogma only as far as the end of the Umayyad period.[17] "The main explanation of this," Wensinck adds, "is that the large mass of materials contained in the canonical collections, though it received its final form in the middle of the third century A.H., covers a period reaching no farther than the beginning of the second century." But this generalization goes beyond the facts of the case, and Wensinck's assumption that the same applies to traditions concerning questions of law, is contradicted by the whole evidence of the ancient texts. That the development of dogmatic traditions was indeed different from that of legal ones becomes obvious, for example, from Shaibani's *Kitab al-Athar*, where the dogmatic sections (pp. 56–60) consist almost entirely of traditions from the Prophet himself, whereas they form only a small minority in the other sections.

Even so, dogmatic traditions from the Prophet ought not to be dated back into the first century indiscriminately. The dogmatic treatise ascribed to Hasan Basri, whether or not it is genuinely his, cannot be later than the very early years of the second century,[18] and it shows that dogmatic traditions on the important problem of free will and human responsibility hardly existed at the time of its composition. There is no trace of traditions from the Prophet, and the author states explicitly: "Every opinion which is not based on the Koran, is erroneous." Two important dogmatic traditions in particular (they occur in the classical collections) cannot yet have existed when the treatise was written. The reasoning of one, "the writing of the recording pens has dried, and on every forehead is written Blessed or Damned," is decried by the author, is an excuse of his opponents for breaking Allah's commands, and the argument, of the other, that one should hobble one's camel but put one's trust in Allah, is used by the author *against* what became later the orthodox doctrine.[19] If we compare the relevant chapters in Malik's *Muwatta'* and in Shaibani's *Kitab al-Athar* (the authors of these two works died in A.H. 179 and 189 respectively), the growth of dogmatic traditions, concerning the same problem, about the middle of the second century becomes obvious.

A field on which the new method can be applied with particular age is the vast field of traditions pertaining to history. The authorities for legal and historical information are to a great extent identical; apart from protagonists such as 'Umar, 'Ali, Mu'awiya, and 'Umar b. 'Abdal'aziz, I will mention only important transmitters of traditions such as 'Urwa and Hisham, of whom I spoke before, Zuhri and Sha'bi. If the family isnad with the names 'Urwa and Hisham in it serves to lend authority to legal traditions put into circulation after the time of Hisham, the same applies to historical traditions with the same isnad. If we can show that the legal opinions attributed to Sha'bi are invariably spurious, that this ancient worthy of Kufa had nothing to do with the nascent religious law of Islam as it was being elaborated in his hometown, and that his name was later claimed by two contending schools of thought we are able to assess his political activity much more objectively than if we looked at it through the colored glass of the religious and legal prejudices of a later generation.

As regards the biography of the Prophet, traditions of legal and of historical interest cannot possibly be divided from one another. The important point is that to a much higher degree than hitherto suspected, seemingly historical information on the Prophet is only the background for legal doctrines and therefore devoid of independent value. For instance, the Medinese regarded the marriage concluded by a pilgrim as invalid, the Meccans and the Iraqians regarded it as valid. The Medinese projected their doctrine back to Ibn 'Umar and, with spurious circumstantial details, to 'Umar himself. The opposite doctrine was expressed in a tradition to the effect that the Prophet married Maymuna as a pilgrim. This tradition was countered, on the part of the Medinese, by another tradition related by Sulaiman b. Yasar who was a freedman of Maymuna, to the effect that the Prophet married her in Medina, and therefore not as a pilgrim, and by a more explicit tradition to the same effect related by Yazid b. Asamm, a nephew of Maymuna.[20] We see that even the details of this important event in the life of the Prophet are not based on authentic historical recollection, notwithstanding the family isnads; but are fictitious and intended to support legal doctrines.

This transformation of legal propositions into pseudohistorical information is one aspect; another is what might be called the independent growth of alleged historical material concerning the biography of the Prophet. We can observe this growth directly over the greater part of the second century in the discussions on the law of war, concerning which the biography of the Prophet was searched for precedents. The polemical nature of these discussions makes it safe to conclude that whenever an author does not mention a relevant historical tradition which agrees with his own doctrine and disagrees with that of his opponents, he was not aware of it, in other words, it cannot have as yet existed in his time. We find new traditions at every successive stage of doctrine, and the lawyers occasionally object to historical traditions adduced by their opponents, because they are unknown to or not accepted by the specialists on the biography of the Prophet. A considerable part of the standard biography of the Prophet in Medina, as it appeared in the second half of the second century A.H., was of very recent origin and is therefore without independent historical value.[21]

But the real test of the new approach to Islamic traditions which I advocate lies not in the negative and critical conclusions derived from it, important and timely as these may be; it lies in the value of the method as a tool for arriving at new and positive results. Here are some of these results in so far as they relate to Umayyad administration. An attentive study of legal traditions reveals by certain indications, that a number of problems of early Muhammadan law arose from

Umayyad administrative practice. If we collect the points on which we must postulate an Umayyad administrative regulation as the starting-point of Muhammadan jurisprudence, we find that practically all fall under the three great headings of fiscal law, law of war, and penal law.

For instance: the Umayyad administration imposed the *zakat* tax on horses; it used to deduct the *zakat* from Government pensions; it levied *zakat* tax on the property of minors. When payments were made in kind, the administration issued assignments on its stores which were considered negotiable. The Government gave detailed regulations on the levying of tolls; as a prospective residuary heir, it restricted legacies to one-third of the estate. As regards the law of war, it was the policy of the Umayyads not to lay waste the enemy country wantonly; the Government controlled the distribution of booty, and recognized the customary right of the killer to the spoils.

The Umayyad administration did not interfere with the working of the old Arab *lex talionis*, it only supervised the payment of weregeld: it deducted the sums due from the pension account of the culprit or of his tribe, if necessary in three yearly instalments, and paid them to the family of the victim; if a Christian was killed, only half the weregeld was paid to his family but the Treasury took the other half. Concerning the purely Islamic *hadd* punishments and similar penalties, the administration took a greater interest, though its practice differed in some respects from that regarded as normal later. The non-Muslim slave who tried to escape to the enemy was killed or crucified at the discretion of the Government, but the Government refused to cut off the hands of slaves who had escaped in Islamic territory and stolen, and reserved to itself the right to carry out all *hadd* punishments for theft on slaves. It was the practice under the Umayyads not to apply *hadd* punishments in the army in enemy country, for fear of desertion, but military commanders were otherwise entitled to apply them, and banishment as part of the punishment for fornication was introduced in the interest of public morals. Traces of Umayyad regulations outside the three fields mentioned are confined to the administration of justice, to the re-marriage of wives whose husbands disappeared and were no more heard of, and to fixing the position of the grandfather in the law of inheritance.

The points I have mentioned are not simple surmises; they are based on positive indications in traditions, if we are prepared to look at them historically and critically. I can fairly claim it as a confirmation of the soundness of my method, that it shows the existence of Umayyad administrative regulations on those subjects on which we should more or less have expected them. But the full inference from the details I mentioned has never been drawn. This is the best proof that a truly historical and critical study of Islamic traditions is not only destructive but constructive, that it helps us not only to demolish the one-sided traditional sham-castle, but to use its materials for building a truer, more adequate, and more satisfactory model of the past.

Since I presented these conclusions to the Twenty-first Congress of Orientalists in Paris, I have found an independent confirmation of them in a paper of R. Brunschvig, "Ibn 'Abdalhakam et la Conquête de l'Afrique du Nord par les Arabes."[22] In this critical study Professor Brunschvig examines "historical" traditions relating to the Arab conquest of North Africa and shows how deeply imbued they are with legal interest, how the seemingly straightforward statements on historical persons and events are often nothing but decisions of legal problems, provided with alleged historical precedents; he concludes that the whole of the "historical" narrative is subject to grave doubts, that only the barest outlines represent, or are likely to represent, authentic historical recollection, and that the details are unreliable.

To sum up: In the field of law, the "Sunna of the Prophet based on formal traditions from him, developed out of the "living tradition" of each of the ancient schools of law, the common doctrine of its specialists. Some of its features might, of course, in the last resort, go back to an early period, but it acquired its superstructure of formal traditions from the Prophet with proper isnads only about the middle of the second century A.H., as a result of the activity of the traditionists. The imposing appearance of the isnads in the classical collections of traditions ought not to blind us to the true character of these traditions, which is that of a comparatively recent systematization of the "living tradition." The same is true in the field of history; here, too, the vague collective memory of the community was formalized, systematized, replenished with details, and shaped into formal traditions with proper isnads only in the second century A.H.

NOTES

1. This paper was read to Section VIII (A) of the 21st International Congress of Orientalists, Paris, July, 1948. I have added notes and a few paragraphs.

2. H. A. R. Gibb, *Mohammedanism* (Oxford: Oxford University Press, 1949), p. 196, calls Goldziher's *Muhammedanische Studien* "the standard critical study of the Hadith."

3. C. H. Becker, *Islamstudien*, vol. 1 (Leipzig, 1924–1932), pp. 522, 526, uses the expressions "der historische Instinkt" and "das historische Gefühl" in an otherwise fair and balanced review of Lammens, *Fatima*. But the reaction to Lammens's one-sided thesis ought not to have led to a reversion from historical criticism, a thing which Becker himself had feared would happen.

4. I borrow this formula from A. N. Poliak, in *AJCL* 57, (1940): 52.

5. See my forthcoming book, *The Origins of Muhammadan Jurisprudence* (Oxford: Clarendon Press).

6. Shafi'i, *Kitab al-Umm* (Cairo: Bulaq Press, 1325/1907).

7. E.g., by C. A. Nallino, *Raccolta di Scritti*, vol. 4 (Rome, 1942), p. 89. Nallino's arguments take no account of the legal texts of the second century A.H.

8. Abu Usuf, *Kitab al-Athar* (Cairo, 1355/1936).

9. Shaibani, *Kitab al-Athar* (Lahore, 1329/1911).

10. Goldziher, *Muhammedanische Studien*,vol. 2 (Halle, 1889–1890), p. 72, rightly emphasizes the fact that only very few decisions of the Prophet on legal subjects can have been current in the Umayyad period.

11. This has already been pointed out by Goldziher in his *Muhammedanische Studien*, ii, p. 157, and in *ZDMG* 1 (1896): 483f.

12. This has already been noticed by Gertrude H. Stern, *Marriage in Early Islam* (London, 1939), pp. 12, 16, although Miss Stern on the whole seems to take isnads too readily at their face value.

13. The most ambitious effort of this kind was made by Prince L. Caetani, *Annali dell'Islam*, vol. 1 (Milan, 1905–1926) Introduction, §§ 19, 24–29.

14. *Muhammedanische Studien*, ii, p. 72f.

15. See C. Brockelmann, *Geschichte der arabischen Litteratur* vol. 1 (Weimer, 1898–1902), (and *Supplementbände*), pp. 64ff. Brockelmann erroneously states that Muhammad b. 'Abdalrahman 'Amiri, one of the reputed earliest collectors of legal traditions from the Prophet, died in 120; he died in A.H. 158 (Ibn Hajar 'Asqalani, *Tahdhib al-Tahdhib*, ix, no. 503).

16. D. S. Margoliouth, *The Early Development of Mohammedanism* (London, 1914), p. 91, referring to Tabari, *Annales*, ii, p. 1918.

17. A. J. Wensinck, *The Muslim Creed* (Cambridge, 1932), pp. 52, 59.

18. Text, ed. H. Ritter, in *Der Islam* 21 (1933): 67ff.; translation and commentary by J. Obermann, in *JAOS* 55 (1935): 138ff.

19. The first tradition has parallels, somewhat differently worded, in Shaibani's *Kitab al-Athar*, pp. 56, 60 (not yet in the *Muwatta'*), and appears for the first time in Ibn Hanbal.

20. See Shaibani, *Muwatta'* (Lucknow, 1297 and 1306), p. 208; Malik, *Muwatta'* (Cairo, 1310), ii, p. 183; Shafi'i, *Kitab Ikhtilaf al-Hadith*, on the margin of his *Kitab al-Umm*, vii, p. 238.

21. This conclusion agrees well with the evidence, correctly interpreted, of the fragments of Musa b. 'Uqba's (d. 141) *Kitab al-Maghazi*. I intend to discuss it in detail in a separate paper.

22. In *Annales de l'Institut d'Études Orientales* (Faculté des Lettres de I'Université d'Alger), vi, 1942–1947, pp. 108–56. The paper is dated January, 1945, and was published in October, 1948.

Chapter 10

Abraha and Muhammad

Some Observations apropos of Chronology and Literary *Topoi* in the Early Arabic Historical Tradition[1]

Lawrence I. Conrad

I t has long been known that the chronological scheme commonly transmitted by the early Arabic sources for events of the latter half of the sixth century C.E. poses a number of major problems. These are sufficiently important to raise serious doubts about the reliability of the traditional chronological framework for the last years of the Jahiliya in general. A key problem is that of the date for *'Am al-fil*, the "Year of the Elephant," so called after the expedition of Abraha into the Hijaz in that year. The early Arabic literary tradition does not specifically date this event:[2] it simply maintains, first, that Muhammad was born in the Year of the Elephant, and second, that he was summoned to act as God's Prophet at the age of forty. Considered together, the many reports to this effect simply based on the prevailing view that the mab'ath is to be dated to approximately 610 C.E.—that both the expedition of Abraha and the birth of Muhammad occurred in about 570 C.E. However, this is contradicted by other evidence from outside the Islamic tradition, and even some reports within it, suggesting that the Abyssinian incursion occurred at a significantly earlier date, and that Muhammad was born at some time other than the Year of the Elephant.

Considering the evidence available in his time, Nöldeke was already prepared to suggest that the dating based on the traditional reports could not be upheld for these events.[3] Lammens went even further and argued that the

Originally published in *Bulletin of the School of Oriental and African Studies* 50 (1987): 225–40. Reprinted by permission of Oxford University Press.

chronology and content of the sira were hopelessly confused and of almost no historical value; therefore, practically nothing could be known about the birth or youth of Muhammad, or about the year to which *'Am al-fil* corresponded.[4] Many other scholars have since expressed similar, if less extreme, reservations. Blachère, for example, raised numerous doubts concerning reports about Muhammad's birth date and his age at various times during his life, and discussed the dates in such reports as indicative of no more than "la chronologie traditionelle [the traditional chronology]."[5] Watt, though prepared to accept as fairly accurate much of the sira tradition, regarded the dating of various events in the early stages of Muhammad's life and career as a problem of such difficulty that in the continuing efforts of scholars to resolve it, "no alternative can have more than a slight degree of probability."

The discovery (in December 1951) and publication of the Murayghan inscription (Ry 506)[7] introduced new complications, since it provoked speculation on whether the expedition mentioned in the inscription was an incursion prior to that of Abraha,[8] the historical basis for what was only a later folkloric tradition about Abraha,[9] or the Expedition of the Elephant itself.[10] Kister adduced evidence indicating that the last alternative was the correct one, but in so doing he implied that the traditional chronology was wrong by almost two decades.[11] And most recently, Crone and Cook have revived Lammens's theories and have argued that the general structure of early Islamic chronology—and indeed, the entire sira tradition—only emerged in later times, when scholars seeking to reconstruct the career of the Prophet from a confused and contradictory array of early reports organized their material within an arbitrary chronological framework that may or may not reflect the true order and timing of events.[12]

Implicit in the discussion about such matters is a recognition that the problem of dating the expedition of Abraha and the birth of Muhammad is of relevance and importance to more than just the fixing of these two events. It is well known that the pagan Arabs of the Jahiliya considered the Year of the Elephant sufficiently significant to make it the starting point for a new chronology of subsequent occurrences in Arabia, so that we commonly find reports dating events to a certain number of years after the *'Am al-fil*. Hence, to the extent that chronology is presented to us at all, it is to a very large degree based upon the date of this single key event. If this date is found to be erroneous, or worse, unknowable from the evidence available to us, then, as Lammens and Von Grunebaum so aptly pointed out, the entire chronology based upon it is necessarily reduced to ruins.[13]

In this contribution to the discussion, I would like to address the problem from two complementary approaches, viewing the question as one of historiography and, at the same time, as one of social perceptions, as reflected by the use of literary topoi to advance subtle arguments in the form of symbolic messages and images. Such an approach will not resolve all of the outstanding difficulties. But much of the confusion can be eliminated by focusing our attention not so much on the historical events themselves as on how these events and the stories about them were perceived in the Near Eastern milieu of early medieval times.

EXTERNAL EVIDENCE FOR THE EXPEDITION OF ABRAHA

Some important evidence for the date of the Expedition of the Elephant can be found in sources outside of the Islamic tradition. Prokopios gives a summary of the career of "Abramos," insofar as it was known in sixth-century Constantinople, in the first book of his military history.[14] In this account he describes Abraha's rise to power as viceroy of Yemen, his overthrow of Abyssinian suzerainty, and the resulting unsuccessful efforts to bring him back under control. This narrative has long been known to modern scholars, but one very important aspect of it seems to have been neglected. At the end of the passage, Prokopios refers to events in the viceroy's life which occurred "at a later time." Such a statement implies that most of the period of Abraha's rule had already passed by 545, when Prokopios was writing this part of his history, or at the latest by 550–51, when the first seven books of it were published.[15] The issue of this Greek historian's competence in matters of Arabian history is an open question;[16] and further, it is possible that the Expedition of the Elephant occurred very late in Abraha's career. But we cannot be too far wide of the mark in accepting Prokopios's testimony as grounds for placing this conflict prior to 555.

This conclusion can be checked on the basis of other external evidence. The Murayghan inscription discovered by Ryckmans describes a campaign in which a part of the army of Abraha operating in the Hijaz defeated the confederation of the 'Amir ibn Sa'sa'a at Turaba, only 100 kilometers east of al-Ta'if. The date for this event is given (lines 9–10) as 662 of the Himyarite era, i.e., 552 C.E. according to the generally accepted basis for conversion of Himyarite dates, or 547 if one accepts Shahid's suggestion for a theoretical base-date five years earlier.[17] It cannot be later than 554, since the inscription mentions (lines 7–8) the Lakhmid ruler al-Mundhir (III) ibn Ma'al-Sama', who was killed in that year. If this is in fact the clash to which Surat al-Fil refers, then the Murayghan inscription confirms the indications from Prokopios.

Such a conclusion is justified by two other factors. First, extant South Arabian records, although fairly substantial in the immediately preceding decade, completely cease within a few years after the date of the Murayghan inscription. Beeston suggests that Abraha's domain would not have continued, for very long after that time, to flourish to the extent necessary to mount a major offensive into the Hijaz.[18] It would be difficult to push such an argument very far, but its implications for the dating of the Expedition of the Elephant would seem to be corroborated by the indications in a second source. Important Arabic literary evidence adduced by Kister provides a chronological list of late Jahiliya events that would date the expedition of Abraha to 552 C.E.[19] These reports do not mention the birth of Muhammad, and so stand apart from the mainstream of accounts in the sira tradition. They appear to be quite early, and would seem to be approximately correct since 552 is precisely the year preferred by most scholars for the date of the Murayghan inscription.

Various aspects of this material, to which I shall return below, are debatable; but in general it does not seem possible to uphold against it any argument placing Abraha's expedition in 570 C.E. This traditional and still very widespread view is further undermined by another consideration of some importance. While it is true that medieval Islam soon came to regard the birth of the Prophet Muhammad in the Year of the Elephant as having occurred forty years before the beginning of his mission, and to compute dates and ages at various other points in his biography accordingly,[20] it is not likely that the earlier authorities following his activities had such chronological precision in mind. The Arabian society in which Islam arose had only a vague and often confused notion of time. Chronology was reckoned according to a great event of the recent past: when that event was overshadowed by another, the old chronology was abandoned and a new one begun.[21] It was, in other words, difficult to maintain any continuous system of reference to time. The South Arabian kingdoms did establish their own continuous dating systems, but modern investigations demonstrate that even there a great deal of ambiguity and imprecision prevailed.[22]

Among the nomadic and seminomadic tribes to the north, there seems to have been little interest in establishing or using any stable chronological system. This is nowhere more clearly illustrated than in the *ayyam al-'arab*, the "battle-days" lore of the Arabian tribes. Narratives on these clashes were an extremely important part of the tribal heritage and already in pre-Islamic times had developed into an extensive oral literature.[23] Yet no effort was made (or expected) to date the *ayyam* or to organize them into a coherent chronological sequence, most obviously because these narratives were related by tribal poets and *ruwat* who were interested in the lore of their own tribe, not in the *ayyam* genre as a whole. It was only after the advent of Islam that the *ayyam* came to be viewed as a distinct corpus of material amenable to comprehensive historical arrangement, and hence only then that the question of chronology arose. But as such considerations became more important in early Islamic times, scholars studying the *ayyam* found it extremely difficult to go beyond stating that the *yawm* under discussion occurred *fi 'l-jahiliya, fi 'l-Islam*, before or after the *mab'ath*, or that it was *min aqdam ayyam al-'arab.*[24]

The same ambiguity applied to the ages of individuals, which were known only in a very general sense. Birth dates in particular were almost never fixed with any accuracy, largely because so little attention was paid to them. One's date of birth was an insignificant and difficult to determine item of information, and was so lacking in social relevance that most individuals had only a vague idea of when they had been born. Even later, when the Hijra calendar made continuous uniform dating possible, birth dates for even eminent persons remained for the most part unknown.[25] This situation did change with the passage of time[26] but it is worth noting that the umma for centuries even resisted the tendency to regard the date of the Prophet's birth as an occasion for special commemoration. The *mawlid al-nabi* festival evolved only in later medieval times, and among conservative "ulama" it was still then staunchly opposed. The Hanbalite Ibn Taymiya (d. 728/1328), for example, condemned the *mawlid* on the grounds that authorities disagreed on the date of the Prophet's birth, that the festival was an imitation of the Christians' Christmas, and that the early Muslims (*al-salaf*) neither commended nor observed it.[27]

This being the case, why should the early narrators of reports about the Prophet have made such a point of drawing attention to his exact age at the time of the first revelations? This element looms too large in the sira literature to be dismissed as a merely trivial detail, and clearly the early narrators transmitted it as a fact of some significance and relevance to their treatment of the *mab'ath*. If these accounts appear anomalous when taken at face value, then they merit not dismissal as erroneous but reconsideration at a subtler level of interpretation. That is, they should be read as symbolic reports making use of literary topoi.

"FORTY" AS A TOPOS OF MULTITUDE AND PREDICTION

Such numbers as "four" and "forty" were eminently suitable for symbolic usage as literary topoi for, as is well known, in both ancient and medieval times they were widely believed to reflect general notions of perfection, completion, or culmination.[28] The symbolism current in medieval Islam, however, was quite elaborate,[29] and bore particular relevance to the specific intent of the early reports about the Prophet's age at the *mab'ath*.

As noticed long ago by such scholars as Goldziher and Caetani,[30] "forty" is often used as a general metaphorical equivalent to "many." Thus, 'Amr ibn al-'As, reporting to the caliph 'Umar on the conquest of Alexandria, is said to have written, "I have conquered a city in description of which I will only say that in it I seized 4,000 villas with 4,000 baths, 40,000 Jews liable for the poll-tax, and 400 royal places of diversion."[31] Likewise, we read that early Kufa had 40,000 fighting men and 4,000 horses available for military operations.[32] The caliph 'Abd al-Malik (r. 65–86/685–705), receiving a sudden spate of letters requesting appointment to the governorship of Isbahan, reportedly said, "What is this Isbahan? Does it grow gold and silver? Forty letters have been written to me about it!"[33] The geographer al-Muqaddasi (wr. ca. 375/985) hears from an old salt of a treacherous channel from which only one ship in forty returns.[34]

In matters involving measurement of time, this usage of "forty" is clearly devoid of specific chronological content. The general notion of a forty-year reign is already prominent in Old Testament accounts of the history of the patriarchs,[35] and also appears to have been common in pre-Islamic Arabia. It has already been mentioned that the *ayyam* lore rarely shows any concern for chronological stability. It does contain, however, what appear to be attempts to specify the duration of certain conflicts or the period of time that elapsed between two events. But these are in most cases expressed in terms of some form of the topos of "four" and "forty": forty nights, four years, forty years, and so forth.[36] In such narratives nothing more than "some time" or "a long time" is meant. Similarly, Kalbite tradition assigns al-Harith ibn 'Amr a period of forty years' dominion over Kinda: the early accounts are simply stating that at-Harith ruled "for a very long time."[37] So also, in a discussion among philologists, Abu 'Amr ibn 'Ala' (d. 154/771) is ranked above al-Kisa'i (d. 189/805) because "he spent forty years living among the bedouins, while al-Kisa-i did not even remain among them for forty days."[38] Examples could be multiplied fortyfold, but these instances give a representative picture of how the general metaphor of "forty" was applied in matters of chronology.[39]

In a religiously oriented culture it was natural that this topos should also assume a more specific character as a symbol indicating the presence of divine or supernatural influences in the course of events, especially in matters involving eschatology or predictions of the future. Hence, a Jew predicts to the Umayyad caliph Yazid ibn 'Abd al-Malik (r. 101–105/720–24) that he will rule for forty years.[40] Two officials in second-/eighth-century Baghdad find a book predicting ten years as the length of the reign of the caliph, who has already ruled for that long; fearing for their sovereign's life, they change the book to read "forty" instead of "ten" years.[41] An engineer in fourth-tenth-century Egypt predicts that a certain disputed and decrepit church will remain intact for forty years, and then collapse.[42] The Umayyad Mosque in Damascus is often cited as a place that will survive for forty years after the end of the world.[43] In early Ottoman times, Ibn Hajar al-Haytam-i (d. 974/1567) was asked for a legal opinion concerning a man who had died forty years earlier, and whose followers now claimed that he was returning as the *mahdi*.[44]

This numerology was particularly prominent in the religious symbolism of Islam, and a plethora of examples could be cited where four or forty are the numbers which determine or express the extent to which certain deeds arouse divine approbation or ire, or simply demonstrate the hand of God at work in the world.[45] Most illustrative of this is the tradition of the forty *abdal*, or "substitutes," a group of unknown saints believed to reside in Syria. They were thought to intercede with God on the people's behalf to provide them with rain, nurture their crops, gain them victory over their enemies, and protect them from calamities. When one of the *abdal* dies God replaces him with another. Without the complete forty the world would perish; and one of the omens indicating that the Last Judgement is nigh will be the death of all forty of the *abdal*.[46] In such uses of the topos, chronological precision is clearly not a matter of concern. This is perhaps most obvious in a tradition cited by Ahmad ibn Hanbal (d. 241/855) in which 'Abd Allah ibn 'Umar predicts that the Anti-Christ will emerge in the umma and remain for forty. Asked for clarification of this reference to forty, he replies, "I do not know whether it will be forty days, years, nights, or months."[47]

"FORTY" AND THE TOPOS OF AKME

Such topoi based on "forty" are of considerable significance for our purposes here, for within this constellation of conceptions was the view commonly held in both pagan Arabian and Islamic culture that a man only reaches the peak of his physical and intellectual powers when he becomes forty years old. In his younger years he lacks the wisdom and self-discipline necessary to control his whims and passions, while in later years these qualities, though fully developed, are vitiated by increasing physical weakness.[48] Between these extremes, the optimum balance of physical strength, emotional maturity, and intellectual vigour is the age of forty.

This notion had a lineage in Near Eastern tradition extending far back into ancient times,[49] and in Greek and Roman culture it was embodied in the idea of akme, which held that the peak potential for achievement is reached in one's fortieth year.[50] We also find its influence reported for pre-Islamic Mecca, where, as later informants tell us, it was stipulated that no one would be admitted into the Dar al-Nadwa unless he were at least forty years of age.[51] Likewise, the distinctive turban (*'imama*) signifying the status of tribal *sayyid* or leader of a raiding party was an honor generally restricted to mature adults, and according to al-Mada'ini (d. 225/839) to those over forty.[52] Islam quite naturally took up this idea, and gave it Koranic sanction in a verse in which the fully grown man is said to be the one who has reached the age of forty.[53] It was the strength of this social perception that accounts for the considerable discontent in Medina when the Prophet appointed Usama ibn Zayd to lead the second expedition to Mu'ta. Usama could claim the right to do so by reason of his father's death at the hands of the Byzantines; but he was still quite young at the time, and many older warriors were insulted at being placed under the leadership of a mere youth (*ghulam*).[54]

This concept remained strong throughout medieval times, and our sources repeatedly and specifically speak of the forty-year-old as an ideal type, an individual at the optimum balance of physical, emotional, and intellectual capability. It is this notion that is evoked when Abu 'Amr al-Shaybani (d. 95/713–14) reportedly declares that on the day of al-Qadisiya, "I reached the end of my youth, being forty years of age,"[55] as also when Qatada (d. 118/736) opines that forty is the age when the wicked mischief of youth ceases.[56] Al-Jahiz considers that a man who does not speak with wisdom by the age of forty will never do so;[57] and al-Tabari (d. 310/923), in his discussions of some of the Koranic materials, sees forty as the age when a man loses the last of his childish ignorance, yet is in complete command of his intellectual capabilities and so fully recognizes his religious and filial obligations.[58] Al-Muqaddasi assures the reader that he did not bring out his geography until he had reached the age of forty, trod the soil of every clime, and served men of both science and religion.[59] We are also told that the idea of akme applied elsewhere: al-Mas'udi (d. 345/956) states that the Indians allow no king to accede to the throne before the age of forty,[60] and Yaqut (d. 626/1229) approvingly relates how in China such a young individual may not even sit in the presence of the ruler.[61]

Viewed in this light, the reports asserting Muhammad's age at the time of the first revelations become quite clear. The earliest authorities on the Prophet's career were proclaiming the message of a new faith; and their legacy to later times, whether in the form of oral tradition or written record, was profoundly kerygmatic.[62] In maintaining that the Prophet was forty when he embarked on his prophetic mission, they intended to symbolize God's own selection of a perfect man for prophethood, one at the peak of his potential for achievement. The point of departure for this theme was probably Surat Yunus (10), v. 17, where God tells Muhammad that to those who doubt that what he bears is really divine revelation, he should say, "Had God willed I would not have recited it to you, neither would He have taught it to you; I abode among you a lifetime before it—will you not understand?" The term for "lifetime" is *'umur*, which, in accordance with the more general symbolism of forty, the medieval exegetes interpreted as a period of forty years.[63] In the context of the *mab'ath* and *bad' al-wahy*, however, the topos became a far more powerful and effective symbol. The connection made between the Prophet's birth, the ideal age of forty, and the Expedition of the Elephant both appealed to the tribal sense of pride in the victories of one's ancestors, and strengthened Muhammad's prophetic credentials by providing yet another indication of God's favor.

As such a claim was not advanced for its literal chronological content, and since chronology itself was so vaguely known at the time, it should come as no surprise to find, as has been noted frequently in the past,[64] that a number of reports in circulation in early Islamic times gave birth dates for Muhammad other than the Year of the Elephant. Muhammad ibn al-Sa'ib al-Kalbi (d. 146/ 763) reports that the Prophet was born fifteen years before 'Aim al-lil.[65] Ja'far ibn Abi 'l-Mughira (d. late first/early eighth century) prefers a date ten years after Abraha's expedition,[66] which may be compared to the report of Bar Hebraeus (d. 685/1286), of unknown provenance, stating that Muhammad was born in the year 892 of the Seleucid era (580 C.E.).[67] A brief and unfortunately anonymous synopsis of sira chronology adds the alternatives of fifteen and twenty years after Abraha.[68] Al-Kalbi transmits yet another opinion, related independently by Shu'ayb ibn Ishaq (d. 189/805), placing Muhammad's birth date twenty-three years after this event.[69] In a cluster of problematic reports, al-Zuhri (d. 124/742) and Musa ibn 'Uqba (d. 141/758) opt for birth dates thirty and seventy years after *'Am al-fil*, while Muhammad ibn Muhammad al-Jazari (d. 833/1429) favors a report of unknown provenance maintaining that the Prophet was born in *'Am al-fil*, "on 20 April in the seventeenth year of the reign of the just king Chosroes Anushirvan (i.e., 547 C.E.), 578 years after Jesus, son of Mary—peace be upon him—was raised to Heaven (circa 608), in the year 909 from Alexander the Greek (597), which is said to have been 6,043 years after the Fall of Adam— blessings and peace be upon him (552)."[70] It should also be noted that recourse to the topos of "forty" was itself unstable in its early stages. Muqatil and the informants of al-Mada'ini place Muhammad's birth (not the *mab'ath*) forty years after the Year of the Elephant.[71] We also find efforts to calculate further from the "forty" topos: hence reports from Sa'id ibn al-Musayyab (d. 94/713) and 'Ikrima (d. 105/723) stating that at the *mab'ath* Muhammad was forty-three years of age,[72] and from al-Hasan al-Basri (d. 110/728) giving his age at the time as forty-five.[73]

That a disparate range of such alternatives was known in the first century A.H.—this is most probable in any case is suggested by an unusual report transmitted through an isnad of Basran authorities and attributed to Zurara ibn Awfa (d. 93/712).[74] Here it is stated that a *qarn* ("century"[75]) is a period of 120 years, and that the Prophet was born within the same *qarn* as the year in which Yazid ibn Mu'awiya died.[76] Calculating back from this caliph's death date (64/683), this report accommodates any alternative for Muhammad's birth from 566 C.E. onward (counting in lunar years), or perhaps as far back as 563 (counting in solar years). It seems to presume a state of serious disagreement, with a birth date in *'Am al-fil*, forty years before the *mab'ath*, as the earliest alternative under consideration. It is likely that this account does represent the view of Zurara, or at least of some other Basran of his era. It does not appeal to the authority of the Prophet, or even to a Companion. Further, it comments on the birth date of Muhammad through reference to the caliph whom the later Iraqi tradition vilifies as bearing responsibility for the massacre at Karbala'. It is, of course, to be noted that the sympathies of al-Kufa were not necessarily shared by al-Basra, and that the latter town was in fact a focus for the sentiments of the 'Uthmaniya. Even so, for a Basran tradition to be so entirely innocent of any sensitivity over a connection of this kind suggests that it is very early. This same attitude is also evident in an early eschatological tradition, also transmitted through a Basran isnad, portraying Yazid as the "Guarantor of Mercy" (*kafl al-rahma*) and successor to his father Mu'awiyas "King of the Holy Land" (*malik al-ard al-muqaddasa*).[77]

Such accounts appear to have lost ground very rapidly, however, for by the time the extant sira and tafsir materials began to appear in the second/eighth century, the appeal and implications of the "forty" interpretation had already begun to relegate dissenting opinions to obscurity. In the mid third/ninth century, however, Khalifa ibn Khayyat (d. 240/854) could still cite a selection of such views as worthy of serious attention, while adding that the "generally held opinion" (*al-mujtama' 'alayhi*) favors forty as the Prophet's age at the *mab'ath*.[78] Later, we find an attitude of more pointed disapproval. Ibn 'Abd al-Barr (d. 463/1070), for example, declares that no dissenting view exists;[79] but were this so, one might wonder why he bothers to insist on the point. Both al-Dhahabi and Ibn Kathir, while citing some of these by then quite anomalous reports, excoriate them as *da'if*, *munkar*, *gharib*, and so forth.[80]

It is worth noting that the use of the topos of "forty" was not unique to the sira or to the Islamic tradition. It was quite common, for example, in ancient Greece. Of the Peloponnesian War, Thucydides says, "I lived through the whole of it, being of an age to understand what was happening, and I put my mind to the subject so as to get an accurate view of it."[81] Based on this statement, Aulus Gellius (d. late second century C.E.) concludes that the renowned historian must have been forty years old when the war began.[82] Likewise, the birth of Aristophanes is given as 445 B.C.E., for the sole reason that his masterpiece, *The Frogs*, was first produced in 405. Aeschylus is assigned a birth date (525 B.C.E.) on such grounds, by counting back forty years from his first victory in the Dionysia.[83] An example of the persistence of this concept of akme may be found in the New Testament. In Exodus 2:11 we are told that "Moses, a man by now, set out at this time to visit his countrymen"; but when this passage is quoted in Acts 7:23, we find: "At the age of forty he [i.e., Moses] decided to visit his countrymen." A similar notion would seem to have prevailed in the Jewish communities of the medieval Near East, if we may generalize from the Babylonian Talmud's reference to forty as the "age of understanding."[84]

One need not search so far afield for parallels, however. The Arabic sources report, for example, that Khadija bint Khuwaylid was forty when she married the Prophet; but an age of twenty-eight is also mentioned, and this is more likely in view of reports that she bore the Prophet at least five children.[85] The renowned Umayyad poet 'Umar ibn Abi Rabi'a (d. ca. 93/712) is said to have wasted his youth in debauchery; but at the age of forty he changed his ways and lived the rest of his life in abstinence from worldly concerns.[86] Hunayn ibn Ishaq (d. 260/873) reports that as yet a young man of twenty he had translated a Galenic text from what he knew was a corrupt Greek manuscript, but at the age of forty his method changed; henceforth, he first collated several Greek exemplars to produce an accurate copy of his own, and then proceeded to the task of translation.[87] Al-Ash'ari (d. 324/935–936) is said to have been forty when he experienced visions of the Prophet, repudiated his Mu'tazilite training, and embraced the antirationalist views of Ahmad ibn Hanbal.[88]

SOME CONCLUDING OBSERVATIONS

A clear understanding of the function of this prominent topos leads to a number of significant conclusions, which most immediately address the specific problem of dating the Expedition of Abraha and the birth of Muhammad. Statements in the early Islamic tradition giving the Prophet's age as forty at the time of the first revelations are of a kerygmatic rather than historical character. They express the message of Muhammad's qualifications for prophethood, and probably originate in application of the topos "forty" to the exegesis of the Koranic reference to his "lifetime" (*'umur*) among his people prior to the *mab'ath*. Though taken literally at a very early point and elaborated into a chronological framework for the sira, these reports cannot serve as reliable historical evidence, especially since they are contradicted by numerous other accounts—albeit scattered and neglected ones— placing Muhammad's birth in years other than 570 or the Year of the Elephant.

There is accordingly no real contradiction between, on the one hand, early Islamic tradition on the expedition of Abraha, and, on the other, the Byzantine, epigraphical, and even Arabic literary evidence placing the Abyssinian incursion sometime before 554. Specifically, the case for a dating of 552, favored by Beeston and Kister, would seem very strong indeed. This would mean that the expedition occurred in a period of declining power and prosperity in Yemen, as indicated by the total cessation of extant South Arabian inscriptions shortly thereafter. Between this campaign and the fall of Yemen to the Persians in 572, there accordingly elapsed not a brief period of only a few years,[89] as one would conclude had Abraha's incursion occurred in 570, but rather a significantly longer span of time during which other regional forces, such as the Quraysh in Mecca, would have been able to extend their influence into areas previously dominated by the now moribund regime on their southern flank.

For the study of the sira and early Islamic history, dating the Expedition of the Elephant to 552 clearly has important implications. These merit further consideration but can be mentioned only briefly here. Pushing *'Am al-fil* back two decades would obviously mean that if it can yet be demonstrated that Muhammad was born in that year, then he was already close to sixty years old at the time of the first revelations in Mecca, and hence far older at the time of his death in 11/632 than is stated in the traditional accounts, most of which hinge on the literal interpretation of the symbolic age of forty for the beginning of his career. This cannot be dismissed as impossible, but seems unlikely in light of the numerous reports, collected by Lammens, indicating that Muhammad died at an age considerably younger, not older, than the traditional chronology allows.[90] Hence it would be useful to investigate further the accounts providing other alternatives for the birth date of Muhammad.

Such an investigation may not, however, do more than demonstrate that the enormously complex undertaking of sorting out pre-Hijra sira chronology is an impossible task. The extent and depth of our uncertainty can be discerned even in the apparently well-founded dating, based upon the investigations of Beeston and Kister, of the Expedition of the Elephant. Here we must look more closely at the evidence adduced by Kister, a report transmitted on the authority of the renowned early traditionist and historian al-Zuhri.[91] The text is as follows:[92]

Quraysh counted, before the chronology of the Prophet, from the time of the Elephant. Between the Elephant and the (battle of the) Fijar they counted forty years. Between the Fijar and the death of Hisham ibn al-Mughira they counted six years. Between the death of Hisham and the building of the Kaaba they counted nine years. Between the building of the Kaaba and the departure of the Prophet for Medina (i.e., the Hijra—K.) they counted fifteen years; he stayed five years (of these fifteen) not receiving the revelation. Then the counting (of the usual chronology) was as follows.

The problem is clear: what are we to make of the "forty" years between the Expedition of the Elephant and the Harb al-Fijar—accept it as proper chronological evidence, or dismiss it as a topos?

In many such cases no answer can be given. But here we are more fortunate. As Kister observes, this report passes over in silence the question of Muhammad's birth date. This suggests that it predates this issue's rise to prominence, and hence that it is very early. Such a conclusion is further reinforced by the fact that the report appears to predate the emergence of another early and important question—that of the Prophet's participation in the Harb al-Fijar. The extant sira and *ayyam* sources show a special concern for the time of this conflict, which is usually said to have occurred when Muhammad was fourteen years old, although fifteen, twenty, and twenty-eight are also ages given.[93] But this is all embellishment that calculates on the basis of the topos of "forty" for the Prophet's age at the *mab'ath*. And the point is, again, kerygmatic rather than historical, for these accounts are interested not in the date of the Harb al-Fijar, but in the question of whether or not the Prophet was an accountable adult—i.e., fifteen years old[94]—at the time. An affirmative conclusion would have been awkward, as it would have made him not only a party to the intertribal strife of the Jahiliya, but also a participant in sacrilege, since the fighting occurred during the sacred months when all hostilities were to be suspended (hence the name Harb al-Fijar, "war of sacrilege"). Arguing that Muhammad was fourteen at the time, and further, that he only participated by giving his uncles enemy arrows to shoot back, is to say that he was a minor not responsible for his actions, and that his participation was in any case purely defensive. Now, had Kister's report emerged in the late Umayyad period, it would have implied that at the time of the Harb al-Fijar Muhammad was not only an accountable adult, but a fully mature one (forty years old, based on a birth date in *'Am al-fil*) as well. It is very doubtful that a report with such implications would have been set in circulation at that stage in the development of sira studies. In all probability it predates the emergence of the Harb al-Fijar issue, as well as that of the Prophet's birth date, and so must be very early indeed. The extent to which its early origin bears on its authenticity, however, is an entirely different matter. And it is also worth noting that although one can in this case at least suggest a solution to a problem of sira Quellenkritik, the process at the same time highlights even more difficult, and perhaps insoluble, problems elsewhere in the tradition.

More generally, the reports discussed above have important historiographical implications that merit further study. It is worth noting that well into the second century A.H. scholarly opinion on the birth date of the Prophet displayed a range of variance of eighty-five years. On the assumption that chronology is crucial to the stabilization of any tradition of historical narrative, whether transmitted orally or in writing, one can see in this state of affairs a clear indication that sira studies in the second century were still in a state of flux. Muhammad's age at the *mab'ath* was one of many points of debate that had yet to be settled.

What is particularly important about all this is the fact that much of the process of historiographical evolution takes place before our very eyes, as it were, in texts either extant or quoted on fairly secure authority. History was undoubtedly a principal forum for debates about the self-image of Islam as reflected in its past. Nevertheless, as it is possible to see much of what was being discussed, as well as how and why these discussions developed as they did, we are not entirely at a loss for the means to try to separate fact from fiction. The historiographical problems are serious and complex, but do not seem to warrant the conclusion that nothing about the sira can be extracted from the Islamic sources,[95] or indeed, from any sources.[96]

Finally, it is worth drawing attention to the problems raised by the topos of "forty" in other contexts, especially where its multiples by ten appear. Frend's important study of the rise of Monophysitism, for example, concludes with a brief account of the beginnings of Arab rule in Syria, in which he describes the conquest as "a cruel business" in which "no quarter was given."[97] This judgement, to which numerous objections can be raised, is based on an early Monophysite chronology reporting that 4,000 people were killed at this time.[98] Following the Latin translation, Frend reads the number as 40,000; but in this case the number is a topos, hence one zero more or less hardly makes any difference. Figures like 4,000 and 40,000 commonly appear in Near Eastern Christian discussions of the Arab conquests and similar military matters, and are, for example, favored figures of Theophanes (or rather, his source) for events of this period.[99] In such cases, as in many others, it should at least be considered whether the figure presented to us is not a statistic, or even a general estimate, but rather a topos bearing the meaning of nothing more specific than the general idea of "many." Depending upon whether or not they are recognized and understood, such topoi can either be very illuminating or very deceiving.

NOTES

1. This study is based upon presentations made at the 195th Annual Meeting of the American Oriental Society, University of Michigan, Ann Arbor, 15 April 1985, and at the Oriental Institute, Oxford University, 29 May 1986. I am grateful to the participants at these meetings for their comments and suggestions.

2. There are, of course, various reports attempting to stabilize the date for *'Am al fil* and the birth of Muhammad by calculating it according to other calendar systems, e.g., the annus mundi, the Seleucid era, the Arabian system beginning from the Hijjat al-Ghadr, and the "years" of Nebuchadnezzar and Chosroes Anushirvan. See, for example, al-Tabari (d. 310/923), *Ta'rikh al-rusul wa-'l-muluk*, ed. Muhammad Abu 'l-Fadl Ibrahim, 2d ed. (Cairo, 1968–69), II, 103: 18–22, 154: 15–18, 155: 14–16 (from Ibn al-Kalbi, d. 204/819); al-Mas'udi (d. 345/956), *Muruj al-dhahab*, ed. Charles Pellat (Beirut, 1966–1979), II, 202: 8–13; 111, 12: 9–13: 2; idem, *Al-Tanbih wa-'l-ishraf*, ed. M. J. de Goeje (Leiden, 1894; *BGA*, Viii), 228: 7–231: 2. But such reports appear only later. They presume the accuracy of the earlier traditions about the Prophet's birth in the Year of the Elephant, forty years before the *mab'ath*; and, rather than proceeding independently, they are based upon such reports. See Theodor Nöldeke, *Geschichte des Qorans*, 2d ed. by Friedrich Schwally, G. Bergsträsser, and O. Pretzl (Leipzig, 1909–1938), I, 68; idem, *Geschichte der Perser und Araber zur Zeit der Sasaniden* (Leiden, 1879), 168, 172, 205; Leone Caetani, *Annali dell' Islam* (Milan, 1905–1926), I, 149–50.

3. Nöldeke, *Geschichte des Qorans*, I, 68; idem, *Geschichte der Perser und Araber*, 205.

4. See Henri Lammens, "Qoran et tradition: comment fut composée la vie de Mahomet," *Recherches de science religeuse* 1 (1910): 27–51; idem, "L'Age de Mahomet et la chronologie de la sira," *Journal Asiatique*, 10th ser., 17 (1911): 209–50. Lammens's well-known hostility to Islam is evident in both essays, particularly in the former, and neither was as well received as might otherwise have been the case. Both, however, offer a number of useful insights.

5. Régis Blachère, *Le Problème de Mahomet* (Paris, 1952), pp. 15, 28, and frequently elsewhere.

6. W. Montgomery Watt, *Muhammad at Mecca* (Oxford, 1953), p. 58. Cf. also pp. 16, 33, 39, 58–59, and his more generally optimistic views in his recent "The reliability of Ibn Ishaq's Sources," in *La Vie du Prophète Mahomet*, ed. Toufic Fahd (Paris, 1983), pp. 31–43.

7. See G. Ryckmans, "Inscriptions sud-arabes: dixième série," *Le Muséon* 66 (1953): 275–84; Jacques Ryckmans, "Inscriptions historiques sabéennes," *Le Muséon* 66 (1953): 339–42; A. F. L. Beeston, "Notes on the Mureighan inscription," *Bulletin of the Society of Oriental and African Studies* 16, no. 2 (1954): 389–92.

8. Werner Caskel, *Entdeckungen in Arabien* (Köln and Opladen, 1954), p. 30. Caskel's theory is somewhat similar to the earlier two-expedition theory of Carlo Conti Rossini. See the latter's "Expéditions et possessions des habasat en Arabie," *Journal Asiatique*, 11th ser., 18 (1921): 30–32; idem, *Storia d'Etiopia* (Bergamo, 1928), pp. 186–95.

9. J. Ryckmans, "Inscriptions historiques sabéennes," p. 342.

10. Franz Altheim and Ruth Stiehl, "Araber und Sasaniden," in *Edwin Redslob zum 70. Geburtstag: eine Festgabe*, ed. Georg Rohde and Ottfried Neubecker (Berlin, 1955), pp. 200–207.

11. M. J. Kister, "The Campaign of Huluban: A New Light on the Expedition of Abraha," *Le Muséon* 78 (1965): 425–28.

12. See Patricia Crone and Michael Cook, *Hagarism: The Making of the Islamic World* (Cambridge, 1977), pp. 3–9, 157 n. 39. Cf. also Patricia Crone, *Slaves on Horses: The Evolution of the Islamic Polity* (Cambridge, 1980), pp. 14–17, 210 n. 82; Michael Cook, *Muhammad* (Oxford, 1983), pp. 63–64.

13. See Lammens, *"L'Age de Mahomet,"* pp. 210, 218–19, 249–50; Gustave von Grunebaum, *Der Islam in seiner klassischen Epoche, 622–1258* (Zurich and Stuttgart, 1963), p. 30.

14. *De bello persico*, I.xx. 3–8; ed. Jakob Haury in the Teubner *Procopius*, 2d ed. by Gerhard Wirth (Leipzig, 1963–1964), I, 107–108.

15. See Jacob Haury, *Procopiana* (Augsburg and Munich, 1891–1893), I, 5–7; Otto Veh, *Zur Geschichtsschreibung und Weltauffassung des Prokop von Caesarea* (Bayreuth, 1951–1953), I, 8, 28; Berthold Rubin, *Prokopios von Kaisareia* (Stuttgart, 1954), pp. 25–26, 122–23; J. A. S. Evans, *Procopius* (New York, 1972), p. 41; Herbert Hunger, *Die hochsprachliche profane Literatur der Byzantiner* (Munich, 1978), I, 293; Averil Cameron, *Procopius and The Sixth Century* (London, 1985), pp. 8–9. Cf. also Nöldeke, *Geschichte der Perser und Araber*, 201.

16. See Cameron, *Procopius and The Sixth Century*, p. 121 n. 65. Prokopios was prepared to become rather credulous where the exotica of distant lands were concerned. See *De bello persico*. i. iv. 17–31 (Haury/Wirth, I, 17–19), where he offers as "not entirely beyond belief" an allegedly Persian tale about an oyster swimming (!) in the sea, accompanied by a jealously protective shark infatuated with the oyster's pearl. But such ridiculous fables are quite the exception in his military history. On the current debate over the reliability of Prokopios for developments along the eastern frontier, there are two useful contributions by Michael Whitby in *The Defense of the Roman and Byzantine East*, ed. Philip Freeman and David Kennedy (Oxford, 1986): "Procopius and the development of Roman defences in Upper Mesopotamia," pp. 717–35, and "Procopius' Description of Dara (*Buildings*, II 1–3)," pp. 737–83. On the question of his reliability more generally, cf. G. Soyter, "Die Glaubwürdigkeit des Geschichtschreibers Prokopios von Kaisareia," *Byzantinische Zeitschriff* 44 (1951): 541–44; Robert Benedicty, "Vzyatie Rima Alarykhom," *Vizantiyskii Vremennik*, n.s., 20: (1961): 23–31; idem, "Prokopios' Berichte über die slavische Vorzeit: Beitrige zur historiographischen Methode des Prokopios von Kaesareia," *Jahrbuch der Österreichischen Byzantinischen Gesellschaft* 14 (1965): 51–78; Evans, *Procopius*, pp. 40–41, 57–59.

17. On South Arabian dating systems see A. F. L. Beeston, "Problems of Sabaean Chronology," *BSOAS* 16, no. 2 (1954): 37–56, esp. 37–40; idem, E*pigraphic South Arabian Calendars and Dating* (London, 1956), pp. 35–38; Irfan Shahid, *The Martyrs of Najran: New Documents* (Brussels, 1971), pp. 235–42.

18. *Encyclopedia of Islam*, 2d ed., vol. 2, pp. 895.

19. Kister, "The Campaign of Huluban," pp. 427–28; Beeston, "Notes," p. 391 n. 2.

20. This trend is already under way in the era of ʿUrwa ibn al-Zubayr (d. 94/712), and fully developed by the time of Ibn Ishaq (d. 150/767). See Ibn Hisham (d. 218/833), *Sirat Rasul Allah*, ed. Ferdinand Wüstenfeld (Göttingen, 1858–1860), I. 1, 102: 9–12, 108: 3–4, 119: 2–3, 122: 8, 150: 8–9, 415: 10–15; al-Tabari, *Taʾrikh*, II, 290: 14–292: 7; III, 215: 7 216u. it also appears to have made its way into the polemical literature of Byzantium. See Euthymios Zigabenos, *Dialexis meta sarakenou philosophou peri pisteos*, ed. J. P. Migne in his *Patrologia Graeca*, 131 (Paris, 1864), col. 33D. This work was commissioned by Alexios I Comnenos (r. 1081–1118).

21 See A. A. Duri, *The Rise of Historical Writing Among the Arabs*, ed. and tr. Lawrence I. Conrad (Princeton, 1983), 14–20.

22. See Beeston, *Epigraphic South Arabian Calendars and Dating*.

23. On the *ayyam*, see Werner Caskel, "Aijam al-ʿarab: Studien zur altarabischen Epik," *Islamica*, 3: Ergänzungsheft, 1930, 1–99; Egbert Meyer, *Der historische Gehalt der Aiyam al-ʿArab* (Wiesbaden, 1970); *ʿAbd al-Jabbar al-Bayati, Kitab ayyam al-ʿarab qabla ʾl-Islam* (Baghdad, 1976). Cf. also *Encyclopedia of Islam*, 2d ed., vol. 1, pp. 793–94 (E. Mittwoch); Duri, *Historical Writing*, index.

24. See, for example, *Naqaʾid Jarir wa-ʾl-Farazdaq*, ed. A. A. Bevan (Leiden, 1905–1912), I, 238: 9–239: 16; II, 790: 8–15, 1020: 10–13; Ibn ʿAbd Rabbih (d. 328/940), *Al-ʿIqd (al-farid)*, ed. Ahmad Amin et al. (Cairo, 1368–1384/1949–1965), V, 206: 14–16, 236: 11–12; Abu ʾl-Faraj al-Isfahani (d. 356/967), *Kitab al-aghani* (Cairo, A.H. 1285), X, 8pu, 12: 6; al-Maydani (d. 518/1124), *Majmaʿ al-amthal*, ed. Muhammad Muhyi ʾl Din ʿAbd al-Hamid (Cairo, 1379/1959), II, 433, no. 2 1; 436, no. 39; 438, no. 57; 441, no. 83. Most of these cases are cited from Abu ʿUbayda (d. 211/826). Ibn al-Athir (d. 630/1232) of course tried to provide a chronological structure for the *ayyam* in his *Al-Kamil fi ʾl-taʾrikh* (Beirut, 1385–1386/1965–1966), I, 502: 1–687u; but this effort was naturally a very arbitrary process and can hardly have produced results superior to those of the sources upon which it was based. Cf. the detailed treatment of chronological difficulties in Meyer, *Der historische Gehalt der Aiyam al-ʿArab*, pp. 8–9, 29, 37, 47, 47–48, 50, 70, 72–73, 76, 77, 83, 91–92, 98–99; also the special cases to be considered below.

25. See the comments on this phenomenon in my "Seven and the Tasbi": On the Implications of Numerical Symbolism for the Study of Medieval Islamic History," *JESHO*, forthcoming. Cf. also Nöldeke, *Geschichte des Qorans*, I, p. 68 n. 2; Lammens, "Qoran et tradition," pp. 33–35; idem, "LʾAge de Mahomet,"pp. 210.

26. Al-Sakhawi (d. 902/1497) gives us an indication of the extent to which such information was available and considered significant in late Mamluk times (at least among the learned), when he ridicules Jalal al-Din al-Suyuti (d. 911/1505), his bitter adversary, for not knowing the date of his own father's birth. See al-Sakhawi's *Al-Dawʾ al-lamiʿ li-ahl al-qarn al-tasiʿ* (Cairo, A.H. 1353–1355), Xi, 73: 2.

27. Ibn Taymiya, *Majmuʾa fatawa . . . Ibn Taymiya* (Cairo, A.H. 1326–1329), I, 312: 1–10, no. 230; idem, *Kitab iqtida al-sirat al-mustaqim mukhalafat ashab al-jabim* (Cairo,

1325/1907), 141: 1–142: 4. Cf. also the study of Eugen Mittwoch, "Muhammeds Geburts-und Todestag," *Islamica* 2 (1926): 397–401. This was of course not the prevailing attitude at this time. Muhammad ibn Muhammad al-Jazari (d. 833/1429), for example, came to Mecca on pilgrimage in 792/1390 and found the *mawlid* to be the town's most lavishly celebrated festival. See his *'Urf al-ta 'rif bi-'l-mawlid al-sharif*, Al-Maktaba al-Khalidiya (Jerusalem), unnumbered ms, fol. 6v: 3–6.

28. See Genesis 7:12, 17; Exodus 34:28; Numbers 14:33; Ezekiel 29:13; 1 Kings 19: 8; Jonah 3: 4; Acts 1: 3. For discussions of this symbolism in the Jewish and Christian traditions, see Eduard König, "Die Zahl Vierzig und Verwandtes," *Zeitschrift der Deutschen Morgenländischen Gesellschaft* 61 (1907): 913–17; *Dictionary of the Bible*, ed. James Hastings (New York, 1901–14), III, 563–64, 565 (Eduard König); *Encyclopaedia Biblica*, ed. T. K. Cheyne and J. Sutherland Black (New York, 1899–1903), III, 3436, 3437–38 (G. A. Barton); *Encyclopaedia Judaica* (Jerusalem, 1971–1972), III, 291–92 (Y. D. Gilat); XII, 1256–58 (Israel Abrahams).

29. Some observations on this were made by Oskar Rescher. See his articles "Einiges über die Zahl Vierzig," *Zeitschrift der Deutschen Morgenländischen Gesellschaft* 65 (1911): 517–20; "Einige nachträgliche Bemerkungen zur Zahl 40 im Arabischen, Türkischen und Persischen," *Der Islam* 4 (1913): 157–59.

30. E.g., Ignaz Goldziher's introduction to his edition of al-Sijistani's *Kitab al-mu'ammarin* in his *Abhandlungen zur arabischen Philologie* (Leiden, 1896–1899), II, 22–23; Caetani, *Annali dell'Islam*, Iv, 175, 357.

31. Ibn 'Abd al-Hakam (d. 257/870), *Futuh Misr*, ed. Charles C. Torrey (New Haven, 1922), 82: 1–4. No source is cited for this, but the greater part of the information in this work comes from either 'Abd Allah ibn Lahi'a (d. 174/790) or al-Layth ibn Sa'd (d. 175/791).

32. Al-Tabarl, *Ta'rikh*, IV, 51: 2–3, from Sayf ibn 'Umar (d. 180/796); 246: 11, from Abu Mikhnaf (d. 157/774). In a recent SOAS lecture, "Reading Between the Lines of Sayf ibn 'Umar in al-Tabar'is *Annales*," G. H. A. Juynboll made special note of the nonstatistical character of many of the figures cited in accounts of early Islamic history, in this case by Sayf. His observations, which in some respects differ from my own, will appear in the appendices to his translation of vol. 13 (A.H. 15–21) in the al-Tabari translation series.

33. Al-Baladhuri (d. 279/892), *Ansab al-ashraf*, v, ed. S. D. Goitein (Jerusalem, 1936), 337: 4–8, citing "Awana ibn al-Hakam (d. 147/764).

34. Al-Mualaddasi, *Ahsan al-taqasim fi ma'rifat al-aqalim*, 2d ed., ed. M. J. de Goeje (Leiden, 1906); *BGA*, III), 12: 17.

35. See I Samuel 4:18; 11 Samuel 5:4, 1 Kings 2:11, 11:42; 1 Chronicles 29:27, 11 Chronicles 24:1. Cf. also Acts 13:21–22.

36. See *Naqaid Jarir wa-'l-Farazdaq*, I 86: 9, 92: 18, 108: 12; Ibn 'Abd Rabbih, Al-'Iqd (al-farid), V, 141: 5–6, 151: 4–5, 152: 1–2, 260: 4, 14; *Aghani*, iIV, 143: 10; al-Maydani, *Majma 'al-amthal*, II, 439, no. 64. These accounts are for the most part taken from Abd 'Ubayda and Ibn al-Kalbi. An exceptional case of some interest is the attempt in these same circles to date Dhu Qar in terms of the chronology of Muhammad's prophetic career

(*Aghani*, Xx, 135: 26–136: 3, 138: 28–139: 1). But this appears to have occurred only because the Sasanian defeat in that battle was made the occasion for predictions by the Prophet of the imminent destruction of the Persians. This, in turn, raised the question of whether Muhammad was in Mecca or Medina at the time, and resulted in a precise answer—the Prophet was in Medina, and Dhu Qar occurred between Badr and Uhud.

37. *Diwan al-mufaddaliyat*, ed. Sir Charles Lyall (Oxford, 1921), 429: 8. The commentary by al-Anbari (d. 304/916) cites Ibn al-Kalbi for this statement. Cf. also Gunnar Olinder, The Kings of Kinda of the Family of Akil al-Murar (Lund, 1927), 54, 56, 92.

38. Al-Zajjaji (d. 337/949), *Majalis al 'ulama'*, ed. 'Abd al-Salam Muhammad Haruin (Kuwayt, 1962), 171: 11–12.

39. For some ancient precedents and parallels from Persian and Turkish usage, see *Dictionary of the Bible*, III, 563.

40. Al-Tabari, *Ta'rikh*, VII, 22: 17–19, from al-Mada'ini (d. 225/839). In the Byzantine tradition Yazid is persuaded to destroy images in the Christian churches by a Jewish magician promising him a reign of forty years if he will do so; see Theophanes (d. 202–203/818), *Chronographia*, ed. Carl de Boor (Leipzig, 1883), 401pu–402: 7. Variants of the tale are very common in the Greek sources.

41. Al-Tabari, *Ta'rikh*, VII, 146: 1–16, from the contemporary Abd Budayl.

42. Ibn Zulaq (d. 386/996), extracts from his *Umara' Misr* ed. Rhuvon Guest in his *The Governors and Judges of Egypt* (Leiden, 1912), 554: 23–555: 9.

43. See, for example, Ibn al-Faqih (wr. circa 289/902), *Mukhtasar kitab al-buldan*, ed. M. J. de Goeje (Leiden, 1885; *BGA*, V), 108: 3–5; Ibn Battuta (d. 770/1368), Rihla, ed. C. Defrémery and B. R. Sanguinetti (Paris, 1853–58), I, 204: 8–9.

44. Ibn Hajar al-Haytam-i, Al-Fatawa al-hadithiya (Cairo, 1356/1937), 31: 9–10.

45. In the Koran, see Surat al-Baqara (2), vv. 51, 226, 234, 260: Surat al-Ma'ida (5), V. 26; Sarat al-A 'af (7), V. 142; Surat al-Tawba (9), VV. 2, 36; Sarat al-Nur (24), vv. 4, 13; Sarat Fussilat (41), v. 10. The materials in Hadith are collected in A. J. Wensinck, *Concordance et indices de la tradition musulmane* (Leiden, 106–69), 11, 214–16.

46. The most detailed account of the abdal, based on a very broad range of informants, is in Ibn 'Asakir (d. 571/1176), *Ta'rikh madinat Dimashq*, I, ed. Salda al-Din al-Munajjid (Damascus, 1371/1951), 277: 1–291u. Cf. also Wensinck, *Concordance*, I, 153; *Encyclopedia of Islam*, 2d ed., vol. 1, 94–95 (Ignaz Goldziher). Ahmad ibn Hanbal, *Musnad* (Cairo, A.H. 1311), II, 166: 18.

47. Ahmad ibn Hanbal, *Musnad* (Cairo, A.H. 1311), II, 166: 18.

48. This is discussed in detail by al-Jahiz (d. 255/868) in several of his essays; see Rasa'il al-Jahiz, ed. 'Abd al-Salam Muhammad Harun (Cairo, 1384–1399/1964–1979), 1, 91: 9–92u, 294: 5–300u.

49. E.g. Joshua 14:7; 11 Samuel 2:10.

50. See Rudolf Hirzel, "Über Rundzahlen," *Berichte über die Verhandlungen der Königlich Sächsischen Gesellschaft der Wissenschaften zu Leipzig, Phil-hist. Kl.*, 37, 1885, 6–62, and esp. 7–14, on the concept of akme. Marcus Aurelius voices this concept when he proclaims that a man of forty is the one who "possesses the most moderate intelligence" (*Meditations*, xi. 1).

51. See al-Jahiz, *Rasail*, I, 300: 10–13; at-Azraqi (d. 250/865), *Akhbar Makka*, ed. Ferdinand Wüstenfeld (Göttingen, 1858), 65: 16–19, from Ibn lshdq and Ibn Jurayj (d. circa. 150/767); Ibn Durayd (d. 321/933), *Kitab al-ishtiqaq*, ed. 'Abd al-Salam Muhammad Harun (Cairo, 1378/1958), 155: 7–8; al-Zubayr ibn Bakkar (d. 256/870), *Jamharat nasab Quraysh wa-akhbajriha*, ed. Mahmud Muhammad Shakir (Cairo, A.H. 1381), 354: 5–7, 376: 4–6, from *Quraysh mashyakha* of the late second century and from al-Dahhak ibn 'Uthman (d. 180/796); Ibn 'Asakir, *Ta'rikh madinat Dimashq*, Al-Maktaba al-Zahiriya (Damascus), MSS *Ta'rikh*, nos. 1–18 and 113, V, 129v: 13–16, from al-Dahhak ibn 'Uthman; = Ibn 'Asakir, *Al-Ta'rikh al-kabir*, unfinished abridgement by 'Abd al-Qadir Badran and Ahmad 'Ubayd (Damascus, A.H. 1329–1351), IV, 421u–422: 2.

52. Al-Waqidi (d. 207/823), *Kitab al-maghazi*, ed. Marsden Jones (London, 1966), II, 560: 20561: 1; III, 1079: 4–7; Abu Hatim al Sijistani (d. 255/869), *Kitab al-mu'ammarin*, ed. Ignaz Goldziher in his *Abhandlungen zur arabischen Philologie*, vol. 2 (Leiden, 1899), 93: 13, the citation from al-Mada'ini, al-Buhturi (d. 284/897), *Kitab al-hamasa*, ed. Louis Cheikho in *Mélanges de la Faculté Orientale* (Université Saint-Joseph), 4, 1910, 55, no. 1079; *Aghani*, X, 10: 29, from Abu 'Ubayda; Wensinck, *Concordance*, Iv, 348–49; R. P. A. Dozy, *Diciionnaire détaillé des noms des vetements chez les Arabes* (Amsterdam, 1845), 306–307. Cf. al-Jahiz, *Al-Balyan wa-l-tabyin*, ed. 'Abd al-Salam Muhammad Harun (Cairo, 1367–1370/1948–1950), III, 105: 3–5, in elucidation of some early verse; Lammens, "L'Âge de Mahomet," p. 227. It was based on this Arabian tribal custom that the *'imama* became an important symbol of the authority of the caliphate; see al-Buhturi, *Diwan*, ed. Hasan Kamil al-Sayrafi (Cairo, 1963–1978), II, 676, no. 268, V. 16; 902, no. 357, V. 9; 993, no. 389, VV.. 14–15; III, 1546, no. 600, VV.. 3–4; 2019, no. 771, V. 7.

53. Surat al-Ahqaf (46), V. 15.

54. See the reports from 'Urwa ibn al-Zubayr in Ibn Hishim, I.2, 1006: 15–1007: 5; al-Waqidi, *Maghazi*, III, 1118: 6–1119: 10; Ibn Sa'd (d. 230/844), *Kitab al-tabaqat al-kabir*, ed. Eduard Sachau et al. (Leiden, 1904–1940), IV.1, 45: 19–48: 17; also al-Tabari, *Ta'rikh*, III, 225pu–226: 16, from al-Hasan al-Basri (d. 110/728); al-Jahiz, Rasa'il, I, 24: 7–8, 296: 12–13; *Encyclopedia of Islam*, 1st ed., vol. 4, pp. 1548–49 (V. Vacca). *Ghulam* is the term frequently used in the *ayyam* lore to denote a man of fighting age, but too young to lead or to merit consultation in serious matters.

55. Ibn Sa'd, VI, 70: 22–5; al-Fasawi (d. 277/890), *Kitab al-ma'rifa wa-'l-ta'rikh*, ed. Akrarn Diya' al-'Umari (Baghdad, 1974), I, 229: 14–16, 231: 12–14; Abu Zur'a al-Dimashqi (d. 280/893), *Ta'rikh*, ed. Shukr Allah ibn Ni'mat Allah al-Quchani (Damascus, 1400/1980), I, 659: 6–8. These reports all originate with Isma'al ibn Abi Khailid (d. circa 146/763).

56. Al-Tabari, *Jami 'al-bayan 'an ta'wil ay al-Qur'an* (Cairo, A.H. 1330), XXVI, 12: 12–13.

57. Al-Jahiz, *Al-Bayan wa-'l-tabyin*, I, 274: 15–16, quoting "the sages" (*al-hukama*). The literary compendia frequently take up this theme. See, for example, Ibn 'Abd Rabbih, *Al-'Iqd (al-farid)*, III, 185: 17–18; Ibn Hibban al-Busti (d. 354/965), *Rawdat al-'uqala wa-nuzhat al-fudala'*, ed. Muhammad Muhyi' l-Din 'Abd al-Hamid (Cairo, 1368/1949), 31: 17-19; *Aghdnf*, XXVI, 45: 1–12.

58. Al-Tabari, *Jami' al-bayan*, IX, 51: 16–18; XXVI, 12: 8–10.

59. Al-Muqaddasi, *Ahsan al-taqasim*, 8u–9: 1.

60. Al-Mas'udi, *Muruj al-dhahab*, I, 92pu.

61. Yaqut, *Mu'jam al-bulda*, ed. Ferdinand Wüstenfeid (Leipzig, 1866–73), III, 449: 1–2.

62. This theme has been elaborated in detail in John Wansbrough's important (albeit, in my view, overly sceptical) study, *The Sectarian Milieu: Content and Composition of Islamic Salvation History* (Oxford, 1978).

63. See, for example, Muqatil ibn Sulayman (d. 150/767), *Tafsir*, Topkapi Sarayi Müzesi Kütüphanesi (Istanbul), MS Ahmet III, no. 74, I, 164r: 16; Ibn Sa'd, I. 1, 126: 25–27, from Sufyan al-Thawri (d. 161/778); Ibn Hanbal, *Musnad*, I, 251: 29–252: 5, 371: 22–30, both reported in the *musnad* of Ibn 'Abbas (d. 69/687); al-Tabari, *Jami' al-bayan*, XI, 68: 6–9, from Qatada; *Blachère, Le Problème de Mahomet*, 15. For Ibn Khaldun (wr. 779/1317), the length of an *'umur*, which he defines as one generation, is a topic of considerable interest and importance. See his *Muqaddima*, ed. E. M. Quatremère (Paris, 1858), I, 257: 6–8, 306: 2–18. On *'umur*, cf. also Lammens, "Qoran et tradition," 34; idem, "L'Age de Mahomet," 221–22, 226–27.

64. See the discussion in Altheim and Stiehl, "Araber und Sasaniden," 203–205; also Nöldeke, *Geschichte der Perser und Araber*, 205; Kister, "The Campaign of Huluban," 427–28; Sulayman Bashir, *Muqaddima fi 'l-ta'rikh al-akhar* (Jerusalem, 1984), 159–60.

65. Khalifa ibn Khayyat (d. 240/854), *Ta'rikh*, ed. Akram Diya' al-'Umari, 2d ed. (Beirut, 1397/1977), 53: 11–12; Ibn 'Asakir, *Ta'rikh* (MS), I, 202r: 4–8; = Badran and 'Ubayd, I, 282: 4–5; al-Dhahabi (d. 748/1348), *Al-Sira al-nabawiya*, ed. Hisaim al-Din al-Qudsi (Beirut, 1401/1981), 6: 14–15; Ibn Kathir (d. 774/1373), Al-Bidaya wa-'l-nihaya (Cairo, 1351–1358/1932–1939), II, 262: 16–17.

66. Ibn 'Asakir, *Ta'rikh* (MS), I, 201vpu–202r: 4; = Badran and 'Ubayd, I, 282: 4; al-Dhahabi, *Sira*, 6: 8–9; Ibn Kathir, *Al-Bidaya wa-'l-nihaya*, II, 262: 12.

67. Bar Hebraeus, *Ta'rikh mukhtasar al-duwal*, ed. Antoine Salihani (Beirut, 1890), 160: 3–4.

68. *Bayan md waqa 'a min al-hawadith min 'am wiladat [al-nabi] . . . ila zaman waf-atihi*, Bibliothèque Nationale (Paris), MS Arabe no. 5051, fol. 17v: 8–9. On this MS, a majmu'a of six short works, see E. Blochet, *Bibliothèque Nationale: Catalogue des manuscris arabes des nouvelles acquisitions (1884–1924)* (Paris, 1925), p. 54.

69. Al-Tha'labi (d. 427/1035), *'Ara'is al-majalis* (Cairo, A.H. 1369), 444: 22; al-Baghawi (d. 510/1117), Ma'alim al-tanzil (Bombay, A.H. 1295), 994: 26–27: al-Tabarsi (d. 548/1153), *Majma'al-bayan fi tafsir al-Qur'an* (Tehran, A.H. 1373–1374), X, 542: 13–14; Ibn 'Asakir, *Ta'rikh* (MS), I, t99v: 27–31; = Badran and 'Ubayd, I, 281: 12–13; al-Khazin (d. circa. 741/1340), Lubab *al-ta'wil fi ma'ani 'l-tanzil* (Cairo, A.H. 1328), IV, 440: 4–5; al-Dahahabi, *Sira*, 6: 10–13; Ibn Kathir, Al-Bidaya wa-'l-nihaya, II, 261: 7, 262: 12–13.

70. Khallfa ibn Khayyat, *Ta'rikh*, 52u; Ibn 'Asakir, *Ta'rikh* (MS), I, 201v: 12–15, 202r: 8–9; = Badran and 'Ubayd, I, 282: 2, 5; Ibn Kathir, Al-bidaya wa'-l-nihaya, II, 262: 13–14; al-Jazari, *'Urf al-ta'rif*, fol. 3v: 11–15. Cf. al-Dhahabi, *Sira*, 6: 3–5.

71. Muqatil, *Tafsir* (MS), II, 252v: 8–9; Khalifa ibn Khayyat, *Ta'rikh*, 53: 1; al-Tha'labi, 'Ara'is al-majalis, 444: 21–22; al-Baghawi, Ma'alim al-tanzil, 994: 26; al-Tabars-i, *Majma' al-bayan*, X, 542: 14; Ibn 'Asakir, *Ta'rikh* (MS), I, 202r: 9–10; al-Khazin, *Lubab al-ta'wil*, IV, 440: 4; Ibn Kathir, *Al-Bidaya wa-'l-nihaya*, II, 262: 14.

72. Ibn Sa'd, I. 1, 151: 5; al-Tabari, Ta'rikh, II, 292: 10–18; III, 215: 17–20; al-Dhahabi, *Sira*, 65: 3–4.

73. Khalifa ibn Khayyat, *Ta'rikh*, 54: 3.

74. On him, see Ibn Sa'd, VII.1, 109: 5–20. Bruno Meissner's reading of the death date on line 15 must be corrected from 73 to 93: the statement that "Zurara ibn Awfa died suddenly in the year 73, in the caliphate of al-Walid ibn 'Abd al-Malik" is impossible, since this caliph ruled from 87/705 until 96/715. See also Ibn Hajar (d. 852/1449), *Tahdhib al-tahdhib* (Hyderabad, A.H. 1325–1327), III, 322: 12–323: 6, no. 598, where Ibn Sa'd is quoted correctly.

75. On the imprecise usage of qarn, see Goldziher, *Abhandlungen*, II, 22–24 in the Anmerkungen (no. 6).

76. Ibn Sa'd, I.1, 127: 25–27. Cf. Eugen Mittwoch's proposed correction of the passage in his Anmerkungen to this volume, p. 41.

77. Nu'aym ibn Hammad (d. 228/843), *Kitab al-fitan*, British Library (London), MS Or. 9449, fol. 24v: 1–2. Cf. also the portrayal of Yazid in the *Continuatio Byzantia Arabica* (wr. circa 123/741), ed. Theodor Mommsen in his *Chronica minora saec. IV. V. VI. VII.* (Berlin, 1894; Monumenta Germaniae Historica, Auctores antiquissimi, XI. 2), 345a: 14–30, no. 27. In an *Epimetrum* to this text (pp. 368–69), Theodor Nöldeke concludes that such information comes from a Syrian Arabic source, probably written in Damascus. On Yazid more generally, see Ignaz Goldziher, "Tod und Andenken des Chalifen Jezid I," Zeitschrift der Deutschen Morgenländischen Gesellschaft 66 (1912): 139–43; Henri Larmmens, "Le Califat de Yazid Ier", *Mélanges de la Faculté Orientale* (Université Saint Joseph) 6 (1913): 449–63; Jibra'-il Jabbur, "Yazid ibn Mu'awiya," *Al-Abadth* 18 (1965): 115–25.

78. Khalifa ibn Khayyat, *Ta'rikh*, 53: 1–2. Cf. also al-Tabari, *Ta'rikh*, II, 290: 14–15, where it is explicitly conceded that earlier generations (*al-salaf*) had disagreed on the age of the Prophet at the *mab'ath*.

79. Ibn 'Abd al-Barr, Al-Isti'ab fi *ma'rifat al-ashab*, ed. 'Ali Muhammad al-Bijawi (Cairo, n.d.), I, 30: 13.

80. Al-Dhahabi, *Sira*, 6: 9, 10, 13, 16, 8: 3–4; Ibn Kathir, *Al-Bidaya wa-'l-nihaya*, II, 262: 15, 17. Al-Dhahabi proposes that the error of those who say that Muhammad was born thirty or forty years after the Year of the Elephant arose because what they really meant to say was "days" (*yawman*), not "years" ('*dman*).

81. *Peloponnesian War*, V.26; tr. Rex Warner (Middlesex, 1954), p. 364.

82. *Noctes Atticae*, XV. 23; ed. Carl Hosius (Leipzig, 1903), II, 150.

83. Richmond Lattimore makes some valuable observations about this practice in the introduction to his translation of the *Oresteia* (Chicago, 1953), 2.

84. See *The Babylonian Talmud*, ed. I. Epstein (London, 1935–1948), *Aboth*, 75–76. Cf. also the significance attributed to the age of forty in *Shabbath*, II, 774, 775.

85. See Ibn Sa'd, I. 1, 84: 1–85: 11; VIII, 7: 23–11: 17, where many of the early reports about this are collected. Also cf. Caetani, *Annali dell'Islam*, I, 169–73; Lammens, "L'Âge de Mahomet,' pp. 212, 241; Watt, *Muhammad at Mecca*, 38; Von Grunebaum, *Der Islam*, p. 31. The tenacious credibility of such claims is illustrated by a later case cited by Keith Thomas for Elizabethan England. The Ealing "census" of 1599 includes a woman who "has two children aged four and one, plus a nurse child of nine months, yet is herself aged 67." See Thomas's "Age and Authority in Early Modern England," *Proceedings of the British Academy* 62 (1976): 206.

86. *Aghani*, I, 36: 29–30, from Muhammad ibn al-Dahhak (d. circa 190/805). See the detailed discussion of these matters in Jibra'il Jabbur, 'Umar ibn Abi Rabi'a (Beirut, 1935–1971) II, 181–95.

87. Hunayn ibn Ishaq, *Risala ila 'Ali ibn Yahya*, ed. and tr. G. Bergsträsser in his *Hunain ibn Ishaq über die syrischen und arabischen Galen-Übersetzungen* (Leipzig, 1925; *AKM*, XVII 3), 4–5, no. 3.

88. See Louis Gardet and M. M. Anawati, *Introduction à la théologie musulmane* (Paris, 1948), p. 53.

89. As Nöldeke observed (*Geschichte der Perser und Araber*, p. 205), this leaves insufficient time for other events prior to the Persian occupation.

90. See Lammens, "L'Âge de Mahomet," pp. 231–39. It is at least worth noting that according to the thirteenth-century Byzantine polemist Bartholomaios of Edessa, Muhammad was thirty-two at the time of the first revelations and spent fifteen years preaching the new faith before his death: i.e., he died at the age of forty-seven. See his *Elegchos Agarenou*, ed. J. P. Migne in his *Patrologia Graeca*, CIV (Paris, 1860), col. 1388 A–B, D. It is unfortunately impossible to determine whether these statements are based on reliable early sources, on the one hand, or baseless anti-Islamic slander, on the other.

91. See Duri, *Historical Writing*, 27–30, 95–121, and the further works cited therein.

92. Kister's translation and glosses. See his "The campaign of Huluban," p. 427.

93. See Ibn Hisham, I. 1, 117pu–118: 1, 118u–119: 3; Ibn Sa'd, I. 1, 80: 17–82: 2; Ibn 'Abd Rabbih, *Al-'Iqd (al-farid)*, V, 253: 7–10; *Aghani*, XVI, 75: 11–16; XIX, 73: 26–75: 3; Ibn al-Athir, *Kamil*, I, 588: 9–595: II.

94. On fifteen as the age of majority, see my "Les Âges de la vie dans l'Islams classique," forthcoming in *Annales*. Cf. also Harald Motzki, "Geschlechtsreife und Legitimation zur Zeugung im frühen Islam," in *Geschlechtsreife und Legitimation zur Zeugung*, ed. Ernst Wilhelm Müller (Munich, 1985), 481–97; idem, "Das Kind und seine Sozialisation in der islamischen Familie des Mittelalters," in *Zur Sozialgeschichte der Kindheit*, ed. Jochen Martin and August Nitschke (Munich, 1986), 423–24.

95. See Crone, *Slaves on Horses*, pp. 3–17, where this position is argued at length.

96. Wansbrough, *The Sectarian Milieu*, esp. II 6–19. For a useful introduction to his hypotheses, see Andrew Rippin, "Literary Analysis of Qur'an, Tafsir, and Sira: The Methodologies of John Wansbrough," in *Approaches to Islam in Religious Studies*, ed. Richard C. Martin (Tucson, 1985), pp. 151–63.

97. W. H. C. Frend, *The Rise of the Monophysite Movement* (Cambridge, 1972), 351–52, 354.

98. *Chronicon miscellaneum ad annum Domini 724 pertinens*, ed. E. W. Brooks in *Chronica minora*, II (Paris, 1904: *CSCO*, 3; *Scriptores syri*, 3), 147: 25–148: 3.

99. See Theophanes, *Chronographia*, 307: 24–25, 316: 13–15, 337: 10–12, 338: 9–10. It should also be noted that in classical and Byzantine Greek, the term "khilias" bears the meaning not just of "a thousand," but also of "many." A number like "40,000" may therefore signify nothing more precise than "very many."

Chapter 11

The Function of *Asbab al-Nuzul* in Koranic Exegesis

Andrew Rippin

I n John Wansbrough's work, *Quranic Studies: Sources and Methods of Scriptural Interpretation*, several theses are put forth regarding the material known as *asbab al-nuzul*, occasions of revelation; the overall view of Wansbrough is one which is derived (critically) from al-Suyuti,[1] which is that the *asbab* material has its primary reference point in works devoted to deriving law from the text of the Koran, that is, halakhic works. He suggests that the presence of *asbab* material as found in a haggadic or narrative tafsir such as that of Muqatil is "accidental" because, while the narrative *asbab* reports serve as anecdotes, they do not fulfil what Wansbrough sees as the "essential function," that of establishing "a chronology of revelation."[2]

The purpose of this study is to pursue a specialized investigation of this function of the *asbab* in exegesis: to pose the fairly straightforward question of what are the *asbab* narratives designed to accomplish? Are they providing history or exegesis? Is that exegesis haggadic or halakhic in character? The question is to be addressed both in terms of direct literary analysis of the narratives themselves and by looking at the use of the material within texts of exegesis. The questions to be posed in this vein are the following: Why within the context of a work such as that of al-Tabari is *asbab al-nuzul* material adduced? What is the

Originally published in *Bulletin of the School of Oriental and African Studies* 51 (1988): 1–20. Reprinted by permission of Oxford University Press.

exegete's purpose in doing so? What does he hope to accomplish by doing so? What does he do with the material after adducing it?

The framework of the investigation is limited to that of exegesis of the Koran written by Sunni authors in Arabic from the early (i.e., pre-sixth-century Hijra) period primarily (although not exclusively), when the literary techniques of exegesis were fairly uncomplicated and uncluttered. The range of exegetical works surveyed includes the early narrative-haggadic types, those of Muqatil (d. 150/767), pseudo al-Kalbi (d. 146/763),[3] Sufyan al-Thawri (d. 161/777), Mujahid (d. 104/772), 'Abd al-Razzaq (d. 211/826), al-Tabari (d. 310/922), and al-Wahidi (d. 468/1075), the legal-halakhic *ahkam* works, those of Muqatil again, al-Jassas (d. 370/981), Ibn al-'Arabi (d. 543/1148) and al-Qurtubi (d. 671/1272), and the *naskh*-abrogation texts of al-Nahhas (d. 338/949), Hibat Allah (d. 410/1019), al-Baghdadi (d. 429/1037), and Makki al-Qaisi (d. 437/1045). The point of employing these three subgenres of tafsir for the investigation is simply because they have been suggested within the context of previous discussions of the role of *asbab al-nuzul* in exegesis primarily as found in both of Wansbrough's recent works, *Quranic Studies* and *The Sectarian Milieu*, but also as indicated within the discussions of the topic by al-Zarkashi (d. 794/1391) and al-Suyuti (d. 911/1505). Once again, the purpose of using these texts is to focus on an essentially literary question: why is the *asbab* material adduced within the context of these works? The results should provide an insight into the exegetical technique or method of literary interpretation employed by these exegetes.

Rather than go through all these texts looking for *asbab* reports, the study places its primary focus upon another exegetical subgenre, that called *asbab al-nuzul*, which is devoted to compiling these reports. Each time a report is cited in this literature as a *sabab* for a verse, the exegetical employment of that *sabab* has been checked within the tafsir literature. The study was limited to sura 2 which presented some 107 verses to be treated. Sura 2 was selected because it contains a near ideal mix of Koranic material, with extensive narrative, polemical, exhortative, and legal material. Ibn al-'Arabi, for example, treats over 80 verses out of the 286 in his *ahkam* text; al-Nahhas discusses 30 verses in the context of *naskh*. This kind of representative selection of verses is important because essentially the final result of the study is statistical; the overall aim of the study is to see which purposes behind adducing the *asbab* material predominate and which are subsidiary. While the precise proportions of the statistical result may well change somewhat if the entire Koran were treated in the same way, sura 2, being a representative cross-section of the whole, should produce fairly accurate results while at the same time not presenting the problem of prejudicing the whole issue by selective citation of verses which happen to be illustrative of certain traits preconceived to be crucial in the role of the *asbab*.

Four *asbab al-nuzul* texts were employed in combination to act as the primary focus. The texts by al-Wahidi (d. 468/1075) and al-Suyuti (d. 911/1505) are famous and should need no further comment. The third text is by Muhammad (or Ahmad) ibn As‘ad al-‘Iraqi who died in 567/1171 or perhaps 667/1268. Entitled *Asbab al-nuzul wa qisas al-furqaniyya*, it is contained in the manuscript copy held by the Chester Beatty Library (no. 5199). The fourth text is found in the Berlin Staatsbibliothek, catalogue no. 3578, and is ascribed to al-Ja‘bari; this ascription has been shown to be incorrect although no other likely writers have arisen to claim authorship. The manuscript itself was written in the year 709.[4]

The actual definition of a *sabab* is a matter which has already been treated in another paper[5] but it is worth emphasizing now that the term has definitely seen a measure of evolution over the years. Indeed, some of the reports studied would often be classified as *akhbar* rather than *asbab*, as al-Suyuti himself argues against al-Wahidi. Suffice it to say here that al-Wahidi did consider such reports to be *asbab al-nuzul* and for this study that is the important point, since the aim is to try to see what the exegetes thought, not whether their categories and understandings conform to our own. Al-Wahidi's conception of a *sabab* seems to revolve around the phrase *al-aya nazalat fi hadha*, "the verse was revealed about such and such" and the like; if a report contained the phrase, then it was *sabab*. Al-Suyuti disagreed.

One result of this study points to an essentially theological rather than literary result. On many occasions it seems that the *asbab* reports are adduced by the commentators for no reason at all; they are cited and then ignored. Of course, for the informed readership of such works, the simple mention of the report may well summon up the related background discussion. But, additionally, such reports are cited in these instances, out of a general desire to historicize the text of the Koran in order to be able to prove constantly that God really did reveal his book to humanity on earth; the material thereby acts as a witness to God's concern for His creation. Indeed al-Suyuti cites this as one of his understandings of the function of the *sabab*[6] and it seems to me to be quite true, and is a statement which underpins the entire phenomenon of the *sabab*. The *sabab* is the constant reminder of God and is the "rope"—that being one of the understood meanings of *sabab* in the Koran[7]—by which human contemplation of the Koran may ascend to the highest levels even while dealing with mundane aspects of the text.

The major literary exegetical role that the *sabab* plays, however, is what could be called a "haggadically exegetical" function; regardless of the genre of exegesis in which the *sabab* is found, its function is to provide a narrative account in which the basic exegesis of the verse may be embodied. The standard interpretational techniques of incorporating glosses, masoretic clarification (e.g., with variants), narrative expansion, and, most importantly, contextual definition predominate within the structure of the *sabab*.

Exegetical glosses provided with the narrative context of the *sabab* may be noted to occur quite frequently: as an example the following treatment of sura 2:44 may be cited. The verse reads: "Do you order right conduct for the people but forget yourselves while reciting the scripture? Will you not understand?"

Al-Wahidi, al-Suyuti, and Berlin 3578, all give the same basic report regarding this verse: "The verse was revealed about the Jews of Medina. A certain man had said to his son-in-law and to his relatives and to those with him (and among them were some who were in foster relationship with the Muslims): 'Be upright in your religion and in what this man—meaning Muhammad—orders you to do! Indeed his command is true?" So they had ordered the people to do that but they did not do it."[8]

Embedded here is the gloss of the Koranic *birr*, "right conduct" as the Sunna of Muhammad. Even the Jews, this *sabab* seems to be arguing, acknowledged the legitimacy of the Sunna, that is, following the orders of Muhammad, although, of course, in their hypocrisy they did not follow it. From the Muslim perspective, as reflected in the entire body of tafsir, here was the evidence of the major sin of the Jewish rabbis, summed up in the term *kitman*: the knowledge of the true status of Muhammad while concealing that fact in order to mislead the entire community.

Closely aligned to the lexical content of the *sabab* is the concern for more literary matters, as in the resolution of ellipsis in sura 2:215: "They are asking you: 'What should they give?' Say: 'Whatever you give of good, that is for parents, relatives, orphans, the poor and the followers of the way; whatever you do of good, God knows of it.' "

Al-Wahidi cites two reports for this verse, one of which is the following: "It was revealed about 'Amr ibn al-Jumuh al-Ansari who was an old man and had a lot of money. He said: 'What shall he [*sic*] give as alms [*bi madha yatasaddaqu*] and to whom shall he give (it) [*'ala man yunfiqu*].' So this verse was revealed."[9] The *sabab*, by employing the keywords of the Koranic phraseology—*madha yunfiquna*—but dividing them into the two parts, serves to make explicit what could be considered as rather elliptical Koranic wording, where the question seems to be *what* to give but the reply more relevant to the question of to *whom* to give it.[10]

Disputes over masoretic matters such as variant readings have also left their trace in the *asbab* material. Sura 2:119 provides a vivid example of this: "Indeed we sent you with the truth as a bringer of good tidings and as a warner. You will not be questioned [*or* Do not ask] about the inhabitants of hell!"

As the translation indicates, two radically different interpretations of this verse can be suggested depending upon the reading of the text. The word in question ‏سل‎ is read according to the *qira'at* literature either in the first form passive *tus'alu* or in the first form imperative *tas'al*.[11] Accompanying these two readings are different *asbab*, each apparently designed to explicate the appropriate meaning and thereby confirm a choice of textual reading.

In explanation of the reading *tus'alu*, the following *sabab* is cited: "The prophet said: 'If God would reveal his strength to the Jews, they would believe.' So God revealed: You will not be questioned about the inhabitants of hell!" i.e., they are not your responsibility.[12] Second, to support *tas'al*, the following report is adduced: "The prophet said one day: 'If only I knew what happened to my parents!' So this verse was revealed: 'Do not ask about the inhabitants of hell!'" [13] Al-Wahidi and Berlin 3578 give both of these *asbab*.[14]

Narrative expansion of a Koranic verse is a more frequent feature in the *sabab*, ranging from the most simple setting of the scene to a full elaboration, spinning an entire narrative structure around a Koranic verse. Often such elaborations revolve around polemical motifs—disputation over sectarian emblems, over the respective values of each religious tradition, over merits of prophets and scriptures, over *tahrif*, *kitman*, and hypocrisy. All these motifs, and many more, are familiar from Wansbrough's analysis of the sira literature[15] and may be illustrated here by the treatment of sura 2:130: "Who could turn away from the religion of Abraham without his soul being foolish? Indeed, We choose him in the world, and in the hereafter he will be among the righteous."

Al-Suyuti and Berlin 3578 quote a *sabab* for this verse, derived from Muqatil's *Tafsir* (according to Berlin 3578). " 'Abd Allah ibn Salam called his brother's two sons, Salama and Muhajir, to Islam. He said to them: 'You know that God said in the Torah: "I am sending from among the children of Ishmael a prophet named Ahmad. He who believes in him will be rightly guided and a true believer; he who does not believe in him will be cursed"' So Salama converted but Muhajir turned away. So God revealed" (2:130).[16]

Exegesis of the verse is provided here with Muhajir obviously representing the foolish one, and Salama the one who sticks with "the religion of Abraham." More important in the *sabab*, it would seem, is the continual motif of Jewish rejection of the alleged prognosis of Muhammad/Ahmad in the Torah—that being the Koranic turning away, made equivalent here to *tahrif/kitman*. The verse is elaborated in a narrative form constructed around standard polemical motifs.

It might also be noted that we seem to have an aetiological narrative here: Salama, the one who is safe and Muhajir, the one who has left.

Other elaborations are not so much polemical as illustrative of the desire to create a good yarn: nowhere is this more apparent than in sura 2:260 and Abraham's questioning. This verse states: "Indeed, Abraham said: 'Lord show me how you gave life to the dead!' He said: 'Do you not believe?' (Abraham) said: 'Why yes, but to satisfy my heart . . . !' He said: "Take four birds, then turn them to you. Then put a part of them in each hill and call them and they will come to you swiftly. Know that God is powerful and wise!'"

For the curious mind, a reading of this verse will raise many questions; it certainly did for the classical exegetes. One major question was what was Abraham supposed to do with the birds? Was he supposed to kill them and cut them up and scatter them around? This is certainly the most popular explanation, although the verse says nothing about killing the birds. Perhaps he was just supposed to take whole birds to the various hills and they would fly back. But wherein is the test in that interpretation? Another question revolves around God's statement, "Do you not believe?" Did God not know whether Abraham believed? Another question, the one that the *asbab al-nuzul* information tries to answer, is why did Abraham ask the question to begin with? Why does Abraham need his heart to be satisfied? It is this situation to which God responds, sending down (*nuzul*!) the instructions, because of Abraham's need or stimulus (*sabab*!).

A majority of the reports concerning Abraham's question revolves around his contemplation of the processes of nature; this situation brought the question to his mind.

> Qatada said . . . Abraham came upon a dead animal which the sea and land creatures were distributing among themselves. So he said: "Lord, show me how you bring life to the dead." Al-Hasan, 'Ata' al-Khurasani, al-Dahhak and Ibn Juraij said that it was a corpse of a donkey on the shore of the sea; 'Ata' said: the lake of Tiberias (i.e., the Sea of Galilee). They all said: (Abraham) saw it, the land and sea creatures devouring it. When the tide came in, the fish and the sea animals came and ate from it: what fell off it became a part of the water. When the tide went out, the beasts of prey came and ate it; what fell off it became a part of the land. When the beasts of prey left, the birds came and ate from it, what was dropped became part of the wind. When he saw that, Abraham was amazed at it and he said: "Oh Lord, You know that it amazes us. Show me how You will bring life to it so I may see it with my own eyes."[17]

Abraham's amazement leads him to question God, and God's response to him is as indicated in the Koranic verse. Another version of the same basic report has

Satan put the evil question into Abraham's mind after witnessing the same events: "How can God gather together all these parts from all these bellies?" This question apparently troubled Abraham's heart, so he asked God.[18]

The second major theme relates to Abraham's adventures with Nimrod-, the account in al-Wahidi, credited to Ibn Ishaq, is also found in similar form in al-Kisa'i's *Qisas al-anbiya'*.

> When Abraham argued with Nimrod he said: "(It is) my Lord who gives life and brings death" (sura 2:258). So Nimrod said: "I give life and bring death" (sura 2:258). He then killed a man and set a man free and said: "I brought death to the former and gave life to the latter." Abraham said to him: "God gives life by restoring the soul to a dead body." So Nimrod said to him: "Have you witnessed that of which you speak?" He was not able to reply, "Yes, I have seen it," so he turned to a different proof. Then he asked his Lord to show him giving life to the dead in order to settle his heart about the argument. So he (Abraham) informed him (Nimrod) of the witnessing and viewing (of the act of God).[19]

The reference in this story to the "different proof" may well be Abraham's demand of Nimrod to make the sun rise from the west if he is so powerful (i.e., sura 2:258); this is an intermediate argument for the power of God which, according to this *sabab*, interrupts the flow of the overall argument between Nimrod and Abraham over life and death. The special quality of this *sabab* is its ability to continue the context of the Nimrod encounter from verse 258 onwards; while the first *sabab* develops in a minor way the theme of the donkey which God "clothes with flesh" in verse 259, the overall Nimrod context is lost in that version. The Nimrod *sabab* is clearly an effort at continual haggadic narrative.

A third option also disregards the context of the passage but tries to explain Abraham's question:

> When God took Abraham as a friend, the messenger of death asked permission of his Lord to go to Abraham and tell him the good news of that. So he went and said: "I come to you bringing you good news that God has taken you as a friend." So he praised God and said: "What is the sign of that?" He said: "That God will answer your call and give life to the dead at your request." Then he proceeded on his way and left. So Abraham said: "Lord, show me how you gave life to the dead." He said: "Do you not believe?" He said: "Why yes, but in order to set my heart at ease by knowledge that you answer when I call and give me what I ask for and that you have taken me as a friend."[20]

This *sabab*, rather cleverly, turns the focus to God: that it was God who put the whole matter to Abraham to begin with. This *sabab* illustrates clearly what is implicit in all the other accounts as well: that Abraham could not possibly have had any doubts in his faith and that the reason for his question was totally innocent. Theological motivation colors the *asbab* material in this, as in other instances, but the main concern is for a good story and, in some cases, the narrative context.

The notion of *ta'yin al-mubham*, identification of the unknown, is, of course, closely related to narrative expansion as well, and is most obviously seen in examples where identification is made of the Koranic "they" which is so frequently left ambiguous in the text, as in, for example, sura 2:116: "They say: 'God has taken a son; glory be to him!' Rather, to Him is what is in the heavens and the earth, each obeying Him."

Al-Wahidi and Berlin 3578 each provide reports for this verse which function to explicate who the "they" of "they say" are: "It was revealed concerning the Jews when they said 'Uzair is the son of God and concerning the Christians of Najran when they said the Messiah is the son of God and concerning the polytheists among the Arabs who said the angels are the daughters of God."[21] As Blachère has stated, the "horror of the uncertain" is the prime motivation in haggadic exegesis,[22] and the *sabab* seems to be a particularly favored and appropriate literary form in which to incorporate such information and thereby quiet restless minds.

It is this kind of interpretation of the motivation behind the citation of the *sabab* which would also seem to explain best the resolution of metaphorical language by means of the *sabab*, which is displayed most clearly in sura 2:19–20: "Or (it is) like rain from the sky in which is darkness and thunder and lightning. They put their fingers in their ears because of the thunderclaps as protection from death. But God encircles the unbelievers. The lightning almost takes away their sight; whenever it gives them light, they walk in it. But when it darkens on them, they stand still. If God wished He would take away their hearing and their sight. Indeed God has power over everything."

Al-Suyuti is alone among *asbab* authors in bringing forth a *sabab* for this verse, and a very extensive one at that; the report is derived from al-Tabari's *Tafsir.*

> Two men of the Medinan hypocrites were fleeing from the prophet to the polytheists when this rain [*matar*] which God mentioned befell them, and in it was loud thunder and thunderclaps and lighting. Every time the thunderclaps befell them, it made both of them put their fingers in their ears out of fear [*faraq*] that the thunderclap would enter their ears [*masami'*] and kill them [*taqtuluhuma*]. When the lightning flashed they walked in its light and when it did not they stood in their place, not walking. They began saying: "If only we had begun by

going to Muhammad and putting our hands in his [i.e., converting]." So they arose and went out and converted to Islam, putting their hands in his. Their conversion was good. So God made the affair of these two fleeing hypocrites into an extended simile [*mathal*] applicable to the hypocrites of Medina.

From here the report goes on to explain the application of this story as a simile:

> When the hypocrites were present at the assembly of the prophet, they put their fingers in their ears out of fear of the speech of the prophet concerning something that was revealed about them or they were reminded of something; so they were killed. (That is) just like those two fleeing hypocrites who put their fingers in their ears. And (the Koranic statement) "Whenever it gives them light, they walk in it," when their property and children increase and they gain booty or win battles. They walk in it and they say: "Indeed Muhammad's religion is true for this time" and they stick to it, just as those two hypocrites walked when the lightning gave them light. And (the Koranic statement) "But when it darkens, they stand still," when their property and children are destroyed and misfortune befalls them, they say: "This is because of the religion of Muhammad" and they fall back into their disbelief, just as those two hypocrites stood when the lightning darkened for them.[23]

Now this *sabab* accomplishes a number of things, very prominently the function of incorporating glosses. But probably most significantly, the *sabab* acts to concretize the simile in human events. As the second half of al-Suyuti's report explains, the verse is normally taken as a simile, the second one in a row after the explicit mention of *mathal* in verse 17, with the resolution of the vocabulary being rain = the Koran, darkness = the disbelievers and so forth. But the *sabab* provides an intermediary stage in the interpretation of the terms of the simile. In fact the *sabab* would seem to suggest that an exemplum may be extracted directly from the wording of the text rather than being taken on a symbolic level. The underlying desire is to read the text as literally as possible. This *sabab* then would seem to be grounded in the basic haggadic notion of removing any ambiguity and at the same time of generating a story for repetition and (edifying) entertainment.

Creating a story not only satisfies a haggadic impulse (along with providing opportunities for lexical and masoretic elaboration) but also performs a basic exegetical function of providing an authoritative interpretational context and determining the limits of each narrative pericope. It has often been remarked that the Koran lacks an overall cohesive structure (albeit that in that very fact may well lie the text's special literary power) and does not provide within itself many keys for interpretation. One of the very basic problems is that it is often impossible to tell where one theme or pericope ends and the next one begins. This has been noted above with regards to sura 2:260 but it is most clearly indicated in the exegetical flurries in the form of *asbab* reports that alight around sura 2:113–121, The questions posed by the exegetes are: Is this one section? Does the one section have the same referent (be it Jews, Christians or pagans)? Those who wish to make legal deductions from sura 2:115 are forced to break up the section and see the referent of the passage as varying; others, from the opposing camp, attempt to maintain one narrative context throughout and downplay any legal implications (or see such as an additional "level" in the reading). The *sabab* plays a central role in supporting exegetical decisions regarding the establishment of context; note, however, the *asbab* information is frequently far too varied and flexible to allow decisions to be based primarily upon it—rather, the exegete clearly makes the decision on the interpretation and supports it ex post facto with the appropriate *sabab*. What does occur, however, is that narratives are adduced, for example, concerning Jewish-Christian disputation in front of Muhammad, and each verse from sura 2:113 through 121 is seen as a response to this disputation by means of the *sabab*.

The reverse situation to this establishing of a context may occur, where a *sabab* is cited in order to defeat the seeming context. An example occurs in sura 2:280: "If he [the debtor] is in difficulty, then (grant him) a delay until (it is) easy (for him). If you give charity, (it is) better for you, if only you knew."

Only one *sabab* is found for this verse; the report continues the saga of Banu 'Amr and Banu'l-Mughira as related in the *asbab* material for verse 278.[24] It is Muqatil who makes the matter clear:[25] verses 278 and 279 are the response which Muhammad sent to 'Attab concerning the situation of the usury. As a result, the following *sabab* arises for verse 280. "Banu 'Amr ibn 'Umair said to Banu'l-Mughira: 'Give us the principal and we will give you the interest.' Banu'l-Mughira said: 'We are in difficulty today; let us delay until the dates ripen.' They refused to postpone (it) for them. So God revealed" (2:280).[26]

So Banu 'Amr, it would seem, agreed to forget the interest (in response to verse 278) but still wanted their principal (*ru'us amwalihim*) which now Banul'l-Mughira decided they could not repay.

Implicit in this *sabab*, and that would seem to be the point, is that the verse refers not to the repayment of usury—which after all, would appear to have been the topic of the pericope—but rather, to the repayment of all debts. The contrary view was argued by some; several reports are found in al-Tabari to the effect that the verse was revealed specifically about usury.[27] But, as al-Nahhas points out,[28] that makes little sense since usury has already been forbidden, a gloss in al-Tabari of "until (it is) easy" as "death" is probably an attempt at maintaining the usury interpretation while recognizing the illegality of the situation to begin with.[29]

An extension of this haggadic notion in the role of the *sabab* is to be detected in a seeming halakhic context as well, that of providing the Jahili background to verses of apparent legal intent. Such *asbab* reports do not, in general at least, function to provide a context from which legal deductions can be made; rather they answer the naturally curious (haggadic) question of why does the Koran say to do (or not to do) such-and-such a thing? Why would anyone have done it (e.g., enter their houses from the rear as in sura 2:189b) anyway? Numerous examples of this occur, as for example in the just cited sura 2:189b: "It is not piety to enter houses from their rear. But piety is the fear of God and entering houses by their doors. Fear God, perhaps you will prosper."

There is a total agreement among the exegetes, in one sense at least, that this verse was revealed about people who did not enter their houses through the door but rather through the rear when they were in the state of *ihram*. Several of the *asbab* reports state precisely no more than that and then imply that this verse was revealed in order to remove any sanction for the necessity of such a practice.[30]

A larger series of *asbab* reports concerned with this verse, however, is found concerning the practices of the pre-Islamic group, the Hums. It has been pointed out especially by Wansbrough[31] that the type of information found concerning the Hums (and other similar pre-Islamic groups) is totally exegetical: what has been "preserved" is only what is relevant to understanding the Koran and Hadith. This is certainly true for any details concerning the Hums and entering houses in *ihram*, and it is a notion which is only emphasized by the discovery that, in fact, contradictory information is preserved concerning the Hums and this activity: they either did or did not enter their houses from the rear, depending on the report. A typical narrative is the following from al-Suyuti: "The Quraysh were called the Hums and they used to enter their houses in *ihram* while the Ansar and the rest of the Arabs did not enter by the door in *ihram*. While the prophet was in a garden, he went out of the door and Qutba ibn 'Amir al-Ansari went out with him. They said: 'Oh prophet, Qutba is an immoral man; he has gone out of the door with you.' (The prophet) said to him: 'What prompted you to do this?' He said: 'I saw you doing it, so I did as you did.' (The prophet) said: 'I am of the Hums,' to which he responded: 'My religion is your religion!' So God revealed" (2:189b).[32]

But precisely the opposite point is made in some sources; one such report is found in al-'Iraqi, al-Tabari, and, most explicitly, al-Azraqi (d. about 220/835) as found in Guillaume's translation of the *Sira*: "If one of (the Hums) before and at the beginning of Islam was in *ihram* and was one of the house dwellers, i.e., living in houses or villages, he would dig a hole at the back of his house and go in and out by it and not enter by the door. . . . The year of Hudaybiyya the prophet entered his house. One of the Ansar was with him and he stopped at the door, explaining that he was one of the Hums. The prophet said: 'I am one of the Hums, too. My religion and your religion are the same,' so the Ansari went into the house by the door as he saw the prophet do."[33]

Exegetically, whether the Hums did or did not enter the doors matters very little of course; the point of the *sabab* is clearly to answer that perpetual question of why: why does the Koran mention such a thing as how to enter one's house, a notion probably quite foreign to those involved in the development of the exegetical tradition? The *sabab*, once again, responds to the basic haggadic impulse.

This adducing of the Jahili "foil" or background is, in my estimation, one of the most significant element of the *asbab* reports. Provided in these reports is an implicit evaluation of the Islamic dispensation; it is saying: "this is how things were before Islam but now Islam has arrived and things have improved substantially." It is to be noted that it is through the complementary notion of the Abrahamic legacy of Islam that this hermeneutical device is able to function almost perfectly. What is carried over from the pagan age is then to be contrasted either positively (in the case of the Abrahamic legacy) or negatively (in the case of the Jahili foil) with the provisions of the Islamic dispensation.

There is implicit in this adducing of the Jahili foil another at least potential function; this is made most explicit, as it happens, by Maimonides in his treatment of the Jewish law. One reason which Maimonides brings forth to provide an explanation of the legal regulations in Judaism (over and above their rational worth) is that they serve to protect the Jews from foreign (i.e., pagan) influence and thereby produce a positive group identity; "You will know from texts of the Torah figuring in a number of passages that the first intention of the Law as a whole is to put an end to idolatry, to wipe out its traces and all that is bound up with it, even its memory as well as all that leads to any of its works—as, for instance, familiar spirits, or as a wizard. . . ."[34]

Only by detailing pagan practice can the accomplishment and the protection implicit in Jewish law be rationally perceived. "As for the prohibition against eating *meat* [*boiled*] *in milk*, it is in my opinion not improbable that in addition to this being undoubtedly very gross food and very filling—*idolatry* had something to do with it. Perhaps such food was eaten at one of the ceremonies of their cult or at one of their festivals. . . . According to me this is the most probable view regarding the reason for this prohibition."[35]

Maimonides, of course, faced problems when he had to deal with an obvious continuation of pagan practice in Judaism, most especially with sacrifice; his only rationale was that sacrifice as a religious rite was too popular to be immediately abolished although eventually it, too, would be declared a part of the pagan heritage (as indeed it became with the destruction of the Temple). Maimonides did not have available to him the exegetical tool with which Muslims were able to approach their legal structure, that of the Islamic-Abrahamic heritage that could be postulated for a continued pagan practice under the new dispensation. Muslims did then face the problem of determining exactly what was Abrahamic and what was not, however, and this problem is nowhere more clearly illustrated than in the various traces of totally opposing opinions which are recorded in the *asbab* information, as, for example, in sura 2:158.[36] Still, the basic point remains that the production of a Jahili background provides a measure by which Islam is evaluated and provides evidence of the protection and of the sense of identity which Islam entails.

Within this notion of the Jahili background it is to be observed quite frequently that there is a flexibility in the identity of the Jahili opponents; both Jews and pagans may perform the function, for example, as in sura 2:26. This would seem to indicate a mixing of apologetical (i.e., as implied in the "evolution" of Islam away from paganism in the Jahiliyya) and polemical (i.e., *tahrif* on the part of the Jews in haggadic-narrative expansion) concerns and in no way can this really be seen to affect the understanding of the basic purpose of such exegesis. sura 2:26 states: "Indeed God is not ashamed to form a simile from the gnat or something higher. Those who believe, they know that it is the truth from their Lord; but those who disbelieve say: 'What does God mean by this parable?'"

A number of *asbab* reports are found for this verse in al-Suyuti, al-Wahidi, and Berlin 3578, all of which basically tell the same story: extended similes included in the Koran were ridiculed by Muhammad's opponents and this verse was revealed as a rebuttal. There is, however, debate over exactly which parables were being ridiculed and exactly who the ridiculing opponents were.

Two choices are presented for which similes are intended; the first makes reference to the two examples previously cited in the sura: the man who kindled the fire in 2:17 and the rain from the sky in 2:19. This solution pays attention to the context and canonical order of the scripture.[37] The alternate choice seems more concerned to do justice to the Koranic phrase *ma ba'uda fa ma fauqaha*, "from the gnat or something higher"; cited are the extended similes of the *dhubab* "fly," in sura 22:73 and the *'ankabut* "spider," in sura 29:41.[38] *Ba'uda* is frequently glossed by exegetes as simply something weak or small;[39] *dhubab* as "fly" certainly fits that category, just as *'ankabut*, spider, fits *fauqaha*, the fly being the favorite food of the spider. The intention of this choice of similes seems exegetical.

The question of which opponents of Muhammad ridiculed him about these extended similes is, it seems, related to the choice of similes as well. One possible opponent group was the Jews and they are always pictured as ridiculing the fly and spider similes by laughing and saying that such talk "does not resemble the speech of God" or asking rhetorically, "Is this supposed to resemble the speech of God?", a gloss of the Koranic "What does God mean by this simile?" The dispute is plainly polemical, over the respective merits of Jewish and Muslim revelation, and does not touch on the meaning of the simile.[40] The other group of opponents to Muhammad, the polytheists, makes exactly the same accusation against the Koran and these extended similes in other versions of the *sabab*; this once again demonstrates the interchangeability of these two groups in the accounts of the life of Muhammad.[41]

That considerations of Koranic context play a role in selecting the examples of similes as being 2:17 and 2:19 is confirmed by the fact that it is always the "hypocrites" who are pictured as confronting Muhammad about these specific similes and verses. "God is above making such similes," the hypocrites are given to say.[42] This would seem to go back to an understanding that verses 7 to 21 of sura 2 were revealed specifically about the hypocrites. Reading scripture in its canonical order and giving consideration to the connection between various pericopes—that is, paying attention to the context—provides the exegetical impulse for the citation of such *asbab* reports. It is to be noted that al-Tabari, and following him al-Suyuti, argues precisely this point, thus giving support to this version of the *sabab*.[43] As well, al-Suyuti considers the mention of the polytheists inappropriate in connection with this verse "because it is Medinan"(!);[44] the introduction of the Jews into al-Wahidi's text he seems to consider a textual error, for he modifies the report which he cites from al-Wahidi to make it read "polytheists" and seems to be able conveniently to ignore the multiplicity of reports in other works which leave little doubt that al-Wahidi did intend to cite the Jews in the passage.[45]

Now all the above cited functions of the *sabab* are interrelated in their basic haggadic nature and, indeed, this, I would argue, seems to be the predominant aspect in all *asbab* reports. It would, however, be totally incorrect to gloss over the situations where quite clearly the *asbab* do have halakhic value as argued by Wansbrough and by Muslim scholars although, even there, whether the chronological aspect is primary in the material here studied, as has been the general assumption, would seem to be quite doubtful.

Halakhic *asbab* material can function in a number of ways. Frequently a *sabab* will provide an appropriate context in which a halakhic meaning may be extracted from the verse: this happens most prominently in sura 2:115 where the incredible multiplicity of material illustrates the point well that the legal meaning to be taken from the verse can be created or destroyed by the *asbab* material.

Sura 2:115 reads: "To God belong the east and the west; wherever you turn, the face of God is there. Indeed, God is omnipresent, all-knowing."

One thing unites all the *asbab* reports adduced for this verse; virtually all of the material is constructed such that the verse is *not* to be included as a part of the kibla controversy. Approximately ten different major themes are found in the *asbab* material each of which suggests a totally different intention behind the verse. Some leave the verse halakhically relevant only in a partial way; this is found in a report which suggests this verse is a continuation of sura 2:114 which concerns the destruction of mosques and thus that this verse, 115, intends that the destruction of mosques does not mean that one can no longer face a kibla.[46] Here, narrative context is the important factor, as suggested previously.

Another series of reports concerns the Najashi, named Ashama or Adhama ibn Abhar and Muhammad's call for a prayer for him. The simplest report is found always attributed to Qatada: "The prophet said: 'Indeed our brother the Najashi has died, so pray for him!' They said: 'Should we pray for a man who was not a Muslim?!' So, 'Among the people of the book are some who believe in God and what has been revealed to you and what has been revealed to them, humbling themselves to God' [sura 3:199] was revealed. So they said: 'But he did not pray toward the kibla.' So God revealed" (2:115).[47]

A variant on this, found only in al-Wahidi and Berlin 3578[48] and attributed to 'Ata', adds the idea of Gabriel communicating the death to Muhammad, removes the revelation of 3:199, and makes explicit that the Najashi had prayed always to Jerusalem and had not been informed of the change of kibla to the Kaaba.[49]

Significant in these reports is the use of kibla as a sectarian emblem. The Najashi is not a Muslim, the claim is, purely because he did not pray to the correct kibla. The overall impact of this report could perhaps be best classified as haggadic elaboration of a polemical motif.

But most important without a doubt are two series of reports which give the verse a definite legal content, but, interestingly enough, make two radically different legal points, each justified by its own *asbab* material. One series of reports is structured with the following elements: (1) travelling either with or without the prophet; (2) the travellers stop at the time for prayer; (3) it is cloudy, dark, or foggy and the kibla cannot be determined; (4) everyone prays towards the direction he thinks best; (5) next morning the error becomes clear; (6) the prophet is asked about it, the verse is revealed.[50]

The elaborations evidenced in these reports all make more plain the halakhic point of the anecdote: that prayer was legally valid, if, out of ignorance, the kibla was not faced. This was the generally accepted ruling among the *madhahib*, according to al-Qurtubi, the exceptions being al-Shafi'i and al-Mughira who considered the kibla a *shart*, i.e., a part of the obligation of prayer.[51] Thus this *sabab* is halakhically relevant and, by establishing the appropriate context for interpretation, it serves to pose the halakhic problem for which the answer is given by scripture; that is, the problem of an undeterminable kibla is posed and, through the interpretational means of a *sabab*, a passage of the Koran is seen to be relevant.

This being the case, one can only express a certain amount of surprise at finding an alternate series of *asbab* for the verse with its own halakhic point to make, the legal implications of which are generally accepted in combination with those of the previous *sabab*. The basic *sabab* is terse but manages to pose the problem of what to do if one is riding a camel at prayer-time—is it necessary to dismount or may one ride and pray in the direction the camel is facing?

Many different variant reports are found but the following from *al-Sahih* of Muslim[52] are typical:

a. From Ibn 'Umar: "The prophet used to pray the *witr* prayer on his camel."

b. From Sa'id ibn Yasar: "I was travelling with Ibn 'Umar on the road to Mecca. When I feared morning (was approaching), I dismounted and prayed the *witr* prayer and then caught up with him. Ibn 'Umar said to me: 'Where have you been?' I said to him: 'I feared dawn (was approaching) so I dismounted and prayed the witr prayer.' So 'Abd Allah (ibn 'Umar) said: 'Is there not in the prophet an example [*uswa*] for you?' I said: 'Indeed, there is by God!' He said: 'Indeed, the prophet prayed the *witr* prayer on his camel.'"

c. From Salim ibn 'Abd Allah: "The prophet used to pray supererogatory prayers on his camel toward whichever direction it faced and he prayed the *witr* prayer on it, although he did not pray the prescribed prayers on it."

d. From Ibn 'Umar: "The prophet used to pray while going from Mecca to Medina on his camel in whatever direction it pointed. He said, 'concerning this was revealed . . .'" (sura 2:115).

The *sabab* is used to support the notion that supererogatory prayers may be said while riding, regardless of the direction faced.[53] Al-Qutubi also uses the verse as an occasion to deal with an analogous situation of those who are sick and being carried.[54] Al-Tabari also considers this verse as related to the "prayer of fear," normally attached to suras 2:239 and 4:101–104.[55]

A second way in which the *asbab* material functions to produce halakhic relevance for the verse is by providing an example of the application of a law as found within the Koran; an example here is sura 2:232: "When you divorce the women and they reach their term, do not prevent them from marrying their husbands if they come to terms between themselves honorably. That is the preaching to those among you who believe in God and the last day. That is cleaner and purer for you. God knows and you do not know."

The *asbab* material for this verse divides between specification of two people who tried to prevent the marriage of a woman under their care. The most popular identification is presented in three different versions by al-Wahidi as well as being cited by al-Suyuti and Berlin 3578. "Ma'qil ibn Yasar narrated: I had given my sister in marriage to a man. He divorced her, then, when her waiting period was over, he came to propose to her. I said to him: 'I let you marry, I supported you and honored you, then you divorced her. Now you come to propose to her. No, by God, you may never return!' He narrated: The man had no objection and the woman wished to return to him. So God revealed this verse. I then said: 'Now I will do it, oh prophet!' So I married her to him."[56]

A clearly less popular although fairly widely circulated report is the following: "Jabir ibn 'Abd Allah al-Ansari had care of the daughter of his uncle, whose spouse divorced her. She completed her waiting period, then he returned wanting her to return to him. Jabir refused. He said: 'You divorced a daughter of our uncle; now you wish to marry her again?' The woman wanted her spouse (again) because she was pleased with him. So this verse was revealed."[57]

Once again, these reports provide the background information of the fact that an act contrary to the Koranic regulation took place but the Koran then corrected the situation. The *sabab* also includes a gloss of the Koranic *'adala* as *mana'a*, "to prevent." But the importance of the reports is much greater than that, and it would seem that they have been tailored to their purpose. Both al-Qurtubi[58] and Ibn al-'Arabi[59] cite the *sabab* of Ma'qil in order to support their position that marriage is not permitted without a guardian to give permission. As al-Qurtubi states: "Marriage is not permitted without a guardian because the sister of Ma'qil was a divorcee and if she had been able to marry by herself, then there would have been no need for Ma'qil."[60] Quite explicitly, the *sabab* establishes the truth of this position for al-Qurtubi. It would thus seem significant that in both versions of the *sabab* a reference is made to the fact that the woman in question wanted to re-marry but could not because of the lack of permission. Such a reference, unnatural to the narrative flow of both reports, is undoubtedly a reference made in the story so that the specific halakhic point can be made.

As is acknowledged by al-Qurtubi, the followers of the legal school of Abu Hanifa do not agree with this ruling; basing themselves on sura 2:230, "if he divorces her, she is not permitted to him after that, until she marries a different spouse and he divorces her," in which there is no mention of a guardian, they reject the entire notion. Al-Jassas,[61] being a Hanafite, represents this position. Toward the end of his multipage argument he mentions the *sabab* of Ma'qil, in two versions, and rejects it on the grounds of its isnad.[62] Isnad criticism is obviously a tool which can be employed when needed and disregarded when not. The fact that the report is found in al-Bukhari makes no difference to al-Jassas who is quite apparently in the position of having to reject the *sabab*.

A *sabab* may also act to deflect exegetically an apparent halakhic content of a verse such as in sura 2:79: "Woe to those who write the book with their own hands and then say: 'This is from God' in order to sell it at a small price. Woe to them for what their hands write and woe to them for what they gain."

Various *asbab* reports are found for this verse, virtually all of which center on the notion of the malicious alteration of Jewish scripture. Al-Wahidi provides the most extensive report: "(The Jews) changed the description of the prophet in their book and made him a man with long hair and of medium brown (coloring). They said to their companions and followers: 'Look at the description of the prophet who is to appear at the end of time; it does not resemble the description of this (man).' The Rabbis and the learned ones used to receive provisions from the rest of the Jews and they feared that they would not receive it if they revealed the (true) description; therefore they changed it."[63]

While similar reports of scriptural falsification are found in al-Suyuti and Berlin 3578 and while the latter adds that the Jews did this out of "distaste" and "envy" (of the Arabs being chosen to receive the final prophet), al-Wahidi's report is unique in that it combines a gloss on the monetary aspect of the Koranic verse with the standard *tahrif* charge; that is, the Jewish leaders "sold," figuratively at least, the description of Muhammad for a small price, their free food-supply.

Notable within various reports given by al-Tabari are some traditions which suggest that what is involved in this verse is not *tahrif*, alteration, of the Torah but rather the writing of entire books and claiming that they are from God (Mishna? Talmud? variations on that polemical theme have certainly been common within the Christian world) which would suggest that the polemic over scripture between Jews and Muslims may have gone further than the charge of alteration and faulty transmission.[64] An isolated report also in al-Tabari pictures the Gentiles (*ummiyyun*) as upset because they had no prophet nor a book, so they wrote a scripture themselves and proceeded to tell a group of "lowly ignoramuses" that the book was from God, in order to be able to sell it to them.[65]

Finally, al-Tabari (followed by al-Qurtubi) has his perpetually impertinent questioner ask: "What is the meaning of 'Woe to those who write the book with their own hands?' "How can one write without the hand?"[66] One should not overlook the distinct possiblity that al-Tabari was endowed with a certain sense of humor, but the point does lead him to a discussion of the difference between author and writer and to state that the verse most certainly intends a stricture upon the Jews and that it does not necessarily imply a restriction upon writing, buying, or selling books. Indeed, the *sabab* in this case serves to remove possible "misinterpretation" with serious legal implications.

On the other hand, *asbab* reports which seem to have halakhic content are on occasion apparently not employed in exegesis in that way, for example in sura 2:230: "If he divorces her, she is not permitted to him after then until she marries a different spouse and he divorces her. There is no sin on the two of them if they return, if they think that they can maintain the rules of God. These are the rules of God (which) he explains to a people who understands."

Al-Suyuti and al-'Iraqi stand alone among the *asbab* books and almost all the exegetical works consulted in citing a *sabab* for this verse. "(The verse) was revealed about Aisha bint 'Abd al-Rahman ibn 'Atik, who was living with Rifa'a ibn Wahb ibn 'Atik (he was the son of her uncle). He divorced her with the final divorce and she married 'Abd al-Rahman ibn al-Zubair al-Qurazi after him. He then divorced her. She then went to the prophet and said: 'He divorced me before having slept with me. May I return to (my) first (husband)?' So . . . [sura 2:230] . . . was revealed. So he slept with her and divorced her after that; thus there was no sin on the two of them when they rejoined."[67]

The same identification of the protagonists is made in al-Kalbi and al-Tabari,[68] and a shortened version of the report is found in Muqatil,[69] although the report is absent from explicit mention in the *ahkam* texts, despite its halakhic relevance. Much debate is conducted in the *ahkam* works concerning whether intercourse is necessary to confirm the legal status of the intervening marriage, the precise point with which this *sabab* is concerned;[70] the appeal to *ijma'* is made by al-Tabari[71] in order to prove the need for intercourse to legalize the marriage. It would seem that a *sabab* may well be halakhic in application or even in origin, but that fact does not necessarily mean that it will actually be advanced for such purposes.

It is within discussions of *naskh* that one intuitively expects to find the majority of the discussions about chronology and one also expects that such discussions will center around *asbab* reports; indeed, this was an emphasized point within most previous scholarly discourses on *asbab*. In very few cases, however, is that discussion about chronology and *asbab* ever carried on in the verses that were examined in this study, at least on an overt level. An example of where it does happen to some extent at least occurs in sura 2:104: "O you who believe! Do not say *ra'ina*! For those who disbelieve, there will be a great punishment."

The numerous *asbab* reports which are connected to this verse all attempt to answer the many questions that arise about this prohibition: Why should it not be said? Why was it said in any case?

The prohibition contained in the verse was seen, quite obviously, as applying to Muslims, so it must have been Muslims who were saying the word at one time;

this assumption is reflected in all the reports. Just where, why, and how the Muslims used this word is a matter of some debate, with three original contexts being suggested by the *asbab* reports:

a. The word was Jewish—perhaps used mockingly—which the Muslims misunderstood and adopted into their speech. Al-Suyuti presents the following report in this vein: "When two Jewish men, Malik ibn al-Saif and Rifa'ibn Zaid, met and talked to the prophet they would say: *ra'ina sam'aka wa-sma' ghair musma'* [compare sura 4:46]. The Muslims thought that this was something that the people of the book (said) to honor their prophets. So they said that to the prophet. So God revealed" (2:104).[72]

Just why it was necessary for the word to be banned is not made clear in this report; another report of al-Suyuti suggests simply that God "detested" the phrase.[73] Al-Tabari's reports, however, state that the Jews said it "to mock" Muhammad and thus it was banned;[74] the Muslims apparently did not realize that this was mockery, an observation which leads al-Tabari to reject the reports since the *ashab* would not have been so careless or foolish as such an oversight would suggest.[75]

b. The word, in the "Jewish language" was a curse, although it was an innocent word in Arabic.

Al-Wahidi, among others, gives an extensive account of this matter: "The Arabs used to say (*ra'ina*) and when the Jews heard (the Muslims) saying it to the prophet they were amazed at that. *Ra'ina* was a severe curse in their language. They said: 'We used to curse Muhammad secretly but now they know the curse of Muhammad because it is (also) in their speech.' They used to come to the prophet and say: 'Oh Muhammad, *ra'ina*,' and then they would laugh. One of the *ansar*, Sa'd ibn 'Ubada who knew the Jewish language, noticed it and said: "Oh enemies of God! May God's curse be on you! By Him who has the soul of Muhammad in His hand, if I hear it from anyone of you, I will break his neck!!" They said: 'Have you not said it to him (yourself)?!' So God revealed" (2:104).[76]

The notion of an interlingual play, perhaps راعِ يْ١ . In, "see" and "evil," is seen to be the reason for the prohibition.

c. The word was a part of Arab-Jahili speech. Al-Suyuti, among others, has the simple report that the Arabs used to say this word in the Jahiliyya and that God then prohibited its use.[77] No further explanation is given; the report is one more of the numerous instances of the flexibility of the motif of opposition to Muhammad.

All these *asbab* reports fulfil a basic haggadic function of providing answers for matters left unstated in the Koran. But the importance of the verse goes somewhat beyond the haggadic level; for one thing, the verse is considered to be a case of abrogation by al-Nahhas, on the basis of the *sabab*.[78] The *sabab* implies for al-Nahhas that at one time it was permitted (*mubah*) to say the word, then that permission was removed or abrogated. This seems significant because many other laws with the Koran are not considered by al-Nahhas as abrogators (food laws for example), rather the assumption seems to be these rulings confirm past practice, but here, on the basis of the *sabab*, prior usage is established and thus the verse enters the realm of *naskh*.

Even more important here is the halakhic significance of the *sabab*. Al-Jassas sees the legal significance of the verse as going beyond merely not saying *ra'ina*; the Jews (or the Arabs) said the word to mock others, according to *sabab*—therefore mockery is not permitted; nor are double entendres permitted (or at least, maliciously intended ones).[79] The wording of the verse is extended in legal application through application of the *sabab*.

While it cannot really be doubted that there is an implicit assumption of the chronological-progressive order of the Koran in the *naskh* texts, it is notable that the discussions themselves do not generally make this point explicit; *naskh*, be it with regards to wine or direction of prayer, always assumes that the present law is known (that is, no wine and facing Mecca), and the verses which agree with that fact are necessarily the valid ones. Any verses which contradict this are necessarily invalid, and thus can be logically arranged according to a basic notion of "progressive revelation." The arguments found in the *naskh* texts are, in short, based on logic not chronology. Where that logic needs backing up in terms of specifics, appeal is generally made to the ordering of suras and, once again, not *asbab* information. Of course, the two notions of ordering suras and the *asbab* interact through the adducing of the *sabab* regarding the *qiyasi* method of sura ordering at sura 2:21.[80] Even there, however, the connection is deflected by al-Wahidi at least who suggests that this *sabab* refers to the people who are addressed (that is, the Meccans or the Medinans) and not the place (and therefore the time!) of revelation.[81] To emphasize the point once more: the bringing forth of the *asbab* as explicit proof of "progressive revelation" within these texts is simply not done very frequently.[82]

A matter which appears not to have arisen in the examination of sura 2 is the explicit question of prophecy; is prophecy in the Koran not closely interrelated with chronology and therefore, one may assume, *asbab*? In the polemical text of Ibn Kammuna, a list of ten verses from the Koran which are traditionally claimed to be prophecies is adduced; cited in it is sura 2:61, which states in reference to the Jews, "struck upon them was humiliation and poverty," about which the argument runs: "[the truth of] this became clear from the fact that after this word no forceful power appeared among the Jews."[83] Now the precise "prophetic" sense of this passage is admittedly vague, but it is worthy of note that no *sabab* is found in the *asbab* texts to support the necessary chronology and interpretation of the assertion. Once again, as far as the verse-prophecy is concerned, the fact is known and not in need of proof. In addition, two instances may be noted in sura 2:142, 189a, where the *sabab* appears to deflect exegetically possible prophetic qualities in the verses concerned.[84]

In conclusion, then, in comparison to Wansbrough's statements, the following may be asserted:

a. The primary (i.e., predominant) function of the *sabab* in the exegetical texts is not halakhic.

b. The essential role of the material is found in haggadic exegesis; that is, the *sabab* functions to provide an interpretation of a verse within a basic narrative framework. I would tentatively trace the origins of this material to the context of the *qussas*, the wandering storytellers, and pious preachers and to a basically popular religious worship situation where such stories would prove both enjoyable and edifying.[85]

REFERENCES

'Abd al-Razzāq. *Tafsir.* Cairo MS *tafsīr* 242.

Al-Baghdādī. *Kitāb al-nāsikh wa'l-mansūkh.* Beyazit MS 445 (also Berlin MS Petermann 555).

Al-Bukhārī. *al-Sahīh.* Cairo, 1378/1958.

Al-Dānī. *al-Taisīr fī'l-qirā'āt al-sab'.* Istanbul, 1930.

Guillaume, Alfred (tr.). *The Life of Muhammad: A Translation of [Ibn] Ishāq's Sīrat rasūl Allāh.* London, 1955.

Hibat, Allāh. *al-Nāsikh wa'l-mansūkh.* Cairo, 1960.

Ibn al-'Arabī. *Ahkām al-Qur'ān.* Cairo, 1959.

Ibn Ishāq. *al-Sīrat al-nabawiyya.* Cairo, 1955.

Ibn Kammūna. *Ibn Kammuna's Examination of the Three Faiths.* M. Perlmann (tr.). Berkeley, 1971; Arabic text, M. Perlmann (ed.). Berkeley, 1967.

Ibn Sa'd. *Kitāb al-tabaqāt al-kabīr.* E. Sachau et al. (ed.). Leiden, 1905–1940.

Al-Jassās. *Ahkām al-Qur'ān.* Istanbul, 1935.

Pseudo al-Kalbī. *Tafsīr;* printed as al-Fīruzābādī, *Tanwīr al-miqbās min tafsīr Ibn 'Abbās.* Cairo, 1951.

Al-Kisā'ī. *Qisas al-anbiyā'.* Leiden, 1922.

Maimonides, Moses. *The guide of the perplexed.* S. Pines (tr.). Chicago, 1963.

Makkī al-Quasī. *al-Idāh li-nāsikh al-Qur'ān wa-mansūkhihi.* Riyad, 1976.

Mujāhid. *Tafsīr.* Qatar, 1976.

Muqātil b. Sulaymān. *Tafsīr.* Ahmed III MS 74.

Muqātil b. Sulaymān. *Tafsīr khams mi'at āya min al-Qur'ān.* I. Goldfeld (ed.). Shefaram, 1982.

Muslim. *Sahīh Muslim. . . bi sharh al-Nawawī*. Cairo, 1390/1970.

Al-Nahhās. *al-Nāsikh wa'l-mansūkh*. Cairo, 1938.

Nwiya, Paul. *Exégèse Coranique et langage mystique: nouvel essai sur le lexique technique des mystiques musulmans*. Beirut, 1970.

Al-Qurtubī. *Al-Jāmi' li-ahkām al-Qur'ān*. Cairo, 1935–1936.

Rippin, Andrew. "The Exegetical Genre *asbāb al-nuzūl*: A Bibliographical and Terminological Survey," *BSOAS* 48, no. 1, (1985): 1–15.

Rippin, Andrew. "al-Zarkashī and al-Suyūtī on the function of the occasion of revelation material," *Islamic Culture* 59 (1985): 243–58.

Rippin, Andrew. "al-Zuhrī, *naskh al-Qur'ān* and the problem of early *tafsīr* texts," *BSOAS* 48, no. 1, (1985): 22–43.

Sufyān al-Thawrī. *Tafsīr*. Rampur, 1965.

Al-Suyūtī. *al-Itqān fī 'ulūm al-Qur'ān*. Beirut, 1983 (4th printing).

Al-Suyūtī. *Lubāb al-nuqūl fī asbāb al-nuzūl*. Cairo, 1382/1962.

Al-Tabarī. *Jāmi' al-bayān 'an ta'wīl āy al-Qur'ān*. Cairo, 1374–1388/1954–1968.

Al-Wāhidī. *Asbāb nuzūl al-Qur'ān*. A. Saqr (ed.). Cairo, 1969.

Al-Wāhidī. *Tafsīr al-wajīz*, on the margin of al-Nawawī, *Marāh Labīd: Tafsīr al-Nawawī*. Cairo, 1972, reprint.

Al-Wāhidī. *al-Wasīt bain al-maqbūd wa'l-basīt*. Berlin Staatsbibliothek MS Sprenger 415.

Wansbrough, John. *Quranic Studies: Sources and Methods of Scriptural Interpretation*. Oxford, 1977.

Wansbrough, John. *The Sectarian Milieu: Content and Composition of Islamic Salvation History*. Oxford, 1978.

Al-Zarkashī. *al-Burhān fī 'ulūm al-Qur'ān*. Cairo, 1957.

NOTES

1. See Rippin, "al-Zarkashi," pp. 248–58.

2. See Wansbrough, *Quranic Studies*, pp. 141–42, 177–85.

3. The text in question here is *Tanwir al-miqbas min tafsir Ibn 'Abbas* referred to by Wansbrough as the tafsir of the al-Kalbi and catalogued in that way in *GAL* and *GAS*; for further details and the argument that the text originated in the third or fourth century, see Rippin, "al-Zuhni," pp. 23–24.

4. On all of these *asbab* texts, see Rippin, "Exegetical Genre," pp. 4–7, 9–10.

5. See Rippin, "Exegetical Genre," pp. 12–15.

6. See Rippin, "al-Zarkashi," pp. 250.

7. See Rippin, "Exegetical Genre," pp. 12–13.

8. Al-Wahidi, *Asbab*, 22, report from al-Kalbi, also *Wajiz*, 12; al-Suyuti, *Lubab*, 19; Berlin 3578, f. 5b, is slightly different: "The Jews said to those from their families who had converted to Islam secretly: 'Be upright in what you are in and do what he

[Muhammad] says, for it is the truth.' So the verse was revealed." Also see al-Qurtubi, I, 365, who adds other reports, found nowhere else, concerning precisely what the Jewish rabbis said.

9. Al-Wahidi, *Asbab*, 60 and *Wajiz*, 57; Berlin 3578, f. 12b; al-'Iraqi, f. 4b, 'Amr asks about gifts for jihad and obedience; also al-Suyuti, *Lubab*, 42, second report, 'Amr asks: "What shall we give from our possession and where shall we put it?" Al-Qurtubi, III, 36, with 'Amr's words in the first person. Muqatil, *Tafsir*, f. 24a, "How much shall we give and to whom shall we give it?"

10. That there appears to be no halakhic input in the *sabab* is apparent from Ibn al-'Arabi, I, 145–46, and al-Jassas, 1, 319–21, who do not cite the *sabab* but rather use only the appeal to the sunna to elaborate the noncompulsory nature of this alms-giving.

11. See e.g., al-Dani, *al-Taisir*, 76, *tas'al* is the reading of Nafi', *tus'alu*, of all the others.

12. Al-Qurtubi, II, 92; also see al-Wahidi, *Wajiz*, 32, the only *sabab* there adduced.

13. Al-Qurtubi, II, 92–93; also al-Tabari, II, 558–89, reports 1875–77; in report 1876, Muhammad repeats the formula: "If only I knew what happened to my parents," *layta shi'ri ma fa'ala abawai*, three times.

14. Al-Wahidi, *Asbab*, 36–37; Berlin 3578, f. 8a; al-Suyuti, *Lubab*, 28, who gives only the one version about Muhammad's parents, in two renditions, equalling al-Tabari's reports 1876 and 1877; both reports al-Suyuti considers *mursal*, incomplete in isnad.

15. See Wansbrough, *Sectarian Milieu*, chap. i.

16. Al-Suyuti, *Lubab*, 29; Berlin 3578, ff. 8a–8b; Muqatil, *Tafsir*, f. 22a.

17. Al-Wahidi, *Asbab*, 79, first report; Berlin 3578, ff. 14b–15a, third report (another possible version: a dead man); Muqatil, *Tafsir*, f. 44b. (donkey corpse); al-Tabari, V, 485–86; al-Qurtubi, III, 300, third report.

18. Al-Wahidi, *Asbab*, 79–80, second report; al-Wahidi's third report, p. 80, is a comment of 'Ikrima on the same subject but with no reference to Abraham.

19. Al-Wahidi, *Asbab*, 80, fourth report; al-Kisa'i, 134–35; Berlin 3578, f. 14b, second report; al-Tabari, V, 487; al-Qurtubi, III, 300, second report.

20. Al-Wahidi, *Asbab*, 80–81, fifth report; Berlin 3578, f. 14b, first report, the angel named as 'Izra'il; al-Qurtubi, III, 300, first report; al-Tabari, V, 487–89.

21. Al-Wahidi, *Asbab*, 36 and *Wajiz*, 31; Berlin 3578, f. 8a.

22. R. Blachère, *Introduction au Coran,* 2d ed. (Paris, 1977), p. 233, cited in Nwyia, 61–64.

23. Al-Suyuti, *Lubab*, 18; also al-Tabari, I, 347–48, report 452 although there are minor differences between the two accounts especially toward the end; there would also appear to be a number of editing or typographical errors in al-Suyuti's report which I have corrected by reference to al-Tabari.

24. Al-Suyuti, *Lubab*, 50, first report; similar reports are found in al-Wahidi, *Asbab*, 87, first report; Berlin 3578, f. 16a, third report; al-Qurtubi, III, 363.

25. Muqatil, *Tafsir*, ff. 47a–47b.

26. Al-Wahidi, *Asbab*, 88; Berlin 3578, f. 16a; al-Qurtubi, III, 37 1; also see Ibn al-'Arabi, I, 245; al-Jassas, I, 473.

27. E.g., al-Tabari, VI, 30, reports 6277, 6279.

28. Al-Nahhas, 83–84; also al-Jassas, I, 473.

29. Al-Tabari, VI, 32, report 6288.

30. Al-Bukhari, *Al-sahih, kitab al-tafsir*, VI, 30: al-Wahidi, *Asbab*, 48, first report and *Wajiz*, 50; al-Suyuti, *Lubab*, 36, first report and third report; Berlin 3578, f. 10b, first report; al-Tabari, III. 556–60, reports 3075, 3076, 3080, 3084, 3088; Ibn al-'Arabi, I, 100–10 but somewhat more extensive; al-Jassas, I, 256.

31. See *Quranic Studies*, 16–17.

32. Al-Suyuti, *Lubab*, 36, second report; al-Wahidi, *Asbab*, 48, second report; Berlin 3478, f. 10b, second report, al-Tabari,III, 559–60, report 3087; Muqatil, *Tafsir*, ff. 29a–29b; al-Qurtubi, II, 345.

33. A. Guillaume, *The Life of Muhammad*, p. 89, somewhat modified; al-'Iraqi, f. 3b; al-Tabari, III, 559, report 3085; also see W. M. Watt, "Hums," *Encyclopedia of Islam*, 2d. ed., vol. 3, pp. 576–77.

34. Maimonides, *Guide*, III, 29, p. 517; the basic point was made in pre-Islamic times as well, e.g., in the *Letter of Aristeas*.

35. Maimonides, *Guide*, III, 48, p. 599; also see Menahem Haran, "Seething a Kid in its Mother's Milk," *Journal of Jewish Studies* 30 (1979): 23–25.

36. See al-Wahidi, *Asbab*, 42, fourth report and in basic thrust, *Wajiz*, 41, but cf. al-Wahidi, *Asbab*, 41, second report; Muqatil, *Khams mi'at aya*, 90, where the tradition is connected to the practice of the Hums.

37. Al-Wahidi, *Asbab*, 21, first report; al-Suyuti, *Lubab*, 18–19, first report; Berlin 3578, f. 5b, second report; al-Tabari, I, 398, the same as al-Wahidi's report.

38. Al-Wahidi, asbab, 21–22, second and third report; al-Suyuti, *Lubab*, 19, second, third, and fourth reports (from 'Abd al-Razzaq in whose tafsir the report would seem not to be found, although there are numerous large water-stains at the beginning of the manuscript making reading difficult); Berlin 3578, f. 5b., first report; al-Tabari, I, 400; Muqatil, *Tafsir*, f. 7a.

39. E.g., al-Tabari, I, 401, 402.

40. Al-Wahidi, *Asbab*, 21, second report; Berlin 3578, f. 5b., first report; Muqatil, *Tafsir*, f. 7a; al-Qurtubi, I, 242.

41. Al-Wahidi, *Asbab*, 21–22, third report; al-Suyuti, *Lubab*, 19, second and third reports; al-Tabari, I, 400; al-Qurtubi, I, 235.

42. Al-Wahidi, *Asbab*, 21, first report; al-Suyuti, *Lubab*, 18, first report; Berlin 3578, f. 5b, second report; al-Tabari, I, 398; al-Qurtubi, I, 241–42.

43. Al-Tabari, I, 400; al-Suyuti, *Lubab*, 19. On the 13 verses of sura 2 as revealed about the hypocrites, see e.g., al-Wahidi, *Asbab*, 19; al-Suyuti, *Lubab*, 17; Berlin 3578, f. 5a; Sufyan al-Thawri, 41.

44. *Lubab*, 19.

45. *Lubab*, 19; compare al-Wahidi, *Wasit*, f. 17b and *Wajiz*, 8, where the Jewish report concerning the parables of the fly and spider is cited. Note that in the order of presentation this is al-Wahidi's second report of three in *Asbab*, yet apparently it is his pre-

ferred one; see also Muqatil, *Tafsir*, f. 7a and not that pseudo al-Kalbi, 5, glosses the party as the Jews.

46. Al-Qurtubi, II, 83.

47. Al-Tabari, II, 532–33. Also see al-Qurtubi, II, 81; Ibn al-'Arabi, I, 35; al-Suyuti, *Lubab*, 27, seventh report taken from al-Tabari. The report is also found in Hadith literature, but not connected to the scriptural verse: see A. J. Wensinck, *A Handbook of Early Muhammadan Tradition* (Leiden, 1960), 175, "Nadjashi." Also see Ibn Ishaq, *Sira*, I, 341.

48. Al-Wahidi, *Asbab*, pp. 35–36, fourth report; Berlin 3578, ff. 7b–8a, second report. Cf. al-Tabari's understanding, II, 532 that the Najashi had not known a kibla at all.

49. Cf. al-Tabari, *Annales* (Leiden, 1879–1901), I, 1473 (as cited in A. Guillaume, *The Life of Muhammad*, pp. 658–59) for the death of Khusro and Muhammad's knowledge of it at the same time as that king's death; also Ibn Sa'd, *Tabaqat*, II, 24–25, the king dies at the same time that a delegation from Persia arrives.

50. Al-Jassas, I, 62, four parallel reports; Ibn al-'Arabi, I, 34, his fourth opinion; al-Qurtubi, II, 79–80, first opinion, two reports; al-Tabari, II, 531–32, reports 1841–43, the most frequent reports from Ibn Rab'ia rejected as weak; al-Wahidi, *Asbab*, 34–35, first two reports and *Wajiz*, 31; al-Suyuti, *Lubab*, 26–27, fourth, fifth, and sixth reports, the sixth report is attributed to al-Kalbi but is much more elaborate than that found in the printed pseudo al-Kalbi text; Berlin 3578, f. 7b, first report.

51. Al-Qurtubi, II, 80; cf. Ibn al-'Arabi, I, 35, who gives the dissenting opinions as the Mu'tazila and al-Shafi'i.

52. Muslim, *Al-sahih*, II, 350–53, reports 26–34. This topic of the "travel prayer" is a complex one, extensively treated in Muslim legal literature. Many different types of "travel prayer" are known, each varying according to the conditions in which it is performed. The selections given here from Muslim does not even scratch the surface of the available material. I would like to thank Dr. J. Burton for drawing this fact to my attention.

53. Al-Qurtubi, II, 80, Ibn al-'Arabi, I, 35, his third opinion, "sound"; al-Jassas, I, 63, sixth opinion, little legal derivation; al-Tabari, II, 530, two reports from Ibn 'Umar. The *sabab* also appears in: al-Wahidi, *Asbab*, 35, third report attributed specifically to *madhhab Ibn 'Umar*; al-Suyuti, *Lubab*, 26, first report; briefly, Berlin 3578, f. 8a, third report. It is to be noted that not all schools of law agreed on the exact restrictions on the practice. See e.g., al-Qurtubi, II, 81.

54. Al-Qurtubi, II, 80–81; see Wansbrough, *Quranic Studies*, 167–69, on '*illa/qiyas* as halakhic deduction.

55. Al-Tabari, II, 530; also al-Qurtubi, III, 80. See e.g., Muslim, *Al-sahih*, II, 489–94, reports 297–305, for "prayer of fear" (i.e., when in fear of being attacked) but note no Koranic prop. Note that al-Wahidi, *Asbab*, quotes no occasion for sura 2:239.

56. Al-Wahidi, *Asbab*, 734, first report, also see his second and third reports, 74–75 and *Wajiz*, 65; al-Suyuti, *Lubab*, 46, first report; Berlin 3578, f. 14a, first report; al-Bukhari, *Al-sahih, kitab al-tafsir*, VI, 39–40; al-Tabari, V, 17–21, reports 4927–4938; Mujahid, 109; pseudo al-Kalbi, 26; Muqatil, *Tafsir*, ff. 37b–38a and *Khams mi'at aya*, 186, with full identification of all the actors.

57. Al-Wahidi, *Asbab*, 75–76, fourth report; al-Suyuti, *Lubab*, 46, second report; Berlin 3578, ff. 14a–14b, second report; al-Tabari, V, 21–22, report 4939.

58. Al-Qurtubi, II, 158, in five different versions.

59. Ibn al-'Arabi, 1, 201.

60. Al-Qurtubi, III, 158–59.

61. Al-Jassas, I, 399–403.

62. Al-Jassas, I, 402.

63. Al-Wahidi, *Asbab*, 24, and *Wajiz*, 21, in more general terms; al-Suyuti, *Lubab*, 20, second report (the first report merely says the verse was revealed about *ahl al-kitab*); Berlin 3578, f. 6a; al-Qurtubi II, 9, from al-Kalbi and Ibn lshaq although I have not located a similar report in the *Sira*. Also see Mujahid, 81.

64. Al-Tabari, II, 270–71, reports 1388, 1393.

65. Ibid., 270, report 1389.

66. Ibid., 272–73; al-Qurtubi, II, 9.

67. Al-Suyuti, *Lubab*, 45–46; al-'Iraqi, f. 6b, somewhat shortened.

68. Pseudo al-Kalbi, 26; al-Tabari, IV, 588–96, especially report 4893.

69. Muqatil, *Tafsir*, f. 37b.

70. E.g., Ibn al-'Arabi, I, 198; al-Qurtubi, III, 147–48. The report is cited in the works of Malik and al-Shafi'i; these later works may well be assuming that their readers are aware of the background to the discussions and thus do not feel there is a need to cite the *sabab*.

71. Al-Tabari, IV, 588–89.

72. Al-Suyuti, *Lubab*, 24; also al-Tabari, II, 460–61, reports 1728–1731, and II, 462–63, report 1738.

73. Al-Suyuti, *Lubab*, 24, fourth report.

74. Al-Tabari, II, 460–61, reports 1728–173 1; also al-Jassas, I, 58.

75. Al-Tabari, II, 465–66.

76. Al-Wahidi, *Asbab*, 31 and *Wajiz*, 28; also al-Suyuti, *Lubab*, 24, second report; Berlin 3578, f. 7a; al-Qurtubi, II, 57; Muqatil, *Tafsir*, f. 19a; also al-Nahhas, 26; Ibn al-'Arabi, I, 32.

77. Al-Suyuti, *Lubab*, 24, reports six and seven and perhaps three; al-Tabari, II, 461–62, reports 1733–37; al-Jassas, I, 58 makes the transferral Jews-Jahiliyya complete by having the expression as one of mockery to the pagan Arabs. Al-Suyuti, *Lubab*, 24, report five, indicates a combination of reports also: the expression was Arabic, the Jews picked it up, so God prohibited its usage; no explanation is given. On this verse, see David Kunstlinger, " 'Ra'ina,' " *BSOAS* 5, vol. 4 (1930): 877–82 and Arthur Jeffery, "The Qur'an as Scripture," *Muslim World* 40 (1950): 260.

78. Al-Nahhas, 26; also see Makki, 107.

79. Al-Jassas, I, 58; also Ibn al-'Arabi, 1, 32; al-Qurtubi, II, 57–60.

80. Al-Wahidi, *Asbab*, 20–1; Berlin 3578, f. 5a.

81. Al-Wahidi, *Asbab*, 21; note that Berlin 3578, f. 5a, presents some alternative identifications for verse 21 as well: the unbelievers (according to al-Suddi) or the hypocrites (according to Muqatil; see his *Tafsir*, f. 6b).

82. Dr. J. Burton has pointed out to me that this apparent lack of halakhic discussion is reflective of the nature of the sources employed in this study; these sources, he suggests, present only a distillation of discussions going on elsewhere, in this case primarily in fiqh literature. This would indicate that there is another entire study to be done, beyond the context of the traditional *'ulum al-Qur'an* to which this study has directed its attention, in order to discover the complete picture of the *sabab* in the Islamic religious sciences, especially as that material relates to halakhic matters.

83. Ibn Kammuna, *Examination of the Three Faiths*, text, p. 87, trans., p. 127.

84. In 2:142 the reference *sa-yaqulu*, "they will say," is not elaborated in the *asbab* material; in 2:189a, the idea of "they will ask you" is likewise not seen as prophetic.

85. This paper is a distillation of chap. 3, part d, of my 1981 McGill dissertation "The Quranic *Asbab al-nuzul* Material: An Analysis of its Use and Development in Exegesis." Thanks are extended to Professor J. Wansbrough, SOAS, and Dr. C. J. Adams, McGill, for their help and encouragement. This paper was read at the Colloquium on Qur'an and Hadith held at University of Cambridge, September, 1985. M. Hinds, P. Crone, and G. Juynboll must be thanked for inviting me to the colloquium; the participants at that meeting, especially Dr. J. Burton, were most helpful with their comments.

Chapter 12

Methodological Approaches to Islamic Studies

Judith Koren and Yehuda D. Nevo

O ver the past few decades the western study of early Islamic history and religion, and of the place of the Koran as a scripture within it, has developed along two distinct paths. One—which we will here call the "traditional" approach—confines its field of enquiry to the Muslim literary sources, which it examines in ways consonant with the premises and traditions of Muslim scholarship. The other analyzes this literature by source-critical methods, and includes as evidence also the relevant contemporary non-Arabic literature, and material remains: the findings of archaeology, epigraphy, and numismatics, which are not generally studied by the "traditional" school. This is usually called the "revisionist" approach, more on the basis of its conclusions than its methods. We dislike this term, but will use it in this article in view of its general acceptance.

The "revisionist" approach is by no means monolithic; works by different authors offer conflicting accounts of the Arab conquests and the rise of Islam. But they share a basic set of methodological premises, which by and large are not accepted by the "traditional" approach; and they tend to lead to conclusions which—however much they conflict with each other—are united in denying historical validity to accounts based purely on "facts" derived from the Muslim literary sources. This being the case, it is not surprising that the rise of "revisionism" has met with considerable opposition. But its opponents do not, in general, argue

Originally published in *Der Islam* 68 (1991): 87–107. Reprinted by permission of Walter de Gruyter and Co.

against its *methods*—which are part of the normal western arsenal for attacking problems of ancient history—or its *evidence*; rather, they tend simply to dismiss its *conclusions*: to ignore "revisionist" publications, or even to reject out of hand the validity of a source-critical study (e.g., by labelling it "anti-Islam") without ever coming to grips with its basic premises, methods, and conclusions.[1] Thus the "traditional" and "revisionist" approaches are, for the most part, parallel strands which never touch, for the latter typically discounts the former's validity as historical enquiry, while the former at best ignores the latter altogether.

This situation was perhaps inevitable, for the premises and methodology of the two approaches actively conflict. The "revisionist" approach classifies the "traditional" as the study of religion and of literature, but not of history, either religious or political; for it maintains that early history can rarely be derived from the Muslim literature, and that attempts to do so are methodologically faulty. This is not an attitude which can be accommodated within the mainstream of traditional Islamic studies: the "traditional" and "revisionist" outlooks are deeply divided on methodological grounds. It is by now clear that the two methods cannot both be valid. The present authors, firm "revisionists," hope in this article to indicate the basic premises of the two approaches (which are usually implicit, more rarely stated openly), and to give a few examples of studies based on the "revisionist" approach. In the course of that survey it should become apparent why we consider this to be the correct method of approaching early Islamic history.

BASIC METHODOLOGICAL QUESTIONS

The "Traditional" Approach

The "traditional" school tends not to discuss questions of methodology. Martin (1985), a first step in that direction, is a reaction to the rise of "revisionism," and it is significant that the most cogent methodological exposition in it is the sole "revisionist" contribution, A. Rippin on Wansbrough. The basic premises of this approach must therefore be inferred from its publications. These premises, insofar as we understand them, may be stated as follows:

a. The enormous body of Muslim literature, dating from the mid-second/eighth century on, does in fact preserve historical facts about the pre-Islamic period, the rise of Islam and the Conquest. Therefore one can, by suitable analysis, construct a historically valid picture of *Jahili* society in the Hijaz, of the rise of Islam and the biography of the Prophet, the Conquest of the Near East and the subsequent early history of the Islamic State, based purely upon these sources.

b. Where accounts of the same event conflict (as they often do), it should be possible, by studying the chains of transmission (isnads) of these accounts and other factors, to decide which is the more likely to be true. One may be sure that "the truth" is hidden somewhere within them.

c. This being the case, there is no need to consider other evidence, which is much more intractable to analysis than written documents. The religious slogans on early Umayyad coins are an example: if they include clearly Muslim phrases, this adds nothing to our knowledge, and if they do not, it proves nothing, for we already know from the literary sources that the Arabs were Muslim from before the Conquest.

d. In general, this school rejects arguments *e silentio*: the lack of material evidence for a historical phenomenon attested by the literary sources does not invalidate these sources. Of course it does not corroborate them either, but this is of little consequence, for no corroboration is required.

e. The Koran is analyzed along the lines of accepted Muslim scholarship, i.e., one may categorize verses as "Meccan" or "Medinan," "early" or "late" revelations, without entering into the question of what "revelation" means outside the framework of Muslim belief.

f. *Linguistic analysis*: the meanings of most semantic elements are accepted from classical Muslim scholarship, so that modern methods of linguistic enquiry are unnecessary, and may safely be disregarded as irrelevant.

The "Revisionist" Approach

An explicit statement of basic methodology has been given by Wansbrough in a 1986 lecture.[2] We may summarize his points, with our own additions and comments, as follows:

a. A written source—any written source—cannot tell us "what really happened", but only what the author(s) *thought* had happened or *wanted to believe* had happened or *wanted others to believe* had happened. Thus before we can consider the historicity of a written account, we have to consider problems of the extent of the author's *knowledge*, and his *intentions*. This is the basic problem in the use of a written text, and outside the field of Arab studies has given rise to its own literature of historical methodology.[3]

b. Only an eyewitness "knows" what he writes (and even this knowledge is subject to conscious and unconscious interpretation which attempts to fit it into his preexisting knowledge). A contemporary chronicler may—perhaps—be accorded near-eyewitness status. Everyone else, writer or reader, has to *accept* that the contemporary account is true, and by extension, that the later accounts supposedly based on it are also true. There are two possible bases for this acceptance. The preferred method is to crosscheck against external evidence: other contemporary accounts (which may, taken together, cancel out the personal biases and defects of any single author), and even better, non-written remains from the period in question. In the absence of such evidence, the other way is to see what other people accept to be true: "one reads the works of one's colleagues, and, sooner or later, something like a consensus emerges."[4] But this approach is problematical, for it is possible by such means to build cloud-capp'd towers on essentially unpinned foundations.

c. Wansbrough sees another problem of written sources, to which we, however, would accord less importance than he does: that the very act of writing distorts "what really happened" by reducing it to a series of words, thus imposing on it an order, linearity, and sequentiality which the events described may not have had.[5]

d. The *transmission history* of an ancient document is open to great doubt. This is not just a question of the usual quota of copyists' errors, but of more insidious divergences from the original; for a writer who was demonstrably working within the framework of an accepted version of history will, even unconsciously, alter older texts in ways that accord with that view. We have therefore to contend with transmitters who interpret the older text in ways that they "know" to be true: by embellishing and explaining, or adding, subtracting, or substituting a word, a phrase or a gloss here and there. An example would be the use of the term "Muslim" where the older text had "Hagarene" or "Ishmaelite" or "Saracen," or the substitution of the word "Muhammad" for an original "the Prophet"; or the assignation of the name of a battle familiar from the Muslim literary sources to the description of a battle originally unnamed, or given a name which does not appear in the "known" version of history.[6] If the older text did not survive independently, it is nearly impossible to detect such tampering with it. We cannot, then, accept an excerpt from an older text found in a later writer as an accurate transmission of the text at this level.

e. The conclusion from the above points is that written sources are deceptive in promising to give us an account of "what really happened"; they cannot, by their very nature, provide "hard facts" but only *the writer's view of what he knows of those facts*—i.e., they are *literature*. The study of them is not *history*, but *literary criticism*.[7] The information they provide must be corroborated by the "hard facts" of material remains, which, as one archaeologist has succinctly put it, "represent what somebody once did, not what some contemporary or later writer says that they did."[8] If this is true even of contemporary accounts, it is truer still of the Muslim literature, which did not start to be recorded till a hundred and fifty years after the events it claims to describe, and most of which was written under a régime with a vested interest to legitimize its own claims to power and to discredit the Umayyads, whose history it purported to record. The " 'Abbasid bias" is well known; that it might have involved rewriting both political and religious history is worth considering. Again, outside of Arab studies the political use of religious belief is accepted as commonplace: it is, for instance, well known "that in order to make them more authoritative [polemical] stories and [political] slogans were often circulated by centers of prophecy or were linked with famous cult centers and that they exploited ancient myths and hallowed traditions."[9] In such cirumstances it is even more important to corroborate the written accounts from outside sources, or else to base one's research on a sound methodology which enables one "to extrapolate from the literary version(s) what is likely to have happened."[10] It is a basic weakness of the "traditional" approach that such a methodological foundation has not been published; rather, the historical value of the Muslim literature seems to be assumed. The need to crosscheck that literature against "concrete facts" has been discounted—which is what Wansbrough means when he says that "the literary account of the Hijaz has gradually assumed the status of an archaeological site."[11] Wansbrough considered that the "hard facts" necessary for comparison are simply not available; we submit that they are, from archaeology, numismatics, and epigraphy, and that research in these fields does not in fact corroborate the "traditional" account of the rise of Islam and the early Arab state, but presents a different picture of seventh-century history, one much more in line with the conclusions Wansbrough himself reached on the basis of source-criticism of the Koran and Muslim literature.[12]

f. There are problems in using material evidence. For one thing, what has been discovered or has survived is always more or less due to chance, and is only a fraction of the whole—but then the same may be said of the written sources. For another, there are no ready-made causal connections: the meaning behind each piece of the jigsaw puzzle, and the links between the different pieces, have to be supplied. Nonetheless this undertaking is less difficult than the prospect of distilling history from a written account, when in order to do so one must allow for the author's degree of knowledge, intelligence, and powers of reasoning and drawing conclusions, his personality, view of history (which will inevitably influence his choice of what to record and how to record it), and aims in writing—none of which are fully known, and some of which may not be known at all. Raw, unsieved evidence is preferable to that selected according to unknown criteria. Thus although it looks easier to get history out of written sources than archaeological ones, it often proves much more difficult. Indeed, the very fact that it does look easy to get history out of a written source is evidence that considerable *literary* efforts have been invested, rather than that the account is "true." Authenticity, as Wansbrough reminds us, "can be as much a result of (successful) narrative technique as of veracity";[13] and with specific reference to the Muslim versions of history, Conrad points out that "such [fragmentary and incomplete] evidence as was available to each authority was pieced together by him with a view to producing a plausible and coherent narrative of events. That the resulting reconstructions appear reasonable simply reflects the purpose of the exercise and proves nothing so far as the historical accuracy of these scenarios is concerned.[14] Nonetheless, the written sources do exist and this approach does not maintain that they should never be used. The point is rather that their versions should always be checked against external (preferably material) evidence, and where the two conflict, the latter should be preferred.

g. Since external evidence is necessary to corroborate a view derived solely from the Muslim literary account, lack of such corroboration is an important argument against that account's historicity. This approach is therefore more open than the "traditional" to acceptance of an *argumentum e silentio*. For if we are ready to discount an uncorroborated report of an event, we must accept that there may be nothing with which to replace it: that the event simply did not happen. That there is no evidence for it outside of the "traditional account" thus becomes positive evidence in support of the hypothesis that it did not happen. A striking example is the lack of evidence, outside the Muslim literature, for the view that the Arabs were Muslim at the time of the Conquest.

h. The Koran is viewed in the same way as the Old Testament has been viewed by biblical scholars for over a century: as a literary source to be critically analyzed in order to ascertain its probable origins and textual history. Moreover its language, too, is open to the same type of critical linguistic analysis as any other: it has no special status.

The "revisionist" approach thus rests essentially on three basic methodological requirements: (1) a source-critical approach to both the Koran and the
Muslim literary accounts of the rise of Islam, the Conquest, and the Umayyad
period; (2) the need to compare these accounts with contemporary ones external
to the Muslim tradition; (3) the use of contemporary material evidence (archaeology, numismatics. epigraphy) and the acceptance that conclusions derived
from it are likely to be more valid than those based on the non-contemporary, literary Muslim accounts of history. We should like to give a few examples of
recent work based on each of these main tenets. Obviously we cannot enter here
into the detailed analysis of the evidence found in each: our point is rather to
indicate the methods used and the *conclusions* reached by using them.

THE USE OF SOURCE-CRITICISM

It is interesting to compare the current situation in Islamic studies with that of
Old Testament studies in nineteenth-century England. As is well known, the
source-critical method of studying the Old Testament—and especially the Pentateuch—developed in Germany, and in England through most of the nineteenth-
century, as a recent study has pointed out, "any theologian with sympathy for
German achievements could be sure of hostility directed from all sides of an
overwhelmingly orthodox establishment."[15] Thus while German scholars were
spending most of the nineteenth century arguing over when the original *Grund-
schrift* of the Pentateuch had been written, how many redactions it had undergone, and what each redactor had added, in England the view that critical scholarship meant unbelief and must therefore at all costs be prevented held sway until
finally swept away by Wellhausen not long before the end of the century.[16]

While England was experiencing the shift of paradigm that followed the
publication of Wellhausen's *Prolegomena* (1885), and following the long tradition in Germany, Goldziher's study of the Muslim literary sources[17] suggested
some conclusions of a "source-critical" nature in this field, too: that the data on
the Umayyad period in the Muslim sources probably do not derive from the times
to which they are ascribed. In other words, the Muslim sources do not faithfully
transmit historical information, but are literary creations based on a transmission
history (isnads) whose validity remains doubtful. They "are primarily documents
which show how the oldest teachers of Islam [!—Goldziher is talking about the
late second-century teachers] set out to teach in the spirit of the founder";[18] they
are full of "unhistorical data invented by philologists and antiquarians of the
second century,"[19] and the picture they provide of Jahili society indicates, not the

situation in the early seventh-century Peninsula, but "the Beduins' reaction to Muslim teaching at a time when the greater part of the traditions came into being—i.e., at a time when Islam was strong, or even dominant."[20] These views Goldziher grounded in an examination of selected Hadith (such as Muhammad's speech in Mecca during his farewell pilgrimage) and themes (e.g., the Beduin aversion to prayer and glorification of wine-drinking). In general, he argued, many Hadith and ascriptions to the Prophet arose from religious or political need—i.e., they are the coinages of polemic.[21] One should date them by reference to cultural or historical events. For instance, suggested Goldziher, foreigners "presumably originated all those traditions which are intent on reinforcing the teaching of the equality of all believers irrespective of race"[22]—mainly in the second century A.H.—whereas the traditions enjoining respect for Arabs date from the fourth century, when Persian influence had become so strong that the Arabs were the ones despised.[23]

Such views met with the same lack of receptivity that previous generations had accorded to Old Testament source-criticism: the new developments in biblical studies did not cross-pollinate the study of Islam. But Goldziher confined his scepticism to questions of the date of origin of Hadith and legal material, otherwise accepting the "traditional" historical framework and the historicity of Muhammad. It was thus possible to select parts of his work and ignore the rest; and Goldziher's more radical views did remain largely ignored until the return, in the last few decades, to the source-critical method of investigating both the Koran—first as the authority for legal material (Schacht 1950), and then as a work of literature and a scripture (Wansbrough 1977, 1978)—and the classical Muslim literature.

The Koran

The main practitioner of source-critical analysis of the Koran to date has been Wansbrough, chiefly in *Qur'anic Studies*. He there concluded that the Koranic material originated as *logia* and pericopes which came to form several different collections over a long period of transmission. The clear evidence of oral delivery does not exclude the possibility that these *logia* and collections also came to exist in written forms. The different collections could have grown up in different geographical areas, one of which war, probably Mesopotamia, and/or in different *sectarian communities*. In other words, they were separated either by differing belief or different locations, or both.[24]

These conclusions are based on an analysis of several aspects of the Koran:

1. Its *thematic content*: Wansbrough isolated four basic monotheistic themes, handled in a very repetitive style, which "could indicate either a long period of oral transmission or an original series of uncoordinated pericopes, or both."[25]

2. Its *vocabulary* and *imagery*, which suggest the latter—that the Koran is a collection of several different collections of *logia*, which developed "from originally independent traditions during a long period of transmission."[26]

3. Its *structure*, which supports the same conclusions. Wansbrough considers that the Koran was canonized only at the end of the second/eighth century.

4. The *variant traditions* it preserves, which do not support the theory that there was one original text, but suggest rather "the existence of independent, possibly regional traditions incorporated more or less intact into the canonical compilation.[27] It is characteristic of the Koran that "a comparatively small number of themes is preserved in varying stages of literary achievement"[28]— for example, the su'ayb traditions in suras 7, 11, 26, and 29, and the descriptions of "two gardens" in sura 55. The Muslim explanation of the existence of variant traditions as due to the chronology of revelation is problematic, and seems to have been invented to explain away a serious obstacle to acceptance of the Koran as God's Word.

5. Its *language*: there are similarities with usages of the cognate Hebrew words in the Pentateuch and, especially, the later prophets; thus the literary history of the Koran leads back to the Judaic and Christian tradition.[29] Similarly, even the most elementary *stylistic analysis* demonstrates that the Koran's audience was expected to be familiar with the stories of Judaic-Christian scripture.[30]

All of these conclusions are based on detailed textual arguments; in order to refute them, one needs to refute these arguments. The "traditional" school has not so far come to grips with this problem. But its own view that the Koran was composed by Muhammad in the Hijaz and canonized within a generation of the Conquest, and that variant accounts are due to the piecemeal way in which the Koran was "revealed" to the Prophet—depends on a priori acceptance of the Muslim sources' version of history. The source-critical method's view of the Koran rests on a surer foundation, for it derives from detailed examination of the text itself, whereas the "traditional" view derives from later exegesis of it. The source-critical approach brings to the study of Islamic materials a basic methodology accepted in the West for the past two centuries for the study of the literary sources of the Judaic and Christian traditions, while basing its choice of the *cri-*

teria to use on the Koranic text itself. Rejection of this approach presupposes that these methods of analysis, so fruitful in the study of one Scripture, are totally worthless for studying another, related one. This assumption remains to be proved, and so far the 'traditionalist" school has not attempted to prove it.

Schacht on Law

Goldziher considered most of the legal material ascribed to the Prophet to be, like the Hadith, of much later date. Following this lead, Schacht (1950) analyzed the development of *legal theory* and *legal traditions* in the Muslim sources. He concluded that "Muhammadan law did not derive directly from the Koran but developed . . . out of popular and administrative practice under the Umayyads, and this practice often diverged from the intentions and even the explicit wording of the Koran . . . norms derived from the Koran were introduced into Muhammadan law almost invariably at a secondary stage."[31] There are a very few exceptions, mainly regarding divorce law, but as Wansbrough points out, these are evidence for the existence, in the Umayyad period, of Koranic material, not for the existence of the canon.[32] There is in fact no contradiction between Schacht's conclusions and Wansbrough's view of the Koran as a late compilation of oral and written pericopes. Wansbrough concludes, from source analysis of the Koran, that it was compiled/canonized at the end of the second/eighth century; Schacht concludes, from analysis of the Muslim legal literature, that law started to be derived from the Koran, as Scripture, in the third/ninth century.

Attitudes to Isnads

"Traditional" scholarship, like Muslim scholarship, devotes much attention to establishing the reliability of chains of transmission (isnads). But a critical approach to them soon leads to the conclusion that they cannot be relied upon to authenticate historical data—a conclusion already reached, again, by Goldziher. As part of his study of law, Schacht examined the growth, back-formation, and lateral spread of isnads, with detailed examples.[33] He concluded that "some of those isnads which [the Muhammadan scholars] esteem most highly are the result of widespread fabrications."[34] Specifically, "wherever the sources available enable us to judge, we find that the legal traditions from Companions are as little authentic as those from the Prophet"—the traditions attributed to particular Companions are "products of schools of thought which put their doctrines under the authority of the Companions in question."[35] One must, for many reasons, accept the fictitious nature of the early sections of isnads, and the much later date of the material to which they are attached, and reject "the uncritical acceptance at their face value of isnads as far back as the time of the Companions."[36] Thus much of the work of the "traditional" approach is unacceptable as historical evidence: "their whole technical criticism of traditions, which is mainly based on the criticism of isnads, is irrelevant for the purpose of historical analysis."[37]

Michael Cook, building on Schacht's work, has examined the growth and especially the spread of isnads occasioned by "the pressure of elegance on truth," and provides detailed examples illustrating the various mechanisms which could be involved.[38] His conclusion is that they are inadmissible as proof of historicity: "the traditions have to be dated on external criteria" (i.e., external to the isnad).[39] Wansbrough characteristically takes the conclusion much further. He argues that the isnads are methodologically impossible to accept, because of their internal contradiction, anonymity, and arbitrary nature: "biographical information on the exegetes [i.e., those mentioned in the isnad] is found exclusively in literature composed to impugn [them] or to vindicate [them] . . . or to assess [their] relative merit . . . and as such constitutes merely a pseudohistorical projection of the acceptance or dismissal of their views."[40] He sees *all* the stories—not just the legal material studied by Schacht—purporting to come from seventh-century figures: Companions and Successors, as well as the Prophet himself, as stories originating at the time they were written, i.e., from the end of the second/eighth century on.[41] Thus, for example, Ibn 'Abbas may reasonably be seen as a personification of consensus (*ijma'*)—if one needed an authority for a point involving the principle of *ijma'*, one could provide it with an isnad back to Ibn 'Abbas, or to one of his disciples transmitting on his authority, which resulted in the proliferation of "companion isnads." Similarly, 'Umar represents an "anti-tafsir" tradition, 'Uthman a "canonization" one. Both were mechanisms designed to give the earliest possible origin to the views of the writer or transmitter of the story or argument. To argue that no works of scriptural comment/interpretation have survived from before the late second century because variant texts were destroyed is "contrived and internally inconsistent": It is much simpler, and therefore more convincing, to conclude that no one commented because nothing existed to comment on. When Scripture and, therefore, commentary arose, a means of proving the authenticity of one's view (as deriving from a known early authority) was necessary, and the isnads filled this need.[42]

As Cook has pointed out,[43] we have here a basic methodological question which depends on one's choice of paradigm. If one accepts the essential authenticity of the isnads preserved in the Muslim literature, then the existence of several different isnads for a single tradition, all deriving from, for instance, the Prophet, is very strong proof that the tradition is authentic—i.e., that the Prophet did indeed relate the Hadith attributed to him. If one accepts that isnads both spread and grow backwards, neither an attribution to the Prophet, nor the existence of several different isnads making this attribution, have any necessary historical value. "On this issue the choice is between Schacht and Shaf'i: there is no methodological middle ground."[44]

Many "traditional" scholars do now accept that many isnads are definitely spurious, and many others probably unreliable, and even that we often cannot tell the status of an isnad. But they have not drawn the conclusion which the "revisionist" approach would regard as inevitable: that the historicity of the data supposedly transmitted by these means is thereby placed in doubt. To accept the arguments without accepting the conclusion is a difficult position to maintain. One suspects that it can only be held because the "traditional" approach continues to reject the basis of both arguments and conclusion: that the "Traditional Account" is only a hypothesis which may be disproved by contrary evidence.

Crone on Trade

It is almost an axiom of Muslim studies that Mecca was the center of an important international trading network, from which its inhabitants gained considerable wealth and a preeminent position in Peninsular politics. The items traded through this network have usually been seen as Arabian spices and incense, with the addition of a transit trade in high-cost, low-bulk luxury wares from India, supplied to the Mediterranean world. Crone (1987) has studied this trade in both the Muslim and non-Muslim literature, and demonstrated that the whole picture is unfounded. Mecca was not on the overland trade route from Southern Arabia to Syria, which in any case was never very important compared to the maritime route through the Red Sea and by the end of the second century A.D., at latest, was no longer in use (chapter 2). A close examination of the Muslim sources themselves shows that, except for Yemeni perfume, the Meccans traded mainly in cheap leather goods and clothing, and, occasionally, in basic foodstuffs (clarified butter and cheese) (chapter 4). These goods were not exported to Syria, which already had plenty of them, but were supplied almost exclusively to inhabitants of the Peninsula (chapter 5). None of the different versions in the Muslim sources support the conclusions reached by early western scholars and accepted since.

Thus far, a "traditionalist" could have produced a work with such a conclusion; and indeed, parts of Crone's analysis are based on the work of Kister (1965). The difference lies in the additional conclusions which an adherent of the "new" approach is prepared to draw. Crone goes on to point out that the traditions in the Muslim account conflict with each other so often and so regularly "that one could, were one so inclined, rewrite most of Montgomery Watt's biography of Muhammad in the reverse."[45] Source-criticism attempting to separate "early" from "late" traditions, and accept the former, leads to the conclusion "that the Meccans did not trade outside Mecca on the eve of Islam."[46] But in fact neither "early" nor "late" traditions were concerned to preserve the truth: they should all be regarded as storytellers' fabrications, whose writers knew little about seventh-century Hijazi trade in general, or Meccan trade in particular. Thus "whether the Meccans traded outside Mecca on the eve of Islam or not is a question that cannot be answered on the basis of these stories. Indeed, the very theme of trade could be legendary."[47] Crone concluded, after examining the variant accounts, that there was no continuous transmission of historical fact through the three generations or so that separated the early first/seventh century from the mid-second/eighth-century (and later) recorders of the tales that had meanwhile grown up. Thus "it was the storytellers who created the tradition; the sound historical tradition to which they are supposed to have added their fables simply did not exist."[48] This could be said of the whole historical tradition, not just of trade—for instance, Crone illustrates it with reference to the date of the Battle of Badr.[49] Crone, then, concludes like Wansbrough that the Traditional Account is literature, not history; and like Goldziher, Schacht, Wansbrough, and Cook, that the lines of transmission from the early first/seventh century are pure fabrications.

EVIDENCE EXTERNAL TO THE MUSLIM ACCOUNT

Contemporary Accounts in Non-Arab Literature

Brock (1982) has considered historical references to the Arabs in seventh-century Syriac works, i.e., those written by the people who witnessed the Arab takeover of the Fertile Crescent. He concluded that the authors did not, at the time, perceive events as an organized conquest, and that only after a decade at least did they become aware that they had witnessed the arrival of an organized Arab kingdom.[50] Moreover they may only have used the term "kingdom" (*malkuta*) because they were accustomed to thinking in biblical terms, and saw the Arab successes as fulfillmerits of prophecy; for it was not till much nearer the end of the seventh century that they conceived of Arab rule as Arab Empire, equating the new political order with the old. Brock notes, similarly, the lack of references to Islam in the literature of the Christian inhabitants—who lived side by side with the newcomers and indeed intermarried with them to an alarming extent—and their late recognition of it as a new religion.[51] And he points out that there are no details of Muhammad's early career in any Byzantine or Syriac sources which predate the Muslim literature on the subject. Brock's field of interest is not the Arabic literature, but the Syriac and Byzantine; thus he makes no attempt to reconcile these facts with accepted Arab history. He confines himself to indicating that these sources' writers did not *perceive*, or *notice*, or *recognize* the fact of Arab rule for the first decade at least, nor the Arab religion for most of the first century. This conclusion is not based on source-criticism, but on a simple examination of what these authors say, and how they say it.

The present authors have studied the political and religious references to the Arabs in all the seventh-century sources that mention them (mainly Syriac, but also Byzantine authors and the Armenian Sebeos).[52] We conclude that the local sources written before the early eighth century provide no evidence for a *planned invasion* of Arabs from the Peninsula, nor for great battles which crushed the Byzantine army; nor do they mention any caliph before Mu'awiya, who by contrast is clearly a historical figure fully attested from several works. The picture the contemporary literary sources provide is rather of raids of the familiar type; the raiders stayed because they found no military opposition. We suggest, on this and other evidence, that what took place was a series of raids and minor engagements, which gave rise to stories among the Arab newcomers of How We Beat the Romans; these were later selected and embellished in late Umayyad and early 'Abbasid times to form an Official History of the Conquest. The *ayyam* nature of these accounts explains why the written versions in the Traditional Muslim account disagree with each other concerning the names of battles, of commanders, the number of participants and casualties, and so on. Furthermore, if we are to judge from this literature, we must conclude that the mass of the Arab tribesmen were pagan at the time of their influx into the Fertile Crescent, and remained so throughout the seventh century; the governing élite adopted a simple form of monotheism, basically Judaeo-Christian, which may be discerned in an account of official Christian dealings with the Arab governor already from the early years of Mu'awiya's rule (the 640s/20s).[53] Neither the references to the Koran nor the accounts of Muhammad in the non-Arab literature predate the writing of the Traditional Muslim account. Moreover one can discern signs, in so late a work as John of Damascus' *De Haeresibus* (743 C.E.), that the Koran had not yet been canonized.

Archaeological Evidence

The archaeological work published on the Byzantine *limes arabicus* over the last decade, mainly by S. T. Parker,[54] has important implications for the history of the

Arab conquest. A survey of the *limes arabicus* in 1976, followed by excavations of the forts along the *limes*, led to the conclusion that Byzantium abandoned most of its fortifications during the fifth and sixth centuries C.E. and withdrew most of the regular troops, leaving frontier defense mainly in the hands of the Arab phylarchs.[55] For instance, the forts of Fityan, Yasir, and probably Bsir were peacefully abandoned before 500 C.E., and Lajun after the earthquake of 551.[56] By the end of Justinian's reign, Byzantium had essentially withdrawn from the Arabian frontier: "both legionary camps, sixteen of twenty-four *castella*, and all twelve watchtowers surveyed were abandoned by the late sixth century," and "the eight watchtowers in the Hisma, were also not occupied."[57] Nor, as far as the archaeological work carried out to date can tell, were any forts or watchtowers from Wadi Hasa to Edom, a ca. 100-km stretch of frontier. Moreover, even the eight *castella* that were occupied were not necessarily being used for military purposes, for the only indication of occupation is Late Byzantine pottery, which could equally have been left by people (monks or desert dwellers) who moved in after the *limes* had been abandoned.[58] In addition, Byzantium also apparently wound down her civilian presence, in the sense that she neither allowed the local authorities to continue to invest in the cities nor did so herself: "there is virtually no evidence of imperial patronage of secular building in sixthcentury Syria. The government took over the finance of building and maintenance of public monuments from the cities and their councils and was then unwilling or unable to sustain its commitments."[59]

Archaeological evidence thus indicates that Byzantium began to withdraw militarily from al-Sham already a hundred years before the Sassanian forays started in 604 C.E. By the mid-sixth century she was no longer interested in the upkeep of civilian settlements either, and by the early seventh century she had physically withdrawn from civilian settlements in al-Sham, leaving only a limited Imperial presence in a few places.[60] The Persians had further continued this trend by deporting large numbers of Melkite Christians. After Heraclius defeated the Persians, he did not return real Imperial forces to any area south of Antioch, nor regarrison or even militarily strengthen the *limes arabicus*. The conclusion this archaeological evidence invites is that Byzantium had made a policy decision, long before the Conquest, that she would not defend al-Sham. This casts some doubts on the historicity of parts, at least, of the Traditional Account of the Conquest. One may try to formulate other accounts of this period which do accord with the archaeological evidence;[61] one cannot simply disregard it.

Another area in which extensive archaeological work has been invested over the past few decades is the Hijaz. Arab and western archaeologists have carried out large-scale, systematic surveys and excavations over the Jordanian desert, the Arabian Peninsula, and especially the Hijaz.[62] They have found Hellenistic, Nabatean, Roman, and early Byzantine remains, but no signs of local Arab cultures from the sixth and early seventh centuries, except for some tumuli in the Jordanian desert, which were not accompanied by any indication of settlement.[63] In particular, no sixth- or seventh-century Jahili pagan sites, and no pagan sanctuaries such as the Muslim sources describe, have been found in the Hijaz or indeed anywhere in the area surveyed. Judging from archaeology, the pagan cults these sources describe were not a Hijazi phenomenon. Furthermore, the archaeological work has revealed no trace of Jewish settlement at Medina, Khaybar, or Wadi al-Qurra. Both these points contrast directly with the Muslim literary sources' descriptions of the demographic composition of the pre-Islamic Hijaz. This is of course an *argumentum e silentio*; but if the Muslim sources really did preserve a historical account of sixth- and early seventh-century Hijazi society, the archaeological work already done should have revealed at least some points of correlation with it.

This lack of material evidence for Jahili paganism in the Hijaz is highlighted by the wealth of such evidence in an area disregarded by the literary sources—the Central Negev. Shrines and stone stelae testify to a continuous cult of stela worship there from the Nabataean period down to the start of the 'Abbasid, i.e., first to mid-eighth century C.E. Judging from the findings of the recent surveys and excavations, active pagans must have formed a considerable part of the Negev population right through the first one-and-a-half centuries of the Muslim era, and paganism apparently reached its zenith in Hisam's reign, when many pagan cultic centers were built. The 1985 surface survey of the Negev discovered some thirty sites of this kind.[64] These pagan centers correlate highly with the descriptions of the Jahili pagan sanctuaries in the Muslim literary sources, especially regarding the topography of the sites and the layout of the buildings.[65] Thus the archaeological evidence indicates that the pagan sanctuaries described in the Muslim sources did not exist in the Jahili Hijaz, but sanctuaries strongly resembling them did exist in the Central Negev until soon after the 'Abbasids came to power. This in turn suggests that the accounts of Jahili religion in the Hijaz could well be back-projections of a paganism actually known from later and elsewhere.

At Sde Boqer the end of the pagan center can be dated to circa 160–170 A.H. Down to this date, over thirty such centers were active in the Central Negev, i.e., they were periodically visited and pagan ceremonies were performed in them. Such a widespread cult with so many centers of worship could not have existed in a barren desert area without the government's knowledge: and since a desert population is not self-sufficient, but depends on economic contact with the surrounding populations of the settled land, one must conclude that its very existence implied acquiescence on the part of the central government, at least under the Umayyads. This again cannot be easily reconciled with the traditional Muslim account. Sooner or later the "traditional" hypotheses regarding the course of early Islamic history will have to be refrained to take account of these archaeological findings.

Numismatics

The use of numismatic evidence is still in its infancy and involves several problems. For instance, most of the work on the early Arab coins to date has been done by numismatists, who are naturally interested in quite different features from those of value to historians. Moreover, coins are published in a wide range of works, varying from auction catalogs to the appendices of reports on archaeological excavations; much of this literature is difficult of access and immensely time-consuming to study. Problems of interpretation also complicate the use of numismatic evidence. On the whole it is best seen as an auxiliary aid, not to be used as the main evidence for a particular reading of history. Nonetheless coins can provide a great deal of evidence. For the historian of the early Arab State, the first task is to become accustomed to the idea of using them as sources of historical data. This is even truer for the historian of the early Arab religion. An important first step in this direction is Bates (1986)—though we cannot subscribe to all of his conclusions—and he, too, argues the need for historians to utilize numismatic evidence. The present authors have also attempted to derive information regarding the progress of the Arab takeover of al-Sham from the early municipal issues of Arab-Byzantine coins.[66] We tentatively concluded that the towns of al-Sham recognized Arab sovereignty gradually over a period of time, starting with Jaras and Baysan in the south in the 630s/10s and extending to Hims and Tartus in the north, possibly as much as a few decades later. It was not until relatively late that a centralized government imposed uniformity of minting processes on the various towns, and this stage may not have been reached till the Battle of Siffin. Moreover, the numismatic data provides no evidence that Mu'awiya at any time controlled the towns of Central Palestine ('Amman—Iliya' [Jerusalem] Bayt Jibrin).

These conclusions are tentative and represent one possible way of reading the evidence. Much less tentative are the conclusions regarding the early stages of the Arab religion. Here the numismatic evidence comes from the Arab-Sassanian coins which, unlike the Arab-Byzantine, routinely bear both dates and religious legends from the earliest issues down to 'Abd al-Malik's reform. Several different religious formulae were used, but until circa 70 A.H. none of them includes either the name Muhammad or any specifically Islamic phrases. Instead, the phrases used (e.g., *bism Allah, bism Allah rabbi/al-malik, rabbi Allah*) are of a general monotheistic nature which the members of any of the area's many monotheistic religions could have accepted.[67] As we mentioned earlier, the "traditional" approach to seventh-century Arab history would consider this fact to be beside the point. We, on the other hand, argue that minting coins is an official act of political as well as economic significance, and that the legends on coins are official pronouncements of current State attitudes (in this case to religion), intended for wide promulgation. Merely placing religious formulae on coins involves a conscious act of choice regarding what to say and what to omit. The religious formulae that the State saw fit to proclaim by such means are therefore an important indication of State religious policy. One cannot, then, brush aside as irrelevant the lack of any apparent State interest in referring to Muhammad or using religious slogans with specifically Muslim content before 71 A.H., especially when such slogans, once introduced, became obligatory on all coins minted over a wide area.

Epigraphy

The Arabian Peninsula and the Syro-Jordanian desert, including the Negev, are strewn with literally thousands of rock inscriptions, at first pagan ones in the various epigraphic Peninsular languages, and later monotheistic ones in classical Arabic in the Kufic script. The "traditional" school approaches these inscriptions from within a clear paradigm: Islam existed from the 620 C.E., therefore all the monotheistic Kufic inscriptions were written by Muslims. This viewpoint obviously sees no need to search in this material for evidence of religious development, nor, conversely, to use the stage of religious development evidenced by an inscription in order to date it. If an inscription is undated (as most are), it is assigned a date on purely palaeographic grounds—a highly risky and imprecise procedure, since early Arabic palaeography is notoriously unreliable, and can date most inscriptions only as "first to third centuries A.H."[68] A "revisionist" approach to the same material would critically analyze the incriptions' religious content in the hope of discerning differences of religious development and determining a chronological sequence.[69] It would, besides, admit as evidence a great deal of background information considered irrelevant by "traditionalists." It would note, for instance, that no inscriptions in Classical Arabic have been found in the Hijaz from before the first years of Mu'awiya's reign. The earliest date from the 40s/660s, and come from the Ta'if area, which Mu'awiya seems to have been interested to colonize around that time. It would further note that there are no pagan inscriptions in Classical Arabic, nor do any Classical Arabic inscriptions make any mention of paganism, or include pagan names, such as are usually found among first-generation converts.[70] This suggests that Classical Arabic arose in a nonpagan milieu and that the owners of the monotheistic Classical Arabic inscriptions were not converts from paganism. The "revisionist" approach would, thirdly, point to the unexplained adoption by Classical Arabic of an Aramaic (twenty-two-letter) script quite unsuited to transcribing Arabic, even though a much more suitable South Arabian script with twenty-eight to twenty-nine letters was being used to write Arabic by the Jahili Peninsular tribes (Tamudians, Safaites, Lihyanites). That the Hijazi Arabs chose an unsuitable northern script in preference to a suitable local one would appear to require some explanation. And fourthly, it would note that Classical Arabic occurs in the Hijaz in a developed form—there are, in that area, no traces of development from an earlier form of either the language or the script. To find such traces one must turn to Syria, where inscriptions in a close variety of Classical Arabic and an early Kufic script appear (e.g., on church lintels) in the sixth century C.E.[71] All these points together suggest, to a "revisionist" that Classical Arabic in fact arose in Syria rather than the Peninsula, and penetrated to the Hijaz only as part of Mu'awiya's colonization efforts in the 40s A.H. Such a conclusion is likely to be rejected out of hand by the "traditional" school, because it is incompatible with the Muslim sources' version of history. But again, this can only be done by ignoring the epigraphic evidence rather than confronting it.

The differences between the two approaches may perhaps be summed up as follows. The ability to derive history from the account of seventh-century events found in the Muslim sources is, for the "traditional" approach, a basic fact, the one firm basis on which to build. For the "revisionist" approach, it is merely a hypothesis which needs to be proved; and the more external evidence one examines, the harder it becomes to prove it. The "traditional' school is methodologically unprepared for these demands to provide proof of initial premises; it therefore tends to disregard them, or even to discount them as occasioned by religious and/or political bias.[71] We consider that in the long run an approach whose methodological foundations are clearly stated and defendable, and whose historical theories are based on the widest possible range of evidence, must prove more attractive than an approach that lacks these attributes.

BIBLIOGRAPHY

Bates, M. L. "History, Geography, and Numismatics in the First Century of Islamic Coinage." *Revue Suisse de Numismatique* 65 (1986): 231–61, Pl. 31. (We owe this reference to Mr. Shraga Qedas.)

Brock, S. P. "Syriac Sources for Seventh-Century History." *Byzantine and Modern Greek Studies* 2 (1976): 17–36.

——— "Syriac Views of Emergent Islam." *Studies on the First Century of Islamic Society*. Edited by G. H. A. Juynboll. Carbondale: Southern Illinois University Press, 1982.

Chabot, J. B. *Littérature Syriaque*. Paris: Bloud and Gay, 1934.

Colt Archaeological Institute. *Excavations at Nessana: Report of the Colt Archaeological Expedition*. Princeton University Press, 1950–1962. 3 vols. (The Arab papyri are in vol. III.)

Conrad, Lawrence I. "The Early Muslim Campaign in Southern Palestine." Typescript.

Cook, Michael. *Early Muslim Dogma: A Source Critical Study*. London: Cambridge University Press, 1981.

Crawford, Michael, ed. Sources for Ancient History. London: Cambridge University Press, 1983.

Crone, Patricia. *Meccan Trade and the Rise of Islam*. Princeton, N.J.: Princeton University Press, 1987.

Goldhizer, I. *Muslim Studies*. Translated by C. R. Barber and S. M. Stern, edited by S. M. Stern. Albany: State University of New York Press, 1966.

Grohmann, Adolf. *Arabic Inscriptions*: Part 2 vol. 1 of *Expedition Philby-Ryckmans-Lippens en Arabie*. Louvain: Publications Universitaires, 1962. *Arabische Paläographie*, Bd. 2, Tl. 2, Wien: Böhlaus, 1971.

Hawting, G. R. "We Were Not Ordered With Entering It." *BSOAS* 47 (1984): 228–42.

Kaegi, Walter E. "Initial Byzantine Reactions to the Arab Conquest." *Church History* 38 (1969): 139–49.

Kennedy, Hugh. "The Last Century of Byzantine Syria: A Reinterpretation." *Byzantinische Forschungen* 10 (1985): 141–83.

Khan, M., and Ali Mughannam. "Ancient Dams in the Ta'if Area 1981 (1401)." *Atlal* 6.

Kister, M. J. "Mecca and Tamim (Aspects of Their Relations)." *Journal of the Economic and Social History of the Orient* 8 (1965): 113–63. Also reprinted in *Studies in Jahiliyya and Early Islam*. London: Variorum, 1980.

Macler, Fréderic, trans. and ed. *Histoire d'Héraclius par l'Evêque Sebeos*. Paris: Imprimerie Nationale, 1904.

Martin, Richard C., ed. *Approaches to Islam in Religious Studies*. Tucson, Ariz.: University of Arizona Press, 1985.

Nau, M. F. "Un Colloque du Patriarche Jean avec l'Émir des Agaréens." *Journal Asiatique* 9ᵉ. sér., 5 (1915): 225–79.

Negev, A. *The Greek Inscriptions from the Negev*. Jerusalem: Franciscan Press, 1981.

Nevo, Yehuda D., and Judith Koren. *Crossroads to Islam*. (Forthcoming).

———. "The Origins of the Muslim Descriptions of the Jahili Meccan Sanctuary." *JNES*, 49 (1990) :23–44.

Nevo, Yehuda D., and A. Rothenberg. *Sde Boyer 1983–84* (Forthcoming).

Parker, S. Thomas. *The Historical Development of the Limes Arabicus*. Ph.D. diss., University of California, Los Angeles, 1979.

———. "The Central Limes Arabicus Project: The 1982 Campaign." *Annual of the Department of Antiquities of Jordan* 27 (1983): 213–30.

————. *Romans and Saracens: A History of the Arabian Frontier*. Philadelphia: America Schools of Oriental Research, 1986.

Peters, F. E. "The Commerce of Mecca before Islam." Edited by F. Kazemi and R. D. McChesney. *A Way Prepared: Essays an Islamic Culture in Honor of Richard Bayley Winder*. New York: New York University Press, 1988.

Rogerson, John. *Old Testament Criticism in the Nineteenth Century: England and Germany*. London: Society for Promoting Christian Knowledge, Fortress Press, 1985.

Rubin, Uri. "The Ka'aba: Aspects of its Ritual, Functions, and Position in Pre-Islamic and Early Islamic Times." *JSAI* 8 (1986): 97–131.

Schacht, Joseph. *The Origins of Muhammadan Jurisprudence*. Oxford: Clarendon, 1950.

Tsafrir, Yoram. Excavations at *Rehovot-in-the-Negev*. Vol. 1, *The Northern Church*, *Qedem*, 25.

al-'Uss, Muhammad Abu al-Faraj. *Kitabat 'arabiyyah gayr mansunah fi Jabal 'Usays* (Arabic Inscriptions from Jabal Usays) *Al-Abhat* 17 (1964): 227–316.

Wansbrough, John. *Quranic Studies: Sources and Methods of Scriptural Interpretation*. Oxford University Press, 1977.

————. *The Sectarian Milieu*. Oxford: Oxford University Press, 1978.

————. "Res Ipsa Loquitur: History and Mimesis." Seventh Einstein Memorial Lecture, Jerusalem, Israel Academy of Sciences and Humanities, delivered 1986, published 1987.

Wellhausen, J. *Geschichte Israels*. Berlin, 1878. 2d. ed: *Prolegomena zur Geschichte Israels*. Berlin, 1883. *Prolegomena to the History of Israel*. Edinburgh, 1885 (English translation).

Winnett, Frederick V. and J. L. Harding. *Inscriptions from Fifty Safaitic Cairns*. Toronto: Toronto University Press, 1978.

NOTES

1. E.g., R. B. Serjeant's review of Wansbrough's *Qur'anic Studies*, *Journal of the Royal Asiatic Society* (1978): 76–78.

2. *Res Ipsa Loquitur*, Jerusalem, published 1987; Rippin's article in Martin (1985), 151–63 is a more discursive presentation of Rippin's interpretation of Wansbrough's methodology.

3. For a useful discussion cf. Crawford (1983), chap. 1; for a basic bibliography, idem pp. 75–79.

4. *Res Ipsa Loquitur*, p. 12.

5. Ibid., p. 14.

6. Even modern scholars are not immune to such tendencies in translating old texts and in drawing conclusions from them. Thus Kaegi (1969) paraphrases the seventh-century Armenian historian Sebeos as accepting that the "Islamic Empire" is here to stay (p. 147), whereas Sebeos in fact mentions only the "kingdom of Ishmael." Macler (1904), chap. 30 ff.

7. *Res Ipsa Loquitur*, p. 14–15. This conclusion leads a Muslim scholar, F. Rahman in Martin (1985), p. 198, to assert that "the strategy adopted by those who uphold Wansbrough's methods is, in effect, to negate history and then apply what they call the 'literary method.'" This is putting the cart before the horse. Those conversant with Wansbrough's work are more likely to agree with Norman Calder's opinion that "J. W.'s caveats about historical reconstruction were a result of literary analysis and not for him, initially, a methodological point, though they may have become one." (Review of Martin (1985) in *BSOAS* 50, no. 3 (1987): 546.

8. A. Snodgrass, in Crawford (1983), p. 139.

9. E. Gabba, in Crawford (1983), p. 15.

10. *Res Ipsa Loquitur*, p. 10.

11. Ibid., p. 22. One could of course retort that the process of an archaeological excavation tends to reduce an archaeological site to the status of a literary account (cf. Crawford [1983], p. 140); but when properly performed, it includes techniques to minimize this danger and enable later crosschecking of the findings.

12. See our paper "The Origins of the Muslim Descriptions of the Jahili Meccan Sanctuary," *JNES*, 1990.

13. *Sectarian Milieu*, p. 39.

14. "Southern Palestine," p. 22.

15. Rogerson (1984), p. 249.

16. Ibid., pp. 252–60, 273.

17. *Muslim Studies* (1966).

18. *Muslim Studies*, p. 71.

19. Ibid., p. 68.

20. Ibid., p. 18.

21. Ibid., p. 86.

22. Ibid., p. 74.

23. Ibid., p. 142.

24. *Qur'anic Studies*, p. 47–50.

25. Ibid., p. 3.

26. Ibid., pp. 4–10, 17.

27. Ibid., p. 21.

28. Ibid., p. 25.

29. Ibid., p. 16.

30. Ibid., p. 20.

31. Schacht (1950), p. 224.

32. *Qur'anic Studies*, p. 44.

33. Schacht (1950), pp. 162–75.

34. Ibid., p. 163.

35. Ibid., pp. 169–70.

36. Ibid., p. 175.

37. Ibid., p. 163.

38. Cook (1981), chapter 11.

39. Ibid., p. 116.

40. *Qur'anic Studies*, p. 140.

41. Ibid., p. 144.

42. Ibid., p. 158.

43. Cook (1981), pp. 115–16.

44. Ibid., p. 116.

45. Crone (1987), p. 111.

46. Ibid., p. 114.

47. Ibid. Cf. also Peters (1988) on the lack of evidence for Meccan trade in contemporary non-Arab sources.

48. Ibid., p. 225.

49. Ibid., pp. 226–30.

50. Brock (1982), p. 20. Brock has also compiled a bibliography of all Syriac sources with any historical bearing on the seventh century: Brock (1976). Chabot (1934) is a more comprehensive compilation of notes on Syriac authors, but includes none of historical interest that cannot be found in Brock.

51. Brock (1982), p. 21.

52. Nevo and Koren, *Crossroads to Islam*.

53. Nau (1915); for discussion see *Crossroads to Islam*.

54. Parker (1979), (1983), (1986).

55. Parker (1979), p. 261; (1983), p. 149.

56. Parker (1983), p. 230.

57. Parker (1979), p. 272.

58. Ibid., pp. 272–73.

59. Kennedy (1985a), p. 19.

60. Parker (1983), p. 230.

61. The present authors suggest such a theory of the transfer of control from Byzantium to the Arabs in *Crossroads to Islam*.

62. This work is published continuously in *ADAJ*, *Abhat* and *Atlal*. For an impressive example of such field work, see M. Khan and A. Mughannam, "Ancient Dams in the Ta'if Area 1981 (1401)," *Atlal* 6.

63. Winnett and Harding (1978).

64. The largest of these, at Sde Boqer, has been partly excavated: for the report see Nevo and Rothenberg, *Sde Boqer 1983–84*. A condensed description appears in Nevo and Koren, *Crossroads to Islam*.

65. For the pagan sites see Nevo and Rothenberg, *Sde Boqer 1983–84*; for the Muslim accounts: Hawting (1984); Rubin (1986); for a comparison of the two: Nevo and Koren (1990).

66. *Crossroads to Islam*.

67. For a detailed analysis and discussion of the religious formulae on early Arab coins and problems of dating them, see Nevo and Koren, *Crossroads to Islam*.

68. For an example of such dating methods, see Grohmann (1962); most of the dates there assigned are simply opinions or intelligent guesses.

69. The present authors apply such methods of analysis to the inscriptions from the Central Negev, in *Crossroads to Islam*.

70. Contrast this with the pagan names of Christians, such as 'Abd al-Ga or 'Amat Ga, included in Christian texts or a list of donors to a Church building in the Negev: cf. Negev (1981); Colt Archaeological Institute, vols. 1 and 3; Tsafrir (1988).

71. The following are so far known and have been collected in Grohmann (1971), pp. 16–17, figs. 7–8: (1) the trilingual inscription from Zebed, southeast of Aleppo, dated 512 C.E.; (2) the bilingual inscription from Harran, dated 568 C.E.; (3) an inscription from Umm al-Jimal II, datable to the sixth centur; (4) an inscription from Jebel Usays, 528 C.E.; originally published by al-'Uss (1964), p. 302, no. 85, reprinted with corrected reading in Grohmann (1971), p. 16, fig. 7d. There is besides a very early (first half of fourth century C.E.?) inscription from the temple of Jabal al-Ramm, which preserves Nabatean forms of Kaf, Mim, and Waw, and thus possibly indicates the transition from the Nabatean to an early Kufic script: Grohmann (1971), p. 16, fig. 7a. The original bibliographic citations may be found in Grohmann.

72. Cf. R. Martin's essay in Martin (1985), pp. 14–15, citing as an example of "less obvious" western bias the "countless articles" of the *Encyclopedia of Islam* in which "traditional and contemporary Muslim views are contrasted with what their sources really say (or fail to say) when they are subjected to historical and textual criticism."

Chapter 13

The Quest of the Historical Muhammad

F. E. Peters

Writing in 1962 Stephen Neill listed twelve of what he regarded as "positive achievements of New Testament studies" over the past century.[1] As an affirmation of progress in a notoriously difficult field of investigation, they make satisfying and even cheerful reading for the historian. Who was Jesus of Nazareth? What was his message? Why was he put to death? Why did his few followers become, in effect, the nucleus of the powerful and widespread community called Christianity? These were the enormously difficult questions that had begun to be posed in a critical-historical way in the mid-nineteenth century, and some of the answers Bishop Neill discerned, though by no means final, represented ground gained and truths won. Neill's widely read book was revised in 1988, and though his optimism was here and there tempered by what had been said and thought in the twenty-five years since the first edition,[2] there was still good reason to think that historians were by and large on the right track in pursuing what Albert Schweitzer described in 1906 as "the quest of the historical Jesus."[3]

The pages of Neill and his redactor Tom Wright are lustrous with congratulation and hope for the various tribes of New Testament critics and historians, but they make dismaying reading for their Islamicist cousins who were not too long ago instructed by one of their own eminences that "there is nothing of which we can say for certain that it incontestably dates back to the time of the Prophet."[4]

Originally published in *International Journal of Middle East Studies* 23 (1991): 291–315. Reprinted by permission of Cambridge University Press.

Indeed, there is much in both the first and second editions of Neill's work to puzzle, and even discourage, the laborers in a neighboring historical field, where scholars engaged in the "quest of the historical Muhammad" share many of the problems, tools, and therefore, one would have thought, some of the same successes as Neill's enterprising investigators. However, even though a great deal of effort has been invested in research into the life and times of Muhammad, the results do not seem at all comparable to those achieved in research on Jesus, and the reasons are not at all clear. It may be useful, then, to look at some recent and representative examples of "Muhammad research" and attempt to discover why this is the case.[5]

Muhammad would appear, at least in theory, to be a far more apposite subject for historical inquiry than the founder of Christianity. The most abiding and forbidding obstacle to approaching the historical Jesus is undoubtedly the fact that our principal sources, the documents included in the New Testament, were all written on the hither side of Easter: that is, their authors viewed their subject across the absolute conviction that Jesus was the Christ and the Son of God, a conviction later rendered explicit in Christian dogma. There is, however, no Resurrection in the career of Muhammad, no Paschal sunrise to cast its divinizing light on the Prophet of Islam. Muhammad is thus a perfectly appropriate subject of history: a man born of woman (and a man), who lived in a known place in a roughly calculable time, who in the end died the death that is the lot of all mortals, and whose career was reported by authorities who share the contemporary historian's own conviction that the Prophet was nothing more than a man. What is at stake in Islam, then, is not dogma as it is in Christianity, but rather piety; obversely, it is the same sense of impropriety that a pre-1850s Catholic might have felt in the presence of a positivist-historical study of Mary.[6]

With Muslim piety and Christian dogma put aside, as the historian insists they must be, there would seem at first glance to be sufficient historical evidence on Jesus and Muhammad from which to at least attempt, as many have done, to take the measure of both the men and their milieu. Indeed, in the view of one early biographer of Jesus, the available sources are even better for Muhammad than for Jesus, since Islam was "born in full view of history."[7] Within twenty-five years after Ernest Renan wrote those words, his optimism regarding Islamic origins—or perhaps simply his pessimism at getting at the historical Jesus—already stood in need of serious revision. History's view of the birth of Islam, it turned out, was neither full nor particularly clear, and the search after Islamic origins had to begin where the search for Christianity's origins had, standing before the evidence for the life of the founder and its milieu.

The question of milieu is a critical one for the historian. Many of Bishop

Neill's underscored gains in New Testament studies have to do with a better understanding of both the Jewish and the Hellenic background out of which Jesus and his movement issued, and it is in that area that arguably the greatest progress has been made—and the greatest number of new hypotheses spawned—in the last quarter century.[8] Moreover, it is here, historians of Muhammad will discover, that the "full view of history" grows exceedingly clouded and that their own inquiry is not going to run on equal stride with the quest after Jesus.

Quite simply, there is no appropriate contemporary and contopological setting against which to read the Koran. For early Islam there is no Josephus to provide a contemporary political context, no apocrypha for a spiritual context, and no Scrolls to illuminate a Palestinian "sectarian milieu." There is instead chiefly poetry, great masses of it, whose contemporary authenticity is somewhat suspect but that was, nonetheless, "the main vehicle of Arab history in the pre-Islamic and early Islamic periods,"[9] and that in any event testifies to a quite different culture. The Koran, in fact, stands isolated like an immense rock jutting forth from a desolate sea, a stony eminence with few marks on it to suggest how or why it appeared in this watery desert. The nearest landfalls for our beatings are the cultures of the Yemen to the south, Abyssinia across the Red Sea, and the distant Jewish and Christian settlements of Palestine-Syria to the north and Christian Iraq to the northeast.[10] It is the equivalent, perhaps, of attempting to illuminate the Gospels solely from Egyptian papyri and Antiochene inscriptions. The fact is that, despite a great deal of information supplied by later Muslim literary sources, we know pitifully little for sure about the political or economic history of Muhammad's native city of Mecca or of the religious culture from which he came.[11] Moreover, to the extent that we are ignorant of that history and culture, to that same extent we do not understand the man or the movement that followed in his wake.

The surviving evidence for both Jesus and Muhammad lies primarily in literary works rather than in material evidence,[12] and in both instances those works include an important body of "teaching." Jesus' teaching is incorporated into, but is not the entirety of, the Gospels, while Muhammad's constitute a separate work, the Koran, both of which have some claim to be regarded as authentic.[13] "Some claim" is not, of course, the same as self-evident, particularly with regard to Jesus, whose words and teachings are embedded in complex Gospel narratives whose purpose is far more than mere reportage. The argument about the reported words of Jesus has been loud and vigorous, and even if many people now seem to be convinced of the authenticity of at least some of what Jesus is alleged to have said, and likely of the very words of its expression, that conviction remains only the first step in a continuing and even more difficult historiographical process centering on Jesus and Muhammad. Granted that there is *something* of these two men in the works said to be about or by them, what precise part, one must then go on to ask, of what is said and done by Jesus in the Gospels is really his own words and deeds? Similarly, what part of what is reportedly said by Muhammad in the Koran and in the extra-Koranic reports circulated under his name are really his words,[14] and which of the deeds ascribed to the Prophet in the Muslim historical tradition actually occurred? The disparity is immediately apparent. Both the life and message of Jesus are contained in the Gospels, while for the events of the life of Muhammad we must turn to sources outside the Koran, what I have just called "the Muslim historical tradition."

At first glance the question of the authenticity of Jesus' sayings would appear to be a relatively simple one since their *final* tradents, the "evangelists," worked, at the furthest remove, no more than forty to eighty), years after the death of Jesus—and quite conceivably even closer, perhaps thirty-five to forty years.[15] Moreover, they give every indication of resting, as Luke maintains quite explicitly in the opening of his Gospel (Luke 1:1–4), upon the testimonies, some recollected, some written, of eyewitnesses themselves. The issue appears no less simple with Muhammad, at least as it concerns the Koran. Parts of that document were apparently written down during his own lifetime, and the finished work, what is essentially our Koran, was finally assembled or "collected" from various sources, some recollected and some written, no more than fifteen years after the Prophet's death.[16]

Why, then, is there such apparent skepticism about retrieving the actual words of Jesus from the Gospels, while there is no similar debate about the Koran, which is generally thought to represent what issued from Muhammad's mouth as "teachings" in the interval from C.E. 610 to 632? Indeed, the search for variants in the partial versions extant before the Caliph 'Uthman's alleged recension in the 640s (what can be called the "sources" behind our text) has not yielded any differences of great significance.[17] This is not to say, of course, that since those pre-'Uthmanic clues are fragmentary, large "invented" portions might well have been added to our Koran or authentic material deleted. This latter charge has, in fact, been made by certain Shiite Muslims who fail to find in the Koran any explicit reference to the designation of Ali as the Prophet's successor and so have alleged tampering.[18] However, the argument of the latter is so patently tendentious and the evidence adduced for the fact so exiguous that few have failed to be convinced that what is in our copy of the Koran is, in fact, what Muhammad taught, and is expressed in his own words.[19]

Why, then, are there these differences in recollection, the fluctuating memory of what Jesus said and the apparently flawless and total recall of the words of Muhammad? To advance what is at this point simply a preliminary con-

sideration, we may point to the fact that the anonymous tradents of the pre-'Uthmanic Koran, Muslims all, were convinced from the outset—the outset being
their own conversion to this belief—that what they were hearing and noting "on
scraps of leather, bone and in their hearts" were not the teachings of a man but
the *ipsissima verba Dei* and so they would likely have been scrupulously careful
in preserving the actual wording. In the case of Jesus, however, whatever the
respect for him as a teacher—a very particular and unique teacher—by the first
auditors of his words, the mere recollection of his teaching, its substance and
gist, was all that was required for their moral instruction. Certain phrases and
images might have lodged in their memories—formulae used in cures, predictions about the destruction of the Temple, the blessing of the bread and wine at
his last supper spring readily to mind—but there is little ground for imagining
that during his actual lifetime there would have been any motive for his followers
to memorize every word that proceeded from the mouth of Jesus of Nazareth.

The four Gospels are not about Jesus of Nazareth, of course, but about Jesus
the Christ, and his sayings and teaching were re-collected after the Resurrection
from a very different perspective, it is true. However, the initial impression had
already been taken, so to speak, and no change in the understanding of what
Jesus *meant* could enlarge the memory of what he had actually *said*. Even then,
however, in the very different post-Easter light that bathes the entirety of the
New Testament, it is not so much the words of Jesus that were illumined as his
deeds. The earliest forms of the Christian *kerygma* (in I Corinthians 15:3–7/8, for
example, or Acts 2:22ff. and 10:36–43) include not Jesus' teachings but the
events of his life: his miracles, his death, and his Resurrection, and Paul's
scanting of Jesus' words is, of course, notorious.

We have touched here on a basic difference between the Christians' regard
of Jesus and the Muslims' regard of Muhammad. For the Christians Jesus was—
whether he intended it or not, the historian carefully adds—an "event." His goal
was achieved by deeds, his redemptive death and the probative miracle of his
Resurrection: "He was declared Son of God by a mighty act in that he rose [was
raised] from the dead" (Rom. 1:4). Jesus did not reveal; he was himself a revelation, and that fact informs our Gospels, which bear witness to the event. More,
the Christian tradents of the words of Jesus who stood behind the canonical
Gospels had no idea, as the early Muslims certainly had, that they were transmitting a revelation, nor did the authors of those same Gospels by any means
understand, as Muhammad's scribes and secretaries were convinced, that they
were writing down Scripture. Indeed, that was the original understanding of the
Arabic word, "a recitation," unmistakably for liturgical purposes.[20] However, for
a considerable time after the completion of the Gospels, the Christians' "Scrip-

ture" continued to be what it always had been for the Jews, including Jesus and his followers, to wit, the Hebrew Bible.

To sum up at this point: the Koran is convincingly the words of Muhammad, perhaps even dictated by him after their recitation,[21] while the Gospels not only describe the life of Jesus but contain some arguably authentic sayings or teachings of Jesus. How does that latter argument proceed? A primary version of it is that devised by Form criticism, and Rudolf Bultmann, one of its masters, formulated the criterion of authenticity with elegant brevity:

> We can only count on possessing a genuine similitude of Jesus where, on the one hand, expression is given to the contrast between Jewish morality and piety and the distinctive eschatological temper which characterized the teaching of Jesus, and where, on the other hand, we find no specifically Christian features.[22]

To take the second point first, where the form of Jesus' reported sayings and stories conform to what we know of contemporary Jewish, that is, rabbinic, didactic forms, the likelihood is strong that they are authentic. The obvious example is, of course, the parables, and whether Jesus is judged a skilled or merely a traditional practitioner of the genre, there are enough rabbinic parables in the Gospels to convince the skeptic that here at least he is face to face with a form of Jesus' teaching that could not, or at least was not, invented by some later Christian pietist. Whether those "rabbis" whose works provide one term of the comparison, namely, the authorities quoted in the Mishna (c. 200 C.E.) onward, may in fact be regarded as Jesus' "contemporaries" for purposes of illuminating either the teachings or the events of the Gospels continues to be a vexing question whose answer is more often assumed than discussed, particularly by Form critics.[23]

Most Form critics have turned with Bultmann from this modest piece of ground gained through "rabbinic parallelism" to the other principal criterion of authenticity, that of "dissimilarity," where the credited sayings can be shown to be unique to Jesus to the degree that we do not find parallels in either the early Church or ancient Judaism. To put it more brazenly: when Jesus sounds like a rabbi, that is authentic; when Jesus does not think like a rabbi, that, too, is authentic. As far as context is concerned, then, originality is a mark of authenticity, and, by way of an aside at this point, very little of Jesus' teaching has been retrieved on the basis of that criterion, not assuredly because he does not often express original notions in the Gospels, but rather because he sounds all too original, in John's Gospel, for example, and Redaction criticism has denied Jesus most of that originality and credited it instead to the first generation of Christians.

What does Muhammad sound like? His contemporaries thought they caught echoes of a number of familiar charismatic types, seers, or poets (sura 52:29–30; 69:41–42), which the Koran stoutly denies, or even a rehash of old stories (25:5). Some modern scholars think the first charge has some merit, though by no means for the entirety of the Koran.[24] However, once again we are limited by an almost total lack of contextual background. We know little or nothing of the utterances of the "seer" (*kahin*); the preserved pre-Islamic poets are patently not the demonic (*majnun*) type to which Muhammad was being compared; and our only contemporary examples of "ancient tales" are precisely those told in the Koran.

There is something curious about the Koran's stories, a quality that once again underlines our inability to penetrate into the milieu. In 1982 Anthony Harvey raised the issue of the "constraints of history" in connection with the study of the life of Jesus:

> No individual, if he wishes to influence others, is totally free to choose his own style of action and persuasion: he is subject to constraints imposed by the culture in which he finds himself. If communication is to take place, there must be constraints recognized by both the speaker and his listeners. . . . Now Jesus . . . succeeded in communicating with his hearers, his followers, and indeed his enemies. To do so he had to speak a language they could understand, perform actions they would find intelligible, and conduct his life and undergo his death in a manner of which they could make some sense.[25]

What was true of Jesus was equally true of Muhammad. He, too, was bound by the "constraints" of matter and style "recognized by both the speaker and his listeners." Now it is clear from the Koran itself that, though there may have been those of his Meccan contemporaries who doubted the supernatural origin of what Muhammad was proclaiming, there was no problem with understanding it, and in understanding it better in many cases than we do today. The Koran is filled with biblical stories, for example, most of them told in an extremely elliptical or what has been called "allusive" or "referential" style.[26] Manifestly, Muhammad's audience was not hearing these stories for the first time, as the remark about "rehashing old stories" itself suggests. These stories were current in Mecca then, though we have little idea how current or for how long, and when Muhammad "retold" them in his allusive style in the Koran to make some other moral point (God's vengeance for the mistreatment of earlier prophets, to cite one common theme), his listeners might not agree with the point but apparently knew well enough to what he was referring.

We, however, do not know since these stories are "biblical" only in the sense that they take characters or incidents from the Bible as their point of departure.

However, their trajectory is haggadic; they are the residue, echo, recollection— we are at a loss precisely what to call it—of what is palpably Jewish *midrashim*, though which they were, or what were their origins, we cannot even guess. We have only one biblical *midrash* current in seventh-century Arabia, and that is the Koran itself.

The accusations of Muhammad's contemporaries that he was no more than a "seer" or a "poet" provided an important guidepost for modern attempts at applying Form criticism to the Koran. The literary forms employed in the book range, we can observe, from brief oaths and mantic utterances, through parables and apocalyptic fragments, to rather extended narratives to illustrate in homiletic fashion what awaits those who ignore or mistreat prophets.[27] There are, as well, a large and generally unconnected body of halakic dicta that obviously date from the Medina period of the Prophet's life and prescribe norms of action and behavior for a community-in-being. The remainder consists of the warnings and threats (many of them repeated catchphrases) and a good deal of polemic, some-times in the form of retorts to questions whose source or thrust we do not know.

However, if Form criticism proved valuable as a clue to the transmission and the secondary *Sitz im Leben* of the New Testament, that is, "the situation in the life of the Church in which those traditions were found relevant and so preserved (as it turned out) for posterity,"[28] it can have no such useful purpose in Islam since there is no conviction that the Koranic material was in any way being shaped by or for transmission. On our original assumption that Muhammad is the source of the work, what is found in the Koran is not being *reported* but simply *recorded*; consequently, modern Form criticism amounts to little more than the *classifica-tion* of the various ways in which the Prophet chose to express himself, a proce-dure that casts no light forward since the Koran was regarded by Muslims as "inimitable,"[29] and none backward where there is, as we have noted, only dark-ness in the religious past of western Arabia—no convenient rabbis, monks, or Arab preachers to whose words or style we might compare the utterances of the Prophet of Islam.

This is not to say that *no* hands have touched the Koranic material. An early investigator of the life of Jesus compared the Gospel stories about him to pearls whose string had been broken. The precious stones were reassembled in the sequel by individuals such as the Evangelist Mark, who supplied both the narra-tive framework and within it the connective links to "restring" them. The Koran gives somewhat the same impression of scattered pearls, though these have been reassembled in quite a different, and puzzling, manner. The Koran as we now possess it is arranged in 114 units called suras connected in no obvious fashion, each bearing a name and other introductory formulae, of greatly varying length and, more appositely to our present purpose, with little internal unity. There is no narrative framework, of course, and within the unconnected suras there are dislocations, interpolations, abrupt changes of rhyme and parallel versions, a condition that has led both Muslim and non-Muslim scholars alike to conclude that some of the present suras or sections of them may once have been joined to others. By whom were they joined? We do not know, nor can we explain the purpose of such rearrangements.[30]

Nor do we know the aim or the persons who arranged the suras in their present order, which is, roughly (the first sura apart), from the longest to the shortest. They are not, in any event, placed in the order of their revelation, as everyone agrees. However, there the agreement apparently ends. Early Muslim scholars settled on a gross division into "Meccan" and "Medinan" suras, which were labeled accordingly in copies of the Koran, and they even determined the relative sequence of the suras. However, this system rested on premises unacceptable to modern western scholars,[31] who have attempted to develop their own criteria and their own dating system, which, though it starts with different assumptions, ends with much the same results as those of the early Muslim savants.[32] This distribution of the suras even into limited categories like "Early-," "Middle-," and "Late-Meccan" or "Medinan" is of critical importance to the historian, of course, since it provides the ground for following the evolution of Muhammad's thought and at the same time for connecting passages in the Koran with events that the ancient Muslim authorities asserted had occurred in Muhammad's lifetime. The highly composite nature of many of the suras makes any such distributional enterprise highly problematic to begin with, but an even more serious flaw is the fact that the standard western system accepts as its framework the traditional Muslim substance, sequence, and dating of the events of the life of Muhammad, an acceptance made, as we shall see, "with much more confidence than is justified."[33]

Redaction criticism, one of the most powerful critical tools developed for an understanding of the Gospels, is founded on the premise that the Gospels are not mere transcripts of Jesus' words or an unretouched photograph of his life, but that both the words and the deeds recorded therein have in the first place been illuminated by the witnesses' belief in his Resurrection, the proof that Jesus was Messiah, Lord, and Son of God: and second, as the Redaction critics have pointed out, the Gospels reflect the perceptions of the Christian community when and where they were written down. Can we make the same assertions with respect to Islam? Does any serious scholar now doubt that the materials in the Koran and/or the *Sira*, the standard life of Muhammad originally composed by Ibn Ishaq (d. 767) and preserved in an edition from the hand of Ibn Hisham (d.

833), were shaped by the needs of the early Islamic community? There is probably no doubt, at least as far as the Sira is concerned,[34] particularly since its re-redactor Ibn Hisham openly admitted as much in the introduction to his reediting of his predecessor's work:

> God willing I shall begin this book with Isma'il and mention those of his offspring who were the ancestors of God's apostle one by one with what is known of them, taking no account of Isma'il's other children, for the sake of brevity, confining myself to the prophet's biography and omitting some of the things which Ibn Ishaq has recorded in this book in which there is no mention of the apostle and about which the Koran says nothing and which are not relevant to anything in this book or an explanation of it; poems which he quotes that no authority on poetry whom I have met knows of; things which it is disgraceful to discuss; matters which would distress certain people; and such reports as al-Bakka'i told me he could not accept as trustworthy—all these things I have omitted. But God willing I shall give a full account of everything else so far as it is known and a trustworthy tradition is available.[35]

As for redaction activity in the Koran, that would depend on when the materials were assembled. On the Burton hypothesis there is no need to search for community shaping; on the Wansbrough hypothesis there must have been a great deal of shaping indeed, but "the Koran as the product of the early Islamic community" is not a proposition that has found a great deal of favor in Islamicist circles. Indeed, there is a notable redactional "flatness" about the Koran. As has already been said, there was no Easter for the Muslims—Muhammad died of natural causes in C.E. 632 and by all reports still rests in his tomb in the mosque at Medina—but the enormous and astonishing expansion of Islam, which was unmistakably underway when the Koran was collected into its final form sometime about 650, is an Islamic event of similar if not identical redactional magnitude to the Christians' Easter. If the almost miraculous success of the movement he initiated did not change the Muslims' essential regard for Muhammad, who was after all, only a man, it could certainly have cast a different light on his version of God's message. However, we find no trace of this in the Koran, no signs that its "good news" was "redacted" in the afterglow of an astonishing politico-military authentication of its religious truths.

Why should this be so? It is probably because of the reason already cited, that the Koran was regarded not as preaching or "proclamation" but as revelation pure and simple, and thus was not so inviting to redaction and editorial adjustment as the Gospels. Indeed, what was done to the Koran in the redactional process appears to have been extremely conservative. The materials were kept, in the words of one modern scholar, "just as they fell,"[36] or assembled in such a mechanical fashion as to exclude redactional bias. Our conviction that either was in fact the case is strengthened when we look to the other source of Muhammad's teachings, the Hadith, or traditions, which even on the Muslims' view constitute Muhammad's words and not those of God.

The Hadith are discrete reports of the words, or less often the deeds, of the Prophet, each generally accompanied by its own chain of tradents: I heard from Z, who heard from Y, who heard from . . . A, who reported that Muhammad, upon whom be peace, said. . . . In other words, each Hadith is arguing its own authenticity, something the Koran and the Gospels do only occasionally.[37] Muslims were alerted, as we are, by this obvious *petitio auctoritatis* in the Hadith, and looked closely at those argumentative chains, accepting many and rejecting a great many more. Modern western scholars may point disarmingly to these earlier Muslim attempts at separating the authentic Prophetic wheat from the chaff of forgery,[38] but they have at their disposal a different heuristic tool in dealing with the Hadith, the now familiar Redaction criticism, which, since the late nineteenth century, they have wielded with enormous and, what should be, at least for the historian, dismaying success. A great many of the prophetic traditions bear on their own bodies what is for the Redaction critic the equivalent of a smoking gun: circumstantial tendentiousness. If certain of the sayings of Jesus in the Gospels show a suspicious, and very un-Jewish, concern for the Gentiles, many Hadith report remarks by Muhammad on personalities, parties, and religious and legal issues that could only have arisen as subjects of community concern after his death, and in some instances, long after his death.[39] If the Gospel critic, or some Gospel critics, think it possible to retrieve a good bit of Jesus' words and at least some of his own authentic teaching from the canonical Gospels, there are only very few modern historians who would make the same claim for Muhammad and the Hadith.

If the Hadith-sayings of Muhammad are suspect—and they are, after all, mostly halakic in content—what of the Prophet's deeds? Have we grounds for a biography? We have none in the Koran, it would appear, since its form is that of a discourse, a divine monologue or catechism so to speak, that reveals little or nothing about the life of Muhammad and his contemporaries. Both the life and the work of Jesus are integrated in the Gospels, and, unlike Paul's letters, which are essentially hermeneutical when they come to speak of Jesus,[40] the Gospels treat both the words and deeds of Jesus in the manner of history; that is, they *describe* events and they *reproduce* teachings, and each is done circumstantially enough for the modern historian to form some kind of unified judgment about the veracity of the first and the authenticity of the second.

For Islam, on the other hand, the pursuit of truth and authenticity is infinitely simpler (though not necessarily more satisfying) since there is a very large gap indeed between the sources for Muhammad's life and those for his teachings. On our assumption that the notions in the Koran are Muhammad's own—there is very little historical evidence that they are anyone else's—one can indeed approach them with much the same questions as one might bring to Jesus' reported teachings in the Gospels. Are these words or sentiments likely to be authentic in the light of, first, the context in which they were delivered, and second, the manner of their transmission? The reader of the Gospels is immediately predisposed to give an affirmative answer to the first question since, as Stephen Neill expressed it, "when the historian approaches the Gospels, the first thing that strikes him is the extraordinary fidelity with which they have reproduced, not the conditions of their own time, but the conditions of Palestine in the time and during the ministry of Christ."[41] The Koran, on the other hand, gives us no such assurance, nor indeed any instruction whatsoever on the context in which its contents were delivered, and no clues as to when, where, or why these particular words were being uttered; it is as little concerned with the events of the life of Muhammad and his contemporaries as Paul was with the narrative life of Jesus. The Holy Book of Islam is text without context, and so this prime document, which has a very strong claim to be authentic, is of almost no use for reconstructing the events of the life of Muhammad.[42]

There is, however, another, somewhat less obvious, facticity that rests between the lines of Islam's sacred book. If the Koran is genuinely Muhammad's, as it seems to be, and if, somewhat less certainly, distinctions between "Early-" and "Late-Meccan" and "Early-Medinan" suras of the Koran hold firm, then it is possible in the first instance to retrieve a substantial understanding of the type of paganism confronting Muhammad in his native city—the primary religious *Sitz im Leben* of the Meccan suras of the Koran—and even to reconstruct to some degree what appears to be an evolution in Muhammad's own thinking about God.

Though later Muslim historians profess to know a good deal on the subject, there exists, as has already been remarked, no physical or contemporary evidence for the worship and beliefs that prevailed at Mecca on the eve of Islam. The Koran, however, averts often to those conditions in its earliest suras. They were, after all, directed toward an overwhelmingly pagan audience whose beliefs and religious practices Muhammad was attempting to change and on which he was not likely to have been misinformed. Since the appearance of his *Muhammad in Mecca* in 1953, Montgomery Watt has concentrated much of his subsequent research on this issue, now summed up in his *Muhammad's Mecca: History in the Qur'an*,[43] and the work has been pushed further, and argued somewhat more rigorously, by Alford Welch.[44] What emerges is not a very detailed picture, but the outlines are clear and distinct.

Muhammad's own beliefs are somewhat less distinct. Welch was not eager to find "evolution" in the ideas of the Prophet,[45] but viewed through the prism of "the historical Muhammad," that is exactly what he discovered. The name "Allah" does not appear in the earliest revelations, as he has pointed out, and Muhammad refers to his God as simply "the Lord." When he does begin to use a proper name, his preference is for *al-Rahman*, "the Merciful," a familiar deity from elsewhere in the Fertile Crescent. It can scarcely be argued that "al-Rahman" is identical with "Allah"; otherwise, why would he have introduced the unfamiliar "Rahman" (17:110, 25:60) for the known and accepted "Allah" except out of personal conviction?

The issue of "al-Rahman" aside, what distinguished Muhammad from his Meccan contemporaries was (1) his belief in the reality of the Resurrection and the Judgment in both flesh and spirit, and (2) his unswerving conviction that the "High God" was not unique but absolute; that the other gods, goddesses, jinn and demons were subject and subservient to Him: Allah's "servants," as he put it (7:194). Muhammad was to go much further than this; as Welch has demonstrated, sometime around the battle of Badr in 624, two years after the Hijra, a fundamental change took place in his thinking: Thereafter, Muhammad was an absolute monotheist. The other gods had completely disappeared and the now unique and transcendental Allah was served only by his invisible host of angels.[46]

This is genuine history, and it is more secure than anything else we know about Muhammad. It is not very "occasional" perhaps—we cannot firmly connect any of these religious changes with external events—and it tells us nothing about the social or economic life of Mecca. Those aspects of his environment will not yield up their secrets to the biographer unless additional context can be supplied from some other source, as Josephus provides the general background for the Gospels, or much as the Evangelists are thought to have done for Jesus himself, where his torical narrative and a "sayings" source like the famous "Q" were integrated into a single Gospel narrative. Mark, the earliest of the Gospels, is already an integrated account of sayings and deeds, and everything else we know indicates that Jesus' followers remembered his sayings, his actions, and what happened to him all in the same context. If events showed that certain of his acts, notably his death and Resurrection, were considerably more consequential than his preaching—witness Paul and the earliest creeds—nonetheless, sayings and deeds were never completely disassociated in the Christian tradition.

Though there is no contemporary Josephus to report on seventh-century western Arabia, there are, in fact, just such integrated, Gospel-like sources in Islam. These siras or traditional biographies of the Prophet, of which the oldest preserved specimen is the *Sira* written by Ibn Ishaq (d. 767), as edited by his student Ibn Hisham (d. 833), provide a richly detailed narrative of the events of Muhammad's career into which at least some Koranic material and other "teaching" has been incorporated at the appropriate places.[47] The "appropriate places" were the subject of a great deal of speculative attention by Muslim scholars who studied them under the rubric of "the occasions of revelations," that is, the particular set of historical circumstances at Mecca or Medina that elicited a given verse or verses of the Koran. The results of this energetic quest are not always convincing. There is very little evidence, for example, that independent sources of information were brought to bear on the enterprise, and the suspicion is strong that medieval Muslim scholars were recreating the "occasion" by working backwards out of the Koranic verses themselves, an exercise at which a modern non-Muslim might be equally adept.[48] If these "occasions of revelation" are strung together in chronological order, a task accomplished by early Muslim scholars by arranging the suras, or part of suras, of the Koran in *their* chronological order, and one which we have already seen rests on extremely problematic grounds, then a semblance of a biography of the Prophet can be constructed, one that covers the ground at least from 610 to 632. This is, in fact, what was done, and the standard "Lives" of the Prophet, Ibn Ishaq's for example, rest on that kind of framework, fleshed out by other material about his early life at Mecca and considerably more elaborate descriptions of his later military expeditions at Medina.[49]

Though the earliest extant lives of Muhammad are far more distant from the events they describe than the Gospels are from the life of Jesus,[50] the Muslim authorities, unlike their Christian counterparts, cite their sources, by name and generation by generation, back to the original eyewitnesses contemporary with Muhammad. Hence, it is not unnatural that historical criticism in Islam has concentrated on those chains of transmitting authorities rather than, as is overwhelmingly the case in early Christian documents, on the matter transmitted. As has already been noted, in the nineteenth century Ignaz Goldziher,[51] and more recently Joseph Schacht,[52] looked more carefully at the accounts themselves and came to the generally accepted conclusion that a great many of the "Prophetic traditions" are forgeries fabricated to settle political scores or to underpin a legal or doctrinal ruling, a situation with no very convincing parallel in the Jesus material.[53] This conclusion was drawn, however, from the analysis of material in reports that are chiefly legal in character, where both the motives and the signs of falsification are often quite obvious; what of the reports of purely historical events of the type that constitute much of the life of Muhammad? The obvious clues to forgery are by no means so obvious here, nor is the motive quite so pressing since it is not the events of Muhammad's life that constitute dogma for the Muslim but the teachings in the Koran.[54] However, so great has been the doubt cast on the bona fides of the alleged eyewitnesses and their transmitters in legal matters that there now prevails an almost universal western skepticism on the reliability of *all* reports advertising themselves, often with quite elaborate testimonial protestations, as going back to Muhammad's time, or even that of his immediate successors.[55]

Though Goldziher and Schacht concentrated chiefly on the legal Hadith, the Belgian Jesuit Henri Lammens argued in a number of works that the historical traditions are equally fictitious, and whatever his motives and his style—Maxime Rodinson, a contemporary biographer of Muhammad, characterized Lammens as "filled with a holy contempt for Islam, for its 'delusive glory,' for its 'dissembling' and 'lascivious' Prophet"—Lammens's critical attack has never been refuted.[56] One of the most notable of Muhammad's modern biographers, W. Montgomery Watt, found no great difficulty in this, however:

> In the legal sphere there may have been some sheer invention of traditions, it would seem. But in the historical sphere, insofar as the two may be separated, and apart from some exceptional cases, the nearest to such invention in the best early historians appears to be a "tendential shaping" of the material. . . . Once the modern student is aware of the tendencies of the historians and their sources, however, it ought to be possible for him to some extent to make allowance for the distortion and to present the data in an unbiased form; and the admission of "tendential shaping" should have as its corollary the acceptance of the general soundness of the material.[57]

While Watt rejected Lammens's criticism of the Hadith, he accepted the main lines of the Jesuit's reconstruction, out of the same type of material, of Meccan society and economy, which in turn provided Watt with the foundation of his own interpretation of Muhammad's career.[58] However, Goldziher, Lammens, and Schacht were all doubtless correct. A great deal of the transmitted material concerning early Islam was tendentious—not only the material that was used for legal purposes but the very building blocks out of which the earliest history of Muhammad and the Islamic community was constructed.[59] "The actual historical material [in Ibn Ishaq's *Life* of Muhammad] is extremely scanty. So the allusions to the Koran are taken and expanded; and, first and foremost, the already existing dogmatic and juristic Hadith are collected and chronologically arranged."[60] This opinion was written near the beginning of the century, and long past its midpoint it was concurred in, as we have seen, by one of Muhammad's most recent biographers, Maxime Rodinson.[61]

Whatever the quality of the material with which he was working, Ibn Ishaq generally hewed much closer than the Gospels to the straight historical line; he was much more a biographer than an evangelist. For one thing, he is excused from presenting the teachings of Muhammad on two grounds. First, according to the Muslim view, there are no "teachings of Muhammad," at least not in any sense in which a Christian would understand that expression as applied to Jesus. There are the enunciations of God, but *they* are in the Koran, and if Ibn Ishaq occasionally reproduces the text of the Holy Book, or paraphrases it, it is generally, if we except the summary types noted above,[62] to set out some particular "occasion of revelation," a circumstance in the life of Muhammad that provided the setting for some particular sura.

The recorded life of Jesus is filled with mysteries, most of which derive not from the fact that we have four disparate written testimonies to what happened— any single Gospel would present the historian with the selfsame problems of interpretation—but because the evangelists were recording events and discourse and at the same time attempting a demonstration. The recording is, in fact, rather straightforward, and apart from certain problems of chronology and the incorporation of what appears to be legendary material (in the infancy narratives, for example), fashioning a biography of the "historical Jesus" from the Gospel materials would pose no unfamiliar or entirely insuperable difficulties for the historian of either Greco-Roman antiquity or post-biblical Judaism.

It is the demonstration that causes the historian's problem. The Evangelists were not simply recording; they were arguing. The conclusion to that argument was already fixed in their minds when they began their work, a fact they made no effort to disguise, namely, that their subject was no mere man but the Messiah of Israel and the Son of God;[63] that he was embarked on a series of events governed not by the historian's familiar secondary causality but by God's provident will; that Jesus was both completing the past—and thus "the Scriptures were fulfilled"—and breaking forth into a new and only gradually revealed eschatological future. Indeed, the death, Resurrection, and Ascension of Jesus do not complete the story; there is more: Pentecost at least, and how much more beyond that no one of the New Testament writers was aware. There is in all the material before the historian an open-ended anticipation that reflects disconcertingly backwards on almost every event in Jesus' life.

Many of the same problems confront the student of the life of Muhammad. Ibn Ishaq's biography of the Prophet begins, at least in the Ibn Hisham version we now possess,[64] much the same way that Mark's Gospel does, with a declaration that "this is the book of the biography of the Apostle of God,"[65] and it has, like Matthew and Luke, a brief "infancy narrative."[66] Moreover, there is a consistent, though low-key, attempt to demonstrate the authenticity of the Prophet's calling by the introduction of miracles, a motif that was almost certainly a byproduct of the eighth-century biographers' contact with Jews and, particularly, Christians.[67] This is sometimes imitative or polemical piety, and sometimes, and perhaps at an even earlier stage, a simple desire to entertain,[68] and its manifestations are not difficult to discern. Moreover, though the sira literature is not used to mask special doctrinal pleading—there are no carefully crafted "theologoumena" on this landscape[69]—there are, in their frequent lists, genealogies, and honorifics, abundant signs of the family and clan factionalism that troubled the first- and second-century Islamic community.[70] Finally, there are chronological questions. The earliest "biographers" of the Prophet, who were little more than collectors of the "raids" conducted by or under him, took the watershed battle of Badr as their starting point and anchor, and dated major events in Muhammad's life from it. However, for the years from Badr (624) back to the Hijra (622) there is great uncertainty, and for the entire span of the Prophet's life at Mecca there is hardly any chronological data at all.[71] The historians' only relief, perhaps (if relief it is), is that they do not have four differing accounts with which to work—all the earliest surviving versions of Muhammad's life rely heavily on Ibn Ishaq's original *Sira*—and that in that *Sira* he is not constrained to grapple with either a prologue in heaven or an eschatological epilogue.

Ibn Ishaq's *Life* is, on the face of it, a coherent and convincing account, and certainly gives historians something with which to work, particularly if they close their eyes to where the material came from. However, as has already been pointed out, the authenticity of the Hadith has been gravely undermined, and a medieval biography of Muhammad is little more than an assemblage of Hadith. Most modern biographers of the Prophet have been willing to close their eyes, and while conceding the general unreliability of the Hadith, they have used these same collections as the basis of their own works which differ from those of their medieval predecessors not so much in source material as in interpretation.[72] This may be a calculated risk based on the plausibility and internal coherence of the material, or it may simply be the counsel of despair. If the Hadith are rejected there is nothing notably better to put in their place.[73]

A few modern biographers, however, have attempted something different, to apply the biblical criteria of Form and Redaction criticism to the basic historical assemblage on which our knowledge of the events of the Prophet's life rests, the *Sira* of Ibn Ishaq. While Watt contented himself with a brief investigation of the "sources of Ibn Ishaq," first Rudolf Sellheim and then, far more thoroughly, John Wansbrough attempted to see the parts in the whole.[74] As Wansbrough explained the procedure, various motifs (the election and call of a prophet, for example) that are common to many religious societies—Judaism, Christianity, and possibly even Arab paganism among them—were adduced as *topoi* as surely in the construction of the "Gospel of Muhammad" as in the parallel lives of Moses and Jesus.[75]

Thus, if we regard the *Life* through Wansbrough's eyes, the "evangelical" materials of Islam were assembled out of standard Jewish and Christian (or other) *topoi* long after the death of Muhammad, and reflect not so much historical data as the political and polemical concerns of the "sectarian milieu" that shaped them. The Islamic "Gospel" was, as a New Testament critic might put it, the product of the Muslim community, and, in its final form, of the ninth-century Muslim community in Iraq, and far removed in time and space from the primary *Sitz im Leben*. There is, unhappily, no documentary hypothesis to explain the content of the framelike *topoi* of the *Sira*, no J or E or P or Q; instead, there are only the discredited bits and pieces of the Hadith, snippets of anecdotes, each with an "eyewitness" attached to the end of a more or less complete chain of transmitters, and with chain and witness sharing the same degree of likelihood or implausibility. "P" was an editor, "Q" the collector of *logoi*, but A'isha was the child bride of Muhammad and Abu Hurayra was a Companion of the Prophet, a man who had the simultaneous reputation of knowing more Hadith than anyone and of being an idle chatterer. Between them they witnessed an enormous number of the tesserae out of which we attempt to reconstruct what happened between 610 and 632.

One effect of Redaction criticism on the study of the life of Jesus has been to direct the emphasis forward from Jesus himself to Paul and the first generation of Christians who shaped the tradition of Jesus. Muhammad died a success and Jesus died a failure; and historians work within those givens. One common position, then, is to maintain that whatever Jesus may have said or done (to put it in its most obviously agnostic terms), Gospel Christianity, whether Mark's early version or John's later one, was the creation of Jesus' followers. In Islam, on the contrary, where historical agnosticism would seem to be equally justified by the sources, the historians' interest remains riveted on Muhammad and what is imagined to have been his own immediate milieu. Muhammad the charismatic, the mystic, the social reformer, and the political genius are all familiar figures in western scholarship—as familiar as the same qualities are alien to the present portrait of the historical Jesus—and there is no Paul nor a "Johannine community" to distract from the Prophet's central, or rather, unique, role in the fashioning of Islam.

A degree of reductionism has occurred, and it can be read between the lines of Wansbrough's reluctance to indicate a single or even principal sectarian influence operating on the *Sira*. In the first half of this century, when there was far greater trust in what the later Muslim sources said about pre-Islamic Arabia, and when there prevailed an innocent freedom to extrapolate from almost any Jewish or Christian source, whatever its date or provenance,[76] the formation of Muhammad had not infrequently been reduced to the sum of the Christian, and particularly the Jewish, influences operating on him,[77] but only to account for the presence in the Koran of pervasive and detailed references to things Christian and Jewish, and never to explain Muhammad's enormous impact on his environment. Jesus, on the other hand, often appears in current historical appreciations, and overwhelmingly so in Jewish ones,[78] as a rather commonplace but politically naive rabbi who was the victim, the dupe, or the ploy of other forces or other men whose agenda were political rather than spiritual; who was caught up, probably unwittingly, in a movement of national liberation and paid for it with his life.

With Jesus we have some hope of coming to an informed judgment, of speaking with a degree of conviction about "Jesus within Judaism," or "Jesus and the Transformation of Judaism," with its corollary of taking the measure not only of Jesus' "traditionalism" but of his "originality."[79] Judgments of Muhammad's originality, on the other hand, founder on our almost absolute inability to measure him against any local or contemporary criterion. As Michael Cook has put it, "to understand what Muhammad was doing in creating a new religion, it would be necessary to know what religious resources were available to him, and in what form."[80] However, we do not know. We cannot tell whether Muhammad is innovating or simply borrowing because, if the Koran is silent on the matter, as it often is, then:

> We are obliged to turn to the theologians of later periods, to the authors of tradition and *fiqh*, who frequently give accounts expressing variant interpretations. Even if these writers are in agreement with each other, often their consensus is still unacceptable to us. Generally, posterity was inclined to trace back to Muhammad all customs and institutions of later Islam. . . . Islamic tradition, however, not satisfied with claiming that the greater part of the cult was introduced by Muhammad, wants to date every institution as early as possible so that in many instances the pre-Islamic Arabs appear as precursors of Islam. This tendency is a consequence of the dogma of the religion of Abraham, the basis of Islam, which Muhammad felt it was his mission to preach.[81]

At every turn, then, historians of Muhammad and of early Islam appear betrayed by the sheer unreliability of their sources. The New Testament documents have their *Tendenz*, as all will quickly concede, and much of the "quest of the historical Jesus" has been in reality a search for a means to get around and behind that historical disability. However, most New Testament scholars also share a conviction that somewhere within the documents at their disposal is a grain or nugget, or perhaps even entire veins of historical truth, and that they can be retrieved. This explains the enormous and ingenious assiduity expended on the quest. Historians of Muhammad entertain no such optimism. They confront a community whose interest in preserving revelation was deep and careful, but who came to history, even to the history of the recipient of that revelation, too long after the memory of the events had faded to dim recollections over many generations, had been embroidered rather than remembered, and was invoked only for what is for historians the unholy purpose of polemic. Islam, unhappily for modern historians, had no immediate need of a Gospel and so chose carefully to preserve what it understood were the words of God rather than the deeds of the man who was His Messenger or the history of the place in which he lived.

Is there anything valuable in this Islamic tradition, which Patricia Crone has pessimistically called the "debris of an obliterated past"? It seems that there must be. It is inconceivable that the community should have entirely forgotten what Muhammad actually did or said at Mecca and Medina, or that the tenaciously memoried Arabs should have allowed to perish all remembrance of their Meccan or west Arabian past, no matter how deeply it might now be overcast with myth and special pleading. Some historians think they can see where the gold lies;[82] what is lacking is a method of extracting that priceless ore from the redactional rubble in which it is presently embedded. Those redactional layers may be later and thus thicker and less tractable than those over the figure of the historical Jesus, but just as the redactional editing of the Gospels was addressed and made to yield substantial results, there is no reason why the enterprise within Islam should prompt either resignation or despair. Faced with his own kind of unyielding tradition, the Islamicist has at least two ways of proceeding, as Julius Wellhausen recognized a century ago in his classic *Prolegomenon* on biblical criticism: either to arrange the accounts, in this instance, the Hadith, in an internationally coherent order that would then represent the growth of the tradition— thus, for pre-Islamic Mecca, M. J. Kister and, after him, Uri Rubin, Michael Lecker, and others[83]—or else to deduce the evolution of matters at Mecca from a comparison with parallels in other religious cultures, a task that carried the biblical critic Wellhausen into his equally classic study of "the remains of Arab paganism."[84] This latter method is the one pursued most recently by G. R. Hawting,[85] and though terribly hypothetical, it has the advantage of forming hypotheses about the religious phenomena themselves and not merely about the traditions regarding those phenomena.[86]

Both methods are painstakingly slow and yield results that are notably more successful in analyzing Jewish influences and cultic practices than in dealing with Christian ideas, and more convincing when applied to pre-Islamic Mecca than to the Prophet's own life. Moreover, in dealing with Muhammad, where the Koran is the historian's chief "document," it is far easier to do as Watt and Rodinson have done and to apply a combination of common sense and some modern heuristic devices to the traditional accounts than to attempt what Griesbach and Wrede did in the nineteenth century with the Gospels, or Streeter or Bultmann in the twentieth. It is easier still simply to give over the "quest of the historical Muhammad" and produce instead *Muhammad, His Life Based on the Earliest Sources* (1983), Martin Lings's uncritical English conflation of the traditional Muslim accounts which is offered without a word of explanation from the author on what he is about, or why, in this curious undertaking. There may be some value in presenting the Prophet of Islam in the same manner one might write a biography of Moses out of Ginzberg's *Legends of the Jews*, but it is not an enterprise likely to summon forth an Albert Schweitzer from the distraught bosom of Orientalism.

NOTES

1. Stephen Neill, *The Interpretation of the New Testament, 1861–1961* (London, 1964), pp. 338–40.

2. Stephen Neill and Tom Wright, *The Interpretation of the New Testament, 1861–1986* (New York, 1988), pp. 360–64.

3. I use this latter expression in the sense isolated by Martin Kähler's famous distinction, first made in 1892 (cf. Martin Kähler, *The So-Called Historical Jesus and the Historic Biblical Christ*, trans. Carl E. Braaten [Philadelphia, 1964]), between the "historical Jesus" and the "historic Christ," the latter being the continuous subject of Christian preaching and the object of both Christian faith and Christian piety. Precisely the same distinction is intended when reference is made here to the "historical Muhammad." While the Prophet's person is not the object of Muslims' faith, as Jesus' is for Christians, his prophethood is, and thus both the person and the role of "the historic Prophet," to adapt Kähler's expression to the Islamic situation, have had an enormous and continuous influence on Islamic piety, practice, and beliefs (cf. Annemarie Schimmel, *And Muhammad Is His Messenger: The Veneration of the Prophet in Islamic Piety* [Chapel Hill, N.C., 1995]), none of which is in question here.

4. Maxime Rodinson, *Mohammed*, trans. Anne Carter from the revised French edition of 1968 (London, 1971), p. xi. This was by way of preliminary to writing a 324-page biography of the Prophet!

5. What follows does not pretend to be exhaustive on either Muhammad or the

Koran, nor does it generally recover—though it occasionally glances at—the ground surveyed by Rudi Paret and Maxime Rodinson down to the early 1960s (Rudi Paret, "Recent European Research on the Life and Work of the Prophet Muhammad," *Journal of the Pakistan Historical Society* 6 [1958]: 81–96; Maxime Rodinson, "A Critical Survey of Modern Studies of Muhammad," first published in *Revue historique* 229 [1963]: 169–220; and translated from French in Merlin Swartz, *Studies on Islam* [New York, 1981], pp. 23–85). The state of Koranic studies through the 1970s is reflected in Alford T. Welch, "Kur'an," *EI²*, vol. 5 (Leiden, E. J. Brill, 1981): 400–432; and, more recently, in Angelika Neuwirth, "Koran," *Grundriss der arabischen Philologie*, vol. 2, *Literaturunvissenschaft*, ed. Helmut Gätje (Berlin, 1987), pp. 96–135.

6. See generally, on what might be called the "irenic approach" to Islam, Andrew Rippin, "Literary Analysis of Qur'an, Tafsir, and Sira: The Methodologies of John Wansbrough," *Approaches to Islam in Religious Studies*, ed. Richard Martin (Tucson, 1985), p. 159.

7. Ernest Renan, writing in 1851, and cited by Maxime Rodinson in "The Life of Muhammad and the Sociological Problem of the Beginnings of Islam," *Diogenes* 20 (1957): 46.

8. Neill and Wright, *Interpretation*, p. 363.

9. Nabia Abbott, Studies in *Arabic Literary Papyri*, vol. 1, *Historical Texts* (Chicago, 1957), p. 18; and compare Frants Buhl, *Das Leben Muhammeds*, translated from the second Danish edition of 1953 by Hans Heinrich Schaeder (rpt. Heidelberg, 1961), pp. 21ff. The pre-Islamic poetry makes its inevitable appearance in modern surveys on the "background sources" on Muhammad (see Rodinson, "Critical Survey," p. 37), but, except for Henri Lammens's work (see notes 11 and 56 below), it is far less in evidence when it comes to actually describing that background.

10. These are all likewise dutifully reported in surveys of the "sources for the life of Muhammad" (see Rodinson, "Critical Survey," pp. 29–39). It is in the north that we come the closest to the environment of Mecca, since both Jewish and Islamic traditions agree that there were Jewish settlements in the northern Hijaz; and, more important, the assertion is confirmed by epigraphical evidence (see Moshe Gil, "The Origin of the Jews of Yathrib," *Jerusalem Studies in Arabic and Islam* 4 [1984]: 203–224). However, the fact remains that there is between the contemporary Greek, Roman, and Sasanian sources about Syria and Arabia and the later Islamic tradition about the same places a "total lack of continuity" (Particia Crone, *Slaves on Horses: The Evolution of the Islamic Polity* [Cambridge, 1980], p. 11).

11. Compare Henri Lammens, *La Mecque à la Veille de l'Hégire* (Beirut, 1924), where the Arab literary evidence is collected (and perhaps distorted), with Patricia Crone, *Meccan Trade and the Rise of Islam* (Princeton, N.J., 1987), passim; and F. E. Peters, "The Commerce of Mecca before Islam," *A Way Prepared. Essays . . . Richard Bayly Winder,* ed. Farhad Kazemi and R. D. McChesney (New York, 1998), pp. 3–26. A more sober approach than that of Lammens to the same pre-Islamic milieu has been taken over the last quarter-century by M. J. Kister of the Hebrew University (see M. J. Kister, *Studies in*

Jahiliyya and Early Islam [London, 1980], and n. 83 below). In the face of the complete dearth of Hijaz evidence, Yehuda Nevo and Judith Koren have recently attempted to extrapolate the pre-Islamic Meccan milieu from what appears to have been a collection of pagan shrines still flourishing in the mid-eighth century at Sde Boqer in the Negev (Yehuda D. Nevo and Judith Koren, "The Origins of the Muslim Descriptions of the Jahili Meccan Sanctuary," *Journal of Near Eastern Studies* 49 [1990]: 23–44). The argument is seductive, but whether the buildings in question were indeed shrines does not appear to be at all clear.

12. For Muhammad, see Buhl, *Das Leben*, p. 366. While there is some material evidence for the Galilee and Jerusalem of Jesus' day, the latter conveniently summarized in John Wilkinson, *Jerusalem as Jesus Knew It: Archaeology as Evidence* (London, 1978), there has been no archaeological exploration in either Mecca or Medina, nor are the prospects good that there will be (F. E. Peters, *Jerusalem and Mecca: The Typology of the Holy City in the Near East* [New York, 1986], pp. 72–74). The almost total absence of archaeological evidence for early Islam is particularly striking when contrasted with the role that the excavation of sanctuaries and the discovery of legal and liturgical inscriptions have played in controlling the purely literary material that constitutes the "Hebrew Epic."

13. In all that follows I have left aside the question of "revelation" and "inspiration" and taken as my starting point the historian's normal assumption that the religious documents in question, the New Testament and the Koran, are entirely and uniquely the products of human agents, whoever those latter may turn out to be.

14. These latter reports are the Hadith or Prophetic traditions allegedly reproducing the actual words of Muhammad on a variety of subjects. Their authenticity, which is of crucial importance to the historian, will be taken up in due course; here it need only be noted that while they do not share the cachet of divine inspiration attached by Christians to the entire New Testament, they have for Muslims a high degree of authority. Though that authority may have originated in their promotion, like that of the Mishna and Talmud, to magisterial authority in legal questions, the Hadith soon began to enjoy the same status as purely historical documents.

15. If anything, the gap between the events of Jesus' life and their final redaction in the preserved Gospels appears to be growing narrower as time passes (see John A. T. Robinson, *Redating the New Testament* [Philadelphia, 1976]; and Neill and Wright, *Interpretation*, p. 361).

16. Conceivably even fewer, or perhaps many, many more. Though the later Muslim tradition came to agree that the "collection" of the Koran took place in the caliphate of 'Uthman (644–656), some early Muslim authorities dated it to the Caliph Abu Bakr (632–634) and others to 'Umar (634–644). This early uncertainty about what would appear to be a critical event in Islamic history is by no means atypical, and two modern scholars have rejected the traditional "'Uthmanic" consensus out of hand. One (John Burton, *The Collection of the Qur'an* [Cambridge, 1977] would make the "collection of the Koran" the work of the Prophet himself, while the other (John Wansbrough, *Qur'anic Studies: Sources and Methods of Scriptural Interpretation* [Cambridge, 1977]) would

postpone it to the ninth century. It is still early in the career of each hypothesis, but neither seems to have been widely embraced.

17. Arthur Jeffery, *Materials for the History of the Text of the Qur'an* (Leiden, 1937); Rudi Paret, "Der Koran als Geschichtsquelle," *Der Islam* 37 (1961): 24–42, cited from its reprint in *Der Koran*, ed. Rudi Paret (Darmstadt, 1975), pp. 141–42.

18. J. Eliash, "The Shi'ite Qur'an: A Reconsideration of Goldziher's Interpretation," *Arabica* 16 (1969): 15–24; E. Kohlberg, "Some Notes on the Imamite Attitudes toward the Qur'an," *Islamic Philosophy and the Classical Tradition: Essays . . . Richard Wither* (Columbia, S.C., 1973), pp. 209–24.

19. As noted, one who has failed to be convinced is John Wansbrough who, in two major studies (Wansbrough, *Qur'anic Studies*, and Wansbrough, *The Sectarian Milieu: Content and Composition in Islamic Salvation History* [Oxford, 1978]) has attempted to demonstrate that (1) the Koran was not finally fixed ("collected") until the early ninth century, and (2) it was shaped out of biblical and other materials by redactors influenced by contemporary Judeo-Christian polemic. For a sympathetic appreciation of Wansbrough's work, see Rippin, "Literary Analysis"; and for a Muslim's criticism of both Wansbrough and Rippin, see Fazlur Rahman, "Approaches to Islam in Religious Studies: Review Essay," *Approaches to Islam in Religious Studies*, ed. Richard Martin (Tucson, 1985), pp. 198–202.

20. William Graham, "Qur'an as Spoken Word: An Islamic Contribution to the Understanding of Scripture," *Approaches to Islam in Religious Studies*, ed. Richard Martin (Tucson, 1985), p. 31: "Fundamentally, the Koran was what its name proclaimed it to be: the recitation given by God for human beings to repeat (cf. sura 96:1)."

21. This is believed according to the universal Muslim tradition (W. Montgomery Watt, *Bell's Introduction to the Qur'an* [Edinburgh. 1970], pp. 37–38).

22. Rudolf Bultmann, *History of the Synoptic Tradition* (New York, 1963), p. 205.

23. See W. D. Davies's judicious remarks (*Paul and Rabbinic Judaism* [Philadelphia, 1980], p. 3): "While it is clear that Rabbinic sources do preserve traditions of an earlier date than the second century . . . it must never be overlooked that Judaism had made much history during that period. It follows that we cannot, without extreme caution, use the Rabbinic sources as 'evidence for first-century Judaism." Study of the life of Muhammad suffers, as we shall see (see note 80), from the selfsame problem.

24. Watt, *Bell's Introduction*, pp. 77–79; compare R. B. Serjeant, "Early Arabic Prose," *Arabic Literature to the End of the Umayyad Period*, ed. A. F. L. Beeston et al. (Cambridge, 1983), pp. 126–27.

25. A. E. Harvey, *Jesus and the Constraints of History* (Philadelphia, 1982), pp. 6ff.

26. Rippin, "Literary Analysis," p. 159, commenting on Wansbrough's delineation of this style (Wansbrough, *Qur'anic Studies*, pp. 40–43, 47–48, 51–52ff.; Wansbrough, *Sectarian Milieu*, pp. 24–25): "The audience of the Koran is presumed able to fill in the missing details of the narrative, much as is true of work such as the Talmud, where knowledge of the appropriate biblical citations is assumed or supplied by only a few words." Far more than this is assumed by the Mishna and Talmud, of course. There, the reader is

expected to understand the lines of both the issues and the current state of the debate on those issues when the text opens.

27. Watt, *Bell's Introduction*, pp. 77–82, 127–35. All these would fall within what the New Testament Form critics would call "Paränesis" or "Sayings and Parables" (cf. Robert H. Stein, *The Synoptic Problem: An Introduction* [Grand Rapids, Mich., 1987], pp. 168–72), though with far greater variety than the Gospel examples show.

28. Neill and Wright, *Interpretation*, p. 264.

29. See, most recently, Issa Boullata, "The Rhetorical Interpretation of the Qur'an: I'jaz and Related Topics," *Approaches to the History of the Interpretation of the Qur'an*, ed. Andrew Rippin (Oxford. 1988), pp. 140–41.

30. For Richard Bell's ingenious but unconvincing hypothesis, see Watt, *Bell's Introduction*, pp. 101–107.

31. Namely, that the present suras were the original units of revelation, and that the Hadith, and the historical works incorporating them, provide a valid basis for dating the suras (cf. Neuwirth, "Koran," p. 100). These premises, which roughly correspond to standard rabbinic theory about the books of the Bible, would, of course, rule out even the possibility of a "documentary hypothesis" for either the Bible or the Koran.

32. The standard statement of what has become the western position is found in the first volume of Theodor Nöldeke's *Geschichte des Qorans* (Göttingen, 1860), revised by Friedrich Schwally in 1909. Others have slightly revised the Nöldeke-Schwally sequence, but it remains the basic sura order used in the West (Neuwirth, "Koran," pp. 117–19).

33. Watt, *Bell's Introduction*, p. 114: "Like all those who have dated the Koran, Bell accepted the general chronological framework [and much else besides] of Muhammad's life as this is found in the *Sira* . . . and other works." The value judgment is that expressed in Welch, "Kur'an," p. 417.

34. This was somewhat disingenuouisly conceded by W. Montgomery Watt (*Muhammad at Mecca* [Oxford. 1953], p. xiii), and, more helpfully, by Rudolf Sellheim ("Prophet, Calif und Geschichte: Die Muhammad Biographie des Ibn Ishaq," *Oriens* 18–19 [1965–1966]: 33–91); and Wansbrough (*Qur'anic Studies* and *Sectarian Milieu*), among others.

35. *The Life of Muhammad: A Translation of Ishaq's "Sirat Rasul Allah", with Introduction and Notes by Alfred Guillaume* (Oxford, 1955), p. 691.

36. Michael Cook, *Muhammad* (New York, 1983), p. 68.

37. See sura 10:38–39, where, as usual, God is speaking:

> This Koran is not such as could ever he invented in despite of God; but it is a confirmation of that which was before it and an exposition of that which is decreed for men—there is no doubt of that—from the Lord of the Worlds. Or do they say he [that is, Muhammad] has invented it? Then say: If so, do you bring a sura like it, and call for help on all you can besides God, if you have any doubts.

For the Gospels, see John 21:24: "it is this same disciple who attests what has here been written. It is in fact he who wrote it, and we know that his testimony is true"; and cf. Luke 1:1–4.

38. Summarily described, from a Muslim point of view, in Muhammad Abdul Rauf, "Hadith Literature—1: The Development of the Science of Hadith," in *Arabic Literature to the End of the Umayyad Period,* ed. A. F. L. Beeston et al. (Cambridge, 1983), pp. 271–88. However, they may have included, even by their own criteria, far more chaff than has been suspected; compare G. H. A. Juynboll, "On the Origins of Arabic Prose: Reflections on Authenticity," *Studies on the First Century of Islamic History,* ed. G. H. A. Juynboll (Carbondale, Ill., 1982), pp. 171–72: "Classical Muslim isnad criticism has not been as foolproof as orthodox circles, and in their wake many scholars in the West, have always thought."

39. Consider, for example, what might be taken, were it genuine, as a prime example of early Islamic *kerygma,* Muhammad's own "farewell discourse" on the occasion of his last pilgrimage before his death. It is reported in substantially similar versions by three major historians, Ibn Ishaq, Waqidi, and Tabari, but, remarked R. B. Serjeant, a generally conservative critic, "patently signs of political ideas of a later age, coupled with internal and external contradicitions, largely discredit the attribution of much of the extant versions to the Prophet" (Serjeant, "Early Arabic Prose," p. 123). For another example, see note 62.

40. This is not to say that, as Wright put it (Neill and Wright, *Interpretation,* p. 362):

It is still universally agreed that our picture of the earliest Church must begin with the study of Paul, and in particular of the letters generally agreed to be authentic. . . . These writings, which almost certainly antedate the earliest written Gospel, remain central for both the theology and history of the period.

Islam lacks a Paul, that is, an authoritative contemporary interpretation of the founder's message. The Islamic sources for early Islam are, like those on the life of Muhammad himself, later by a century and a half. Paul may have done theological mischief in the Christian context by providing an interpretation before the message, but all in all, it is better to have Paul than Tabari, as either a historian or an exegete.

41. Neill and Wright, *Interpretation,* p. 294.

42. Buhl, *Das Leben,* p. 366. Michael Cook succinctly summed up the contemporary historical data provided by the Koran:

Taken on its own, the Koran tells us very little about the events of Muhammad's career. It does not narrate these events, but merely refers to them: and in doing so, it has a tendency not to name names. Some do occur in contemporary contexts: four religious communities are named (Jews, Christians, Magians, and the mysterious Sabians), as are three Arabian deities (all female), three humans (of whom Muhammad is one), two ethnic groups (Quraysh and the Romans), and nine places. Of the places, four are mentioned in military connections (Badr, Mecca, Hunayn, Yathrib), and four are connected with the sanctuary (Safa, Marwa, Arafat, while the fourth is "Bakka," said to be an alternative name to Mecca). The final place is Mount Sinai, which seems to be associated with the growing of olives. Leaving aside the ubiquitous Christians and Jews, none of these names occurs very often: Muhammad is named four or five times (once as

"Ahmad"), the Sabians twice, Mount Sinai twice, and the rest once each."
(Cook, *Muhammad*, pp. 69–70)

43. W. Montgomery Watt, *Muhammad's Mecca: History in the Qur'an* (Edinburgh, 1988), especially pp. 26–38. Alford T. Welch ("Muhammad's Understanding of Himself: The Koranic Data," *Islam's Understanding of Itself*, ed. Richard G. Hovannisian and Speros Vryonis [Malibu, Calif, 1983], pp. 15–52) has likewise attempted a biographical sketch of Muhammad's "self-understanding" as revealed by the Koran.

44. Alford T. Welch, "Allah and Other Supernatural Beings: The Emergence of the Qur'anic Doctrine of Tawhid," *Studies in Quran and Tafsir*, ed. Alford T. Welch, *JAAR Thematic Issue* 47 (1979, 1980): 733–58.

45. Welch, "Muhammad's Understanding," p. 16; and compare the significant omission of the personal pronoun in "A thorough analysis of the Koranic contexts involving Allah, other deities, and the 'lower' members of the spirit world shows a clear and unmistakable development of ideas or teachings" (Welch, "Allah," p. 734).

46. Ibid., pp. 751–53.

47. On the genre, see M. J. Kister, "The *Sira* Literature," *Arabic Literature to the End of the Umayyad Period*, ed. A. F. L. Beeston et al. (Cambridge, 1983), pp. 352–67.

48. The consensus opinion—and reservations—are rendered in Welch, "Kur'an," p. 414. Similar, and stronger, reservations are expressed by Wansbrough (*Qur'anic Studies*, p. 141); Cook (*Muhammad*, p. 70); and Rippin ("Literary Analysis"), who wrote:

> Their [the "occasions of revelation" narratives] actual significance in individual cases of trying to interpret the Koran is limited: the anecdotes are adduced, and thus recorded and transmitted, in order to provide a narrative situation in which the interpretation of the Koran can be embodied. The material has been recorded within exegesis not for its historical value but for its exegetical value. Yet such basic literary facts about the material are frequently ignored within the study of Islam in the desire to find positive historical results. (p. 153)

49. On Koranic exegesis posing as biography, see W. Montgomery Watt, "The Materials Used by Ibn Ishaq," *Historians of the Middle East*, ed. Bernard Lewis and P. M. Holt. (London, 1962), pp. 23–34; and on the "raids of the Prophet," which Watt regards as the "essential foundation for the biography of the Prophet and the history of his times," see ibid., pp. 27–28, and also J. M. B. Jones, "The Maghazi Literature," *Arabic Literature to the End of the Umayyad Period*, ed. A. F. L. Beeston et al. (Cambridge, 1983), pp. 344–51.

50. Alternatively, as Patricia Crone dramatically stated it (*Slaves on Horses*, p. 203 n. 10), "consider the prospect of reconstructing the origins of Christianity on the basis of the writings of Clement or Justin in a recension by Origen."

51. Ignaz Goldziher, "On the Development of the Hadith," *Muslim Studies*, ed. S. M. Stern, vol. 11 (London, 1971), pp. 17–254; originally published in 1890.

52. Joseph Schacht, *The Origins of Muhammadan Jurisprudence* (Oxford, 1950).

53. Compare Stein's recent assessment of the materials attributed to Jesus in the Gospels: "The lack of such material [dealing with the most pressing problems facing the

earliest Christian communities] in the Gospels witnesses against the idea that the church created large amounts of the gospel materials and in favor of the view that the church tended to transmit the Jesus traditions faithfully." Moreover, citing G. B. Caird, "There is not a shred of evidence that the early church ever concocted sayings of Jesus in order to solve any of its problems" (Stein, *Synoptic Problem*, p. 189).

54. Thus argues W. Montgomery Watt in *The History of al-Tabari*, vol. 6, *Muhammad at Mecca*, trans. and annotated W. Montgomery Watt and M. V. McDonald (Albany, N.Y., 1988), p. xviii.

55. On these latter see the trenchant Form criticism analysis by Albrecht Noth, *Quellenkritische Studien zu Themen, Formen, und Tendenzen frühislamischen Geschichtsüberlieferung*, vol. 1, *Themen und Formen* (Bonn, 1973).

56. On Henri Lammens's approach, see "Qoran et tradition: Comment fut composée la vie de Mohamet?" *Recherches de Science Religieuse* 1 (1910): 25–61, and *Fatima et les filles de Mahomet* (Rome, 1912); and compare C. H. Becker, "Grundsdtzlichen zur Leben-Muhammadforschung," *Islamstudien*, 2 vols. (Leipzig, 1924; rpt. Hildesheim, 1967), vol. 1, pp. 520–27, and K. S. Salibi, "Islam and Syria in the Writings of Henri Lammens," *Historians of the Middle East*, ed. Bernard Lewis and P. M. Holt (London, 1962), pp. 330–42; for Rodinson's characterization, see Rodinson, "Critical Survey," p. 26, and compare Buhl, *Das Leben*, p. 367: "H. Lammens . . . dessen Belesenheit und Scharfsinn man bewundem muss, der aber doch oft die Objectivität des unparteischen Historikers vermissen lässt."

57. Watt, *Muhammad*, p. xiii, and compare Watt, "Materials," p. 24. Kister's cautiously worded opinion seems similar:

> The development of Sira literature is closely linked with the transmission of the Hadith and should be viewed in connection with it . . . . Although some accounts about the recording of the utterances, deeds and orders dictated by the Prophet to his companions are dubious and debatable and should be examined with caution (and ultimately rejected), some of them seem to deserve trust." (Kister, "Sira Literature," p. 352)

58. Compare Rodinson, "Critical Survey," p. 42: "Orientalists are tempted to do as the Orientals have tended to do without any great sense of shame, that is, to accept as authentic those traditions that suit their own interpretation of an event and to reject others." Rodinson, who, as we shall see shortly, had even less faith than Watt in the source material, may have himself done precisely that in his own biography of the Prophet.

59. Crone, *Slaves on Horses*, pp. 14–15:

> Among historians the response to Schacht has varied from defensiveness to deafness, and there is no denying that the implications of his theories are, like those of Noth, both negative and hard to contest. . . . That the bulk of the Sira . . . consists of second-century Hadiths has not been disputed by any historian, and this point may be taken as conceded. But if the surface of the tradition consists of debris from the controversies of the late Umayyad and early Abbasid

period, the presumption must be that the layer underneath consists of similar debris from the controversies that preceded them, as Lammens and Becker inferred from Goldziher's theories.

According to Crone, Watt "disposes of Schacht by casuistry," but Shaban, Paret, Guillaume, and Sellheim have likewise been unwilling to deal squarely with the critical issue he has raised (ibid., p. 211 n. 88). Watt's brief rebuttal is in his "The Reliability of Ibn Ishaq's Sources," *La vie du prophète Mahomet* (Colloque de Strasbourg, 1980; Paris, 1983), pp. 31–43; and Watt and McDonald, *Muhammad*, pp. xvii–xix.

60. Becker, "Grundsätzlichen," p. 521, cited in Watt, "Materials," p. 23.

61. Cited in note 4 above; compare his similar remarks in note 58 above and, earlier, Buhl, *Das Leben*, pp. 372–77.

62. The earliest example of such a summary, in both the serial and the absolute chronology, appears in Ibn Ishaq's *Life* (1:336) on the occasion of some Muslims emigrating to Abyssinia in 615, when the ruler there was given a summary presentation of Islamic "good news." This apparently early Muslim "kerygma" has been analyzed in Wansbrough, *Qur'anic Studies*, pp. 38–43, and Wansbrough, *Sectarian Milieu*, pp. 100–101. That author concludes (*Qur'anic Studies*, p. 41) that "the structure of the report suggests a careful rhetorical formulation of Koranic material generally supposed to have been revealed after the date of that event," and, even more sweepingly (*Sectarian Milieu*, p. 100), "save for the Meccan pilgrimage, no item in these lists falls outside the standard monotheist vocabulary, and is thus of little use in the description of origins."

63. From Mark onward—"Here begins the Gospel of Jesus Christ the Son of God"—all the Gospels make a similar declaration at their outset.

64. In Ibn Ishaq's original "world history" version, before Ibn Hisham removed the "extraneous material," the story began with Creation, and Muhammad's prophetic career was preceded by accounts of all the prophets who had gone before. The life of the man was the "seal" of their line (see Abbott, *Studies*, pp. 87–89). This earlier, "discarded" section of Ishaq's work can be to some extent retrieved (Gordon Darnell Newby, *The Making of the Last Prophet: A Reconstruction of the Earliest Biography of Muhammad* [Columbia, S.C., 1989]), and while its remains are revealing of Ibn Ishaq's purpose and the milieu in which the work was finally composed (Abbott, *Studies*, p. 89), they add nothing of substance to the portrait of the historical Muhammad.

65. Ibn Ishaq 3 in Guillaume, *Life of Muhammad*, p. 3.

66. Ibid., pp. 102–7 in Guillaume, *Life of Muhammad*, pp. 69–73: and compare what Ibn Ishaq calls "Reports of Arab Soothsayers, Jewish Rabbi, and Christian Monks" about the birth of the Prophet (ibid., pp. 130ff. in Guillaume, *Life of Muhammad*, pp. 90ff.).

67. Sellheim, "Prophet," pp, 38–39, 59–67; Kister, "Sira Literature," pp. 356–57; and, for a more general consideration of "polemic as a history-builder," see Wansbrough, *Sectarian Milieu*, pp. 40–45, and note 77 below.

68. Kister, "Sira Literature," pp. 356–57, on the early sira of Wahb ibn Munabbih (d. 728 or 732) and the "popular and entertaining character of the early sira stories, a blend of miraculous narratives, edifying anecdotes and records of battles in which sometimes

ideological and political tendencies can be discerned." (Compare Cook, *Muhammad*, p. 66.)

69. The New Testament critic Joseph Fitzmyer defined a "theologoumenon" as "a theological assertion that does not directly express a matter of faith or an official teaching of the Church, and hence in itself is not normative, but that expresses in language that may prescind from facticity a notion which supports, enhances or is related to a matter of faith" (Joseph A. Fitzmyer, "The Virginal Conception of Jesus in the New Testament," originally published in 1973. Reprinted in Joseph A. Fitzmyer, *To Advance the Gospel* [New York, 1981], p. 45).

70. Sellheim, "Prophet," pp. 49–53; Kister, "Sira Literature," pp. 362–63.

71. Wansbrough, *Sectarian Milieu*, p. 35; and compare Noth, *Quellenkritische Studien*, pp. 40–45, 155–58. The reason for the vague "distributional chronology," as Wansbrough called the pre-Hijra system, was certainly not, as Watt has suggested (in Watt and McDonald, *Muhammad*, p. xxi), that "there were fewer outstanding events." The call of the Prophet, the earliest revelation of the Koran, and the making of the first converts would all appear to be supremely important, though the Muslim tradition had little certainty, chronological or otherwise, about them (ibid., pp. xxii, xxv–xii), likely because there was either no way or no reason to remember the date.

72. Crone, *Slaves on Horses*, p. 13:

> The inertia of the source material comes across very strongly in modern scholarship on the first two centuries of Islam. The bulk of it has an alarming tendency to degenerate into mere arrangements of the same old canon—Muslim chronicles in modern languages and graced with modern titles. Most of the rest consists of reinterpretation in which the order derives less from the sources than from our own ideas of what life ought to be about—modern preoccupations graced with Muslim facts and footnotes.

73. One attempt to substitute "genuine" eyewitness testimony (if not to Muhammad himself, then to the first appearance of the Islamic movement on the early seventh-century Near East) has been Patricia Crone and Michael Cook's *Hagarism: The Making of the Islamic World* (Cambridge, 1977), and while a brave and provocative book, it has tempted few others to follow its suggestion: "The historicity of the Islamic tradition is . . . to some degree problematic: while there are no cogent internal grounds for rejecting it, there are equally no cogent external grounds for accepting it . . . . The only way out of the dilemma is thus to step outside the Islamic tradition altogether and start again" (p. 3). What the external testimony to early Islam amounts to (and it is not a great deal) is summarized in Cook, *Muhammad*, pp. 73–76; and the limitations of this approach are underscored in Wansbrough, *Sectarian Milieu*, pp. 115–16.

74. Watt, "Materials"; Sellheim, "Prophet"; Wansbrough, *Qur'anic Studies*; Wansbrough, *Sectarian Milieu*.

75. Wansbrough, *Qur'anic Studies*, p. 66.

76. See note 90 below. Michael Cook (*Muhammad*) reflects the far more modest aims of contemporary searchers after "influences":

For the most part we are reduced to the crude procedure of comparing Islam with the mainstream traditions of Judaism and Christianity, and trying to determine which elements came from which. The answers are often convincing, but they fail to tell us in what form those elements came to Muhammad, or he to them. (p. 77)

77. This was done as early as Abraham Geiger's *Judaism and Islam* (originally published in Latin in 1832; reprinted from the translation published in 1898 [New York, 1970]); and then later, Charles Cutler Torrey, *The Jewish Foundations of Islam* [New York, 1933; reprinted New York, 1967]). There have been a number of suggestive portraits of the "Jewish Muhammad," followed by the arguments of Richard Bell, *The Origin of Islam in Its Christian Environment* (London, 1926; reprinted London, 1968). Karl Ahrens, "Christliches im Qoran" (*Zeitschrift der Deutschen Morganlandischen Gesellschaft*, 84 [1930], pp. 15–68, 148–90); and Tor Andrae, *Les origines de l'Islam et le Christianisme* (Paris, 1955), for a "Christian Muhammad."

78. The political hypothesis, first argued by Eisler and Brandon, took this more recent form in Hyam Maccoby, *The Mythmaker: Paul and the Invention of Christianity* (New York, 1987):

Though all these [just cited Jewish] writers have their individual approaches, it is characteristic of the school as a whole to use the Talmud to show that Jesus' life and teaching are entirely understandable in terms of the Judaism of his time, particularly rabbinical or Pharisaic Judaism. The corollary is that, since Jesus did not conflict with Judaism, his death took place for political reasons, later camouflaged as religious by the Christian Church in its anxiety to cover up the fact that Jesus was a rebel against Rome. (pp. 208–209)

Cf. Ernst Bammel, "The Revolutionary Theory from Reimarus to Brandon," *Jesus and the Politics of His Day*, ed. Ernst Bammel and C. D. F. Moule (New York, 1984), pp. 11–68.

79. Harvey, *Jesus*, p. 6, was cited in note 25 above on the "constraints of history." However, he went on to add:

This is not to say, of course, that he [Jesus] must have been totally subject to these constraints. Like any truly creative person, he could doubtless bend them to his purpose. . . . But had he not worked within them, he would have seemed a mere freak, a person too unrelated to the normal rhythm of society to have anything meaningful to say.

80. Cook, *Muhammad*, p. 77. Moreover, it is here that the Islamicist, like the New Testament scholar (see note 23), runs into the problem of the usefulness of the "rabbinic sources": to what extent can the Mishna, the Talmud, and the Midrashim (many of these latter sources being, in fact, post-Islamic and so possibly influenced by, rather than influencing, early Islam) be used to illuminate the pre-Islamic milieu of Mecca? Geiger, Torrey (*Jewish Foundations*, p. 34), and, notoriously, Abraham Katsh, *Judaism in Islam: Biblical*

and Talmudic Backgrounds of the Koran and Its Commentaries. Surahs II and III (New York, 1954), invoked them almost as if Muhammad had a personal yeshiva library at his disposal, or, as Torrey thought, even a rabbinic teacher (*Jewish Foundations*, pp. 40–42).

81. Arent Jan Wensinck, *Muhammad and the Jews of Medina*, with the excursus, *Muhammad's Constitution of Medina* by Julius Wellhausen, trans. and ed. Wolfgang Bohn (Freiburg, 1975), p. 73.

82. Paret, *Der Koran*; Watt, "Materials," p. 28; Watt and McDonald, *Muhammad*, pp. xxi–xxv; Sellheim, "Prophet," pp. 73–77; Kister, "Sira Literature," pp. 352–53.

83. Kister and his students have painstakingly compared variants in early, and largely unpublished, Muslim traditions on various topics—thus, for example, his analysis of a rather mysterious prerevelation religious practice of Muhammad called *tahannuth* ("Al-Tahannuth: An Inquiry into the Meaning of a Term," *Bulletin of the School of Oriental and African Studies* 31 (1968): 223–36—and attempted to construct the original understanding behind them, on the assumption that the "original" tradition derived, to some degree, from a historical "fact." They did not, however, directly address the critical question of the authenticity of any of the Hadith materials with which they are so scrupulously dealing, though Kister for one, as we have seen (note 68 above), was well aware of the historiographical problems posed by the inauthenticity of the Hadith.

84. Julius Wellhausen, *Reste arabischen Heidentums*, 2d ed. (Berlin, 1897).

85. G. R. Hawting, "The Origins of the Islamic Sanctuary at Mecca," *Studies on the First Century of Islamic History*, ed. G. H. A. Juynboll (Carbondale, Ill., 1982), pp. 25–47.

86. It is instructive of the two methods to compare Hawting, "Origins," with Uri Rubin, "The Ka'ba, Aspects of Its Ritual, Functions, and Position in Pre-Islamic and Early Islamic Times," *Jerusalem Studies in Arabic and Islam* 8 (1986): pp. 97–131, both of which deal with the pre-Islamic sanctuary at Mecca.

Chapter 14

Recovering Lost Texts: Some Methodological Issues*

Lawrence I. Conrad

A recent attempt to reconstruct the initial and now lost section of Ibn Ishaq's biography of Muhammad raises some important methodological issues as to how early Islamic authors and transmitters quoted their sources, and the problems these citations pose to any effort to use them to reconstruct otherwise lost texts. This review article stresses that while some such efforts may well prove successful, the task is not a straightforward one and requires the collection of potentially useful material on a large scale and careful attention to a wide range of historiographical questions.

T he prospect of recovering lost Arabic texts from later sources which quote from them is one which has long tantalized modern scholars,[1] and in *The Making of the Last Prophet* Gordon D. Newby takes up the task of reconstructing a book of particular interest, the *Kitab al-mubtada'* of Muhammad ibn Ishaq (d. 150/767). As Newby quite rightly argues in his introduction, the recovery of this work would provide many important insights into how early Muslims viewed Islam's relation to Judaism and Christianity. Newby's reconstruction, offered here in English translation, consists of twenty-nine narratives in *qisas al-anbiya'*

---

*Originally published in *Journal of the American Oriental Society* 113, no. 2 (April/June 1993): 258–63. Reprinted by permission of the American Oriental Society. This article is a review of *The Making of the Last Prophet: A Reconstruction of the Earliest Biography of Muhammad* by Gordon Darnell Newby.

style, each introduced by an analysis pointing to Judeo-Christian parallels and suggesting how such a text would have been regarded in Muslim society in Ibn Ishaq's own time. There are also interesting observations on the role of the *qass* and on the possible function of the text in moralizing to the crown prince and future caliph al-Mahdi (pp. 161, 194)—assuming, as Newby does, that one is to accept the view that Ibn Ishaq wrote his *Sira* at al-Mansur's behest and for the purpose of instructing his son.[2]

The principles governing the process of reconstruction, however, are never set forth clearly—a brief explanation on page 16 states that the order of material in each story is determined by considerations in the following descending order of priority: Koranic order, al-Tabari's order, biblical or historical order, and as a last resort, "an attempt to present a coherent whole." What this means in practice (more on this below) is that the traditions in al-Tabari's *Ta'rikh* which deal with *qisas al-anbiya'* figures, and which bear isnads in which Ibn Ishaq is named, are all assumed to come from Ibn Ishaq's *Kitab al-mubtada'* and form a kind of base text. To this is added anything on the subject which is to be gleaned from traditions in al-Tabari's *Tafsir* which also bear the name of Ibn Ishaq in their isnads. Some further traditions are added from the *Qisas al-anbiya'* of al-Tha'labi, *Al-Bad' wa-l-ta'rikh* by al-Maqdisi, and the *Tafsir* of Khazin (called "al-Baghdadi" in this book). Al-Azraqi's *Akhbar Makka* is occasionally used (see below), and Ibn Sa'd and the *Kitab al-mu'ammarin* of Abu Hatim al-Sijistani are each cited once. The stories are presented in English translation only, with the sentences "reordered . . . to follow more closely the expectations of one who is reading only in English" (p. xi). Each story ends with a list of the sources used to reconstruct it, but there are no notes or other means to find out exactly how the editor is proceeding and why.

A proper discussion of why this method is problematic and unlikely to produce any demonstrably close approximation to the original *Kitab al-mubtada'* (a perhaps vexed concept in any case; see number 4 below) would take many pages, and here a few summary points may serve to indicate the key problems:

1. *The Making of the Last Prophet* is founded on an extremely narrow range of source material. The basis for any reconstruction would of course have to be not al-Tabari, however important he may prove to be in other respects, but the early *mubtada'* material by Ibn Ishaq himself,[3] and by other early authors on this subject who may either comprise one of his sources, such as Wahb ibn Munabbih (d. 114/732),[4] or quote him, such as Abu Hudhayfa (d. 206/821)[5] and 'Umara ibn Wathima al-Farisi (d. 289/902).[6] It is sources of this kind that would provide the clearest and most reliable picture of the probable structure, range, and agenda of the *Kitab al-mubtada'*. The relevant materials in early tafsir, *qisas al-anbiya'*,

and Hadith, all ignored by Newby, would also have to be consulted. A broadly based corpus is essential for addressing some of the problems to be discussed below, and without it progress is possible only through means which are essentially arbitrary.

2. It is fallacious to suppose that everything on subject X in which scholar NN figures as a transmitter must have come from the book which NN is known to have written on this subject. That is, it is obviously wrong to assume that Ibn Ishaq never transmitted or taught anything relevant to the topic of *mubtada'*, except what he included in his book entitled *Al-Mubtada'*. What one must reasonably expect is that the book represents a selection from a much larger body of available material, and in the case of Ibn Ishaq it is fairly clear that this larger body of material was very large indeed.[7]

An all-inclusive method must also be queried on the grounds that there are many instances in which a *mubtada'*-style tradition in fact figures elsewhere in the *Sira*. To take but one example of many, the activities of Adam and Abraham are obvious *mubtada'* topics, but are also discussed at length by Ibn Ishaq in the *mab'ath* part of his biography, when his attention turns to the pre-Islamic history of Mecca and the *Ka'ba* (but see number 5 below). This includes some of the material which Newby has included in his reconstruction of the *Kitab al-mubtada'*, because the subject is indeed *mubtada'*.[8] In the final analysis it must be stressed that thematic categories, as conceived by the early transmitters of Arab-Islamic tradition, were simply not so insulated and clear-cut as to justify the methodological assumptions which Newby brings into play in this book.

3. Equally, one cannot gratuitously jettison important early material which does not seem to "fit" into the framework established, by privileging the material cited by al-Tabari. If the papyrus fragments identified by Abbott[9] as part of the *Kitab al-mubtada'* correspond to nothing in the reconstruction, then this obviously places in doubt either the reconstruction or the attribution of these fragments to Ibn Ishaq and his *Kitab al-mubtada'*.[10] In any case, one cannot simply attribute the fragments to a lacuna in the reconstruction (i.e., they belong to the text), and at the same time discard them (i.e., they don't belong to the text, p. 16). Likewise, if the *Kitab al-aghani* contains possible passages from the text, these must be included in the corpus and subjected to criticism along with everything else—this alone will determine whether the passages should or should not figure in the reconstruction. In *The Making of the Last Prophet* one sees no indication that these passages have actually been identified, collected, and studied (ibid.).

4. One cannot assume that citations from the *Kitab al-mubtada'* in later works will correspond to what Ibn Ishaq originally wrote—this for several rea-

sons. First, if Ibn Ishaq wrote not as a neutral dispassionate observer, but, as Newby concedes, as an active voice in the debates of his day, and if his *Sira* involved a great deal of image-making in an era in which "both the image of Muhammad and the nature of the Koran appear to have been in flux" (pp. 3–4), then in later times, when Islamic society's conception of its spiritual roots was far more stable and developed, many formulations which had been perfectly acceptable in Ibn Ishaq's own day would appear offensive, erroneous, or otherwise open to doubt and suspicion. Here we need to recall that when Ibn Hisham followed through on his intention to omit from Ibn Ishaq's *Sira* everything which he regarded as irrelevant, dubious, disgraceful, embarrassing, or untrustworthy,[11] he dropped the *Kitab al-mubtada'* in its entirety. While al-Tabari's opinion of the book was obviously much higher than Ibn Hisham's, here too personal criteria of selection and al-Tabari's explicitly stated intention of giving versions of events which enjoyed the general assent of the Community[12] would lead us to expect from him not a verbatim transcription of the text, but a redaction which Muslims in the late third century A.H. would have found appropriate and useful.

This observation leads us, secondly, to the very well-known problem that Ibn Ishaq's numerous students and their successors took what they received from the master and redacted and transmitted it in different ways. Witness, for example, the differences between Ibn Hisham, the quotations in al-Tabari, the recension of Yunus ibn Bukayr, and that of Muhammad ibn Salama al-Harrani. As different lines of transmission represent potentially different redactions, efforts to reconstruct the original form of a text cannot simply combine quotations from different lines of transmission, as if Ibn Ishaq's students and their successors were making no revisions or changes of their own. In medieval times the importance of distinguishing between one *riwaya* of a text and another was very well known, and it is this problem of multiple versions which renders the task of reconstructing the *Kitab al-mubtada'* particularly complex. Newby argues that reconstructing on the basis of al-Tabari is justified because his source was Salama ibn al-Fadl al-Abrash, who was Ibn Ishaq's closest pupil, heard all the material from his master, had his notes checked, and received his teacher's lecture notes (p. 15). But Ibn Bukayr makes similarly legitimating claims for his own version,[13] and in fact both students were acting within their proper bounds, though the result for us is that they (and others) confront us with multiple and differing recensions.[14] Here one must bear in mind that what we encounter in the various recensions of Ibn Ishaq's *Sira* was absolutely typical of *akhbar* historiography in the second century A.H. in general. Transmitters did not limit themselves to passing on what they had received from their teachers, but rather laid claim to the role of adapting and revising their materials as they saw fit, not just by the well-known means of the collective isnad, but also by rearranging, abbreviating, expanding, and recasting.[15]

The notion of an "authoritative" version of a master's book is thus one which, however common it may have become later, is difficult to accept for the second century. And even if one student did happen to receive an "authoritative" version, this would guarantee verbatim transmission of that version neither by the student in question nor by any of the transmitters through whom it might happen to pass over the next several generations. The same applies to the passages cited from all of the other six sources used for the reconstruction, especially al-Maqdisi and al-Tha'labi, who often relate composite traditions containing material from other tradents in addition to Ibn Ishaq, or traditions for which attribution is uncertain or unknown.

Third, the possibility must at least be noted that the considerable variations among the various recensions of Ibn Ishaq's *Sira* spring from a practice by Ibn Ishaq of repeatedly revising his materials, in which caste he would not have taught the same *text* (as opposed to subject) to all his students. If this was so, then comparison of the recensions made by these students will lead the investigator back not to a stable archetype attributable to Ibn Ishaq, but rather, and only, to a fluid corpus of notes and teaching materials either taught to students in different ways or given specific form by these students in different ways. A much less complicated example of this would be the case of al-Zuhri, to whom tradition attributes a *Kitab al-maghazi*, while at the same time insisting that he "had no book other than a book on the genealogy of his people."[16] The problem disappears, however, when one sees in the *Musannaf* of 'Abd al-Razza al-San'ani that al-Zuhri's *Kitab al-maghazi* was actually a loose corpus given definite shape by his student Ma'mar ibn Rashid, who augmented the content of the book by about 50 percent.[17]

5) It is more likely an error (and a serious one) to reconstruct the *Kitab al-mubtada'* into chapters all of which have the lives of specific individuals as their primary themes. The most obvious objection to this arrangement is that it eliminates the subject of Creation itself, a primary theme throughout the extant literature relevant to *mubtada'*, but one for which Newby has only two pages, incorporated into his chapter on Adam (pp. 34–36). Al-Tabari of course devotes many pages to *bad' al-khalq*, but has little from Ibn Ishaq—not because the latter ignored Creation, but rather because his traditions on this subject seem to have lacked isnads, a serious shortcoming in the eyes of al-Tabari.[18] Another example is the topic of *bina' al-Ka'ba*, which is primary in al-Tabari[19] and elsewhere, but is subsumed within the chapter on Abraham by Newby (pp. 73–76).[20]

6) To return to a point (number 1) made above: without a broadly based

corpus of material one simply has none of the tools or data necessary to make the fine textual comparisons and distinctions which alone can determine what should be included in the reconstructed text and where it should go.[21] Where this is lacking, its replacement is arbitrary fiat. A few examples may indicate the extent of this in *The Making of the Last Prophet*.

At a general level, the reader, having been informed that the Koran was still in a state of flux in the time of Ibn Ishaq, may well wonder how one can uphold "Koranic order" as the most crucial factor reflecting the order of the traditions comprising the qisas of the original *Kitab al-mubtada'*—no such order would yet have existed in Ibn Ishaq's time. If one holds to the view of a Koran stable from the time of 'Uthman, we are still left with the question of how the notion of "Koranic order" can be interpreted to dictate any given order of traditions in Ibn Ishaq's book. Authors of this sort of text often did, it is true, link their stories to verses of the Koran; but these verses were themselves discrete blocks of narrative which could be and often were treated separately and out of order; and in the formative era represented by the career of Ibn Ishaq, an author could tell his story in a broad variety of ways (as discussed above, number 4), citing the Koranic references wherever the opportunity arose, irrespective of whatever Koranic order there may have been in his day. In his *Tafsir*, of course, al-Tabari could not do this, but what this has to do with the original order of the *Kitab al-mubtada'* would have to be investigated and demonstrated, rather than simply declared by privileging "the order found in al-Tabari," whether in the *Ta'rikh* or in the *Tafsir*. In any case, "the order found in al-Tabari" is in elusive concept and in the construction is often abandoned. That is, the order of passages in both the *Ta'rikh* and *Tafsir* is often rearranged by Newby (why and to what end we are not told), and there are four entire stories (pp. 58–61, 154–56, 172–73, 193–200) which are interpolated from the *Tafsir* into the framework of the *Ta'rikh*, and so on.

So far as reordering the sentences to suit the expectations of the English-only reader is concerned, one need only pose a few questions. Doesn't a reader coming to a new literary tradition need to deal with that tradition in its own terms? Exactly what order or arrangement is it that suits the expectations of the English reader? If these expectations require alteration to the text, does this not compromise the reconstruction?

At the level of specific narratives one again finds a highly arbitrary methodology in play. To illustrate this, as well as some points already made above, the occasional citations from al-Azraqi's *Akhbar Makka* will suffice.

On page 38, lines 30–36, a passage from al-Azraqi[22] is attached to the end of a completely different passage cited from the "People of the Torah," thus implying that the entire paragraph has been taken from a Jewish source or infor-

mant. In fact, in the Arabic text as given by al-Azraqi, Ibn Ishaq gives no specific
source at all for the interpolated lines, and reads only, *ballaghani,* "It has come
to my knowledge. . . ." Here the arbitrary connection is clearly misleading.

On page 49, al-Azraqi is cited for a passage about Noah. The text is in fact
a composite tradition from Ibn Ishaq and Ibn Jurayj (Ibn Ishaq's contemporary
and a rival authority based in Mecca),[23] and deals with Qusayy. I did not find it
in Newby's chapter on Noah, nor would one think that it would belong there in
the first place.

On page 76, lines 8–32, in the chapter on Abraham, a long passage from al-
Azraqi[24] is attached to a short text stating that Adam established the foundations
of the Kaaba, and that later prophets made the pilgrimage to the shrine. The interpolated passage, however, states that Abraham built the Kaaba. One would thus
suspect that if the two passages do indeed go together, their context would more
likely be a chapter on "Building of the Kaaba" rather than "Abraham." Further,
sira specialists will immediately recognize this as a composite tradition created
by combining various older *akhbar* into a single long narrative about how
Abraham summoned the men and *jinn* from everywhere on earth to perform the
pilgrimage to Mecca, and then led them through the various stations. At least one
of the older traditions, though dealing with Abraham, comes from Ibn Ishaq's
Mab'ath and not, so far as one can tell, from the *Mubtada'.*[25] The reason for the
creation of the composite is transparent: 'Abd Allah ibn al-Zubayr asks about the
pilgrimage, and the response is that Abraham came from Syria to Mecca on pilgrimage and then returned to Syria. This clearly implies the priority of Mecca
over Syria as a goal for pilgrimage, and therefore suggests that old traditions
were being gathered and recast for arguments over sacred places. The fact that
Ibn al-Zubayr is given the role of putting the question in the first place further
suggests that the formulator of the composite had the Second Civil War in mind.
As would have been entirely normal in his time, Ibn Ishaq seems to have transmitted both the composite and its constituent sources. But if we decline to privilege the transmission of al-Tabari and check through a broader range of material, it is no longer immediately apparent which of these traditions should be
assigned to the original *Kitab al-mubtada'* and where in the text they would have
been situated.

At page 78, line 33 to page 79, line 18, also taken from a passage in al-
Azraqi,[26] we have what appears to be the only place in Newby's corpus where a
tradent specifically ascribes a passage to the *Kitab al-mubtada'.* But only the first
two lines, naming Abraham's wife, are to be so assigned. The rest of the passage
is from a different source, Ibn Jurayj citing Ibn 'Abbas, as is stated five times in
the Arabic text, but dropped each time in the English.

Within ten pages of al-Azraqi there are at least five other passages[27] which are cited in Newby's lists of sources at the ends of various narratives, which in fact never appear in the English text (so far as this reader could see).

In addition to the above, it must be said that the text bears numerous printing errors. Proper transliteration of Arabic is usually dispensed with altogether—an extraordinary lapse in a work seeking to recover a lost Arabic text—and where transliteration is provided it is highly erratic and occasionally quite wrong.

As more early Arabic source material becomes available, it becomes possible to investigate with greater confidence of success questions concerning the character and content of works now lost in their original forms, but frequently cited and sometimes copied in large blocks by writers whose books are extant. The importance of this work is evident from the results of some recent efforts in this direction,[28] but there can be no doubt that such research leads into very complicated and elusive difficulties, and that it is essential that the results of one's work indicate as clearly as possible—and at every step of the way—how conclusions have been reached and upon what evidence they rest. Where this is done, new ground is broken and new possibilities are opened for work on other texts; but it is only in this way that progress is achieved, and only in this way that one can judge whether one is penetrating back into the era of the Umayyad-period tradents and compilers, or simply adding a new and modern text, at our own end, to the venerable corpus of traditional Islamic scholarship.

NOTES

1. For a survey of past scholarship in this vein, see Ella Landau-Tasseron, "On the Reconstruction of Lost Sources," in *History and Historiography in Early Islamic Times: Studies and Perspectives*, ed. Lawrence I. Conrad (Princeton: Darwin Press, 1992).

2. On this controversial question, we Johann Fück, *Muhammad ibn Ishaq: Literarhistorische Untersuchungen* (Frankfurt am Main, 1925), 33; Josef Horovitz, "The Earliest Biographies of the Prophet and Their Authors," *IC* 2 (1928): 172; Nabia Abbott, *Studies in Arabic Literary Papyri*, vol. 1 (Chicago: University of Chicago Press, 1957–1972): 89–90. Rudolf Sellheim, "Prophet, Chalif und Geschichte: Die Muhammad-Biographic des Ibn Ishaq," *Oriens* 18–19 (1967): 39, 43; Albrecht Noth, *Quellenkritische Studien zu Themen, Formen und Tendenzen frühislamischer Geschichtsüberlieferung*, vol. 1, *Themen und Formen* (Bonn: Selbstverlag des Orientalischen Seminars, 1973), p. 45.

3. See the edition of fragments of Ibn Ishaq's *Sira* by Muhammad Hamid Allah (Ribat: Ma'had al-dirasat wa-l-abhath lil-ta'rib, 1396/1976). The attribution to Ibn Ishaq is, however, uncertain and merits investigation.

4. For a detailed discussion of the *Mubtada'* of Wahb, see Raif Georges Khoury,

Wahb ibn Munabbih (Wiesbaden: Otto Harrassowitz, 1972), 1:222–46. Material from Wahb is extant, not only in al-Tabari's *Ta'rikh* and *Tafsir*, but also in such sources as Ibn Hisham's *Kitab al-tijan*, ed. Fritz Krenkow (Hyderabad: Da'irat al-ma'arif al-'uthmaniya, A.H. 1347); and Ibn Qutayba's *Kitab al-ma'arif*, ed. Tharwat 'Ukasha, 2d ed. (Cairo: Dar al-ma'arif, 1969). The *Tijan* is listed in Newby's bibliography, but not used in any reconstructed narrative.

5. From his *Al-Mubtada'* there survive an incomplete manuscript in Damascus and quotations in later texts, and the papyri identified by Abbott as belonging to the *Mubtada'* of Ibn Ishaq have been assigned to that of Abu Hudhayfa by Albert Dietrich. See *GAS*, 1:294.

6. His *Kitab bad' al-khalq wa-qisas al-anbiya'* has been edited in Raif Georges Khoury, *Les Légendes prophétiques dans l'Islam depuis le 1er jusqu'au IIIe siècle de l'Hégire* (Wiesbaden: Otto Harrassowitz, 1978). Ibn Ishaq is frequently quoted for *mubtada'* material in this text.

7. On the enormous overall scale of Ibn Ishaq's transmission, see, for example, Ibn Hajar, *Tahdhib al-tahdhib* (Hyderabad: Da'irat al-ma'arif al-nizamiya, A.H. 1325–1327), 9:41, 11. 10–12.

8. See Ibn Ishaq, *Kitab al-siyar wa-l-maghazi*, recension of Yunus ibn Buqay, ed. Suhayl Zakkar (Damascus: Dar al-fikr, 1399/1978), 94, 11.1–101, 1. 7.

9. Abbott, *Studies in Arabic Literary Papyri*, 1:32–37.

10. See n. 5 above.

11. Ibn Hisham, *Sirat Rasul Allah*, ed. Mustafa al-Saqqa, Ibrahim al-Ibyari, and 'Abd al-Hafiz Shalabi (Cairo: Mustafa al-Babi al-Halabi, 1375/1955), 1:4,11. 5–15.

12. Al-Tabari, *Ta'rikh al-rusul wa-l-muluk*, ed. M. J. de Goeje et al. (Leiden: E. J. Brill, 1879–1901), 1:6, 1. 17–7, 1. 7; 56, II. 12–17. For further discussion, see this writer's "The Conquest of Arwad: A Source-Critical Study in the Historiography of the Early Medieval Near East." in *The Byzantine and Early Islamic Near East*. I: *Problems in the Literary Source Material*, ed. Averil Cameron and Lawrence I. Conrad (Princeton: Darwin Press, 1992), pp. 392–93.

13. Ibn Ishaq, *Al-Siyar wa-l-maghazi*, 23, 11. 1–3.

14. According to Fück, *Muhammad ibn Ishaq*, page 44, there were at least fifteen students who transmitted versions of Ibn Ishaq's work. In the more recent study of Muta' al-Tarabishi, "Ruwat al-maghazi wa-l-siyar 'an Muhammad ibn Ishaq," *RAAD* 56 (1981): 533–609. this number increases to sixty-one and the complexity of the situation becomes far more evident.

15. See Conrad. "Im Conquest of Arwad," 349–401; Stefan Leder, *Das Korpus al-Haitam ibn 'Adi* (st. 207/822): *Herkunft, Überlieferung, Gestalt früher Texte der Ahbar Literatur* (Frankfurt: Vittorio Klostermann, 1991).

16. See A. A. Duri, *The Rise of Historical Writing among the Arabs*, ed. and trans. Lawrence I. Conrad (Princeton: Princeton University Press, 1983), pp. 95–121, esp. pp. 113–14.

17. 'Abd al-Razzaq al-San'ani, *Kitab al-musannaf*, ed. Habib al-Rahman al-A'zami (Karachi: Al-Majlis al-'ilmi, 1390–1392/1970–1972), 5:313, 1. 1–492, 1. 3.

18. See al-Tabari, *Ta'rikh*, 1:33, 11. 16–19.

19. Ibid., 1:274, 1. 10.

20. For illustrative outlines of what the *Mubtada'* of Ibn Ishaq's older contemporary Wahb ibn Munabbih might have looked like, see Duri *Historical Writing among the Arabs*, pp. 128–29; Khoury, *Wahb ibn Munabbih*, 1:227–46.

21. See, for example. Landau-Tasseron, "On the Reconstruction of Lost Sources."

22. Al-Azraqi, *Akhbar Makka*, ed. Ferdinand Wüstenfeld (Leipzig: F. A. Brockhaus, 1858), 9, 1. 18–10, 1. 1

23. See ibid., 65, 1. 16: *thumma raja'a ila hadith Ibn Jurayj wa-ibn Ishaq.*

24. Ibid., 36, 1. 8–37, 1. 4; parallel in al-Tabari, *Ta'rikh*, 1:287, 1. 11–288, 1. 18.

25. See lbn Iskaq, *Al-Siyar wa-l-maghazi*, 94, 1. 15–95, 1. 1.

26. *Akhbar Makka*, 24, 1. 21–25, 1. 20.

27. Ibid., 37, 11. 4–7, 43, 1. 10–44, 1. 2; 46, 1. 16–49, 1.5 (possibly to 50, 1. 9).

28. See. for example, Harald Motzki, *Die Anfänge der islamischen Jurisprudenz: Ihre Entwicklung in Mekka bis zur Mitte des 2/8. Jahrhunderts* (Stuttgart: Franz Steiner Verlag, 1991).

PART FIVE

THE SIGNIFICANCE OF JOHN WANSBROUGH

Chapter 15

The Implications of, and Opposition to, the Methods and Theories of John Wansbrough[1]

Herbert Berg

This article serves as an introduction to Wansbrough's methods and theories for the study of the Koran, its tafsir, the sira, and other early Islamic texts. Muslim and most non-Muslim scholars work within essentially the same framework: one which reads the literature of early Islam as history. Wansbrough has demonstrated that what these sources provide is not history per se, but salvation history, and that methods appropriate for the study of this genre are not source critical but literary critical. Through the application of these methods Wansbrough has postulated theories, which, if correct, radically alter our understanding of Islamic origins. Islamicists have tended to fixate on these theories at the expense of the methodological approach from which they are derived. Judging by the arguments raised thus far by these opponents of Wansbrough, I suggest that their aversion to his work stems as much from the unwillingness of Islamicists to accept the uncertainty inherent in his methods and the political incorrectness associated with his theories as from their theoretical conservatism and methodological naivete.

1. INTRODUCTION

It has been two decades since John Wansbrough[2] published his *Quranic Studies: Sources and Methods of Scriptural Interpretation*. This work and his *Sectarian*

Originally published in *Method and Theory in the Study of Religion* vol. 9–1 (1997): 3–22. Reprinted by permission of Brill Academic Publishers.

Milieu: Content and Composition of Islamic Salvation History, published a year later in 1978 are, arguably, the two most significant contributions made to the study of Islamic origins since Ignaz Goldziher and Joseph Schacht. The former argued that the Sunna, the words and deeds of Muhammad as preserved in authentic Hadiths (reports or traditions about Muhammad), was more valuable as a historical source for the theological and legal debates of the early centuries of Islam than as a source for the life of Muhammad and the early Muslim community (Goldziher 1971, p. 19). The latter, looking specifically at the history of the development of Muslim jurisprudence which is primarily based on the information found in Hadiths—with complete and proper chains of authorities (isnads) guaranteeing authenticity—concluded that "[t]he more perfect the isnad, the later the tradition" (Schacht 1949, p. 147). Together, Goldziher and Schacht dissociated the Sunna from Muhammad; Wansbrough has gone much farther; he has severed both the Koran and the Sira (the biography of the Prophet) from the figure Muhammad and even from Arabia.

Since the works of Goldziher and Schacht met (and still continue to meet) with stiff opposition both from Muslim and non-Muslim scholars, it is hardly surprising that Wansbrough's methods and theories have come under an even stronger and more vehement attack. This reaction is due in part, no doubt, to the larger scope and religiously and historically more critical foci of his studies. Muslim scholars have always admitted the possibility that at least some Hadiths were fabricated. They have developed a whole science of scrutinizing the transmitters found in isnads and thereby determined the authenticity of the Hadiths. According to Muslim scholars Goldziher, Schacht, and others of their "ilk" have simply been negligent in their reading of the texts (e.g., Azami 1992). Wansbrough's work cuts the very bases of Islam, the Koran, and the Prophet, and so he cannot be dismissed as merely negligent. This is not a particularly unexpected reaction; that the reaction of non-Muslim Islamicists has been, for the most part, no more receptive is. If the source of the latter's hostility was simply that of scholars being conservative and loathe to sacrifice their familiar ideas, it would hardly be noteworthy for the study of religion. In time, the subsequent generations of Islamicists would be more willing to consider and employ a new paradigm. However, the problem is much more insidious: the debate, at least in veiled form, revolves around the questions of what are "sources" and what is "history"?

2. APPROACHES TO EARLY MUSLIM TEXTS

Methodological questions are not often broached in the study of Islam. The method employed by Muslim scholars is essentially one of ascription. That is to say, the extant body of literature that began to emerge at the end of the second and beginning of the third century of Islam is held to transmit faithfully the earlier events, including (and particularly) those of Muhammad's life. Western scholars have brought to this material source critical methods, which, in the context of Islamic origins, often involves the analysis of the isnads attached to the material (as if each isnad represents an independent recension). Their results confidently depict "what really happened." Nevertheless, the Koran and sira, and even largely the Sunna, are treated by western scholars in a manner not significantly different from that of Muslim scholars and theologians. The Koran's purported chronology has been analyzed in terms of the Meccan (early) and Medinan (later) suras, though western scholars have developed subcategories (e.g., Nöldeke 1909–1926 and Bell 1953), which continue to be thought of as definitive (e.g., Neuwirth 1993 and Welch 1983, respectively).[3] The meaning of a Koranic word or passage is to be found in the classical Koranic commentaries, most of which were produced at least three centuries after the fact. The biography of the Prophet is assumed to give a fairly reliable picture of Muhammad's life (e.g., Watt 1953; 1956). More scepticism is evident when working with the Sunna because of the doubts raised by Goldziher and Schacht, but not much more: even if one cannot be sure if any one Hadith is authentic, as a whole they converge to produce a fairly accurate picture of what Muhammad said and did (Juynboll 1983, p. 6). The net result of all this scholarly activity has been to produce an account of Islamic origins which scarcely differs from that constructed by Muslims. Like Wansbrough, I would not want to suggest that this "impressive unanimity in their assent to the historical 'fact' " is the product of collusion (1987, p. 9), at least not at a conscious level. Rather, what we have is a case of a shared epistemological framework and methodology producing largely similar results.

This situation, in itself, would not be problematic but for the presence of two factors. First, as Wansbrough notes, "[b]ereft of archaeological witness and hardly attested in pre-Islamic Arabic or external sources, the seventh-century Hijaz owes its historiographical existence almost entirely to the creative endeavour of Muslim and Orientalist scholarship" (1987, p. 9). That is to say, all Islamicists acknowledge that all the information we have about the first two centuries of Islam comes from compilations and writings whose present recensions date from little earlier than the third Islamic century (i.e., 800 C.E.). Many Islamicists recognize the implications of this lacuna in the extant sources, but attempt to circumvent it by placing their faith in the general veracity of the claims of the later sources to preserve earlier ones in a reasonably reliable manner. Although the later works might have "tendentially shaped" the earlier material, it is maintained that the kernel of "what really happened" is retained and can be discovered by carefully sifting through the material (e.g., Watt 1953, xiii–xiv). This type of argument is at least plausible and, in the absence of any other reason to doubt the claims of accurate transmission of originary "facts" by the extant literature, perhaps even probable. However, there is a second factor, an extremely critical one, to which Wansbrough draws attention: the Koran, its commentaries (tafsir), the biographies of the Prophet, and the Sunna—all early Muslim literature—are sacred, or salvation history. In other words, it is not history, not even tendentially shaped history. "What really happened" might possibly be congruent with what they say, but all we have is what the Muslim community of two centuries later in the continuing process of self-definition "*thought* had happened or *wanted to believe* had happened or *wanted others to believe* had happened" (Koren-Nevo 1991, p. 89).[4] This distinction is one that seems to be lost on the opponents of Wansbrough. But if one recognizes it as a valid distinction, then methodological implications are simple, but enormous.

If "what we know of the seventh-century Hijaz is the product of intense literary activity, then that record has got to be interpreted in accordance with what we know of literary criticism" (Wansbrough 1987, pp. 14–15). Salvation history,[5] even in the guise of "scientific" history, is literature. The methods most appropriate for its analysis are form criticism, redaction criticism, and literary criticism, just as they have been in the study of early Christianity and Judaism as pioneered by Rudolf Bultmann and Jacob Neusner. Wansbrough is opposed "to that school of sanguine historiography in which the pursuit of reconstruction is seldom if ever deflected by the doubts and scruples thrown up in recent (and not so recent) years by practitioners of form-criticism, structuralism and the like" (1980, p. 361). Why Islamicists have, however, shied away from such methods is a question to which I shall return.

3. A SUMMARY OF WANSBROUGH'S THEORIES AND THEIR IMPLICATIONS

Although literary methodological issues are paramount for Wansbrough, they are intimately connected to his theories on Islamic origins. "Wansbrough, after all, is also a historian: . . . his extensive exercises in literary criticism are part of an effort to tell the history of a community. His objections are to the arbitrarily privileged position of 'reality,' the tyranny of some narrative structures, the eschewal of interpretative versatility, and a lack of methodological and literary selfconsciousness" (Calder 1994, p. 40). It is as a historian that he has gained his notoriety, for from this application of literary analysis to the texts of early Islam emerges a radically new model for Islamic origins.

Both Wansbrough's analysis and model were first introduced in his *Quaranic Studies*. Its main concern is the development of Koranic exegesis. By way of introduction, however, Wansbrough provides three chapters entitled "Revelation and Canon," "Emblems of Prophethood," and "Origins of Classical Arabic" which explore the development of the scripture, prophetology, and sacred language in early Islam.[6] In the first chapter (1977, pp. 1–52) Wansbrough demonstrates that the themes of retribution, sign, exile, and covenant compose a major portion of the Koranic message. The literary forms of these themes are apodictic formulae, supplicatory formulae, and narrative. Wansbrough suggests that "taken together, the quantity of reference, the mechanically repetitious employment of rhetorical convention, and the stridently polemical style, all suggest a strongly sectarian atmosphere, in which a corpus of familiar scripture was being pressed into service of as yet unfamiliar doctrine" (1977, p. 20). These features, along with the Koran's referential nature, place the Muslim scripture in the literary tradition of Christian and Hebrew scriptures, though it is clearly neither a calque nor reformulation of them. As for the origin of the material in the Koran, factors such as the composite (and often contradictory) nature of the Koran, the incidental role of the Koran in the formulation of Muslim jurisprudence, the absence of reference to the Koran in an early Muslim creed from the middle of the eighth century, and the lack of masoretic exegesis before the ninth century, suggest the prophetic *logia*[7] underwent a significant period of organic growth and oral transmission before they were codified. Certainly these factors belie the tradition of the systematic collection and canonization of the Koran in the first decade(s) after the death of Muhammad.

Wansbrough's chapter on Islamic prophetology (1977, pp. 52–84) focuses on both the Koranic material and the biographical material (what he calls the Muhammadan *evangelium*). The historical value of the Koran is not as a source of biographical details, but "as a source for the concepts eventually applied to the composition of the Muslim theology of prophethood" (1977, p. 56). In fact, it was the earliest exegesis that was responsible for linking the anonymous Koranic material (the prophetic *logia*) to the figure of the independent Arabian prophet;[8] this early exegesis produced the biography of Muhammad. The *logia's* contribution to this process was to give the Arabian Prophet a distinctly Mosaic character while the *evangelium* placed the *logia* in the Hijaz (the Western region of Arabia containing the cities of Mecca and Medina).

Wansbrough examines the development of the Islamic *lingua sacra* in his third chapter (1977, pp. 85–118) and argues that it is wrong to see classical Arabic as standing at the beginning instead of the end of a "long and varied linguistic evolution" (1977, p. 87). Classical Arabic is traditionally thought of as being embodied within the Koran and pre-Islamic [*sic*] poetry, and therefore it must be assumed that this Arabic served not only as the *lingua sacra*, but also as a Bedouin *lingua franca* in Arabia and that it is the (hypothetical) source of modern sedentary vernaculars. Wansbrough suggests an alternative: the process of Arabicization closely followed the Arab conquests. To suggest otherwise would mean to

> assent to a period of from 150 to 200 years between textual stabilization of the Koran and analysis of its contents in the formulation of Arabic grammar. The implication must be that the text of scripture, like those of pre-Islamic poetry, was faithfully transmitted and intelligently understood read/recited and heard for a very long time indeed, without once provoking the questions about its meaning and its form with which the literature of the third/ninth century is filled. (1977, p. 101)

This is particularly odd, since the Koran seems not infrequently anomalous with the rules of classical Arabic grammar.

In the fourth and main chapter of *Quranic Studies* (1977, pp. 199–246), Wansbrough demonstrates that on the basis of function and style it is possible to distinguish between five types of Koranic exegesis (tafsir). The first, haggadic exegesis (narrative) is typified by the use of prophetic tradition, identification, and anecdote. The second, halakhic (legal) exegesis uses analogy, abrogation, and circumstance of revelation (though narrative often is used to provide a chronological framework for apparently contradictory Koranic passages). The third, masoretic exegesis employs the variant reading of the Koran, poetic exemplifications, and lexical and grammatical explanations. The fourth and fifth are rhetorical and allegorical exegesis. The final type was particularly popular in sectarian movements. Moreover, these types of exegesis emerged chronologically in the order specified, and so allow at least the relative dating of texts and an alternative to dating texts by ascription. For example, the lack of references to the Koran and of other indications of a stable scriptural text in halakhic arguments suggests that the establishment of the Koran as a source of law antedated and contributed to the canonization of a *ne varietur* text, rather than the other way around (1977, p. 202). That the Koran could not have been canonized much before the emergence of masoretic exegesis is further supported by the characteristically masoretic practice of explicating the whole of the Koran in its proper order (1977, p. 226).

The theories which emerge from this analysis are, in Wansbrough's own words, "conjectural" (1977, p. xi), "provisional" (1977, ix), and "tentative and emphatically provisional" (1978, p. x). Nevertheless, the implications are enormous: neither the Koran nor Islam is a product of Muhammad or even of Arabia. During the early Arab expansion beyond Arabia, there is no evidence that the conquerors were Muslim. Almost 200 years later "early" Muslim literature began to be written by the Mesopotamian clerical elite. The implication may be that the hitherto secular polity discovered and adopted a new movement which, though a non-Jewish, non-Christian movement, was a product of a Judaeo-Christian sectarian milieu. This movement and its history were soon Arabicized. The Koran, however, took somewhat longer to be canonized—not until circa 800 C.E. This process has been (tentatively) described as the

> attribution of several, partially overlapping, collections of logia (exhibiting a distinctly Mosaic imprint) to the image of a biblical prophet (modified by the material of the Muhammadan evangelium into an Arabian man of God) with a traditional message of salvation (modified by the influence of Rabbinic Judaism into the unmediated and finally immutable word of God). The process was accompanied by a grammatical effort "to relate the anomalies of the lingua sacra to the demands of a normative description of language." (Mallat 1994, p. 166)

In *The Sectarian Milieu*, Wansbrough continues his literary analysis by examining the subjects of historiography, authority, identity, and epistemology in early Islamic literature. In the first chapter he focuses primarily on the early haggadic exegesis, the biography of Muhammad, and argues that it is not history but salvation history. Its narrative techniques are: exegetical, in which serial or isolated Koranic extracts provide the framework for a longer narrative; parabolic, in which the narrative itself is the source for frequent allusion to *logia* (not verbatim, but in terms of diction and imagery); and paraphrastic, in which *logia* are presented in the form of anecdotes replete with scriptural keywords. In this way, salvation history was produced. Wansbrough sees some twenty-three *topoi* in this literature, all of which derive from a Judaeo-Christian sectarian milieu. In his chapter on authority,[9] he argues that Islamic salvation history invests the word of Allah, that is, the revelations to Muhammad, with authority. On the other hand, the Sunna, a completely separate body of early Muslim literature, places authority in the paradigmatic conduct of the Prophet. By placing all ritual and legal commands in the mouth of Muhammad, this latter literature became the main source for Islamic law. (Of course, considerable effort was expended on elaborating and harmonizing these originally disparate scriptural and apostolic forms of authority.) In the following chapter, Wansbrough examines Islam's quest for identity and self-definition and highlights the polemical nature of this quest which is so characteristic of a sectarian movement. His final chapter explores the "role of that historically fixed theophany in the organization of communal and individual experience" (1978, p. 130).

These two monographs, as well as a few articles and book reviews, comprise the sum total of Wansbrough's publications in Islamic origins. In them, he has rewritten almost every "historical fact" of Islamic origins. He is, I would venture, less concerned with the accuracy or inaccuracy of the historical implications of his work than with its methodology; his opponents reverse the priorities. That is not to say that the two are unrelated for either Wansbrough or his opponents. Presumably, neither is so naive. For Wansbrough, his radical reinterpretation of Islamic origins is the outcome of what he considers the only proper approach to the extant texts. The approach is correct, his preliminary results may or may not be (though it is fairly clear that he thinks the historical conclusions he has drawn are largely correct). His opponents have focused on these conclusions because it is these that they find offensive. However, it seems that his methods are considerably less assailable. Certainly the concerted attack on the historical implications can be seen as a means by which to delegitimize his methods, but it is more likely that the relatively few and feeble attacks on his methods are attempts to delegitimize the implications thereof.[10]

4. OPPOSITION TO WANSBROUGH

The Islamicists who oppose Wansbrough do so rather vehemently, even questioning whether he and his allies merit the dignity of a collected set of essays on their ideas. Perhaps this attitude accounts for the paucity of articles and chapters, much less monographs, in which his opponents tackle the issues raised by Wansbrough. Their main arguments can only be gleaned from reviews of *Quranic Studies* and *The Sectarian Milieu*, and from passing remarks in publications devoted to other topics. Though worded in numerous ways, these arguments are surprisingly few in number (four) and are found in at least nascent form in the comments made by Fazlur Rahman.[11] He also epitomizes the tendency to sidestep serious discussion when he suggests that "[m]y disagreements with Wansbrough are so numerous that they are probably best understood only by reading both this book and his" (1989, p. xiv).

Rahman sees in Wansbrough's theory of the origin of the Koranic material in a Judaeo-Christian sectarian milieu evidence that he stands at the "logical end of the line for Jewish apologists" (1989, p. xiii). This line has its origin in the late-nineteenth century in works such as *Was hat Mohammed aus dem Judenthume aufgenommen?* (1902) by Abraham Geiger and *Jüdische Elemente im Koran*

(1878) by Hartwig Hirschfeld.[12] In his review of *Quranic Studies* R. B. Serjeant echoes this accusation, calling it "a thoroughly reactionary stand in reverting to the over-emphasis of the Hebrew element in Islam . . . [and] one has the sense of a disguised polemic seeking to strip Islam and the Prophet of all but the minimum of originality" (1978, p. 76). Both Rahman and Serjeant use a thinly veiled *ad hominem* argument, but, because of the prevalence of the irenic approach to the study of Islam (see below [p. 508]), the argument seems to carry some weight. I do not believe this aspect of the argument merits refutation, except to say that it has no bearing on the validity of Wansbrough's methods and the veracity of his conclusions. (A more serious problem with this suggestion is its misunderstanding of the role of the sectarian milieu, a problem discussed in G. R. Hawting's article [see chapter 16 in this volume].)

Rahman also states that "[t]he development [of the Koranic teaching on miracles] is intelligible only in the context of a unified document gradually unfolding itself. It cannot be understood as a composite of different and contradictory elements" (1989, xiii). In other words, Muhammad's life is so intimately and obviously intertwined with the material of the Koran, that it must be genuinely connected to him; the Koran can only be understood if it is read with the life of the Prophet as the backdrop. A strong supporter of this view is Alford T. Welch. After dismissing Wansbrough's "radical hypothesis" as unconvincing because of the valid "historical memory" retained despite contradictory accounts, he states:

> A distinctive feature of the Koran that cannot be ignored if the Muslim scripture is to be understood fully is its close relationship to the life of Muhammad and his contemporaries. . . . [T]he Koran is a historical document that reflects the prophetic career of Muhammad and responds constantly to the specific needs and problems of the emerging Muslim community. It abounds in references and allusions to historical events that occurred during the last twenty or so years of Muhammad's lifetime, a period during which it was itself a history making event. (Welch 1980, p. 626)

For Welch, the Koran serves perhaps as the only reliable source for information about Muhammad and his understanding of himself and his mission (1983). This argument is couched in many other forms. Serjeant castigates Wansbrough for his neglect of "the vital Arabian element" in the Koran and "the plain and uncontested evidence . . . that the Hijaz was its birthplace" (1978, p. 76). When Juynboll highlights "the obvious disparity in style and contents of Meccan and Medinan suras" (1979, p. 294) or when Burton (1995) adduces the "embarrassing" contradictions in the Koran, they, too, are suggesting that the geographical, cultural, religious, and political landscape influenced Muhammad.

To illustrate the basis of this ubiquitous argument consider the following two examples. The story of Noah, which is adduced or alluded to several times in the Koran, is assumed to reflect Muhammad's life. The opposition faced by Noah, for that matter, Abraham, Moses, and all the other Koranic prophets is no different than that faced by Muhammad in the city of Mecca. These stories are thought to have been revealed/produced to encourage Muhammad or his followers and to warn his opponents that the messengers of Allah have always been opposed by their people and that Allah will mete out punishment soon enough. For the second example, consider the following "(auto)biographical" Koranic passage.

> Your lord has not forsaken you, nor is your lord displeased with you.
> The hereafter will be better for you than the present.
> Your lord will give you [that which] will please you.
> Did he not find you an orphan and shelter you?
> Did he not find you straying and guide you?
> Did he not find you poor and enrich you? (sura 93:3–8)

How is this passage to be understood if not in reference to the period known as the *fitra*, which occurred after the first revelation and during which Muhammad was distressed because he received no further revelations? And, was not Muhammad an orphan? Was he not guided by Allah? And was he not destitute until the wealthy, Khadija married him?

While this argument of Rahman, Welch, and many others is internally consistent, it seems a product of a superficial reading of Wansbrough. The argument assumes the epistemological and chronological priority of the events in Muhammad's life over the passages in the Koran. If, as Wansbrough suggests, the biography of the Muhammad is the product of a narrative exegesis of the prophetic *logia*, the priority should be reversed. If opposition to, and vindication of, the messengers were simply some of the many schemata and *topoi* associated with them, would not an exegetical account of the Arabian Prophet be constructed on similar lines? Thus, it is hardly surprising that the stories of Noah and Muhammad parallel each other. The Koranic passage adduced above in and of itself contains nothing which requires perforce that it be read as addressed to Muhammad or any other particular individual. However, any haggadic commentator might find it convenient to draw upon this otherwise ambiguous passage. In so doing, the passage and the "history" corroborate each other: the former is "explained" and the biography receives a framework upon which to construct an Arabian Prophet's story. A passage historicized in this manner naturally appears (auto)biographical.

The third major argument was first alluded to by Graham in his review of *Quranic Studies* (1980, p. 140) and rests on the assumption that Wansbrough's historical reconstruction of early Islam requires a massive conspiracy—an inconceivable scenario to Rahman (1985, p. 201). This line of reasoning is more fully developed by Versteegh. Of Wansbrough he says:

> [O]ne needs a conspiratorial view of the Islamic tradition, in which all scholars are assumed to have taken part in the same conspiracy to suppress the real sequence of events. . . . It may be true that sometimes an opinion becomes fashionable for religious, political or even social reasons, and is then taken over by most people. But the point here is that if one particular interpretation or point of view prevails, there are bound to be some dissenters and in important issues, such as the ones we are dealing with here, it is inconceivable that tradition could manage to suppress all dissenting views. (1993, p. 48)[13]

A conspiracy of the magnitude needed to account for Wansbrough's conclusions about the extended process of scriptural canonization and historicization and Arabicization of the prophetic *logia* does seem unlikely. If the choice were simply between historicity and conspiracy, the former would certainly seem more plausible. However, these are not the only two choices. Recourse to a conspiracy theory exhibits a rather simplistic understanding of how literature and particularly salvation history are produced. The authors of the texts of early Islam were all working in more or less the same cultural milieu. Their perceived unanimity on the "facts" of early Islam need not be the result of collusion to fabricate an Islam to their liking or which served their religious, political, or ethnic objectives. When the traditions of Islam began to be recorded around 800 C.E., it was done in a manner that the Muslims of that time believed, or needed to believe, that events had been. And in so doing, the beliefs became "facts." Wansbrough says "that historiography is primarily a form of literature, is a step seldom and then only very reluctantly taken in the field of Islamic Studies. . . . [T]he language of a historical report is also the language of fiction. The difference between the two is a psychological assumption shared by writer and reader, and it is from that assumption that the historical report acquires significance, is deemed worthy of preservation and transmission" (1978, pp. 118–19). Hence, there are no "truths" that had to be suppressed in favour of "falsehoods." The version of the origins of Islam which has come to us is therefore the one which the later community "knew" to be the truth. However, a conspiracy there may be, but not as Rahman and Versteegh would envision it. "With neither artifact nor archieve, the student of Islamic origins could quite easily become victim of a literary and linguistic conspiracy. He is, of course, mostly convinced that he is not. Reason for that must be confidence in his ability to extrapolate from the literary version(s) what is likely to have happened" (Wansbrough 1987, p. 10).

These three preceding arguments have focused on Wansbrough's theories and not his methodology. The only challenge to the latter is that which questions the value of abandoning the "historical method"—by which is meant "ascription"—and turning to literary analysis.[14] Rahman argues that the historical method works, and that "Wansbrough's methods of literary analysis . . . are so inherently arbitrary that they sink into the marsh of utter subjectivity" (1985, p. 199). Serjeant also refers to "his untenable subjective theories" (1978, p. 77). While it seems doubtful whether Rahman or Serjeant are trying to offer a serious argument against Wansbrough on this point—their statements are brief, polemic, and undeveloped—this issue of subjectivity is not an unimportant one. Trying to avoid lapsing into an epistemological debate over "objectivity" and "subjectivity," I would simply point out that what Rahman and others seem to overlook is that the unquestioned apriorism of accepting the sources at face value is no less subjective. What we can be certain of is that a body of literature emerged circa 800 C.E. that purported to describe events some 150 years earlier. The subjectivity of these ninth-century authors cannot be transformed into objectivity merely by the passage of time. A more "objective" approach would clearly be to treat the literature as literature and not as an archeological site (born out of the perennial urge to turn literary convention into historical "reality") (Wansbrough 1987, pp. 12, 22).

5. FACTORS CONTRIBUTING TO OPPOSITION AND HOSTILITY

My purpose in attempting to refute these four arguments is not to champion the methods and conclusions of Wansbrough nor to imply they should not be challenged. In labelling his own work as experimental, Wansbrough invites such challenges. Rather it is to demonstrate that the main lines of these critical arguments tend to be based on either misconceptions of Wansbrough or on circular arguments. As such, they are not particularly compelling. Some scholars have, however, taken issue with Wansbrough on somewhat firmer grounds. For example, evidence suggesting the existence of a Koranic canon prior to 800 C.E. is problematic. Newly discovered papyri with short fragments of the Koran from the late Umayyad period (which ended in 750 C.E.) and administrative letters and treatises from the same period are replete with Koranic illusions and/or quotations. They may suggest that 800 C.E. as the date for the canonization of the Koran is somewhat late (Crone 1994, p. 18; Qadi 1992).[15] Cook rightly points out that the sources we have, though they are relatively late, do not preclude that other texts were written which simply did not survive (1980, p. 181). However, these letters, treatises, and (hypothetical) texts need not be at odds with Wansbrough's theory. These early Koranic references might only suggest that some of the *logia* were in circulation and that they may even have had a measure of authority: it need not suggest the existence of a recognized canon. The *logia* would have had a long life prior to their final canonization.[16] Thus, this evidence is not conclusive. And, other scholars have sought and discovered archeological, numismatic, and epigraphical evidence in support of Wansbrough (Koren-Nevo 1991, pp. 100–106).

That Muslim scholars take offense at Wansbrough's work is to be expected. The more interesting question remains, why would non-Muslim scholars feel likewise? What is at stake for them? Surely the threat to faith is not the problem. Rippin has already suggested several factors which seem to contribute to the reluctance of Islamicists to accept Wansbrough methods and theories (1985).

First, historians are in the business of determining what really happened and why it happened. Wansbrough has suggested that we may never know what has really happened, and "to historians the factor of ambiguity is not especially welcome" (1987, p. 15). Unfortunately, for the first two centuries of Islam, the required material is not extant. Without blind faith in the reliability of the sira, for example, there is little for the scholar who wants to study the life of Muhammad in his early seventh-century Arabian context to do or say.

Second, Schacht, while assessing Islamic studies and the impact of his own work, said that Islamicists were characterized by an "intellectual laziness" which gradually undermined the progress made in the field. This happened first to Goldziher's work, then his own. Perhaps Wansbrough's work will also fall victim. This "intellectual laziness" manifests itself primarily in an unwillingness to be sceptical and methodologically and theoretically sophisticated. As Wansbrough observes:

> As a document [i.e., the Koran] susceptible of analysis by the instruments and techniques of Biblical criticism it is virtually unknown. The doctrinal obstacles that have traditionally impeded such investigation are, on the other hand, very well known. Not merely dogmas such as those defining scripture as the uncreated Word of God and acknowledging its formal and substantive inimitability, but also the entire corpus of Islamic historiography, by providing a more or less coherent and plausible report of the circumstances of the Koranic revelation, have discouraged examination of the document as representative of a traditional literary type. (1977, p. ix)

It is much easier (and productive from a quantitative, not qualitative, perspective) simply to accept the literature at face value. Treated as reliable historical records, the methods and results are relatively straightforward. There is virtually no need to depend on literary theory and analysis, which only obscure as much as they reveal. (That is, Wansbrough's methods destroy the hitherto "historical facts" of Islamic origins without replacing them with new ones. For example, we used to "know" that Muhammad produced the Koran, perhaps with the help of some Jews and/or Christians, but we have no names for the individuals or communities which produced the *logia*).

Third, Islamicists have become too narrowly focused. Competency in Arabic and familiarity with Arabia on the eve of Islam are considered the only requisite skills needed for a "proper" investigation of Islamic origins. "For the most part, there are few scholars active today who can move with equal agility throughout the entire western religious framework and its necessary languages" (Rippin 1985, p. 159).

Fourth, today's Islamicists seem on the whole very reluctant to say anything which might be interpreted as critical of Islam, including its own sacralized "origins" and "history." Prior to the publication of *Quranic Studies*, Charles Adams noted that "[i]n the years since World War II there has grown up a distinctive movement in the West, represented in both religious circles and the universities, whose purpose is the greater appreciation of Islamic religiousness and the fostering of a new attitude toward it" (1976, p. 38). The works of such scholars as Wilfred Cantwell Smith and W. Montgomery Watt exemplify this irenic approach to the study of Islam. The phenomenological approach to the study of Islam, though purportedly less theological in its intent, results in much the same attitude. It emphasizes the "experience of the believer" and, in the case of the study of Islam, has been seen as "the key to making restitution for the sins of unsympathetic, hostile, or interested approaches that have plagued the tradition of Western Orientalism" (Adams 1976, p. 50). Modern Islamicists are perhaps more inclined to adopt these approaches because a sense of collective guilt. That Islamicists have been culpable has been convincingly demonstrated by Edward Said (1978). The sins of our ancestors in the study of Muslim peoples has made modern Islamicists wary of committing the "sin of orientalism" and rightly so. However, if the result is a fear of asking and answering potentially embarrassing questions—ones which might upset Muslim sensibilities—this "restitution" is disturbing.

The popularity of an antitheoretical and sensitive approach in order to atone for or allay some perceived guilt is not exclusive to Islamicists. The work of early cultural anthropologists also contributed the colonial oppression of the people they studied. The response of many of today's anthropologists is described by

Lawson and McCauley as "throw[ing] the scientific baby out with the colonialist bath water" (1993, 202). They argue that

> this strategy for reconceiving cultural anthropology as humanistic inquiry in the hermeneutic mode may buy sensitivity and moral rectitude, but at the cost of forfeiting its place among the sciences. What is missing is the recognition that the connection between scientific aspirations for anthropological research and collusion with imperialism is not a necessary one. (1993, pp. 203–204)

Islamicists, too, have failed to recognize the nature of this connection. As a result, their scholarship remains narrowly focused and antitheoretical, and, "in order to remain true to the 'faith of other men,' is doomed most of all to avoid asking the basic question: How do we know?" (Rippin 1985, p. 159).

6. CONCLUSION

Many non-Muslim scholars of Islamic origins continue to operate in a Muslim theological framework for the reasons outlined above. But in so doing, they risk forfeiting their status as scholars. Bruce Lincoln, speaking of the study of religion generally, suggests:

> When one permits those whom one studies to define the terms in which they will be understood, suspends one's interest in the temporal and contingent, or fails to distinguish between "truths," "truth-claims," and "regimes of truth," one has ceased to function as historian or scholar. In that moment, a variety of roles are available: some perfectly respectable (amanuensis, collector, friend and advocate), and some less appealing (cheerleader, voyeur, retailer of import goods). None, however should be confused with scholarship. (Lincoln 1996, p. 227)

Wansbrough's greatest contribution to Islamic origins may be his summons for Islamicists to return to scholarship.

While my counterarguments have not necessarily refuted objections raised by the opponents of Wansbrough, they do demonstrate that these objections are far from convincing. Wansbrough's experiment is not yet complete, but the initial results are certainly positive. Whether Wansbrough has initiated a paradigm shift in the study of Islamic origins and provided "an outline of future studies in Islam, the directions in which they should go" (Rippin 1981, p. 166) remains to be seen. But no longer can it be said that Wansbrough's "*implication[s]* and *logic* are his alone" (Juynboll 1979, p. 294).

REFERENCES

Adams, Charles J. "The Islamic Religious Tradition." In *The Study of the Middle East: Research and Scholarship in the Humanities and Social Sciences*, edited by Louis Binder, 29–95. New York: John Wiley & Sons, 1976.

Azami, Mohammad Mustafa. *Studies in Early Hadith Literature: With a Critical Edition of Some Early Texts*. 3d ed. Indianapolis: American Trust Publications, 1992.

Bell, Richard. *The Origin of Islam in its Christian Environment*. London: Frank Cass, 1968.

———. *The Qur'an: Translated, with a Critical Re-arrangement of the Surahs*. 2 vols. Edinburgh: T & I Clark, 1937.

———. *Introduction to the Qur'an*. Edinburgh: University of Edinburgh Press, 1953.

Brett, M., and G. R. Hawting. "Published Writings of J. E. Wansbrough." *Bulletin of the School of Oriental and African Studies* 57 (1953): 4–13.

Burton, John. "Rewriting the Timetable of Early Islam." *Journal of the American Oriental Society* 115 (1995): 453–62.

Calder, Norman. *Studies in Early Muslim Jurisprudence*. Oxford: Clarendon Press, 1993.

———. "The Barahima: Literary Construct and Historical Reality." *Bulletin of the School of Oriental and African Studies* 57 (1994): 40–51.

Cook, Michael. Review of *The Sectarian Milieu: Content and Composition of Islamic Salvation History*, by John Wansbrough. *Journal of the Royal Asiatic Society* (1980): 180–82.

———. *Early Muslim Dogma: A Source-Critical Study*. Cambridge: Cambridge University Press, 1981.

Crone, Patricia. "Two Legal Problems Bearing on the Early History of the Qur'an." *Jerusalem Studies in Arabic and Islam* 18 (1994): 1–37.

Geiger, Abraham. *Was hat Mohammed aus dent Judenthume aufgenommen?* 2d ed. Leipzig: M.W. Kaufmann, 1902.

Goldziher, Ignaz. *Muslim Studies*. 2 vols. Edited by S. M. Stern and translated by C. R. Barber and S. M. Stern. London: George Allen and Unwin, 1971.

Graham, William A. Review of *Quranic Studies: Sources and Methods of Scriptural Interpretation*, by John Wansbrough. *Journal of the American Oriental Society* 100 (1980): 137–41.

Hirschfeld, Hartwig. *Jüdische Elemente im Koran: Ein Beitrag zur Koranforschung*. Berlin: Selbstverlag, 1878.

Juynboll, Gautier H. A. Review of *Quranic Studies: Sources and Methods of Scriptural Interpretation*, by John Wansbrough. *Journal of Semitic Studies* 24 (1979): 293–96.

———. *Muslim Tradition: Studies in Chronology, Provenance, and Authorship of Early Hadith*. Cambridge: Cambridge University Press, 1983.

Koren, J., and Y. D. Nevo. "Methodological Approaches to Islamic Studies." *Der Islam* 68 (1991): 87–107.

Lawson, E. Thomas, and Robert N. McCauley. "Crisis of Conscience, Fiddle of Identity:

Making Spaces to a Cognitive Approach to Religious Phenomena." *Journal of the American Academy of Religion* 61 (1993): 201–23.

Lincoln, Bruce. "Theses on Method." *Method and Theory in the Study of Religion* 8 (1996): 225–27.

Mallat, Chibli. "Readings of the Qur'an in London and Najaf: John Wansbrough and Muhammad Baqir al-Sadr." *Bulletin of the School of Oriental and African Studies* 57 (1994): 159–73.

Neuwirth, Angelika. "Images and Metaphors in the Introductory Sections of the Makkan Siras." In *Approaches to the Qur'an*, edited by G. R. Hawting and Abdul-Kader A. Shareef, 3–36. London: Routledge, 1993.

Nöldeke, Theodor. *Geschichte des Qorans*. 2d rev. ed.; vols. 1 and 2 revised by Friedrich Schwally; vol. 3 revised by G. Bergstrasser and O. Pretzl. Leipzig: Dieterichische Verlagsbuchhandlung, 1909–26.

Qadi, Wadad al. "Early Islamic State Letters: The Question of Authenticity." In *The Byzantine and Early Islamic Near East: Problems in the Literary Source Material*, edited by Averil Cameron and Lawrence I. Conrad, 215–75. *Studies in Late Antiquity and Early Islam*, no. 1, vol. 1. Princeton: Darwin Press, 1992.

Rahman, Fazlur. *Major Themes of the Qur'an*. 2d ed. Minneapolis: Bibliotheca Islamica, 1989.

———. "Approaches to Islam in Religious Studies: Review Essay." In *Approaches to Islam in Religious Studies*, edited by Richard C. Martin, 189–202. Tucson: University of Arizona Press, 1985.

Rippin, Andrew. Review of *The Sectarian Milieu: Content and Compositium of Islamic Salvation History* by John Wansbrough. *Journal of Semitic Studies* 26 (1981): 164–66.

———. "Literary Analysis of Qur'an, Tafsir, and Sira: The Methodologies of John Wansbrough." In *Approaches to Islam in Religious Studies*, edited by Richard C. Martin, 151–63. Tucson: The University of Arizona Press, 1985.

———. Letter to Herbert Berg. 1 April 1996.

Said, Edward. *Orientalism*. New York: Random House, 1978.

Schacht, Joseph. "A Revaluation of Islamic Tradition." *Journal of the Royal Asiatic Society* (1949): 143–54.

———. *The Origins of Muhammadan Jurisprudence*. Oxford: Clarendon Press, 1959.

Serjeant, R.B. Review of *Quranic Studies: Sources and Methods of Scriptural Interpretation* by John Wansbrough and *Hagarism: The Making of the Islamic World* by Patricia Crone and Michael Cook. *Journal of the Royal Asiatic Society* (1978): 76–78.

Versteegh, C. H. M. *Arabic Grammar and Quranic Exegesis in Early Islam*. Leiden: E. J. Brill, 1993.

Wansbrough, John. *Quranic Studies: Sources and Methods of Scriptural Interpretation*. Oxford: Oxford University Press, 1977.

———. *The Sectarian Milieu: Content and Composition of Islamic Salvation History*. Oxford: Oxford University Press, 1978.

———. Review of *Anfänge muslimischer Theologie: Zwei antiqadaritische Traktate aus dem ersten Jahrhundert der Higra* by Josef van Ess. *Bulletin of the School of Oriental and African Studies* 43 (1980): 361–63.

———. *Res Ipsa Loquitur: History and Mimesis.* Jerusalem: The Israel Academy of Sciences and Humanities, 1987.

Watt, W. Montgomery. *Muhammad at Mecca.* Oxford: Oxford University Press, 1953.

———. *Muhammad at Medina.* Oxford: Oxford University Press, 1956.

Welch, Alford T. "Qur'anic Studies—Problems and Prospects." *Journal of the American Academy of Religion* 47 (1980): 620–34.

———. "Muhammad's Understanding of Himself: . . . 'The Koranic Data.' " In *Islam's Understanding of Itself,* edited by Richard G. Hovannisian and Speros Vryonis Jr., 15–52. Malibu: Undena Publications, 1983.

Yapp, Malcolm. "John E. Wansbrough." *Bulletin of the School of Oriental and African Studies* 57 (1994): 1–4.

NOTES

1. I want to thank Professors Willi Braun, Jane D. McAuliffe, Russell McCutcheon, and Andrew Rippin for reading earlier versions of this paper and for their many helpful comments and suggestions.

2. A brief biography (Yapp 1994, pp. 1–4) and a complete bibliography of the books, articles, and reviews (Brett-Hawting 1994, pp. 4–13) of John Wansbrough can be found in the preface of a recent *Festschrift* for him in the *Bulletin of the School of Oriental and African Studies.*

3. Richard Bell, who sought to employ the methods of the Documentary Hypothesis (1937; 1953), nonetheless "worked wholly within presuppositions of the Islamic tradition" (Rippin 1985, p. 158) and so it is hardly surprising that his conclusions differ from those of Muslim accounts at best only superficially. In many ways this approach to the material is so ubiquitous that it hardly requires me to adduce specific examples. However, these examples do demonstrate the extent to which the traditional approach forms the basis for virtually all work on the Koran, the Sira, and the Sunna.

4. Koren and Nevo also correctly point out that the transmission of these materials is extremely problematic:

> This is not just a question of the usual quota of copyists' errors, but more insidious divergences from the original; for a writer who was demonstrably working within the framework of an accepted version of history will, even unconsciously, alter older texts in ways that accord with that view. We have therefore to contend with transmitters who interpret the older text in ways that they "know" to be true: by embellishing and explaining, or adding, subtracting or substituting a word, a phrase or a gloss here and there. An example would be

the used of the term "Muslim" where the older text had "Hagarene" or "Ismaelite" or "Saracen," or the substitution of the word "Muhammad" for an original "the Prophet"; or the assignation of the name of a battle familiar from the Muslim literary sources to the description of a battle originally unnamed, or given a name which does not appear in the "known" version of history. If the older text did not survive independently, it is nearly impossible to detect such tampering with it. We cannot, then accept an excerpt from an older text found in a later writer as an accurate transmission of the text at this level. (1991, p. 90)

Moreover, the texts in question were written at least 150 years after the events they purport to describe, and written under the rule of the 'Abbasid dynasty who had to legitimize itself to its Muslim, Jewish, Christian subjects, Arab and non-Arab.

5. Wansbrough is well aware that "salvation" is a Christian concept that is not wholly applicable to Islam. The term "election history" is a more accurate one (1978, p. 147). His use of "salvation history" is designed to emphasize the literary genre of this material and the methods appropriate to the study of such a genre. My use of the term is meant to emphasize that the literature itself may claim to be a reliable account of the origin of the Muslim community, but that it is in fact the product of a community which has sacralized its origin.

6. Wansbrough explains his categorization thus:

In order to deal with the reports of seventh-century Arabia, I divided the field into constants and variables: the former representing the "basic categories" common to most descriptions of monotheism; the later representing "local components" that give each version its special character. Recourse to this simple taxonomy seemed to facilitate a discussion of Islamic origins in terms that would make sense to any student of religion, in short, to make the unfamiliar an intelligible unit of study. The constants were prophet, scripture, and sacred language; the variables were the specifically Arabian features of these, together with such traces of local usage as could be inferred from its later abrogation by the new faith (e.g., in ritual practice and civil law) (1987, pp. 11–12).

He recognizes the possibility of polygenesis of these "constants." However, polygenesis does not account for the presence of a Mosaic exemplar for Muhammad in the Koran (just as it does not account for a Davidic genealogy for Jesus in the Gospels) (1987, p. 12).

7. "Prophetic *logia*" is Wansbrough's term for the elements out of which the Koran would eventually emerge. He suggests that these *logia* developed as a series of uncoordinated pericopes to meet the liturgical and didactic needs of a group or communities in a sectarian milieu within mainstream Semitic monotheism. The period of organic growth and oral transmission led to a gradual juxtaposition of the *logia* in separate collections. The repetitions and apparent contradictions within the Koran may indicate that the *logia* achieved a measure of canonicity in several communities prior to the canonization of the Koran itself (1977, pp. 2, 50–51). "The entire process of canonization will thus be seen as a protracted one of community formation (*Gemeindebildung*)" (1977, p. 51).

8. Wansbrough points out that "the role of the Koran in the delineation of an Arabian prophet was peripheral" (1977, p. 56). The doctrine which grants the Arabian Prophet superiority over other messengers mentioned in the Koran is not attested in the scripture and is a later development.

9. By "authority" Wansbrough means "the immediate and tangible instruments of legitimation: those means by which the sanctions of the transcendent deity are realized in practices, those terms within which a theodicy becomes credible and workable" (1978, p. 50).

10. Naturally, there are Islamicists who are intrigued, perhaps even convinced, by Wansbrough's method, but not by his conclusions. For instance, Graham suggests: "The literary perceptions [of Wansbrough] . . . do not obviously demand the postulated historical conclusions" (1980, p. 140).

11. Fazlur Rahman (d. 1988) was both a modernist Muslim (too modernist for his native Pakistan) and a professor at McGill University and the University of Chicago. His arguments seem to encapsulate both Muslim and non-Muslim opposition to Wansbrough.

12. As Rahman points out, this is not a strictly Jewish activity. Richard Bell's book, *The Origin of Islam in its Christian Environment* (1968; first edition 1926), is one of the many, but perhaps the most respected, attempts to attribute much of Islam to the influence of Christianity upon Muhammad. The "Judaeo-Christian" elements in the Koran result from a difference process according to Rahman. Jewish and Christian ideas and stories, if not the religions themselves, had penetrated Arabia as deep as Mecca long before the appearance of Muhammad. They had been Arabicized. Furthermore, Rahman argues, "the starting point of the Koranic teaching was not biblical controversies but existential problems within Meccan society itself. During its course, not doubt, the Koran picked up a great amount of Judeo-Christian tradition" (1985, p. 201).

13. This argument is not a new one in the study of early Islamic texts. Azami (1992, pp. 130–47) attacked Schacht's scepticism about the authenticity of the Hadith corpus by attempting to demonstrate that some Hadiths were transmitted by many Muslims from every generation and in numerous regions in the Islamic empire. As Michael Cook points out, "that each of them should put about the same fabricated tradition presupposes a level of conspiratorial action which is historically quite implausible" (1981, p. 115). This argument seems irrefutable unless one accepts the possibility of massive fabrication of Hadiths. Either Schacht is correct, or the traditional Muslim approach is correct; "there is no methodological middle ground" (Cook 1981, p. 116). Schacht (1959), Calder (1993, pp. 161–97, 236–37), and Cook (1981, pp. 107–16) have all suggested milieux in which such fabrication seems quite plausible, even probable.

14. Both Wansbrough and his opponents speak of history and texts and in that sense both use historical methods and literary analysis. The distinction lies in reading early Islamic texts as literature deeply invested in a sacralized origin and as a product of a religious community in the process of developing its self-identity. Though they do not read these texts literally, his opponents use "scientific" methods to extract the actual "history" of the origins and development of the Muslim community.

15. Numismatic and epigraphical evidence such as that on the Umayyad coinage (from 695 C.E. onward) and the Dome of the Rock (691 C.E.), hardly attest to a *ne varietur* canon. These passages are short and the inscriptions on the Dome of the Rock mix up verses that are (now) part of different suras (Crone 1994, pp. 17–18 n. 48).

16. As Rippin points out, "that's the significance of tafsir: it provides the date at which we have demonstrable evidence of the existence of a full canon (and even arguments about its canonical shape)" (1996).

Chapter 16

John Wansbrough, Islam, and Monotheism

G. R. Hawting

ABSTRACT

John Wansbrough has elaborated a model of the emergence of Islam, one of the chief merits of which is to place Islam squarely within the development of Semitic or Middle Eastern monotheism. This article draws attention to the way in which Islam's own tradition about its origins, and most modern scholarship which has worked within the framework provided by Muslim tradition, has the effect of distancing Islam from the development of the wider stream of monotheism—especially by—explaining it as the result of an act of revelation which occurred in a remote region of inner Arabia. By insisting that Islam developed and came to fruition in the Middle East outside Arabia following the Arab conquest of the region and that its account of its own origins has to be understood in the same context, Wansbrough has increased our understanding of the nature of Islam's own tradition and what can and cannot be done with it. The article attempts to put him in a scholarly context and to contrast his approach with more usual modern scholarly discussion of the origins of Islam.

O f all people, John Wansbrough would be aware that, however careful the choice of words in which they are expressed, ideas, once published, are likely to be subject to reinterpretations, distortions, and misunderstandings. The

Originally published in *Method and Theory in the Study of Religion* vol. 9–1 (1997): 23–38. Reprinted by permission of Brill Academic Publishers.

more complex and subtle the thought, the more certain it is to be understood (or misunderstood) in different ways. Although I have been exposed to Wansbrough's ideas and arguments in a variety of formal and informal settings over many years, I do not claim to have any especially authentic version of them or to be able to communicate them without introducing my own shifts of emphasis, glosses, and distortions. I do not, therefore, want to attempt here a summary or repetition of his words in my own. My aim is to put his work in the context of the history of the study of the emergence of Islam and to indicate what I see as the most important way in which it advances scholarship. I want to focus on the seriousness with which he situates Islam within the tradition of Semitic monotheism.[1]

1. CONSEQUENCES OF THE VIEW
THAT ISLAM ORIGINATED IN ARABIA

That Islam is a monotheistic religion related to Judaism and Christianity is a generally accepted commonplace, although the fact may be emphasized or toned down in different circumstances. However, although the interrelationship of the three monotheistic religions is generally accepted in principle, Islam has often continued, both at the scholarly and at the popular level, to be treated as something rather distinct from the other two, even when there is no discernible polemical motive for doing so. At the popular level one reason for this seems quite obvious: historical developments led to the association of Islam with Asia and Africa and thus to its identification as something essentially nonwestern. More significant at a scholarly level is the account of its origins which Islam itself developed and which has largely been accepted by non-Muslims.

In its equation of the origins of Islam with the career of Muhammad and its detailed depiction of Muhammad's life in Mecca and Medina, Muslim tradition effectively dissociates Islam from the historical development of the monotheist stream of religion as a whole. Islam is shown to be the result of an act of divine revelation made to an Arab prophet who was born and lived most of his life in a town (Mecca) beyond the borders of the then monotheistic world.

A number of modern scholars have speculated about, or claimed to have found evidence of a Jewish or Christian presence in Mecca in the time of Muhammad. For example, Reinhart Dozy (1864) postulated the migration of an Israelite tribe to Mecca in the pre-Temple period, Richard Bell (1926, p. 105) speculated about contact between Muhammad and a Christian Abyssinian slave, while Tor Andrae (1955, pp. 206–208) referred to reports in quite late Muslim sources that Muhammad had heard the famous (and perhaps legendary) Christian Arab Bishop, Quss b. Sa'ida, preaching at the market of Ukaz near Mecca. These and other such theories can be understood as reactions to an awareness of the close similarity of Koranic ideas and stories to those known in Judaism and Christianity and a feeling that Muhammad must have got his materials from somewhere. But Muslim tradition really tells us nothing about this and emphasizes the dominant polytheism and idolatry of the Meccans. Islam is shown primarily as an appeal to the pagan Arabs to abandon their corrupt way of life and to recognize the existence of the one true God, with all that that implies.

It is true that the tradition tells us that there were individuals among these Arabs who had abandoned the paganism of their ancestors and contemporaries (Watt 1954, pp. 165–66), but there is no suggestion that Muhammad was in any way indebted to them for his own religion. It is also true that in the last ten years of his life, after his move from Mecca to Medina in 622 C.E., Muhammad is shown to have had frequent and increasingly acrimonious contact with a significantly large community of Jews and that his relationship with the Jews of Medina had some consequences for the direction in which Islam developed (Wensinck 1975; Lecker 1995). Again, however, there is no suggestion in the tradition that Muhammad borrowed anything from these Jews. In tradition his contact with them is important but not fundamental for the origins of Islam. One can speculate about and search for evidence concerning the earthly sources of Muhammad's doctrine, but none of the work along those lines can be said to have achieved very concrete results or been widely accepted in scholarship. They are a testimony, in fact, to the strength of the tradition's depiction of Muhammad's original milieu as pagan and remote from the world of monotheism.

The idea that Islam was essentially in existence by the time of Muhammad's death in 632 C.E. rests on a number of traditionally accepted facts. Although it has been generally agreed that the revelation given to him, the Koran, was not collected and written down until a (relatively short) time after his death, the revelation is—as a result of the way in which it is traditionally interpreted—closely associated by tradition with the events of Muhammad's life.[2] The Koran is presented as the source of some of the basic Muslim beliefs and rituals, to the extent that there is a tendency to identify the Koran with Islam. Traditionally the essence of Islam is held to reside in the "five pillars," and these rituals and associated beliefs are all traced in tradition to the life of the Prophet. In addition, Muhammad is said to have founded and led the first and only true Islamic state in history.

Although the Sunni tradition grants some positive value to the time of the early caliphs who succeeded the Prophet as leaders of the Islamic state, in general the subsequent period is seen as one of decline from a golden age, especially since it was after the Prophet that internal dissension led to the division of the community and the emergence of sects. This, too, reinforces the impression that true Islam is synonymous with the time of the Prophet. It is recognized, of course, that some positive and valuable developments took place considerably later than the time of the Prophet—for example, the composition of the books of law and collections of Hadiths which, alongside the Koran, are seen as fundamental to Islam. But these works are regarded simply as the systematization or elaboration of principles which had been there from the start. At the basis of everything there is the Koran and the model practice of the Prophet—his Sunna.

Above all, it seems to be the Arabian background and Arab associations of Islam which make it different and difficult to understand as an integral part of the monotheistic tradition in the same way as Rabbinic Judaism and Christianity. The traditional approach tells us that it originated in Arabia and was spread by the Arab conquerors of the Near East. The language of its scripture, law, and theology is Arabic. Its sanctuary is in Mecca in the Hijaz and its direction of prayer is towards this sanctuary. The traditional lives of Muhammad portray him as the prophet of the Arabs and a large number of the institutions of Islam (for example, its calendar [Hartner 1913–1938] and its system of polygamy [Schacht 1913–1938]) are traditionally explained against the background of pre-Islamic Arabia. Islam is traditionally understood in terms of the rejection, adaptation, or acceptance of features of the Arabian background. Thus from the very beginning there seems to be something which makes Islam stand apart from its monotheistic ancestors with whom, however, as is evident from the Koran and Muslim tradition, it shares so much.

The Arabian setting, the fundamental importance of divine revelation, and the view that Islam was essentially in existence by the time of the Prophet's death, therefore, support the idea that Islam originated in a way which was different from other forms of the monotheistic tradition. Whereas Rabbinic Judaism and Christianity emerged in the strongly monotheistic regions of the Near East and the Mediterranean world, Islam is seen as having originated and undergone its basic formation outside it. Whereas Rabbinic Judaism and Christianity (and other, less long-lived variants) emerged as a result of redefinitions of a common tradition to which they constantly refer, Islam seems to begin as an attack on traditional Arab idolatry and polytheism which it completely rejects.[3] Rabbinic and Christian concern with the polytheistic element in the world in which the two religions were developing seems less important than their concern with the monotheistic tradition and with one another (see Lieberman 1950, pp. 115–27, 128–38; Kaufmann 1960, especially pp. 7–20; Halbertal-Margalit 1992 for the metaphorical and transferred character of the concept of "idolatry" in monotheistic usage). Muslim concern with the monotheistic element (usually identified as the Jews of Medina) in the world in which it was developing, if one accepts the traditional accounts, was secondary in relation to its concern with Arab paganism.

While there may be nothing inherently implausible or incoherent in this traditional version of the origins of Islam, it ought at least to arouse comment among Islamicist scholars coming to the study of Islam from a background in Judaism or Christianity. The fact that it generally does not may be due to the power and effectiveness of Muslim tradition, to the lack of critical acumen on the part of the scholars, or to a mixture of both. Wansbrough's approach, it seems to me, assumes that, as the third major variant within the monotheist tradition, the origins of Islam are not likely to be, *mutatis mutandis*, significantly different in character from those of Rabbinic Judaism, Christianity, or other variants. In large part, his achievement consists in having shown that it is possible to analyze the origins of Islam along the same lines as those of other forms of Semitic monotheism.

2. WESTERN APPROACHES TO THE PROBLEM OF THE ARABIAN ORIGINS OF ISLAM

Acceptance of the framework and much of the data provided by Muslim tradition has meant that western scholarly explanations of the origins of Islam have largely been attempts to explain how an Arab form of monotheism might have developed in the early seventh-century Hijaz. A common pursuit has been to account for it in terms of the impact of the outside world on the milieu of Muhammad, and in this respect trade routes have been a favorite explanatory mechanism. A major international trade route running through western Arabia has been discerned by several modern scholars and held to have had important social consequences which somehow account for the appearance of the new religion and help to explain its success (e.g., Wolf 1951; Watt 1953). Patricia Crone (1987) has demonstrated the questionable character of the evidence on which the theory has been based and has pointed out logical inconsistencies in the way that it has been used.

Another common approach has been to propose an internal religious evolution, usually expressed in terms of a decline of native Arabian polytheism and the emergence, persistence, or revivication of a distinctive Arab form of monotheism. Versions of this theory rest on outmoded schemes of religious development, usually on the assumption that monotheism is an evolutionary advance on polytheism and that all societies will eventually evolve from the latter to the former (Wellhausen 1897, pp. 215–24). Sometimes the persistence of a primordial monotheism (Urmonotheismus) in Arabia has been used to account for the development of Islam as a specifically Arab form of monotheism (Brockelmann 1922; Watt 1970; 1976; 1979).

Recently some scholars (Cook 1983, pp. 81, 92; Crone 1987, pp. 190–91 n. 104; Shahid 1989, pp. 167–72; Rubin 1990, p. 99 n. 68) have suggested an alternative mechanism for the introduction of monotheistic ideas (including the idea that the Arabs were descendants of Abraham) into north and central Arabia by reference to a passage in the *Ecclesiastical History* of the fifth-century C.E. Sozomen of Ghaza. Sozomen talks of certain Arabs learning through contact with Jews of their common descent from Abraham and their consequent adoption of certain Hebraic practices such as circumcision. An isolated and question-begging text has come to carry a lot of weight.

These approaches and theories reflect the willingness of modern non-Muslim scholarship to work within the framework provided by Muslim tradition. The tradition tells us that Islam arose with the preaching of Muhammad in Arabia but most western scholars are unable to accept that that was the result of an act of divine revelation and engage, therefore, in the search for influences on Muhammad and for political, social, and economic explanations for his success. The results have not been compelling, although the erudition and interpretative ingenuity often demonstrated should not be underestimated.

The main reason why most scholars have been willing to accept the traditional Muslim accounts as the framework within which to work is that those accounts provide us with an explicit and very detailed version of the Prophet's life, the historical circumstances in which he lived, the revelation made to him, what happened after his death, etc. The tradition is not entirely consistent—within a generally accepted framework it contains numerous variant accounts, inconsistencies, and contradictions—but, compared with the amount of detail it offers and its transparency, other evidence appears fragmentary and opaque. The result has been that for the most part the Muslim traditional accounts have been seen as a repository of facts to be quarried by historians seeking to reconstruct the origins of Islam, and all other evidence, archaeological or literary, has been read and interpreted in the light of the data provided by the tradition. (See Rippin [1991] for an illustration of the circular argumentation which often results.)

In general such interpretations seem arbitrary and lacking in any real methodology for assessing which items of tradition are to be accepted as of value and which are to be discarded. They often resort to speculation, their interpretation of evidence is far from compelling, and the logic of the arguments used sometimes does not stand up to critical scrutiny. Above all, they discuss the origins of Islam in abstraction from the wider history of the monotheistic tradition, speculating about how "influences" from one monotheistic group or another might have percolated into Arabia and influenced the thought of Muhammad or how Islam arose in Arabia from the development of a native tradition of monotheism.

3. LATE SOURCES AND THE COMPLEXITY OF ISLAM

Wansbrough's work embraces and stresses two incontrovertible facts, neither of which were previously unknown in the field of Islamic studies. But the rigour with which he allows for them and the consequences which he draws from them make his work distinctive. One is that there is no Muslim literature which can be dated, in the form in which it is available to us, earlier than about 800 C.E. (end of the second century of the Islamic era); the other is that Islam is a complex phenomenon the development of which must have taken many generations and occupied an extended geographical area before it attained a form resembling that which we know today.

Although it is true that there are a few traditional texts conventionally attributed to figures who died before 800 C.E. (notably Ibn Ishaq and Malik b. Anas), we only have those works in recensions made by Muslim scholars of later generations, and none of the works available to us were put into the form in which we know them earlier than the ninth century C.E. (the third century of Islam). We have no biography of Muhammad, no commentary on the Koran, no law book, no collection of Hadiths, no history of early Islam, etc., which can be said to predate, in the form in which we have it, the beginning of the third Islamic century. And, given the impulse in traditional Islamic scholarship to attribute to great figures of the past texts which have been formed over a considerable period of time and which stabilized comparatively late, it may be suspected that the conventional attribution to "authors" living in the early ninth century of a number of important works may be too generous (see further Calder 1993).

What is still a matter of scholarly debate and controversy is how far one can push back beyond these works to recover the earlier layers of tradition on which they are based and which they frequently cite extensively. The aim of much modern research has been to establish the form and the wording of the sources on which our sources drew, a project which looks feasible because it is a characteristic of Muslim traditional literature that each work is usually made up of hundreds or thousands of relatively short and discrete reports or units of tradition, and each of these is prefaced by a chain of the authorities responsible for having transmitted it. These chains of authorities, the isnads, offer the prospect, therefore, of tracing the material at our disposal back through the generations, in many cases to the Prophet himself. (For a recent example of an attempt to recover early legal material from a relatively late source, see Motzki 1991.)

Wansbrough's work exhibits severe scepticism about these attempts to push our Muslim sources back earlier than the form in which we know them and he shows no interest in reconstructing or analyzing the isnads. His position seems to be that even were it possible to accept the accuracy and authenticity of the isnads (which seems doubtful for the most important, earliest, alleged links in the transmission), there would nevertheless be little possibility of assessing the transformation of the accompanying traditions as they were subject to the vicissitudes of transmission over many generations. Variant wording, the introduction of glosses, the removal of material from its original context, abbreviation, summary and expansion, incomplete transmission, and other features can all be assumed to have taken place. Above all, even though our earliest Muslim literature undoubtedly recycles and reworks material which originated much earlier, that material exists because it answers to the needs of the generations in whose work we find it.

Wansbrough's position on this question can to some extent be understood as a logical extension of the work of Ignaz Goldziher and Joseph Schacht. The former's study (1889–1890) of the traditional reports which purport to contain eyewitness accounts of what the Prophet said or did in particular circumstances (the Hadiths), demonstrated that large numbers of them should be understood as the reflection of the political, religious, and social concerns of Islam as it developed over several generations following the death of the Prophet and the Arab conquest of the Middle East. The debates and arguments within the emerging religion and society were projected back into the time of the Prophet and support for one party or another was put into the mouth of the Prophet. As a general principle, therefore, the Hadiths should not be regarded as evidence for the time to which they explicitly refer—the time of the Prophet—but for the circles and times in which they were produced.

Schacht (1949; 1950; 1964) pushed Goldziher's conclusions further, especially in the field of law. He outlined a theory, which makes sense of the evidence, about the rise, in the second century of Islam, of the idea of prophetic authority and the subsequent growth in the number of traditions which reported the Prophet's views, words, and practice. He pointed out the weakness of traditional approaches to the analysis of the isnads and stressed their limited value for an investigation of the sources of the Hadiths. Furthermore, he showed how legal concerns permeated all fields of literature and affected, for instance, the biographical material on Muhammad.

The other important fact which serves as the starting point for Wansbrough's approach is the complexity of Islam. As already explained, Muslim tradition and, following it, much modern scholarship tends to equate the origins of Islam with the activity of Muhammad and to regard Islam as substantially in existence by the time of his death. In spite of a theoretical recognition that some important features of Islam as we know it developed substantially later than the time of the Prophet, there is a tendency to regard them as secondary features or elaborations of the fundamental elements which had been created by Muhammad. It is this which makes it possible for scholars (Donner 1975; Kaegi 1992) to continue to refer to the Arab conquest of the Middle East as a Muslim conquest—somehow the motive for that conquest, it is thought, was the expansion of Islam.

On the other hand, it has long been recognized, in theory at least, that Islam is something more than a religion in the sense in which that word is usually understood—Islamic law, the fundamental institution of Islam, attempts to regulate such things as social life, political theory, economic activity, and penal law, as well as matters of ritual and cultic behavior. In a wider sense, Islam refers to a culture and a civilization, as well as to a religion. Even on a more specifically religious level, it involves a complex of theological and other beliefs, ritual behaviour, and associated institutions like a central sanctuary, mosques, scripture (not only the Koran) and its interpretation, and a sacred language. In addition, naturally, it needs a significant number of adherents who identify themselves as Muslims and have some understanding of what that identification involves, Given this, it is difficult to see in what sense Islam could be said to be in existence by the time of the death of Muhammad or even at the time of the Arab conquest of the Middle East. Schacht's work documents the slow and relatively late emergence of Muslim law and jurisprudence and without its law it is difficult to envisage what Islam might be.

Wansbrough gives due weight to the complexity of Islam and works with the idea of a religion, society, and state developing in the Middle East over several generations following the establishment of Arab political control. In this he develops a framework sketched out most explicitly by Carl Becker (1910; 1913), who argued that Islam should be understood as the end product of social and cultural changes which had been taking place in the Middle East even before the Arab conquests and which were intensified as a consequence of those conquests. In the elaboration of the new religion and culture, the contribution of the conquered, originally non-Arab peoples, was probably of greater importance than that of the conquerors.

In this scheme of things, Islam is a part of the historical development of the Middle East as a whole from the Hellenistic period onwards. In Becker's celebrated phrase: "So bizarr es klingt: ohne Alexander den Grossen keine islamische Zivilisation!" The more traditional approach, emphasizing the origins of Islam in western Arabia in the time of Muhammad, has the effect of presenting Islam as an element of discontinuity in the history of the Middle East, as something which originates from a remote and isolated region, as something essentially Arab, and, from the traditional point of view, as something which literally came about as a result of Allah's immediate intervention in the historical process.

Furthermore, the approach suggested by Becker partly resolves the problem, inherent in traditional accounts of the rise of Islam, of why the Arab conquerors of the Middle East were not absorbed by the societies and cultures over which they established their political domination. In broad terms the Arab conquest of the Middle East seems comparable to numerous other instances of the conquest by "barbarian" outsiders of lands with a strong cultural tradition and an established system of government. In the other cases, although the "barbarians" may have achieved military conquest and political domination, the culture of the conquered peoples proved more resilient and to some extent absorbed the conquerors. In particular the religion and, to some extent, the language of the conquered often overcame those of the conquerors and eventually led to their assimilation into the general population. The pattern is variable, according to different historical conditions, but generally recurrent (e.g., the various barbarian invasions of Roman western Europe, the Islamic Middle East, and China).

At first sight, and according to the traditional approach, the Arab conquest of the Middle East has a radically different outcome. Instead of the Arabs losing their identity and becoming, say, Greek-speaking Christians, it looks as if the conquered peoples accepted the identity of their conquerors and became (mainly) Arabic-speaking Muslims. According to the traditional approach, this happened because, already by the time of their military triumph, the Arabs had a strong religious and linguistic identity which was impervious to the counterattractions of the religions and languages of the conquered.

The approach urged by Becker argues that this is too simple and moves the Arab conquest of the Middle East closer to the general model. The religion and culture of Islam was not something brought out of Arabia by the conquering Arabs and either imposed on the peoples of the Middle East by force or willingly accepted by them in a passive fashion. Rather it gradually evolved from the interaction of the Arab conquerors and those over whom they ruled. Weight is given to the diversity of the culture of the Middle East which the Arabs conquered and the slow process of the reassertion of local provincial cultures at the expense of the once-dominant Hellenistic culture. This process had been under way for some centuries before the Arabs arrived on the scene and the rise of Islam can be understood as its continuation with the addition of elements brought on to the scene by the Arab conquest.

4. SOME FEATURES OF WANSBROUGH'S MODEL FOR THE ORIGINS OF ISLAM

In general Wansbrough's work can be understood as a logical extension of some of the principles which had been developed by scholars such as Goldziher, Schacht, and Becker and as the application to the study of early Islam of some of the methods and concepts generated in the study of other branches of monotheism and in cultural studies more widely. While limiting himself to the facts about the tradition itself (and not attempting to discuss the facts which the tradition tells us about), he is yet able by his application of conceptual models to relate the tradition to the question of the emergence of Islam.

Perhaps the most notable feature of his work for those coming to it from the more traditional approaches to the problem of the emergence of Islam is what it does not attempt to do. In contrast with most other works on the origins of Islam, Wansbrough's books and articles tell us nothing about the personality of the Prophet, his actions and their motives, the milieu in which he lived, the history of the early caliphate, etc. Nor do they attempt to reconstruct the state of the historical tradition in a form prior to that in which we know it from the texts at our disposal. While not denying the importance of establishing the lines of transmission and sources of our texts, he rejects the assumption, held by most of the proponents of the source-critical method, that one can move easily from the earliest version of a particular report available to us to acceptance of the facts which it purports to recount. He accepts that on its own terms the traditional account of the origins of Islam in Arabia is reasonably coherent and displays considerable doubt about whether it is possible to go beyond it using the source-critical methods which have been commonly espoused since the time of Wellhausen and Caetani.

This refusal to be drawn into attempts at historical reconstruction on the basis of sources which are much later than the events they report reflects not only a recognition of the work of Goldziher and Schacht but, even more, an appreciation of the literary character of the texts. Wansbrough's work has always displayed an awareness of the literary nature of the sources used by most historians, even when those sources are archive documents or inscriptions, and he has insisted that without a proper analysis of such things as form and genre, *topoi* and rhetorical conventions, we will not understand our sources properly. His analysis of early Muslim historical tradition in *The Sectarian Milieu* (1978) as a form of salvation history is the most important reason for his avoidance of historical reconstruction. This type of historical literature, with its inherent message concerning Allah's control of and intervention in the historical process is even more problematic than normal secular historiography for the historian concerned to recreate the events which it recounts. Beyond that, Wansbrough has expressed philosophical scepticism about the idea of history as the reconstruction of the past *wie es eigentfich gewesen war* ["as it actually was"] and a distaste for conventional narrative history as an outmoded form.

But the eschewal of traditional narrative and reconstruction is only one aspect of an approach which offers a way out of what had become a scholarly impasse. The concept of Islam as an evolution from the sectarian monotheism of Mesopotamia in the wake of Arab migration and the establishment of Arab rule; the analysis of that evolution as a gradual elaboration of a series of ideas, practices, and institutions expressive of the independent identity of the community; and the understanding that an elaboration of an account of its own origins is a part of that evolution; these seem to me to be the especially liberating aspects of Wansbrough's approach.

To attempt to link Islam with one or more forms of sectarian monotheism has been common in discussions of the origins of Islam. Usually the discussion is framed in terms of the way in which a particular sectarian group may have influenced Muhammad, and this sometimes involves speculation about the existence of a community of these sectarians in Arabia. This is another example of the speculation, which I referred to above, about how monotheistic influences may have reached Muhammad in inner Arabia. Among the groups most often mentioned are Samaritans (Finkel 1933; Crone-Cook 1977), Judaeo-Christians such as the Elkasaites or Ebionites (Schlatter 1918; Schoeps 1949), or a sect related to that responsible for the production of the Qumran documents (Rabin 1957; Philonenko 1966; 1967; 1972). The evidence on which such discussions usually depend is a perceived or real similarity between a Muslim idea or practice and one attested for the group which is being put forward as the key influence on the development of Islam.

Wansbrough's distaste for the speculative and inconclusive nature of most of these discussions is obvious. Similarity does not necessarily indicate borrowing or influence. Using the same basic ideas and materials, monotheistic groups are likely to evolve some of the same or similar ideas, practices, and institutions. Indeed one of the problems with the various attempts to posit this or that sectarian group as the decisive influence on Islam is that certain things, such as ideas pertaining to prophetology, are held by more than one of them. Nor is it clear how one could distinguish a decisive influence on a complex religion which has emerged over a long period of time and in an extended geographical area.

These problems do not mean that the discussion is of no value. Islam is obviously a part of the Semitic monotheistic tradition and must have arisen within its matrix, and it is not futile to attempt to define rather more precisely how that happened. Wansbrough does not talk in terms of influence on Muhammad but envisages the generation of what would become Islam within sectarian monotheist groups in Mesopotamia following the Arab conquest of the region. Koranic christology seems to point to the importance of Judaeo-Christianity, but his concern is less with identification of the precise group than with understanding how an ultimately distinct and independent religion could emerge from such a milieu.

The gradual development of new versions of some of the features required of a religion in that historical setting is the essence of the process. *Quranic Studies* focuses on the composition of the Koran and its acceptance as scripture by the emerging community, but also has much to say about the identification of a sacred language (classical Arabic) and the elaboration of an image of an Arabian Prophet. *The Sectarian Milieu* contains a more theoretical account of the process whereby the building blocks common to the tradition as a whole are chosen, molded into new forms, and put together in a distinctive pattern by a group emerging out of Semitic monotheism. It seems that above all it is the need to establish and define its independent identity which motivates the community's development of such things as its own calendar, sanctuary, and theological ideas. Only when a significant number of such essential features have been developed can one talk about Islam meaningfully. The community itself develops by reformulating already existing features and tendencies in the monotheistic communities of the Middle East, and a new and independent religion within that monotheist tradition can be said to have emerged when a range of rituals, beliefs, and institutions has developed in a distinctive form and been put together in a distinctive combination.

What seems to me to be most fruitful part of Wansbrough's analysis here is his view that Islam's account of its origins and of the life of its founder and Prophet must be understood as a part of the same process and therefore reflect the same motivation. The beginning of the stabilization of Muslim tradition in the form of the texts available to us in the period after 800 C.E. is, in this perspective, not a more or less fortuitous result of such things as the increasing sedentarization of the Arabs and the growing inadequacy of oral transmission. Indeed the tradition is unlikely to have been the product of the originally nomadic Arabs. Rather it is one of the things which, like the canonization of the

Koran as scripture, marks the transition of Islam from its formative to what might be called its classical stage—the stage when it begins to crystallize as Islam as we know it.

Like other institutions, the historical tradition takes time to evolve and cohere and like other institutions it is a reworking of the common stock of the Semitic monotheist tradition. Since the tradition reflects the evolving awareness of the community of its distinctiveness within monotheism, and of its independence from other forms of monotheism, it follows that it will be characterised by retrojection. The events of the past will be interpreted and reinterpreted from later points of view and later conditions will be read back into the past. Essentially this is what makes it so difficult to use the tradition to reconstruct the past.

But above all it is the Arabian setting of the account of its origins which establishes the distinctiveness of Islam and its independence of the wider tradition of Semitic monotheism. According to its own accounts, Islam did not, as Wansbrough envisages, emerge from and develop slowly among a complex of monotheistic religions and sects in the regions under Arab rule, but as a result of a revelation given to an Arab prophet living among mainly polytheistic Arabs in inner Arabia. Wansbrough's analysis of the tradition illustrates how this Arabian background is constantly emphasized and imposed on what otherwise is a repertory of common monotheistic themes and arguments. In spite of a multitude of inconsistencies and even contradictions on point of detail, the thrust of the tradition is to establish that Islam began in Arabia.

It follows from what has already been said that one cannot disprove the tradition or show that the image it presents is misleading or false. On its own terms it is coherent and it reflects the community's understanding of its origins. What one can do is to propose alternative models and to ask whether the available evidence is consistent with these. It seems to me that that is what Wansbrough has done. He has set out a scheme for the emergence of Islam which does justice to Islam as a complex religion and culture and which provides a framework within which much of the evidence can be reinterpreted. Evidence does not speak for itself and especially in the study of religions it is difficult to separate it from the interpretation which accompanies it. What is especially persuasive about Wansbrough's model for me is the consistent way in which it reinstates Islam as the third major constituent of the tradition of monotheism which has its roots in the ancient Middle East.

REFERENCES

Andrae, Tor Efrem. *Les origines de l'Islam et le Christiamsme*. Translated by Jean Gaude-froy-Demombynes. Paris: Adrien-Maisonneuve, 1955.

Becker, Carl Heinrich. "Der Islam als Problem." *Der Islam* 1 (1910): 1–21.

———. "The Expansion of the Saracens." In *The Rise of Saracens and the Foundation of the Western Empire*, 329–390. Cambridge Mediaeval History, vol. 2. Cambridge: Cambridge University Press, 1913.

Bell, Richard. *The Origin of Islam in its Christian Environment*. London: Macmillan, 1926.

Brockelmann, Carl. "Allah und die Götzen: Der Ursprung des islamischen Monothe-ismus." *Archiv für Religionswissenschaft* 21 (1922): 99–121.

Burton, John. *The Collection of the Quran*. Cambridge: Cambridge University Press, 1977.

Calder, Norman. *Studies in Early Muslim Jurisprudence*. Oxford: Oxford University Press, 1993.

Cook, Michael. *Muhammad*. Oxford: Oxford University Press, 1983.

Crone, Patricia. *Meccan Trade and the Rise of Islam*. Princeton: Princeton University Press, 1987.

Crone, Patricia, and Michael Cook. *Hagarism: The Making of the Islamic World*. Cambridge: Cambridge University Press, 1977.

Donner, Fred McGraw. *The Early Islamic Conquests*. Princeton: Princeton University Press, 1975.

Dozy, Reinhart. *Die Israeliten zu Mekka von Davids Zeit bis in's fünfte Jahrhundert unsrer Zeitrechnung*. Leipzig: W. Engelman, 1864.

Finkel, Joshua. "Jewish, Christian, and Samaritan Influences on Arabia." In *The Mac-donald Presentation Volume* (1933): 145–66. Princeton: Princeton University Press, 1933.

Goldziher, Ignaz. *Muhammedanische Studien*. 2 vols. Halle: Max Miemeyer, 1889–1890.

Halbertal, Moshe, and Avishai Margalit. *Idolatry*. Cambridge: Harvard University Press, 1992.

Hartner, Willi. "Zaman." In *Encyclopedia of Islam*, 4, no. 2: 1207–1212. Leiden: E. J. Brill, 1913–1938.

Kaegi, Walter. *Byzantium and the Early Islamic Conquests*. Cambridge: Cambridge University Press, 1992.

Kaufmann, Yehezkel. *The Religion of Israel from its Beginnings to the Babylonian Exile*. Translated by Moshe Greenberg, trans. Chicago: University of Chicago Press, 1960.

Lecker, Michael. *Muslims, Jews, and Pagans: Studies on Early Islamic Medina*. Leiden: E. J. Brill, 1995.

Lieberman, Saul. *Hellenism in Jewish Palestine*. New York: The Jewish Theological Seminary of America, 1950.

Motzki, Harald. *Die Anfänge der islamischen Jurisprudenz*. Stuttgart: Franz Steiner, 1991.

Philonenko, M. "Une tradition essenienne dans le Coran." *Revue de l'histoire des religions* 170 (1966): 143–57.

———. "Une expression qoumranienne dans le Coran." *Atti 3. cong. studi arabi e islamici, Ravello 1966*, 1967.

———. "Une regle essenienne dans le Coran." *Semitica* 22 (1972): 49–52.

Rabin, Chaim. *Qumran Studies*. Oxford: Oxford University Press, 1957.

Rippin, Andrew. "RHMNN and the Hanifs." In *Islamic Studies Presented to Charles J Adams*, edited by Wael B. Hallaq and Donald P. Little, 153–68. Leiden: E. J. Brill, 1991.

Rubin, Uri. "Hanifiyya and Ka'ba: An Enquiry into the Arabian Pre-Islamic Background of *din Ibrahim.*" *Jerusalem Studies in Arabic and Islam* 13 (1990): 85–112.

Schacht, Joseph. "Nikah." In *Encyclopedia of Islam* 3, no. 2: 912–14. Leiden: E. J. Brill, 1913–1938.

———. "A Revaluation of Islamic Tradition." *Journal of the Royal Asiatic Society* (1949): 143–54.

———. *The Origins of Muhammadan Jurisprudence*. Oxford: Oxford University Press, 1950.

———. *Introduction to Islamic Law*. Oxford: Oxford University Press, 1960.

Schlatter, D. A. "Die Entwicklung des jüdischen Christentums zurn Islam." *Evangelisches MissionsMagazin*, Neue Folge 62 (1918): 251–64.

Schoeps, Hans Joachim. *Theologie and Geschichte des Judenchristentums*. Tübingen: J. C. B. Mohr (Paul Siebeck), 1949.

Shahid, Irfan. *Byzantium and the Arabs in the Fifth Century*. Washington: Dumbarton Oaks, 1989.

Wansbrough, John. *Quranic Studies: Sources and Methods of Scriptural Interpretation*. Oxford: Oxford University Press, 1977.

———. *The Sectarian Milieu: Content and Composition of Islamic Salvation History*. Oxford: Oxford University Press, 1978.

Watt, W. Montgomery. *Muhammad at Mecca*. Oxford: Oxford University Press, 1953.

———. "Hanif." In *Encyclopedia of Islam* 3: 165–66. Leiden: E. J. Brill, 1954.

———. "The 'High God' in Pre-Islamic Mecca." In *Actes du ve congrès international d'arabisants et islamisants*, 499–505, 1970.

———. "Pre-Islamic Arabian Religion in the Qur'an." *Islamic Studies* 15 (1976): 73–79.

———. "The Qur'an and Belief in a 'High God.'" *Der Islam* 56 (1979): 205–211.

Wellhausen, Julius. *Reste arabischen Heidentums*. 2d ed. Berlin: Georg Reimer, 1987.

Wensinck, Arent Jan. *Muhammad and the Jews of Medina*. Translated by Wolfgang H. Behn. Berlin: Adiyok, 1975.

Wolf, Eric R. "The Social Organization of Mecca and the Origins of Islam." *Southwestern Journal of Anthropology* 7 (1951): 329–56.

NOTES

1. Wansbrough's use of "Semitic" to qualify the tradition of monotheism to which Judaism, Christianity, and Islam belong is, perhaps, open to question, but it is difficult to suggest another expression which is not equally debatable. The use of the term is, I think, intended to avoid the implication that there is only one legitimate form of monotheism. His work is not concerned to define "monotheism" or to distinguish it from any other ideal type of religion.

2. Wansbrough (1977) suggests an alternative to the traditional account of the collection and composition of the Koran. John Burton, a former student of Wansbrough, was occupied with the same question at the same time and his very different conclusions (he argued that the Koran had been collected and composed in the lifetime of Muhammad) appeared in the same year (1977).

3. Where non-Muslim scholarship has seen the persistence of pre-Islamic pagan Arab practices in Islam (notably in the Kaaba at Mecca and the ceremonies associated with it), the Muslim tradition has perceived a restoration and purification by Islam of practices which had originally been monotheistic but which had been corrupted over time.

Glossary

Abul Qasim. Father of Qasim, i.e., Muhammad, the Prophet; a *kunya* for Muhammad, the Prophet.

adab. Belles-lettres; refinement, culture.

'adalah. Probity; synonym of **ta'dil**.

adib. Writer of **adab**; man of letters.

'ahd. Covenant, treaty, engagement.

Ahl al-Bayt. The people of the house, Muhammad's household (the Family of the Prophet).

ahl al-Hadith. Those collecting and learned in the **Hadith**.

Ahl al-Kitab. "People of the Book," especially Christians and Jews.

ahl al-ra'y. People of reasoned opinion; those using their own opinion to establish a legal point.

ahl as-suffa (ahl al-suffa). The people of the bench, of the temple at Mecca; they were poor strangers without friends or place of abode who claimed the promises of the Apostle of God and implored his protection.

akhbar. Reports, anecdotes, history.

a'lam. Signs, marks, badges.

aman. Safe conduct.

amarat al-nubuwwa. Marks of Prophethood.

527

ansars. The helpers; early converts of Medina, and then later all citizens of Medina converted to Islam; in contrast to the Muhajirun or exiles, those Muslims who accompanied the Prophet from Mecca to Medina.

aqiqah. The custom, observed on the birth of a child, of leaving the hair on the infant's head until the seventh day when it is shaved, and animals are sacrificed.

'asabiyyah. Tribal solidarity.

asbab al-nuzul. The occasions and circumstances of the Koranic revelations

ashab al-nabi. Companions of the Prophet (a single companion is a **sahabi**).

asharah mubashsharah (mobassara). The ten who received glad tidings. Ten of the most distinguished of Muhammad's followers whose certain entrance into Paradise he is said to have foretold: Abu Bakr, 'Umar, 'Uthman, 'Ali, Talhah, az-Zubayr, 'Abd ar-Rahman, Sa'd ibn Abu Waqqas, Said ibn Zayd, Abu Ubaida ibn al Jarrah.

Awa'il. The Ancients; the first people to do something.

ayah (pl. **ayat**). Sign, miracle; verse of the Koran.

ayyam al-Arab. "Days" of the Arabs; pre-Islamic tribal battles.

bab. Subchapter, especially in **Hadith** literature.

basmalah. The formula "In the name of God, the Merciful, the Compassionate" (*bi-'smi 'illahi 'l-Rahmani 'l-Rahim*).

bint. Daughter of.

daif (pl. **du'afa**). Weak, as classification of a **Hadith**; Traditionist of dubious reliability.

dala'il. Proofs, signs, marks.

dar. Abode.

Dar al-Harb. The Land of Warfare, a country belonging to infidels not subdued by Islam.

Dar al-Islam. The Land of Islam, The Islamic World.

dhimmah. Security, pact.

dhimmi. A non-Muslim, living as a second-class citizen in an Islamic state; a Christian or Jew.

din. Religion.

diwan. Register; collection of poetry by a single author or from a single tribe.

dua. Prayer; generally used for supplication as distinguished from **salat** or liturgical form of prayer.

fada'il. Merits.

fakhr. Boasting, self-glorification, or tribal vaunting.

faqih (pl. **fuqaha'**). One learned in **fiqh**.

fatihah. The first **sura** of the Koran.

fiqh. Islamic jurisprudence.

al-fitahl. The time before the Flood.

fitnah. Dissension, civil war; particularly the civil war ensuing on the murder of the Caliph 'Uthman.

fusha. The pure Arabic language.

futuh. Conquests; the early Islamic conquests.

gharat. Raids.

gharib. A rare, uncommon word or expression; a rare tradition, or traditions that are isolated, and do not date from one of the companions of the Prophet, but only from a later generation.

ghazwah (pl. **ghazawat**). Early Muslim military expeditions or raiding parties in which the Prophet took part; synonym of **maghazi**.

habl. Covenant, treaty, engagement.

Hadith. The Corpus of Traditions of the sayings and doings of the Prophet;.

Haggada. *See* **Midrash**.

Hajj. The annual pilgrimage to Mecca in the month of Dhu '-Hijjah.

Halakha. *See* **Midrash**.

halal. Licit, permitted; opposite of **haram**.

hanif. A Koranic term applying to those of true religion; seeker of religious truth.

haram. Sacred enclave; especially those of Mecca and Medina.

haram. Forbidden, illicit; opposite of **halal**.

hasan. Category of **Hadith** between sound (**sahih**) and weak (**daif**)

Hijra. Muhammad's migration from Mecca to Medina in 622 C.E.

hima. (Lit. "guarded," forbidden.") A portion of land reserved by the ruler of a country as a grazing ground.

hukm. Judgment.

ibn. Son of.

ijaz. Inimitability of the Koran.

ijazah. Licence given by a scholar to his pupil, authorizing the latter to transmit and teach a text.

ijma'. Consensus; the consensus of the Islamic community.

illah (pl. **ilal**). Cause or defect, especially a gap in the chain of authentic transmission of a **Hadith**.

imam. Leader, especially a religious leader; leader in communal prayer.

Injil. The Gospel.

isnad. Chain of authorities; in particular in **Hadith** and historical writings.

isra'. Journey by night; the famous night-journey of Muhammd to Jerusalem.

Jahiliyyah. Period before Muhammad's mission; era of ignorance; pre-Islamic period.

jihad. Holy War.

jizyah. Poll-tax; capitation tax.

kafir. Unbeliever.

kahin. Pre-Islamic soothsayer.

kalam. Scholastic theology.

kergyma. (Greek for "preaching.") The element of proclamation of religion (preaching of the Christian Gospel in particular) as opposed to its didache or its instructional aspects.

khabar (pl. **akhbar**). Discrete anecdotes, reports.

khassiya,khasa'is. Privilege, prerogative, feature, trait.

khatib. Orator; person pronouncing the Friday **khutbah**.

khulq. Disposition, temper, nature.

khutbah. Oration; address in the mosque at Friday prayers.

kiblah. Direction of prayer.

kissa. *See* **qissa**.

kitab (pl. **kutub**). Writing; scripture; book; in *Hadith*, a division approximating to a chapter.

kufic. Style of Arabic script, used in early Koran codices.

kunya (konia, kunyah). A patronymic or name of honor of the form Abu N or Umm N (father or mother of N).

kussas. *See* **qissas.**

mab'ath. Sending; The Call, when Muhammad was summoned to act as God's Prophet.

maghazi. Early Muslim military expeditions or raiding parties in which the Prophet took part.

majlis. Meeting, assembly, council. In Iran used for "parliament."

manaqib. Virtues, good qualities.

mansukh. Abrogated

mashhur. Well known, widely known.

mathalib. Defects.

matn. Main text; narrative content.

mawla (pl. **mawali**). Client, non-Arab Muslim.

Midrash. (Hebrew for "exposition or investigation.") A Hebrew term for the method of biblical investigation or exegesis by which oral tradition interprets and elaborates on the scriptural text. This investigation became necessary because the Written Law in the Pentateuch (the first five books of the Old Testament) needed to be reinterpreted in the light of later situations and disagreements. The Midrashim are usually divided into two broad groups:

1. **Halakha Midrash**, which is the scholastic deduction of the Oral Law (Halakha) from the Written Law; the totality of laws that have evolved since biblical times regulating religious observances, and conduct of the Jewish people; tend to be rather dry and legalistic.

2. **Haggada Midrash**, which consists of homiletic works whose purpose is edification rather than legislation; while less authoritative than halakhic ones, they are often highly imaginative stories, with a great deal of charm.

miraj. Ascent; the Prophet's vision of Heaven.

Mu'allaqah (pl. **Mu'allaqat**). A collection of pre-Islamic poems.

mubtada'. Beginnings.

mubassara. See **asharah mubashsharah**.

Mufakharah. Contests of vaunting; a war of words constituting a literary genre.

muhadith. **Hadith** scholar, collecting and studying the **Hadith**.

muhajirun. Those who went with the Prophet from Mecca to Medina at the time of the **Hijra**.

muruwwah. Manliness, chivalry, prowess; the qualities of the ideal pre-Islamic Arab.

musannaf. Classified, systemized compilation; **Hadith** compilations arranged according to subject matter.

mushaf. Koran codex.

musnad. Work of **Hadith** in which individual *Hadith* can be attributed to the Prophet himself.

mut'ah. Temporary marriage.

mutakallim. Scholastic theologian.

Mu'tazilah. Theological school which created speculative dogmatics of Islam.

mutawatir. Handed down successively.

nabi. Prophet.

nahdah. Renaissance.

nasab (pl. **ansab**). Genealogy.

nasikh. Passage in the Koran or Sunna which abrogates another passage.

Qaddarites. A group of teachers during the Abbasid period who championed free-will against the theory of predestination.

qadi. Judge of a shariah court.

qara'a 'ala. Literally, to read aloud to; study under.

qari' (pl. **qurra**). Reader, reciter of the Koran.

qira'ah. Recitation of the Koran; variant reading of the Koran.

qissah (pl. **qisas**). Story, fable, narrative tale; the narrative tales of the Koran.

qiyas. Analogy; the process of arriving at a legal decision by analogy.

qussas. Storytellers, relaters of **qisas**.

rajul (pl. **rijal**). Literally, man; trustworthy authorities in **Hadith** literature.

Rashidun. The first four caliphs (the orthodox or rightly guided caliphs), that is, Abu Bakr, 'Umar, 'Uthman, and 'Ali.

rasul. Messenger; apostle.

rawi (pl. **ruwah**). Reciter, transmitter.

ra'y. Opinion.

Ridda. At the death of Muhammad, Abu Bakr took over. But many outlying tribes of Bedouins refused to recognize Abu Bakr as successor and considered their former allegiance to, and contract with, the Prophet null and void. This led to the Wars of the the Ridda (wars of apostasy), as Abu Bakr eventually re-imposed the central authority of Mecca on the whole of the Arabian peninsula.

risalah (pl. **rasa'il**). Epistle.

riwayah. Transmission, especially of a non-religious text; recension; variant reading in poetry.

Sadaqa. Alms, charitable gift; almsgiving, charity; legally prescribed alms tax.

Sahabah. The group of the Companions of the Prophet.

sahifah (pl. **suhuf**). Page leaf; in the plural: manuscripts, documents containing **Hadith** material.

sahih. Sound (category of **Hadith**); name of the **Hadith** collections of al-Bukhari and Muslim.

saraya. Early Muslim military expeditions at which the Prophet was not present.

shadhh. Peculiar, especially unacceptable variants of the Koranic text.

shama'il. Good qualities; character, nature.

Sharia. The corpus of Islamic law.

shawahid. Piece of evidence or quotation serving as textual evidence.

Shia. Sect, who hold that the leadership of the Islamic community belongs only to the descendants of 'Ali and Fatima.

Shu'ubiyyah. Anti-Arab political and literary movement, especially strong in Iranian circles.

sira. Biography, especially of the Prophet.

THE QUEST FOR THE HISTORICAL MUHAMMAD

Sitz im Leben. (German, lit. "situtation in life." The context, or background, especially the context of origins of some phenomena.

Sunna. Way, path; customary practice, usage sanctioned by tradition; the sayings and doings of the Prophet which have established as legally binding.

sura. A chapter of the Koran.

tabaqat. Historical works organized biographically.

tabi (pl. **tabi'un**). Followers, the generation after the Prophet's Companions (**sahabah**).

ta'dil. Confirming the credibility of a **muhaddith**.

tafsir. Koranic exegesis.

tanzil. The divine revelation incorporated in the Koran; occasionally the inspiration of soothsayers.

tarikh. History.

tawhid. The doctrine of the unity of God.

ummah. Folk; the Islamic community.

usul. The fundamentals of jurisprudence.

warraq. Paperseller, stationer, bookseller, copyist.

wazu, wuzu. Ablution.

zakah. Alms-tax of prescribed amount.

zuhd. Asceticism.

Abbreviations

JESHO	*Journal of the Economic and Social History of the Orient*
JNES	*Journal of Near Eastern Studies*
JPHS	*Journal of the Pakistan Historical Society*
JRAS	*Journal of the Royal Asiatic Society*
JSAI	*Jerusalem Studies in Arabic and Islam*
JSS	*Journal of Semitic Studies*
MW	*Muslim World* (Published as the *Moslem World*, 1911–1947.)
RHR	*Revue de l'histoire des religions. Annales du Muséé Guimet*
RSO	*Revista degli studi orientali*
RSR	*Revue des sciences religieuses*
SI	*Studia Islamica*
WI	*Die Welt des Islams*
WZKM	*Wiener Zeitschrift fur die Kunde des Morgenlandes*
ZDMG	*Zeitschrift der deutschen Morgenlandischen Gesellschaft* (Journal of the German Oriental Society)

Dramatis Personae:
Explanatory List of Individuals
and Tribes[1]

Abbas ibn 'Abd al-Muttalib, of the Meccan clan of Hashim, paternal uncle of Muhammad, was the most celebrated of the Companions of the Prophet, and founder of the Abbasid dynasty, father of **Fadl ibn Abbas**, the celebrated authority on Islamic traditions.

'Abd, all names with *'Abd* mean the "servant" or "slave of x," where x used to refer to a pagan divinity, until the arrival of Islam when the names of God were used instead, e.g., *'Abd ullah.*

'Abd Manaf, the common ancestor of many Quraysh clans, forming the ethnic group of the Banu 'Abd Manaf.

'Abd al-Muttalib ibn Hashim, the grandson of 'Abd Manaf, and Muhammad's grandfather and his guardian for two years. He died, aged 82, in 578 C.E. His sons were Abdullah (Muhammad's father), al-Haris, az-Zuhair, Abu Talib, Abu Lahab, al-Abbas, and Hamza. His descendants are considered by some to be a special ethnic group, the Banu 'Abd al-Muttalib. Aloys Sprenger thinks he is possibly a mythical personage.

'Abd ar-Rahman ibn Auf (or 'Abd ar-Rahman ibn Awf), was one of the Companions who embraced Islam at a very early stage, and was one of those who fled to Ethiopia/Abyssinia. He also accompanied Muhammad in all his battles, receiving many wounds at Uhud. He was of the Zuhra clan.

537

'Abd Shams ibn 'Abd Manaf, the ancestor of a major Quraysh clan including the Banu Umayya.

Abdallah ibn 'Abd al-Muttalib, the father of Muhammad. Much that is recounted by Tradition of his life is worthless legend. It is possible he died before the birth of Muhammad.

Abdallah ibn Muhammad, a son of Muhammad, who died in infancy.

Abdallah ibn Sa'd, the secretary of Muhammad, foster brother of 'Uthman ibn Affan, a Qurayshite.

Abdallah ibn Ubayy, a Medinan chief of the Khazrajite clan of Auf. Among Muslim authors, he is regarded as the head of the hypocrites (*munafikun*).

Abraha, an Ethiopian, Christian governor of Yemen about the middle of the sixth century C.E. Said to have led a campaign against the Persians using elephants in the year 570 C.E., the traditional date for the birth of Muhammad.

Abu, meaning father, e.g., "Abu l Qasim" means "the father of Qasim"; it is then the *kunya*. It can also mean "the man of . . ." or "the man with . . .", e.g., Abu Himar, literally, "the father of the donkey," but meaning "the man with the donkey."

Abu Afak, a Medinan elder and anti-Muslim poet, who was assassinated under Muhammad's orders.

Abu Amir, ar-Rahib, the monk, a Medinan monotheist opposed to Muhammad.

Abu l-As ibn ar-Rabi, a nephew of Khadija, he married his cousin on his mother's side, Zaynab bint Muhammad, and was thus Muhammad's son-in-law.

Abu Bakr ibn Abi Quhafa, of the Taym clan, one of Muhammad's first Companions, his father-in-law (being the father of Aisha). He was the first Khalifah or successor of Muhammad; often referred to as the Veracious (*siddiq*) because of the purity of his life.

Abu Jahl, of the Makhzum clan, an influential Qurayshite, and an implacable enemy of Muhammad. Abu Jahl is a nickname meaning "Father of Folly." He is supposed to be alluded to in the Koran, sura 22: 8: "There is a man who disputes concerning God without either knowledge or direction." According to Muslim writers, Abu Jahl was a vain and debauched man. He died in the battle of Badr.

Abu Lahab, a nickname meaning "Father of the Flame," was one of the sons of Abu Muttalib and Muhammad's uncle. He was bitterly opposed to Islam. Zayd and Abu Lahab are the only relatives or friends mentioned by Muhammad in the Koran, the latter in sura III. He died soon after the battle of Badr.

Abul Qasim, a kunya for Muhammad, the Prophet.

Abu Sufyan Sakr ibn Harb, an enemy of Muhammad, of the Qurayshite clan of Abd Shams, a grandson of Umayya, husband of Hind, father of Muawiya, Yazid, and Umm Habiba (one of Muhammad's wives). Became head of all the Qurayshites.

Abu Talib, Muhammad's uncle and guardian, father of 'Ali and Aqil. Though he remained Muhammad's friend and guardian all his life, Abu Talib is said to have died an unbeliever.

Abu Ubayda, one of the Companions, who was with the Prophet in all his wars, and distinguished himself at the battle of Uhud.

Abul Walid, a kunya for Utba ibn Rabia.

Ad, a mythical tribe of South Arabia, to which the prophet Hud is said to have been sent (sura 7:63).

Aisha bint Abi Bakr, daughter of Abu Bakr, and Muhammad's child-bride of nine.

Al, Arabic definite article which sometimes becomes ar-, az-, as-, at-, and so forth, or may be shortened to l-.

'Ali ibn Abi Talib, son of Abu Talib, and cousin, and later son-in-law, of Muhammad, having married the Prophet's daughter, Fatima. Father of Hasan and Husayn, he was to be the fourth Caliph. The Shias hold that on the death of Muhammad, 'Ali was entitled to the Caliphate, and the respective claims of Abu Bakr, 'Umar, and 'Uthman on the one hand and of 'Ali on the other, gave rise to the Shia schism. Persians call him Sheri-Khuda, The Lion of God.

Allat, a pre-Islamic Arab goddess (*See* **Lat**).

Amina bint Wahb, a Qurayshite of the Zuhra clan, wife of Abdallah ibn 'Abd al-Muttalib. Mother of Muhammad, died before her son claimed the position of Prophet.

Ammar ibn Yasir, a confederate of the Banu Makhzum, one of the earliest converts to Islam.

Ansars, The Helpers, Muhammad's Medinan followers in contrast to the muhajirun.

Al-Arqam ibn 'Abd Manaf, a Qurayshite of the Makhzum clan, who offered his house to the Muslims as a meeting place.

Asma bint Marwan, poetess from Medina, who wrote verses mocking the Muslims, and as a consequence was assassinated on Muhammad's orders.

Attab ibn Asid, a governor established by Muhammad in Mecca.

Awf, a Medinan clan of the Khazraj tribe.

Aws, one of the two great Medinan tribes.

Aws Manat, a group of Medinan clans of the tribe of Aws.

Banu, meaning "sons of," can be put in front of names of tribes, e.g., Banu Quraysh, though they may be called just "Quraysh" or "Qurayshites." In each case what is meant is the tribe, clan, or family which considers itself the descendants of Quraysh. Other well known tribes include, Banu Najjar, Banu Quraizah, Banu Kinana, Banu Nazr, Banu Umayya, and so forth.

Banu Bakr ibn 'Abd Manat, a section of the Kinana tribe whose land bordered on Mecca.

Banu ibn Wail, a big tribe from northeast Arabia.

Bilal, a black slave, one of the early converts to Islam, and the first *muezzin*, the person giving the call to prayer.

Dhu Nuwas, a Judaizing king of South Arabia in the sixth century.

Fadl ibn Abbas, or Ibn Abbas, son of Abbas, a cousin of Muhammad, and the source of many traditions.

Fatima bint Amr, of the Qurayshite clan of Makhzum, wife of 'Abd al-Muttalib, mother of Abu Talib and also of Abdallah, the Prophet's father.

Fatima bint al-Khattab, a sister of 'Umar.

Fatima bint Muhammad, a daughter of Muhammad the Prophet and Khadija; wife of 'Ali, and mother of Hasan and Husayn.

Fazara, a tribe from northwest Arabia.

Ghassan, the Ghassanids, a Christian Arab dynasty from Syria, subjects of the Byzantine Empire.

Ghatafan, nomad tribe from northwest Arabia.

Hafsa bint 'Umar, daughter of 'Umar ibn al-Khattab; wife of the Prophet.

Hala bint Khuwaylid, of the Asad clan, sister of Khadija, and mother of Abu l-As ibn ar-Rabi.

Hala bint Wuhayb, of the Zuhra clan, wife of Abd al-Muttalib, and cousin of Amina, the Prophet's mother.

Halima bint Abdallah, of the Sad clan of the Hawazin tribe; the Prophet's nurse.

Hamza ibn 'Abd al-Muttalib, Muhammad's uncle; was present at the battle of Uhud, and killed Usman, one of the leaders of the Quraysh, but was killed himself soon afterward.

Hanif, those Arabs tending to monotheism without belonging to either Judaism or Christianity.

Hanifa, a tribe of the Yamama in central Arabia.

Al-Harith ibn Jabala (Arethas in Greek), Ghassanid chief and vassal of Byzantium (ca. 539–570).

Hashim, a clan of the Quraysh tribe to which Muhammad belonged; founded by Hashim, father of 'Abd al Muttalib.

Hasan, son of 'Ali and Fatima, thus Muhammad's grandson; brother of Husayn. Poisoned by his wife, on Yazid's insistence.

Hawazin, a large tribe from northern and western Arabia.

Himyar, Himyarites, principal tribe in south Arabia from the beginning of the Christian era onward.

Hind bint Utba, daughter of Utba ibn Rabia, wife of Abu Sufyan, mother of Muawiya, implacable enemy of Muhammad.

Hubal, god of Mecca, represented by a red cornelian idol.

Hud, mythical prophet sent to the people of Ad.

Hudayl, a confederation of western Arabian tribes.

Husayn, son of 'Ali, brother of Hasan, grandson of the Prophet, and fourth caliph. Killed in the most gruesome manner possible at the battle of Karbala.

Imrul Qays ibn Amr, of the tribe of Lakhm, "king of all Arabs," died in 328.

Imrul Qays ibn Hujr, king of Kinda, and a considerable Arab poet (first half of sixth century C.E.).

Jafar ibn Abi Talib, son of Abu Talib, brother of 'Ali, cousin of Muhammad.

Juwayriyya bint al-Harith, daughter of the chief of the Banu l-Mustaliq, wife of Muhammad.

Kab ibn al-Ashraf, a half Jew from Medina, murdered on Muhammad's command; one of eighty assassinations carried out on the Prophet's orders.

Kalb, a largely Christian Arab tribe living in Syria.

Khabbab ibn al-Aratt, an early convert to Islam, confederate of the Banu Zuhra.

Khadija bint Khuwaylid, of the clan Asad, a rich widow who married Muhammad; mother of Fatima and other of his children.

Khalid ibn Said ibn al-As, of the clan Abd Shams, a young Qurayshite, a convert to Islam.

Khalid ibn al-Walid, of the clan of Makhzum, a Qurayshite general. At first fought against Muhammad at Uhud, but later converted to Islam, and led many successful expeditions in Iraq and Syria.

Khatma, a Medinan clan of the Aws Manat group.

Khazraj, one of two main non-Jewish tribes of Medina.

Khuza'a, an Arab tribe from the area around Mecca.

Lakhm (Banu), Lakhmids, an Arab family of the Tanukh tribe which founded the kingdom of Hira; subject to the Sassanid Persians.

al-Lat, an idol worshipped by the ancient Arabians, and is mentioned in the Koran in conjunction with two other idols, al-Uzza and Manat. (sura 53:19–20). Waqidi and Tabari tell the story of the "Satanic Verses," when the Devil tempted the Prophet to compromise with idolatry. The Prophet proclaimed, "These are exalted females, and verily their intercession is to be hoped for," but later retracted these words.

Makhzum, a Qurayshite clan.

Maslama, the prophet of the Banu Hanifa in the Yamama in central Arabia; often referred to as Musaylima.

Maymuna, the sister-in-law of Abbas, a widow, wife of Muhammad.

Mazdaeans, Zoroastrians.

Mu'awiya ibn Abi Sufyan, son of Abu Sufyan and Hind; brother of Yazid, Muhammad's secretary and later Caliph (661–680), founder of the Umayyad dynasty and enemy of 'Ali.

muhajirun, literally "the Emigrants," name applied to Muhammad's supporters aamong the Qurayshites of Mecca who "emigrated" with him to Medina.

Musab ibn Umayr, a Qurayshite Muslim, lieutenant of the Prophet in Medina before the Hijra.

Nadir (Banu), one of three great Jewish tribes of Medina.

Qasim, son of Muhammad and Khadija; died very young.

Qaynuqa, Jewish tribe of Medina.

Quraysh, the eponymous ancestor of the tribe; lived in Mecca. Also name of tribe, which was made up of shepherds and robbers who terrorized the pilgrims to Mecca.

Qurayza, Jewish tribe from Medina.

Rayhana bint Zayd, a Jewess of the Nadir tribe, taken by Muhammad as concubine after the slaughter of her husband and all other males of the tribe, Banu Qurayza.

Ruqayya bint Muhammad, daughter of Muhammad and Khadija; first married a son of Abu Lahab, and then 'Uthman ibn Affan.

Sa'd (Banu), a clan of the Hawazin tribe to which Muhammad's nurse belonged.

Sa'd ibn Mu'adh, a Medinan chief of the Abd al Ashhal clan of the Aws tribe.

Safwan ibn al-Mu'attal as-Sulami, a young Muslim who found Aisha when she was lost; the incident caused great scandal.

Sa'ida, a clan of the Medina tribe of Khazraj.

Sajah, a prophetess of the tribe of Tamim; originally a Christian who came to receive revelations in rhymed prose.

Sassanids, the dynasty that ruled the Persian Empire fromm 224 to the Arab Conquest (636–651).

Suhayb ibn Sinan, the Rumi (from Byzantine), a freedman, an early convert to Islam.

Talha ibn Ubaydallah, a Qurayshite of the Taym clan, an early convert to Islam.

Tamim, Arab tribe from north eastern Arabia of Meccan origin who fought by the side of Muhammad at Mecca and Hunain.

Thamud, a people of ancient Arabia; various monuments are attributed to them.

Thaqif, a tribe from the town of Taif.

Tubba', the ancient kings of South Arabia.

'Umar ibn al-Khattab, a Qurayshite of the Adi clan, father of Hafsa, father-in-law of Muhammad, and second Caliph, assassinated by a slave. Responsible for the spread of Islam.

Umayya ibn Abd Shams, a Qurayshite grandfather of Abu Sufyan and ancestor of the Umayyad family.

Umayyads, family of the descendants of Umayya, of the Qurayshite clan of Abd Shams. Under Mu'awiya, they became the ruling dynasty of the Muslim world.

Umm Habiba bint Abi Sufyan, daughter of Abu Sufyan, who became a Muslim, and eventually married Muhammad.

Umm Kulthum, daughter of Muhammad and Khadija, wife of 'Uthman.

Usama ibn Zayd, the son of Zayd ibn Haritha and an Abyssinian freedwoman; much loved by Muhammad.

Usayd ibn al-Hudayr, chief of the 'Abd al-Ash'hal clan of the Medina tribe of Aws.

Utba ibn Rabia, a Qurayshite of the 'Abd Shams clan, father of Hind, the wife of Abu Sufyan; killed at Badr.

'Uthman ibn Affan, of the Umayya family, an early convert to Islam, married Ruqayya, Muhammad's daughter and after her death, her sister Umm Kulthum. Third Caliph, 644–656. Assassinated by Abu Bakr's son.

'**Uthman ibn Mazun**, a Qurayshite of the Jumah clan, an early convert to Islam.

Uzza, an Arab deity. *See* **al-Lat**.

Al-Walid ibn al-Walid, a Qurayshite of the Makhzum clan, early convert to Islam.

Waraqa ibn Naufal, cousin of Khadija, a Qurayshite of the Asad clan; a hanif.

Yazid ibn Abi Sufyan, son of Abu Sufyan, brother of Mu'awiya; became governor of Tayma and a general.

Zayd ibn Haritha, of the Kalb tribe, a slave of Khadija freed by Muhammd and later adopted as a son by him (hence known as Zayd ibn Muhammad); married Zaynab bint Jahsh and was father of Usama.

Zaynab, a Jewess from Khaybar who tried to poison Muhammad.

Zaynab bint Jahsh, a cousin of Muhammad on his mother's side, daughter of 'Abd al-Muttalib, married Zayd ibn Haritha, then Muhammad.

Zaynab bint Khuzayma, of the tribe of Amir ibn Sa'sa'a, the wife of a Qurayshite, then of his brother, then Muhammad.

Zaynab bint Muhammad, daughter of Muhammad and Khadija; married Abu l-As ibn ar-Rabi.

Az-Zubayr ibn al Awamm, one of the first converts to Islam, a nephew of Khadija and a cousin of Muhammad.

Zuhra, a Qurayshite clan.

NOTE

1. I have relied on the *Encyclopaedia of Islam*, 1st and 2d eds., *Dictionary of Islam*, ed. Thomas P. Hughes (Delhi, 1988); and Maxime Rodinson, *Mohammed* (New York, 1980). However, it should be pointed out from the outset that many of the personages and even the biographical details of historical persons in this list may well be fictitious without any foundation in history, given the nature of our very suspect sources.

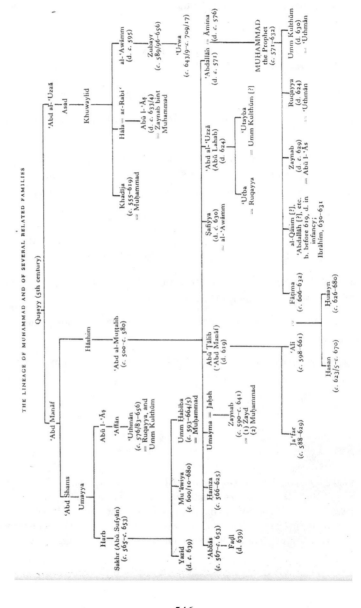

THE LINEAGE OF MUHAMMAD AND OF SEVERAL RELATED FAMILIES

Quṣayy (5th century)

Western Asia and Arabia *c.* A.D. 630

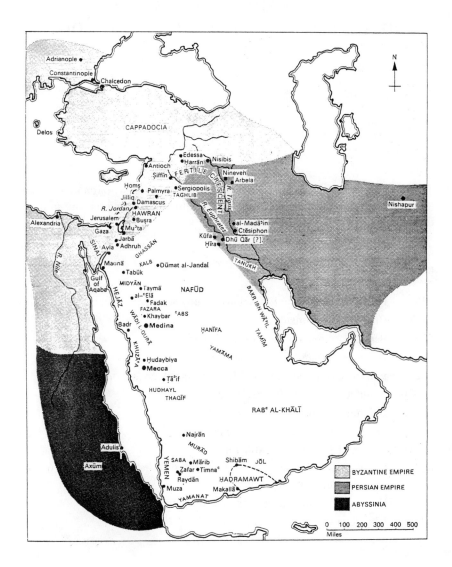

Adrianople

Constantinople
Chalcedon

Delos

CAPPADOCIA

Edessa
Harrān   Nisibis
Antioch   Nineveh
Şiffīn   FERTILE CRESCENT   Arbela

Homs   Sergiopolis
Jillīq   Palmyra   TAGHLIB
R. Jordan   Damascus
Jerusalem   HAWRAN   Nishapur
Gaza   Buşra
Muʾta   al-Madāʾin
Jarbā   Kūfa   Ctēsiphon
SINAI   Ayla   Adhruh   Ḥīra   Dhū Qār [?]
Maanā   KALB   Dūmat al-Jandal   GHASSĀN
R. Nile   Tabūk   TANŪKH
Gulf of Aqaba   MIDYĀN
Ṭaymā   NAFŪD
al-ʿElā   BAKR IBN WĀʾIL
Fadak
FAZARA   ʿABS   TAMĪM
Khaybar
Badr   Medina
WĀDĪ L-QURĀ   ḤANĪFA
YAMĀMA
KHUZĀʿA
Ḥudaybiya
Mecca
Ṭāʾif
HUDHAYL
THAQĪF

RABʿ AL-KHĀLĪ

Najrān
MURĀD
Adulis   YEMEN   SABA   Mārib   Shibām   JŌL
Axūm   Zafār   Timnaʿ
Raydān   HADRAMAWT
Muza   Makallā
YAMANAT

N

Alexandria

R. Tigris

R. Euphrates

Nishapur

BYZANTINE EMPIRE
PERSIAN EMPIRE
ABYSSINIA

0   100   200   300   400   500
Miles

547

Chronological Table
and the Islamic Dynasties

These are traditional dates; in recent years not only have many of them been contested, but some of the putative events (battles, treaties, conquests, and so forth) themselves have been discredited.

C.E.

525 Fall of Himyar—the Ethiopians occupy southern Arabia.

ca. 570 Birth of Muhammad.

575 Persian occupation of southern Arabia.

576 Death of Muhammad's mother, Amina.

602 End of Arab principality of Hira, on Iraq-Arabian borderlands.

ca. 610 Beginning of Call, first revelation.

ca. 613 Beginning of public preaching.

Flight of Muhammd's followers to Ethiopia.

ca. 619 Deaths of Khadija and Abu Talib

620 Muhammad's reputed "Night Journey" from Mecca to Jerusalem, and thence to the Seventh Heaven.

Hijra of Muhammad from Mecca to Medina.

622 Islamic era begins July 16.

The Quraysh are defeated by the Muslims at the Battle of Badr.

Muslims are defeated at the Battle of Uhud.

The Jewish tribe of al-Nadhir is crushed and expelled.

Meccans attack Muslims in Medina but are driven off during "The War of the Trench."

627   The Jewish tribe of the Qurayza is attacked by Muhammad.

The Treaty of Hudaybiyya; truce with the Quraysh.

The Jews of Khaybar are exterminated.

630   Muhammad conquers Mecca.

632   March, Pilgrimage of farewell.

632   Death of Muhammad. Abu Bakr becomes first Caliph.

633–37 Arabs conquer Syria and Iraq.

636   Battle of Qadisiyya, decisive defeat of the Persians.

639–42 Conquest of Egypt.

650   Fall of island of Arwad.

656   Murder of 'Uthman—beginning of the first civil war in Islam.

657–59 Battle of Siffin.

Murder of 'Ali—beginning of Umayyad dynasty.

Massacre of Husayn and Alids at Karbala.

683–90 Second civil war.

685–87 Revolt of Mukhtar in Iraq—beginning of extremist Shia.

'Abd al-Malik introduces Arab coinage, as part of reorganization of imperial administration.

Muslims land in Spain.

Fall of Umayyads, accession of Abbasids.

Arabs capture Chinese paper-makers, use of paper spreads.

Umayyad prince 'Abd ar-Rahman becomes Amir of Cordova.

762–63 Foundation of Baghdad by Mansur.

Harun ar-Rashid deposes Barmecides.

809–13 Civil War of Amin and Ma'mun.

813–33 Reign of Mamun—development of Arabic science and letters.

THE CALIPHS

The Orthodox or Rightly Guided Caliphs (Al Khulafa ar-Rashidun), 11–40/632–61

11/632 Abu Bakr
13/634 'Umar
23/644 'Uthman
35–40/656–61 'Ali

The Umayyad Caliphs, 41–132/661–750

41/661 Mu'awiya I
60/680 Yazid I
64/683 Mu'awiya II
64/684 Marwan I
65/685 Abd al-Malik
86/705 al-Walid I
96/715 Sulaiman
99/717 'Umar b. Abd al-Aziz
101/720 Yazid II
105/724 Hisham
125/743 al-Walid II
126/744 Yazid III
126/744 Ibrahim
127–32/744–50 Marwan II al-Himar

The Abbasid Caliphs (in Iraq and Baghdad)

132–656/749–1258
132/749 as-Saffah
136/754 al-Mansur
158/775 al-Mahdi
169/785 al-Hadi
170/786 Harun ar-Rashid
193/809 al-Amin
198/813 al-Mamun

List of Contributors

LAWRENCE I. CONRAD (1949–), Historian of Near Eastern Medicine at the Wellcome Institute for the History of Medicine (London, U.K.) and Lecturer, University College, London, received his Ph.D from Princeton University. He is the author of numerous studies on medieval Near Eastern social history, Arabic-Islamic medicine, and Arabic, Greek, and Syriac historiography. He collaborated with Albrecht Noth on the important second edition of *The Early Arabic Historical Tradition: A Source-Critical Study* (1994).

JOSEPH SCHACHT (1902–1969), Schact was professor of Arabic and Islamics at Columbia University, New York. He was the leading Western scholar on Islamic Law, whose *Origins of Muhammadan Jurisprudence* (1950) is still considered one of the most important works on the subject ever written, essential for all advanced studies. The author of many articles in the various editions of the *Encyclopedia of Islam*, Schacht also edited *The Legacy of Islam* for Oxford University Press. Other books include *An Introduction to Islamic Law* (1964).

ARTHUR JEFFERY (18??–1952). Jeffrey was professor of Semitic Languages at Columbia University and Union Theological Seminary. Apart from numerous articles in learned journals, Jeffery wrote two works that are considered definitive in their respective domain: *Materials for the History of the Text of the Qur'an: The Old Codices* (1937), and *The Foreign Vocabulary of the Quran* (1938). The latter was a tour de force that reviewed about 275 words in the Koran that were regarded as foreign. This survey led Jeffery to examine texts in Ethiopic, Aramaic, Hebrew, Syriac, Greek, Latin, and Middle Persian, among other languages. His research led him to look for and at manuscripts in the Middle East, including Cairo. He was also the author of *The Qur'an as Scripture* (1952).

ERNEST RENAN (1832–1892). Renan was born at Tréguier in Brittany, France. Albert Schweitzer sum up his life thus: "Intended for the priesthood, he entered the seminary of St. Sulpice in Paris, but there, in consequence of reading the German critical thoelogy, he began to doubt the truth of Christianity and of its history. [After studies in Italy, he wrote *Averroes et l'Averroisme* (Paris, 1852)]. In 1856 he received from Napoleon III the means to make a journey to Phoenicia and Syria. After his return in 1862 he obtained the professorship of Semitic Languages at the College de France. But the widespread indignation aroused by his *Life of Jesus*, 1863 [which looked at Jesus Christ as a purely historical figure, shorn of all the supernatural elements], forced the Government to remove him from office. In politics, as in religion, his position was somewhat indefinite.In religion he was no longer a Catholic; avowed free-thought was too plebeian for his taste, and in Protestantism the multiplicity of sects repelled him. [When asked by someone whether it was true that he had, on abandoning Catholicism,embraced Protestantism, Renan replied testily, "It was my faith that I lost and not my reason."] . . . At bottom he was a sceptic."

ANDREW RIPPIN (1950—   ). Rippin is associate professor of Religious Studies at the University of Calgary, with a particular interest in the Koran and Koranic exegetical literature. Professor Rippin is the author of numerous articles and reviews, and has also written widely acclaimed introductory books on Islam such as *Muslims, Their Religious Beliefs and Practices* (2 vols., 1990, 1993). He also edited *Approaches to the History of the Interpretation of the Quran* (1988), and co-edited with Jan Knappert, *Textual Sources for the Study of Islam* (1986), which has become a standard textbook. He is at present supervising the new series of scholarly works on the Koran, *Curzon Studies in the Quran*.

HENRI LAMMENS (1862–1937). Born in Ghent, Belgium of Catholic Flemish stock, Henri Lammens joined the Jesuit order in Beirut at the age of fifteen, and settled in Lebanon for good. During his first eight years there Lammens mastered Arabic, Latin, and Greek. His first work of scholarship was a dictionary of Arabic usage (1889). He edited *al-Bashir*, the Jesuit newspaper of Beirut, and after much travelling, he began his career as an Orientalist at the School of Oriental Studies at the Jesuit College in 1907. He published a series of studies on the Umayyads, and several on pre-Islamic Arabia: *Etudes sur le regne du calife Omaiyade Mo'awia Ier* (1908), *Le berceau de l'Islam; L'Arabie occidentale a la vielle de l'Hegire* (1914). He contributed many articles to the first edition of the *Encyclopedia of Islam*, as well as various learned journals. It is universally acknowledged "that Lammens provided the study of the sira with a new basis; and none would underestimate his contributions on the history of the Umayyads."

G. R. HAWTING (1944–) is currently Senior Lecturer in the History of the Near Middle East at the School of Oriental and African Studies (SOAS). Apart from numerous articles in various journals, Dr. Hawting has written *The First Dynasty of Islam* (1986), translated two volumes in the *Tabari Translation Project* (vols. 17, 20), edited together with Abdel Kader Shereef, *Approaches to the Quran* (1993), and in 1999 Cambridge University Press published his new book, *The Idea of Idolatry and the Rise of Islam: From Polemic to History*.

HERBERT BERG is assistant professor in the Department of Philosophy and Religion, University of North Carolina at Wilmington. His most recent publication is *The Development of Exegesis in Early Islam: The Debate over the Authenticity of Muslim Literature from the Formative Period*.

F. E. PETERS is professor of Middle Eastern Studies at New York University, his major interests being Muhammad, Jesus, Jerusalem, Mecca, and Comparative Judaism. After a degree in Classics, and an M.A in Philosophy and Greek, Peters obtained his doctorate in Islamic Studies from Princeton. Apart from articles in many journals, Professor Peters's works include *Muhammad and the Origins of Islam* (1994), *Mecca: A Literary History of the Muslim Holy Land* (1994), *The Hajj: The Muslim Pilgrimage to Mecca and the Holy Places* (1994), and *Judaism, Christianity, and Islam: The Classical Texts and Their Interpretation* (3 vols. 1990).

Y. D. NEVO AND J. KOREN. Yehuda Nevo was a freelance archaeologist who discovered Kufic inscriptions in the Negev desert in Israel, four hundred of which were published in *Ancient Arabic Inscriptions from the Negev*. This led him and Judy Koren to reexamine the origins of Islam, and early Islamic history. At his death, Nevo left the manuscript of *Crossroads to Islam*, which Judy Koren is revising for publication soon. Judy Koren worked with Nevo on the archaeological sites in Israel, and at present teaches at Haifa University. Koren and Nevo have also published together *The Origins of the Muslim Descriptions of the Jahili Meccan Sanctuary* (*Journal of Near Eastern Studies*, 1990, no 1).

C. H. BECKER (1876–1933). Becker was a great German specialist on Islam, with many articles in the first edition of the *Encyclopedia of Islam* to his credit. Many of his other important articles were collected together in *Islamstudien: Vom Werden und der islamischen Welt* (2 vols., 1924–1932). Other works include *Beitrage zur Geschichte Agyptens unter dem Islam* (2 vols., 1902–1903), and *Papyri Schott-Reinhardt: Veroffentlichungen aus der Heidelberger Papyrus-Sammlung*, vol. 3 (1906). Becker developed the idea that the "bursting of the Arabs beyond their native peninsula was, like earlier irruptions in which the religious element was totally lacking, due to economic necessities."